SECOND EDITION

ATTITUDES AND OPINIONS

Stuart Oskamp

Claremont Graduate School

PRENTICE HALL, Englewood Cliffs, New Jersey 07632

Library of Congress Cataloging-in-Publication Data

OSKAMP, STUART.
    Attitudes and opinions / Stuart Oskamp.—2nd ed.
        p. cm.
    Includes bibliographical references and indexes.
    ISBN 0-13-050592-7
    1. Public opinion. 2. Attitude (Psychology) 3. Public opinion
polls. I. Title.
HM261.O75 1991
303.3'8—dc20   90-45391
                                                          CIP

Box 5–4 extracts from Wheeler (1976, pp. xv–xvii, 23–37, 245–255). Reprinted from *LIES, DAMN LIES, AND STATISTICS: The Manipulation of Public Opinion in America*, by Michael Wheeler, by permission of Liveright Publishing Corporation. Copyright © 1976 by Michael Wheeler.
Table 9–1 adapted and expanded from McGuire (1972, p. 112) in *Experimental Social Psychology* by Charles G. McClintock, copyright © 1972 by Holt Rinehart and Winston, Inc., reprinted by permission of the publisher.

Editorial/production supervision and
    interior design: *Joan L. Stone*
Cover design: *Carol Ceraldi*
Prepress buyer: *Debbie Kesar*
Manufacturing buyer: *Mary Ann Gloriande*

 ©1991, 1977 by Prentice-Hall, Inc.
A Paramount Communications Company
Englewood Cliffs, New Jersey 07632

Printed in the United States of America

10 9 8 7 6 5 4 3 2

ISBN 0-13-050592-7

PRENTICE-HALL INTERNATIONAL (UK) LIMITED, *London*
PRENTICE-HALL OF AUSTRALIA PTY. LIMITED, *Sydney*
PRENTICE-HALL CANADA INC., *Toronto*
PRENTICE-HALL HISPANOAMERICANA, S.A., *Mexico*
PRENTICE-HALL OF INDIA PRIVATE LIMITED, *New Delhi*
PRENTICE-HALL OF JAPAN, INC., *Tokyo*
SIMON & SCHUSTER ASIA PTE. LTD., *Singapore*
EDITORA PRENTICE-HALL DO BRASIL, LTDA., *Rio de Janeiro*

My attitudes—

Gratitude and love to Catherine,
Pride and love for David and Karen,
Appreciation to all who have smoothed my path.

Contents

Preface

Revising this book has taken a major portion of my energy and devotion for the last several years—as long to revise it as to write the first edition! It has been a labor of love, in which I tried to find and include all of the best recent work in the very broad areas which this volume covers. I hope that I have succeeded so that you, the reader, will find your main interests in the topic satisfied.

The first edition achieved a popularity and longevity far beyond my initial expectations, and I hope that this one will be equally well received. The major changes in it are a whole new chapter on social perception and social cognition, including attribution theory, and major new sections on cognitive response theories of attitude change, on systems for prediction of behavior and behavioral intentions, and on increases in citizens' ideological thinking. In addition, there is updated and expanded coverage of the research topics in every chapter, especially in the substantive attitude topics of Part Two of the volume.

Attitudes and opinions are crucial aspects of people's daily lives, and they influence the affairs of groups, organizations, and nations. They comprise the general area that has been most studied by social psychologists over the years, and yet they are often given a skimpy coverage in psychology textbooks. Attitudes and opinions are also central to the concerns of other academic disciplines, including sociologists, political scientists, communications researchers, and other social scientists. Methodologically, they have been studied by descriptive researchers, measurement specialists, public opinion pollers, theorists, and experimentalists.

The first main goal of this book is to present a broad coverage that includes the key contributions and concerns of all of these fields and approaches, and thus to help bridge the gaps between them. I have tried to avoid the one-sided emphasis of many texts, which may concentrate solely on the area of attitude change, or attitude theories, or attitude measurement. The book covers those topics in some depth, but it also includes major sections on the structure and functions of attitudes, the nature of public opinion, public opinion polling, attitude formation, communication of attitudes and opinions, attitude-behavior relationships, and the content of public opinion on several of the most socially important topics. Among the key themes of the volume are the usefulness of attitudes in our everyday lives, their relationship to the processes of social perception and social cognition, the persuasion processes that lead to attitude change, and the social impact and policy implications of attitudes and opinions.

A second major aim of this book is relevance to people's lives and key concerns. It stresses principles and research findings on topics that are salient and recurrent to citizens today. In particular, Part Two of the volume covers many important contemporary social issues, including political attitudes and voting behavior, international attitudes, racism and prejudice, and sexism and gender role attitudes. Instructors may want to supplement these chapters with readings from other valuable contemporary sources such as *Public Opinion Quarterly*, the *Gallup Poll Monthly*, and the *Harris Survey*.

This book is intended primarily for upper-division or graduate students in courses on Attitudes, on Survey Research, on Public Opinion, or on Persuasive Communication. Such courses presuppose an introduction to the principles of social science research, and they might be offered in departments of psychology, sociology, political science, communication, anthropology, or public policy. However, the book should also be understandable and relevant to many general readers outside of those fields, for I have aimed to make the writing style readable and interesting. Each chapter has a clear organizational structure, with important terms set off in bold face, and many figures and boxes that add interesting details about major people and research findings in the field.

To serve the needs of advanced students for a scholarly reference work, I have included a very large number of citations to the research literature (over 1500 references).

Thanks

I can't begin to recall or acknowledge all the intellectual debts I have contracted in the years of working on this volume. Foremost in my gratitude are the psychology faculty, graduate students, and administration of Claremont Graduate School, which has been a congenial and supportive intellectual home for me for 30 years. Other friends and colleagues elsewhere have made many relevant contributions in their research findings and conceptual ideas, which I have selected and summarized herein. I am also grateful to four collaborators who contributed chapters to the first edition: Catherine Cameron, Mark Lipsey, Burton Mindick, and Theodore Weissbach. The reviewers who offered helpful criticisms and suggestions (many of which I took to heart) were Eugene Borgida, University of Minnesota, and James Olson, University of Western Ontario. Other instructors who read the first edition also made useful constructive comments. Jane Gray and B. J. Reich helped to organize all the text and references that my trusty word processor churned out, and Joan Stone supervised the production details with aplomb. Finally, my wife and children are the ones whose love and support I counted on to make life meaningful during my work on this volume and in the many years before that. Thanks to you all.

Stuart Oskamp
Claremont, California

1

Background
History
and Concepts

Attitude. It's the current buzzword. It's also one of the most important factors of success, according to more than 1,000 top- and middle-level executives of 13 major American corporations. . . . Your attitude can make or break your career.—Allan Cox, 1983, p. 11.

What are laws but the expressions of the opinion of some class which has power over the rest of the community? By what was the world ever governed but by the opinion of some person or persons? By what else can it ever be governed?—Thomas B. Macaulay, 1830.

As these quotations illustrate, attitudes and opinions are important. They can help people, they can hurt people, they have influenced the course of history. Novelists and poets describe them, historians weigh and assess them, average citizens explain people's behavior in terms of their attitudes, politicians attempt to understand and shape public opinion. Consequently social psychologists, too, have long had a great interest in attitudes and opinions and have devised many ways of studying them. This book will describe these research methods, summarize the important findings on major aspects of attitudes and opinions, and try to clarify the many current theories and controversies in the field.

WHY STUDY ATTITUDES?

One long-standing controversy has been whether to study attitudes or behavior. This debate goes back to the early years of social psychology, when it was just beginning to be differentiated from other areas of psychology and sociology. For instance, the well-known sociologist Read Bain (1928, p. 940) wrote, "The development of sociology as a natural science has been hindered by . . . too much attention to subjective factors, such as . . . attitudes." Behaviorists, following the lead of psychologists such as B. F. Skinner (1957), have generally tried to avoid use of "mentalistic concepts" like attitude, and to study observable behavior instead.

However, the majority view among social psychologists was best expressed in

1

Photograph courtesy of Harvard
University News Office. Reprinted by
permission.

Box 1–1   GORDON ALLPORT, *Champion of Attitudes*

*Gordon Allport (1897–1967) was one of the most famous and beloved social psychologists
of his day. He received his B.A., M.A., and Ph.D. from Harvard and taught there continuously since 1930. He served as chairman of Harvard's psychology department, president of
the American Psychological Association, editor of the major journal in social psychology for
12 years, and member of numerous national and international committees.*

*Allport's interests within social psychology were broad. He wrote several major textbooks
on personality, as well as* The Psychology of Rumor, The Nature of Prejudice, The Psychology of Radio, *books on religion, expressive movement, and research methods, and also over
200 articles. An authority on attitudes, he wrote classic chapters covering that topic in
three successive editions of the* Handbook of Social Psychology *(1935, 1954, and 1968),
and his final chapter was reprinted in the 1985* Handbook.

a landmark handbook chapter by Gordon Allport, one of the founders of the field,
who stressed the central importance of attitudes. In 1935 he wrote:

> The concept of attitude is probably the most distinctive and indispensable concept in
> contemporary American social psychology. . . . This useful, one might almost say
> peaceful, concept has been so widely adopted that it has virtually established itself as
> the keystone in the edifice of American social psychology. (1935, p. 798)

Though there have been some periods since then when research in other areas of
social psychology, such as small-group dynamics, has somewhat overshadowed the
amount of work on attitudes, by and large the study of attitudes and related topics
has remained dominant (McGuire, 1985). Herbert Kelman, who succeeded Allport
as a professor at Harvard, has written: "In the years since publication of Allport's
paper, attitudes have, if anything, become even more central in social psychology"
(1974, p. 310). Recent reviews of the field agree that the high interest in attitude
research seems likely to continue in the foreseeable future (Cooper & Croyle, 1984;
Chaiken & Stangor, 1987; Tesser & Shaffer, 1990).

Nonscientists, as well as scientists, frequently use the concept of attitude in
their descriptions and explanations of human behavior. For instance, "She has a
very good attitude toward her work." Or, "His suspicious attitude made me want
to avoid him." In everyday conversation we often speak of a person's attitude as

the cause of his actions toward another person or an object; e.g., "Her hostile attitude was shown in everything she did." Similarly, in his 1935 review, Allport concluded that the concept of attitudes was "bearing most of the descriptive and explanatory burdens of social psychology" (Allport, 1935, p. 804).

Why is attitude such a popular and useful concept? We can point to several reasons:

1. "Attitude" is a *shorthand* term. A single attitude (e.g., love for one's family) can summarize many different behaviors (spending time with them, kissing them, comforting them, agreeing with them, doing things for them).

2. An attitude can be considered the *cause* of a person's behavior toward another person or an object.

3. The concept of attitude helps to explain the *consistency* of a person's behavior, since a single attitude may underlie many different actions. (In turn, Allport says, the consistency of individual behavior helps to explain the stability of society.)

4. Attitudes are *important in their own right,* regardless of their relation to a person's behavior. Your attitudes toward various individuals, institutions, and social issues (e.g., a political party, the church, capital punishment, the President of the United States) reflect the way you perceive the world around you, and they are worth studying for their own sake.

5. The concept of attitude is relatively *neutral and acceptable* to many theoretical schools of thought. For instance, it bridges the controversy between heredity and environment, since both instinct and learning can be involved in the formation of attitudes. It is broad enough to include the operation of unconscious determinants and the dynamic interplay of conflicting motives, which have been stressed by Freud and other psychoanalysts. At the same time it provides a topic of common interest to theorists as diverse as phenomenologists, behaviorists, and cognitive psychologists.

6. Attitude is an *interdisciplinary* concept. Not just psychologists but also sociologists, political scientists, communication researchers, and anthropologists all study attitudes. In particular, the subarea of public opinion—the shared attitudes of many members of a society—is of great interest to students of politics, public affairs, and communication.

Yet, in spite of the popularity and apparent utility of the concept of attitude to lay people and scientists alike, some theorists have challenged the value of the concept. Some of the crucial issues in this debate are definitional, and they are discussed later in this chapter. Other chapters analyze other aspects of the debate, as will be outlined a little later on.

Five Ways of Studying Attitudes

Five different ways of studying attitudes and opinions have typified most of the research studies in the area. Surprisingly, there has been very little overlap or interaction between the adherents of these five approaches, so that in most cases their work has been carried on with little cross-fertilization from the methods or findings of the other groups of researchers. The five different approaches are:

Description.   Attitude describers typically study the views held by a single interesting group of people (for instance, recent immigrants, or state legislators). Or they may compare the opinions of two or more groups (for example, the attitudes of white-collar workers versus those of blue-collar workers on the topic of labor unions). To some extent they may overlap with the next two groups of researchers (the measurers and the pollers), but the describers are usually less concerned with sophisticated quantification than are the measurers and less concerned with representative sampling than are the pollers. They are also less interested in understanding and explaining the underlying bases for attitudes than are the theorists and experimenters.

Measurement.   Attitude measurers have developed many highly sophisticated methods for quantifying and scaling attitudes. The best-known methods of building attitude scales are discussed in Chapter 3. It is surprising, but true, that public opinion pollers and attitude experimenters have made very little use of these sophisticated measurement methods, and attitude describers have made only a little more use of them.

Polls.   Public opinion pollers are generally concerned with the attitudes on important social issues held by very large groups of people (for instance, the voting intentions of all registered voters of a state, or the opinions about crime and punishment held by adult citizens). The procedures and problems of public opinion polling are discussed in Chapter 5. At their best, polls are careful to *sample* systematically or randomly (rather than haphazardly) from the total population so that their results will be *representative* of the opinions of the total population.

Theories.   Attitude theorists are primarily concerned with explaining the basic nature of attitudes, how attitudes are formed, and how they can be changed. In most cases they have not been concerned with the precise measurement of attitudes nor with their content, socially important or not. However, since they need to demonstrate the correctness of their theories through experimental evidence, there has been more overlap and interaction between the theorists and the experimenters than between any of the other groups. Chapters 9 and 10 will discuss both theories and research on attitude change.

Experiments.   By definition, experiments involve manipulating a situation so as to create two or more different levels of the independent variable (for instance, two different kinds of persuasive message) and observing their effect on the dependent variable. Attitude experimenters have concentrated on investigating the factors that can produce attitude *change* and on testing the hypotheses of the attitude theorists. They have usually been relatively unconcerned with sophisticated measurement methods, and they generally choose to experiment on attitude topics of little importance or relevance to their subjects, since such attitudes can more easily be changed in a short-term laboratory situation. However, there have also been a number of experiments done on topics of greater social importance, such as basic personal values, racial attitudes, or health-care practices.

Themes of This Book

There are a number of general themes that recur throughout this book and help to organize the information in the various content areas. The major ones are:

• Social cognition processes. **Social cognition** refers to our thought processes about people and social situations. It includes the ways we gather social information, organize it, and interpret it. Thus social cognition processes are important in determining the way our attitudes and opinions are formed, strengthened, and changed over the course of time.

• Functions of attitudes and opinions. Our attitudes and opinions are *useful* to us. They are convenient aids to our thinking, decisions, and actions in innumerable social situations. They summarize and organize our thoughts and reactions to other people, situations, objects, and ideas.

• Attitude measurement and research methods. Many specialized ways of measuring attitudes and opinions have been developed, and distinctive research methods have also been established, particularly in the areas of survey research and attitude change.

• Attitude formation and transmission. The processes by which attitudes and opinions are formed are important topics in many sections of this volume, as are the ways that attitudes and opinions are communicated, both through the mass media and through personal communication.

• Persuasion and attitude change. This is one of the areas most heavily studied by social psychologists, so portions of the immense research literature are discussed at many points in the text.

• Attitude-behavior relationships. As mentioned earlier, the choice of attitudes versus behavior as a major focus of study has long been a controversy in social psychology, and the question of how closely people's attitudes and behavior are related is a key issue in the field—one which is crucial in attempts to predict, understand, and/or change people's behavior.

• Social impact and policy implications of attitudes and opinions. This theme shows up at many points, in discussions of the structure of public opinion and of how (if at all) public opinion influences public policy or is influenced by it.

DEFINITIONS OF "ATTITUDE"

So far we have been using the term "attitude" without defining it. Since it is a common term in the English language, every reader will probably have a notion of its meaning. Unfortunately, however, there may be relatively little overlap between your notion and that of other readers. Indeed, there has sometimes been little overlap between the definitions of "attitude" suggested by different social scientists.

Originally the term "attitude" referred to a person's bodily position or posture, and it is still sometimes used in this way—for instance, "He sat slumped in an attitude of dejection." There is a marvelous example in Gilbert and Sullivan's operetta, *H.M.S. Pinafore*, in which the proper stance for a British tar is described (Gilbert, 1932, p. 31):

> His foot should stamp and his throat should growl,
> His hair should twirl and his face should scowl;
> His eyes should flash and his breast protrude,
> And this should be his customary attitude.

FIGURE 1-1 A British tar.

In social science, however, the term has come to mean a "posture of the mind," rather than of the body. In his careful review, Allport cited many definitions with varying emphases and concluded with a comprehensive definition of his own which has been widely adopted. The aspects stressed in the various definitions include attitude as a mental set or disposition, attitude as a readiness to respond, the physiological basis of attitudes, their permanence, their learned nature, and their evaluative character. Sample definitions illustrating each of these points are presented in Box 1–2, together with Allport's comprehensive definition. Though Allport's definition may seem unduly complex, careful thought will show that each of its phrases makes a specific and important contribution to understanding the concept. Interested readers might want to consult McGuire's classic chapter for a detailed presentation of the implications of every aspect of the definition (McGuire, 1969, pp. 142–149).

The central feature of all these definitions of attitude, according to Allport, is the idea of **readiness for response**. That is, an attitude is not behavior, not something that a person does; rather it is a preparation for behavior, a predisposition to respond in a particular way to the attitude object. The term **attitude object** is used to include things, people, places, ideas, actions, or situations, either singular or plural. For instance, it could be a group of people (e.g., teenagers), an inanimate object (e.g., the city park), an action (e.g., drinking beer), an abstract

---

Box 1–2 *Differing Definitions of "Attitude"*

*Many different aspects of the concept of "attitude" have been stressed in definitions offered by different authors:**

> *SET—[An attitude] denotes the general set of the organism as a whole toward an object or situation which calls for adjustment. (Lundberg, 1929)*

> *READINESS TO ACT—Attitude . . . a condition of readiness for a certain type of activity. (Warren, 1934)*

> *PHYSIOLOGICAL BASIS—The attitude, or preparation in advance of the actual response, constitutes an important determinant of the ensuing social behavior. Such neural settings, with their accompanying consciousness, are numerous and significant in social life. (F. H. Allport, 1924)*

> *PERMANENCE—. . . a more or less permanently enduring state of readiness of mental organization which predisposes an individual to react in a characteristic way to any object or situation with which it is related. (Cantril, 1934)*

> *LEARNED NATURE—An attitude, roughly, is a residuum of experience, by which further activity is conditioned and controlled. . . . We may think of attitudes as acquired tendencies to act in specific ways toward objects. (Krueger & Reckless, 1931)*

> *EVALUATIVE NATURE—An attitude is a tendency to act toward or against something in the environment, which becomes thereby a positive or negative value. (Bogardus, 1931)*

> *COMPREHENSIVE DEFINITION—An attitude is a mental or neural state of readiness, organized through experience, exerting a directive or dynamic influence upon the individual's response to all objects and situations with which it is related. (G. W. Allport, 1935)*

*The sources of all these definitions are fully referenced in Allport (1935).

Source: Extracts from pages 804, 805, and 810 of Allport, G. W., Attitudes. In C. Murchison (Ed.), *A Handbook of Social Psychology.* Worcester, Mass.: Clark University Press, 1935.

concept (e.g., civil rights), or an idea linking several concepts (e.g., rights of teenagers to drink beer in the city park).

Another point to note is the **motivating** or driving force of attitudes. That is, attitudes are not just a passive result of past experience. Instead they have two active functions, described by Allport as "exerting a directive or dynamic influence." "Dynamic" indicates that they impel or motivate behavior: i.e., they can be what behaviorists or psychoanalysts call "drives." "Directive" indicates that attitudes guide the form and manner of behavior into particular channels, encouraging some actions and deterring others.

The **relatively enduring** nature of attitudes is also important. This stability was illustrated by a study during the height of the Vietnam War when the feelings of college students were being hammered by dramatic and highly publicized events such as antiwar protests, U.S. troops crossing the Vietnam border to invade neutral Cambodia, and American National Guardsmen killing and injuring some students on two U.S. college campuses. For three years in a row Thistlethwaite (1974) measured many different attitudes of men enrolled at 25 American universities, and he found quite small average effects of even these dramatic events on the relevant social attitudes of the students. In other research, even over periods as long as *20 years*, people's values and vocational interests have been shown to have a high degree of stability, though other kinds of attitudes are apt to display greater fluctuations (Kelly, 1955).

In recent years the **evaluative** aspect of attitudes has been increasingly stressed. That is, an attitude is now generally seen as a disposition to respond *in a favorable or unfavorable manner* to given objects. For example, in many studies the evaluative dimension of Osgood's Semantic Differential (Osgood, Suci, & Tannenbaum, 1957) is used *alone*, without other dimensions, as the sole measure of attitudes. This emphasis is clearly shown in Bem's simple definition: "Attitudes are likes and dislikes" (1970, p. 14). Though this statement is an oversimplification, it emphasizes the central importance of the evaluative aspect of attitudes.

Since all of these aspects of attitudes are important, a comprehensive definition of the concept will be used in this book. A useful example of such a comprehensive definition of attitude is offered by Fishbein and Ajzen (1975, p. 6): "a learned predisposition to respond in a consistently favorable or unfavorable manner with respect to a given object."

THEORETICAL VIEWS ON ATTITUDE COMPONENTS

Tri-Componential Viewpoint

There are two main theoretical viewpoints about the essential nature of attitudes. The older one, called the **tri-componential viewpoint**, holds that an attitude is a single entity but that it has three aspects or components, as follows (see Figure 1–2):

1. A **cognitive** component, consisting of the ideas and beliefs which the attitude-holder has about the attitude object. For example, let us take Martians as an attitude object (you can substitute any other group if you wish). Examples of the cognitive component of an attitude would be:

> "Martians look strange—they have green skins and antennae coming out of their foreheads."
>
> "Martians can read your thoughts."

2. An **affective (emotional)** component. This refers to the feelings and emotions one has toward the object. For instance:

> "Martians make me feel uncomfortable—I hate to think of them reading my mind."
>
> "I don't like Martians."

3. A **behavioral** component, consisting of one's action tendencies toward the object. For example:

> "If I saw a Martian, I'd run away as fast as I could."
>
> "I certainly wouldn't let one into my club nor allow my daughter to marry one."

This conceptual distinction between thoughts, feelings, and actions as separate but interrelated parts of an attitude has a long history in philosophy. Though the term "attitude" was first used by Herbert Spencer in 1862 (Allport, 1985), the thought-emotion-behavior distinction is essentially identical with one made by Plato, who used the terminology of cognition, affection, and conation.

However, honored as this tripartite division is in tradition, and clear as it seems conceptually, there is still an important question about its *empirical* validity

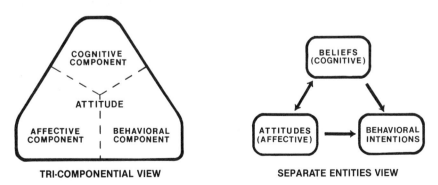

TRI-COMPONENTIAL VIEW **SEPARATE ENTITIES VIEW**

FIGURE 1-2 Two viewpoints on components of attitudes.

and usefulness. The view of attitudes as having separate cognitive, affective, and behavioral components raises the question of consistency between these components. This view requires a relatively high (but not perfect) degree of consistency. If there is little or no consistency among them, there is no reason to consider the three components as aspects of the same concept (attitude); instead they would have to be viewed as entirely independent entities. On the other hand, if they are perfectly correlated, they cannot be separate components; in this case they would merely be different names for the same thing.

McGuire (1969, p. 157) concluded, after surveying the literature, that the three components have proven to be so highly intercorrelated that "theorists who insist on distinguishing them should bear the burden of proving that the distinction is worthwhile." However, an opposite conclusion was reached by Krech, Crutchfield, and Ballachey (1962), who favor the tripartite view. On the basis of their review of the literature, they stated that there is only a "moderately high" relationship between the three components (typically, a correlation coefficient of about +.5); and they even cited evidence from one study showing a relationship as low as $r = +.2$ or $+.3$ between the cognitive and behavioral components. More recent studies have confirmed the view that there is generally a moderately strong relationship among the three components (Bagozzi, Tybout, Craig, & Sternthal, 1979; Breckler, 1984).

Separate Entities Viewpoint

The newer theoretical view of attitudes is that the three components described above are distinct, **separate entities** which may or may not be related, depending on the particular situation (see Figure 1–2). This viewpoint has been strongly advocated by Fishbein and Ajzen (1975). They suggest that the term "attitude" be reserved solely for the affective dimension, indicating evaluation or favorability toward an object. The cognitive dimension they label as "beliefs," which they define as indicating a person's subjective probability that an object has a particular characteristic (for example, how sure the person feels that "This book is interesting," or that "Smoking marijuana is no more dangerous than drinking alcohol"). The behavioral dimension they refer to as "behavioral intentions," defined as indicating a person's subjective probability that (s)he will perform a particular behavior toward an object (e.g., "I intend to read this book," or "I am going to write my congressperson about legalization of marijuana").

Fishbein and Ajzen point out that a person usually has various beliefs about the same object and that these beliefs are not necessarily related. For instance, if someone believes "This book is interesting," that person may or may not also believe that "This book is attractively printed" or that "This book is inexpensive." The same situation also holds true for behavioral intentions. "I intend to read this book" does not imply "I am going to buy this book" nor even "I am going to study this book carefully." By contrast, these authors say, all measures of a person's *affect* toward a particular object should be highly related. "I like this book" *does* imply "I enjoy reading it," and such responses should be quite consistent with the same person's answers to an attitude scale evaluating the book.

A final point about the separate entities viewpoint is that there is no necessary congruence among beliefs, attitudes, and behavioral intentions, which the tricomponential viewpoint would consider all aspects of the same attitude. "I like this book" (attitude) does *not* necessarily imply "This book is inexpensive" (belief), nor does it imply "I am going to buy this book" (behavioral intention). Thus these distinctions provide a justification for treating the three concepts as entirely separate entities. This viewpoint seems to have both theoretical and empirical advantages over the older tripartite view of attitude components, and it is the viewpoint endorsed by this text.

The conflicting findings mentioned above about the varying degrees of relationship among the three attitude "components" in different studies give support to the separate entities viewpoint because it does not require a necessary connection among these concepts but does allow for a strong relationship under certain specified conditions. Fishbein and Ajzen (1972) point out that most attitude scales are made up of several items stating various beliefs and/or intentions about the attitude object. However, many beliefs or intentions will not make satisfactory items for such a scale. Examples include beliefs which are so widely agreed upon that they are not held differentially by people with different attitudes ("President Bush is a Republican"); or statements whose evaluative significance is ambiguous (e.g., "As a national leader, President Bush's performance was about average"—disagreement here might indicate either a high or a low evaluation of Bush). Thus, it is only when an "attitude scale" has been carefully constructed from several well-chosen belief or intention items that we should expect it to correlate highly with other standard attitude measures. And in any case there will always be many possible items about particular beliefs and/or behavioral intentions which will not correlate highly with such a scale (e.g., "I believe President Bush is the Messiah," or "I am going to write President Bush a letter").

RELATED CONCEPTS

Having defined "attitude," we need now to present brief definitions of several other terms that are related to the concept of attitude, or are sometimes even used synonymously with it. You should keep in mind that each of these terms has been used and defined in various ways, and that there is never complete agreement with any given usage. However, these definitions will help to clarify the distinctions between these terms and the concept of attitude.

Belief

We have seen that Fishbein and Ajzen (1975) define **beliefs** as statements indicating a person's subjective probability that an object has a particular characteristic. Another way of putting this is that they assert the truth or falsity of propositions about the object, or that they state a relationship between the object and some characteristic. For instance: "This book is informative," "Einstein's theory of relativity is important," "My boss is easygoing." This viewpoint is advantageous in that it distinguishes clearly between beliefs and attitudes: Beliefs are cognitive—thoughts and ideas; whereas attitudes are affective—feelings and emotions.

This raises a question, however, about how to treat an intermediate category which we may call **evaluative beliefs**: that is, beliefs which state a value judgment about an object. For instance: "My boss is a nice guy," or "Freedom of the press is a good thing." Clearly, evaluative beliefs are closely linked to attitudes of liking or disliking, and sometimes they are almost indistinguishable from them. For instance: "My boss is a nice guy" (evaluative belief), and "I like my boss" (attitude). A good resolution of this issue is to consider that *a person's attitude toward an object is a summary of all of his or her evaluative beliefs about the object*.

An alternative approach is to consider beliefs, both evaluative and nonevaluative, as the cognitive component of attitudes (cf. Krech, Crutchfield, & Ballachey, 1962, p. 178). However, this approach may produce problems because it implies a necessary consistency between the three components of attitudes. As mentioned in the previous section, often beliefs and attitudes are not completely consistent, and sometimes they are not even closely related. Thus, this approach is less desirable than drawing a clear distinction between beliefs and attitudes.

Opinion

As the title of this book indicates, **opinion** is an important concept and one closely related to the concept of attitude. Sometimes the two terms have been used synonymously, leading McGuire (1969, p. 152) to characterize the situation as "names in search of a distinction, rather than a distinction in search of a terminology." However, more often, distinctions have been made between attitudes and opinions, though there are many different views as to what the nature of the distinction should be.

The viewpoint that we prefer is that *opinions are equivalent to beliefs*, rather than to attitudes. That is, they are usually narrower in content or scope than the general evaluative orientation which we call an attitude, and they are primarily cognitive rather than emotion-laden. Another way of putting this is that opinions involve a person's judgments about the likelihood of events or relationships, whereas attitudes involve a person's feelings or emotions about objects or events. Thus, in this view, "I think this book is interesting" is an opinion or belief, whereas "I like this book" is an attitude.

A distinction that has occasionally been proposed is based on overtness versus covertness of expression. The ultimate extension of this view is to regard an opinion as merely the overt verbal or written expression of an underlying, covert attitude (e.g., Childs, 1965). However, if that is the only distinction, there is no need for two different terms, since one can just as easily use the term "attitude statement" instead of opinion. Also, this distinction is undesirable because it is contrary to the common-sense notions that a person can hold an opinion without expressing it, and that a person can state an attitude in words.

McGuire (1985) warns about definitional distinctions such as the ones we have been considering, emphasizing that in order to be useful they must have clearcut empirical consequences. He questions the value of distinguishing between attitudes and opinions, saying:

> Distinctions deserve to be made only insofar as they make a difference such that the distinguished variables relate differently to third variables of interest. (p. 241)

In our conceptual view, the nature of "opinions" is identical to that of "beliefs." Since there are now extensive research findings showing differential relationships of beliefs and attitudes to other concepts (e.g., Fishbein & Ajzen, 1975), it is important to make a clear distinction between attitudes and opinions.

Nevertheless, the term "opinion" continues to be used synonymously with "attitude," particularly in the area of survey research and polling. There the phrase **public opinion** is the commonly accepted term to designate the shared attitudes *and* beliefs of large segments of a society. We will discuss public opinion further in a later section of this chapter.

Value

There is more general agreement about the relationship of values to attitudes than about the previous terms. The most common view is that a **value** is an important life-goal or societal condition desired by a person (Rokeach, 1968). Values are usually broad abstract concepts like freedom, justice, beauty, happiness, or service to others, though sometimes they are more concrete, such as money or material possessions. Values are ends rather than means—the goals a person strives to reach rather than the methods that (s)he uses to get there.

Since values are a person's goals or standards in life, it is clear that individuals will have strong positive attitudes toward the values they hold. Thus values can be viewed as very special attitude objects—situations where strong favorable attitudes are directed toward abstract concepts concerned with one's major goals for oneself or for the world. In addition, values are very important and central in a person's whole system of attitudes and beliefs—that is, they are resistant to change, and they influence many other beliefs and attitudes (Rokeach, 1979; Kahle, 1983; Tetlock, 1986). For instance, if you have a key value of piety, it will influence your views about many religious concepts and issues, as well as your attitudes toward national leaders, friends, activities, and so on. On the other hand, if patriotism is your main value, you will favor different activities and leaders: you will wave the flag, go to July 4th parades, and applaud patriotic speeches, rather than spending your time in religious services, prayer, or listening to broadcast evangelists.

Habit

Habits can also be easily distinguished from attitudes. They are frequently-repeated patterns of behavior, whereas attitudes are not behavior. Habits are usually quite automatic and standardized in their manner of performance, but they require the presence of the appropriate stimulus object in order to occur (e.g., saying "sir" to a superior officer in the armed forces). By contrast, attitudes may be expressed in many different ways, and even in the absence of the stimulus object (e.g., I like to watch snow falling even though, as a Southern Californian, I haven't seen any close-up in several years). Like attitudes, habits are learned through experience, but unlike them, they are frequently nonevaluative in nature. For instance, a habit of scratching one's head or of saying "you know" frequently in conversation does not necessarily imply a favorable attitude toward these activities. However, some habits are evaluative; for instance, a habit of voting Democratic probably would imply a favorable attitude toward the Democratic Party (Allport, 1935).

ATTITUDES ARE INFERRED

We have defined attitudes as constituting a readiness for response, but we stated that they are not behavior per se. Thus, it follows that they cannot be directly observed, as habits or other responses can be. How then can we reach conclusions about them? Only through a process of inference, based on the study of responses which *are* observable. Allport (1935) phrased the situation clearly:

> how does one know that [attitudes] exist at all? Only by necessary inference. There *must* be something to account for the consistency of conduct. It is the meaningful resemblances between activities and their congruence with one another that leads the psychologist inescapably to postulate some such generalized forms of readiness as the term "attitude" denotes. (p. 836)

Campbell (1963) stated a similar view: "A social attitude is (or is evidenced by) consistency in response to social objects" (p. 96).

Thus an attitude has the status of an **intervening variable**: that is, an attitude is a theoretical construct which is not observable in itself, but which mediates or helps to explain the relationship between certain observable stimulus events (the environmental situation) and certain behavioral responses. For instance, the concept that a man has a prejudiced attitude can help to explain the relationship between such an antecedent event as his being seated next to a black person and such responses as an increase in his galvanic skin response (GSR) measure, or his getting up and moving to a different chair. Similarly, a women's political attitudes can help to explain why she would go to hear and cheer a speech by one political candidate, but turn off the TV when a different candidate was on the air.

A diagram of this view of attitudes is shown in Figure 1-3. It indicates that a person's attitudes are the result of his or her past experiences (both vicarious and

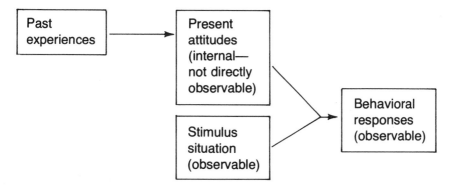

FIGURE 1–3 Attitudes are unobservable intervening variables which influence the relationship between stimulus events and behavioral responses.

actual), and that they combine with the present stimulus situation to determine the person's responses.

Latent Process Viewpoint. This definition of attitude as an unobservable intervening variable has also been termed the "latent process" viewpoint (DeFleur & Westie, 1963). That is, this viewpoint postulates a hidden process occurring within the individual, which we call an attitude; and it uses this attitude as an explanation of the relationship between stimulus events and the individual's responses.

Probability Viewpoint. Another viewpoint on the nature of attitudes is the behavioristic, or positivistic, one. This viewpoint avoids all intervening variables and insists on direct operational measures of all concepts used. In this framework "attitude" would be defined as a particular type of response, rather than as a readiness to respond. For instance, a woman's attitude might be operationally defined as her response to a specific question, or to a set of questions about her likes and dislikes, or as an increase in her GSR measure, or as her willingness to be photographed in a social situation with a black man. DeFleur and Westie (1963) have called this the "probability" definition of attitude—defining it in terms of the *probability of occurrence* of a particular response or type of response.

There are a number of difficulties presented by the probability position. First, a habit is a typical response or behavior pattern of an individual, and its probability of occurrence can be determined. But, as mentioned in the previous section, many habits are nonevaluative in nature and hence cannot be considered as attitudes. Thus the occurrence of such kinds of habitual responses could not be used as an indication of a person's attitude, and the same thing is true of many isolated nonhabitual responses. As Fishbein and Ajzen (1972) have pointed out, "if a single belief or intention is to be used as an index of attitude, evidence has to be provided for a high correlation between responses to that item and some standard measure of attitude" (p. 496).

A second difficulty with the probability or behavioristic viewpoint has been noted by McGuire (1985, p. 240), who raised the objection that in practice it would be exceedingly inefficient. This is so because it requires that the relationship between each antecedent measure and each response measure must be separately established, instead of linking each antecedent measure to just one intervening variable (the attitude) and then in turn linking the single attitude to the various response measures. For instance, antecedent variables for a racially prejudiced attitude might include parental teaching, bad personal experiences with blacks, growing up in the South, etc. Under the probability viewpoint, each separate type of response must be considered as a separate attitude (e.g., telling antiblack stories or jokes, not sitting next to blacks, increases in GSR in their presence, etc.). Thus, without the convenience of considering attitude as an intervening variable, there would be an overwhelming number of relationships to measure between all the antecedent variables and all the response variables.

Finally, Campbell (1963) has pointed out that in actual practice the behaviorists follow the same procedure as other investigators by *inferring* attitudes from a pattern of responses:

> even those whose behavioristic orientation leads to a rejection of such mentalistic definitions as Allport's . . . in research practice do not equate *isolated* responses with attitudes; but on the contrary, look for the appearance of *response consistencies*. (p. 96)

Thus, in practice, there is little if any difference in the way that latent process theorists and probabilistic theorists actually measure and study attitudes.

WHAT IS PUBLIC OPINION?

You are undoubtedly familiar with public opinion polls such as those of George Gallup and Louis Harris, and you know that they involve asking questions of large groups of people. However, you might be surprised to learn that the term "public opinion" is one which has led to just as many difficulties in definition as the term "attitude" (Bennett, 1980).

In general, **public opinion** refers to the shared opinions and attitudes of large groups of people (sometimes called "publics") who have particular characteristics in common—e.g., all registered voters in Illinois, or all small business owners in a particular city. However, there are some aspects of more complete definitions which have provoked debate for 200 years or more. In the very first issue of the *Public Opinion Quarterly*, Floyd Allport (1937) presented a seminal discussion of problems in defining the concept of public opinion. Harwood Childs (1965) reviewed these debates and problems in detail and concluded that it is unwisely restrictive to include additional specifications in defining "public opinion," such as the particular public involved, the subject matter of the opinions, or the extent of consensus, etc. Box 1–3 contains a sample of specific definitions of "public opinion," presented both for their great variety and their historical interest. The list concludes with Child's general definition, which is recommended as the most useful one for our purposes because of its breadth and lack of restrictions.

Historically, public opinion polls were used to get indications of the strength

---

Box 1–3   *Differing Definitions of "Public Opinion"*

Many varied definitions of the concept of "public opinion" have been suggested by different authors over the years, emphasizing the following specific aspects:*

RATIONALLY FORMED—*Public opinion is the social judgment of a self-conscious community on a question of general import after rational public discussion. (Young, 1923)*

WELL-INFORMED (ELITE GROUP)—*Public opinion may be said to be that sentiment on any given subject which is entertained by the best informed, most intelligent, and most moral persons in the community. (MacKinnon, 1828)*

HELD BY SECONDARY GROUP—*When the group involved is a public or secondary group, rather than a primary, face-to-face group, we have public opinion (Folsom, 1931). What the members of any indirect contact group or public think or feel about anything and everything. (Bernard, 1926)*

IMPORTANT TOPIC—*The attitudes, feelings, or ideas of the large body of the people about important public issues. (Minar, 1960)*

EXTENT OF AGREEMENT—*. . . a majority is not enough, and unanimity is not required, but the opinion must be such that while the majority may not share it, they feel bound, by conviction, not by fear, to accept it. (Lowell, 1913)*

INTENSITY—*. . . public opinion is more than a matter of numbers. The intensity of the opinions is quite as important. Public opinion is a composite of numbers and intensity. (Munro, 1931)*

MODE OF RESPONSE—*Public opinion consists of people's reactions to definitely worded statements and questions under interview conditions. (Warner, 1939)*

EFFECTIVE INFLUENCE—*Public opinion in this discussion may simply be taken to mean those opinions held by private persons which governments find it prudent to heed. (Key, 1961)*

GENERAL DEFINITION—*The study of public opinion is, therefore, the study of collections of individual opinions wherever they may be found. (Childs, 1965)*

*The sources of all these definitions are fully referenced in Childs (1965).

of political candidates as early as 1824. In that year newspapers reported two straw votes, one in Delaware and one in North Carolina, where select groups of citizens were asked who they preferred for President. Interestingly enough, Andrew Jackson won both of these "polls," though it was not until 1828 that he gained wide enough support to be elected President (Roll & Cantril, 1980).

We will take up the characteristics of modern public opinion polls, as well as issues and problems involved in such polling, at length in Chapter 5. Building on that background, Chapter 6 will describe the structure of public opinion, and Chapter 11 will discuss the relationship of public opinion to public policy.

APPROACHES TO ATTITUDE AND OPINION RESEARCH

Different disciplines have typically approached the study of attitudes and opinions in rather different ways. The four major disciplines which treat attitudes and opinions as part of their subject matter are sociology, communication research, political science, and psychology. In each field there have been many scientists who have done excellent, highly regarded work on attitudes and opinions, utilizing a variety of approaches. Though it is dangerous to overgeneralize, some of the five ways of studying attitudes mentioned early in this chapter are more common in each field than are others.

In sociology, the most frequently used method of attitude research has been *description* of various social groups. Quite often the choice of groups to study has been based on variables such as social class or position in an organization (e.g., supervisors, or blue-collar workers). To a lesser extent such research also usually involves some emphasis on attitude *measurement* through written questionnaires or interviews.

In communication research, the typical approach has also involved *description* as well as *measurement*, but the subject matter is usually written or spoken messages. Here the method of study is generally **content analysis,** a careful systematic method of describing the manifest and/or latent content of written or oral communications (cf. Krippendorff, 1980).

In political science, the most common approach has been *polling*, though again some workers have used other methods, particularly *description*. A predominant interest in political science has been the study of public opinion, and the most common way of determining public opinion is to use a face-to-face interview, asking many detailed questions of a large sample of people from the relevant classification (e.g., voters, PTA members, or business executives).

In psychology, the most common way of studying attitudes has been *experimentation*, though each of the other approaches has had its adherents. Usually the focus of experiments has been on attempts to change an attitude by manipulating one or more situational factors and/or measuring individual differences (such as personality dimensions) which are related to attitude change. Very often the attitude chosen for changing is one that is unimportant or even completely new to the subjects, so that it can be influenced more easily, and generally only immediate or short-term attitude change has been studied.

We will see many of these research features and the approaches typical of each discipline illustrated in the ensuing chapters.

SUMMARY

The concept of attitude was a very important one in social psychology's formative years and still remains so today. Though many conflicting definitions have been offered, in general, an attitude can be defined as a readiness to respond in a favorable or unfavorable manner to a particular class of objects. Attitudes have been studied using five relatively independent approaches: description, measurement, polls, theories, and experiments. A traditional view of attitudes is that they have three interrelated components: cognitive, affective, and behavioral. However, a preferable newer approach is to consider these three aspects as separate and distinct entities, calling them beliefs, attitudes, and behavioral intentions.

Beliefs, opinions, values, and habits are concepts which are related to the concept of attitude, but are not synonymous with it. Whereas an attitude is a general evaluative orientation toward an object, a belief or an opinion is narrower in scope and more cognitive in nature. "Public opinion" refers to the shared opinions and attitudes of many members of a society.

It is universally agreed that attitudes and opinions are inferred from behavioral responses. However, there are conflicting views as to whether they should be considered theoretically as unobservable intervening variables (the "latent process" viewpoint, which is favored in this text) or merely as probabilistic summaries of a person's consistency in making a particular response.

2

Social Perception and Social Cognition

The human understanding when it has once adopted an opinion draws all things else to support and agree with it.—Francis Bacon, 1620.

Thinking is the hardest work there is, which is the probable reason why so few engage in it.—Henry Ford.

Think of a woman whom you met for the first time recently. When you first set eyes on her, you recognized her as being a person and a woman, and you noted certain facts about her—perhaps her height, build, and hair color, or the type of clothes she was wearing. You may have inferred other facts about her—estimated her age and activities from her behavior, or guessed where she grew up from her accent. In addition, you probably made other, more subjective judgments about her—her personality, interests, attractiveness, intelligence, friendliness, and so on. Some of your judgments may have been influenced by stereotypes that you already held about different categories of people—about Southerners, overweight people, athletic types, or socialites. All of these types of perception and judgment fall in the realm of social cognition.

Social cognition refers to our thought processes about other people, ourselves, and social situations—that is, how we understand and make sense of social stimuli. Social cognition includes the ways in which people gather social information, organize it, and interpret it. It is intimately related to the topic of attitudes, for social perceptions, beliefs, and attributions comprise the cognitive components on which attitudes are based. As a research area, social cognition has experienced an explosion of activity since about 1975 (Wyer & Srull, 1984; Higgins & Bargh, 1987).

CHARACTERISTICS OF PERCEPTION

The first stage of social cognition is **perception**, the reception and organization of sensory information about people or social situations. Social perception, like our perception of any object or situation, has a number of important character-istics (Schneider, Hastorf, & Ellsworth, 1979). We can illustrate these characteris-tics by considering a concrete situation: you have just entered an office and you see another person seated behind a desk.

1. Perception is *immediate*. As you first glance into the room, you are immediately aware of the person there. There is no apparent delay in this process of awareness.

2. Perception is *selective*. Your attention focuses on only a few objects out of the multitude that are within your sensory range. For instance, you may note the person and the desk but ignore the walls, the floor covering, pictures, and other objects in the room, even though they impinge on your sense organs just as much or even more than the person or the desk. Thus perception is an *active* process, not just a passive receptive process.

3. Perception is *structured*. Though your eyes merely receive light waves of various frequencies and degrees of brightness, you organize that complex stimula-tion into a pattern of shapes, colors, and sizes. The separate groups of stimuli—hair, face, clothes, hands, etc.—are integrated into a structured whole: you perceive a person.

4. Perception is *stable*. This is best illustrated by our experience of **constan-cies** in perception: the apparent size, shape, and color of objects remain constant even though we view them from different distances and angles and in different amounts of light. For example, as you approach the person and the desk, their images on your retina increase in size, but you don't perceive them as growing taller or wider.

5. Perception is *meaningful*. In interpreting a pattern of stimuli as a person, you have already imparted meaning to the sensory experience, but you don't stop there. You immediately integrate aspects of their facial features, body build, cloth-ing, hair style, and so on, and you perceive the person as male or female, young or old, tall or short, stout or thin. Similarly, animals are perceived as being cats or dogs, birds or reptiles, and objects are understood as boxes, bricks, or houses. Thus our perceptual experience is organized into meaningful categories.

Social Perception

There are also some ways that perception of people is unlike perception of objects (Schneider et al., 1979). We perceive people (and sometimes animals, but not inanimate objects) as causal agents. They do certain things, and they have various intentions and personal traits, whereas objects are not perceived as having intrinsic causal efficacy, intentions, or traits. (The issues of causality, intentions, and personal characteristics are central to the topic of attribution, which is dis-cussed later in this chapter.) Second, we perceive personal interactions as being dynamic. That is, unlike objects, other people adjust their behavior in response to us, and vice versa. Third, because we expect other people to have basic human characteristics like our own, we typically perceive them as having specific emo-tions and attitudes that are not directly observable.

Our perception of the world around us is usually quite accurate, or **veridical**. If it were not, our lives and welfare would constantly be endangered by our mistakes in judging the height of curbs, the speed of approaching cars, the heat of stoves, and so on. However, we know that sometimes our senses can be fooled, as they are in the misleading perceptual situations that we call **illusions**. Similarly, the visual cues that we all normally rely on can sometimes mislead us. For instance, the clarity of outlines helps us determine the nearness of objects; but when visibility is poor, as in foggy weather, the distance of objects is often overestimated because their outlines are blurred, and as a result our chances of crashing into the car ahead of us are increased. On the other hand, when visibility is unusually good, the contours of objects are seen very sharply, and consequently the objects seem much closer than they really are, like mountains in clear desert air (Tversky & Kahneman, 1974).

Though physical perception is occasionally mistaken, *social* perception is much more likely to be inaccurate, for it suffers from numerous sources of subjectivity and unreliability. We turn now to a discussion of some of the main sources of potential error.

COMMON THOUGHT PROCESSES

There are many thought processes that people use to simplify and give order to their everyday decisions and interactions with others. In recent years these processes of social cognition have been much studied by both cognitive psychologists (Tversky & Kahneman, 1974) and social psychologists (Ross, 1977). We will discuss two aspects of such thought processes, heuristics and biases.

Heuristics

The adjective *heuristic* means "helpful in discovering things." As described by Tversky and Kahneman (1974), **heuristics** are convenient, informal guides that people find helpful and often follow in making decisions or predictions. Among the most important and frequently used ones are the availability, adjustment, and representativeness heuristics.

The Availability Heuristic. This is the use of readily available (salient) information about events, such as instances that are easily remembered or imagined. It is often used in making estimates of the frequency or probability of events. For example, if you were asked what percentage of people have serious automobile accidents each year, an easy and convenient basis for making your estimate would be to think of how many accidents you could remember among your friends or relatives. If you could easily recall several serious crashes, you would probably give a higher estimate than if you could remember no auto accidents among your acquaintances.

In general, use of the availability heuristic aids people in making accurate estimates (Hogarth, 1981), for when examples of some kind of event (such as thunder showers) can be remembered easily, that type of event may have been quite frequent. However, the availability heuristic can and often does lead people to incorrect judgments as well. For instance, hearing news reports of a violent crime—a dramatically available, salient bit of information—leads people to increase their estimates of the frequency of such crimes, and as a consequence they often substantially overestimate the occurrence of crimes (Doob, 1982; Wolfgang & Weiner, 1982). The selective emphasis of media coverage often contributes to such erroneous estimates. Careful studies have shown that people underestimate the frequency of fatal diseases, which are relatively rarely reported in U.S. newspapers, and overestimate the frequency of accidents, fires, tornadoes, murders, and other violent causes of death, which are much more often reported in the media. Thus, media coverage of such events contributes to their salience in people's awareness, and subjective judgments of their frequency are correlated as much as .70 or more with the amount of media coverage (Slovic, Fischhoff, & Lichtenstein, 1980).

Availability also enters into the estimation of risks involved in possible future courses of action. Use of one's imagination to construct scenarios of possible future events has been termed the **simulation heuristic** (Kahneman & Tversky, 1982). A typical example can be seen in the planning of the abortive attempt to rescue the U.S. hostages held in Iran in 1980. The planners of the expedition could easily imagine the many dangers involved in the final stage of achieving surprise and reaching the hostages before they could be moved or killed by their captors, and they laid elaborate plans to overcome those problems. What they failed to anticipate were the more-mundane, less-salient difficulties that could be caused by dust storms and failures of helicopter parts in the earlier stages. Thus they provided too few extra helicopters, and the mission had to be canceled before it reached its difficult final stage. Janis (1985) has referred to this kind of problem as the "unsqueaky wheel trap," because the unsqueaky wheel gets little attention.

The Adjustment Heuristic. This approach involves making estimates or predictions by starting with some salient initial value (an **anchor**) and "adjusting" it upwards or downwards. However, the adjustments that people make are usually too small, and the result is an **anchoring effect**, in which the initial value overinfluences the subsequent predictions (e.g., Peake & Cervone, 1989). A common situation where this heuristic is displayed is in people's predictions of the future range of some index, such as the Dow-Jones stock market average's range during the coming year. Most people apparently start with the current level as their initial value, and they frequently underadjust, thus predicting a range which is narrower than the values that actually occur.

Apparently the anchor that individuals use for estimating the behavior of other people is frequently their own norms or habits. We may know intellectually that many other people don't feel or act as we do, and yet we are still unlikely to

Photo courtesy of Daniel Kahneman.
Reprinted by permission.

Photo courtesy of Amos Tversky.
Reprinted by permission.

Box 2–1   DANIEL KAHNEMAN and AMOS TVERSKY, *Analysts of Judgment and Decision Making*

Daniel Kahneman and Amos Tversky are unique in being the first team of unrelated psychologists to be jointly honored with the American Psychological Association's Distinguished Scientific Contribution Award. In their collaboration they originated the concept of heuristics as aids to people's judgments about uncertain events, and they developed "prospect theory" as an alternative to the classical rational theory of choice among risky options. Their partnership began at the Hebrew University in Jerusalem in 1969 and has continued to the present in North America, resulting in one joint book and more than 17 joint articles.

Both Kahneman and Tversky were born in Israel in the 1930s, attended Hebrew University, spent a period in military service, earned their Ph.D.s in the United States in the 1960s, and soon returned to teach at Hebrew University. Kahneman's doctorate is from Berkeley, Tversky's from the University of Michigan, but both specialized in mathematical and statistical aspects of psychology. Both spent separate periods as Fellows at Harvard's Center for Cognitive Studies and a joint period at the Oregon Research Institute. In the late 1970s, Tversky moved to Stanford, and Kahneman moved to the University of British Columbia and later to Berkeley.

Each of them has also maintained independent research programs and published several other books and many articles—Kahneman on the topics of attention and perception, Tversky on mathematical psychology and measurement. Though an early colleague predicted that their collaboration wouldn't last long "because of differences in temperament and style," they found that they greatly enjoyed their tenacious arguments about the best way to express their ideas. For several years they spent up to half of their working time together, carefully choosing every word of their joint papers, and they marvel at their good fortune in finding "that serious work could be so much fun."

adjust our estimates of their behavior far enough away from the anchor provided by our own standards. In a clever demonstration of this phenomenon, students were asked if they would be willing to walk around their college campus for 30 minutes wearing a large advertising placard saying "Eat at Joe's." Some students agreed to do so, while others were unwilling. Then they were asked to estimate what percentage of their classmates would have made the same decision they did. Those who had agreed to wear the sandwich board estimated that 62% of other students would also agree, while those who refused estimated that only 33% of students would agree to the task (Ross, Greene, & House, 1977).

Other experiments have established the important finding that anchoring effects can positively or negatively influence estimates of one's own abilities, and those estimates in turn can affect one's later behavioral persistence in a task, becoming "self-fulfilling prophecies" (Cervone & Peake, 1986). Such effects may be one of the sources of "learned helplessness"—clarifying, for instance, why children from deprived backgrounds become discouraged from trying to go on to higher education.

The Representativeness Heuristic.   This is a method of making judgments or predictions about probability by relying on bits of information that you consider representative (typical) features of a group or category. For instance, you might believe that librarians are typically neat and tidy people. Then, if you were asked to guess whether various individuals were librarians or not, you might look for evidence about whether they were neat and tidy. While using these limited cues, people commonly ignore other useful data such as the amount of evidence available, the reliability and/or validity of the evidence, the likelihood of statistical regression effects, and **base-rates** of the behavior being predicted (i.e., its probability in the population at large, or "prior probability"—Tversky & Kahneman, 1974, 1982).

To take an example, suppose you were told that Joe Green had been a star Little League ballplayer, and you were then asked to predict whether he was now a professional baseball player or a business executive. Since being a star athlete as a child is a common or representative characteristic of later professional athletes, you might rely on that cue and predict that Joe became a pro player. However, such a procedure would overlook the scantiness of the single predictor cue, the fact that *many* star Little Leaguers do not go on to big league sports, and the base-rate information that there are many more business executives than professional baseball players. Thus being a star youth athlete is not a very valid predictor of later professional status, and the base-rate probabilities strongly suggest that many more youthful stars become business executives than become pro athletes.

Biases

Biases of common thought processes often result from or are combined with the above heuristics in people's decisions or predictions, producing many errors in judgment. Among the important biases that we will discuss are: the "fundamental attribution error," underestimation of role-related behavior, the false consensus bias, overlooking nonoccurrences, reliance on vivid or concrete evidence, ignoring base-rates, making overly extreme predictions, and the persistence of initial impressions (Ross, 1977; Nisbett & Ross, 1980). Note that we are dealing here with purely cognitive sources of bias, not *motivational* ones such as the phenomenon of wishful thinking—increased belief in the likelihood of something desirable because we *want* it to be true (Tversky & Kahneman, 1974).

The Fundamental Attribution Error. The so-called fundamental attribution error is the widespread human tendency to overestimate the importance of personal characteristics as the causes of other people's behavior and to underestimate the importance of situational influences. For instance, if you observe one person hurting another, you are more likely to explain it in terms of the first person having a hostile or sadistic personality than to attribute it to situational conditions that forced the first person's actions. This was demonstrated experimentally in Bierbrauer's (1973) reenactment of the classic Milgram (1963) study where subjects supposedly delivered strong shocks to a victim. In the reenactment, even participants who had taken the role of the person giving the shock overlooked the strength of the situational forces compelling that behavior and dramatically underestimated the percentage of people who would yield to those situational forces. In a real-life situation, the same tendency was seen in people's condemnation of Patti Hearst for yielding to the persistent, overwhelming threats of her Symbionese Liberation Army captors, as if submitting indicated a defect in her personality.

Underestimation of Role-Related Aspects of Behavior. This is a common tendency that is closely related to the fundamental attribution error. Holding a social role such as teacher, boss, or member of the upper class confers considerable control over one's personal interactions and thus offers many opportunities to display one's strengths and conceal one's weaknesses. The cognitive tendency to overlook the extent of role-related behavior adds to our overestimation of the importance of personal characteristics. For instance, a teacher can appear very knowledgeable by confining class discussions to topics that he or she knows a lot about and avoiding other topics. An experimental demonstration of this principle required one participant to think up questions on any esoteric informational topic, which another person had to try to answer. In this situation, both the answerers and uninvolved observers typically overestimated the difference in the two individuals' knowledge, saying that the questioner was much more knowledgeable than the answerer. Thus they overlooked the impact of the participants' roles in the situation (Ross, Amabile, & Steinmetz, 1977).

The False Consensus Bias. This is one result of the availability heuristic discussed above. It is displayed in the fact that most people overestimate the frequency of other people's acting or thinking the same way as themselves (Fields & Schuman, 1976; Ross, Greene, & House, 1977). For instance, if you have recently fed pigeons in the park, learned to ski, gone to an art exhibit, or taken some other distinctive action, you will usually remember having done so and consequently tend to overestimate how often other people do the same things. In addition to the availability of such memories, there are several other cognitive tendencies which all tend to push people's judgments in the direction of the false consensus effect (Zuckerman, Mann, & Bernieri, 1982; Deutsch, 1989). For a review of research in this area, see Marks and Miller (1987).

Overlooking Nonoccurrences.   Also related to the availability heuristic is people's tendency to overlook nonoccurrences because they are less salient, less easily classified and remembered than occurrences. For instance, you meet a new acquaintance briefly and afterwards you try to decide whether she liked you. The things she said and did may be easily remembered and interpreted, but the equally informative things she did *not* do and say are apt to be too little noticed to be weighted properly in your judgments. Examples would include if she did *not* prolong the encounter, nor listen attentively to you, nor smile at you frequently, and so on. This typical cognitive tendency was illustrated in a Sherlock Holmes story by Dr. Watson's comment that nothing unusual had happened during the night. However, Holmes overcame this cognitive set, noticed the fact that a particular dog did *not* bark at the nighttime intruder, and used this insight to help solve one of his cases (Ross, 1977).

Reliance on Vivid or Concrete Information.   Another common human characteristic, which is also related to the availability heuristic, is too much reliance on vivid or concrete information, such as that provided by a specific instance. For example, suppose you are trying to decide what college courses to take or what kind of car to buy. If you are like most people, you will tend to be strongly influenced by vivid bits of specific information from a friend or acquaintance—for instance, that they took a particular course and thought it was terrific, or they bought a particular make of car and got a lemon. People typically pay much more attention to such information than to general, but abstract, information such as the ratings of courses in university-wide student handbooks or the repair records of cars published by *Consumer Reports*, which of course have much more general validity (Borgida & Nisbett, 1977; Nisbett & Ross, 1980).

Ignoring Base-Rate Information.   The reverse side of that cognitive bias is the widespread pattern of ignoring **base-rate** information (relevant data on large groups of cases), which is almost always presented in abstract or "pallid" form. However, summaries of base-rate probabilities, such as frequency-of-repair records for thousands of cars, usually provide the best predictor information available as to how any one car will perform. Nevertheless, in their passion for vivid, concrete information, most people largely or entirely disregard the much more useful base-rate information (Hamill, Wilson, & Nisbett, 1980).

Making Overly Extreme Predictions.   Another important type of cognitive error is making overly extreme predictions. For instance, suppose you were given individual students' mathematical aptitude test scores and were asked to predict the same students' verbal aptitude test scores. There are two biases that operate here, both of which foster overly extreme predictions. First, most people assume a stronger relation between the two variables (in this case, math and verbal aptitude) than actually exists. Second, utilizing the adjustment heuristic, most people make predictions on the dependent variable that are nearly as extreme as the scores on the predictor variable (e.g., if Joe is at the 90th percentile in math, they predict that he will be close to the 90th percentile in verbal aptitude). This procedure is contradicted by the phenomenon of **statistical regression**—the fact that on any imperfectly correlated dimensions, most people's scores will be much closer to the mean on the second variable than they are on the first one. However, even students and professionals who are familiar with the concept of regression tend to ignore it and make predictions that are too extreme. As a result, Ross (1977, p. 203) has concluded:

> It is difficult to resist the blunt summary that, when it comes to predictions, a little knowledge (i.e., knowledge of a weakly related predictor variable) is a dangerous thing.

Persistence of Initial Impressions.   This is the final cognitive bias that we will discuss here. Even though initial impressions are subject to all of the sources of error we have discussed, nevertheless people tend to cling to them much too fervently. That is, when presented with additional information that should change their initial judgments, people tend to make grossly insufficient adjustments. Like the bias involved in making extreme predictions, this is an example of the adjustment heuristic and the anchoring effect, for our initial impression provides an anchor that prevents our later judgments from shifting as far as the evidence warrants. This phenomenon has been shown in many types of social psychological situations and tasks, going back as far as Asch's (1946) classic study of first impressions. It is apt to occur even in controlled experiments where the initial information is later completely discredited (Anderson, Lepper, & Ross, 1980). Moreover, ambiguous new information is often interpreted by recipients as credible support which strengthens their original beliefs (Lord, Ross, & Lepper, 1979). Thus this cognitive tendency may help to explain the persistence of laymen's beliefs and also of scientists' theories, even in the face of seemingly contradictory evidence.

STEREOTYPES AND SCHEMAS

As discussed in Chapter 1, we all use convenient shortcuts in our thoughts and decisions. One of the most common of these shortcuts is the use of stereotypes. This term originally referred to a metal printer's plate, which could faithfully print thousands of copies of a picture, all exactly alike. Later the word was borrowed by Walter Lippmann (1922), the famous author and commentator on public affairs. He used it to mean "pictures in our heads" about various racial, national, or social groups—that is, perceptions of members of a given group as all being identical copies of each other, all having the same characteristics and traits.

Though the term **stereotype** has become widely used, various social scientists have defined it in somewhat different ways. We will define it simply as a mental image or set of beliefs which a person holds about most members of a particular social group. Of necessity such beliefs are highly simplified, and they may be highly evaluative and rigidly resistant to change (e.g., "most dogs are vicious," "women are irrational"). Note that this definition does not specify that stereotypes must be inaccurate, as some authors do. The reason for this omission will become clear in the following paragraphs. Note also that the definition does not specify that stereotypes must be shared beliefs—an individual can have his or her own idiosyncratic stereotype of another group of people (e.g., "women are highly logical"), though when we speak of *social* stereotypes, we mean ones which are shared by many individuals.

Stereotypes develop and persist because they are useful. They reduce the tremendous complexity of the world around us into a few simple guidelines which we can use in our everyday thought and decisions. If we "know" that "all politicians are crooked," we can dismiss government scandals without having to think very hard about what should be done to prevent or control them. Similarly, if we believe that "women are irrational," we won't hire one to be our lawyer. Unfortunately, however, the simpler and more convenient the stereotype, the more likely it is to be inaccurate, at least in part.

The inaccuracy of stereotypes has been much emphasized, particularly in the field of racial attitudes, where the terms "stereotype" and "prejudice" have taken on derogatory connotations. In one classic study the stereotype shared by citizens of Fresno, California about the local Armenian minority group was shown not only to be false, but to be opposite to reality on many characteristics—e.g., Armenians were actually more law-abiding than average rather than less so (LaPiere, 1936). However, several authors have pointed out that many stereotypes (though not necessarily all) have a *kernel of truth* in them (e.g., Brigham, 1971; Triandis, 1977). Campbell (1967) has convincingly presented the reasons for a possible kernel of truth, stressing that the traits which are most important to a perceiving group and the traits on which it differs most from another group will be likely to enter into its stereotype of the other group. To take one example, since cleanliness is an important characteristic to most Americans, and relatively unimportant to many primitive societies, it is more apt to enter into Americans' stereotypes of primitive societies than into those societies' stereotypes of Americans. Thus, paradoxically, a stereotype is *determined largely by the nature of the perceiving group*, and relatively little by the nature of the group which it ostensibly describes.

Formation of Stereotypes

Much recent research on stereotypes treats them as a result of people's normal cognitive processes of learning and adapting to the world around them (Hamilton, 1981a; Miller, 1982; Hamilton & Trolier, 1986). It should be emphasized that, like other beliefs and attitudes, a person's stereotypes are often not the product of personal experience with the group in question. They may also derive largely, or entirely, from one or more of the following three sources:

1. Explicit teaching. Particularly when children are young, they are frequently given explicit stereotypic information by their parents as they are taught about life ("kitties are nice," "damn politicians," "dirty commies," "honest cops," or "police brutality"). Later on, peers and teachers may also pass on stereotypes directly. However, this explicit transmission of stereotypes is augmented by two other processes which occur with much less conscious awareness.

2. Incidental learning, particularly from the mass media. This is typically a process of associative learning, in which members of a social group are repeatedly paired with particular personal characteristics. For instance, time after time, images in old movies have shown blacks as lazy or stupid, American Indians as bloodthirsty or treacherous, women as subservient housewives, and so on. Though more recent movies and TV shows have included a wider range of behaviors for these groups, there are still subtle forms of racism in their portrayal of blacks (Pierce, 1980), and non-Americans and Chicanos are typically depicted in lower-status activities (Seggar & Wheeler, 1973). On children's TV programs, more than half the villains have accents, typically German or Russian (Mendelson & Young, 1972). The repeated portrayal of such characteristics as being typical of particular social groups is a potent source of stereotypes among the mass media audience.

3. Illusory correlation. In contrast with the above two processes, where stereotypic information is actually presented as being differentially associated with various social groups, in the process of **illusory correlation** people come to perceive a correlation of particular traits with a given social group even where they have not been differentially associated. Experiments on social cognition have shown that this illogical process often occurs in situations where subjects are presented with instances in which two groups of different size (a majority group and a minority group) are paired with two or more kinds of traits or behaviors having different frequencies (a common one and a rare one, such as being honest or a criminal). In this situation, even when there is no differential association of any trait with any group, subjects nevertheless typically tend to see an association of the *small* group with the *rare* trait (Hamilton 1981b; Hamilton, Dugan, & Trolier 1985), though there is still debate about the pervasiveness of this effect (McArthur & Friedman, 1980; Pryor, 1986). In a real-life situation, this phenomenon would mean that individuals would generally form a stereotype associating a minority group (or any outgroup that was seldom contacted) with various uncommon traits or behaviors. Some of these traits could be favorable ones, but since negative traits like criminality are generally quite rare, stereotypes are usually composed mostly of negative traits.

Illusory correlation seems to be an example of the availability heuristic at work. The rare, extreme behavior is apt to be more memorable than more common traits (Rothbart, Fulero, Jensen, Howard, & Birrell, 1978). When it is paired with members of a majority group, the perceiver has plenty of contrary examples to counteract the association, but when it is occasionally paired with a member of a rarely encountered outgroup, the association of two rare categories is salient and its frequency tends to be exaggerated by the perceiver. This process can be seen not only in the formation of stereotypes, but also in maintaining and strengthening them once they are formed. That is, even in sets of data where there is no differential association of an outgroup with one of its established stereotypic traits, perceivers tend to see one as being present (Hamilton & Rose, 1980). Other studies show that stereotypes serve as hypotheses about new acquaintances, but that people test them out in a biased manner by looking solely for confirmatory information, and thus they rarely ever learn about instances in which the stereotypes are false (Darley & Gross, 1983; Kulik, 1983). In such cases, instead of "seeing is believing," people's behavior indicates that "believing is seeing" (Hamilton, 1981b).

Social Schemas

In addition to stereotypes, social schemas are another type of shortcut device which people use to help them operate efficiently in their social interactions. A **schema** is an abstract, general expectation about how some part of the world operates, built up on the basis of our own past experience with specific examples. Social schemas provide patterns of expectations that help us to function in social situations on the basis of typical, expected interaction patterns without thinking in detail about the characteristics of the particular individuals or occasions that we are dealing with. In using schemas, perceivers actively create their own versions of reality. Research has shown that schemas (also called "schemata") "guide the perception of new information, memory for old information, and inferences that go beyond both" (Fiske & Taylor, 1984, p. 139).

There are five general types of social schemas, as follows. **Role schemas** describe the norms and behavior expected of people in various social categories based on age, sex, race, occupation, and so on (e.g., grandmothers, or missionaries). Stereotypes can be viewed as a particularly important subcategory of role schemas. **Person schemas** summarize your actual or vicarious experience concerning the characteristics of broad types of people or of specific individuals (e.g., extraverts, or your roommate). **Self-schemas** are simplified conceptions that people hold about their own key traits, goals, feelings, and behavior. Different individuals' self-schemas stress different dimensions (e.g., their weight, or their sense of humor) and omit many other dimensions. **Event schemas** comprise knowledge about the normal sequence of events in familiar social situations, such as baseball games, buying groceries, or asking for a date. Event schemas are also called **scripts** and, like actors' scripts in the theater, they include props, roles, typical actions, and rules for the sequence of events (Abelson, 1981). Finally, **procedural social schemas** are relatively content-free rules for how pertinent information is to be sought and linked together. The most-studied type is causal schemas (ways of explaining the causes of events), which are discussed later in this chapter as an aspect of attribution theory. The use of any of these types of schemas can make learning, memory, and inference faster and easier, but it often also makes them less accurate.

Schema research has cast important light on the process of stereotyping. For instance, studies have shown that role schemas can influence the earliest stages of perception, and thus it is possible for someone's very first impressions of an outgroup member to be mistaken and to omit many of the person's true characteristics (Klatzky, Martin, & Kane, 1982). In general, people perceive any **outgroup** (i.e., a group which they don't belong to) as being more homogeneous, less variable than their own membership groups; and they consistently evaluate their own ingroups as being better on many different dimensions. This is true not only for racial, occupational, and gender groups, but also for such trivial characteristics as eye color or alphabetical position of one's name, and even for arbitrary assignments to groups such as children's teams (Wilder & Cooper, 1981; Park & Rothbart, 1982). As a result of these tendencies, people are often willing to make rash inferences about outgroups concerning whom they have very little information—sometimes even on the basis of a single instance. Similarly, people tend to remember information about individuals better when it confirms their stereotype of the group (Rothbart, Evans, & Fulero, 1979), and they particularly remember the negative actions of outgroup members (Wilder, 1981).

Though schemas can change over time, one of their main features is their perseverance, even when the evidence that produced them is completely discredited (Anderson et al., 1980). When discrepant information is encountered, a schema about an individual is more likely to change than is a stereotype about a whole social group (Wyer & Gordon, 1982). The most likely kind of change in a group stereotype is the formation of a subtype to contain the discrepant individual (e.g., a brilliant janitor), with no change in the schema for the group as a whole (Weber & Crocker, 1983).

ATTRIBUTION PROCESSES

Our next topic, attribution processes, has been by far the most studied aspect of social cognition in recent years. In fact, it has been the most popular research topic in all of social psychology. Various reviewers have termed it "the single most pervasive influence upon social psychology in the past decade" (Cialdini, Petty, & Cacioppo, 1981, p. 389) and "the leading theoretical concern and dominant empirical topic of the field" (Fiske & Taylor, 1984, p. 20).

What do we mean by **attribution**? Essentially, it refers to our process of making inferences about the unobservable characteristics of other people, ourselves, objects, or events. By far the predominant aspect of attribution processes that has been studied is the topic of perceived causality: that is, how we decide about the causes of behavior or events. Another important aspect is the attribution of responsibility: i.e., our judgments about whether people are responsible for particular events, and how we assign praise or blame for their actions. In addition to these central topics, attributional concepts and principles have been applied to many different social psychological topics, such as perceptions of freedom, physical attractiveness, success or failure, and depression. Interested readers may want to consult one of the longer recent discussions of attribution theory and research (e.g., Jaspars, Fincham, & Hewstone, 1983; Fiske & Taylor, 1984; Harvey & Weary, 1985; Ross & Fletcher, 1985).

Heider's Theory of Naive Psychology

There is not just one attribution theory but several parallel and partly overlapping approaches. In origin, they all stem from Fritz Heider's (1944) early paper on phenomenal causality, that is, on how people make inferences or attributions about the causes of events. Later Heider (1958) expanded his attribution principles in his book on interpersonal perception, which is also the source of many of the central principles of consistency theory.

Heider proposed to build a theory of causal inference from studying people's "naive psychology"—that is, their everyday ways of thinking about events and

Photograph courtesy of Fritz Heider.
Reprinted by permission.

Box 2–2   FRITZ HEIDER, *Father of Attribution Theory*

Fritz Heider's career was greatly influenced by the school of Gestalt psychology. Born in Vienna, Austria in 1896, he took a Ph.D. in psychology at the University of Graz in 1920. Later he attended lectures by Lewin, Köhler, and Wertheimer at the University of Berlin, translated one of Lewin's books, and wrote about Gestalt theory and Lewinian theory. After three years of teaching at the University of Hamburg, he came to America in 1930 to do research and teach with Koffka at Smith College. He remained there, doing much of his research on problems of deafness, until moving to the University of Kansas in 1947.

Heider is famous for his development of both attribution theory and consistency theory. His major work, The Psychology of Interpersonal Relations *(1958), has much in common with Lewin's field theory, and the following year he was honored with the Lewin Memorial Award by the Society for the Psychological Study of Social Issues. Among his other honors is the American Psychological Association's Distinguished Scientific Contribution Award for his work on social perception. Retired in 1967, he lived in Lawrence, Kansas, until his death in 1988.*

making sense out of the world. He felt that individuals necessarily developed some causal notions about events and behavior because such notions were crucial in their attempts to understand, predict, and control the world around them. In contrast to the previously discussed emphasis on heuristics and biases, Heider and the other early attribution theorists tended to see people as making their judgments and inferences in a relatively logical and rational manner—as "intuitive scientists."

Heider was interested primarily in the conditions under which attributions about the stable dispositions of people (e.g., their friendliness, honesty, likes and dislikes, etc.) would be made, based upon information about their actions. This is a question which we all try to answer for ourselves many times every day (e.g., "I wonder why (s)he smiled at me"), so it has great practical as well as scientific interest. Depending upon the situation, attribution processes may result in attitude formation, attitude change, or support for one's existing attitudes.

Heider (1958) distinguished between internal attribution and external attribution. **Internal attribution** concludes that the cause of an individual's actions is a personal disposition—for example, "she smiled because she is friendly." **External attribution** concludes that the cause of a person's actions is a factor outside the person—e.g., "He succeeded because of good luck, or because the task was easy." Thus we may attribute the cause of a person's actions to his(her) own characteristics, to situational factors, or to a combination of both. How do we arrive at this conclusion in any given instance? Heider says that we consider three factors: the person's ability, intention, and exertion. We evaluate ability in relation to the difficulty of the task, and we evaluate exertion by observation of the person's apparent effort. Intention is the hardest factor to evaluate because many actions have both intended and unintended consequences; therefore, it is difficult to determine the person's intentions from observing the consequences of his(her) actions. Nevertheless, Heider concluded that only when we perceive the person as intending the action's consequences do we infer **personal causality** and make internal attributions about the person's dispositions or traits.

Heider also discussed the perception of people's responsibility for social outcomes. This is often the next question raised after the determination of causality—i.e., first, what caused an event? and then, who was responsible? For instance, suppose your car hit a parked car; who was responsible for the accident? Heider posited five different levels or aspects of responsibility that are considered in a sequential fashion in order to determine a person's accountability for such an event. First, **association** is mere linkage in time and space. If you were in the car, whether or not you were driving, you would be associated with the accident, and at a primitive level you might be considered at least partially responsible. Second, **commission** means that you carried out or caused the action. It would be present if you were the driver. Third, **foreseeability** concerns whether or not you could foresee the outcome. If you had just come over the crest of a hill and found the other car parked right ahead of you in the middle of the road, foreseeability would be absent, and you would be held less responsible. Fourth, **intentionality** may be present or absent even when you could foresee the outcome. If a chuckhole in the pavement made you swerve and hit the other car, the crash would be an unintentional one. Finally, **justification** may sometimes be present even where the action was intentional. For instance, you would be justified (and therefore less responsible legally or morally) if you intentionally chose to hit the car rather than to run down a child who dashed out in front of you. As these examples suggest, not only do people consider such factors in their personal judgments about responsibility, but they are also built into our society's moral codes and legal procedures—e.g., the various gradations of homicide from murder through negligent manslaughter to justified self-defense.

Jones and Davis's Theory of Correspondent Inferences

Heider's discussion of attribution principles has been extended in many directions by several groups of theorists, of whom the most influential have been Jones and Davis (1965) and Kelley (1967). Jones and Davis focused on the process of making *internal* attributions about personal casuality, while Kelley concentrated largely on *external* attributions about impersonal situational causes.

Jones and Davis (1965) hold that when people act, the causal sequence is that their dispositions (long-term, stable personal characteristics) lead to their intentions, which in turn produce their actions. That is:

CAUSATION: dispositions → intentions → actions

However, in making inferences about personal causation, this process is reversed, as follows:

CAUSAL INFERENCE: observed actions → intentions → dispositions

Thus Jones and Davis propose that people first observe another person's actions and the effects of those actions, then use that information to infer the person's intentions, and finally make attributions about the person's traits or dispositions on the basis of the inferred intentions. This is called the **theory of correspondent inferences** because the perceiver is trying to form an inference that the person's behavior and the intentions that led to it *correspond* to an underlying, stable personality characteristic. This inference process is a tricky one because the evidence is often unclear or incomplete, and the perceiver has to act like a detective or a scientist in puzzling out the true causal factors behind events.

Jones and Davis's theory suggests four factors that help to increase the correspondence of inferences (that is, the strength and confidence of people's causal attributions): lack of social desirability, noncommon effects, hedonic relevance, and personalism.

1. The **social desirability** of a person's actions decreases the strength of our attributions about them, whereas socially undesirable actions give us more confi-

dence in our attributions (Skowronski & Carlston, 1989). This is true because most people follow social norms and act in socially desirable ways most of the time, and thus it is unclear whether such behavior reflects their real dispositions or merely their understanding of what is expected of them. If a wife gives her husband a peck on the cheek in public, this in-role behavior doesn't tell us much about her true feelings, but if she hits him in public, her behavior is much more informative.

2. The **noncommon effects** resulting from a chosen and an unchosen action are also informative about the chooser's motives and dispositions, whereas the effects that the two actions have in common don't help us make such attributions. Suppose a friend of yours is trying to decide between two summer jobs. If both would require him to live in a city, both involve desk work, and both are well paid, these common effects don't help you to understand his motives. However, if one is near his girlfriend's home while the other is far away, and he chooses the nearby job, that noncommon effect of the chosen and unchosen alternatives strengthens the inference that being near his girlfriend is important to him. If the two choices have more than one noncommon effect (for instance, one job also requires mathematical skills and the other doesn't), then your attribution about the real reason for his choice will be less clear and less confident.

It is also possible to observe a person's successive actions over a period of time and make inferences about their underlying dispositions (Jones & McGillis, 1976). The flip side of the noncommon effects principle is that, when a person has taken *both* of two actions, their *common effects* are informative about the person's motives, whereas their noncommon effects are irrelevant. If your friend had held several very different jobs in turn, and the only thing that they had in common was that they all paid very well, that common effect would be a factor allowing you to make confident attributions about your friend's goals in life.

3. The **hedonic relevance** of a person's actions means the degree to which they are beneficial or harmful to the perceiver. In general, greater hedonic relevance produces stronger and more confident attributions. If I am careless about paying back my debts, you will be more inclined to condemn me as dishonest if you have lost some of your own money in this way than if the loser was someone else.

4. The **personalism** of a person's actions means the degree to which they are viewed as being aimed specifically at the perceiver. Personalism is roughly equivalent to intentionality, and it also increases the strength of attributions. If I not only failed to pay back your loan to me, but in addition you believe that I intended not to pay it back, your conclusion about my dishonesty will be even stronger.

Jones and his colleagues have suggested a few other factors that influence the attribution process. One key requirement for making correspondent inferences is the presence of some freedom of *choice* in the actor's behavior. In contrast, it is not safe to make dispositional attributions if the person's actions are situationally constrained in some way, such as being required by law or performed under the shadow of threats. (Again this principle indicates that people should not have

Photograph courtesy of Edward E. Jones.
Reprinted by permission.

Box 2–3   EDWARD E. JONES, *Researcher on Attribution and Self-Presentation*

Edward E. (Ned) Jones was born in Buffalo in 1926 and studied history at Swarthmore and social psychology at Harvard, where he also earned his Ph.D. following some postwar military service in Japan. In 1953 he took his first faculty position at Duke University, where he spent 24 happy years and developed a strong social psychology program. In 1977 he moved to Princeton to accept an endowed professorship and won the American Psychological Association's award for Distinguished Scientific Contributions.

Jones was an early convert to the experimental side of social psychology, and his dissertation was an experimental study of authoritarianism as a determinant of first impression formation. He is co-author of a noted social psychology textbook and wrote a prize-winning research monograph on ingratiation in self-presentation. His central contributions to attribution theory include classic papers with Keith Davis on correspondent inferences and with Richard Nisbett on actor-observer differences. Most recently he has co-authored or authored books on social stigma, minority-group mental health, and interpersonal perception.

labeled Patti Hearst a criminal because her antisocial actions were performed under the threat of injury or death.) Another factor that prevents confident attributions is behavior that is part of a *social role*. As suggested above regarding social desirability, in-role behavior is not a good basis for dispositional attributions, but out-of-role behavior or role-inconsistent behavior is. Finally, our *prior expectations* about a person are attributions that develop as a result of our past experiences with him or her, and later behavior that departs from them can give us a basis for refining these dispositional attributions (Jones & McGillis, 1976). For instance, if your normally unflappable roommate got very excited when running for a student office, you might conclude that the social approval involved in winning the election was one of her most highly valued goals. However, if a person's behavior departs too much from your expectations, *skepticism* is likely to be aroused—if your roommate got too hyper, you might suspect that she was really putting on an act.

In conclusion, it can be seen that Jones and Davis's attribution theory presents a rational cognitive model of how people make causal inferences about people and events around them, and it largely ignores affective and motivational bases of the perceiver's judgments. It focuses mainly on the logical, rational processes that people *should* use in making attributions, as Kelley's parallel theory likewise does, and for this reason these theories have been termed **normative models** or guidelines for how social cognition should proceed (Fiske & Taylor, 1984). However, as we have seen earlier in this chapter, there are many pervasive biases and sources of error that cause people's inferences to depart in certain ways from the normative models specified by these theories.

Kelley's Theory of Covariation

Harold Kelley's (1967) covariation theory of attribution is complementary to Jones and Davis's approach. While Jones and Davis focus on internal attributions about personal causality, Kelley's theory deals mainly with *external* attributions about objects and stimuli in the environment; however, it can also be applied to self-perception and to internal causal inferences about other people's behavior. It concerns situations where one has repeated observations of behavior or events, whereas Jones and Davis's original formulation was limited to inferences about single actions.

Kelley (1967) proposed that people make causal inferences by using the principle of covariation in much the same way that scientists use analysis of variance (ANOVA) to determine which of several possible independent variables actually affects a set of repeated observations. The **covariation principle** posits that an effect will be attributed to a causal factor that is present when the effect is present and absent when the effect is absent. For instance, if my wife rarely ever complains, but protests every time I wear my old threadbare jacket, there is a covariation between wearing the jacket and her complaints, and it is likely that something about the jacket causes the complaints. By contrast, if her protests occur approximately equally whether I am wearing my old jacket or my new one, it is unlikely that the old jacket is the cause of the complaints.

According to Kelley's theory, there are three kinds of possible causes for such social effects: persons, entities (environmental objects), and times (occasions or situations). How can people know whether they have correctly attributed a given effect to a particular cause? Kelley suggests that, in assessing covariation, they consider three key dimensions of information about the possible causes: namely, distinctiveness, consistency, and consensus information. To see how this works, imagine that your friend Steve has told you he loved the movie *Vampire's Castle*. This effect could be due to the movie's excellence (an external attribution) or to Steve's poor taste regarding movies (an internal attribution). An external attribution that the movie was a good one would be strengthened by information on these three key dimensions:

1. **Distinctiveness**—Was Steve's reaction to this movie distinctively different from his feeling about other movies, or does he love almost any movie he sees?

2. **Consistency**—Was Steve's response to the movie similar when he saw it at other times and under other conditions (e.g., with and without his girlfriend)?
3. **Consensus**—Did Steve's reaction resemble the consensus of other people who saw the movie?

If your analysis found high distinctiveness, high consistency, and high consensus, you would be very confident in concluding that the movie was a good one (an external or entity attribution). Another pattern that would be clearly interpretable is low distinctiveness, high consistency, and low consensus, leading to a person attribution—i.e., Steve enjoys any old movie at any time, but others don't agree with him, so he must be undiscriminating (McArthur, 1972). Other patterns of information can lead to an attribution of joint responsibility for the effect (e.g., it's a good movie, but Steve is a poor judge of movies), or to ambiguous causal conclusions.

As you might expect from the section earlier in this chapter on ignoring base-rate information, research has shown that people's attributions often rely relatively little on consensus information (Kassin, 1979; Borgida & Brekke, 1981), but cues of distinctiveness and consistency are quite generally utilized (Kelley & Michela, 1980).

Discounting. In another paper Kelley (1972a) suggested a principle which may be brought into play when you are trying to understand a single event and you have no evidence about distinctiveness, consistency, or consensus. The **discounting principle** posits that the importance of any given cause in producing a particular effect will be discounted in a situation where there are other plausible causes. For instance, if a college classmate gave you an unexpected compliment, you would ordinarily be tempted to believe it; but you would be much more inclined to discount its sincerity if you discovered that the classmate was hoping to get on your good side and borrow your car for the weekend. The discounting principle is similar to Jones and Davis's notion of noncommon effects, for each noncommon effect between two actions constitutes a plausible cause for the chosen action, and strength of inference is greater whenever the number of plausible causes (and thus, noncommon effects) is small. Research studies have generally supported both the discounting and noncommon effects principles (Kelley & Michela, 1980).

Augmentation. In a situation where there are multiple plausible causes for a given effect, some possible causes might facilitate the effect whereas others might inhibit it (make it less likely). In such cases the **augmentation principle**, which is roughly opposite to the discounting principle, may be applied. It holds that if an effect occurs in the presence of a plausible inhibitory cause, people will attribute more strength to the facilitative cause than if it were operating in the absence of an inhibitory cause. In other words, the facilitative cause is seen as having to be stronger in order to overcome the opposite effect of the inhibitory cause. For example, if your friend buys tickets to a rock concert despite their very

high price, you would conclude that he really liked the musicians, whereas if he
went to a low-priced concert, you'd be less sure of his degree of enthusiasm for
those performers. There is also research support for this augmentation process
(Ginzel, Jones, & Swann, 1987).

Causal Schemas

In another later paper, Kelley (1972b) departed from the earlier emphasis on
people as being logical and rational, proposing that much of our causal attribution
is not done in the careful, full-scale manner described in his covariation or

Photograph courtesy of Harold H. Kelley.
Reprinted by permission.

Box 2–4   HAROLD H. KELLEY, *Analyst of Attribution and Personal
Relationships*

*Harold Kelley began life in 1921 in Idaho and grew up in California's central valley. After
two years at Bakersfield Junior College, he transferred to Berkeley where he took a B.A.
and M.A. in psychology. During World War II he served in the Aviation Psychology program, and following the war he earned his Ph.D. in Kurt Lewin's newly formed Research
Center for Group Dynamics at MIT. When the Center moved to the University of Michigan
in 1948 following Lewin's untimely death, Kelley took his first faculty position there. In
1950 he became an assistant professor at Yale, where he did research in Carl Hovland's
Attitude Change Program and was co-author of the classic volume* Communication and
Persuasion. *In 1955 he moved to the University of Minnesota and in 1961 to UCLA, where
he remains. He has been honored with the American Psychological Association (APA)
Distinguished Scientific Contribution Award and elected President of the APA Division of
Personality and Social Psychology and of the Western Psychological Association.*

*Kelley's early interest in social perception led to his dissertation on first impressions.
Later he worked closely with John Thibaut on small-group and interpersonal phenomena,
and they have jointly authored* The Psychology of Groups *(1959) and* Interpersonal Relations: A Theory of Interdependence *(1978). Co-author of eight books and nearly 100
articles, Kelley is perhaps best known for his contributions to attribution theory, detailed in
this chapter. More recently, he has written several books analyzing the structure and
processes of close personal relationships.*

ANOVA model. Oftentimes there isn't enough information available, or we don't have the time or interest to do a complete causal analysis. In such situations we may use causal schemas as a shortcut to make causal inferences. Kelley identified two main types of causal schemas: (1) The **multiple necessary causes schema** applies to tasks that are very difficult, such as winning an Olympic gold medal. Here many causes are necessary for success (ability, training, effort, etc.), so success tells us that all of these causes were present, but failure would not tell us which was missing. (2) The **multiple sufficient causes schema** applies to tasks that are very easy, such as winning a game against a small child. Here any one of several causes might be sufficient for success (ability, effort, experience in the game), so failure tells us that none of them were present; however, success would not tell us which one(s) were missing, and so we would tend to use the discounting principle in assessing them (Fiske & Taylor, 1984). It is also sometimes possible to use the strength of effects (e.g., how close the contest was) to infer how strong some of the causal factors were (e.g., how much ability or effort the winner displayed). For a review of research in this area, see Fiedler (1982).

Bem's Self-Perception Theory

A fourth theorist who has made important contributions, particularly in the area of self-attributions, is Daryl Bem (1967, 1972). Bem stated that his self-perception theory derived from a radical behaviorist position, based on B. F. Skinner's (1957) operant behavioral analysis of human verbal behavior; and he originally presented his ideas as a critique of and an alternative to cognitive dissonance theory (a controversy that we will discuss in a later chapter). However, because of his focus on the previously neglected area of how people make inferences about *their own* intentions, goals, and traits, his work has been acknowledged as an important addition to the field of attribution theory.

Bem holds that people are not nearly as aware of, nor as clear about, their own internal feelings and beliefs as they think they are. Bem's **self-perception principle** states that:

> Individuals come to "know" their own attitudes, emotions, and other internal states partially by inferring them from observations of their own overt behavior and/or the circumstances in which this behavior occurs. Thus, to the extent that internal cues are weak, ambiguous, or uninterpretable, the individual is functionally in the same position as an outside observer, an observer who must necessarily rely upon those same external cues to infer the individual's inner states. (1972, p. 2)

In the beginning, Bem says, every child learns about his external environment through discrimination training by the adults and other children around him. By verbal labeling and corroboration or correction, children learn to distinguish between dogs and cats, for instance, and between anger and happiness in other people. In the same way, says Bem, through self-perception we also learn to label our own inner feelings of hunger, anger, anxiety, or liking. To use his favorite example, we decide that we like brown bread by observing the fact that we eat a lot of it. The other factor that is important in determining our self-attributions is whether the external circumstances constrain our behavior. If we realize that the only bread our mother serves us is brown bread, we will be less likely to conclude that our eating it indicates great fondness for it.

In his first theoretical papers, Bem (1967) stated even more strongly the dramatic and unorthodox claim that people don't really know their attitudes and beliefs until they act, that they can only infer these internal states from their behavior, and that they even may be unable to remember any internal states that are discrepant from their behavior (Bem & McConnell, 1970). Later he retreated from this extreme position and only claimed that individuals use *partially* the same external evidence as outside observers, as quoted above. However, his theory does not tell us how to determine whether a person's internal cues are "weak, ambiguous, or uninterpretable" in a given situation (though he suggests that that is very often true), so there is no clear way to determine how much the person has to rely on external cues. Also, his theory does not contain any motivational principles about why or when people will make attributions. Nevertheless, Bem's focus on inferences about the self and his emphasis on one's own behavior as an important inferential cue have stimulated much important attributional research.

Bem has also applied his theory to attitude change, positing that it occurs in reaction to self-observed behaviors *combined with* observation of external cues which indicate whether or not the behavior is apt to be valid or truthful. For instance, if an actor in a TV commercial says "I like Busy Bakers' brown bread," but we know that he was paid to make the commercial, we may doubt whether that is his true attitude. On the other hand, if a person is subtly induced to say something contrary to his former opinion under conditions which suggest truthfulness, he is apt to decide that he really believes the statement which he has made.

As a real-life instance of this process, Bem (1970) has asserted that police-station interrogation conditions constitute a truth-telling situation for most people, and that in such situations certain wily interrogation procedures can induce prisoners to make *and to believe in* false confessions about crimes which they have not really committed. This is a particularly surprising and dramatic example of attitude change, and Bem has backed up his claims with clearcut evidence from a laboratory experiment which showed exactly this process at work. However, it should be noted that other investigators have had difficulty in replicating these results (Kiesler & Munson, 1975).

In comparison to Kelley's or Jones and Davis's attribution theories, Bem's theory is a very simple one, and it proposes that people normally do very little cognitive work in making their attributions. Some experimental findings suggest that this is true in situations where the consequences for the social perceiver are minimal, but that in more important situations more time and information will be used in determining one's attributions and attitudes, and consequently more use will be made of internal cues and less of external ones (Taylor, 1975). However, in its emphasis on the simple, shortcut nature of social cognition, Bem's theory is consistent with the work on heuristics and biases described earlier in this chapter. Thus it anticipated the currently popular **cognitive miser** view of social cognition—the conclusion that people's attributions often do not follow the normative models of rational inference processes, but rather take shortcuts that require as little time and effort in information processing as possible (Taylor, 1981).

Actor-Observer Differences

In the vast research literature on attribution, one of the most important topics is actor-observer differences. Here the term *actor* means a participant who has taken part in some social interaction, while an *observer* is an uninvolved individual who has merely watched the interaction. Jones and Nisbett (1972) proposed that actors tend to attribute their actions to situational factors, whereas observers of the same actions tend to attribute them to stable personal dispositions of the actor, including abilities, traits, and attitudes (the fundamental attribution error again). There is a large body of support for this principle, though some exceptions have also been found (Kelley & Michela, 1980; Watson, 1982). The difference has been summed up provocatively in Triandis's (1977) comment that actors seem to believe Skinnerian theory, while observers appear to prefer Allport's trait theory.

What might be the reasons for this pervasive finding? One factor is the amount of knowledge that each person has about the actor's past behavior: the observer who has seen the actor in only one situation may assume that her behavior in other situations is consistent and so make a dispositional attribution, whereas the actor is aware of much variability in her past behavior, depending on the situation that she was in. Research has confirmed that, as we know a person longer, we tend to make fewer trait attributions and give more situational explanations for his or her behavior (Nisbett, Caputo, Legant, & Marecek, 1973; Goldberg, 1981).

Another factor is visual salience or focus of attention, due to the differing visual perspectives of the actor and the observer. In the typical experimental situation the observer is watching the actor's behavior while the actor is attending to incoming situational stimuli related to his task. In an experiment that made a clever use of videotape feedback, Storms (1973) showed that when these visual perspectives were reversed, the types of attributions made by the actor and observer were also reversed. When the actor who had just completed a short conversation saw a replay of his behavior from the visual perspective of the observer, his attributions became less situational; and when the observer saw a replay of the discussion made from the actor's visual perspective, his attributions became *more* situational than the actor's revised ones. Another study showed that observers' attributions can also be made more situational by instructing the observers to empathize with the actor (Regan & Totten, 1975).

Motivational factors may also enter into this phenomenon. One motivation that has been suggested for observers' tendencies to use trait attributions is the need for personal control: If they think that other people's behavior is consistent, they will have a better chance of predicting it and perhaps also of influencing it in the future (Miller, Norman, & Wright, 1978).

Certain exceptions to the actor-observer pattern also seem to stem from motivational factors. In line with a self-esteem or egotism hypothesis, it has been found that actors give more internal attributions for their own positive behaviors and less internal explanations for their negative behaviors, such as harmful actions or failures (Taylor & Koivumaki, 1976; Burger, 1986). Contrariwise, observers give more internal attributions for actors' harmful actions than for their beneficial ones. In competitive games it has been found that winners tend to give dispositional explanations for their success, but losers (who are also actors) attribute the outcome more to external factors, particularly luck (Snyder, Stephan, & Rosenfield, 1976; Lau & Russell, 1980).

The general pattern of actor-observer differences in attribution is well established, and these latter studies show the recent turn toward investigating when and why it occurs and its resulting effects. This is a very important area of research, with many practical implications for relationships between managers and workers, husbands and wives, and parents and children (Harvey & Weary, 1981). For example, extending the actor-observer relationship by analogy to ingroups and outgroups in the area of intergroup prejudice, Aboud and Taylor (1971) found that people typically explain the behavior of members of their ingroup by using role

FIGURE 2–1 An example of actor-observer differences. Observers often attribute behavior to internal characteristics of the actor, whereas the actor often attributes it to situational pressures.

(external) attributions, whereas they use (internal) ethnic personality traits to explain the behavior of outgroup members. Furthermore, as in the egotistically motivated differential attribution patterns mentioned above, people have been found to attribute their own ethnic group's desirable behavior to internal factors and its undesirable behavior to external causes, whereas they do just the opposite in explaining outgroups' desirable and undesirable behavior (Taylor & Jaggi, 1974).

Self-Attributions, Self-Esteem, and Self-Presentation

In addition to the above research on actors' attributions about their own behavior, there has been considerable other work on self-attributions. Bem's self-perception theory, which was discussed earlier, was modified by Nisbett and Valins (1972) to indicate that people infer their beliefs and attitudes from their behavior *only if* they perceive the behavior to have resulted from their true feelings toward the attitude object, but not if they perceive their behavior to have been constrained by some other aspect of the situation (for instance, norms, roles, or instructions). Since the actor-observer literature shows that people frequently see their own behavior as being determined by some aspect of the situation, it follows that Bem's self-perception theory will only hold true some of the time.

In this area of research, we deal with *motivational* aspects of attribution, as opposed to strictly cognitive (informational) processes. That is, people's motivation to maintain or enhance their self-esteem can influence the attributions they make. In general, people usually take more causal responsibility for their favorable outcomes than for their unfavorable ones—e.g., they make internal attributions for their own success and external ones for their failure. A popular explanation for this pattern is the operation of **self-serving biases** or ego-defensive biases (Greenwald, 1980; Weary, 1980).

Self-serving attributive biases have been found to occur when subjects' outcomes and attributions are entirely private, so they cannot be due solely to attempts to impress others (Riess, Rosenfeld, Melburg, & Tedeschi, 1981; Greenberg, Pyszczynski, & Solomon, 1982). People usually display self-serving biases on tasks which are stereotypically expected of their sex, but not on tasks expected of the opposite sex (Mirels, 1980). Real-world demonstrations of self-serving biases have been shown in coaches' and athletes' attributions for athletic performance (Lau & Russell, 1980; Peterson, 1980), in premed students' attributions for their admission or rejection by medical schools (Smith & Manard, 1980), and in corporation officers' reports to their stockholders (Bettman & Weitz, 1983). Thus people clearly do slant their attributions to make themselves feel good. However, further research shows that they do so less on dimensions where their own positions are objectively clear (e.g., income—Marks & Miller, 1988).

A related form of attributional bias is aimed at making a favorable *self-presentation* to others, not just to oneself. This is an aspect of **impression-management theory**, which has become a popular topic in social psychology in recent years (Schlenker, 1980; Jones & Pittman, 1982). A typical research design in this area compares attributions under relatively private conditions with those made under identical but public conditions. When college students make attributions in front of student peers, they typically further embellish their private self-serving attributions (Weary, 1980). However, individuals who are high in social anxiety and those who expect their behavior to be reviewed by prestigious or expert evaluators are likely to reverse the self-promotional approach and accept more responsibility for failure than for success (Arkin, Appelman, & Burger, 1980; Greenberg et al., 1982). This modesty effect, though it underplays one's accomplishments, may ultimately gain more approval from others than boastfulness would.

Evaluation of Attribution Theory

Attribution theory has passed its twenty-fifth birthday, and since the early 1970s it has maintained its position as the most prolific research area in social psychology. A number of important attributional theories have been proposed, many research areas have been identified and explored, and attribution concepts have begun to be applied to a host of social issues such as helping behavior, romantic attraction, and treatment of various clinical problems (e.g., Frieze, Bar-Tal, & Carroll, 1979). Yet there is still much that we don't know about attributions.

One danger of the many fascinating offshoots of attribution theory is that concentration on them will distract researchers and prevent them from ever constructing a firm and unified framework for the theory. Among the important topics that need concentrated study are: when and why attribution processes are set in motion, what determines whether they will be extensive or shortcut procedures, establishing criteria for determining the accuracy of attributions, understanding attribution in its everyday natural contexts, and clarifying connections of cognitive attribution processes to motivations and emotions, as in the study of self-presentation. Related issues are whether attributions mediate behavior, as is widely assumed but not yet well demonstrated, and what are the other long-range consequences of various types of attributions (Kelley & Michela, 1980).

In some areas there have been encouraging linkups of attributional concepts with other theoretical viewpoints, such as learned helplessness (Abramson & Martin, 1981) and symbolic interactionism from sociology (Stryker & Gottlieb, 1981). Despite its problems and unfilled gaps, attribution theory has clarified many cognitive processes as well as common biases, and it remains a central focus in the field of social cognition.

SUMMARY

Social cognition is the process by which we understand people and social situations, and it forms the cognitive basis of our attitudes. It begins with perception, which selects stimuli and imparts meaning to them; but, particularly in the social realm, perception can also introduce error into our thinking. In their usual thought processes, people often use convenient, shortcut guides for making decisions or predictions, such as the availability, adjustment, and representativeness heuristics. These heuristics often result in, or are combined with, various cognitive biases, and the result is many errors of human judgment.

Stereotypes are images or beliefs that a person holds about most members of a particular social group. Though useful in simplifying our everyday thought and decisions, they are overly simple, evaluative, and resistant to change, and they are very often inaccurate, though they may contain a "kernel of truth." They may be derived from explicit teaching, from incidental learning such as we gain from the mass media, or by incorrectly perceiving illusory correlations in events.

Attribution is the process of making inferences about the unobservable characteristics of people, social objects, or events—especially the perception of causality in events or behavior. Since about 1970, attribution theory has become the most popular research topic in social psychology. It was initiated by Fritz Heider, whose approach has been extended by Jones and Davis's theory of correspondent inferences, Kelley's covariation theory and causal schema concepts, Bem's self-perception theory, and others—each being a particular version of attribution theory with its own set of principles. Though there is still no single, unified attribution theory, various attribution concepts have provoked extensive research in many areas, and attribution ideas have been applied to a wide variety of real-world social issues.

3

Measurement of Attitudes

Man, that Michael is a livin' doll.

Auto dealers are just out to make a quick buck, and they'll rip off their customers every time they get a chance.

That proposed law is a bad idea because it doesn't treat everybody equally.

These are all expressions of attitudes. They describe a person's feelings toward another person, a group, a situation, or an idea. Attitudes can be expressed in many ways—with different words, different tonal inflections, and different degrees of intensity. Some of the color and richness of the ways in which attitudes and opinions are often expressed is captured in the quotations from actual public opinion interviews shown in Box 3–1.

How can statements like these be studied scientifically? In order to compare them in any systematic way, they have to be at least **classified** into two or more categories (e.g., pro or anti concerning some group or idea) or, preferably, **measured** on a quantitative scale (e.g., indicating *degree* of favorability or unfavorability). Furthermore, the classification or measurement must be **reliable**, that is, consistent. Reliability means (a) that two different raters agree on their classification of the statements most of the time, and also (b) that on two different occasions the respondents' statements are generally consistent. Reliability and validity of measurement are discussed later in this chapter.

TYPES OF ATTITUDE QUESTIONS

There are two basic types of questions which are used to obtain statements of attitudes and opinions. Some of the interview questions quoted in Box 3–1 are **open-end** questions, ones which give the respondent a free choice of how to answer and what to mention (e.g., "What do you think was the main cause of these disturbances?"). Other questions are **closed-end**, that is, ones which present two or more alternative answers for the respondent to choose between (e.g., "Have the disturbances helped or hurt the cause of Negro rights?"). Often an interview

Box 3-1 Examples of Opinion Interview Responses

The following responses are selected quotations from public opinion interviews conducted in 1968 by the Survey Research Center at the University of Michigan on the subject of white attitudes toward blacks, and particularly toward the urban riots of the preceding year. Here are some quotes from one respondent:

Q. What do you think was the main cause of these disturbances?

A. Nigger agitators. Martin Luther King and Rap Brown and that black bastard Carmichael.

Q. Have the disturbances helped or hurt the cause of Negro rights?

A. Hurt. Whites are starting to wise up what a danger these people can be. They are going to be tough from now on. People are fed up with giving in and giving them everything their little black hearts want.

Q. What do you think the city government could do to keep a disturbance from breaking out here?

A. Ship them all back to Africa. Lock up all the agitators and show them we mean business.

Q. Would you go along with a program of spending more money for jobs, schooling, and housing for Negroes . . . or would you oppose it?

A. I'd oppose it. They're getting too much already. If they want something they can damn well work for it. The government would just waste the money anyway. . . .

Q. That finished the interview. Is there anything you would like to add to any of the subjects we've discussed?

A. I just want to say that I don't have anything against Negroes as long as they don't get pushy and stay in their place. One of my best buddies is a nigger so I don't have anything against them.

By contrast, here are some answers from a second respondent:

Q. What do you think was the main cause of these disturbances?

A. Dissatisfaction. They are dissatisfied with the way they live, the way they are treated and their place in the social structure of America.

Q. Have the disturbances helped or hurt the cause of Negro rights?

A. They have helped because they have forced white people to pay attention and have brought the subject out into the open and you can't ignore it anymore. They haven't helped yet but overall it will help. . . .

Q. What do you think the city government could do to keep a disturbance from breaking out here?

A. Not only promise but actually improve conditions, education, housing, jobs, and social treatment. . .

Source: Campbell, A. (1971). *White attitudes toward black people* (pp. 2–4, 17). Ann Arbor: Institute for Social Research, The University of Michigan, Copyright © August 1971.

will use both types of questions because they have complementary advantages and disadvantages.

Open-end questions have the advantages of eliciting the full range, depth, and complexity of the respondent's own views, with minimal distortion, in his or her own words. They reduce the likelihood of overlooking important possible viewpoints which the investigator has not thought of or not included in the questionnaire. For these reasons they are often used as introductory questions to open up a topic, which will subsequently be probed more deeply and intensively with closed-end questions. (This is the **funnel sequence** of questioning.) The chief disadvantages of open-end questions are the difficulty and frequently the unreliability of scoring or **coding** them. That is, trying to decide how the response should be classified or what quantitative point on a scale it best represents can be difficult and time-consuming, and sometimes it cannot be done with adequate agreement between raters. For instance, how would you score the second respondent's answer in Box 3–1 that the disturbances "have helped. . . . They haven't helped yet but overall it will help. . . ."?

For these reasons closed-end questions are likely to make up a large majority of the items on most interviews and questionnaires. They have the advantages of being easy to score and relatively **objective**. That is, independent observers or scorers can reach a high percentage of agreement on which response was given or on what score should be assigned to the response. Of course, unlike open-end questions, they have the possible disadvantage that they may force the respondent to use the concepts, terms, and alternative answers preferred by the investigator, rather than expressing his own ideas and preferences (Schuman & Presser, 1981b; Sudman & Bradburn, 1982; Converse, 1984).

Closed-end questions have to be very carefully written so as not to lead to biased answers. Without such care in item construction, the results will be far less reliable, and sometimes they may be so slanted that they are seriously misleading. For instance, here are two biased items that were on questionnaires sent out by two political lobbying groups.

Are you in favor of allowing construction union czars the power to shut down an entire construction site because of a dispute with a single contractor, thus forcing even more workers to knuckle under to union agencies?   YES_____   NO _____
(Sudman & Bradburn, 1982, p. 2)

The Soviets and other Communist countries have a record of breaking one treaty after another. They not only shoot down unarmed passenger planes but lie about it afterwards. Do you agree with those Congressmen who want a so-called political solution based on signing agreements with Communist forces in Central America?
YES_____   NO_____

Obviously, these questions are worded so as to encourage a "No" answer. Consequently, the response percentages reported by their sponsoring agencies will markedly exaggerate citizens' real feelings about these issues. The moral of these examples is that one should always look at the question wording before making or accepting an interpretation of the meaning of survey response figures.

The most common way of measuring attitudes is to combine several items on the same topic to form a **scale** (e.g., a scale of political liberalism versus conservatism), and to compute a single score for each respondent for the group of items. In the following section we will describe the major ways of constructing such attitude scales.

ATTITUDE SCALING METHODS

During the late 1920s and early 1930s a number of attitude scaling methods were developed which are still in common use today, and more recently a few additional methods have been developed. Each of the major attitude scaling techniques will be discussed below rather briefly, primarily to clarify their major characteristics and points of difference. This will not prepare you to use these methods yourself to build an attitude scale, but it will provide you with enough information to understand references to such methods later in this book or in the research literature.

In 1925 Bogardus was one of the first individuals to use quantitative measurement methods in the field of social psychology. Thus, surprisingly, the quantitative study of attitudes is about 65 years old, even though quantitative research in psychology goes back over 110 years to the founding of Wundt's laboratory in 1879, though the term "attitude" has been used in the psychological sense for well over a century, and though cognition, affect, and conation have been discussed by philosophers ever since the time of Plato. It is no wonder, considering this relatively short history of quantitative research on attitudes and opinions, that many questions remain to be answered.

Bogardus's Social Distance Scale

Bogardus (1925) proposed a scale of **social distance** that could be used to determine attitudes toward various racial or nationality groups, many of which at that time were relatively recent immigrants to the United States. Judgments were obtained using the following instructions:

> According to my first feeling reactions, I would willingly admit members of each race (as a class, and not the best I have known, nor the worst members) to one or more of the classifications under which I have placed a cross.
> 1. To close kinship by marriage
> 2. To my club as personal chums
> 3. To my street as neighbors
> 4. To employment in my occupation in my country
> 5. To citizenship in my country
> 6. As visitors only to my country
> 7. Would exclude from my country

By using this scale, people's attitudes toward Englishmen, Germans, Turks and many other groups could be compared.

As can be seen, the scale points progress systematically from acceptance of members of the racial or national group into the most intimate family relationships, down to complete exclusion of the group. The respondent's attitude score toward that group is taken as the closest degree of relationship which he or she is willing to accept. Some early findings showed that, to the average American, Englishmen were the most accepted national group and Turks were one of the least accepted groups (Bogardus, 1928). A recent study using a social distance scale, conducted among Arabs living in Israel, showed how close various respondents felt to Jews (Lever & Smooha, 1981).

Variations of this technique have allowed measurement of attitudes toward any social group, not just racial or nationality groups, and have also broadened the range of response options. Triandis (1964) has done extensive work in this area. Using factor analysis, he has found five relatively independent dimensions of attitudes toward social classifications of people, and he has developed a scale having several items to measure each dimension. The five dimensions are listed below, together with a sample item for each (Triandis, 1971, p. 53):

1. Respect—admire the ideas of this person.
2. Marital Acceptance—fall in love with this person.
3. Friendship Acceptance—eat with this person.
4. Social Distance—exclude this person from my neighborhood.
5. Superordination—command this person.

This scale represents a considerable advance over the original social distance measures, since it reflects some of the complexity of human social behavior. For instance, a person may feel very differently about relations with members of another race in intimate areas such as friendship and marriage than in more formal areas such as working together. (As one example, see Minard's [1952] data on the social relations of white and black coal miners in Chap. 11, Box 11–2.)

Thurstone's Method of Equal-Appearing Intervals

Thurstone (1928) proposed the next attitude scaling method. In contrast to the Bogardus scale, where the scale points were not necessarily considered as equidistant, Thurstone attempted to develop a method which would indicate rather precisely *the amount* of difference between one respondent's attitude and another's. The method that he developed is rather complex.

First, the investigator collects or constructs a large number (100 or so) of opinion statements representing favorable, neutral, and unfavorable views about the topic of interest (for instance, Thurstone studied attitudes toward the church, Negroes, capital punishment, birth control, etc.). Then the investigator must obtain a large group of people to serve as judges and rate each statement's favorability or unfavorability toward the topic. Each judge sorts the statements into eleven equally spaced categories, disregarding his (her) own attitude toward the topic, and considering only how *favorable* or *unfavorable* the statement is toward the attitude object. Statements about which different judges show substantial disagreement are discarded as ambiguous; other items may be discarded as irrelevant to the topic; and judges who make too few differentiations are omitted from later computations. The remaining statements are assigned **scale values** based on the median favorability rating of the judges. From these statements a final scale of about 20 items (or sometimes more) is selected, using two criteria. The aim is to choose items having (a) scale values at approximately **equal intervals** along the 11-point scale of favorability, and (b) high agreement among the judges' ratings (that is, low spread or variability of their ratings).

After the items for the final scale have been chosen, they are randomly arranged on the questionnaire form without any indication of their scale values. Respondents check only the items they agree with and leave the others blank. A person's attitude toward the topic can then be defined as the mean (or the median—both methods have been used) of the scale values of the items which he

---

Box 3–2 A Thurstone Scale of Attitudes Toward Using Contraceptives

A selection of about half of the items from a contemporary Thurstone scale is shown below. Although the items are arranged here in the order of their scale values, on the actual questionnaire they would be arranged in a mixed-up order, and the scale values would not be shown. Respondents are to check or circle the numbers of the items with which they agree.

Scale value	Item no.	Item
1.28	5	I detest the very word birth control.
2.23	13	I am afraid to use birth control.
3.00	3	My feelings would be hurt if someone advised me to practice birth control.
4.17	6	I am sorry for those who practice birth control.
5.06	11	It frightens me to think that the overcrowding is going to force birth control on us whether we want it or not.
7.38	10	It saddens me that so many persons are ignorant of the advantages of birth control.
8.37	9	I am happy about the positive effects of birth control.
9.37	12	I am so glad people are beginning to accept birth control.
10.77	1	It is a wonderful feeling to take advantage of birth control.

Source: Kothandapani, V. (1971a). *A psychological approach to the prediction of contraceptive behavior* (pp. 26, 69–70). Chapel Hill: University of North Carolina, Carolina Population Center.

or she has checked. A more recent example of a Thurstone scale is shown in Box 3–2.

Thurstone's method makes the important assumption that the opinions of the judges do not affect the scale values of the items obtained from their judgments. This assumption has been shown to be reasonably correct when the judges do not have extreme views on the topic. However, if many of the judges have extreme views or are highly ego-involved in the topic, the obtained scale values of the items will be affected (Hovland & Sherif, 1952). Specifically, judges who are highly favorable to a topic rate only a few of the most extreme statements as favorable, and they displace their ratings of most of the statements toward the unfavorable end of the judgment scale. The opposite is true for judges who are highly unfavorable toward a topic.

The other major drawback of Thurstone's method is that it is time-consuming and tedious to apply (Webb, 1955). For that reason it is used much less extensively than the method described next.

Likert's Method of Summated Ratings

Shortly after Thurstone's work, Likert (1932) proposed a simpler method of attitude scale construction which does not require the use of judges to rate the items' favorability. Better still, the reliability of Likert scales has been shown to be at least as high as that of the more difficult-to-construct Thurstone scales (Poppleton & Pilkington, 1964).

Likert's method was the first approach which measured the *extent* or *intensity* of the respondent's agreement with each item, rather than simply obtaining a "yes-no" response. In this method, again, a large number of opinion statements on a given topic are collected, but each one is phrased in such a way that it can be answered on a 5-point rating scale. For instance, here is an example from Likert's original scale of internationalism (Likert, 1932)—it is interesting to note how many of these attitude items still have an up-to-date ring:

> We should be willing to fight for our country whether it is in the right or in the wrong.
> _____ Strongly approve
> _____ Approve
> _____ Undecided
> _____ Disapprove
> _____ Strongly disapprove

Respondents check one of the five choices, which are scored 1, 2, 3, 4, and 5 respectively. (Of course, items on the opposite end of the continuum—ones expressing a favorable attitude toward internationalism—would be scored in reverse: 5, 4, 3, 2, and 1 respectively.) This method uses only items that are clearly positive or negative toward the attitude object, whereas Thurstone's method also requires some relatively neutral items.

As the name "summated ratings" indicates, respondents' attitude scores are determined by adding their ratings for all of the items. This procedure is based on the assumption that all of the items are measuring the same underlying attitude. As a consequence of this assumption it follows that all the items should be positively correlated, in contrast to the Thurstone method, which does not impose this requirement. Though the correlations between items are not usually high, since each item is measuring its own unique content as well as the general underlying attitude, the assumption can be, and should be, checked. The usual way to do this is to correlate the score on each item with the total score for the whole pool of items

Photograph courtesy of Rensis Likert.
Reprinted by permission.

Box 3–3   RENSIS LIKERT, *Attitude Measurement Pioneer*

Rensis Likert's distinguished career included pace-setting work in four major areas: attitude measurement, survey research methodology, research on organizational management, and applications of social science to important social problems. Beginning with an interest in engineering at the University of Michigan, he shifted to a Ph.D. in psychology at Columbia. His dissertation research, published in 1932, developed the attitude measurement technique which bears his name. After teaching briefly at New York University, he moved to full-time research on organizational management. In 1939, as founding director of the Division of Program Surveys for the U.S. Department of Agriculture, he began making major contributions to methods of survey interviewing, probability sampling, and wartime public opinion research.

Following World War II, Likert founded the University of Michigan's Survey Research Center and later the Institute for Social Research, which under his leadership became the largest university-based social science research agency in the U.S. After retiring, he started a consultation and research firm on organizational management and headed it until his death in 1981. Author of over 100 articles and six books, including New Patterns of Management *and* The Human Organization, *he was also elected President of the American Statistical Association, and a director of the American Psychological Association, and he received the highest research award of the American Association for Public Opinion Research.*

combined; any items with correlations near zero are discarded since they are not measuring the common factor shared by other items.

A great strength of the Likert method is its use of **item analysis** techniques to "purify" the scale by keeping only the best items from the initial item pool. A common way of accomplishing this is to compare the groups of respondents scoring highest on the total pool of items (say, the top 25%) with the group scoring lowest (the bottom 25%), thus eliminating the middle group whose attitudes may be less clear, less consistent, less strongly held, and less well informed. If a particular item does not **discriminate** significantly between these groups—that is, does not have significantly different mean scores for the top and bottom groups—it is clear that it is measuring some other dimension than the general attitude involved in the scale. For example, in a scale of internationalist attitudes, a nondiscriminating item might be concerned with a hope for world peace, because high scorers (internationalists) and low scorers (isolationists) might both share this hope.

The Likert method of attitude scale construction quickly became and remains the most popular method, and a number of variations of it have also gained wide usage. One variation is to eliminate the "Undecided" or "Neutral" category, thus forcing respondents to choose between favorable and unfavorable stances. For instance, an item from the California F Scale, for measuring authoritarian or "fascist" attitudes, is scored as follows (Adorno, Frenkel-Brunswik, Levinson, & Sanford, 1950):

An insult to our honor should always be punished.

+ 1: slight support, agreement   − 1: slight opposition, disagreement
+ 2: moderate support, agreement   − 2: moderate opposition, disagreement
+ 3: strong support, agreement   − 3: strong opposition, disagreement

A more serious, and unfortunate, departure from Likert's procedure is the frequent omission of an item analysis. When this occurs, there is no empirical evidence that the items are all measuring the same underlying attitude, nor that they are useful, discriminating items. This situation is often signaled by use of the term "Likert-type" scale, which is apt to be an indication of hasty, slipshod research, quite out of keeping with Likert's own procedures.

Guttman's Cumulative Scaling Method

One of the limitations of both the Thurstone and Likert techniques is that the respondent's attitude score does not have a unique meaning. That is, any given score can be obtained in many different ways. On a Likert scale, for instance, a mid-range score can be obtained by giving mostly "Undecided" responses, or by giving many "Strongly approve" responses balanced by many "Strongly disapprove" responses, or by both "Approve" and "Disapprove" responses, etc.

Guttman (1944) proposed a method in which scores would have unique meanings. This was to be accomplished by ensuring that response patterns were **cumulative**. That is, in the Guttman method, a respondent who is moderately favorable to the attitude object should answer "yes" to all of the items accepted by a mildly favorable respondent *plus* one or more additional items. Similarly, a strongly favorable respondent should endorse all the items accepted by moderately favorable respondents *plus* additional one(s).

This reasoning can be clarified by some examples. Actually, the steps on the Bogardus Social Distance Scale apparently meet these requirements, as can be seen on page 51. A respondent who was very unfavorable toward Cubans, for instance, might be willing to accept them to citizenship in the country but not to the higher categories. Another person might agree to citizenship and also to equal employment. A favorable respondent might accept both of these items and also endorse accepting Cubans into his neighborhood and his social club; and so on, up to respondents who agreed with all the items.

Guttman suggests that if a scale displays the cumulative pattern just described, we can be sure that it is **unidimensional**—i.e., that it is measuring just one underlying attitude. By contrast, Thurstone and Likert scales may be measuring two or more underlying dimensions, and Triandis's (1964) expansion of the social distance scale illustrates the possibility of several related but different dimensions in one measure (see page 52).

Guttman has proposed a quantitative index for determining the unidimensionality of a scale, and as a consequence Guttman scales are apt to be quite short (perhaps 4–10 items) and restricted to a narrow topic. Box 3–4 presents an example of a Guttman scale constructed to measure attitudes toward politicized religious fundamentalism or the "religious right" (the attitude object). Notice that all six items are on a rather narrow topic, concerning various signs of religious fundamentalism, while many other aspects of religiosity are not represented. Of course, if desired, they could be measured by other Guttman scales on such topics as specific religious beliefs, frequency of religious activities, or degree of ethical behavior.

In order to develop a unidimensional scale by Guttman's procedure, an initial pool of items is given to a large group of respondents, each item being stated in a "yes-no" or "agree-disagree" format. Next, the items are arranged according to the number of respondents agreeing with them. In this procedure, by definition, the item agreed to by the fewest respondents is the item most favorable toward the attitude object (e.g., the "Moral Majority" in the scale shown in Box 3–4); that is, it is the most-difficult-to-accept item. Each respondent's score is then determined very simply: it is merely the rank number of the most favorable item which he endorsed (answered in the scored direction). The answers of each respondent are examined separately (usually by computer nowadays). This is done in order to discover all instances of inconsistent response patterns: that is, cases where a respondent endorses an item and fails to endorse one of the less-favorable items. According to the theory of measurement underlying this scaling method, each such

---

Box 3–4   An Example of a Guttman Scale

Attitudes toward religious fundamentalism and its role in current American politics were measured in a study of the 1980 U.S. election conducted by the Center for Political Studies at the University of Michigan. Responses to interview questions were obtained from a representative national sample of over 1200 white adults.

   The six-item Guttman scale which was constructed from the survey responses is shown below. Items are listed here in rank order of the percent of respondents agreeing with them, but in the actual interview they were arranged in a mixed-up order. The index of reproducibility of the scale was .925 (only 7½% inconsistent responses). This is a Guttman scale because of the decreasing percentages of profundamentalist answers on the successive questions (though it is unusual to have two items as close together in percentage of agreement as questions 3 and 4 here) and because most respondents who agreed with any given item also agreed with all of the lower-numbered items (as shown by the index of reproducibility).

   Some evidence of the scale's validity is that, of 11 current political issues, its highest correlations were with opposition to abortion and support for school prayers.

Items (in rank order, not in their order in the interview)	% agreeing
1. Religion is an important part of one's life.	73
2. The Bible is God's word and all it says is true.	44
3. I feel favorable toward evangelical groups like the Moral Majority.	30
4. Religion provides a great deal of everyday guidance.	28
5. I am born again.	21
6. I feel close to evangelical groups active in politics such as the Moral Majority.	6

Source: Miller, A. H., & Wattenberg, M. P. (1984). Politics from the pulpit: Religiosity and the 1980 elections. *Public Opinion Quarterly, 48*, 301–317. Copyright 1984 by The Trustees of Columbia University. Reprinted by permission of the University of Chicago Press.

---

instance is considered a response error, and no more than 10% of inconsistent responses are allowed if a scale is to be considered unidimensional. (Guttman refers to this as an **index of reproducibility** of .90 or higher.) Items which have many inconsistent responses are probably measuring a different underlying dimension, and accordingly they are deleted from the pool of items. After a number of rounds of computation and discarding of items, a short scale may be developed which meets Guttman's criteria for unidimensionality. However, critical analyses have demonstrated that even more procedural safeguards than those recommended by Guttman are necessary in order to be sure that a truly unidimensional scale has been developed (Dawes & Smith, 1985).

Osgood's Semantic Differential

In contrast to the above methods of constructing attitude scales, Osgood's Semantic Differential is actually a scale in itself. But it is a scale of such a general sort that it can be applied to any concept at all. This has the great advantage that one does not have to construct and try out a new scale every time one wants to study a new topic. No doubt this convenience is a major reason for the sustained popularity of the Semantic Differential since it was introduced (Osgood, Suci, & Tannenbaum, 1957).

The reason for the name "Semantic Differential" is that the technique attempts to measure the **connotative meaning** of the concept or object being rated: that is, its implied meaning, or differential connotations to the respondent. In contrast with the other major attitude scaling methods, the Semantic Differential does not consist of opinion statements about the attitude object. Instead it uses a series of 7-point scales with two opposing adjectives (e.g., "good" and "bad") at the ends of each scale. Respondents check the point on each scale which corresponds to their impressions of or feelings about the object or concept being rated. An abbreviated example of the instructions and the rating form is shown in Box 3–5.

Osgood, Suci, and Tannenbaum (1957) have reported a great deal of research on the application of this Semantic Differential approach to the measurement of a wide variety of concepts, and it has been applied in many different cultures and subcultures (Osgood, 1965; Cronkhite, 1977). Using the method of factor analysis, Osgood and his colleagues have studied the underlying dimensions in connotative meaning, and time after time they have come up with generally similar results. They have concluded that there are three basic dimensions on which people make semantic judgments, and these are applicable quite universally to varied concepts, varied adjectival rating scales, and various cultures. The three dimensions are as follows: (a) the **evaluative** dimension, involving adjectives like good-bad, beautiful-ugly, kind-cruel, pleasant-unpleasant, and fair-unfair; (b) the **potency** dimension, marked by adjectives like strong-weak, large-small, and heavy-light; and (c) the **activity** dimension, identified by adjectives like active-passive, hot-cold, and fast-slow.

Of these dimensions, the one most heavily weighted in people's judgments is evaluation. Osgood (1965) has recommended using it as the prime indicator of attitude toward the object. Clearly it is an affective dimension whereas the other two seem more cognitive in nature. Normally each dimension can be measured reliably by the use of only three or four adjective scales, so use of the Semantic Differential is simple and convenient for the investigator and relatively easy for respondents as well.

A modification of the Semantic Differential which has gained some attention is the Behavioral Differential (Triandis, 1964). This is a way of analyzing the behavioral component of attitudes, or behavioral intentions. It illustrates the great

---

Box 3–5 An Example of a Semantic Differential Rating Task

Both the instructions and the rating form are substantially shortened in this demonstration example. Ordinarily many concepts to be rated would be presented to each respondent in a stapled booklet, one concept on each page; and more adjective scales might also be used for each concept. Note that the end of the scale representing the positive pole on the dimension is systematically varied between left and right.

INSTRUCTIONS: The purpose of this study is to measure meanings of certain things to various people by having them judge them against a series of descriptive scales. In taking this test, please make your judgments on the basis of what these things mean to you.

Here is how you are to use these scales: If you feel that the concept at the top of the page is very closely related to one end of the scale (for instance, very fair), you should place your check mark as follows:

fair <u>X</u> :__:__:__:__:__ unfair

If you feel that the concept is only slightly related to one or the other end of the scale (for instance, slightly strong), you should place your check mark as follows:

weak __:__:__:__:<u>X</u> :__:__ strong

The direction toward which you check, of course, depends on which of the two ends of the scale seem most characteristic of the thing you're judging.

If you consider the concept to be neutral on the scale, both sides of the scale equally associated with the concept, or if the scale is completely irrelevant, unrelated to the concept, then you should place your check mark in the middle space.

Rate the concept on each of these scales in order, and do not omit any. Please do not look back and forth through the items. Do not try to remember how you checked similar items earlier in the test. Make each item a separate and independent judgment. Work at fairly high speed throughout this test. Do not worry or puzzle over individual items. It is your first impressions, the immediate "feelings" about the items, that we want. On the other hand, please do not be careless, because we want your true impressions.

SEPARATION OF CHURCH AND STATE *(Dimension)**

good __:__:__:__:__:__ bad	(evaluative)	
weak __:__:__:__:__:__ strong	(potency)	
active __:__:__:__:__:__ passive	(activity)	
large __:__:__:__:__:__ small	(potency)	
slow __:__:__:__:__:__ fast	(activity)	
unfair __:__:__:__:__:__ fair	(evaluative)	

*Of course, the dimensions are not shown on the respondents' forms.

Source: Adapted from Osgood, C. E., Suci, G. J., & Tannenbaum, P. H. (1957). *The measurement of meaning* (pp. 36–38, 82–84). Urbana: University of Illinois Press.

flexibility of the Semantic Differential in allowing modifications for various specific purposes. In it, the respondent is presented with a brief description of a category of persons (e.g., a black male street cleaner, a 50-year-old Jewish physician, etc.), and he is asked to rate the probability of his engaging in a long list of behaviors with that type of person. For instance:

A 50-year-old Jewish physician

would ___:___:___:___:___:___:___:___ would not
       have a cocktail with this person

would ___:___:___:___:___:___:___:___ would not
       vote for this person

As mentioned earlier, by using this approach Triandis has demonstrated that there are at least five basic factors involved in behavioral intentions toward other people.

Final Comments on Attitude Scales

This work by Triandis illustrates the possibility of multidimensional scaling of attitudes. Though most attitude scales have concentrated on measuring the **magnitude** of attitudes—that is, their degree of favorability or unfavorability (also sometimes called their **valence**)—several other dimensions of attitudes have been suggested as worthy of study. In particular, these dimensions include the **complexity** or elaboration of attitudes, their **centrality** or importance to the person who holds them, and their **salience** (closeness to awareness, or readiness for expression). The structure of attitudes will be considered in more detail in Chapter 4.

It should also be emphasized here, as was mentioned in Chapter 1, that carefully constructed attitude scales have been little used by researchers and only occasionally utilized by attitude pollers for practical assessment. Instead, their major contribution has been to provide theoretical understanding of specific domains of attitudes.

A number of other attitude scaling methods have been proposed (e.g., Edwards & Kilpatrick, 1948; Coombs, 1950). However, no methods other than the "big five" described above appear at all frequently in the attitude and opinion research literature. Though these five scaling methods are different in structure, they generally yield scores which are quite highly correlated with the other methods—Fishbein and Ajzen (1974) reported typical intercorrelations of around $+.7$, though Tittle and Hill (1967) found lower figures averaging around $+.5$. Both studies showed the Likert scale to be most highly correlated with the various other attitude measures.

A common limitation shared by all attitude measurement methods is that the scales which they produce are **ordinal** scales rather than equal-interval scales. This means that respondents can successfully be placed in their *rank order* on the attitude dimension, but we cannot be sure that the actual attitudinal distance between two values on the scale is equal to the distance between two other values. For instance, on a Likert scale, is the distance between "Undecided" and "Approve" (3 and 4) the same as the distance between "Approve" and "Strongly approve" (4 and 5)? The two distances are numerically equal, but they may not be psychologically equal. Even though Thurstone's method strives to achieve "equal-appearing intervals," it is nevertheless an ordinal scale rather than an interval scale.

Technically, ordinal scales should be treated with nonparametric, distribution-free statistical techniques involving measures such as the median. For this reason it is statistically improper to add or multiply scores together, compute mean scores, use t-tests, analysis of variance, etc. However, these restrictions are almost universally disregarded, largely because statistical research has shown that in most instances violations of the assumptions underlying the use of parametric techniques do not lead to serious distortions of their results. Thus, scores are customarily added, means computed, and t-tests and F tests used on attitude scale results. It is well to keep in mind, however, that occasionally, when distributions are markedly skewed or variances are grossly different, use of parametric techniques may produce misleading conclusions (Dawes & Smith, 1985).

RELIABILITY AND VALIDITY OF MEASUREMENT

There are two essential characteristics for attitude scales, as for all other types of measurement: reliability and validity. **Reliability** means consistency of measurement. A measurement that is unreliable is like an elastic tape measure, which stretches a different amount every time it is used. Two kinds of reliability are commonly reported: **internal consistency** measures, showing the amount of agreement between different items intended to assess the same concept; and **stability** measures, indicating the consistency of scores on the same scale at two different points in time. Both kinds are generally reported in terms of correlation coefficients. Internal consistency measures include *split-half* coefficients, *alternate-form* agreement, and the *alpha coefficient* of internal homogeneity of items (Cronbach, 1984). Stability is usually reported as *test-retest* correlations for the same group of subjects taking the same test or other measurement at two points in time. For verbal attitude or information measures, these two occasions need to be far enough apart that subjects are unlikely to remember their previous answers and simply repeat them on the second measurement occasion—usually a week or two at a minimum.

Unreliability of measurement in verbal scales can often be combatted by several means. Sometimes it results from very coarse measurement (e.g., simply "Agree" or "Disagree"), and this problem can usually be reduced by increasing the number of response alternatives (e.g., several degrees of agreement or disagreement). Thus, even if a person gives a slightly different response on another occasion, she will not have shifted from one end of the dimension to the other.

Another common source of unreliability in multi-item attitude scales is that items are not "pure" measures of the characteristic that one is attempting to measure, and thus they are often only weakly or moderately correlated with each other. The customary way to solve this problem is to add more items of the same sort to the scale, because statistical principles of measurement guarantee that, for any given level of item intercorrelation, a longer scale will be more reliable than a shorter one. This approach is limited only by the availability of appropriate items and the feasible length of the scale. Other ways of reaching sounder statistical conclusions by improving measurement reliability are discussed by Cook and Campbell (1979) and Cronbach (1984).

Validity means accuracy or correctness of measurement. Measuring instruments can be reliable without being valid—for example, a bathroom scale that consistently gives too heavy readings. However, they cannot be valid if they are not reliable—for instance, the many different readings given by an elastic tape measure would almost all (or all) be wrong, and thus the tape measure would not be a valid instrument.

The validity of a measuring instrument is often determined by comparing its results to a **criterion**—an accepted, standardized measure of the same characteristic. For example, butchers' scales are calibrated and tested against a very accurate master instrument. In psychological measurement, a criterion may be a well-established instrument, as in using the Stanford-Binet intelligence test as a standard of comparison for the results of a newly devised IQ test. However, in many cases there may be no well-established criterion instrument for the characteristic being measured, as when research begins on a new topic that hasn't been measured before. This is frequently true in the area of attitudes, and it necessitates an approach similar to pulling oneself up by one's bootstraps. The typical approach here is termed **construct validation**, which involves computing a network of relationships between the new measure and other relevant characteristics and comparing the obtained correlations with those expected on a theoretical basis. If there is generally good correspondence, that constitutes support for the instrument's validity. Other aspects of validity will be discussed in Chapter 4, and extensive elaborations of threats to validity in reaching conclusions from psychological data and ways of counteracting these threats may be found in Cook and Campbell (1979) and Cronbach (1984).

PROBLEMS AFFECTING THE VALIDITY OF ATTITUDE SCALES

Pause for a moment, and think in detail about what respondents have to do in the process of answering an attitude question:

Respondents first interpret the attitude question, determining what attitude the question is about. They then retrieve relevant beliefs and feelings [from their memory]. Next they apply these beliefs and feelings in rendering the appropriate judgment.

Finally, they use this judgment to select a response. (Tourangeau & Rasinski, 1988, p. 299)

Problems can occur at each of these stages which may reduce the validity of respondents' answers.

The *wording* of attitude questions is one of the main factors affecting the validity of attitude scales. However, since principles regarding the wording of attitude questions are also applicable to the wording of public opinion interviews, they are discussed in detail in Chapter 5.

The major problem to be discussed here is the ways in which **response sets** can invalidate attitude questionnaire answers. Response sets are systematic ways of answering which are not directly related to the question content, but which represent typical behavioral characteristics of the respondents. Several types of response sets are mentioned below and some possible solutions to them discussed.

Carelessness

When respondents are unmotivated or careless, their answers will be variable and inconsistent from moment to moment or from one testing session to another. Such a situation will reduce the questionnaire's reliability, and unreliable questionnaires are necessarily low in validity.

Some carelessness and low motivation can be minimized by building good rapport, stressing the importance of the task, and engaging the respondent's interest in it. However, despite such precautions, some respondents may still answer carelessly or fail to follow directions through misunderstanding or poor comprehension. Therefore, the response sheets are usually scanned visually, and the data are either discarded or analyzed separately for respondents who (a) omit answers to many items, (b) answer almost all items in the same way, or (c) show systematic patterns of responding (for example: a, b, c, d, a, b, c, d).

Social Desirability

The social desirability response set is the tendency to give the most socially acceptable answer to a question, or to "fake good." It operates both in attitude scales and public opinion interviews. For example, people will rarely describe themselves as dishonest, even though almost everyone occasionally fudges on the truth or cheats a little bit (by glancing at an opponent's cards, etc.). In extensive studies on this topic Edwards (1964) has shown that personality characteristics which are considered as desirable in our culture are also ones which are claimed by most respondents as applying to themselves, and vice versa. In one study of 140 items, the correlation was +.87, an almost perfect relationship. Edwards (1964) has developed a personality scale which indicates the degree of an individual's tendency to give socially desirable answers about himself, and other authors have done research with similar scales that they have constructed (Crowne & Marlowe, 1964; Schuessler, Hittle, & Cardascia, 1978).

To control for social desirability responding, Edwards has advocated the use of **forced-choice** items. In this technique of scale construction two items of approximately equal social desirability, but indicating, for instance, two different social needs, are paired together; the respondent has to pick the one which is most true of himself. This was a creative proposal, but unfortunately the evidence of its success in solving the problem of social desirability responding is disappointing (Barron, 1959, p. 116; Scott, 1968, p. 241). Consequently, only a few scales have been built in this way, the best-known of which is Rotter's (1966) scale of internal versus external locus of control.

None of the available methods for combatting social desirability responding is entirely satisfactory. The techniques which are most often used are: (a) selecting innocuous items, where social desirability seems not to be an issue, (b) providing anonymity for the respondents, (c) stating that there are no right or wrong answers since the items cover matters of opinion rather than fact, (d) urging respondents to answer honestly and stressing that it is their own opinions which are desired, (e) use of the forced-choice technique of item construction, discussed above, and (f) auxiliary use of personality scales to identify respondents who are particularly high or low in social desirability responding.

Extremity of Response

An extremity response set can only occur on items where there are more than two alternative answers. For example, on a Likert-type scale having responses scored from $+3$ to -3, an extremity response set would be demonstrated by a respondent who picked mostly $+3$ and/or -3 answers. Its opposite, a mid-range response set, would be shown by a large number of $+1$ and/or -1 answers. In one nationwide study of high school students, black students were found to give many more extreme responses than whites (Bachman & O'Malley, 1984).

There has been little study of the effects of extremity response sets or mid-range response sets on questionnaire validity. Their effects can be reduced if equal numbers of items on a scale are keyed in the positive and negative directions, for then the $+3$ answers of an extreme responder will tend to counterbalance his -3 answers (and similarly for the $+1$ and -1 answers of a mid-range responder). Another possible remedy is to eliminate extremity response set altogether by using items with only two alternatives (Yes-No, or Agree-Disagree).

Acquiescence (Yea-Saying)

The most thoroughly studied aspect of acquiescence is **agreement** response set, or yea-saying, defined as a tendency to agree with any questionnaire item regardless of its content. It has been studied extensively in the California F Scale measure of authoritarianism (Adorno et al., 1950), but it also is an issue in many other attitude and personality scales, particularly in the Minnesota Multiphasic Personality Inventory (Bradburn & Sudman, 1979). An example of agreement responding is answering "Yes" to both of the following items: "Jews are more willing than others to use shady practices to get ahead" and "Jews are just as honest as other businessmen" (Jackman, 1973). Such patterns of response have been found to be more common among lower education and income groups (Ware, 1978).

The fact that acquiescence is a problem on the California F Scale is the result of a poor decision regarding the construction of the scale. All 28 items were worded in such a way that agreement indicated authoritarianism and disagreement indicated lack of authoritarianism; that is, all items were keyed in the positive direction. At the time that the authoritarianism studies were being formulated, this was not recognized as a major issue in scale construction, but it has since become so.

It is relatively easy to rid a scale of agreement response bias effects during its construction stages by *reversing the wording and the keying* of half of the items from that of the other half. The result is called a **balanced scale**—that is, one having half of the items on the scale scored if the answer is "true," and half scored if the answer is "false." If the two groups of items are equally good, are positively intercorrelated, and have an equal spread of responses, this procedure will cause any agreement response effect to cancel out on the two groups of items.

However, this was not done on the California F Scale, and debates raged for years about the resulting problems. One group of authors (e.g., Bass, 1955; Campbell, Converse, Miller, & Stokes, 1960) claimed that the scale was more a measure of acquiescence than of authoritarianism. Another group, using different statistical methods, concluded that there was little relationship between authoritarianism and acquiescence (Couch & Keniston, 1960). A third group (e.g., Christie, Havel, & Seidenberg, 1958) found that there was some admixture of acquiescence in F Scale scores, but argued that there *should* be because agreeing with an authoritatively worded statement is really one aspect of being an authoritarian.

For investigators who want to eliminate agreement response set from their studies, there is a relatively simple solution: use a balanced scale. Procedures for developing such a scale and controlling for agreement response set have been described by Winkler, Kanouse, and Ware (1982). For those who want to study agreement responding, alone and unconfounded, Couch and Keniston (1960) have developed a relatively pure scale of "agreeing response set." Thus this problem has been largely resolved, though other well-known attitude scales are still being built without balanced scoring, such as Rokeach's (1960) Dogmatism Scale and the Survey Research Center's Index of Political Efficacy (Wright, 1975). Indeed, Rokeach (1967) has argued that there are some circumstances under which balanced scales may not be desirable.

A nay-saying or disagreement response set—i.e., a tendency to disagree with any item regardless of its content—is the other end of the agreement dimension. It is relatively rare and has been little investigated. One study found the disagreement response set more common among Republicans than among Democrats (Milbrath, 1962).

Conclusion

In summary, it seems clear that response sets do affect the answers of some respondents on attitude scales, particularly when the items are ambiguous in meaning or unimportant to the respondent. We have also seen that there are ways in which each kind of response set can be at least partially controlled or overcome.

OTHER WAYS OF MEASURING ATTITUDES

An important approach to improving attitude measurement that has been frequently suggested (but less frequently implemented) is to utilize other methods of measuring attitudes *in addition to* attitude scales. Though these methods are often experimental and admittedly imperfect, it would be desirable for any attitude study to use some of them in conjunction with verbal attitude scales.

In general, most of the following approaches have been used only experimentally rather than in any large-scale measurement program. Some of them have limited areas of applicability, and others are based on questionable or unestablished assumptions. In comparison to the well-known attitude scaling methods considered above, most of these approaches have yet to prove their usefulness, and their reliability and/or validity is often unknown. Nevertheless, they can be very helpful when used in conjunction with verbal attitude scales, because multiple measurements through different methods can add greatly to the depth and richness of our understanding of attitude patterns and variations.

Unobtrusive Measures

One of the most promising ways of supplementing attitude scale scores is the use of **unobtrusive measures** of behavior (observations made without attracting the attention of the people being studied), as suggested in a fascinating paperback book by Webb, Campbell, Schwartz, Sechrest, and Grove (1981). Such measures may be direct observations of behavior, such as standing in a high lookout and counting the number of students taking different paths across campus, or watching children's aggressive behavior in a schoolyard. However, several types of unobtrusive measurement can also substitute for tedious long-term observation as indicators of attitudes: (1) Direct measures of **preference** can be counted, such as candidate bumper stickers in a parking lot (Wrightsman, 1969). (2) **Byproducts** or waste products can show people's attitudes; for instance, counts of beer cans and liquor bottles in trash can gauge the amount of drinking and the preferred beverages in an area (Rathje & Ritenbaugh, 1984). (3) Measures of **erosion**; for instance, paths worn in the grass across campus, or the rate of emptying of ice cream tubs, can indicate preferred routes or flavors. (4) Measures of **accretion**; people's interests can be estimated from the amount of dirt on pages of library

Photograph courtesy of Lehigh University.
Reprinted by permission.

Box 3–6   DONALD CAMPBELL, *Methodologist and Attitude Researcher*

Donald Campbell has received nearly every major honor which psychology has to offer—notably, election to the National Academy of Sciences, the presidency of the American Psychological Association (APA), and the Distinguished Scientific Contribution Award of the APA. He has been honored as a methodologist and a philosopher, a field researcher and a laboratory experimenter, and for work in anthropology, political science, and sociology as well as psychology.

Born in 1916, Campbell took his B.A. and Ph.D. at the University of California at Berkeley, where his dissertation was a noteworthy study of the consistency of racial attitudes. After short periods of teaching at Ohio State and the University of Chicago, he settled in 1953 at Northwestern, where he remained until 1979, when he moved to Syracuse and later to Lehigh University.

Campbell is widely known as coauthor of books on unobtrusive measures and on quasi-experimental research methods. Among his 150 articles, one on indirect methods of measurement is particularly relevant to the topic of this chapter. Chapter 4 cites his research on attitude consistency; and in Chapter 11 his critique of attitude-behavior pseudo-inconsistency is described, and his call for planned experimentation on social and governmental programs is seconded.

books or the number of fingerprints and nose smudges on glass cases in museums (Webb et al., 1981).

Another good example of unobtrusive measures used in recent studies is the percentage size of tips left for waitresses (Crusco & Wetzel, 1984). Similarly, the forwarding of letters in the **lost letter technique**, in which stamped and addressed letters are dropped in shopping areas, can gauge community sentiment toward local organizations or election issues (Simmons & Zumpf, 1983). Further use of such imaginative approaches could help to solve the problems inherent in interpreting the results of attitude-scale and opinion-interview research.

A wide range of indirect methods of measuring attitudes has been described in various reviews (see Kidder & Campbell, 1970; Dawes & Smith, 1985). It is possible to classify all attitude measurement methods into five broad categories, as suggested by Cook and Selltiz (1964), and these categories will provide the framework for our following discussion:

1. Measures utilizing self-reports of beliefs, feelings, or behavior.
2. Measures involving observation of behavior toward the attitude object.
3. Measures of reactions to or interpretations of relevant partially structured stimuli.
4. Measures involving performance on relevant objective tasks.
5. Measures of physiological reactions to the attitude object.

In using measures from any of these categories, it should be emphasized that the researcher's conclusions about people's attitudes is an inference from the particular measures taken. This is true even where the measure used is individuals' self-reports of their own attitudes, for the researcher still has to decide whether the respondents truly are aware of their own attitudes and are reporting them accurately.

Self-Report Measures

This category contains all of the attitude scaling methods described above. Since they have already been discussed at some length, only one additional type of self-report measure will be mentioned.

Taylor and Parker (1964) have suggested use of an "attitude report question." This is merely a single general question such as, "In general, how do you feel about politicians?" combined with a graphic rating scale (a line with words at each end such as "Very favorable" and "Very unfavorable," and numbers below it indicating its units) where the respondent marks his (her) degree of favorability. Surprisingly, for such a simple technique, it has been found to be as reliable as 5- or 6-item Guttman scales. Of course, even more than most self-report measures, responses to it can be easily faked. Its virtues are its directness and simplicity, but a resulting drawback is the impossibility of measuring different aspects or dimensions of the general attitude with this technique. For some types of attitudes and some people, an overall global attitude measure may be quite sufficient because there is little differentiation of nuances and details; but for other attitudes and/or other people, **multidimensional** attitude scaling may demonstrate a much more complex pattern of attitudes.

As mentioned above, the validity of self-report measures is always open to question. However, their validity can sometimes be increased by using them in conjunction with a related objective measure. For instance, in a study of adolescents' self-reports of smoking, the amount of smoking reported was significantly higher when reports were taken after a demonstration that recent smoking could be detected from the presence of carbon monoxide in their breath (Bauman & Dent, 1982). This carbon monoxide measure was a true indicator of smoking, but the same effect of increased validity should occur if respondents merely *believe* that there is a true measure of their behavior or feelings available. That principle is the basis of the so-called **bogus pipeline**, in which subjects are falsely convinced that some elaborate electronic apparatus can detect their true feelings; and this technique typically results in their giving increased reports of various socially undesirable attitudes or behaviors such as racial prejudice (Jones & Sigall, 1971; Quigley-Fernandez & Tedeschi, 1978; Liebhart, 1979). Of course, the same principle may help to account for whatever accuracy the polygraph or "lie detector" may possess (see the final section of this chapter for more details).

It should be emphasized that using techniques such as the bogus pipeline—indeed, all of the following four categories of indirect attitude measurement—raises certain ethical questions. To some extent, each such technique poses issues of invasion of privacy, informed consent, deception, and/or debriefing. However, these are not black-white issues, and authorities differ on how they should be resolved. Much of the behavior that might be studied observationally by researchers is public and thus open to anyone's view. Similarly, minor deception is often socially acceptable (as in conventional politeness and "little white lies"), and debriefing may sometimes do more harm than good. Dawes and Smith's (1985) review recommends following social norms about what is considered ethical outside of the laboratory, and using deception only where it seems so innocuous that no debriefing should be needed. A fuller discussion of ethical issues in research will be found in Chapter 11.

Observations of Behavior

Compared with verbal self-report measures, behavioral measures of attitudes have been very little used and consequently are poorly developed and crude in their methodology. In large part this is because they are difficult, time-consuming, and expensive to utilize.

The most straightforward type of behavioral observation is one made in a natural setting, such as watching for aggressive episodes in a schoolyard. However, the time-consuming, tedious nature of such observation has led to use of more standardized situations which are structured so as to elicit the behavior of interest more easily. Cook and Selltiz (1964) have described three different types of such standardized approaches: (a) apparently unstaged standardized situations in which a subject's behavior can be observed, (b) staged role-playing situations in which the subject is asked either to respond as (s)he would in real life, or to take the part of a particular other person, and (c) use of sociometric choices which the subject believes will have real-life consequences (e.g., choice of members of a group to work with on a joint task). In all three of these approaches, of course, the situation chosen is one in which the attitude objects (e.g., children of a different racial group) are presented in some way. A key advantage of this approach is that *subjects can be convinced that there will be real-life consequences* flowing from their responses (e.g., they will actually get to work with the classmates they choose). It is also possible to represent the attitude objects only *symbolically* (i.e., in words or pictures) rather than having them physically present. However, this procedure studies the respondents' behavioral intentions (what they *say* they would do) rather than their actual behavior toward the attitude object—thus it is a return to a self-report form of measurement.

Since Fishbein and Ajzen (1972) have reported very high correlations between behavioral intentions and behavior, the use of behavioral-intention measures may be justifiable here. Cook and Selltiz (1964) have defended it on the grounds that it is less subject than real-life behavior to a variety of extraneous influences. However, we should emphasize that it is sometimes possible to observe actual behavior in situations where extraneous influences are relatively inoperative. For instance, slight vertical or horizontal head movements are good indicators of a person's attitude toward a persuasive message (Wells & Petty, 1980). Similarly, in a small-group discussion situation, choice of a seat next to a crippled person rather than one farther away could indicate a person's attitude toward cripples. Since Wicker (1969) and others have shown that there is often little relationship between verbal self-report attitude measures and behavior, the use of actual behavior measures here may be preferable to behavioral intention measures.

One famous example will illustrate the types of behavioral intention measures which have been used. DeFleur and Westie (1958) have developed a method in which white subjects, after seeing some relevant interracial slides, are asked whether they would be willing to be photographed with a black person of the opposite sex. The subjects are also requested to sign a "standard photograph release agreement" indicating which of a variety of purposes they would be willing to have such a photograph used for—from showings solely to professional sociologists for research purposes, to a nationwide publicity campaign in favor of racial integration. The number of uses that they check is taken as an indicator of favorableness toward blacks.

Reactions to Partially Structured Stimuli

This measurement approach involves the use of **projective techniques**. The stimuli are not clearly structured, i.e., they do not provide sufficient information to determine a person's response. Therefore, subjects must draw on their own needs and dispositions in interpreting or describing the characteristics of the attitude object. For instance, a picture of the head of a black girl may be presented, and the subject be asked to describe her characteristics or to make up a story about her. The task is usually presented as a test of imagination or social sensitivity or some similar concept, rather than as a measure of the subject's attitudes.

Obviously, in a sense this approach uses the subject's verbal self-report, and so is similar to that measurement approach. The primary differences are the use of the somewhat ambiguous stimulus instead of an explicitly named attitude object, and the disguised goal of the measurement (e.g., as a test of ability to judge people's characteristics rather than an attitude measure). It is assumed that these aspects of the technique decrease the likelihood of subjects distorting their true feelings in an attempt to present themselves in a favorable light to the investigator. However, the literature on projective techniques is full of critiques questioning the validity of their results (e.g., Anastasi, 1979). It is clear that projective responses may reflect an individual's attitude; but they may also merely indicate a person's awareness of the common cultural patterns of response, such as unequal treatment of various minority groups.

As a result of these limitations, systematic use of projective techniques in the study of attitudes and opinions has been rare. One successful example was the study by Riddleberger and Motz (1957) which found that relatively prejudiced and unprejudiced subjects (as measured by a self-report instrument) differed in their interpretations of a pictured interracial group. Partially structured projective pictures can also be used as stimulus materials to obtain responses on typical attitude scales such as the Semantic Differential, as was done in a study by Perlman and Oskamp (1971).

Performance on Objective Tasks

This measurement approach has been used somewhat more widely than the previous ones. Cook and Selltiz (1964) describe it as follows:

> Approaches in this category present the respondent with specific tasks to be performed; they are presented as tests of information or ability, or simply as jobs that need to be done. The assumption common to all of them is that performance may be influenced by attitude, and that a systematic bias in performance reflects the influence of attitude. (p. 50)

Thus, in a sense this approach is similar to observations of behavior. It differs in that the task is structured for the subjects, and that the relevance of their performance to measurement of their attitudes is usually quite thoroughly disguised.

Some examples may clarify how this can be done. Hammond (1948) devised an "information" test with alternative answers that were equally far on either side of the correct response (which was not provided as an alternative). He showed that the subjects' choices of erroneous responses were generally consistent with their own attitudes. For instance, a prounion subject would generally choose an answer which overestimated labor unions' membership size, rather than an answer which underestimated it, while the opposite would usually be true for an antiunion subject. Similarly, Brigham and Cook (1970) had subjects judge the plausibility of pro-integration and anti-integration arguments, and the judgments were treated as indicators of the subjects' own attitudes toward racial integration.

Two problems are present in interpreting measures of this sort. If a person shows a consistent bias in performance, it seems safe to infer that the individual's attitudes are responsible. However, if a consistent bias is not shown, it may not be safe to infer that the person's attitude is a weak one, for we do not know how sensitive such measures are. Second, a particular bias in response might reflect either the subject's wishes or fears; "a member of the Communist party may overestimate the number of Communists in the United States, but so may a member of the John Birch Society" (Cook & Selltiz, 1964, p. 51). Thus, additional information may be needed to determine the direction of the subject's attitude from a biased performance.

Physiological Reactions

A fairly wide variety of physiological reactions have been used as indicators of attitudes: galvanic skin response (GSR), blood vessel constriction, heart rate, dilation of the pupil of the eye, and even the conditioned response of salivation in humans. For instance, Westie and DeFleur (1959) showed subjects pictures of whites and blacks in social situations and found a relationship between GSR, blood vessel constriction, and a verbal measure of attitudes. Hess (1965), using careful eye photograph techniques, reported pupillary expansion in response to interesting or pleasing stimuli and pupillary constriction as a response to unpleasant stimuli. However, most later studies have not been able to replicate these pupillary findings (Woodmansee, 1970).

In these techniques it is assumed that the amount of the physiological reaction indicates the extent of the subject's arousal, the intensity of his feelings, and hence the extremity of his attitudes. However, physiological measures are generally **nondirectional** in nature; that is, they do not indicate whether the feeling involved is a pleasant or unpleasant one. Thus, additional information is usually necessary in order to interpret them adequately.

There are two physiological measures that give promise of being directional indicators of attitudes. The first is **electromyograph (EMG)** recordings of invisible movements of the facial muscles. Cacioppo and Petty (1979b) have shown that electrical recordings of activity in these muscles can distinguish the direction of people's feelings toward a persuasive message, but it is not yet known whether this measure can indicate the strength (intensity) of feelings as well. The second measure that may be able to show both direction and intensity of attitudes is **generalization of conditioned GSR** responses, demonstrated in the area of racial attitudes by Tognacci and Cook (1975). Their procedure was to give electrical shocks to a subject accompanying non-race-related statements that the individual had previously evaluated as "bad." After a conditioned GSR response was developed, it was found to generalize to race-related statements. However, this effect was significant only for equalitarian subjects and not for mildly prejudiced ones, so its extent of applicability is still unclear.

Sensitive electronic recordings of this sort are also used in the most familiar physiological indicator of emotional reactions, the **polygraph** machine or "lie detector." The use of "lie detector" tests has been increasing rapidly in industry, government, and law enforcement—for instance, to screen job applicants for honesty, or to identify guilty criminals (Beach, 1980). However, at the present state of our knowledge, there is very little empirical support for their use, either as a screening device or to indicate guilt; and as a result most courts will not admit polygraphic evidence (Saxe & Dougherty, 1985). A variety of other applications of physiological measures to social behavior is presented in a volume by Cacioppo and Petty (1983).

The purpose of physiological measurements may or may not be disguised. It usually makes little difference to the results, for normally these physiological reactions are not under the conscious control of subjects. Thus, even if they knew the purpose of the study and wanted to present a particular impression of themselves, they probably could not modify their responses accordingly. However, unfortunately, physiological responses are sensitive to many other variables, such as stimulus characteristics and environmental factors, in addition to the subjects' attitudes. Therefore, particularly careful control of the measurement situation is needed, and this generally restricts the use of these measures to experimental laboratory studies.

SUMMARY

Attitudes and opinions may be expressed in many colorful ways, but for purposes of scientific study, they must be classified into categories or measured on a quantitative scale. The development of attitude scaling methods in the 1920s was the first major application of quantitative measurement in the field of social psychology. In terms of the frequency of their use, the "big five" of attitude scaling methods are Bogardus's scale of social distance toward various ethnic groups, Thurstone's method of equal-appearing intervals, Likert's method of summated ratings (the most popular of all), Guttman's cumulative scaling method of constructing a unidimensional scale, and Osgood's scale of connotative meaning, the Semantic Differential. All of these methods produce scales which are ordinal in nature, and therefore some caution must be exercised if parametric statistics are used in analyzing their results.

It is essential for attitude scales, like all measurement methods, to be both reliable (consistent) and valid (accurate) in their results. Problems which affect the validity of attitude scales include the response sets of carelessness, social desirability, extremity, and acquiescence (yea-saying). With due care in constructing and interpreting attitude scales, all of these problems can be at least partially overcome.

In conjunction with attitude scales, it is recommended that other less-common methods of studying attitudes also be more widely used in research, in order to provide a broader multidimensional measurement approach. These additional methods include other self-report measures, observations of behavior (particularly unobtrusive observations), reactions to partially structured stimuli such as projective techniques, measures of performance on objective tasks in attitude-relevant situations, and physiological reactions to attitudinal stimuli.

4

Structure
and Functions
of Attitudes
and Beliefs

*My attitude is my greatest asset. As long as a person has a positive attitude,
he can always make it.*—Glenn Turner, millionaire super salesman.

*If a man would register all his opinions upon love, politics, religion, and
learning, what a bundle of inconsistencies and contradictions would appear at
last.*—Jonathan Swift.

*Belief in the general credibility of our senses is the most central belief of all;
nearly all of our other beliefs rest upon it, and to lose our faith in it is to lose
our sanity.*—Daryl J. Bem.

What do attitudes and opinions do for the person who holds them? Some
people feel that their favorite football team is the best in the country; others are so
negative toward racial minorities that much of their identity is based upon their
prejudiced attitudes. Do the attitudes that you hold help you to live your daily life,
to fulfill your psychological needs, and to get along effectively in your world?
Social scientists have traditionally answered these questions with a resounding
"Yes." Your attitudes and opinions may not make you wealthy, as the above
quotation from a super salesman suggests, but they can at least help to make you
healthy and wise. Let us take a closer look at the functions of attitudes.

FUNCTIONS OF ATTITUDES

Major theorists who have proposed functional views of attitudes are Smith,
Bruner, and White (1956) and Katz (1960). The former group used a detailed case-
study approach to analyze individuals' personality characteristics and salient attitudes, and they showed that nationalistic and internationalistic attitudes about the

United States and the Soviet Union often seemed to reflect the holder's personality needs, values, and defenses. Similarly, attitudes about any topic that a person feels strongly about may serve important functions in his or her life.

Katz (1960) has suggested that there are four major functions which attitudes perform:

1. Understanding. Many attitudes help us to understand our world and to make sense of occurrences around us. They provide consistency and clarity in our explanation and interpretation of events. This has also been called the **knowledge** function of attitudes, but that term does not imply that attitudes provide a factually truthful picture of the world—merely one that is meaningful and understandable to the particular individual who holds them. For one person, the events of the Watergate cover-up might be understood in reference to an attitude that "Republicans are no damn good." Another person might relate the same facts to the belief that "Power tends to corrupt." In each case the person's beliefs or attitudes provide a context for the new information, aiding in its interpretation and assimilation into the person's belief system.

2. Need Satisfaction. Many attitudes are formed as a result of our past rewards and punishments for saying or doing particular things. Once formed, these attitudes usually continue to be useful in helping us to satisfy our needs or to reach our goals. These attitudes have also been termed **adjustive** in the sense of helping us to adjust to life situations, or **utilitarian** in the sense that they are useful in reaching our goals. Examples would include the attitudes of a worker who favors a political party because he believes it will "do more for the working man," or the pupil who comes to like language classes because she has done well in them in the past and been rewarded by the teacher's praise and her own feeling of competence.

3. Ego Defense. Attitudes can also help to enhance our self-esteem and to defend us against the "thousand slings and arrows" of life. All people use defense mechanisms to some extent, but they are used much more by individuals who are insecure or feel inferior or who have deep internal conflicts. Prejudiced attitudes are often used as a crutch to bolster the self-esteem of the holder, a phenomenon which has been called the "scapegoat view of prejudice." Similarly, the employee who shrugs off criticism from the boss by saying "The boss is always bad-tempered" may be using an unrealistic ego-defensive attitude to avoid thinking about his (her) own failings.

4. Value Expression. A value-expressive attitude is one which helps to establish a person's self-identity, which portrays the sort of person (s)he is, which says in effect "This is the way I am." Examples include the motorcyclist's liking for his black leather jacket, and the teenage girl's preference for her favorite color in all of her wardrobe. More important attitudes often express an individual's basic values, as with the conscientious objector's aversion to all aspects of warfare and violence.

These four types of needs which attitudes can serve for a person are useful in classifying and understanding attitudes. But they also have other uses. As Katz pointed out, they can also help to explain the types of situations in which different attitudes will be aroused, and the types of influences which will be effective in changing different attitudes.

Attitude Arousal

Each of us has hundreds of attitudes toward hundreds of different attitude objects, but they are not all active at the same time. Most of the time most of our attitudes are lying dormant while only a few are in the focus of our conscious attention or directly influencing our behavior. It requires the onset of a particular psychological need or a relevant environmental cue to **arouse** into an active state a particular attitude which we hold. And, importantly, the question of what type of internal need or external cue will arouse a particular attitude is largely determined by the function which that attitude serves for the individual concerned.

To illustrate this relationship, consider a common attitude, that of racial prejudice, which involves negative feelings toward blacks. This attitude could serve any of the functions mentioned above, but Katz has emphasized that the conditions necessary to arouse the attitude would be different for the different functions. Attitudes serving the understanding function are apt to be aroused by a cognitive problem while attitudes serving the adjustment function may be prompted by a social need. Ego-defensive attitudes can be aroused by threats to the holder's security or by appeals to hate feelings, whereas value-expressive attitudes may be aroused by appeals to a person's ideals or self-image.

Many attitudes serve more than one of the types of functions discussed above, and consequently they can be aroused in several different ways. For instance, one attitude may serve both an understanding and a need-satisfaction function for a person. Still, it is important to know which functions the attitude is serving for the individual in order to know what external cues or internal needs will arouse the attitude into an active state.

Attitude Change

As with attitude arousal, it takes different forces and pressures to *change* attitudes that are serving different functions. For example, the conditions that might lead to changing a person's understanding-oriented attitude may be quite different than the conditions necessary for changing an ego-defensive attitude.

Understanding-oriented attitudes are most likely to change in situations which have become ambiguous for the attitude-holder due to new information or a

Photograph courtesy of Daniel Katz.
Reprinted by permission.

Box 4–1   DANIEL KATZ, *Attitude Theorist and Researcher*

Widely respected and honored as a social psychologist, Daniel Katz is Professor Emeritus at the University of Michigan. His B.A. was earned at the University of Buffalo and his M.A. and Ph.D. at Syracuse. Before moving to Michigan he taught at Princeton, was chairman of the psychology department at Brooklyn College, and served in the Office of War Information in World War II.

In this chapter, Katz's theory of the functions of attitudes is prominently mentioned. He has also been influential as a researcher in many different attitude areas and as editor of the outstanding journal in social psychology from 1962 to 1967. He has been elected president of three different divisions of the American Psychological Association and served on its Board of Directors. His early research on racial stereotypes is mentioned in Chapter 14, and he has also done cross-national research in Norway, Denmark, Greece, and Yugoslavia.

changed environment. For example, prejudiced individuals may learn about the achievements of black doctors, scientists, statesmen, or authors. If the prejudiced attitudes had been serving the understanding function, they would probably then be changed in order to establish a more consistent, complete, and logical cognitive structure.

Need-oriented attitudes, on the other hand, are likely to change only if the holder's goals or needs have changed or if the person's needs are no longer being satisfied by the attitude in question. An example would be the prejudiced merchant who realizes that the hiring of black employees and the serving of black customers can increase profits. If the merchant's attitudes toward blacks were utilitarian in nature, they would be very likely to change.

Ego-defensive attitudes are unlikely to be changed by the procedures which work with other types of attitudes, such as providing new information or offering positive incentives for change. Since ego defenses are erected to protect the person from threats and conflicts, it is necessary first to remove the threat or conflict before attitude change can occur. This can sometimes be done by establishing a supportive atmosphere, as in a long-term therapy situation; or individuals may gradually outgrow the emotional conflicts which underlie their prejudices, or they may acquire insight into their defense mechanisms.

Value-expressive attitudes are also usually difficult to change because people's values are apt to be very important and central parts of their cognitive structure. White supremacists whose prejudiced attitudes express some of their most strongly held values are unlikely to change those attitudes. However, change could occur if they were to become seriously dissatisfied with their self-concept or former values, as for instance if they underwent a religious conversion. A more common way in which value-expressive attitudes may change is by the holders becoming aware that the attitudes don't really fit with their values. For example, Rokeach (1971) found that experimental subjects' prejudiced attitudes and behavior were changed following a dramatic demonstration that they were really inconsistent with one of the subjects' basic values, the idea of equality for all.

Evaluation of Functional Viewpoints

Evaluation of functional theories of attitudes is difficult. On one hand, the theoretical stance seems very plausible, and it is consistent with the ideas of many authors. On the other hand, for about 25 years after the early statements about attitude functions, very little research was done specifically to test their theoretical hypotheses. As psychological theories, these statements have a number of serious problems (Kiesler, Collins, & Miller, 1969). They are an eclectic compendium of ideas from many past thinkers and researchers (for instance, the ego-defensive function comes directly from psychoanalytic theory), but as a result many of their concepts are ill-defined and their hypotheses therefore are not clearly testable. Undoubtedly the greatest problem is in measuring individual differences in the functions that a particular attitude (e.g., racial prejudice) serves for a particular person. Until there is a clear way of measuring those functions, the functional viewpoint will have mainly suggestive value rather than predictive power or practical usefulness.

During the middle 1980s there was a resurgence of interest in studying attitude functions, and a number of researchers carried out studies relating some of the traditional attitude functions to various objective measures. Fazio (1988) has emphasized the understanding or "object appraisal" function as primary because it is applicable to all attitudes whereas the other functions apply to only some attitudes. Notable advances in operationalizing aspects of functional theories have been made by Herek (1986), Snyder and DeBono (1987), and Shavitt (1988). Herek has developed a new instrument, the Attitude Function Inventory, to measure a somewhat revised set of attitude functions. He postulates three types of expressive functions, two of which are similar to Katz's concepts: *defensive, value-expressive*, and *social-expressive* attitudes. The latter term refers to attitude expression which is motivated by a need for acceptance by other people in one's social environment. Three other functions, which are all based on the utility of the attitude object (or person) to the attitude holder, Herek refers to as *evaluative* attitudes; as a group, they are similar to Katz's need-satisfaction function. It is too early to tell how successfully Herek's inventory can measure these different functions, but the effort is well worthwhile.

THE STRUCTURE OF BELIEFS

We will turn now from the topic of function to that of structure—from the question of how attitudes work to how they are built. In doing this, we will consider first the structure of beliefs and belief systems, drawing upon the thinking of Rokeach (1968) and of Jones and Gerard (1967).

Centrality and Intensity of Beliefs

What factors determine how important a belief is to the person who holds it? The concept of a *belief system* may help to answer this question. A system is a set of interconnected parts which function in relationship to each other. Just so, beliefs and attitudes do not exist in isolated separateness, but they are connected with many other beliefs in an organized system.

The **centrality** of a belief, that is, its importance in the person's belief system, may be defined in terms of its degree of connectedness with other beliefs—the number of "implications and consequences it has for other beliefs" (Rokeach, 1968, p. 5). Rokeach has suggested four principles which spell out the concept of centrality in more detail:

1. Beliefs about one's **self**, one's existence and identity, are much more central than other beliefs.
2. **Shared** beliefs about one's existence and self-identity are more central than unshared beliefs (ones held only by oneself).
3. Beliefs which are **derived** from other beliefs (rather than from contact with the object of belief) are *less* central than underived beliefs.
4. Beliefs concerning **matters of taste** are *less* central than other beliefs. They are usually seen by the holder to be arbitrary in nature, and thus they are relatively inconsequential in their impact on other beliefs.

The **intensity** of a belief refers to how strongly the belief is held, or how sure the person is about it. Central beliefs are usually intensely held, but the opposite does not follow. Beliefs concerning matters of taste may be intensely held even though they are not central. I may like pistachio ice cream with a passion (intensely), but that fact probably does not affect my attitude toward people who prefer vanilla or my beliefs about the nutritive value of pistachio nuts. My belief in the tastiness of pistachio ice cream is not central in my belief system because it does not influence other beliefs, and if it were to change, there would be few consequences for my other beliefs.

Primitive Beliefs

Rokeach (1968, p. 6) has suggested the term **primitive beliefs** for ones which are very central and which "have an axiomatic, taken-for-granted character." They are generally formed through direct contact with the object of belief (that is, they are not derived beliefs), and they are "psychologically incontrovertible because they are rarely, if ever, experienced as subjects of controversy." Such beliefs are the person's "basic truths" about the world, about other people, and about one's self. Examples would be: "My name is _____." and "Water is wet." However, they do not have to be shared beliefs. They can be based solely on one's own experience, and thus they can include pathological beliefs such as phobias, delusions, and hallucinations. Examples of unshared primitive beliefs would be: "No matter what others may believe, I know that my mother doesn't really love me" and "I believe I am Jesus Christ returned to earth."

The importance of primitive beliefs to the individual holding them can be demonstrated by challenging them and observing the person's response. An effective challenge may produce astonishment, disbelief in the challenge, anger, intense anxiety, or even pathological symptoms of withdrawal and confusion if continued long enough. The humor in the television show *Candid Camera* often came from seeing the astonishment of persons whose primitive beliefs were being challenged, for instance by seeing water apparently running uphill or an inanimate object apparently talking or moving under its own power. Rokeach has observed that when a parent unexpectedly calls a young child by a name which isn't its own, the child will first enjoy it as a new game; but if the parent continues, the child will soon ask for reassurance that it really is a game, and before long intense anxiety will result, with tears, panic, and desperate attempts to get the parent to stop.

Daryl Bem (1970) has described primitive beliefs in an entertaining selection which is reprinted in Box 4–2.

Box 4–2 *Types of Primitive Beliefs*

Many beliefs are the product of direct experience. If you ask your friends why they believe oranges are round, they will most likely reply that they have seen oranges, felt oranges, and that oranges are, indeed, round. And that would seem to end the matter. You could, of course, ask them why they trust their senses, but that would be impolite.

Consider a more complicated belief. If you ask your friends why they believe the asteroids are round (that is, spherical), the more sophisticated among them might be able to show how such a conclusion is derived from physical principles and astronomical observations. You could press them further by asking them to justify their belief in physical principles and astronomical observations: Whence comes their knowledge of such things? When they answer that question—perhaps by citing the New York Times—you can continue to probe: Why do they believe everything they read in the Times? If they then refer to previous experience with the accuracy of the Times or recall that their teachers always had kind words for its journalistic integrity, challenge the validity of their previous experience or the credibility of their teachers.

What you will discover by such questioning—besides a noticeable decline in the number of your friends—is that every belief can be pushed back until it is seen to rest ultimately upon a basic belief in the credibility of one's own sensory experience or upon a basic belief in the credibility of some external authority. Other beliefs may derive from these basic beliefs, but the basic beliefs themselves are accepted as givens. Accordingly, we shall call them "primitive beliefs."

Source: From *Beliefs, Attitudes, and Human Affairs*, by Daryl J. Bem, page 5. Copyright © 1970 by Wadsworth Publishing Co., Inc. Reprinted by permission of the publisher, Brooks/Cole Publishing Co., Monterey, Calif.

Bem divided primitive beliefs into two categories. **Zero-order beliefs** are so taken for granted that they are normally out of our awareness—"the nonconscious axioms upon which our other beliefs are built" (p. 6). They are mostly beliefs about the trustworthiness of our senses, the size and shape constancy of objects, and the validity of particular authoritative sources of knowledge such as the Bible or the dictionary. **First-order beliefs** are ones based directly on our sensory experience or on an unquestioned authority. They are normally in our awareness, and we can imagine alternatives to them, but they require no justification other than a citation of our experience or of the relevant authority (e.g., oranges are round, not square). Bem (1970, p. 7) concluded:

We all hold primitive beliefs. It is an epistemological and psychological necessity, not a flaw of intellect or a surplus of naiveté. We all share the fundamental zero-order beliefs about our senses, and most of us hold similar sorts of first-order beliefs. For example, we rarely question beliefs such as "This woman is my mother" and "I am a human being." Most of us even treat arbitrary social-linguistic conventions like "This is my left hand" and "Today is Tuesday" as if they were physical bits of knowledge handed down by some authority who "really knows." Finally, most religious and quasi-religious beliefs are first-order beliefs based upon an unquestioned zero-order faith in some internal or external source of knowledge. The child who sings "Jesus loves me—this I know, / For the Bible tells me so" is actually being less evasive about the metaphysical—and hence nonconfirmable—nature of his belief than our founding fathers were when they presumed to interpret reality for King George III: "We hold these truths to be self-evident . . ."

Empirical evidence that there really is a difference between the various types of beliefs discussed above has been presented by Rokeach (1968). He showed that primitive beliefs which are shared with other individuals were most resistant to change, followed by primitive beliefs which are not widely shared. Next in resistance to change came beliefs about authority, such as "The Pope is infallible in matters of faith and morals" or "The philosophy of Karl Marx is basically a sound one, and I am all for it." Next came derived beliefs, such as "Birth control is morally wrong" or "The Russians were justified in putting down the Hungarian revolt in 1956." Finally, easiest to change were inconsequential beliefs concerning matters of taste, like "I think summertime is a much more enjoyable time of the year than winter" or "There is no doubt in my mind that Elizabeth Taylor is more beautiful than Dinah Shore."

Syllogistic Structure of Beliefs

We have seen that nonprimitive beliefs such as the ones just quoted can be derived from other beliefs which we hold. Beliefs exist in interconnected networks, and a useful way of thinking about their connections is to use the syllogistic model proposed by McGuire (1960) and Jones and Gerard (1967)—also termed the **probabilogical model** by McGuire (1985). As you may remember from studying logic, a syllogism is a set of three statements, two of which (the first and second premises) lead logically to the third (the conclusion). For example:

1st Premise:	Using birth control protects a woman from getting pregnant.
2nd Premise:	I want to be protected from getting pregnant.
Conclusion:	Therefore, I should use birth control.

The conclusion is a derived belief, and in this case both premises are also derived from other beliefs. Let us trace a possible chain of derivations for this conclusion back to a primitive belief. The next step back toward the source might be:

My doctor says that using birth control protects a woman from getting pregnant.

My doctor is an authority about medical matters.

Therefore, using birth control protects a woman from getting pregnant.

Here the second premise is a belief about authority, and for many people this step in reasoning might end the matter. They trust their doctor as a reliable source of facts about medical matters, though of course they wouldn't necessarily accept the doctor as an authority in other fields such as car repair or politics. If this is the end of a person's chain of reasoning, then we have arrived at one of her primitive beliefs, an idea so self-evident to her that she takes it for granted: "My doctor knows about medical matters."

The Vertical Structure of Beliefs.   Another person, however, might have a longer, more elaborate chain of reasoning, one with more links between the ultimate conclusion and the underlying primitive belief. This characteristic of the belief system has been called its **vertical structure**. The conclusion of each syllogism can be used as a premise in the next syllogism above it. Tracing the chain of reasoning back several more steps, a person might have beliefs about the doctor's candor and about his source of information:

My doctor believes that using birth control protects a woman from getting pregnant.

My doctor says what he really believes.

Therefore, my doctor says that using birth control protects a woman from getting pregnant.

Scientific studies show that using birth control protects a woman from getting pregnant.

My doctor believes scientific studies.

Therefore, my doctor believes that using birth control protects a woman from getting pregnant.

The journal *Science* has reported scientific studies showing that using birth control protects a woman from getting pregnant.

Science is an authoritative source of accurate information.

Therefore, it is true that scientific studies show that using birth control protects a woman from getting pregnant.

Again we have reached a primitive belief about authority as the underlying premise in this chain of reasoning. No matter how wise or well-informed we are, many of our beliefs ultimately rest on our faith in some authority: the Bible, the *New York Times, Time* magazine, the encyclopedia, the President, or some other source of information which we trust.

The Horizontal Structure of Beliefs.   Fortunately, most of our beliefs do not rest on just one line of reasoning nor stem from just one authority. There are usually several different routes to the same conclusion. The breadth of support for a given belief has been called its **horizontal structure.** For instance, there may be several other chains of reasoning leading to the same conclusion about personal use of birth control. One such chain, starting from its most central end, might be:

World overpopulation leads to famine.

Famine is bad.

Therefore, world overpopulation is bad.

World overpopulation is bad.

Birth control programs can reduce world overpopulation.

Therefore, birth control programs are good for the world.

Birth control programs are good for the world.

I should take part in programs which are good for the world.

Therefore, I should use birth control.

Another part of the horizontal structure might be:

Using birth control produces a more enjoyable sex life.

I want an enjoyable sex life.

Therefore, I should use birth control.

Of course, these supporting chains of beliefs are not necessarily in the person's awareness at any given time, and the person may not even be able to verbalize them without extensive self-searching and introspection. Also, a person's beliefs are rarely all consistent in leading to the same conclusions. There are usually some contradictory beliefs also present, such as:

Using birth control has some medical hazards.

I don't like to run the risk of medical hazards.

Therefore, I shouldn't use birth control.

The question of the amount and importance of consistency in a person's belief systems is one which has been widely debated by attitude theorists, as we will see in Chapter 10.

"Psycho-Logic" in Belief Systems.   It is important to realize that, though we have used logical syllogisms to indicate the structure of belief systems, a person's beliefs are not completely logical or rational. In fact, some of the syllogisms quoted above would not meet the rigorous specifications of a logician. The following reasoning is no more illogical than the first syllogism supporting birth control above, but it would probably be much less acceptable to most women:

Never associating with men can prevent a woman from getting pregnant.

I don't want to get pregnant.

Therefore, I should never associate with men.

Not only may the basic reasoning process be faulty, but even if the reasoning is correct, false premises may lead to incorrect conclusions. Also, even if the premises and the reasoning within each chain are correct, different lines of thought can lead to contradictory conclusions, so a person's higher-order beliefs are often inconsistent with each other.

Thus, the typical state of people's belief systems is a kind of rough, partial consistency rather than complete logical rationality. If we look closely, there are usually many gaps, overlaps, and conflicts among the beliefs which we hold. Abelson and Rosenberg (1958) coined the term **psycho-logic** to describe the way in which people's beliefs are based on ideas and concepts which seem to "go together" comfortably from their subjective viewpoints rather than being derived by strict deductive logic. If there are inconsistencies or contradictions, they can often be avoided by denial, or by redefining concepts, or by other cognitive mechanisms, or simply by refusing to think about the conflict.

Finally, there is evidence that people often choose their beliefs in order to support their feelings about a topic. McGuire (1960) called this process "wishful thinking" in his extensive experimental study which clearly demonstrated the prevalence of such nonlogical thinking side by side with more logical reasoning processes. Other studies have suggested that people may selectively search for information supporting their feelings or selectively avoid contrary information, rather than rationally considering all the evidence. This common phenomenon of beliefs supporting feelings leads us to our next topic, the question of the relationship between the cognitive (thinking), emotional (feeling), and behavioral aspects of attitudes.

THE STRUCTURE OF ATTITUDES

We move now from discussion of the structure of beliefs to the structure of attitudes, a topic which has had a resurgence of attention in recent years (cf. McGuire, 1985). We will begin by distinguishing between two important dimensions: the valence and complexity of attitudes.

Valence and Complexity of Attitudes

Attitudes are, by many definitions, intrinsically evaluative; that is, they involve positive and/or negative feelings toward the attitude object. The **valence** of an attitude is the degree of favorability or unfavorability of the person's feelings toward the object. (As in chemistry, the valence is a combination of the attitude's **direction**—pro or con—and its **extremity**—*how much* pro or con.) An example of valence would be how favorable or unfavorable one feels toward the Democratic Party. It is this evaluative dimension of attitudes which is usually measured by the type of scales which we discussed in Chapter 3.

Another, less-commonly-measured characteristic of attitudes is their **complexity**, that is, the number of elements which they contain. Each of the three aspects or components of an attitude can range from being very simple to very complex. For instance, in the area of political attitudes, the cognitive component for active members of a political party is likely to be highly differentiated (complex)—i.e., composed of many different beliefs. In the United States a party member is apt to have information and beliefs about several potential candidates for President, about many issues important to the party's platform, about a number of Senators, Representatives, and other party figures, about important events in the party's history, etc. By contrast, many Americans probably have very simple belief systems regarding Britain's Conservative Party, perhaps even just a single dim impression that its leader was Margaret Thatcher.

Similarly, the affective component of attitudes can range from simple liking or disliking for a distant acquaintance to a very complex set of feelings toward someone we know well. Close associates of a political leader such as a U.S. presidential candidate might hold a complex mixture of feelings toward him, possibly including admiration, supportiveness, envy, resentment, amusement, and occasional anger. Likewise, the third component of attitudes, behavioral tendencies toward such a public figure, might range from simply intending to vote for him, to the other end of the scale, where one might be ready to carry out a complex set of actions such as advising him, helping to write his speeches, soliciting public support from his colleagues, running errands, and even taking the blame for his political mistakes.

A number of researchers have devised various measures of cognitive or attitudinal complexity, based on different assumptions and approaches (Streufert & Streufert, 1978). One psychologist who has studied complexity extensively is Tetlock (1985, 1986), who has developed a system for coding what he calls "integrative complexity" from written materials such as diplomatic communications, speeches by U.S. Presidents, or Supreme Court decisions. A particularly interesting application of this system studied official American and Soviet foreign policy statements from 1945 to 1983 (Tetlock, 1985). The study predicted and found that higher integrative complexity accompanied periods of coordinative policy initiatives by the two governments, whereas lower integrative complexity was associated with competitive national actions such as military or political interventions in other countries.

Another use of this system studied the complexity of people's ideas about political issues involving conflicting values (e.g., opening public park lands to mining). Findings showed that people display more complex reasoning and attitudes in situations where they see two approximately equally important values in conflict with each other (Tetlock, 1986). Another way of stating this relationship is that complex beliefs are generally accompanied by relatively moderate, rather than extreme, evaluative attitudes (Linville, 1982).

Relationship of Cognitive and Affective Components

The studies on complexity described just above have carried us over into a heavily studied topic concerning attitude structure: the relationship of the cognitive and affective aspects of attitudes.

Research Methods.   Three major types of research methods are often used in the attitude area. The first is **correlational** studies, defined as ones which measure the *naturally occurring* covariation in two or more variables. (The term "correlational" is not limited solely to studies which use correlation coefficients as their statistical procedure.) The second type is **experimental** studies—ones which *manipulate* one or more independent variables and observe their effects on one or more dependent variables. For instance, they may influence one attitude component by an experimental procedure and observe the resulting effects on a different attitude component. The third research method is **quasi-experimental** research, defined as studies where the investigator does *not* have full control over the independent variable and therefore cannot assign subjects randomly to conditions, but *does* have control over how and when the dependent variable is measured, and usually also over what groups of subjects are measured (Campbell & Stanley, 1966; Cook & Campbell, 1979). The most common forms of quasi-experiments are nonequivalent control group studies (where the research groups are not equated by randomized assignment to conditions), and time-series studies (where a group is measured at several successive points in time, and thus it can serve as its own control). Donald Campbell has pioneered the concept of quasi-experiments and has stressed that, by a careful choice of measurement procedures and additional comparison groups, one can construct research designs that are almost as powerful and rigorous as true experimental designs.

Early Research.   Empirical study of the relationship of attitude components has been going on since the beginnings of attitude measurement in the 1930s, and there have been three successive waves of such research. The first wave was part of the great burst of empirical research in social psychology which followed World War II, and it was typified by correlational studies. A good example is a study by Campbell (1947), who investigated attitudes toward five different ethnic minority groups (Negroes, Jews, Japanese, etc.) among non-minority-group college students and high school students. He measured the behavioral component of attitudes with a social distance scale, which indicated tendencies to avoid contact with members of each minority group. The affective component was measured by feelings of liking or disliking for each group, and the cognitive component was measured by three scales indicating beliefs in each group's competence, morality, and degree of blame for social problems. In general, the several dimensions for each group were found to correlate around +.5, showing a substantial positive relationship, but not a complete identity.

Experimental and Quasi-Experimental Research.   The second wave of research on attitude components, which peaked in the 1960s, was more experimental in character and typically studied attitude change as a dependent variable. One of its hallmark volumes was produced by the Yale University research group headed by Carl Hovland (Rosenberg, Hovland, McGuire, Abelson, & Brehm, 1960) and contained several studies showing the influence of one attitude component on other components. In it, Rosenberg (1960) demonstrated that hypnotically induced changes in the *affective* component (i.e., feelings about a social issue) could create continuing parallel changes in the cognitive components of value importance and perceived instrumentality.

Another study in this same volume (McGuire, 1960) began by assessing subjects' beliefs in many different propositions, which included dispersed subgroups of statements having a clearcut, syllogistic logical relationship to each other. McGuire found a high degree of consistency in beliefs about these cognitive elements, but the consistency was far from perfect because of tendencies toward "wishful thinking" and toward cognitive isolation of inconsistent opinions in "logic-tight compartments." One part of the study demonstrated a so-called **Socratic effect**, showing that the Socratic method of inquiry (merely asking subjects to think about and state their beliefs) was sufficient to produce greater cognitive consistency on a retest one week later. Another portion of the study provided evidence for both *wishful thinking* (a conclusion's desirability influencing belief in its probability) and, on the other hand, for *rationalization* (a conclusion's probability influencing belief in its desirability).

Recent Analytical Research. The third wave of research on attitude components accompanied the upsurge of interest in social cognition in the late 1970s and 1980s. These studies have gone into great analytical detail concerning the conditions that influence various components and their interrelationships. Some examples of such research were mentioned in the earlier section on cognitive complexity.

Another example of analytical research is recent studies investigating conditions under which the inconsistency-reducing Socratic effect occurs. In general, it is a robust phenomenon, found under most conditions and methods of study (Tesser, 1978; McGuire, 1985), but it is strongest when related belief statements are initially presented in nonsyllogistic order (conclusions mixed with premises) and interspersed with unrelated statements, and when the interval between the original presentation and the retest is short (O'Malley & Thistlethwaite, 1980). Studies using improved measurement methods have indicated that early research may have overestimated the extent of people's "wishful thinking" about such belief statements (C. Miller, 1980). Other research on attitude components has concluded that cognitive-affective consistency is a good indicator of well-defined attitudes, which tend to be resistant to outside attempts to change them (Chaiken & Baldwin, 1981). In Chapters 9 and 10 we will go into more detail on theories and findings concerning attitude change.

From findings such as those above, McGuire (1985, p. 245) has derived several postulates of nonlogical thinking that amplify the "psycho-logic" viewpoint discussed earlier in this chapter:

1. A person's attitude on one issue is affected by his or her attitudes on other related issues *only* insofar as they are momentarily salient (e.g., the Socratic effect).
2. Loose linkages in belief chains cause persuasive impacts to be progressively smaller on more remote related issues (McGuire calls this "spatial inertia").
3. Persuasive impacts on unmentioned related issues filter down gradually over time ("temporal inertia").
4. Due to the loose linkages in belief chains, persuasive effects on a target attitude must exceed some *threshold* amount before change will be induced in remote related attitudes.
5. There is a tendency for one's beliefs and one's desires on any given issue to converge ("hedonic consistency").

Prediction of Behavioral Intentions

Another key question about attitude structure is how closely the behavioral component, often called "behavioral intentions," is tied to the other components.

We will discuss some of the many systems that have been proposed to try to predict behavioral intentions from beliefs, attitudes, and other factors. In turn, behavioral intentions have been used as predictors of actual behavior, but we will save that important topic for extended discussion in Chapter 11.

Fishbein and Ajzen's Theory of Reasoned Action. The most widely cited approach in this area is a theory which has been developed and tested over the past 20 years by Fishbein and Ajzen (1975; Ajzen & Fishbein, 1980). Their name for it, the "theory of reasoned action," emphasizes the principle that people act on the basis of their beliefs and available information, though it does not imply the use of strictly logical reasoning. The theory holds that a person's behavioral intention is normally the best predictor of how (s)he actually will behave, and that behavioral intentions in turn can be predicted by knowing the person's relevant attitudes and beliefs. Specifically, the behavioral intention to perform a certain behavior (for instance, to take a particular college course) is a weighted additive function of two factors: the person's own *attitude toward*

Photograph courtesy of Martin Fishbein.
Reprinted by permission.

Box 4–3 MARTIN FISHBEIN, *Founder of Reasoned Action Theory*

Martin Fishbein has been doing research on the relationship of attitudes to beliefs, intentions, and behavior for over 25 years, and his theory of reasoned action is the best known one in this area. After earning his bachelor's degree at Reed College, he took his Ph.D. at UCLA in 1961 and has served on the psychology faculty of the University of Illinois ever since.

Fishbein is the author or editor of five books and nearly 100 journal articles and book chapters. He has received awards for his scientific contributions from the American Marketing Association and the Interamerican Psychological Society. Among many other consulting positions, he has given advice on attitude and behavior change to the Congressional Office of Technology Assessment, the Center for Disease Control's Office on Smoking and Health, and the NIMH AIDS Policy Subcommittee. As mentioned in this chapter, he has had a long and fruitful collaboration with Icek Ajzen, which has resulted in their joint authorship of two books and over two dozen articles and book chapters.

the behavior and his or her *subjective norm* about what relevant other people think he or she should do. Each of these factors is computed using an **expectancy x value** model—that is, each is a compound involving a series of salient beliefs, with the individual's perceived probability (or expectancy) of each belief statement being multiplied by an evaluative term (the perceived value of that outcome to the individual).

Thus, a person's attitude toward the behavior is composed of behavioral beliefs (beliefs about the consequences of performing the behavior), each of which is multiplied by the person's evaluation of that consequence; the attitude toward the behavior is the sum of these products. Similarly, the subjective norm is made up of normative beliefs (beliefs about what each "significant other" thinks the person should do), each of which is multiplied by the person's motivation to comply with that other; again the products are summed to yield the subjective norm. These computations are shown symbolically by the formulas in the left side of Table 4-1.

Triandis's Model of Interpersonal Behavior. Triandis (1977) has proposed a model closely related to Fishbein and Ajzen's, but with some interesting variations. It is shown symbolically in the right side of Table 4-1, using a notation that clarifies its similarities to and differences from Fishbein and Ajzen's system.

Triandis's first equation agrees that intentions are important in predicting behavior, but it introduces two additional factors: habits and facilitating conditions. One reason that Fishbein and Ajzen do not include these two factors as predictors

TABLE 4-1 Comparison of Two Systems for Predicting Behavior from Attitudes, Beliefs, and Intentions

Fishbein & Ajzen (1975, pp. 301–303)	Triandis (1977, pp. 9–19)
1. $B \sim I$	1. $P_B = (Hw_H + Iw_I)\,F$
2. $I = (A_B)w_1 + (SN)w_2$	2. $I = (S)w_S + (A)w_A + (C)w_C$
3. $A_B = \Sigma\, b_i e_i$	3. $C = \Sigma\, b_i e_i$
4. $SN = \Sigma n_i m_i$	4. S includes norms, roles, social contracts, self-monitoring, and self-concept influences

where B = behavior
 I = intention
 w = empirical weight
 A_B = attitude toward the behavior
 SN = subjective norm
 b_i = behavioral belief that behavior B leads to consequence i
 e_i = evaluation of consequence i
 n_i = normative belief that group or individual i thinks I should (or should not) perform the behavior
 m_i = motivation to comply with group or individual i

where P_B = probability of a behavior
 I = intention
 w = empirical weight
 H = habit of performing the behavior
 F = facilitating conditions (including ability, arousal, and knowledge)
 S = social factors (see above)
 A = affect about the behavior
 C = evaluation of consequences of the behavior
 b_i = belief that the behavior leads to consequence i
 e_i = evaluation of consequence i

may be that their system is designed to predict behavior that is under "volitional control," rather than automatic (e.g., breathing) or required or prevented by outside forces (e.g., involuntary crying, or immobility enforced by a straightjacket). Within these extremes, however, there are various degrees of voluntary behavior, some of which could well be influenced by learned habits or by facilitating conditions. Some later studies have shown the value of habit as a variable in predicting behavior, in situations ranging from donating blood to attending college classes to wearing automobile seat belts (Bagozzi, 1981; Fredricks & Dossett, 1983; Wittenbraker, Gibbs, & Kahle, 1983).

Jumping down to the third equation, we can see that Fishbein and Ajzen's "attitude toward the behavior" is structurally identical to Triandis's "evaluation of consequences of the behavior." Also, on the fourth line, Triandis mentions several social factors without specifying how they should be weighted and combined, and some of them are similar to those used in computing Fishbein and Ajzen's subjective norm. Thus, the most clearcut difference in predicting intentions (equation 2) is that Triandis includes a separate term directly measuring affect toward the behavior, whereas Fishbein and Ajzen expect that affect will be subsumed under the attitude term, which they generally measure by cognitive rather than affective items.

In short, Triandis's system is similar in structure to Fishbein and Ajzen's, but it includes several additional terms which may add to its predictive power. On the other hand, Fishbein and Ajzen emphasized the superior parsimony of their system, claiming that it can predict just as well with fewer variables. Of course, the predictive power of these models is an empirical question, and we will summarize some of the quantitative findings below.

First, however, let us mention a few other researchers who have suggested the use of other variables in predicting intentions. Some studies have shown that a variable of *personal moral obligation* adds to predictability of intentions in morally relevant situations (e.g., returning an undeserved tax refund or using contraception—Gorsuch & Ortberg, 1983; Pagel & Davidson, 1984). Somewhat similarly, Budd and Spencer (1984) demonstrated that the centrality and the certainty of people's attitudes contributed to the predictability of their intentions. Sheth (1974), like Triandis, has proposed another related prediction system, primarily for use in predicting consumer buying intentions and actual purchasing behavior. The system is complex; it includes measures of habits, evaluative beliefs, the general social environment, the anticipated situation, and unexpected events, in addition to affect, behavioral intentions, and behavior. Using this model to predict purchases of a newly introduced instant breakfast product by a sample of 954 housewives, Sheth found quite high relationships—multiple correlations of almost +.70 with behavioral intentions and almost +.50 with purchase behavior.

Quantitative Prediction of Intentions.   Sheth's level of success in predicting behavioral intentions is quite impressive, and both of the other systems have reported comparable levels of predictive power. Fishbein and Ajzen (1975, p. 310) summarized the findings of 13 studies involving a wide variety of intentions, ranging from engaging in premarital intercourse to buying eight consumer products. In these studies the average multiple correlation for predicting intentions was a very high figure of +.75, and in 10 later studies the average multiple correlation was +.80 (Ajzen, 1988, p. 119). Triandis (1977, p. 208) has also reported average multiple correlations, using his system, in the .70s. Thus, it is clear that high levels of prediction of intentions can be attained, and the three systems seem to be roughly equivalent in their predictive ability.

However, it is possible that more precise comparative studies may show some differences among the systems, and a few such studies have been done. In research on three different family-planning intentions, Jaccard and Davidson (1975) found the Fishbein and Ajzen system very slightly better than Triandis's system. On the other hand, Brinberg (1979) found Triandis's model superior in predicting intentions to attend church regularly (though Fishbein and Ajzen's system did better at predicting actual church attendance—i.e., behavior). Feldman and Mayhew (1984) studied people's meat and salt consumption using a variation on Triandis's model and found that its additional components made it superior to Fishbein and Ajzen's system in predicting both intentions and self-reported behavior. In summary, no system has been demonstrated to be consistently better, but there is clear evidence that additional predictor variables can add significantly to predictability *in some situations*. Whether this potential improvement outweighs the decrease in parsimony is a matter of personal judgment.

A final interesting point concerns the relative weights of the attitude component versus the subjective norm component in predicting intentions. Fishbein and Ajzen's theory specifies that these weights should vary with the behavior involved, with the surrounding social situation, and for different people. A few findings will illustrate how these weights can provide meaningful interpretive information. In a study concerning intentions to engage in premarital sexual intercourse during a college semester, the subjective norm component (what other people expect) carried all of the predictive power for men, whereas the attitudinal component (summarizing likely consequences) was the major predictor of intentions for women (Fishbein & Ajzen, 1975, p. 311). In cooperative types of interpersonal situations, the normative component is typically the main predictor of behavioral intentions, whereas in competitive situations the attitudinal component is much more important (Ajzen & Fishbein, 1970). Intentions to attend classes regularly during a college summer session were much better predicted by attitudes than by subjective norms (Fredricks & Dossett, 1983), and the same was true for predicting intended church attendance for both Catholics and Protestants, but not for Jews (Brinberg, 1979).

Overview

From this review of research on the components of attitudes, it should be clear that, though there is some general consistency of the three components, nevertheless many situations have been found where there are meaningful distinctions and differences among them (e.g., Bentler & Speckart, 1981).

Finally, consistent with the preceding discussion, an early article by Katz and Stotland (1959) suggested that some attitudes have mostly cognitive elements, others mostly affective elements, and others mostly behavioral elements. This viewpoint can be linked to the question of attitude functions with which this chapter began, for understanding-oriented attitudes might be more likely to be largely cognitive, while value-expressive attitudes might be largely behavioral, etc. Furthermore, ego-defensive attitudes seem most likely to have components which are not consistent, whereas other types of attitudes are more likely to have consistent components (Katz & Stotland, 1959).

A DIFFERENT APPROACH—ATTITUDE LATITUDES

A rather different approach to the structure of attitudes has been taken by Muzafer Sherif and his colleagues (Sherif & Hovland, 1961; Sherif, Sherif, & Nebergall, 1965). Sherif has called his viewpoint a social judgment approach, emphasizing that the process by which a person makes judgments about social objects (other people, objects, events, issues, etc.) is both affective and cognitive at the same time. That is, it involves both evaluation of the objects and categorization of them as similar to or different from other objects. Thus he stresses that the "cognitive" and "affective" aspects of attitudes are inextricably intertwined.

Sherif's major contribution to attitude theory and measurement is the concept of **latitude**, that is, a range of attitudinal positions which a person may accept or reject concerning a given issue. Sherif stresses that *a single score cannot give us sufficient information* about a person's attitude. Since most attitude-measurement techniques yield a single score for each respondent, Sherif feels that they are inadequate to the job of fully understanding attitudes. Though they may be

> . . . useful for locating individuals who take a stand on one or the other side of a controversial issue, [they] tell us very little about the person who adopts a moderate or neutral position. They tell us little about the subject's possible susceptibility to change, the direction in which change is most likely, how tolerant the individual is of other positions, or how committed he is to his own stand. (Sherif et al., 1965, p. 21)

How does Sherif propose to determine all this? First, by measuring the individual's latitudes of acceptance, rejection, and noncommitment, and second, by developing an indicator of his **ego-involvement**, that is, his personal commitment to his own stand on the issue. The **latitude of acceptance** is the set of positions on an issue (or toward a person or object) which a person finds acceptable. The **latitude of rejection** is the set of positions which the person finds objectionable. The **latitude of noncommitment** is any other positions on the issue, which the person neither accepts nor rejects. Research findings have led Sherif to the conclusion that the best measure of ego-involvement is the breadth of the person's latitude of rejection. (Highly ego-involved people reject more positions as personally unac-

Photograph courtesy of Muzafer Sherif.
Reprinted by permission.

Box 4–4   MUZAFER SHERIF, *Proponent of Attitude Latitudes*

Born in Turkey in 1906, Muzafer Sherif did graduate work at the University of Istanbul, Harvard, the University of Berlin, and received his Ph.D. from Columbia in 1935. His dissertation research, published as The Psychology of Social Norms, *achieved fame as a pioneering experimental study in social psychology. Returning to Turkey, he taught at Ankara University, conducted research on social judgment and on adolescence, and translated many American psychological works into Turkish.*

Following World War II, Sherif held research fellowships with Hadley Cantril at Princeton and Carl Hovland at Yale. Each of these collaborations resulted in a well-known book. From 1949 to 1966 he was Professor of Psychology at the University of Oklahoma, and subsequently Professor of Sociology at Pennsylvania State University. His 100 publications include over 24 books which he has written, co-authored, or edited; and in 1968 he received the American Psychological Association's highest honor, the Distinguished Scientific Contribution Award. Retired in 1972, he continued to contribute to social psychology until his death in 1988. His major recent research concentrated on intergroup conflict and cooperation, and on processes of social perception and judgment. His social judgment theory of attitude change is discussed in Chapter 10, and his contributions to attitude measurement are pointed out in this chapter.

ceptable than do uninvolved individuals.) In short, Sherif holds that these three latitudes comprise a *set of categories* that an individual uses in evaluating attitude objects.

The procedure for measuring the three latitudes requires subjects to make judgments about the acceptability and then the unacceptability of a fairly large number of attitude positions. In a typical study concerning a presidential election, Sherif et al. (1965) used nine positions ranging from strongly pro-Republican positions, through milder ones, to neutrality, and on to strongly pro-Democratic positions. As examples, here are positions number 1, 3, and 5 in the sequence of 9:

1. The election of the Republican presidential and vice-presidential candidates in November is absolutely essential from all angles in the country's interests.

3. It seems that the country's interests would be better served if the presidential and vice-presidential candidates of the Republican party were elected this November.

5. From the point of view of the country's interests, it is hard to decide whether it is preferable to vote for presidential and vice-presidential candidates of the Republican party or the Democratic party in November.

A typical subject might check position number 2 as most acceptable and numbers 3 and 4 as also acceptable, check positions 6, 7, 8, and 9 as unacceptable, and leave positions 1 and 5 unchecked. Thus, according to Sherif's definitions, this person would have a latitude of acceptance of three positions, a latitude of rejection of four positions, and a latitude of noncommitment of two positions (see Figure 4–1). This measurement technique has also been used with many other issues, such as drinking alcoholic beverages (Budd & Spencer, 1984) and family size preferences (Granberg, 1982).

Research Findings on Attitude Latitudes

What would you guess about the relative size of the three latitudes? Would you expect people to accept more positions than they rejected, or vice versa? And what kind of people reject the most positions? Results from extensive studies using the latitude concept, summarized by Sherif et al. (1965), are intriguing. They found, first of all, that no matter what the person's own position on the issue was, the average size of the latitude of *acceptance* was about the same (approximately three positions). Second, the latitude of *rejection* was the largest of the three latitudes and, as predicted, its size was greater for subjects holding extreme positions than for more moderate or neutral subjects. Third, as predicted, the latitude of *noncommitment* was largest for individuals holding a neutral viewpoint and considerably smaller for ones with extreme positions. Thus extreme Republicans

POSITION	SUBJECT'S RESPONSE		RESULTING MEASURES
	ACCEPT	REJECT	
1			
2	XX		LATITUDE OF ACCEPTANCE = 3
3	X		LATITUDE OF NONCOMMIT-MENT = 2
4	X		
5			
6		X	
7		X	LATITUDE OF REJECTION = 4
8		X	
9		XX	

FIGURE 4–1 Responses of a hypothetical respondent, showing computation of attitude latitudes.

and extreme Democrats were found to be nearly identical in their attitude structure (the number of positions which they accepted, rejected, and were noncommittal about) despite their opposition in attitude content. Also, the extreme party supporters on both sides were markedly different in attitude structure from the more moderate supporters of the same party.

These interesting results are graphically displayed in Figure 4–2. Very similar results have been found for some other issues such as right-to-work legislation and federal farm policy questions.

These findings suggest that moderates on any issue typically accept about the same number of positions that they reject. However, people with extreme viewpoints ("far out" on either fringe) typically reject substantially more positions than the number that they accept. There are also usually a few individuals with roughly neutral positions who nevertheless hold to their positions very strongly; for instance, in the political arena such individuals would be dedicated independents. Unlike other neutral or "undecided" respondents, they typically reject nearly as many positions as do the extreme partisans. Sherif et al. (1965, p. 59) concluded that "attitude research has concentrated too exclusively on the subject's agreements or acceptances and far too little on what he rejects."

Assimilation and Contrast

Two additional concepts which are vital to Sherif's theory of social judgment are the principles of *assimilation* and *contrast* (Sherif & Hovland, 1961). These principles derive from research findings in the area of psychophysics, which studies human perception and judgment of physical stimuli like weights, colors, sounds, etc. Just as these physical stimuli can be judged on scales of heaviness, brightness, or loudness, so can social stimuli like people or political viewpoints be judged and ranked on attitude scales. For instance, political candidates can be ranked (with some disagreement between judges, of course) on a scale of liberalism-conservatism, or they could be ranked on other more specific scales concerning their stands on civil rights, military spending, welfare programs, etc. The rater's

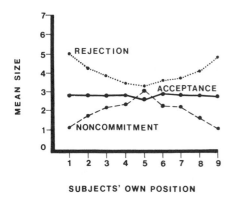

FIGURE 4-2

Average size (number of positions) of latitudes of acceptance, rejection, and non-commitment for persons endorsing different positions as most acceptable in the 1960 presidential election. Positions along base line range from 1 (most extreme Republican) through 5 (nonpartisan) to 9 (most extreme Democrat).

Source: Adapted from Sherif, C. W., Sherif, M., & Nebergall, R. E. (1965). *Attitude and Attitude Change: The Social Judgment-Involvement Approach.* Philadelphia: Saunders, p. 52.

own attitude on the particular issue serves as an important **anchor**, or reference point for judgment, in making such scale rankings.

The principle of **assimilation** states that social stimuli, such as political candidates or persuasive messages, which are within a person's latitude of acceptance will be assimilated. This means that they: (a) will be seen as closer to the person's own attitude than they actually are, (b) will be favorably evaluated, and (c) will produce some change in the person's attitude in the direction advocated by the message. The principle of **contrast** states that when social stimuli are within a person's latitude of rejection, contrast will result. That is: (a) they will be seen as farther from the person's own attitude than they actually are, (b) they will be unfavorably evaluated, and (c) they will produce either no attitude change or, in some cases, attitude change opposite to the direction advocated (a "boomerang effect"). Stated in other words, when an attitude object is close to our own attitude, we tend to see it as more similar to our attitude than it really is (assimilation), and when it is quite far from our own attitude, we tend to see it as even farther away than it really is (contrast).

A clear example of assimilation and contrast effects is shown in Figure 4–3,

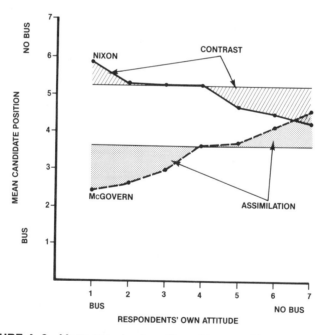

FIGURE 4–3 Mean perceived position of two presidential candidates on the busing issue for McGovern voters who varied in their own attitude toward busing.

Source: Adapted from M. King (1977–78, p. 519). Copyright 1978 by Columbia University Press. Reprinted by permission of the University of Chicago Press.

based on a representative national sample of voting-age Americans in the 1972 election between Nixon and McGovern (King, 1977–78). The figure shows findings for just one of the many issues investigated—attitudes toward busing to achieve school integration—and for only the respondents who actually voted for McGovern. Thus, for these voters, McGovern was clearly in their latitude of acceptance, and Nixon was probably in their latitude of rejection. The seven pairs of data points on the graph represent seven subgroups of McGovern voters whose own attitude toward busing ranged from highly favorable (on the left) to highly unfavorable (on the right). If all voters, regardless of their own attitude toward busing, had perceived a candidate's position on the issue similarly, the plot of data points on the graph would have been horizontal, like the two hypothetical light lines. On the other hand, if there was complete assimilation of the candidate's position to the respondent's own attitude, the plot for McGovern would have been a 45° ascending line; and if there was complete contrast, the plot for Nixon would have been a 45° descending line. What the results actually showed was that these McGovern voters substantially assimilated McGovern's perceived position on busing toward their own attitude (indicated by the stippled areas), and they also contrasted Nixon's position away from their own attitude (the areas with slanted parallel lines).

Though both assimilation and contrast effects were clearly displayed on this issue for these McGovern voters, assimilation was a much stronger and more pervasive finding across all the issues studied and for both Nixon and McGovern voters in this research (King, 1977–78). The greater prevalence and strength of assimilation has been a typical finding in most other studies as well, some of which have even failed to find any evidence for contrast effects (Brent & Granberg, 1982; Granberg, 1984). However, other studies have found substantial contrast effects (e.g., Granberg & Robertson, 1982); and Judd, Kenny, and Krosnick (1983) have argued that common methodological inadequacies have led to underestimation of the strength of contrast effects. Thus both assimilation and contrast seem to be customary ways that we deal with our social world, leading to greater consistency and comfort in our perceptions of people and issues with which we have contact (Manis, Nelson, & Shedler, 1988).

We will return to Sherif's social judgment theory in Chapter 9 and examine its performance in the area of attitude change research.

SUMMARY

In this chapter we have seen that attitudes and beliefs can perform several different functions for the person who holds them. They aid in *understanding* of situations and events; they provide *satisfaction of needs* by helping their holder to adjust to his environment; they form a bulwark of *ego defense* against threats to the person's self-esteem; and they provide a channel for *expression of values* which are important to him. A particular attitude may serve one or several of these functions, and different forces and pressures are necessary in order to change attitudes which serve different functions.

The *centrality* of a belief is its importance in the person's belief system, while a belief's *intensity* is how strongly it is held. *Primitive beliefs* are, by definition, very central in the person's belief system, and they are so much taken for granted that the holder hardly ever has reason to question them. Primitive beliefs are formed either through direct contact with the object of belief or through accepting the statement of an unquestioned external authority such as Mommy or the Bible. Derived beliefs, on the other hand, can be built up from basic underlying beliefs in a syllogistic type of structure. Despite their syllogistic structure, beliefs are not usually completely logical or rational. They are built up of elements which "go together" comfortably in the person's belief system, in accordance with a principle of "psycho-logic" or rough consistency, rather than following the rules of strict deductive logic.

The *valence* of an attitude is its degree of favorability or unfavorability toward the attitude object, and its *complexity* is the number of elements which it contains. Research on the relationship between the cognitive and affective components of attitudes has shown that there is very often a general consistency between them, but also many situations where they differ in meaningful ways. Various theories have been developed to predict the behavioral intention component, of which Fishbein and Ajzen's theory of reasoned action is the best-known.

A different viewpoint on the structure of attitudes rejects the notion that a person's attitude can be adequately represented by a single point on a scale. Sherif and his colleagues have emphasized the concept of *latitude:* the range of positions which a person accepts or rejects on a given issue. Research has shown that the width of the latitude of rejection on an issue is a good measure of a person's *ego-involvement* in the issue. Extremists typically reject more positions than they accept. In judging social stimuli within their latitude of acceptance, people commonly *assimilate* them toward their own attitudinal position, whereas stimuli within their latitude of rejection are often *contrasted* (perceived as farther from the person's own attitude than they really are).

5

Public Opinion Polling

I never paid any attention to the polls myself.—Harry S Truman.

During the first 29 months of the Reagan administration the president's long-time pollster, Richard Wirthlin met with Ronald Reagan more than 25 times to discuss politics and polls.—Richard S. Beal & Ronald H. Hinckley.

Public opinion polls have come to have a pervasive and often dangerous impact in America, an impact which has gone largely unrecognized and uncorrected.—Michael Wheeler.

Polls can help make government more efficient and responsive; . . . they can make this a truer democracy.—George H. Gallup.

In this chapter and the following one we turn to a consideration of public opinion polling—first its procedures and problems, and then its findings about the structure of public opinion.

Public opinion polling is certainly the aspect of psychological measurement with which the general public is most familiar. The major commercial polls, such as Gallup's and Harris's, appear every week or so in hundreds of newspapers throughout the country. Particularly at national election times, there are almost daily reports about the voting intentions of some part of the public, and many aspiring politicians hire private polling firms to help determine their "name recognition" and support by voters.

Other groups of pollers are located in academic research institutions, the best-known of which are the Survey Research Center at the University of Michigan and the National Opinion Research Center (NORC) at the University of Chicago. They usually do large-scale and carefully designed research studies that have less pressing deadlines than those under which the commercial polling firms must operate. For a history of U.S. public opinion research, see Sudman and Bradburn (1987) or Converse (1987).

How valid are the results of public opinion polls? The answer to this question depends on several factors, which are discussed in the following sections. Certainly some politicians have concluded that they are not valid. For instance, in 1960 vice-presidential candidate Henry Cabot Lodge said in a campaign speech: "people are going to look back on these polls as one of the hallucinations which the American people have been subjected to. . . . I don't think the polls are here to stay" (Hennessy, 1975, p. 56). On the other hand, President Lyndon Johnson often pulled the latest poll out of his pocket to show visitors his popularity rating, when it was favorable (Altschuler, 1986). It appears that most politicians, whether they complain about the polls or praise them, nevertheless still pay close attention to poll results.

Despite the wide circulation of opinion-poll information, there are still many widespread misconceptions about the methods, results, and uses of polls. There have even been attempts by legislators to ban opinion polls as being undemocratic! (*Los Angeles Times*, 1973). The following section will try to dispel some of the common misconceptions about polls and polling.

CHARACTERISTICS OF OPINION POLLS

Opinion polls are sometimes taken on street corners or in shopping malls, but more often over the telephone or in face-to-face interviews held in the respondent's home. The interview usually contains many questions and may take as long as an hour or more to complete, depending on the topic and type of interview. Commercial pollers usually use shorter interviews than do academic researchers, but both groups find that most respondents are glad to spend time talking about their opinions, once any initial resistance or suspicion which they may have is dissipated. However, in recent years, the number of potential respondents who refuse to be interviewed has been increasing (Steeh, 1981), and this poses a problem in knowing how much confidence to put in the obtained poll results.

The content of interviews may be highly varied. There are usually questions about attitudes and opinions on important public issues, of course, and questions about demographic characteristics such as the respondent's age, occupation, and voter registration status. Other kinds of information which may be sought include respondents' extent of knowledge on a given topic, typical behavior patterns, personal experiences, and life circumstances. Thus, many factors may be examined together as possible causes or effects of the respondents' attitudes and opinions. Rather than being merely descriptive, in-depth surveys usually study a variety of possibly causal factors by means of correlation techniques or by cross-tabulation of one factor against another. Examples of typical opinion interview questions have already been given in Box 3–1.

The **population** (or **public**) is the whole group of people in which the poller is interested—usually a very large one. It might be the registered voters of a given state, or all citizens over age 18, or a particular class of citizens such as medical doctors. When such a large population is concerned, it is usually neither necessary nor desirable to contact every member—(the national census is probably the only major exception). Instead, a **sample** of respondents is chosen, whose interview responses will be used as an estimate of the views of the whole population.

Therefore, the essential characteristic of any sample is **representativeness**, that is, the degree to which it is similar to the whole population.

A sample does *not* have to be extremely large in order to be representative, but it does have to be very carefully chosen. Of course, there is always some degree of error in any estimate, and the use of a sample necessarily entails some **sampling error** in estimating the population's views. However, in a careful probability sample, the degree of error of the estimate can be computed beforehand by means of a statistical formula, and the sample can be chosen in such a way as to yield any desired degree of precision. Contrary to some people's impressions, the factor determining the degree of precision is the size of the sample, *not* the size of the population. This means that just as large a sample is needed to represent a small population as a large population. Thus, a sample of 1500 respondents will estimate the views of the whole nation just as accurately as it will estimate the views of a single city's residents. How successfully? Well, a randomly chosen probability sample of 1500 cases should not miss the true population value by more than 2$\frac{1}{2}$% in either direction. For example, if 55% of such a sample say they favor establishing full diplomatic relations with mainland China, the true percentage in the overall population is almost surely between 52.5% and 57.5%.

A sample size of about 1500 cases is typical for most of the U.S. national polls. The decision about sample size is necessarily a compromise between the cost (in time, effort, and money) and the degree of precision desired in the final data. More important usually than the size of the sample is the care with which it is chosen, and this is a place where many surveys go astray. Some of the major considerations in choosing the sample are discussed next.

Sampling Procedures

There are many different types of sampling procedures. We will distinguish four main categories here: haphazard sampling, systematically biased sampling, quota sampling, and probability sampling.

Haphazard sampling is an unsystematic, capricious choice of respondents, selected according to the interviewer's whim, or according to who happens to be available. It is the approach customarily used by "inquiring reporters," who often post themselves on a street corner and ask questions of convenient passers-by. It is, most emphatically, *not* identical with random sampling, though "haphazard" and "random" are sometimes used as synonyms in everyday speech. Because of its unsystematic nature, haphazard sampling is not representative of any population, and it therefore has no scientific value.

Systematically biased sampling is also an approach to be avoided. As the name implies, it involves systematic errors in a sample that was intended to be representative. Some examples of biased samples are ones which include too many old people, too many college graduates, too few minority group members, etc. The classic example of this kind of error was made in the 1936 presidential election poll conducted by the magazine *Literary Digest*. The magazine sent ten million postcard ballots to citizens all over the country, and it received well over two million replies. Since 59% of the replies favored the Republican candidate, Alfred Landon, the magazine predicted his election. Instead, however, Franklin D. Roosevelt won re-election in a landslide, carrying all but two states, and Landon got only 37.5% of the votes.

The source of bias in the sample was that the respondents' names were taken from automobile registration lists and telephone books; and in the depression year of 1936, people who could afford to own cars or even have telephones were systematically different in their presidential voting preferences from their poorer neighbors. Interestingly, this bias had been less marked in 1932 and previous elections, when similar sampling methods had correctly predicted the winners (Shively, 1971; Cahalan, 1989). However, ironically, the magazine could have corrected for the sampling bias since it had been pointed out in scientific articles, and George Gallup even predicted the extent and direction of the error four months before the election (Gallup, 1980). After the 1936 fiasco, confidence in the *Literary Digest* was so badly shaken that the magazine died two years later. One clear lesson from this affair is that *a large sample is not necessarily a good sample!*

Quota sampling is the basic method used by many commercial polls. It achieved sudden prominence in the 1936 election, when several young pollers (George Gallup, Archibald Crossley, and Elmo Roper) all used it to predict Roosevelt's re-election, in dramatic contrast to the *Literary Digest* poll's failure. Many refinements have been added since 1936, but the basic principle is unchanged. This approach tries to achieve a representative sample by choosing respondents whose characteristics correspond to those of the national population on several important dimensions. For instance, the dimensions chosen might be geographic region of the country, urban versus rural residence, sex, age, and race. Then an interviewer in Chicago (Midwestern region, urban location) might be assigned a *quota* of respondents with the following characteristics: 10 respondents, all local residents, 5 women and 5 men, 2 of the women and 3 of the men to be black and the other 5 respondents white, 1 woman and 1 man to be in each age decade between 20 and 70. The interviewer may be given a free hand as to how and where she finds these respondents, or in some cases there may be further restrictions on where she goes and whom she chooses to interview. (The word "she" is used here because a very large proportion of poll interviewers are women, employed only part-time. This imbalance in the sex of interviewers may, however, sometimes be a source of bias in their results.)

The quota method of sampling avoids the most obvious sources of systematic bias in the sample, and therefore it is much more likely to yield accurate results than either haphazard sampling or systematically biased sampling. However, it does not avoid more subtle forms of systematic bias which may be inherent in the interviewer's choice of respondents within the limitations of her assigned quota. For

Photograph courtesy of George Gallup.
Reprinted by permission.

Box 5-1 GEORGE GALLUP, *Public Opinion Poller*

The best-known figure in public opinion polling, George Gallup was born in Iowa in 1901 and took his B.A. and Ph.D. at the University of Iowa. Before entering the polling field, he taught journalism and psychology at Iowa, Northwestern, and Columbia. He then began doing commercial research on reader interest in newspapers and magazines and audience interest in radio and motion pictures.

In 1935, Gallup founded the American Institute of Public Opinion, which is now directed by his son, George, Jr., to measure public attitudes on social, political, and economic issues. Using the quota system of sampling, he and several other early pollers became famous by predicting President Roosevelt's surprising landslide in the 1936 election, and he also correctly predicted how far wrong the prestigious Literary Digest *poll would be. Since then, he pioneered many new trends and improvements in survey research, including use of some aspects of probability sampling, and regular research by The Gallup Poll has spread to 32 foreign countries.*

Gallup published many articles and 10 books on public opinion. Among his many honorary degrees and awards were election as President of the American Association for Public Opinion Research and receipt of its award for distinguished achievement. He remained actively involved in polling until his death in 1984.

instance, it is common and understandable that interviewers avoid the "seedy" areas of town, choose to interview only at certain times of the day, and bypass individuals whose looks or behavior they find offensive. Unfortunately, however, by doing so they also may be systematically excluding as respondents poor people, night-shift workers, young "hippies," or other classes of citizens. As a result, the accuracy of the poll's results is diminished.

Probability sampling avoids all of these problems. By definition, it requires that every individual in the population must have a known probability (which may or may not be an equal probability) of being chosen as a respondent. This in turn requires that there be a complete list of the population or a breakdown of the total population by cities and counties such as is provided in the national census. With this breakdown as the starting point, the investigator can choose a sample in such a way that all segments of the population are included proportionally to their size (e.g., different sections of the country, different sizes of cities, various racial groups, etc.).

There are several ways of obtaining a probability sample. The simplest is **systematic sampling**, choosing every *n*th name from a list, such as a college student directory. Next easiest is **random sampling**, drawing from a container whose contents have been thoroughly mixed (as in a properly run Bingo game), or from a table of random numbers. Both of these methods require a complete list of the members of the population, which is not feasible for any population larger than a small city.

For polls of a larger city, a state, or of the whole nation, the probability method usually used is **area sampling** (which is one type of **stratified random sampling**). In this method the total population is broken down into small homogeneous units, such as counties, and a relatively few counties are chosen randomly to be in the sample. In this way the sample includes a group of counties which are typical of the whole country in characteristics such as income and educational level, racial makeup, degree of urbanization, etc. The chosen counties are then broken down into smaller units such as precincts or census tracts (the second level of sampling), and again a few tracts from each chosen county are randomly selected to be in the sample. A similar random procedure may be used to select a few blocks or other geographic areas from each chosen tract. For each of these final areas chosen to be in the sample, a field worker called an enumerator is sent out to list every dwelling unit in the area (including apartments over stores, cottages behind main houses, and all divided-up residences). With this list in hand, the sampling staff randomly chooses a few dwelling units from each sample area, and interviewers are sent to those specific dwellings. This method is also referred to as **cluster sampling** because a geographically contiguous "cluster" of people is chosen at each level of sampling.

As the final stage of this process, in each selected dwelling unit the interviewer is instructed to interview a specific person, who is determined by a final random procedure. If the designated person is not at home, interviewers are instructed to come back, several times if necessary, in order to complete the interview. Thus, a stratified random sample uses random selection procedures within each level of the sampling process.

This description suggests how difficult, time-consuming, and expensive a probability sample is. As a result, this method in its entirety is not used by commercial polls, but only by academic survey researchers. The great advantage of probability sampling methods is that the expected amount of sampling error in the results can be stated exactly; it is an ˙inverse function of the size of the sample (more precisely, of the square root of the sample size). As mentioned in the previous section, the expected error for a sample of 1500 cases would be no more than plus or minus 2½%. By comparison, for a sample of 500 cases, the expected error would be plus or minus 4½%; for a sample of 5000 cases, it would be plus or minus 1½%.

Probability sampling has the smallest amount of sampling error of any sampling method. Moreover, it is the only method where the expected amount of sampling error can be specified. With the sampling methods used by commercial pollsters such as Gallup, Roper, and Harris, one can only guess at the likely amount of error in their results. Thus, though complete probability sampling is expensive and slow, it is the only way to ensure that a sample is really representative of a large population.

Following their incorrect predictions in the 1948 presidential election, several of the major commercial polling firms adopted some aspects of probability sampling in their procedures for selecting areas within which to interview (Perry, 1960, 1979). These changes have undoubtedly improved the representativeness of their samples, but they generally still allow the interviewer some discretion in choosing respondents, as in the quota method of sampling. Interestingly, in England, most election polls still continue to use quota sampling methods, and studies there have found their election predictions to be just as accurate as those using probability sampling (Worcester, 1980).

Telephone Polling

A method of polling which has had rapid growth since the 1970s is interviewing by telephone. It has great advantages in terms of interviewer convenience, reduced costs, increased speed, and closer supervision. Though it was earlier thought that telephone interviews could not be as long as face-to-face ones nor address sensitive subjects with equal validity, most of the doubts about their value have been allayed by careful research (Groves & Kahn, 1979; Schuman & Kalton, 1985). They may obtain less complete answers, but on the other hand, they sometimes yield higher response rates in large urban areas.

In the U.S., over 90% of people have phones in their home, and some of the rest have access to a telephone nearby; thus, the bias due to unreachable respondents is a relatively small one. A potentially more serious issue is the number of unlisted phones, which exceeds 40% in some metropolitan areas (Groves & Kahn, 1979; Lavrakas, 1987). However, this problem can be completely overcome by a technique called **random digit dialing (RDD)**, which uses random methods to determine the numbers to be called. This technique has many variations, but they all have the effect of making all telephone numbers accessible, including those that are unlisted. Thus telephone surveys can use excellent probability sampling procedures.

Another innovation that has gradually followed the wider use of telephone surveys is computer assisted telephone interviewing (CATI). In this system, telephone interviewers read the questions from a computer-controlled video display terminal and punch the responses directly into a computer data file. This makes interviewing easier and more accurate, and it also completely eliminates the steps of coding and cleaning the data, thus greatly speeding up data analysis (Groves & Mathiowetz, 1984).

Historical Highlights

Polling history in the U.S. began in the 1820s, when a few newspapers started to ask interested local citizens or political delegates which candidate they favored for President. These were **straw polls**, named for the practice of tossing up a straw to see which way the wind was blowing. Their samples were haphazard, and their main purpose was to sell more newspapers. Many papers adopted this practice, and by 1904, a poll by a New York newspaper sampled as many as 30,000 registered voters. Two other forms of polling—market research and questionnaire surveys of magazine readers—were first tried out in 1911, and house-to-house interviewing began soon thereafter (Crespi, 1980; Beniger, 1983).

In 1886 a magazine called *Public Opinion* was founded, which addressed major public issues of the day by abstracting and reprinting newspaper editorials from around the nation, influential political speeches, and quotes from public figures, all arranged under broad subject-matter headings. In 1906 it was taken over by the *Literary Digest*, which later became the largest mass-circulation magazine of its era (Sheatsley, 1977). In 1916 the *Literary Digest* conducted the first of its citizen polls, sending postcards to its subscribers in five key states, asking their preferences for President, and publicizing the results. In each succeeding election, the magazine sent out presidential preference ballots to lists of citizens obtained from telephone books and automobile registration records, increasing the number sent to 20 million by 1932. This was largely a circulation boosting tactic, for each postcard included a subscription blank. Though the ballots which were returned always correctly picked the election winner—until 1936—they usually overestimated the Republican vote by a large margin (Gallup, 1980; Squire, 1988; Cahalan, 1989).

In the 1930s the development of large-scale statistical sampling theory set the stage for more scientific polling, first with the quota method used in the 1936 election polls of Gallup, Crossley, and Roper, and later with probability sampling (Rossi, Wright, & Anderson, 1983). In 1937 the influential scientific journal *Public Opinion Quarterly* began publication. In 1939 the first private polling was done for potential presidential candidates, and President Roosevelt asked the help of academic pollers in gauging the public's acceptance of his preparations for possible U.S. involvement in World War II (Gallup, 1976). This brief chronology brings us up to the date of another polling fiasco.

PROBLEMS IN PUBLIC OPINION POLLING

Famous Polling Failures

In 1948 President Truman was running for re-election against Governor Dewey of New York, and all the major polls reported Dewey as the probable winner. Partly for that reason, most people in the country seemed to expect Truman to lose, and the *Chicago Tribune* even hit the streets with a postelection headline proclaiming "Dewey Defeats Truman." Yet when the votes were all counted, Truman won. Whereas the Gallup poll, for instance, had predicted that Truman would receive only 44.5% of the vote, he actually won 49.5% of the vote in a four-party race.

Similarly, in the 1970 British elections the Labour Party led by Prime Minister Harold Wilson was widely expected to win. All except one of the major British polling organizations predicted a Labour win with a vote margin of anywhere from 2% to 9%. Yet on election day the Conservative Party led by Edward Heath scored a smashing upset, winning by a margin of nearly 5%.

These two instances represent the most-dramatic failures of scientific polling methods since the prescientific era of 1936 when the *Literary Digest* poll failed so ignominiously. You may have heard the 1980 U.S. presidential election described as a polling error, but actually it was not. Many of the major national polls were reporting the race as "too close to call" through the end of October, but all of them picked Reagan as the expected winner in their final pre-election report, though they underestimated the margin of his victory over Carter. Careful research has shown that there was a large closing surge in Reagan's voter support due to three factors: an especially large number of undecided voters in that multiparty election; concurrent developments concerning the American hostages in Iran; and public reaction to the final candidate debate, held just one week before the election (Ladd & Ferree, 1981). Thus, all the major national polls were on the right track in 1980.

How can the actual failures of 1948 and 1970 be explained? Both elections have resulted in much scrutiny of the polls, and some of the lessons that have been learned are reported later in this chapter. Before trying to explain these failures, we will discuss some of the basic factors which produce problems in constructing polls and in obtaining valid results. The most important of these factors are: sampling, question wording, respondents' lapses of memory and motivated inaccuracy in reporting, failure to obtain data from some of the designated sample, nonanonymity of responses, interviewer effects on responses, and other practical problems.

Sampling Problems

Many of the problems in quota sampling procedures have been touched on in the previous section. The most important result of these problems is that the commercial polls, due to their sampling methods, cannot specify the expected amount of sampling error in their data.

In really close elections, such as the 1968 race between Nixon and Humphrey, the margin between the two candidates' popular vote totals is clearly less than the expected sampling error of the polls, and consequently the pollsters have had to admit that their data are not precise enough to be sure of picking the winner. That is a lesson which they learned from their fiasco in 1948 when, to their sorrow, they failed to exercise an equal degree of caution.

Also, it should be kept in mind that the commercial polls indicate the expected percentage of people voting for a presidential candidate nationwide (the **popular vote**). By contrast, the **electoral college vote**, which determines the winner, is based on the popular vote winner in each state separately. Thus it is conceivable in a close election that the polls could correctly predict the popular vote totals but fail to pick the winning candidate, who was elected by carrying states with a majority of electoral votes. An outcome like this occurred in the British election of February, 1974. There, most of the polls predicted a Conservative victory, and the Conservatives actually won the popular vote, but the Labour Party won more seats in Parliament and so named the next Prime Minister (Worcester, 1980).

Despite the few famous polling failures described above, the overall record of the national commercial polls in predicting election results has been very good. For instance, in the 1950–1988 period, the Gallup Poll's average error in predicting 20 congressional and presidential elections was only 1.5% (*Gallup Report*, 1988, No. 279). In considering the accuracy of poll results, however, it is important to keep in mind the differences in careful sampling procedures and in objectivity between the major national and statewide polls, the often less-sophisticated newspaper polls, and the privately sponsored partisan polls, which sometimes "leak" or distort their results to achieve a political advantage. In other words, not all polls are equally believable. Findings in the 1970s showed that careful statewide polls had a good prediction record, even in volatile, multiple-candidate presidential primary contests, and that polls taken just before the elections spotted last-minute trends quite well (Felson & Sudman, 1975). However, in some 1980s statewide elections, there were major prediction errors even by some of the most respected commercial and newspaper polls (Roper, 1983; Goldhaber, 1984). These were probably due in part to a trend toward greater volatility in American voting patterns.

Exit Polls.   Also in the 1980s, a new polling technique was widely used on election day, due to the television networks' insatiable desires to be first with their reports of the election victor. So-called **exit polls** are ones which interview a relatively crude sample of voters as they leave selected polling places, asking them to fill out a brief anonymous ballot indicating whom they actually voted for and their views on a few campaign issues. The sample is crude because voters may leave by different exits or in bunches, making systematic selection very difficult, and because different demographic groups tend to vote at different times of day (Busch & Lieske, 1985). Other voters refuse to be polled because they are in a rush or don't want to divulge their vote, even anonymously, and some who do respond apparently falsify their answers. Each couple of hours the interviewer phones the obtained ballot totals in to the network computer room, and by early afternoon the networks may begin to predict expected winners in statewide or congressional races that seem to be lopsided (Levy, 1983).

Two major issues have been raised about exit polls. One, the effect of the broadcast reports on citizens who have not yet voted, is discussed later in this chapter. The other issue is the accuracy of exit polls, especially in view of their questionable sampling methods. Some of them have displayed acceptable accuracy (Levy, 1983; *Public Opinion*, 1989, No. 5). However, the evidence is clear that exit polls contributed substantially to the networks' errors in election-night projections in a number of races, in both England and the U.S., though other, more-careful polls were also wrong in some of these races (Worcester, 1980; Roper, 1983; Steinberg, 1983).

Call-In Polls. Another apparently modern polling technique is really a throwback to the old, unscientific straw polls. **Call-in polls** are ones where respondents phone in their opinions to a special telephone number after a newsworthy event like a presidential candidate debate or a social-issue television documentary. The problem with such audience-response techniques is that there are absolutely no scientific controls on the sample that is obtained. Respondents are self-selected, and a vociferous minority can easily stack the results, as frequently happens in the similar voting for All-Star major-league baseball players. Despite the large response

Photograph courtesy of Howard Schuman.
Reprinted by permission.

Box 5–2   HOWARD SCHUMAN, *Survey Research Authority*

Howard Schuman is Professor of Sociology at the University of Michigan, where he has taught since 1964. He earned an A.B. at Antioch College, an M.A. at Trinity University, and a Ph.D. at Harvard, and then briefly directed field research in Pakistan and India. He has become widely known for his research on survey research methods and on racial attitudes, which is cited in this chapter and in Chapter 15.

Schuman has co-authored seven books, including Questions and Answers in Attitude Surveys, Black Racial Attitudes: Trends and Complexities, *and* Racial Attitudes in America. *In addition to these topics, his 80 published papers include notable contributions concerning the attitude-behavior relationship; religious attitudes; attitudes toward the Vietnam War, gun control, and abortion; and technical issues of question wording and context effects in surveys. He has served as editor of the journals* Sociometry *and* Public Opinion Quarterly *and been elected President of the American Association of Public Opinion Research.*

totals and the flashy gimmicks of immediate computer feedback of results, such polls are just as unscientific as the old *Literary Digest* reports. With the recent proliferation of many different kinds of "polls," it is particularly important for the poll consumer to attend to the sampling methods used and to distinguish the relatively trustworthy, scientific polls from crude, pseudo, or "phony" polls (Orton, 1982; Frankel & Frankel, 1987). Readers beware!

Question Wording and Context

Planning and constructing a public opinion interview is a very large and complex task, about which whole books have been written. As early as 1932, Wang had presented a comprehensive list of recommendations on the construction and wording of attitude and opinion questionnaires. Due to space limitations, our presentation here can only briefly list the most prominent considerations in wording interview questions. Fuller treatments of a practical sort can be found in excellent volumes by Payne (1951), Dillman (1978), Sudman and Bradburn (1982), and Converse and Presser (1986). In addition, the results of extensive research on question wording and question order are summarized by Schuman and Presser (1981b) and Schuman and Kalton (1985).

1. Rapport. The interview usually should begin with an explanation of its purpose and sponsorship and then some comments intended to put the respondent at ease as much as possible. The first questions are usually rather simple and factual ones which will be easy for respondents to answer and which will not threaten them in any way.

2. Format of Questions. They may be either multiple choice, or open-ended ones, which respondents answer in their own words. Both kinds have important and legitimate uses, and many interviews use some of each.

3. Order of Questions. Considerable thought must be given to having the questions in a logical order and to avoiding any influence of earlier questions (i.e., context) on later answers, which can sometimes produce differences in response as great as 20% (Turner & Martin, 1981; Tourangeau & Rasinski, 1988). A common method which aims toward these goals is the **funnel sequence** of questions: asking broad, open-ended questions first, followed by somewhat more limited ones, and finally focusing very specifically on narrow aspects of the topic.

4. Vocabulary Used. When interviewing a representative sample of citizens, it must be remembered that many respondents will have little education, limited vocabularies, and rather poor understanding of technical terms. In addition to wording the questions carefully, it is essential to **pretest** them with a preliminary sample in order to determine how they are interpreted by typical respondents. An amusing example of this is provided by an item from a widely used standard scale which asked whether "the lot of the average man" was getting worse or better.

Pretesting of this item in a recent study showed that this usage of *lot* was not familiar to many respondents. "The question was variously interpreted to refer to a lot of average men, to the size of housing lots, and even in one case to cemetery lots!" (Schuman & Kalton, 1985, p. 643), so it had to be reworded.

5. Clarity. Ambiguity can be avoided in the following ways:

a. Keep the questions simple, clear, and direct.

b. Normally keep the questions short, but add repetition or paraphrasing if it will increase understanding.

c. Make the questions as specific as possible (e.g., asking about behavior in a particular time period, such as the last month).

d. Avoid the use of negatives and especially of double negatives.

e. Avoid use of the passive voice.

f. Avoid questions that may be interpreted in more than one way.

g. Avoid "double-barreled" questions which express two ideas (e.g., Do you favor stronger efforts to eliminate smog and water pollution?—The respondent may have different views on the two topics.)

h. Avoid having so many alternative answers that the question is confusing.

i. Avoid having so few alternative answers that the list is incomplete.

6. Biased Questions. The questions should be as neutral as possible. In order to avoid **acquiescence effects** (respondents agreeing with the position stated or implied in the question), survey questions should normally present both sides of an issue rather than just one side (Bishop, Oldendick, & Tuchfarber, 1982)—for instance: "Do you favor or oppose increases in the defense budget?" To see why this is important, note the discrepancy in responses to the following two questions (Schuman & Presser, 1981b, p. 221):

a. Do you agree or disagree with this statement: Most men are better suited emotionally for politics than are most women.—47% agreed.

b. Would you say that most men are better suited emotionally for politics than are most women, that men and women are equally suited, or that women are better suited than men in this area?—33% said men are better.

Another example of how small changes in question wording can produce major differences in responses is seen in the following two items (Schuman & Presser, 1981b, p. 277):

a. Do you think the United States should forbid public speeches against democracy?—21% said yes (forbid).

b. Do you think the United States should allow public speeches against democracy?—48% said no (not allow).

This difference is due to the tone of the verbs—actually the opposite of an acquiescence effect, since fewer people said yes to either item than would be expected from responses to the other version (Hippler & Schwarz, 1986). Fortunately, this is one of the largest effects ever found as a result of apparently nonsubstantive wording differences, and most experiments with the "forbid-allow" terms have yielded much smaller response discrepancies. For instance, questions about the government forbidding or allowing the showing of X-rated movies produced only a 5% discrepancy (Schuman & Presser, 1981b, p. 282).

Most response effects due to wording differences stem from more substantive differences in question wording or context. An understandable example is seen in responses to these two items, asked by different polling organizations in November 1973, the month after President Nixon had fired Archibald Cox as the special Watergate prosecutor (Lang & Lang, 1984, p. 140):

a. If the Senate Watergate Committee decides that President Nixon was involved in the coverup, do you think Congress should impeach him, or not?—53% said impeach.

b. Would you like to see Nixon continue in office, decide to resign, or be impeached?—10% said be impeached (20% more said resign).

Question-biasing techniques which should be carefully avoided include the use of emotionally laden words or phrases (e.g., "communist agitators," "police brutality") and the use of prestige names or symbols in the question. For instance, if an idea is attributed to a well-known and respected person (e.g., "President Reagan's policy"), more people will generally agree with the idea than if the prestige name is omitted from the question.

7. Incomplete Specification.   It has been said that people will answer what they think you mean rather than what you actually say. In large part, this is a problem of interviewer and respondent having different frames of reference, and it can often be counteracted by asking supplementary questions. (The question "Why?" is often particularly valuable in determining the frames of reference or reasons behind a respondent's attitudes.)

A classic example of the frame of reference problem was provided by Bancroft and Welch (1946) from results of Bureau of the Census interviews designed to determine the number of employed persons in the U.S. The original question used was, "Did you do any work for pay or profit last week?", and it consistently underestimated the employed population. Apparently this occurred because many people such as housewives or students answered it in terms of their main occupation, overlooking the explicit term "any work." The solution adopted was to ask two questions: the first about the respondent's major activity, and a second one (for persons giving "nonworker" responses) as to whether they did any work for pay in addition to their major activity. As a result of this simple change, the official estimate of employment was raised by more than a million persons.

In summary, problems related to question wording and/or context are apt to be the largest source of error in survey results—often much larger than sampling errors.

> It is far more important in assessing the accuracy of a survey to know the wording of the questions asked than the magnitude of the statistical sampling error. (Roper, 1984, p. 24)

Ignoring the possibility of question-wording and context effects may be viewed as an instance of Ross's (1977) "fundamental attribution error," which was discussed in Chapter 2. That is, it is an overestimation of personal, dispositional factors in the respondent's behavior and an underestimation of situational influences (Schuman & Kalton, 1985).

Memory Errors

We know that human memory is fallible, and many studies have been done to investigate the degree of interviewing errors due to faulty memory. In general they show that less important facts are forgotten more quickly than more important facts, and that memory becomes less accurate as the time interval from the event becomes longer. As one example, a survey of known crime victims found that 69% of the crime incidents occurring 1 to 3 months previously were reported to interviewers, whereas only 30% of incidents occurring 10 to 12 months previously were reported (Turner, 1972). Even important past information is apt to be distorted by later events; for instance, reports of past years' income are often distorted in the direction of the respondent's current income. There is also a common phenomenon known as *forward telescoping*, in which past events are recalled as happening more recently than they actually did (Neter & Waksberg, 1964).

A number of means can be used to increase respondents' motivation to remember events accurately and to assist them in their efforts. One common method is to use questions that tap recognition memory rather than unaided recall—for instance, by giving respondents a list to respond to (e.g., illnesses they might have suffered). Other methods include alerting them to the problem of bias in memory so that they can intentionally combat it in their answers, providing contextual information in the question which will help respondents locate an event in time or space, and asking them to consult or keep relevant records (income tax forms, diaries of television viewing, etc.). Cannell, Miller, and Oksenberg (1981) have also recommended giving special instructions about the need for complete and accurate answers, using longer questions which help to symbolize the importance of the topic, asking respondents to sign a pledge of thoroughness, and rewarding their complete answers with verbal approval.

Social Desirability Needs of Respondents

Interview questions are often worded with the implied assumption that the respondent knows something about the topic: "How do you feel about the government's farm policy?" Wanting to be obliging, and not wanting to show their ignorance, many respondents are inclined to fake a knowledge and interest that isn't real: "I think it's pretty good." Often as many as one-third of the respondents will state such uninformed opinions, and this may seriously distort the survey findings (Bishop, Tuchfarber, & Oldendick, 1986). One desirable safeguard is to use **filter** questions to learn the degree of respondents' interest in or knowledge about a topic before asking them detailed questions about it.

However, social desirability bias is much more pervasive than just the nuisance of over-obliging respondents. On any topic where society's norms point to one answer as more socially desirable than another, we can expect an overreporting of the "good" behaviors and an underreporting of the "bad" ones. This tendency is stronger for respondents who are young and/or of lower socio-economic status (Cahalan, 1968), and it seems to show up most strongly and consistently in questions about voting and voter registration, especially among highly educated respondents who firmly believe in voting (Silver, Anderson, & Abramson, 1986). Some examples of social desirability bias in interview responses are shown in Box 5–3.

Biased responses are particularly likely on sensitive topics—ones that may be embarrassing, threatening, or incriminating to respondents—as illustrated by the large underreporting of drunk driving charges and bankruptcies in Box 5–3. However, a review of research on reporting accuracy found surprisingly little systematic denial of undesirable behaviors (Marquis, Duan, Marquis, & Polich, 1981). Sometimes, motives to shock or impress interviewers, or conform to subcultural norms, lead to *over*reporting of apparently undesirable behavior. For instance, in research interviews with ex-heroin addicts, many of whom had substantial criminal records, roughly equal percentages overstated and understated their number of past arrests (Wyner, 1980).

Many standard survey techniques help to combat social desirability response bias. First, in wording questions, one can use neutral (unbiased) wording, present two or more opposing alternatives for the respondent to choose between, state that the question is a matter of opinion with no right or wrong answer, etc. Also, the interviewer should establish good rapport, reassuring the respondent by a supportive manner that any type of response will be perfectly acceptable in the interviewing situation. Detailed **probes** (additional questions following up on a more general one) may often turn up inconsistencies and avoid some overreporting. On the basis of extensive research, Sudman and Bradburn (1982) have made other recommendations about the best ways to ask questions on sensitive or threatening topics.

Box 5–3   *Examples of Social Desirability Bias in Interview Responses*

1.   *Voter registration—12% overreported (falsely said they were registered), 3% underreported (falsely said they were not registered). Based on 1976 National Election Study of 2865 respondents (Katosh & Traugott, 1981).*

2.   *Voting in presidential election (1 month previous)—12% overreported, 1% underreported. Same study as #1.*

3.   *Voting for the winner—14% net overreporting. Based on 1964 national survey; 64% of respondents said they had voted for Kennedy four years before in 1960, but he only received 50% of the vote (Mueller, 1973).*

4.   *Donations to community chest—34% overreported, 0% underreported. Based on survey of 920 Denver adults (Parry & Crossley, 1950).*

5.   *Possession of driver's license—10% overreported, 2% underreported. Same study as #4.*

6.   *Possession of library card—20% overreported, 0% underreported. Based on probability sample of 190 Chicago adults, half interviewed by phone and half face-to-face (Bradburn & Sudman, 1979).*

7.   *Voting in last primary election (8 months previous)—35% overreported, 0% underreported. Same study and interview methods as #6, different probability sample of 157 adults.*

8.   *Recent declaration of bankruptcy—30% underreported. Same study and interview methods as #6, different sample of 79 known recent bankruptcies.*

9.   *Recent drunk driving charge—46% underreported. Same study and interview methods as #6, different sample of 98 respondents all charged with drunk driving 6–12 months previously.*

Of course, in all such checks of official records, it must be realized that sometimes the records may be incorrect, or unavailable because of misfiling, etc. (Marquis, 1978).

Nonresponse Rate

Surveys always fail to obtain data from some of the designated sample members, and the size of this **nonresponse rate** affects the validity of the findings. Nonresponse would not matter if the omitted respondents were just like those who answered, but that is never a safe assumption because they usually are systematically different—e.g., poorer, more transient, busier, less cooperative, or less often at home, etc. Thus, their loss reduces the representativeness of the obtained sample (Stinchcombe, Jones, & Sheatsley, 1981).

The group of nonrespondents is usually composed of about two-thirds refusals, about one-third not-at-homes who cannot be contacted, even after several attempts, and a few cases lost due to language or health problems (Schuman &

Kalton, 1985). Nonresponse rates for national face-to-face surveys with call-backs are apt to be 25%–30%, and refusal rates have been rising in recent years, especially in central city areas (Steeh, 1981). Telephone surveys using random digit dialing may have nonresponse rates of 40% or higher, partly because of their unique problem that an unknown percentage of the persistent unanswered calls may be nonworking numbers not currently assigned to anyone (Groves & Kahn, 1979).

To reduce the nonresponse rate it is important not only to call back persistently, but also to explain the survey as clearly and nonthreateningly as possible. Helpful techniques include sending letters in advance explaining the research, and having well-known and prestigious sponsoring organizations for the survey (Fox, Crask, & Kim, 1988). Wherever possible, the demographic characteristics of nonresponders (e.g., their census tract, or quality of housing) should be obtained for comparison with those of respondents, as an estimate of the amount of bias due to nonresponse. Very often, differential statistical weights are applied in the data analysis phase as a way of compensating for nonresponses.

Nonanonymity of Responses

Another problem that can distort survey findings, especially on sensitive or threatening topics, is lack of anonymity of responses. Though most respondents apparently do answer honestly under normal conditions, some studies have indicated that anonymity of responses will somewhat increase the accuracy of survey findings. Consequently, a number of the major polling organizations have adopted a "secret ballot" format for obtaining respondents' voting intentions (Perry, 1979).

However, several studies suggest that anonymity may seldom be necessary in order to obtain honest responses, even on sensitive topics. For instance, without anonymity, adolescents and young adults will usually give full reports of socially undesirable behavior such as delinquent acts or drug use (King, 1970; Malvin & Moskowitz, 1983).

When anonymity seems crucial, a relatively new method for ensuring it is the **randomized response technique (RRT)**. In it, the respondent is given two yes-no questions, one threatening (e.g., Have you ever had a venereal disease?) and one innocuous (e.g., Is your birthday in May?). The respondent determines which question to answer by means of a private, random technique such as a coin flip or a choice of different colored beads from a box. Thus, the respondent's anonymity is ensured because neither the interviewer nor the researcher can know which question is being answered. However, the innocuous question has a known probability of "yes" answers (about 1/12 in the case of birth month), so a simple mathematical calculation will reveal what percentage of a group of respondents have said "yes" to the threatening question. However, as this description indicates, RRT can only provide meaningful data *for a group of respondents* and not for any given individual, so its use sacrifices any individual-level analysis of the threatening items. More information about RRT is given by Dawes and Smith (1985), Schuman and Kalton (1985), and Fox and Tracy (1986).

Validation studies have shown that RRT does indeed increase the reporting of socially undesirable behavior such as bankruptcies or abortions (e.g., Tracy & Fox, 1981; Himmelfarb & Lickteig, 1982), though it does not eliminate all underreporting (e.g., Bradburn & Sudman, 1979). However, its complexity makes it hard for interviewers to explain, and quite a few respondents remain unconvinced that the randomizing technique will really keep them anonymous (Edgell, Himmelfarb, & Duchan, 1982). In view of these limitations of the RRT method, it is encouraging to remember that many studies have shown relatively little denial of undesirable behaviors or attitudes (Marquis et al., 1981). One reason for this may be the false consensus effect, discussed in Chapter 2—many respondents assume that their own attitudes and behavior are shared by most other people, and so they are not hesitant to express them.

Interviewer Effects on Responses

A vast body of scientific studies shows that the interviewer's behavior and personal characteristics can affect a respondent's answers. Some of the most interesting and most pervasive factors producing interviewer effects are listed briefly below:

1. Lack of Personal Sensitivity and lack of ability to build rapport with respondents. There is unanimous agreement that such interviewer characteristics can lead to invalid responses (in fact, often to no responses at all).

2. Inadequate Training. Great improvement in interviewing performance can be produced by careful training in field research methods (e.g., Cannell et al., 1981; Billiet & Loosveldt, 1988).

3. Variations in Putting Questions. Even carefully trained interviewers have been found to vary in minor ways in their reading of questions (Bradburn & Sudman, 1979). Unfortunately, such variation in questions often produces variation in answers. Furthermore, the rules for using additional follow-up questions **(probes)** can never be completely structured, so additional variability in interviewers' behavior occurs here.

4. Variations in Reacting to Respondents' Answers. For instance, an interviewer's reinforcement of answers by frequently saying "good" can systematically influence a respondent's later answers (Cannell et al., 1981).

5. Interviewers' Expectations. One common expectation is that a respondent's answers to related questions will be consistent, and so interviewers often fail to notice inconsistencies which are present. Other expectations about respondents (e.g., that all businessmen are conservative) can also distort survey results, but recent research suggests that this effect is not strong enough to have much effect on validity (Bradburn & Sudman, 1979).

6. Interviewers' Attitudes. Numerous studies show that interviewers may tend to get (or hear) an excess of responses which are similar to their own attitudes and opinions. Thus the results obtained by interviewers with opposing opinions often vary noticeably (Phillips & Clancy, 1972).

7. Interviewers' Social Class. Some early research indicated that interviewers from working-class backgrounds tend to get more radical opinions from respondents on some economic questions than do middle-class interviewers (Katz, 1942), but this issue has not had much attention recently.

8. Interviewers' Age. This factor may influence the information obtained, particularly across the "generation gap." For instance, when interviewing adolescent girls, older interviewers obtained fewer reports of behavior considered undesirable by middle-class adult standards (Ehrlich & Riesman, 1961).

9. Interviewers' Race. Many studies agree that black respondents tend to give different answers to white interviewers than to black interviewers when the topic is race-related. Such differences in interracial responding generally seem to reflect deference or politeness toward the interviewer. Thus, white interviewers talking to black respondents typically receive fewer indications of distrust of whites or resentment over racial discrimination than do black interviewers (Anderson, Silver, & Abramson, 1988). Parallel findings show that white respondents also avoid offending black interviewers (Hatchett & Schuman, 1975; Campbell, 1981), and similar results have been found for other ethnic minority groups (Weeks & Moore, 1981; Reese, Danielson, Shoemaker, Chang, & Hsu, 1986).

Finding solutions to these problems of interviewer effects is not easy. Sensitive and well-trained interviewers are a first requirement but one that many smaller polling organizations fail to meet. Training can at least reduce variability in reading questions, in the use of probes, and in the amount of verbal reinforcement used by interviewers. To some extent training can also help interviewers to avoid expectational "halo effects." The effects of interviewers' attitudes, social class, sex, and age can be handled by the principle of "balanced bias," that is, by attempting to get approximately equal numbers of interviewers from each class, age group, etc. Unfortunately, however, this is rarely done, and the majority of opinion poll interviewers are middle-aged, middle-class women. The problem of respondents' race, and often of their age and social class, can best be met by using interviewers who have the same race, age, and/or social class as the respondents, and this procedure is often followed when interviewing in ethnic minority areas.

In telephone interviews, interviewers' demographic characteristics present less of a problem, though racial effects may still occur due to recognizable accents

(Cotter, Cohen, & Coulter, 1982). Other bases for interviewer effects, such as expectations or variable interviewing behavior, can operate in telephone surveys (Singer, Frankel, & Glassman, 1983). However, one great advantage of telephone interviewing is the possibility of close monitoring and supervision, which should substantially increase the standardization of interviewer behavior (Schuman & Kalton, 1985).

Other Practical Problems

Public opinion polling is a very complex business, whether done by commercial firms or academic research institutions. Between the time of choosing the initial topic for study and the distribution of the final report of findings, there are many phases of the polling operation, each of which can pose its own problems and difficulties. One way of considering these difficulties is in terms of the skilled workers who are needed at the different phases. In addition to the field interviewers, whose characteristics, training, and behavior were discussed in the preceding section, many other talents are needed. First there is the planning staff who develop the interview schedule and specify how and where the sample of respondents will be obtained. Then there are field supervisors who oversee the work of the interviewers. Next, coders in the main office transform the interview responses into quantitative scores on dozens or hundreds of items, and keypunchers transfer these scores into computer data files. Then computer experts are needed to process the data, and finally analysts and writers make a coherent picture out of the computer output and prepare a written report of their conclusions.

Another major problem is the cost of polling research. For face-to-face household surveys, the fieldwork costs for interviewers, supervisors, call-backs, and travel typically run $150 or more per interview, and these costs increase each year (Schuman & Kalton, 1985). Interviewing costs depend partly on the length of the interview as well as on the location to which the interviewer must travel, and they are markedly increased when the survey design requires call-backs to find previously not-at-home individuals. Consequently, methods have been developed to weight more heavily the viewpoints of less-frequently-at-home individuals who were successfully interviewed, as a substitute for the more expensive call-back procedure. High-quality telephone surveys with call-backs typically cost about half as much as face-to-face interviews, and they can be completed much more quickly if a large enough squad of interviewers is employed. However, between 5% and 10% of the U.S. population do not have access to a phone and so are overlooked in telephone surveys, and this group is disproportionately poor, nonwhite, young, less educated, rural, and southern (Roll & Cantril, 1980). Mailed surveys have the lowest data-collection costs, but their nonresponse rate is usually correspondingly higher, even after follow-up reminders are sent.

Because of the high costs of survey research and the skilled personnel which it requires, very careful advance planning and specification of detailed research goals is essential. A very helpful book which stresses the how-to-do-it approach is *Survey Research* by Backstrom and Hursh-Cesar (1981), and a recent handbook discusses all aspects of survey research in detail (Rossi, Wright, & Anderson, 1983). Hyman (1972) has written a volume on principles and procedures for **secondary analysis** of survey data which were originally collected by someone else for a different purpose—a very economical procedure compared to fresh data collection. Also, Sudman (1967) has described numerous methods which have been used by the National Opinion Research Center to hold down survey costs.

REASONS FOR FAMOUS POLLING FAILURES

Some of the major reasons why opinion polls have sometimes failed to predict election results correctly are end-of-campaign changes in voting intentions, the undecided vote, people who are not at home when the interviewer calls, differential voter turnout, and the effects of the polls themselves on voter behavior.

Late changes in voting intentions were apparently the main factor causing the incorrect predictions in the 1948 election when Truman defeated Dewey (Mosteller et al., 1949). In that year, as in previous elections, some polls stopped interviewing several weeks before the election date. Since that fiasco, the major commercial polls have extended their interviewing as late as possible, and many have adopted a "last-minute" poll taken on the weekend before the election. Thus, by keeping their staffs up all night, they can make the Monday papers with their final predictions on the day before the election. Even then, a late surge in one candidate's strength could catch them flat-footed, as very nearly happened in Humphrey's uphill fight against Nixon in 1968, and did happen with Reagan's widening lead in 1980.

The undecided vote was also an important factor in the 1948 election, for an unusually high 19% of the voters were still undecided one month before the election (Campbell, Gurin, & Miller, 1954). The usual assumption made is that undecided respondents will divide their votes in the same proportion as those who have already decided, but in 1948 most of those votes apparently went for Truman.

Potential respondents who are not at home are always a headache for the polls, for people who cannot be interviewed until the second, third, or fourth visit are apt to be systematically different from respondents who are home on the interviewer's first visit. In one study, the not-at-homes were more likely to be young adults, employed outside the home, with smaller families, and renters rather than homeowners (Hilgard & Payne, 1944). The moral is clear: In order to get an adequate sample, it is essential to use **call-backs** to reach those who are less often at home, or some other procedure (e.g., weighting of responses) which gives them fair representation.

Differential turnout seems to have been a major reason for the polls' incorrect predictions in the 1970 British election (Abrams, 1970), and another factor was the lack of last-minute polls to spot late shifts in voting intentions (Worcester, 1980). Whether a particular respondent will actually vote when the election occurs is always a difficult prediction to make. Useful methods for predicting voter turnout have been developed (Perry, 1979) but were little utilized in the 1970

British election. The only polling firm which correctly predicted the Conservative Party to win did so by making a large correction for Labourite voters' traditionally lower turnout.

The effects of the polls themselves on voters have not been thoroughly studied, but they are widely believed to have an effect on voter turnout and on the undecided vote. This was illustrated in the 1970 British election when many Labour voters stayed home, trusting in the polls' prediction that their party would win. An even more striking example occurs regularly in the United States because of the differential in time zones between the east and west coasts. In the last several elections, the national television networks have predicted the winning party on the basis of east coast votes well before the close of voting on the west coast. In 1980, President Carter even broadcast his concession speech over an hour before the voting deadline in the West, and this early concession was apparently a factor in the narrow defeat of several Democratic Congressmen, many of whose supporters gave up at that point and failed to vote (Kinder & Sears, 1985). Since 1980, early election reports have become even more pervasive as the TV networks have competed to be first to announce the winners on the basis of their election-day exit polls, which potentially allow the "outcome" to be broadcast as early as noon.

The possible impact of such early broadcasts of election results on the turnout and voting choices of late voters is an important and controversial public issue, and legislation has been proposed to prevent their future occurrence (Milavsky, Swift, Roper, Salant, & Abrams, 1985). Indeed, France and West Germany have banned publication of poll results during the *two weeks* before an election, and similar legislation has been introduced in England (Worcester, 1980; Lang & Lang, 1984). The evidence on the size of this effect, however, is equivocal. Several studies of the influence of early election-day projections on west coast voting have not shown any clearcut effects (see Tannenbaum & Kostrich, 1983; Lang & Lang, 1984; Epstein & Strom, 1984; Adams, 1985). However, there are major problems of research design in finding a sample of late voters large enough to yield significance and in choosing a comparison group of other voters which will provide an objective test of the question. Other studies (Wolfinger & Linquiti, 1981; Jackson, 1983; Sudman, 1986) have found evidence that early election returns or projections can reduce turnout by several percentage points, at least under the following special conditions:

> Exit polls appear to cause small declines in total voting in areas where the polls close [later than 8 P.M. EST] for those elections where the exit polls predict a clear winner when previously the race had been considered close. (Sudman, 1986, p. 331)

IMPACT OF POLLS IN POLITICS AND GOVERNMENT

There are many types of polls and innumerable uses for poll information. One type which we haven't discussed previously is government polls to establish necessary facts about the population's economic and social circumstances, working conditions, health, and so on. The granddaddy of such surveys is the U.S. census, taken every ten years since 1790. In addition to the census, the government conducts well over 200 other regular surveys, and these total over 5 million of the estimated 20 million survey interviews conducted with the American public each year (Turner & Martin, 1981). A major purpose of these government surveys is to provide a statistical basis for allocation of government funds to different geographic areas and programs in order to meet demonstrated public needs. In 1979, over $120 *billion* of the federal budget were allocated on the basis of such statistical data (Beal & Hinckley, 1984).

Most of the nongovernment surveys are conducted for business rather than political purposes. In 1980, one company alone (AT&T) conducted about 5 million survey interviews—about the same number as the entire federal government (Turner & Martin, 1981). Most business surveys are **proprietary**—that is, for the sole use of the sponsor—so their results are seldom made public. There are about 1000 polling firms doing these kinds of surveys in the U.S. (Wheeler 1976). In 1986 the top 44 polling companies in the U.S. earned more than $1.5 billion for commercial survey research—mostly consumer research on advertising and marketing issues (Siwolop, 1987). Of that total, political polling represented only a few percent, but this tiny fraction was by far the most visible part (Field, 1983).

In this political polling area, the total expenditure for polling on candidates and issues in the 1980 election was about $20 million. This represented about 2000 separate polls, of which perhaps one-quarter were sponsored by the media (newspapers and television networks), with the rest being private polls commissioned by candidates and political committees. Over $2 million were spent by the two presidential candidates alone (Roll & Cantril, 1980; Field, 1983). Every U.S. President since F. D. Roosevelt has had his own private poller (Worcester, 1987). Since about 1960, most politicians have come to consider poll information as essential in their election campaigns. Privately commissioned polls have become commonplace in races for major state and national offices. One study showed 90% of U.S. senators and governors using private polls, and up to 80% of newly elected congressmen (King & Schnitzer, 1968). Many of the ways that polls have been used in congressional and state elections have been described by Declercq (1978) and Conway (1984).

Obviously, political polling has become big business. But the question remains: Is it good for the country? Oftentimes excessive public relations zeal can lead to merchandising political candidates in the same way that toothpaste is advertised. A political consultant in Los Angeles advertised: "You can be elected state senator; leading public relations firm with top flight experience in statewide campaigns wants a senator candidate." This firm's approach was to choose a catchy campaign slogan, give it saturation exposure, and keep the candidate from making speeches or personal appearances. Unfortunately, this approach works all too often (Bogart, 1972a, p. 8).

However, such excesses cannot all be blamed on public opinion polling. And when criticisms of polls are made, it is important to distinguish between several types of polling organizations. The major commercial polls, such as Gallup, Harris, Roper, and a number of statewide polls, use large samples and established scientific methods, and they do not sell their services to individual candidates. By contrast, the thousand or so firms that do private political and market polling vary widely in the carefulness and scientific adequacy of their procedures, and some unfortunately have been known to succumb to pressures for biased samples, slanted reports, or other unethical procedures (e.g., Shamir, 1986; Krosnick, 1989). A third group of polls are those conducted by newspapers or radio or TV stations, which again vary greatly in the scientific adequacy of their sampling, interviewing, and reporting.

There is an unfortunate tendency for the news media to concentrate very largely on who is ahead in the political polls—"horse-race journalism"—rather than on public opinion about the current issues and reasons for voter opinions. The various types of polls have differing levels of predictive success, which have been summarized in a number of reports (Felson & Sudman, 1975; Sudman, 1983; Crespi, 1988). In general, prediction of election results is much better when the polls are taken only a few days before the election, and when the level of voter interest and turnout is high.

In the following sections we will consider, first, the major criticisms, and second, some of the arguments in favor of modern public opinion polling in politics. We will concentrate our discussion mainly on evaluation of the major commercial polls, but with some attention to the merits and abuses of private political polling.

Criticisms of Political Polling

As mentioned earlier in this chapter, opinion polls have been accused of influencing the preferences and the turnout of voters. They have also been criticized as "undemocratic" and elitist, since they report the views of only a small and not-wholly-representative sample of citizens. On the opposite flank, polls have been accused of destroying the courage and independence of political leaders and enshrining the conventional and unconsidered opinions of the poorly informed "average man." This reduction of political opinion to the lowest common denominator, it is alleged, may keep good men and women from running for office or prevent incumbent politicians from telling the public unpleasant truths or from adopting unpopular positions. On still another front, polls have been criticized for making little contribution to the essential democratic processes of discussion and reconciliation of opposing viewpoints, because they often emphasize divergence in opinions and thus may discourage compromise or consensus. Obviously, these are all controversial viewpoints, with persuasive arguments on both sides.

Summaries of these arguments against polling have been presented by Bogart (1972a) and Wheeler (1976), and pointed extracts of the criticisms are highlighted in Box 5-4. Many national politicians have shared these concerns, including Con-

Box 5-4   A Modern Critique of the Polls

"The polls have a tremendous impact on our political system and other aspects of our life. That the polls can so often be wrong makes that impact all the more disturbing. . . .

Public opinion polls determine who runs for political office and, often, who wins. They also influence the tone and content of debate on great national issues. . . .

The influence of polls extends far beyond elections and government policy-making. The little boxes in twelve hundred homes selected by the Nielsen Company register an electronic thumbs up or down on the television programs which will be watched by the entire country. A shift of a rating point or two can determine whether a program lives or dies, yet each rating point represents only a dozen Nielsen households. . . .

All of these polls are subject to error and manipulation. Even polls which are published in good faith can be dangerously misleading, and of course not all polls are legitimate. . . .

So much now depends on the opinion polls—political candidacies, policies, profits—that there is great pressure on the pollsters to manipulate their surveys. It is not hard to rig a poll. . . . Simply by subtly altering the wording of a question, 'you can come up with any result you want.'. . .

The high rate of refusals and not-at-homes is just one of the many technical problems which pollsters face, but it strikes at the very heart of public opinion polling, for if a great number of people are not answering the pollster's knock on the door, then opinion surveys cannot be truly representative of the entire population. . . .

The percentages which are printed in banner headlines appear precise and scientific but in fact are based on a great deal of personal judgment. The pollster must decide who is likely to vote and who is not; he must determine which way people are leaning; and he must allocate the undecideds to one candidate or the other. In all of these matters there is more guesswork than science. . . .

Sampling error could throw a poll off by several points either way, but that really is insignificant compared to other sources of error. 'Question error—the bias or loading in question wording, or the error that results from the context in which the unbiased question may occur—can cause errors of ten, thirty, or even more percentage points.' . . .

In primaries, where a vote is not considered as important, or in early trial heats, when the candidates have not become fully known, people are far less certain of their preferences for the simple reason that they have given them little thought. . . .

The primary results tell us little of national preferences and attitudes, yet the press plays them up. Reporters handicap the candidates like racehorses, picking favorites according to the polls. . . .

Politicians and the press should disregard these early surveys, but because they do not, such polls can easily become self-fulfilling prophecies. . . .

'Polls obviously have an effect. They have a clearer, more dramatic effect on the financial people who give support to the candidates and on the campaign workers, either boosting morale or undercutting it, making the money flow or drying it up, than they do on the electorate directly.'. . .

Poor polls kill contributions. Without cash it is hard to get the kind of exposure that will keep the candidate from dropping even further back. It is the Catch-22 of politics. . . .

The polls have come to have a far-reaching and often dangerous impact, largely because the pollsters have intimidated most of their potential critics. The pollsters would have us believe that to criticize their calling is to oppose democracy. . . ."

Source: Extracts from Wheeler (1976, pp. xv-xvii, 23–37, 245–255). Reprinted from *LIES, DAMN LIES, AND STATISTICS: The Manipulation of Public Opinion in America*, by Michael Wheeler, by permission of Liveright Publishing Corporation. Copyright © 1976 by Michael Wheeler.

gressman Lucien Nedzi (1971), who proposed and held hearings on a "truth-in-polling" bill, calling for public disclosure of the detailed methodology and sponsorship of every published poll. These proposed requirements were much like the voluntary standards that have been adopted by the polling industry (see below); however, the bill never got to the House floor for a vote, though a similar law has been passed in New York (Wheeler, 1976). Another strong critic of political polling was Senator Albert Gore, Sr., (1960), who raised a commonly heard criticism of the polls about which there is much misunderstanding—the question of how large their samples need to be:

> As a layman, I would question that a straw poll of less than 1 percent of the people could under any reasonable circumstances be regarded as a fair and meaningful cross section test. This would be something more than 500 times as large a sample as Dr. Gallup takes. (Gore, 1960, p. 16962)

For a country like the United States with a population of 240 million, such a procedure would require a sample of nearly two million adult respondents, which would be impossibly costly in time, effort, and money. By contrast, we have pointed out in an earlier section that a carefully chosen probability sample of 1500 cases will produce results with an expected error of only $\pm 2\frac{1}{2}\%$. Thus a sample of 1000 or more cases can be used to predict the total national vote. However, if it is desired to predict the vote *in each state separately,* 50 separate samples each containing 1000 or more cases would be needed. Since the electoral college vote, which determines the winner in presidential elections, is based on the plurality of votes in each state separately, the interest of politicians in having large samples has some justification. However, they have often failed to understand that predicting electoral college returns would require not just one large sample, but a separate large sample for each of the 50 states. Instead of attempting this overwhelming task, Gallup and the other political pollers have limited themselves to predicting the candidates' percentages of the total national vote.

A final accusation which has very often been made against the commercial opinion polls is that early poll results start "band-wagon" movements toward the leading candidate. It is surprising that this criticism still persists, for very few studies have found support for it (cf. Skalaban, 1988). Truman's underdog win in 1948 and Humphrey's comeback near-win in 1968 are dramatic illustrations disputing the band-wagon myth, and there is an abundance of other research evidence against it as well (Roll & Cantril, 1980; Ceci & Kain, 1982).

Some of the unfortunate uses and ethical abuses of private political polls have been described by Roll and Cantril (1980, pp. 12–38). For instance, it is not unheard of for some firms to slant their "findings" in a direction favorable to their customer, and it is common for findings to be "leaked" in attempts to gain political advantage. Early poll results on popularity or "name-recognition" (which are likely to change greatly with time and active campaigning) have nevertheless often discouraged well-qualified candidates from running. Early poll results often set unrealistic goals for a candidate to reach a certain percentage of the vote in the "numbers game" of presidential primary elections; and they are also apt to turn on or off the sluice gates of supporters' financial backing and of media attention. Thus there may well be a band-wagon effect among financial contributors and political reporters, if not among voters themselves. As pollster Samuel Lubell has written:

> Events, not polls, affect people. Polls influence politicians most of all, and, secondly, they influence political writers, and last of all—if at all—they affect the people. (quoted in Roll & Cantril, 1980, p. 28)

Defenses of Political Polling

In response to these criticisms of polling, many supporting arguments have been raised. Roll and Cantril (1980, pp. 39–64) have cited many ways in which private polls can be genuinely useful to political candidates. They can inform candidates about the public's concerns and indicate which arguments on an issue will probably be best received. They can demonstrate trends in public support or recognition and help to show where campaign efforts will be most effective. Further, they can pinpoint aspects of the candidate's own public image, the opponent's weaknesses, and the likely effects of other candidates and issues (cf. Declercq, 1978). In addition, Altschuler (1982) notes that polls can help target specific demographic subgroups for campaign advertising that is particularly relevant to their concerns, and also can help candidates play the "expectations game" of publicizing a conservative estimate of their expected vote in the coming primaries.

One way that polls should *not* be used by candidates is in deciding whether to run at the beginning of the campaign, because at that time most candidates are still unknown and key campaign issues have not yet crystallized (Altschuler, 1982). Levy (1984) has given an overview of how pollsters have helped the campaigns of U.S. presidential candidates, and Sudman (1982) and Beal and Hinckley (1984) have described a number of effective ways that polls have been used by Presidents after they were elected to office.

Early defenders of commercial political polls, though readily admitting that polling methods and results were not perfect, were quick to take issue with many criticisms. Some of their major arguments are stated in George Gallup's (1948) vigorous defense of the polls, summarized in Box 5–5. Another major contribution of public opinion polls is an educational one: they encourage both respondents and readers of the results to think about the issues raised. Polls have opened up formerly hush-hush topics, such as birth control and mental illness, for public discussion. The main limitation of polling is due to the nature of people's opinions, which are often inconsistent and/or shifting, based on their varied roles and conflicting loyalties—a mixture of desires and fears, prejudices and ideals. If this limitation is kept in mind, the polls can perform a very useful public service.

To improve the quality of polling procedures and reporting, the American Association for Public Opinion Research (AAPOR) and the National Council on Public Polls (NCPP) have adopted codes of professional ethics and practices. These standards specify that any reports of poll results prepared for publication should include information on the poll's sponsor, wording of questions, method and time

Box 5–5 *George Gallup Defends the Polls*

"Students of government have noted many contributions to our democratic process made by polls. . . .

1. Public opinion polls have provided political leaders with a more accurate gauge of public opinion than they had prior to 1935.

No responsible person in the field of public opinion research would assert that polling methods are perfect. On the other hand, . . . the indices which were relied upon most in the past—letters, newspaper editorials, self-appointed experts, and the like—have been found to be highly inaccurate as guides to public opinion.

2. Public opinion polls have speeded up the processes of democracy by providing not only accurate, but swift, reports of public opinion. . . .

In fact in many situations—particularly those in which a substantial portion of the population fails to take the trouble to vote—the poll results might be even more accurate as a measure of public sentiment than the official returns.

3. Public opinion polls have shown that the common people do make good decisions. . . .

4. Public opinion polls have helped to focus attention on major issues of the day. . . .

5. Public opinion polls have uncovered many 'areas of ignorance.'. . .

6. Public opinion polls have helped administrators of government departments make wiser decisions. . . . based upon accurate knowledge of public attitudes. . . .

7. Public opinion polls have made it more difficult for political bosses to pick presidential candidates 'in smoke-filled rooms.'. . .

8. Public opinion polls have shown that the people are not motivated, in their voting, solely by the factor of self-interest, as many politicians have presumed. . . .

9. Public opinion polls constitute almost the only present check on the growing power of pressure groups. . . .

Poll results show that pressure-group spokesmen often represent only a minority of those within their own groups, and prove baseless their threats of political reprisal if legislators do not bow to their wishes. . . . more important, [polls] can reveal the will of the inarticulate and unorganized majority of the citizens. . . .

10. Public opinion polls help define the 'mandate' of the people in national elections. . . .

At the same time that the views of voters are obtained on candidates, the views of these same voters can be recorded on issues. In this way, election results can be interpreted much more accurately than in the past. . . .

A true statesman will never change his ideals or his principles to make them conform to the opinions of any group, be it large or small. Rather, such a leader will try to persuade the public to accept his views and his goals. In fact, his success as a leader will in large part be measured by his success in making converts to his way of thinking. . . .

Leaders who do not know what the public thinks, or the state of the public's knowledge on any issue, are likely to be ineffective and unsuccessful leaders, and eventually to lose their opportunity to lead. . . .

Great leaders will seek information from every reliable source about the people whom they wish to lead. . . . The public opinion poll will be a useful tool in enabling them to reach the highest level of their effectiveness as leaders."

Source: *A Guide to Public Opinion Polls* (rev. ed.). Selections from George Gallup. Copyright 1944 by Princeton University Press. © 1972 renewed by Princeton University Press, pp. ix–xii, 5, 8. Reprinted by permission of Princeton University Press.

of interviewing, the population sampled, sample size, likely sampling error, and other details. However, it is unfortunately true that most poll reports in newspapers, much less in radio or TV broadcasts, still do not include much of this necessary interpretive information (Turner & Martin, 1981; Miller & Hurd, 1982). Usually this is because editors have trimmed the longer reports prepared by the polling organizations, but sometimes it is because incomplete or "leaked" reports have purposely omitted such facts. Adherence to these standards by all pollsters and journalists would be one of the most important possible steps toward making survey findings meaningful and useful to the public.

It is interesting to note that public opinion polling has spread even to the USSR and the Communist countries of Eastern Europe, where Americans often think of citizens' personal viewpoints as being ignored by the government (Welsh, 1981). As a final argument in favor of polls in democratic countries, Gallup has claimed:

> that legislators do not follow poll results, and that we would have appreciably better government if they did. As Bryce pointed out, the people are better fitted to determine ends than to select means. The task of the leader is to decide how best to achieve the goals set by the people. . . . In the last thirty years [polls] have tried out hundreds of proposals, many of which are widely approved but may have to wait for years until Congress catches up with the people. (Gallup, 1965, p. 463)

SUMMARY

The accuracy of public opinion poll results depends on many factors, but most importantly on the representativeness of the sample of respondents chosen. The commercial polling organizations generally use various modifications of the quota sampling procedure, which is faster and less expensive but also less accurate than probability sampling. However, despite occasional failures the major polls have a very good overall record in predicting election results. Recently, polling by telephone has replaced face-to-face interviews as the predominant method since it is cheaper, faster, and generally able to produce equally high-quality data.

In addition to sampling procedures, another problem in public opinion polling involves the wording of questions, which is extremely important to the validity of both interview and questionnaire results. Memory errors and social desirability needs of respondents can also distort poll results, as can high rates of refusals or nonresponse, nonanonymity of responses, and variations in interviewers' behavior or characteristics. With proper procedures, there are ways of reducing all of the potential sources of error in poll results.

The main reasons why political polls have sometimes failed to predict election results correctly are last-minute changes in voting intentions, the undecided vote, failure to interview "not-at-homes," the possible effects of the polls themselves on the final vote, and differential voter turnout on election day. Although political polling has become a pervasive part of the American scene, it has both critics of its undesirable consequences and defenders of its valuable contributions.

6

The Structure
of Public Opinion

Q. *What do you believe is the most important problem facing the country right now?* (early 1960s)
A. *Cuba.*
Q. *Why do you think Cuba is the most important problem. . . ?*
A. *We should blast Cuba off the map. I don't care why. Just do it. It should be obvious why.*
Q. *What do you think the government should do about this situation?*
A. *It's hard to say really. I am really not one to say like my husband was. We should stop sending all our money to the Commies. And we should make all the draft dodgers and those Commies at (state university) fight on the front lines some day. My ex-husband was a retired Army man, you know. . . .*—John H. Kessel (1965, pp. 378, 381).

Q. *What do the terms liberal and conservative mean to you?*
A. *Not too much really. For some reason conservative gets identified with the South—identified with drabby looking clothes vs. more something I would wear, drabby clothes, too, but it is just a different type.*—W. Russell Neuman (1986, p. 19).

The above responses (which were actually given by two survey respondents) are not conspicuous for their informational content nor their logical consistency. Yet they were fairly typical of a substantial portion of respondents in these two studies, which were conducted in largely middle-class, metropolitan areas.

According to the theory of democratic government, an informed populace is the bulwark of freedom. It is the citizen's duty to form an opinion about public affairs and to express it at the ballot box. And democratic governments are expected to be responsive to public opinion on important issues.

But are the average citizen's attitudes on major public issues well-informed? Are they internally consistent? Are they responsive to new information and new situations? And do they have an effect on public policy? The answers to these questions bear on some of the most central assumptions underlying the democratic form of government.

Many authorities have concluded that the populace is ignorant rather than informed. As far back as 1947, Hyman and Sheatsley concluded (p. 412): "There exists a hard core of chronic 'know-nothing's'" in the American population. More recently Converse (1964, p. 245) wrote, "large portions of an electorate do not have meaningful beliefs. . . ." Yet there are arguments and evidence supporting the opposite viewpoint as well, so this issue is by no means a simple one to settle. In this chapter we will examine first the extent of public information on current affairs, next the evidence for the elitist view of public opinion, and finally the evidence for the mass politics view of public opinion.

THE EXTENT OF PUBLIC INFORMATION

As a college student, learning is a part of your life. You are used to taking in information every day, discussing it, and (we may hope) using it in your regular activities. Most of your friends are probably also students, or at least educated individuals with an interest in current affairs. From such a position in life, it is often very hard to remember that you are not a typical member of society. Even in this age of mass education, only about half of the population ever attends college, and only 25% graduate from college. Of the total adult population, less than one-third have had any college education at all (Newspaper Enterprise Association, 1985).

These facts are important because one's level of education is a very strong determinant of how much one knows. Of course there are "self-educated" men and women but in general, college-educated individuals have a much larger store of factual knowledge than persons with less education. To take only one example, a national poll in 1975 asked respondents to identify ten famous men ranging from Columbus (the best known with 92% correct identification) through Shakespeare, Napoleon, Freud, Karl Marx, Leo Tolstoy, to Rubens (known by only 24%). The average score for the ten famous men was 54% correct (Gallup, 1978, p. 596). Moreover, the effect of different levels of education on a task like this is dramatic. In an identical previous survey the figures were: college-educated respondents 77% correct, high school-educated ones 51% correct, and grade school-educated ones only 26% correct (Erskine, 1963a).

So you are not a typical member of society in your level of information. How much does the "average citizen" know, and on what topics is (s)he likely to be well-informed or poorly informed? Findings from many different national polls give a rather pessimistic overall picture.

First, let us look at the area of general information. Some items of knowledge are very widespread in our country, but most are not. In a 1982 poll on religious knowledge, 70% of the respondents knew where Jesus was born; but only 42% knew who delivered the Sermon on the Mount, and only 46% could name the four gospels (*Gallup Report*, 1985, No. 236).

Many information items which you might expect to be almost universally known are not (Sudman & Bradburn, 1982, pp. 109–110). For instance, the best-known of many famous statements in the late 1950s was "Hi Yo, Silver!", but only 71% of the population knew who said it (the Lone Ranger). Bugs Bunny's greeting, "What's up, Doc?", was identified by only 40%. Similarly, only 40% of the population knew who wrote *Huckleberry Finn* (Mark Twain), and only 22% knew who wrote A *Tale of Two Cities* (Charles Dickens).

However, there are some items of information which are known to most Americans. We may call these **salient** items, meaning that they are in the focus of people's attention. In 1986, 98% of the population had heard or read about the disease called AIDS (*Gallup Report*, 1986, No. 247), and 92% knew about the recent return of Halley's Comet, though only 7% claimed to have seen it themselves (*Gallup Report*, 1986, No. 246). Following the nuclear accident at Three Mile Island, 96% of a national sample had heard of it (*Gallup Opinion Index*, 1979, No. 165); 93% of the population knew about the national plan to inoculate Americans against an expected epidemic of "swine flu" in 1976; and 90% were aware of the proposed Equal Rights Amendment to the U.S. Constitution when it was being debated throughout the 50 states (Gallup, 1978).

What do these items of widely known information have in common? First, they are topics which have been very prominently *in the news*—in many news broadcasts, on the first page of newspapers, and therefore in the conversation of many people. Some, like the swine flu inoculations, have also been the subject of nationwide *action* which might affect almost every family. Second, each of these topics is quite *unique*, a one-of-a-kind item which stands out in the news because there is nothing else like it with which it can be confused. Third, most of these topics have *continued* to be in the news day after day and month after month so that it would be almost impossible for anyone except a mental hospital patient or a hermit to escape contact with them.

Knowledge about Public Affairs

Let us compare these data on general information with evidence on citizens' knowledge about public affairs—the facts on which public opinion and political attitudes should be based.

Here again we find there are a few facts which are known to almost everyone. One kind of information which is widely held is **exposure** to terms and issues, as contrasted with knowledge about them. In answering questions of this type respondents merely have to say, "Yes, I've heard of that," rather than giving correct information about the topic. Consequently, percentages of people "knowing" about the topic are usually much higher than for questions which require correct information in the answer. In 1986, 76% of Americans reported having followed the events of the recent revolutionary change of government in the Philippines (*Gallup Report*, 1986, No. 246), and 67% said they had followed the Reagan administration's so-called "Star Wars" proposal for a space-based nuclear defense system (*Gallup Report*, 1985, No. 234). About 70% of the population were familiar with the Peace Corps shortly after it was founded, and a similar percentage had heard of the United Nations in its initial years (Erskine, 1963b). These highly familiar events and organizations share the same characteristics mentioned above as causes of perceptual salience—they are unique, and they have been in the news prominently and repeatedly. By contrast, the European Common Market clearly had not achieved that degree of public exposure in 1961 (only 22% of Americans had heard of it), probably in large part because it was seen as a foreign issue which did not directly affect Americans.

Turning to items of substantive **knowledge**, rather than merely exposure to terms or issues, one category of information which is widely known is the names of the very top level of national leaders. In recent years, the only Americans correctly identified by more than 90% of our population have been the current and past Presidents. The best-known Senators and Cabinet members typically receive between 40% and 60% correct identification (Gallup, 1978). Billy Graham's name was recognized by 85% of respondents in 1957, but only 56% could name General Franco's country, and only 43% could identify Marshal Tito. Most less-illustrious mortals are recognized by only a tiny fraction of the public; for instance, the first U.S. ambassador to the United Nations was known by only 11% of Americans in 1947 (Erskine 1962). (Do you know who the current U.S. ambassador is?)

Only a very few other items of information are widely shared by the U.S. population. About three-quarters of Americans can name our national anthem or identify the meaning of the initials "F.B.I." About four-fifths can correctly point out California or Texas on the map, but only three other states (Pennsylvania, New York, and Illinois) were correctly pointed out by as many as half of the respondents. Similarly, only 65% of people could point out England on a map of Europe, and only 60% could show Brazil's position in South America, while most other countries were located correctly by less than one-third of the respondents (Erskine, 1962, 1963b).

Specific **factual details** are even less well comprehended by most people. Even after several Mid-East wars, 40% of respondents mistakenly thought that Israel was an Arab country (Hechinger, 1979); and when the Panama Canal treaty was being debated, well over half of Americans incorrectly believed that the biggest U.S. aircraft carriers and supertankers used the canal, not realizing that they were too large to do so (*Gallup Opinion Index*, 1978, No. 153). Though four-fifths of Americans know what famous event occurred in 1492, only 10% know what happened in 1066 (the Battle of Hastings, in which William the Conqueror gained control of England). Similarly, three-quarters know what the metric system is, but only 13% can correctly state about how many inches there are in a meter (Gallup, 1978). Even during the height of an election campaign, less than one-quarter of U.S. adults can correctly identify either the Democratic or Republican congressional candidates in their own district (Kinder & Sears, 1985).

When we turn to public **issues** about which one might expect citizens to be well-informed, that expectation is rudely shattered. There is rarely ever an issue about which even half of the populace is correctly informed even at the most elementary level. In the midst of the "cold war" between the U.S. and Russia, barely over half of Americans could state the meaning of that term in a reasonably correct fashion. Civics teachers would shudder still more to learn that less than one-quarter of our population can correctly describe any of the contents of the Bill of Rights. Other fascinating examples of the level of knowledge or ignorance on public issues are given in Box 6–1, which presents the most recent available collection of many such factual items.

These examples of the low level of public information provide the factual background for our next topic, the **elitist** viewpoint concerning public opinion. This view maintains that coherent systems of political beliefs and attitudes are held by only a small minority of citizens, an "elite" group. In considering this viewpoint, it is important to realize that it is descriptive rather than *pre*scriptive. That is, it does not advocate nor defend elite control of public opinion; it merely seeks to describe the way that these processes actually operate, but does not hold that they *should* operate that way.

THE ELITIST VIEW OF PUBLIC OPINION

A definitive statement of this viewpoint has been given by Philip Converse (1964) in an influential chapter which effectively established the terms of debate

---

Box 6–1   *The Informed (?) Populace*

The following items from national public opinion polls indicate typical degrees of citizen knowledge about public issues that were currently important when the questions were asked. The number after each item is the percentage of respondents who were reasonably correct.

Will you tell me what the term "cold war" means?	*55%*
Can you tell me what the term "filibuster" in Congress means to you?	*54*
Just in your own words, will you tell me what is meant by the term "farm price supports"?	*54*
How many U.S. Senators are there from your state?	*49*
When you hear or read about the Fifth Amendment, what does it mean to you?	*42*
What does the expression "welfare state" mean or refer to, as you understand it?	*36*
What is meant by the electoral college?	*35*
Will you tell me what the North Atlantic Treaty Organization is?	*35*
What are the first 10 amendments in the Constitution called?	*33*
Can you recall the names of your Senators?	*31*
When you hear or read about the term "bipartisan foreign policy," what does that mean to you?	*26*
What do you know about the Bill of Rights? Do you know anything it says?	*21*
What are the three branches of the Federal Government called?	*19*

Source: Erskine (1962, 1963a).

for most subsequent work in this area, and which provides much of the source material for this section. Converse's major conclusions have also been largely reinforced and extended by several later studies (Converse, 1975; Converse & Markus, 1979; Converse & Pierce, 1985; Neuman, 1986).

After describing the typical low level of citizens' information about public affairs, Converse pointed out the resulting consequences for individuals' political belief systems. His major thesis was that, as one moves down the information scale from the best-informed "elites," individuals' *understanding* of public affairs fades out very rapidly. Also, the *objects of belief* which are central in the individuals' belief system

> shift from the remote, generic, and abstract to the increasingly simple, concrete, or "close to home." Where potential political objects (of belief) are concerned, this progression tends to be from abstract, "ideological" principles to the more obviously recognizable social groupings or charismatic leaders and finally to such objects of immediate experience as family, job, and immediate associates. (Converse, 1964, p. 213)

Furthermore, these differences in belief systems seem crucial in understanding different individuals' political behavior.

What evidence did Converse have for these conclusions? Most of it came from a series of major research studies concerning U.S. national elections conducted every two years by the Survey Research Center at the University of Michigan. These studies polled national samples of 1000 to 1800 citizens and were reported in a very important volume called *The American Voter* (Campbell et al., 1960). Converse stressed several different types of findings from these studies.

Use of Ideological Concepts

The first finding concerned the amount of use of ideological dimensions in understanding public affairs. By **ideological dimension** Converse means a basic principle (such as conservatism or internationalism or socialism) that underlies and helps to determine an individual's beliefs on many different political issues. The respondents in the Survey Research Center studies were asked open-ended interview questions which allowed them to evaluate current political issues and candidates in their own words, showing what evaluative dimensions they used spontaneously. Almost the only ideological dimension used was the *liberal-conservative one*, and only 2½% of the population used any such dimension in a clear and consistent way. A second group of respondents (about 9%) mentioned such an ideological dimension but used it very little or were unclear in their use and understanding of the term. A third group of respondents (the largest one— 42%) evaluated political candidates and parties in terms of their expected favorability toward particular subgroups within the nation (e.g., "A Republican victory will be better for farmers").

A fourth group of respondents with even less concern for broad considerations of political policy were those (about 24%) who emphasized only a single narrow issue, such as social security, war versus peace, or past associations of one of the political parties with national prosperity or depression. Finally, a fifth group of respondents (22½%) entirely ignored policy issues in making political evaluations. They might mention personal qualities of the candidates (e.g., "honest," or "handsome"), or favor a party without showing any knowledge of its program, or be completely uninterested in politics. The distribution of these groups in the national population is depicted in Table 6–1, which also shows that the more ideological groups were more likely to have voted in the previous presidential election. The dramatic conclusion from this table is that no more than 10–15% of the population, at most, thinks about political questions in terms of broad public policy principles or ideological dimensions which underlie many different specific issues.

Converse went on to present evidence that the level of education declines quite regularly from the first to the fifth category. More important for our purposes, the level of political activity also declines dramatically in the same direction. On the average, the first category of respondents had over three acts of political participation (e.g., party membership, campaign contributions, attendance at political rallies, etc.) in addition to voting, while the fifth category of respondents had less than one such act.

A number of later studies have used a variety of methods to compare more recent levels of ideological thinking with Converse's findings. For instance, Neuman (1986) found a somewhat similar distribution of people in the five ideological categories, but a substantial increase in the top category (13% used ideological concepts clearly) and a decrease in the bottom category (only 8% ignored issues completely).

Relationships between Beliefs about Specific Issues

A second major finding in Converse's chapter concerned what he called **constraints** among respondents' beliefs on various political issues. That is, are

TABLE 6–1 Use of Ideological Concepts Among Total National Sample and Among Voters in Last Presidential Election

Ideological category	Total sample	Voters
1. Used ideological dimension clearly	2½%	3½%
2. Mentioned ideological dimension (unclear)	9	12
3. Stressed interests of a particular group	42	45
4. Emphasized a single narrow issue	24	22
5. Ignored policy issues completely	22½	17½
	100%	100%

Source: Adapted and reprinted with permission of Macmillan Publishing Co., Inc. from Converse, P. E. "The nature of belief systems in mass publics," in D. Apter (Ed.), *Ideology and Discontent*, p. 218. Copyright © 1964 by The Free Press of Glencoe, a Division of The Macmillan Co.

beliefs interconnected ("constrained") in logically or psycho-logically meaningful patterns? Or, on the contrary, are an individual's beliefs on different political issues isolated into separate clusters—even "logic-tight compartments"—such that beliefs about one issue do not affect beliefs on another issue, even where they may be logically contradictory? This latter viewpoint is the one which Converse emphasized, and it is very similar to Abelson's (1968) theory of isolated "opinion molecules" about a given topic which are not logically interconnected to opinion molecules on other topics.

To support this viewpoint, Converse cited correlational data relating beliefs about seven different political issues in (a) a national cross-section sample, and (b) an elite sample made up of congressional candidates in the 1958 election. There were four domestic issues and three foreign-affairs issues, as follows:

1. Federal programs for full employment
2. Federal aid to education
3. Federal funds for public housing and electric power
4. Federal F.E.P.C. to prevent discrimination
5. Foreign economic aid
6. Foreign military aid
7. Isolationism vs. commitments abroad

In addition, the respondents' party preferences were obtained. Scores on these eight variables were interrelated using a statistic called tau-gamma, which yields results similar to but somewhat smaller than conventional correlation coefficients. A summary of the results is shown in Table 6–2.

In interpreting these results, it is important to remember that the cross-section sample contained its fair share (about 10%) of "ideologues" and "near-ideologues," the first two categories of people in Table 6–1, and the structure of their political belief systems might be much more like that of the elite sample than

TABLE 6–2 Average Relationships ("Constraints") Between Beliefs on Various Political Issues and Party Preference in Two Samples

Sample	Among domestic issues	Between domestic and foreign issues	Among foreign issues	Between 7 issues and party preference
Elite	.53	.25	.37	.39
Cross-section	.23	.11	.23	.11

Note.—Coefficients are tau-gammas.

Source: Adapted and reprinted with permission of Macmillan Publishing Co., Inc. from Converse, P. E. "The nature of belief systems in mass publics," in D. Apter (Ed.), *Ideology and Discontent*, p. 229. Copyright © 1964 by The Free Press of Glencoe, a division of The Macmillan Co.

that of the remainder of the cross-section sample. Thus, the difference between the two samples was undoubtedly diminished by the inclusion of some "elites" in the cross-section sample. In spite of that, the difference between the samples was marked. The elite sample showed a much greater degree of structure, that is, higher relationships between beliefs about different issues. The elite sample also showed a markedly higher relationship between party preference and beliefs on the seven issues than did the cross-section sample.

In sum, this finding and many similar ones have led Converse to conclude that elites do have a meaningful structure for their political belief systems, but that the "common man" generally does not. Other experts on political behavior have agreed with this point of view. For instance, a similar comparison of 1978 congressional candidates with voters in that election found a much higher level of relationship among attitudes toward various issues in the candidate group than in the general electorate (Bishop & Frankovic, 1981). Hennessy (1970) has even gone so far as to state that

> political attitudes are an elite phenomenon. Most people do not have political attitudes. Even in modern high-energy societies most people do not have political attitudes. (p. 463)

Importance of Groups in Political Belief Systems

If it is true that most people don't have clearly structured political attitudes, do they have any substitute for them? Or are they completely without political belief systems? Converse would not be willing to carry his argument that far, primarily because of the importance of **reference groups** (either positive or negative) which provide a basis for the belief systems of many people.

Take the case of a lathe operator who works in a large factory, has several children to educate, has a large mortgage on the family home, and has occasionally been laid off from work for several months when the company was having financial troubles. This person is apt to organize many beliefs around "what is good for workers" (just as the boss may organize many beliefs around "what is good for industry"). Thus, if asked, the lathe operator might favor reducing taxes, but might also favor increasing unemployment benefits, since both of these measures would be good for workers, his(her) reference group. That would be logical from this person's standpoint, and it would demonstrate at least a rudimentary type of political belief system. But note a discrepancy here: the worker's two answers fall on opposite sides of the major ideological dimension underlying American political positions, liberalism-conservatism (reducing taxes is a "conservative" position, while welfare measures like unemployment benefits are "liberal" programs). Thus, on Converse's scale, this worker would not be classified in the top two ideological categories, but in category 3, the group-benefit category (along with about 40% of the total population—see Table 6–1).

Converse proposed that below the well-informed and ideologically oriented top 10% of the population, the major organizing principle underlying individuals' political beliefs is their attitudes toward major societal groups. That is, whatever political beliefs such individuals have are apt to be organized around their concept of the interests of their own most important reference group, be it a social class, an ethnic or nationality group, a religious group, a regional group (e.g., Easterners), or an occupation (e.g., farmers).

This third major point in Converse's argument has a further aspect which explains why, below the top 50% or so of the population, the importance of groups in determining individuals' political beliefs drops off quite rapidly. Converse suggested that this finding is due to the very low level of political information held by these individuals. They literally know so little about most political issues that they can't determine how the issue would affect their own group, even when they are aware of being a member of a group that has common interests. As an example, many Americans who know that they are members of the working class have so little information about the political party platforms and policies that they cannot tell whether a Democratic or a Republican victory would benefit them. As a result, they form their political opinions on the basis of isolated issues, such as which party will lower taxes (these individuals fall in category 4 of Table 6–1), or on the basis of such factors as the candidate's attractiveness (these people fall in category 5).

Stability of Beliefs over Time

A fourth major finding which supports the elitist theory of public opinion concerns the stability of particular political beliefs over time. Saying that a person has a "belief system" implies that most of his or her beliefs will be relatively stable and unchanging over a few-year period, rather than fluctuating markedly from time to time. This question was studied by a longitudinal design in which the same panel of respondents was reinterviewed several times about two years apart. They were questioned about political issues such as those listed on page 138. The results were dramatic:

> Faced with the typical item of this kind, only about thirteen people out of twenty manage to locate themselves even on the same *side* of the controversy in successive interrogations, when ten out of twenty could have done so by chance alone. (Converse, 1964, p. 239)

By contrast, Converse has deduced from repeated congressional roll-call votes on comparable bills that an elite office-holder sample would show stable opinions over time for about 18 out of 20 respondents. Thus, you can see that there is a marked difference in the temporal stability of political beliefs, with elites being highly stable in beliefs and mass samples being quite changeable over time. This conclusion has recently been corroborated in a comparison of political elites and members of the mass public in France (Converse & Pierce, 1985).

A further question may be raised as to which beliefs are most stable and which most changeable. Of all the items reported, one was by far the most stable—party preference, with a tau-beta reliability coefficient of more than +.7. This stability of people's party identification was one of the major findings of *The American Voter.* By contrast, all of the seven issues listed on page 138 had tau-beta reliability coefficients close to +.3 or +.4, indicating some continuing temporal stability but also a great deal of change over the two-year period. The issue which had the highest stability (close to +.5) was an item about federal action to promote school desegregation, and the next highest in stability were the items concerning a federal F.E.P.C. and federal programs for full employment. Converse concluded that

> stability declines as the referents of the attitude items become increasingly remote, from jobs, which are significant objects to all, and Negroes, who are attitude objects for most, to items involving ways and means of handling foreign policy. (1964, p. 241)

When a third interview was held with the respondents, four years after the first interview, another fascinating finding emerged. Studying the "turnover correlations" between the same beliefs at three different points in time, it was found that these correlations remained very nearly the same from one time to the next. This meant that a person's opinions at time 3 could be predicted just as well from her opinions at time 1 as from her opinions at time 2. This was a surprising finding because test-retest correlations usually tend to decrease with longer time intervals between the original test and the retest, as one would expect if opinion change is a relatively steady or continuous process.

Analyzing the obtained pattern of turnover correlations further with complex statistical techniques, Converse found that they could be explained quite well by an "all or none" model of stability. That is, the model postulated that some respondents had clearcut opinions which were perfectly stable over time, while others (a much larger group) had no opinion in any meaningful sense and were just as likely to change their response randomly upon reinterviewing as to give the same response a second time. The "all or none" model fit the obtained pattern of turnover correlations on one issue perfectly, and it came close to a perfect fit on the other issues as well. Converse suggested that it needed only a slight modification, adding the postulate of a *small* third group of genuine converts, to make it fit the data for all the issues measured.

This is a very important finding, for it indicates once again in a new way that on any given issue the public can be meaningfully divided into a small elite group of the well-informed and a large mass of politically naive individuals. Moreover, this finding goes a step further and says that most of the latter group have *no meaningful opinions at all* since the changes in their responses over time were completely random in nature. As Converse summarized the conclusion,

> large portions of an electorate do not have meaningful beliefs, even on issues that have formed the basis for intense political controversy among elites for substantial periods of time. (1964, p. 245)

Photograph courtesy of Philip Converse.
Reprinted by permission.

Box 6–2   PHILIP CONVERSE, *Analyst of Political Attitudes*

Widely known for his research on political behavior, Philip Converse is the director of the Center for Advanced Study in the Behavioral Sciences at Stanford University. Until 1989 he was Professor of Sociology and Political Science at the University of Michigan, and had served four years as director of the Center for Political Studies and three years as director of its parent body, the Institute for Social Research. Born in 1928 in New Hampshire, he earned a B.A. at Denison University, studied in France, and took his Ph.D. in social psychology at the University of Michigan. He remained there on its faculty for over 30 years, authoring numerous, widely cited books and articles.

Converse is most famous for his books written with Campbell, Miller, and Stokes: The American Voter, *and* Elections and the Political Order, *which are cited in Chapters 12 and 13 and elsewhere in this book. He has also co-authored a social psychology text with Newcomb and Turner, written pivotal papers on the structure of public opinion which are described in this chapter, and collaborated on* The Quality of American Life, *cited in Chapter 12. Converse's scholarly contributions have been acknowledged by his election to the American Academy of Arts and Sciences and the National Academy of Sciences (an especially rare honor for a social scientist). He has also been elected president of the American Political Science Association and the International Society of Political Psychology, and has received the distinguished achievement award of the American Association for Public Opinion Research.*

More recent analyses of political opinion stability over the 1972–1974–1976 elections have produced similarly low stability estimates for the overall population, though some moral attitudes (e.g., toward marijuana or abortion) were found to have higher stability, and party. identification remained very stable (Converse & Markus, 1979). Studies by Abramson (1983) also agree that there has been little change in the stability of political opinions since Converse's early research.

Every Issue Has Its Own Public

The final major conclusion of Converse's paper was that there is not just one political elite group, but there are different **issue publics** for different topics. This means that each important political issue has its own group of interested citizens, partially unique and partially overlapping other issue publics. These issue publics vary in size from about 20% to about 40% of the total population. A tiny group of people were found to be members of all eight issue publics which Converse studied, and many individuals were not concerned nor informed about any of the issues. Most people were members of only a few of the issue publics; for instance, they might be concerned about racial issues but not about economic ones nor about foreign affairs.

The contrast between elite and mass opinion and the concept of issue publics, who are selectively oriented to some political issues but not to others, were beautifully illustrated in the issue of domestic Communism which was raised by Senator Joseph McCarthy in the early 1950s. Though this controversy was long-continued and heavily emphasized by the news media and political leaders, there is evidence that it was much less salient to the mass public than other political issues of that period such as "corruption" in Washington or the Korean War. Converse concluded:

> The controversy over internal communism provides a classic example of a mortal struggle among elites that passed almost unwitnessed by an astonishing portion of the mass public. (1964, p. 251)

THE MASS POLITICS VIEW
OF PUBLIC OPINION

Having discussed the major research findings supporting the elitist view of public opinion, we turn now to its antithesis, which we will call the **mass politics** viewpoint. Here some of the best-known contributions have been Robert Lane's (1962) book, *Political Ideology,* and his later writings (1973). Lane believes that common men and women do have political ideologies, though they may not be expressed as easily and articulately as the elites'. However, as he himself recognizes, his method of intensive depth interviews with a few individuals can only provide suggestive evidence but not prove his case (1962, p. 4). Other researchers have found support for the same theoretical viewpoint with empirical work in several areas.

In general, adherents of the mass politics view do not dispute most of the evidence concerning political belief systems which we have summarized above. Rather, they interpret its meaning differently and present additional evidence which tends to throw a different light on the question. They comprise a diverse collection of critics of the elitist view, each stressing certain kinds of arguments. The several types of research evidence that are discussed below can be classified as having one or another of three main bases: (a) the pluralism or variety of ideologies, (b) methodological problems and refinements, or (c) changes in the political characteristics of the American public (Neuman, 1986).

A Search for Other Ideological Dimensions

Perhaps the smallest departure from the elitist viewpoint has been to search for alternative ideological dimensions, other than the liberal-conservative one, around which individuals' political beliefs might be organized. Since only 10% or 15% of the population is even reasonably articulate about their ideological viewpoints, as Converse has shown, this search has usually taken the form of examining empirical correlations between different political beliefs in a large population, rather than asking people directly about their ideologies.

An increasingly widespread methodological approach used in many such studies is **secondary analysis** of data already collected and analyzed in other ways by another investigator. The huge repository of successive national sample survey data collected by the Survey Research Center (SRC) and the Center for Political Studies (CPS) at the University of Michigan, which formed the basis for *The American Voter* (Campbell et al., 1960) and other later books, has generously been made available to many other researchers for secondary analysis, as have data from many of the commercial polls of Elmo Roper and of George Gallup.

A good example of a secondary-analysis study which focused on ideological dimensions was conducted by Axelrod (1967), using SRC data from the 1956 election. In that survey a national sample of nearly 1800 persons had been asked, among many other questions, about their beliefs on 16 political issues, including the seven listed previously in this chapter. Campbell et al. (1960) had reported the results in terms of two clusters of issues, a welfare scale and a foreign policy scale, both of which had rather weak interrelationships among their several items (the average r between items within each cluster was less than $+.3$). Moreover, there was no relationship at all between these two scales (average r very close to 0.0). This finding had demonstrated once again that there was no clear liberal-conservative dimension underlying most people's political views, since a liberal on welfare issues was no more likely to be liberal on foreign-policy issues than he was to be conservative on them.

In his reanalysis of these same 16 political issues, Axelrod found a single cluster of interrelated items which he termed a **populism** cluster because of its similarity to the principles of the American Populist political movement of the 1890s. This cluster included more issues (six), and the issues had slightly stronger intercorrelations than either of the clusters analyzed by Campbell et al. The American Populist movement was concerned with domestic social reform but was opposed to foreigners and to U.S. foreign involvement. Similarly, Axelrod's populist cluster of items favored federal programs for full employment, aid to education, and medical care, but also favored tax cuts and the firing of suspected Communists, and opposed U.S. foreign involvement. Perhaps most surprisingly, this cluster of issues had its strongest intercorrelations for the subsample of *nonvoters* in the total sample. The cluster was less coherent for more politically active and informed individuals, and it had the lowest intercorrelations for the college graduate subsample.

Axelrod emphasized that for a large segment of the American public, "domestic liberalism is not correlated with internationalism," and his evidence for the populism dimension of political attitudes showed that "much of the public views policy questions as they were seen in the 1890s and not the 1930s" (1967, p. 59).

A more recent study of people's attitudes toward 12 political issues, using the statistical technique of cluster analysis, found, rather than a single liberal-conservative dimension, a variety of ideological patterns (Fleishman, 1986). In addition to liberals and conservatives, it identified distinct groups of people who were primarily prolabor, or who advocated limited government, or who were middle-of-the-road on government economic policies. Other authors have suggested other underlying dimensions of attitudes (e.g., McGuire, 1981).

Consistency within Single Individuals

A methodological objection to the evidence for the elitist viewpoint has been offered by Bennett (1975), following the conceptual approach of Lane (1973). Both authors stress that various individuals may organize their political attitudes in different ways—that is, using a variety of dimensions, not just liberalism-conservatism or populism. Also, for each person, some topics may represent

Photograph courtesy of Robert Lane.
Reprinted by permission.

Box 6–3 ROBERT LANE, *Proponent of Mass Political Ideology*

The best-known advocate of the view that most people have their own political ideology, Robert Lane is Professor Emeritus of Political Science at Yale University. Born in 1917, he did all his undergraduate and graduate work at Harvard, with time out to serve in the Army in World War II. In 1948 he was appointed to the faculty at Yale, where he spent his whole teaching career. He has been awarded fellowships and grants from numerous organizations and spent many periods as a visiting scholar in England, Australia, Italy, and The Netherlands.

Among Lane's widely cited books are Political Ideology: Why the American Common Man Believes What He Does, Political Thinking and Consciousness, *and* Political Man. *He has been honored by election to the presidency of the American Political Science Association, the Policy Studies Organization, and the International Society of Political Psychology.*

"nonissues"—questions that the individual hasn't thought about and has no opinion about. This individualistic conception of belief organization suggests the need for a different research methodology to investigate it. Whereas Converse studied the consistency of attitudes on *each separate issue* across a large number of people, Bennett advocated studying the consistency of attitudes *within each person* on a large number of political issues. The difference in results for these two methods is dramatic. Using 20 specific political issues including Converse's familiar seven, Bennett found test-retest stability figures *across people* which were very similar to Converse's (1964) findings—correlations ranging from about $+.1$ to $+.4$, even though the respondents were college students and the retest was only three weeks after initial testing. However, looking at the stability of attitudes *within individuals* (that is, stability in which ideas they evaluated most favorably and most unfavorably), the average test-retest correlation was an impressively high $+.74$. Bennett concludes that "not all people make sense of politics in the same way, but most people make sense of politics in some way" (p. 25).

Emphasis on Parties Instead of Issues

A third line of attack on the elitist viewpoint has been to downgrade the importance of *policy issues* as major aspects of political attitudes. For instance, Wilker and Milbrath (1970) have argued that people's attitudes on political policy issues are not the only basis for belief systems. Instead of being oriented around policies or issues, the mass public's belief systems are more rudimentary, less detailed, and less differentiated. They are apt to be organized around individuals' *party identification* (Democratic or Republican) or their loyalty to one or another group (unions, farmers, Catholics, blacks, etc.) whose perceived interests influence their vote and their political attitudes.

The importance of a person's party identification for his or her political belief systems has also been stressed by Kirkpatrick (1970a, 1970b). Reanalyzing data from SRC election surveys, he developed a measure of an individual's "total partisan affect" (the number of things which (s)he liked better about one party and its presidential candidate than about the other party and candidate). Then, following a balance theory model, he showed that there was a high degree of consistency between individuals' party identification, their total partisan affect, and the candidate for whom they intended to vote. In a sample of more than 1500, 86% of individuals were consistent and only 14% were inconsistent (for instance, one inconsistent pattern would have been Republican party identification, but partisan affect favoring the Democratic side, and an intention to vote for the Democratic presidential candidate). Thus, Kirkpatrick has shown that when party identification is considered instead of specific policy issues, an overwhelming majority of the population have consistent political attitudes. A similar conclusion was reached by Key and Cummings (1966) in a reanalysis of Gallup Poll data for the 1960 election.

Kirkpatrick (1970a) carried the emphasis on parties as a source of attitude consistency a step farther by relating (a) individuals' *issue* positions to (b) their party identification, and (c) their beliefs about the parties' stands on the same issues. He reanalyzed SRC election survey data for four of the domestic issues discussed earlier in this chapter, examining the responses of relatively small subsets of the total population who had an interest in one or another of these issues ("issue publics"). Within these select groups, he found that consistency among the three belief elements ranged from 83% to 90% for different issues.

From the above studies the conclusion seems clear that party preference forms the foundation for consistent political attitudes in a large majority of the population, regardless of whether or not these individuals have information or beliefs about specific issues. Similarly, people's liking or disliking for other groups in society (e.g., racial or religious groups) has been shown to help determine their political attitudes on particular issues (Brady & Sniderman, 1985). Of course, Converse would classify such group- or party-linked political attitudes at the third level of Table 6–1, as group-related rather than ideological. In Chapters 12 and 13 we will consider further data from recent studies comparing party identification, policy issues, and candidate images as influences on individual voting decisions.

Attitude Structure on Local Issues

A fourth objection to the elitist viewpoint stresses that average citizens may be a good deal more interested in local issues than they are in national or international ones. For instance, Luttbeg (1968) studied attitudes toward ten issues such as urban renewal, bringing in new industry, annexation of suburbs, creation of a metropolitan park along the major river in the area, etc. He sampled over 1200 representative citizens in two Oregon cities and 117 community leaders from the same two cities, who were selected by a reputational technique. Using the technique of factor analysis, he found that five different conceptual dimensions were needed in order to explain the structure of attitudes on these ten issues. These five factors did explain a large amount of the variance (74%) in the attitudes of community leaders, but they also explained nearly as much (65%) of the variance in the citizens' attitudes. Luttbeg concluded, contrary to the elitist viewpoint, that community leaders' attitudes on these local issues were complex (based on several different dimensions) rather than being unidimensional (e.g., based on a single liberal-conservative continuum), and second, that average citizens' attitudes on local issues were very nearly as highly structured as the leaders' attitudes.

In a later article, Luttbeg (1970) did report some differences between the leaders' and citizens' attitudes on these issues, but not differences in degree of structure. He found that the community leaders tended to be more liberal than the overall population and to support these local programs more strongly than did the average citizen.

Salient Issues—A Better Methodology

Another objection to the elitist viewpoint is that most studies have not allowed respondents to specify issues which were important (salient) to them

(Litwak, Hooyman, & Warren, 1973). In 1960 the SRC election surveys rectified this situation by adding to their previous closed-ended (multiple-choice) questions a new set of open-ended questions. These questions asked respondents to describe in their own words any "problems you think the government in Washington should do something about," how worried they were about these problems, and which party they thought would be most likely to do what they wanted done about the problems. The subjects' free responses were coded into about 25 different categories, and the results have been studied by RePass (1971).

RePass analyzed primarily the high-salience issues, that is, ones which respondents were very worried about. He did this because he found that below this level of salience there was a lower level of information about the issue and a poorer perception of party differences concerning it. Thus he was essentially dealing solely with a concerned "issue public" on each issue, and one that had volunteered its concern without any prior cues from the interviewer. It is interesting to note the content of these high-salience problems. In 1960, 62% of them were in the area of foreign affairs and defense (largely problems in relation to Communism), whereas in 1964, 60% concerned domestic issues (most prominently, racial problems).

In general these issue publics perceived differences in the party positions concerning the issues which they mentioned, and they showed a fairly accurate perception of these party differences despite some tendency toward distorted perception favoring their own preferred party. As shown in Table 6–3, there was a very strong relationship between their party identification and their perception of which party could handle their salient issues better; however, a minority of individuals from each party perceived the other party as better on the issues than their own party. It is interesting to note that among respondents for whom this "issue advantage" strongly favored the other party, over 90% ended up voting against their own party. In other words, when issues are important to individuals, and when they can see a clear difference between party positions on these issues, they do tend very strongly to vote in accordance with their issue beliefs.

TABLE 6–3 Relation of Party Identification to Perception of Party's "Issue Advantage" in 1964 Election

Party having perceived "issue advantage"	Party identification				
	Strong Dem. (N = 332)	Weak Dem. (N = 308)	Indep. (N = 272)	Weak Repub. (N = 175)	Strong Repub. (N = 150)
Democratic	78%	53%	39%	26%	7%
No perceived difference	14	26	26	27	11
Republican	8	21	35	47	82
	100%	100%	100%	100%	100%

Source: Adapted from RePass (1971, p. 399).

The overall relationship between these individuals' perception of a party's "issue advantage" and their presidential vote was +.57 (tau-beta). By way of comparison, the relationship between their vote and their overall attitude toward the candidates was almost identical (tau-beta = +.60); and this was in 1964, when attitudes toward the candidates were unusually salient (Kessel, 1968). RePass concluded:

> When we allow voters to define their own issue space, they are able to sort out the differences between parties with a fair degree of accuracy. . . . we have shown that the public is in large measure concerned about specific issues, and that these cognitions have a considerable impact on electoral choice. (1971, p. 400)

Very similar conclusions were reached in an entirely different study by Litwak et al. (1973).

Increases in Ideology

Another basis for criticism of the elitist viewpoint is the claim that the American public has become much more ideological since the 1950s, when Converse's original research was done. Those were the years of Eisenhower's presidency, when partisan politics and ideological disputes were quite muted in comparison to later elections. Several research teams have provided evidence that the number of Americans who used ideological concepts increased markedly in the elections of 1964 through 1972 (Field & Anderson, 1969; A. Miller, W. Miller, Raine, & Brown, 1976; Nie, Verba, & Petrocik, 1979, 1981). This change paralleled the sharply increased issue-based voting produced by the ideological disparities between the candidates and platforms in those elections (particularly in the 1964 contest between Johnson and Goldwater, in George Wallace's third-party candidacy in 1968, and in the 1972 election between Nixon and McGovern).

The strongest proponents of this increased-ideology viewpoint were Nie, Verba, and Petrocik (1979), in their book *The Changing American Voter.* They computed the percentage of ideologues and near-ideologues (the top two levels in Converse's classification) as totaling over 45% in each of these three elections (Nie et al., 1981). However, their coding scheme was substantially different from the one used by Converse, and most analyses by other researchers have reached less-extreme conclusions, putting the total figure for ideologues and near-ideologues for those years close to 25%. This is about twice the 1956 level reported by Converse (1964), and he agrees that there was a substantial increase in Americans' ideological thinking in the 1960s and 1970s (Converse, 1975). This increase was probably due in part to the rising educational levels of the populace and in part to the political battles of the 1960s over civil rights and the Vietnam War. The level of ideological thinking in the American public seems to have stabilized and then decreased somewhat since 1972 (Abramson, 1983).

Increases in Attitude Consistency and Stability

Because Converse (1964) stressed how low were the typical levels of political attitude consistency ("constraint") and stability over time, critics of the elitist view have presented research findings disputing both of these conclusions. Taking consistency first, Nie and Andersen (1974) and Nie et al. (1979) demonstrated that the average relationship between attitudes on different issues (i.e., "constraint") rose markedly between 1960 and 1964, stayed high through 1972, and declined somewhat in 1976. However, the importance of this finding has been challenged because there was a concurrent change in 1964 in the response format and wording of the questions used by the Survey Research Center to measure respondents' issue attitudes (from a 5-choice Likert format to a dichotomous pro-con choice). Though these changes seemed innocuous at the time, careful later experiments with question wording proved that they were sufficient to account for all of the apparent increase in issue consistency (Bishop, Oldendick, Tuchfarber, & Bennett, 1978; Sullivan, Piereson, & Marcus, 1978).

Nie and his colleagues now agree that their earlier finding was a methodological artifact, and that there hasn't been any long-term increase in citizens' issue consistency (Nie & Rabjohn, 1979). Because neither question format is clearly better, it is hard to say whether the "true" level of consistency of the population is as low as Converse's research with the original items indicated, or as high as the more-reliable new items suggest. However, the recent review by Kinder and Sears (1985) favors the newer items and the conclusion that, all along, the American public has *not* been so distressingly low in issue consistency. Likewise, appreciable levels of ideological consistency have been reported in the British populace (Himmelweit, Humphreys, Jaegers, & Katz, 1981).

The stability of these issue attitudes over time has also been the subject of controversy. The main issue here is whether and how to correct for the unreliability of measurement of respondents' issue attitudes, in order to determine what the "true" stability of attitudes would be if they were measured without any error. There are several complex statistical ways of estimating such corrections, and all of them that have been tried yield substantially higher estimates of attitude stability—in other words, lower estimates of the number of respondents whose attitude reports are haphazard or meaningless (Erikson, 1979; Judd & Milburn, 1980; Inglehart, 1985). Here is an example of such conclusions:

> Both the highly educated and the uneducated public show evidence of an underlying ideological predisposition, show remarkable stability in their attitudes, and show equal consistency or constraint between different attitude areas. (Judd & Milburn, 1980, p. 627)

However, these various statistical techniques produce somewhat differing results, and their application has provoked sharp controversies in the research literature (e.g., Converse, 1980; Judd, Krosnick, & Milburn, 1981). Converse and Markus (1979) have analyzed the most recent longitudinal data from the CPS 1972–1974–

1976 election panel study, and concluded that there has been little change in the political-attitude stability of the American public since the 1950s. However, this historical comparison too is tenuous due to the intervening changes in item response format and wording (Abramson, 1983). Kinder and Sears (1985) have concluded that findings of attitude instability partly indicate a real phenomenon, but are also partly due to difficulties in accurate attitude measurement.

RESOLUTION OF THE CONTROVERSY

It is possible to resolve this controversy between the elitist and mass-politics viewpoints, at least in part. Converse himself has emphasized that he is *not* claiming that

> poorly educated people have no systems of beliefs about politics. . . . We do not disclaim the existence of entities that might best be called "folk ideologies," nor do we deny for a moment that strong differentiations in a variety of narrower values may be found within subcultures of less educated people. (1964, pp. 255–256)

Rather, he holds that, below the top elite fraction of the population (10% to 25%, depending on one's calculations):

> Instead of a few wide-ranging belief systems that organize large amounts of specific information, one would expect to find a proliferation of clusters of ideas among which little constraint is felt, even, quite often, in instances of sheer logical constraint. (p. 213)

What can supporters of the mass-politics view add to this conclusion? First, they would agree strongly that the average person does have beliefs, values, and ideas about some aspects of public affairs. Second, they would probably agree that on national and international issues of government policy, the average person's attitudes are less clear and consistent than the elite's, and less likely to be organized along a liberal-conservative dimension. Third, they would point to the presence of a populist ideology or other ideological dimensions among many members of the mass public, and to the importance of political parties and other reference groups as central elements around which many average citizens organize a consistent set of political attitudes. Fourth, they would point to local issues, and also issues which are highly salient to the individual, as areas where the mass public's political attitudes are apt to be very nearly as well-organized and coherent as the elite's. Fifth, they would cite the increasing education levels of the American public (Bishop, 1976) and the issue-oriented character of the elections after 1960 as two factors which have raised the overall level of ideological thinking of the populace. Sixth, they would claim that consistency of political attitudes among the mass public has always been higher than Converse concluded, but that this fact was obscured by the unfortunate choice of attitude measures used in the early studies. Also, they would stress that, when computations are corrected to compensate for unreliability of measurement, the stability of political attitudes over time is substantially higher than earlier reported. All of these points tend to support the view that many common citizens do have a meaningful political ideology.

Finally, a resolution between the elitist view and the mass-politics view of public opinion might point out that in our complex modern world no one can be well-informed in all the areas which touch on one's daily life, so a large degree of ignorance is inevitable for everyone. In this situation, it makes sense to concentrate on the knowledge and opinions which are important in one's own job and to turn over most responsibility for other areas of life to people who are seen as experts in those areas (doctors in health questions, legislators in politics, community leaders in local issues, etc.). It is simply not functional for most people to develop an integrated system of political information and attitudes concerning issues which do not closely affect their everyday lives. This viewpoint has been stressed by Lane (1973) and by Litwak et al. (1973), who give the following example of the unmanageable complexity of modern life:

> To deal with the problems of water supply in a city like New York, knowledge of at least five major bureaucracies is necessary. If someone had no water, he would contact the health department; if not enough water—the department of water supply; if no hot water or water leaks—the buildings department; if these were major water leaks—the department of water supply; if water was overflowing from the apartment above—the police department; if there was water sewage in the cellar—the sanitation department. (p. 330)

Tying the above points back to our discussion of attitude structure and functions in Chapter 4, we can conclude that attitudes serve the same general functions for members of the mass public as for political elites. However, it is much less likely (and less necessary) for political beliefs and attitudes to be central and salient in the belief systems of the average citizen than in those of the highly educated, of community leaders, and of people who are employed in politics or active in political affairs.

SUMMARY

Though the "informed citizen" is often claimed to be a necessary ingredient of democratic government, most citizens in our society are not very well-informed. A few items of knowledge are very widespread, but most are not. The *salient* bits of information which are known to almost everyone are ones which have been very prominently in the news, which are unique and different from other events, and which have continued to receive public attention over long periods of time.

In the field of public affairs, *exposure* to terms and events (such as the Watergate scandal or the war in Nicaragua) is much more widespread than factual knowledge about them, and knowledge about specific public issues and policies is almost always confined to a minority of the population, and often a very small minority.

The *elitist* view of public opinion holds that only the "elite," the top 10% to 25% of the public, have political attitudes and belief systems which provide a broad and coherent basis for understanding public affairs. Only these elites use ideological concepts (such as liberalism-conservatism) in discussing public affairs, and only they show a clear and meaningful pattern of relationships between their beliefs about various political issues and policies. Below this elite level, attitudes toward major societal groups (e.g., farmers, blacks, the working class) provide a major focus for organizing whatever political attitudes are present.

The *mass-politics* view of public opinion generally does not dispute the facts cited by the elitist proponents, but does interpret them differently and add many other sorts of evidence. Methodological studies have shown high consistency in political attitudes within individuals, though different individuals may differ widely in the dimensions they use to judge political issues. Political party preference is a very important factor which forms the foundation for consistent political attitudes in a large majority of the population, many of whom are not concerned about specific policy issues. Other evidence shows that for local community issues, and for issues which are highly salient to the individuals concerned, the mass public's attitudes are apt to be very nearly as well-organized as are the elite's. Also, there is general agreement that the U.S. public's level of ideological thinking increased substantially in the 1960s and 1970s. These types of findings have helped to diminish and resolve the controversy over the political attitudes of the elite versus those of the average citizen.

7

Formation
of Attitudes
and Opinions

The greatest part of mankind have no other reason for their opinions than that they are in fashion.—Samuel Johnson.

Opinions should be formed with great caution and changed with greater.—Josh Billings.

Attitudes and opinions are learned—that much is agreed upon by all authorities. But how are they learned? The processes of attitude formation, and the factors which are most important in the development of attitudes, are still subjects of debate. Some authorities stress family influences in the child's early years, others underline the importance of the educational system or of peer-group pressures, while still others emphasize the mass media of communication, particularly television. Undoubtedly all of these factors play a part in attitude formation, and the research summarized in this chapter has begun the task of classifying and understanding the processes and the determining factors involved.

The term **attitude formation** refers to the initial change from having *no* attitude toward a given object to having *some* attitude toward it, either positive, negative, or in between. But what is it like to have no attitude toward an object? For an infant, the situation was described by William James as a world of "blooming, buzzing confusion" where all stimuli are new and strange. For adults to have no attitude may mean that they have never had any experience, either direct or vicarious, with the object (for instance, your attitude toward "Cromelians," a group of people you have never heard of), or simply that they have never thought evaluatively about it (an example might be your attitude toward the planet Jupiter).

Starting from this zero point, what determining factors can cause a person to acquire an attitude toward Cromelians or toward Jupiter? In answering that question we will consider several different factors, starting with internal and personal determinants and moving toward external influences. Then in the latter part of the chapter we will briefly examine the various *processes of learning* by which a new attitude or opinion may be acquired.

First, one distinction is needed. Attitude formation and attitude change are often hard to distinguish from each other and are therefore often spoken of together, as if they were synonymous. Indeed, many of the same processes and influences are at work when attitudes and opinions are being changed as when they were originally formed. However, the research literature on attitude change, which is voluminous, involves a variety of issues and methods that differ from much of the work on attitude formation. Since the topic of attitude change is taken up in two subsequent chapters, this chapter focuses primarily on attitude formation. However, in some cases where the amount of available research evidence is scanty, we will occasionally cite studies of attitude change in this chapter as well.

WHAT LEADS TO ATTITUDE FORMATION?

Since an attitude is a learned predisposition to respond favorably or unfavorably toward a given object (person, idea, etc.), you can't have an attitude until you have some feeling about the object in question, and feelings are usually based on at least some fragmentary information. Thus an attitude *may* be formed if your early experience with an object elicits a favorable or unfavorable feeling about it. However, oftentimes early experience and information concerning an object may not be accompanied by evaluative feelings, and if so, no attitude would yet exist toward the object. What then would lead an attitude to form?

In a recent theoretical analysis of attitude and opinion formation, Gerard and Orive (1987) stress that a key circumstance for attitude formation is that the person expects to interact with the object and needs to be prepared for that interaction. They posit that when a person expects to interact soon with an object, the person feels an "opinion-forming imperative," which motivates him or her to form a relatively clearcut evaluative stance toward the object. For instance, you may have met several other students once or twice and noticed a few facts about them without having formed any particular favorable or unfavorable impression. But now if you learn that one of them will be paired with you as a lab partner, you will be motivated to decide which ones you like or dislike. In doing so, Gerard and Orive say, you will try to reduce ambivalence toward them; and they make the further point that, as your attitude becomes clearer, it will tend to get more strongly favorable or unfavorable.

Similarly, Jamieson and Zanna (1988) have described the "need for cognitive structure" as an important factor in attitude formation. An interesting example of this principle was seen in people's reactions to the campaign debates of the U.S. presidential candidates in the 1984 election. There, despite the vivid and dramatic nature of the debates, formation of attitudes about campaign issues was less closely linked to having *watched* the debates than to participating in discussions about them—with or without having watched them (Kennamer, 1985). It appeared that, when people anticipated discussing the debates with someone else, they had to form attitudes about the issues involved. Or it may be that those who had not formed such attitudes avoided discussions. In either case, the findings were consistent with Gerard and Orive's point that attitudes are functional and necessary in preparing us for our daily interactions.

As a related point, Tybout and Scott (1983) have made a useful theoretical distinction. When individuals have direct sensory information about an object, their attitude toward it will normally be determined by adding up that information, for instance in ways specified by the theories of Fishbein and Ajzen (1975) or Triandis (1977). However, if their internal knowledge is weak or ambiguous, they may infer their attitude from observation of their own behavior and the surrounding circumstances, as specified in Bem's (1972) self-perception theory. These points tie our discussion of attitude formation back to the attitude theories that were discussed in Chapters 2 and 4.

Though formation of an initial attitude is usually based on some information (either sensory or cognitive or both) about the object in question, Zajonc (1980) has pointed out that sometimes attitudes may be based entirely on affective feelings, without any supportive information being necessary. As he put it, "preferences need no inferences" (p. 151).

Given these principles and circumstances regarding attitude formation, let us consider the various factors that determine what particular attitudes an individual will form.

GENETIC AND PHYSIOLOGICAL FACTORS

The first type of factor which we will consider is a surprising one because it is rarely mentioned in discussions of attitude formation. Since attitudes are generally agreed to be learned, citing genetic or physiological factors in their formation may sound like support for the fallacious viewpoint that acquired characteristics can be inherited (the discredited theory of the Russian geneticist Lysenko). However, McGuire (1985) has pointed out that it is often wise to question any universally accepted principle—at the very least, it may have some exceptions which have been overlooked.

In the case of genetic factors in attitude formation, the most plausible way they might operate would be in establishing a *predisposition* for the development of particular attitudes. For instance, there is good evidence for genetic factors determining an organism's general level of aggressiveness, as in Scott and Fuller's (1965) studies of different breeds of dogs. In humans, the person's level of aggressiveness might help to determine his or her attitudes of hostility to outgroup members, which could be seen in prejudice against other groups (for instance, Jews or foreigners or teenagers). Such intergroup hostility may once have had survival value, though it appears counterproductive in our nuclear age. Another example of possible genetic influences is the widespread human characteristic of feeling nurturant toward individuals with large head-to-body-length ratios—i.e., infants (Alley, 1981). It is important to realize that the notion of genetic determinants of some

Photograph courtesy of Yale University Office
of Public Information. Reprinted by permission.

Box 7-1   WILLIAM McGUIRE, *Systematizer and Gadfly*

William McGuire has made a multiple reputation in social psychology as an experimentalist, theorist, systematizer, editor, and administrator. Born in New York in 1925, he served in the Army in World War II, and then received his B.A. and M.A. from Fordham. Moving to Yale for his Ph.D., he was one of the fruitful group of scholars who worked with Carl Hovland in experimental research on communication and attitude change. Following brief periods of teaching at Yale and Illinois, he spent longer periods on the faculty of Columbia and the University of California at San Diego before returning to Yale as chairman of the psychology department in 1971.

McGuire was influential as editor of the major journal in social psychology from 1968 through 1970. He has already been cited in Chapters 1 and 4 as author of a landmark handbook chapter on attitudes and attitude change, and Chapters 9 and 10 describe his theoretical contributions to consistency approaches, personality research, and resistance to attitude change, as well as his role as a gadfly and prophet for the field.

attitudes does not imply that those attitudes could not be changed under the right environmental conditions, though it may make the change process more difficult.

Physiological factors in attitude formation can be seen particularly in such conditions as aging, illnesses, and the effects of various drugs. For instance, the general conservatism often found in old age is likely to affect new attitudes, such as the person's feelings toward a new political candidate. Daily, weekly, and monthly body rhythms often affect people's moods (such as "blue Monday"), and research has shown parallel changes in attitudes toward events and objects at those times (Gatty & Mack, 1979). Certain illnesses are frequently associated with predispositions to particular attitude states: encephalitis often increases general aggressiveness, while tuberculosis paradoxically seems to increase optimistic attitudes. Such effects are more understandable in light of the attitudinal effects of certain drugs which are clearly physiological in nature. The euphoria produced by marijuana and the opiate drugs is well-known, as are the calming and anxiety-reducing effects of tranquilizers; so both of these are conducive to forming more favorable attitudes. In sum, it is clear that physiological states can influence people's general levels of aggressiveness and persuasibility and their readiness to adopt certain attitudes.

DIRECT PERSONAL EXPERIENCE

The earliest and most fundamental way in which people form attitudes is through direct personal experience with the attitude object. For example, an infant who is given orange juice to drink for the first time is apt to like it because it is sweet, flavorful, pleasantly cool, and filling. Following that encounter, the infant has an attitude toward orange juice which is likely to be confirmed and strengthened with further experience.

Attitudes formed through one's own personal experience with the attitude object are generally stronger than those formed through indirect or vicarious experience (Fazio, 1988). For instance, research shows that they are more likely to influence one's behavior, and more resistant to counterinfluence. As indicated in Chapter 4, a major reason for this is that attitudes based on one's own sensory experience are apt to involve primitive, first-order beliefs. Here we will discuss two aspects of personal experience in the formation of attitudes: salient incidents and repeated exposure.

Salient Incidents

Many authors have stressed the importance of salient incidents, particularly traumatic or frightening ones, in the development of attitudes. Psychoanalysts and clinical psychologists have described many phobias which originated in a single traumatic experience, for instance with a runaway horse or a fierce dog. Other examples of single incidents markedly affecting attitudes can be seen in religious conversion experiences (Paloutzian, 1981), which were written about by William James as long ago as 1902, and in the clinical descriptions of war neuroses (e.g., Sargant, 1957). A typical case is that of a naval pilot who crashed in flames on an aircraft carrier's deck, was rescued with relatively minor injuries, but was never able to approach a plane again because of extreme, uncontrollable fear and trembling.

It is easy to understand the importance of traumatic incidents as influences on attitudes (Read, 1983). Fishbein and Ajzen's (1975) attitude theory posits that a person's attitude toward an object at any given time is based upon a few (perhaps 5–10) salient beliefs that he or she holds about the object. Obviously, a belief like "It almost killed me" is likely to remain very salient and very powerful in determining the person's attitude for a long time.

In the attitude-change literature, a number of studies have shown marked changes in public opinion stemming from a single dramatic event such as President Nixon's precedent-setting trip to mainland China or the assassination of Martin Luther King, Jr. (e.g., Riley & Pettigrew, 1976). However, even the effects of dramatic or traumatic incidents are often counterbalanced by the cumulative effect of other events, leading attitudes to return to their earlier levels.

Repeated Exposure

Another way in which attitudes are often formed is through repeated exposure to an object (or person or idea) over time. The research literature on this topic has been thoroughly summarized by Zajonc (1968a), who has also done a series of experimental studies with his coworkers to clarify how this effect occurs. Zajonc has emphasized that mere exposure to a stimulus object without any associated reinforcement or tension reduction is sufficient to enhance a person's attitude toward the object. This effect operates most strongly during the first few exposures, but attitudes continue to increase in favorability at a gradually slower rate over any number of exposures (see Figure 7-1). In fact, the effect can even occur in situations where people are not aware of being exposed to the stimulus object (Wilson, 1979; Zajonc, 1980). A number of different theoretical explanations of the mere exposure effect have been critically analyzed by Grush (1979).

The attitude-enhancing effect of repeated exposure is not confined to the research laboratory. It has been found also in field studies, such as in elections, where the relative amount of candidates' name exposure often closely predicts the election results (Grush, 1980; Schaffner, Wandersman, & Stang, 1981). Indeed, this principle seems to underlie much commercial advertising and political campaigning. A rather frightening corollary of this principle is that a harmful product

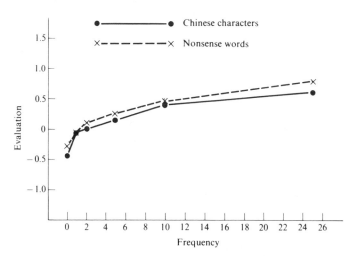

FIGURE 7–1 Relationship between frequency of mere exposure of an object and attitude toward it.

Source: Data from Zajonc (1968a); figure reprinted from Fishbein & Ajzen (1975, p. 282). Reprinted by permission of Addison-Wesley Publishing Co.

or a political demagogue can become more popular just by getting more public exposure, despite their injurious nature.

However, this alarming prospect has been shown to be unlikely, for several studies have demonstrated that the attitude-enhancement effect holds only for positive and neutral stimuli, and it may even be reversed for repeated exposure to stimuli which were originally negative in their impact on the individual (Perlman & Oskamp, 1971; Grush, 1976). In addition, it should be remembered that the mere exposure effect is only one of many influences on attitude formation, and it would not be expected to be as strong as many others, for instance the effect of *reward or punishment* associated with exposure to the stimulus. Thus, if the voice of a particular politician always grates on your ears, or you dislike his insincere manner, you are very likely to become less fond of him with repeated exposure, rather than more fond of him.

Another area where repeated exposure has been studied is in the effect of interracial or international contact on attitude change (Stephan, 1985). In this area, also, repeated contact can lead to more favorable or less favorable attitudes, depending on the presence or absence of several crucial factors. These factors, therefore, are very important to the success of programs aiming at school desegregation or international understanding (cf. Bochner, 1982; Patchen, 1982; Miller & Brewer, 1984). A number of authors have emphasized that interracial contact is more likely to lead to increased friendliness if it has most or all of the following characteristics: if it is (a) continued over a long period, (b) felt to be voluntary, (c) in relatively close relationships, (d) in cooperative activities, between individuals having (e) equal status, (f) common or supportive goals, and (g) similar belief systems, and in situations which are (h) supported by authorities or by social custom. (Chapters 14 and 15 present more information about the details of international and racial attitudes.)

PARENTAL INFLUENCE

The amount of parental influence over a young child's behavior and attitudes is so great that some authors have referred to childhood as a "total institution," comparable in its degree of control to confinement in a penal institution or a concentration camp. Parents have almost total control over the young child's informational input, the behaviors demanded of the child, and the rewards and punishments meted out. Thus they have great power to shape the child's attitudes, particularly because the infant has no preexisting attitudes which would be contrary to the parental influence.

A child's attitudes are largely shaped by its own experience with the world, but much of this experience is comprised of explicit teaching and implicit modeling of parental attitudes (e.g., "Nice kitty. Kitty won't hurt you. Pet the kitty gently."). Thus many childhood attitudes are probably a combination of the child's own experience and what (s)he has heard parents say or seen them do. However, there are many other areas where the average child has no direct experience at all, and in these areas parental influence on the child's attitudes may be very great. Examples include attitudes toward war, toward foreigners, toward other countries, toward political parties and candidates, and toward abstract concepts like freedom and justice.

Gender role attitudes are greatly influenced by parents' teaching and examples. For instance, children of mothers who were employed outside the home generally have less traditional attitudes about gender roles than those whose mothers were housewives (Vogel et al., 1970). Daughters whose fathers encouraged their independence and achievement are more likely to undertake and succeed in demanding careers (Hoffman, 1977). Similarly, adolescents' cigarette smoking attitudes and practices are related to those of their parents (Chassin, Presson, & Sherman, 1984). (For a full discussion of gender role attitudes, see Chapter 16.)

Prejudice and racial attitudes are prominent areas where parental influence has been studied. A long series of studies shows that in general children's level of prejudice is related to their parents' prejudice and that, at least in part, they take over that prejudice directly (Ashmore & Del Boca, 1976). In addition, it is quite possible for children to learn from parental behavior indirectly and without any intentional teaching. Once learned, prejudiced attitudes tend to be. generalized to many outgroups, so there are high positive correlations among the levels of prejudice toward various different minority groups such as blacks, Chicanos, Jews, Japanese, etc. (Frenkel-Brunswik & Havel, 1953). However, as children grow older, there are many other influences on their attitudes in addition to their parents, and by adolescence the degree of parent-child similarity is only a low positive one.

Many studies have attempted to trace children's development of prejudice to the child-rearing methods used by their parents. There is general agreement that emotionally cold, status-oriented parents who stress obedience, discipline, and physical punishment are likely to have highly prejudiced and authoritarian children (Adorno et al., 1950). Triandis and Triandis (1962) found that this relationship held in Greece as well as in the United States. However, research has not clarified whether this effect occurs indirectly, through the psychodynamic mechanisms posited in *The Authoritarian Personality*—i.e., that harsh child-rearing produces children with low tolerance for frustration and high repressed hostility, which later generate prejudiced ethnic attitudes. A plausible alternative view is that these children learn their prejudice directly by identifying with and copying their parents' attitudes and behavior (for a fuller discussion, see Harding, Proshansky, Kutner, & Chein, 1969).

Development of Political Attitudes

The area where children's attitudes and parental influence have been most extensively studied is in the development of political attitudes—a topic known as

political socialization. Because of the large amount of research in this area, we will summarize some of the most interesting findings. For more extensive reviews of political socialization, see Renshon (1977), Abramson (1983), or Kinder and Sears (1985).

The first major finding is the early age at which political attitudes begin to develop. As early as age six or seven many children have developed strong emotional and cognitive associations about their nation, its leaders, and national symbols such as the flag (Lambert & Klineberg, 1967).

Youthful Chauvinism and Idealization. A second finding is the very high degree of chauvinism displayed by young children. For instance, in Hess and Torney's (1967) large nationwide sample of white children from grades two through eight, over 95% of the children at every grade level agreed that "the American flag is the best flag in the world," and that "America is the best country in the world."

Third, this positive view of the nation extends to attitudes of idealization toward the government and toward specific leaders. For instance, 77% of fourth-graders in another study agreed that "the government usually knows what is best for people" (Easton & Dennis, 1965). Idealization of the President occurs not only in the United States, but also in Puerto Rico, Australia, Chile, and Japan (Hess, 1963). Though the President is rated highest, other political leaders are also favorably evaluated by children, being seen as less selfish than most people, more honest, and almost always keeping their promises. Not surprisingly, these positive views in the early grade-school years are accompanied by relatively little factual information about the government and how it works. This first stage of attachment to the system involves an undifferentiated view of one's own nation and its leaders as "good," and associating them with conventional national symbols (e.g., for U.S. children, the flag, the Statue of Liberty, and George Washington).

By junior high school ages, children's chauvinistic attitudes become much more differentiated, and they typically state reasons for their national pride such as "freedom," "democracy," and "the right to vote." They also idealize the President less and become more cynical and doubting of politicians (Hess & Torney, 1967). By about this same time, many of them begin to develop partisan political preferences, which are discussed below.

Amount of Parent-Child Correspondence. Though parents are quite influential in children's earliest political attitudes, during the school years other sources of attitudes are added and parents' degree of influence wanes. By college age, the correspondence in political attitudes between parent-child pairs from the same family is typically fairly low (Niemi, Ross, & Alexander, 1978). A particularly thorough study was done by Jennings and Niemi (1968), who independently interviewed a representative national sample of over 1600 high school seniors and their parents. Their findings conclusively showed rather low positive correlations (between 0.0 and + .4) for parent-child pairs on about 15 measures of political attitudes (political cynicism, attitudes on specific issues and toward various groups, etc.). However, there was one measure with a notably higher relationship, which is discussed next.

Party Identification. The single high relationship in the political area found by Jennings and Niemi was between parents' party identification and their child's party identification—a product-moment correlation coefficient of about + .6. This finding is quite consistent with Converse's (1964) finding, described in the previous chapter, of singularly high stability over time for the party identification measure. In addition to being stable, party identification is a highly salient attitude in the American political system. As a result, it turns out to be the only political attitude transmitted very effectively from parents to their children, though even here there are many cases of noncorrespondence.

The prominence of party identification as an attitude transmitted by parents is paralleled by findings from the area of religious attitudes. There parent-child correspondence in denominational preference was found to be quite high (about 74%, yielding a contingency coefficient of + .88, the highest relationship reported by Jennings & Niemi, 1968). However, just as in the political arena, parent-child agreement on other religious questions displayed a very modest positive relationship. Thus, we may conclude that transmission of parental values is only apt to be noticeably successful when they deal with simple and highly visible questions of group membership.

Disaffection Toward Government. An exception to the general findings of idealization mentioned earlier in this section is the fact that some groups of children have been found to be far less favorable toward the government and political leaders than the typical picture among American middle-class youth. For instance, Abramson (1972) has summarized a number of studies showing greater feelings of political powerlessness among black children and a marked decrease in their political trust following the urban ghetto riots and assassinations of political leaders in the late 1960s. These beachheads of disaffection toward government increased and spread among children as a result of the controversy over the Vietnam War and the Watergate scandal that led to President Nixon's resignation from office.

In a longitudinal follow-up of their former high school seniors, Jennings and Niemi (1973) found that both they and their parents had increased considerably in political cynicism. Though studies of early grade-school children still found considerable idealization of the government, political disaffection was much more common among various demographic subgroups of older children (Tolley, 1973). During the 1980s, approval of President Reagan was relatively high among middle- and upper-class youth, but substantially lower among racial minority groups and poor children (Kinder & Sears, 1985). It now appears that, to a greater extent than formerly thought, children's attitudes toward political institutions are shaped by the events of the times rather than being invariably positive and idealistic.

GROUP DETERMINANTS OF ATTITUDES

Another important influence on the formation of attitudes is the pressure of various groups. We will touch briefly on four kinds of group pressure: school indoctrination, peer groups, conformity pressures in general, and reference groups.

Schools

Second only to parental influences in determining children's attitudes are school teaching and indoctrination. This has become especially clear in the area of political attitudes, where many studies have emphasized the importance of school influence (e.g., Torney, Oppenheim, & Farnen, 1975; Rutter, Maughan, Mortimore, & Ouston, 1979; Schonbach, 1981). The highly favorable attitudes mentioned above which young children develop toward government and their idealization of the President and other leaders (even down to the local policeman) are undoubtedly largely due to schoolroom teaching.

We have all experienced this kind of indoctrination, but it is easy to forget or overlook how hard the schools work to instill patriotism. For example, Hess and Torney (1967) found that teachers, especially in the lower grades, consciously tried to "emphasize the positive" and to avoid discussion of conflict within the country. They reported that 99% of their sample of teachers displayed the American flag

FIGURE 7-2
The schools instill prosystem attitudes.

prominently, over 85% at each grade level required the Pledge of Allegiance to be said daily, and in the lower grades most classrooms spent some time every day singing patriotic songs. Though children may not always understand the words ("one nation, invisible"), it is no wonder that they get the message clearly—"my country, right or wrong."

Peer Groups

Following family and school, the next major determinant of attitudes, both chronologically and in relative importance, is the child's peer group. From the end of grade school onward, peer-group contacts become increasingly important and time-consuming (Renshon, 1977). Where peer-group norms agree with parental or school standards, previously existing attitudes and values may be strengthened (Youniss, 1980). However, peers also frequently introduce and reinforce new viewpoints, attitudes, and behavioral patterns, ranging from fads like hairstyles through preferences for particular music, films, or political parties, to lifestyle choices involving career planning, drug use, and sexual behavior (Conger, 1981; Yankelovich, 1981).

The many "generation gap" differences in attitudes between youth and the older generation are undoubtedly due in part to youthful peer-group influences. Some typical examples of research findings concerning generation differences are young people's greater political liberality, toleration of nonconformity, advocacy of civil liberties, and racial tolerance (e.g., Jennings & Niemi, 1968). That such generational differences are related to peer-group influences was shown in an interesting study of moral attitudes in Israeli *kibbutzim*. There the age-group system of child-rearing produced greater differences in attitudes between parents and children than were found with more traditional family living arrangements (Rettig, 1966). However, it is also true that many attitude differences between generations are due to having grown up under the impact of differing overwhelming societal forces (e.g., the Great Depression, World War II, the civil rights movement, or the Vietnam War—Abramson, 1983).

Conformity Pressures

Not only peer groups, but a variety of other conformity pressures can lead to attitude formation and change. One major example is the impact of major societal events of the era, such as wars or depressions, as mentioned just above. As another example, the overall cultural context within which we live can provide a set of assumptions and salient "facts" which determine the attitudes we will develop, without our even being aware of any influence. For example, Pettigrew (1971) estimated that about three-fourths of Americans who are racially prejudiced are simply reflecting the assumptions and norms of their culture. Moreover, almost everyone believes that others are more prejudiced than themself—a phenomenon termed **pluralistic ignorance**—and this creates added resistance to change in attitudes or behavior (Taylor, 1982).

However, intergroup contact under the right conditions can ameliorate such prejudice, especially when cooperative efforts toward common goals are required by the circumstances. Such beneficial effects of intergroup contact have been demonstrated in preschool children (Crooks, 1970) and in boys' summer camp groups when conditions conducive to cooperation rather than competition were established (Sherif, Harvey, White, Hood, & Sherif, 1961).

Changes in social roles can often exert powerful influences on attitudes, such as when a prounion worker is promoted to the management job of foreman (Lieberman, 1956). Even more far-reaching changes in attitudes and behavior can be induced when there is relatively complete control over the social environment, rewards, and punishments, as in Marine Corps basic training, in some religious cults, or in brainwashing of political prisoners (Lifton, 1963; McEwen, 1980; Pavlos, 1982). See Moscovici (1985) for a recent summary of experimental research on conformity situations.

Reference Groups

A milder form of influence on attitudes, and one which is often unintentional, is seen in **reference groups**. These are groups whose standards and beliefs one accepts and measures oneself against, regardless of whether one is a member of the group or not. For many teenagers, movie stars or rock musicians serve this function, while for others, the "in crowd" at school serves as a reference group.

The point which is central here is that reference groups often influence people's attitudes, even without any overt attempts to do so. In various studies this effect has been found for racial and religious issues, for economic and political attitudes, and for authoritarian attitudes (Pettigrew, 1967). One of the most important studies of reference groups was the famous Bennington College study by Newcomb (1943). Bennington began as a very liberal college during the depression years, but its incoming students were mostly from upper-class highly conservative families. Thus there was a conflict between the college community's standards and those of the new students. Though some students retained their family as their reference group, most of the students resolved this conflict by adopting the faculty and advanced students as their reference group and gradually changing their own attitudes in a more liberal direction throughout their stay in college. A typical student comment describes this process:

> It's very simple, I was so anxious to be accepted that I accepted the political complexion of the community here. I just couldn't stand out against the crowd unless I had made many friends and had strong support. (Newcomb, 1943, p. 132)

A follow-up study 25 years later showed that a surprisingly large amount of the Bennington graduates' college-induced liberalism had persisted for that long period of time (Newcomb, Koenig, Flacks, & Warwick, 1967). Apparently this occurred largely through the women's choices of postcollege social environments (e.g., friends, jobs, and husbands) that were supportive of their attitudes.

MASS MEDIA

The final factor in attitude formation which we will discuss is effects of the mass media—newspapers, magazines, books, movies, radio, and television. There is no doubt that these media have had enormous impact on our society and on other societies where they have been introduced. Just try to imagine what your life would be like if there were no TV or radio, for instance! Yet there is much less hard evidence on their precise effects than we would like.

We know that American children typically spend two to three hours per day watching television, and that by the time they finish high school they will have spent more hours in front of the TV set than in school classrooms, churches, and all other educational and cultural activities combined (Comstock et al., 1978; Timmer, Eccles, & O'Brien, 1985). Thus the *informational* impact of TV, and to a lesser extent of the other media, is potentially very great. By age 10, TV and school have replaced the family as the most frequently mentioned sources of children's information; and attention to news media then becomes the most important influence on children's political socialization (Conway, Wyckoff, Feldbaum, & Ahern, 1981; Garramone & Atkin, 1986). Adults, too, generally say that they rely on television for most of their daily information (Comstock et al., 1978). A major British study of the impact of TV reported that the carefully planned BBC programs broadened children's views of other nations and peoples, making them more objective and less evaluative. The programs also had their greatest effect on children who were not already familiar with their subject matter (Himmelweit, Oppenheim, & Vince, 1958).

These findings are relevant to attitude formation, since people's information and beliefs are important factors in their attitudes. However, the media do not simply transmit infomation. By selecting, emphasizing, and interpreting particular events, and by publicizing people's reactions to those events, they help to structure the nature of "reality" and to define the crucial issues of the day, which in turn impels the public to form attitudes on these new issues (Kinder & Sears, 1985; Roberts & Maccoby, 1985).

Though mass communication persuasion campaigns often have only minor effects (McGuire, 1985), they are most likely to be effective in creating opinions and attitudes on *new issues* where there are no predispositions to be changed, or on topics or political candidates about which current attitudes are weak (Patterson, 1980; Kazee, 1981). For example, research on the national publicity campaign to "take a bite out of crime," which featured the cartoon dog character "McGruff," showed that it had considerable effects on viewers' beliefs, attitudes, and behaviors about crime prevention (O'Keefe, 1985). Similarly, children's viewing of specific types of TV entertainment programs has been shown to affect their racial and gender role attitudes (Zuckerman, Singer, & Singer, 1980; Morgan, 1982).

The topic of media effectiveness will recur again at greater length in the following chapter on attitude communication. In the meantime we will consider the various learning processes by which attitudes can be formed.

LEARNING PROCESSES IN ATTITUDE FORMATION

This section briefly examines seven different learning processes which can be involved in attitude formation. A concrete example is given to clarify the nature of each process, and research studies done using each paradigm are cited as a resource for readers who want to study these approaches more thoroughly.

Classical Conditioning

Classical conditioning is the process investigated by Pavlov, who presented meat powder and the sound of a bell to dogs and observed that later the bell alone would cause the dogs to salivate. The paradigm uses a stimulus, called the unconditioned stimulus, which automatically elicits a response from the organism. Another stimulus which does not automatically elicit that response is presented simultaneously with or just before the unconditioned stimulus on several trials. To test the presence of learning, the unconditioned stimulus is then omitted. If the response is given to the other stimulus alone, we say that the response has been conditioned to that stimulus, which is termed the conditioned stimulus.

Applying this paradigm to attitude formation, we might consider a parental spanking as the unconditioned stimulus, which would automatically produce negative, unhappy feelings in a child. If a spanking is applied every time the child reaches for or touches a valuable vase, the vase will soon become a conditioned stimulus which will by itself produce negative feelings (an attitude). Of course, positive attitudes (for instance, toward a particular medicine) can be produced in the same way by frequently pairing the object with unconditioned stimuli, like tasty food or a hug, which make the child feel good (see Figure 7–3). This paradigm is most relevant to formation of the evaluative or feeling aspect of attitudes.

The classical conditioning paradigm has been used in attitude research by many investigators, involving topics such as the meaning of adjectives, opinions about future scientific discoveries, and children's racial attitudes (e.g., Weiss, 1968; Zanna, Kiesler, & Pilkonis, 1970; Parish & Fleetwood, 1975). The major question in its use is whether subjects are *aware* of the S-R connection which the investigator is trying to establish. If so, the subjects' learning may be of an instrumental sort (trying to do what will gain the investigator's approval), or alternatively it may be of a cognitive, information-processing sort, rather than being classical conditioning (Page, 1974).

Stimulus Generalization

Generalization is a process which occurs after an S-R connection has been established by conditioning. It is usually found that the conditioned response can be elicited, not just by the conditioned stimulus, but by other similar stimuli (for instance, a bell of a different pitch in Pavlov's experiments). An example in attitude formation might be the establishment of a negative reaction to one particular black man, an attitude which would then generalize to other men and women having similar skin color or appearance. Moreover, through the use of language, humans can display **semantic generalization** to other stimuli having similar *meanings*. So, for instance, a negative attitude might further generalize to the words "Negro" and "black" and to other words or objects which had a similar meaning. Examples of research studying this process with attitudes toward people include Edwards and Williams (1970) and Bleda (1976).

Instrumental Conditioning

This process, sometimes called **operant conditioning**, is the kind of learning stressed by Skinner and his followers. It is called *operant* because the organism is allowed to operate freely on its environment instead of being constrained to make one particular response to one particular stimulus. It is *instrumental* in the sense that the organism's behavior is instrumental; that is, the behavior is the means by which reward or punishment is achieved. The researcher does not usually know or care what the original stimulus was for the organism's behavior. Instead, he waits until the organism makes a desired response (say, scratching its ear) and then immediately *reinforces* the response by presenting a food pellet or a piece of candy (see Figure 7–3).

In human attitude formation, the reinforcer is apt to be verbal—either praise or criticism—or nonverbal signs of approval or disapproval. For instance, a child might say "dirty communists" and be rewarded by an approving smile from the parent. As a result, the child would not only be likely to say "dirty communists" more often in the future, but also to form a negative attitude toward communists. Attitude research using this paradigm has been done on opinion statements (Insko, 1965; Weiss, 1968), liking for stimulus persons (Byrne, 1971), and children's racial attitudes (Williams & Morland, 1976).

Selective Learning

An extension of instrumental conditioning called **selective learning** has also been studied experimentally by Weiss (1968). In this situation the organism has several alternative responses, and they are differentially reinforced by using different degrees of reward or punishment. As a result, the more-reinforced responses increase in their likelihood of being emitted. An example in the attitude area might be a youthful baseball fan who has expressed liking for several different teams on different occasions. If one attitude ("I like the Dodgers") was reinforced more quickly, more strongly, or more frequently than his statements favorable to other teams, his favorable attitude toward the Dodgers would gradually be selected as his dominant attitude on the topic of baseball teams. Like instrumental conditioning, this paradigm is most directly relevant to formation of the behavioral aspect of attitudes.

Imitation or Modeling

A common type of learning that can occur without any external reinforcement is **imitation** of the behavior of another person who serves as a model. Parents

FIGURE 7-3 Classical conditioning (top) pairs a new stimulus object (the pill) with one which already produces a response from the person, and eventually the new object will produce the same response. Instrumental conditioning (bottom) applies a reinforcer (such as a reward) after the person has made a particular response, and as a result the person's tendency to make that response is strengthened.

are often disconcerted to find that their children imitate not only their admirable behavior (e.g., helping to feed the baby) but also their antisocial acts (e.g., swearing at the disliked neighbors). In many such modeled actions, the behavioral aspect of attitudes begins to be formed without any explicit instruction or reinforcement by the parent. In fact, children will often imitate what they see their parents practice instead of what they preach (Rushton, 1975). Much research has shown the effectiveness of models in shaping attitudes and behavior, both in the area of aggression (Scientific Advisory Committee on Television and Social Behavior, 1972; Bandura, 1977) and in the area of helping behavior (London, 1970; Berkowitz, 1972).

Persuasion

Persuasive communication is probably the most common way of trying to change a person's attitude, and it will be taken up at length in Chapters 9 and 10. It can also be used to form attitudes for the first time, as when a friend tells you the good or bad points about a local political candidate of whom you knew nothing before. The typical contents of such a persuasive message include one or more suggested conclusions or recommendations for action, usually together with some supporting facts or arguments (e.g., "She's a good candidate because she's honest and won't make any political deals to get elected"). The format of persuasive messages can be infinitely varied: long or short, logical or emotional, organized or disorganized, etc. They are apt to influence the cognitive aspect of attitudes most directly, and sometimes also the behavioral aspect. Some of the most influential work in this area was done by the group of researchers who worked with Carl Hovland at Yale (e.g., Hovland, Janis, & Kelley, 1953; Rosenberg et al., 1960).

Information Integration

The final type of attitude formation process to be discussed here, **information integration**, is emphasized by many cognitive theorists and researchers. They stress that a person's attitude toward an object is based on the beliefs that (s)he holds about it, some of which may be favorable and others unfavorable. In forming their attitudes, people must integrate the beliefs about the object which are salient to them into an overall impression. For instance, your friend may tell you that an unfamiliar political candidate is honest, unwilling to make any deals to get elected, but not a good speaker. To form an attitude toward the candidate, you then have to combine those beliefs (and perhaps also your opinion of your friend's political judgment) in some way. Of course, the evidence on political attitudes cited in Chapter 6 indicates that many people are relatively inattentive and/or inconsistent in their reaction to political information. However, theorists have constructed many different models suggesting ways in which such sets of beliefs are typically combined: additive models, averaging models, weighted-average approaches, and expectancy-value models. The latter type combines the person's degree of belief in each of the attitude object's characteristics with his(her) evaluation of those characteristics, as described in Chapter 4. Major contributors to research on information integration have been Anderson (1971), who favors weighted-averaging approaches, and Fishbein and Ajzen (1975), whose theory of reasoned action is an expectancy-value model using additive formulas.

It should be stressed that the seven learning processes which we have just described are not antagonistic, mutually exclusive theories of attitude formation. Several or all of these processes may take place in the acquisition of various attitudes, depending on the stimulus situations which a person is exposed to.

SUMMARY

Attitude formation, the step from no attitude to some attitude toward a given object, is similar but not identical to attitude change. It is agreed that attitudes are learned, but many different factors can operate in the acquisition process. Genetic and physiological factors, though seldom mentioned in this connection, may establish a predisposition for the development of particular attitudes.

Direct personal experience, either in salient incidents or in repeated exposure over time, is the most fundamental factor in attitude formation. Parental influence is very great in forming the child's early attitudes, as shown in extensive studies of prejudice and of political attitudes. However, by high school age the parent-child similarity is only a low positive one, except on measures of party identification and religious denomination preference, where it remains high.

Studies of political socialization have found that most young children display strong positive attitudes toward the government and national leaders, but older children in some population subgroups display greater disaffection, indicating that idealization of government is largely a middle-class phenomenon.

The schools are very important in instilling attitudes favorable to the political system. Other group determinants—peer groups, conformity pressures in general, and reference groups—become more important as the child grows older. Finally, the mass media not only provide much of our information, but also help to form our attitudes, particularly on new issues where no attitudes existed before.

There are many different learning processes by which attitude formation may occur. Classical conditioning, stimulus generalization, instrumental conditioning, and selective learning are processes which all rely on the effects of reinforcement—reward or punishment. Imitation or modeling of attitudes, on the other hand, often occurs without any reinforcement nor any explicit instruction. Explicit persuasion attempts are one of the commonest methods of attitude change, but they are equally applicable to attitude formation. Information integration is a cognitive process of combining one's salient beliefs into an overall attitude toward an object.

8

Communication of Attitudes and Opinions

Every new opinion, at its starting, is precisely in a minority of one.—Thomas Carlyle.

In the United States, the majority undertakes to supply a multitude of ready-made opinions for the use of individuals, who are thus relieved from the necessity of forming opinions of their own. —Alexis de Tocqueville.

All effective propaganda must be limited to a very few points and must harp on these in slogans until the last member of the public understands what you want him to understand.—Adolf Hitler.

In the United States, communication and advertising campaigns through the mass media cost over *$50 billion* per year (McGuire, 1985). That's over $200 for every man, woman, and child in the country, spent to persuade them to change their attitudes and actions—more than the total per capita income of some developing countries!

What do the advertisers get for all their expenditures? Do mass media campaigns successfully sell products or attract voters? Do people rely on the media for information and advice, or do they turn to their families, friends, and neighbors? What are the communication processes by which mass information, propaganda, and advertising efforts are spread and transformed into individual beliefs, attitudes, and actions?

This chapter will consider these questions regarding the communication of attitudes, beginning with a very brief sketch of the history of communication research.

EARLY STUDIES OF COMMUNICATION AND PROPAGANDA

Much of the early research on communication was motivated by deep concern over the effects on society of political propaganda. By the 1930s numerous demagogues had attained political power, in part through the clever use of propaganda techniques: Hitler and Goebbels in Germany, Mussolini in Italy, Huey Long as Louisiana governor and senator in the United States. Radio broadcasting had begun in 1920, and by the 1930s the widespread U.S. ownership of radios made possible a mass audience of millions for propagandists like the American priest, Father Coughlin. There was deep fear that democracy could not withstand this onslaught, for the propaganda analysts of that era assumed that the millions listening to demagogic broadcasts were an easily swayed, captive, and gullible audience. It was also assumed "that propaganda could be made almost irresistible with sufficiently clever use of propagandistic gimmicks in the content of the communication" (Sears & Whitney, 1973, p. 2). An analysis of Father Coughlin's radio speeches made by the Institute for Propaganda Analysis (Lee & Lee, 1939) ascribed his persuasiveness to tricks like name-calling, use of "glittering generalities," a "plain folks" approach, and "card-stacking" techniques of argument. Other fascinating analyses were made of the principles involved in Goebbels's propaganda campaigns (Doob, 1950) and of the successes and failures with the use of Allied propaganda leaflets in World War II (Herz, 1949).

Gradually it became apparent that these propaganda efforts were not nearly so successful as had first been thought. For instance, careful experimental studies of army orientation films showed that they failed to achieve many of the attitude and motivational changes which were intended (Hovland, Lumsdaine, & Sheffield, 1949). Similarly, the first major field study of American voting behavior showed amazingly small effects traceable to the large amount of media exposure during the political campaign (Lazarsfeld, Berelson, & Gaudet, 1948). Also, in commercial advertising it has become clear that, instead of a captive, easily persuaded, and gullible audience, the communicator is faced by an inattentive, difficult-to-persuade, "obstinate audience" (Bauer, 1964).

Two major changes in the orientation of research occurred as a result of these findings. First, attention largely shifted from mass communication to face-to-face interpersonal communication, which was felt to be considerably more influential in affecting people's attitudes and behavior. Second, attention shifted from the content of the communication to other factors in the communication process, such as the source and the audience. In order to understand these trends in research, we need to describe briefly the various factors in the persuasive communication process.

FACTORS IN PERSUASIVE COMMUNICATION

There are two sets of factors to be considered here: independent variables and dependent variables. Independent variables are the elements of the persuasion situation which can be varied or manipulated in some way. The dependent variables are the various aspects of the persuasion process which may occur in response to the communication, that is, the effects of communication.

Independent Variables. The process of communication can be analyzed in terms of who says what to whom, how, with what intent, and with what effect. The final item, "with what effect," summarizes all of the dependent variables, while the other five items constitute the major independent variables in communication. More frequently used terms for the major independent variables are **source**, **message**, **medium**, **audience**, and **target behavior** variables.

Source variables are characteristics of the source of the message, such as its expertness, credibility, etc. Message variables include both the content and structure of the message, how it is organized, its use of emotional appeals, etc. Media variables include the printed word, radio, television, and face-to-face interpersonal transmission. Audience variables are characteristics of the people who are receiving the message, their personalities, interests, involvement in the communication process, etc. Target behavior variables are the goals of the communicator, which parallel the possible dependent variables. That is, sometimes the goal may be merely to convey knowledge (comprehension); more often it is to change attitudes, or to instigate action; or it may be to create resistance to later persuasion. Reviews of the research findings on all of these variables have been provided by McGuire (1985) and Roberts and Maccoby (1985).

In this chapter we will confine our attention primarily to *media* factors, particularly stressing mass communication media versus personal face-to-face persuasion. Chapters 9 and 10, on attitude change, will present considerable detail on source, message, audience, and target variables.

Dependent Variables. In the process of persuasion there are at least six distinguishable steps which must occur in sequence, each one involving a separate stage of persuasive effect. These steps may be termed **exposure, attention, comprehension, acceptance, retention**, and **action**. Other authors have used other terms, for instance **reception** to include both attention and comprehension, and **yielding** instead of acceptance.

Whatever terms are used, it is important to be clear about which stage is being studied in any given research. For instance, the television Nielsen ratings and newspaper circulation figures pertain to the first stage, exposure to the communication. Research on readership of magazines or recall of TV commercials is using the

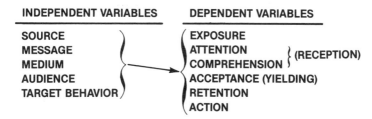

FIGURE 8–1 The major independent variables and dependent variables which are involved in the study of persuasive communication.

second stage, attention, as the dependent variable—a common procedure because it can be much more easily and precisely measured than other variables at later stages. Studies of the amount of information obtained from messages are relevant to the third stage, comprehension. Most experiments on persuasive communication or attitude change measure the fourth stage: yielding, or acceptance of the message. Experiments with delayed posttests can study the fifth stage: retention of the information or the attitude change. Finally, voting research or studies using advertising sales data are dealing with the sixth stage: action.

Importance of Specifying Variables. These distinctions are quite clear conceptually but are often forgotten when authors make generalizations about the effectiveness of persuasive communication. A message may be quite effective at one of the early stages but ineffective at some of the later stages. Success at each stage is generally necessary but not sufficient for effectiveness at each following stage. Hence it is essential to specify, for any given study, what the dependent variables were and which ones showed significant effects.

To illustrate these points, think of a persuasive message in a television commercial. Many homes will not be tuned in, or no one will be in front of the set, so the residents will not be exposed to the message. Among the thousands of viewers of that TV program, many will not pay attention to the commercial. Of those who do, some will not understand it for one reason or another. Many of those who understand the message will not agree with it nor yield to its suggestions. Further, those who are persuaded may not remember the suggestions for more than a short time. And finally, even those who are persuaded and remember the message may not act on it. An important point to notice in this example is that different variables may help to determine which viewers will pass from one stage to the next in the persuasion process. For instance, other activities such as visiting the bathroom may prevent exposure to the message, distraction may hinder attention to it, while low intelligence may decrease comprehension. On the other hand, high intelligence or a high level of knowledge about the topic may reduce yielding to the message. Interference from other messages and activities may decrease retention of the message, while lack of opportunity or lack of money may prevent acting on the suggestion. Thus the effects of persuasive communication are the complex result of many different variables working in interaction with each other.

A Different Approach—Uses and Gratifications of Mass Media. The mass media serve many functions for people—not just providing new information or attitudinal persuasion. This fact has been recognized and studied by the approach called "uses and gratifications" research (McLeod & Becker, 1981). Among the other basic needs which the mass media serve, three main clusters stand out: the media help to provide self-identity (e.g., comparing oneself with media characters), social contact (e.g., discussing recent episodes with friends), and diversion and entertainment (Murray & Kippax, 1979). Of these, *entertainment* is the reason most often given by people for their media attention, though social scientists have studied it much less than the persuasive (attitude change) function (cf. Tannenbaum, 1980).

The uses and gratifications approach differs markedly from the early communication studies which worried about the effects of propaganda on a passive and gullible audience. In contrast, it stresses the active role of viewers or readers in choosing what media to "consume" and in interpreting the content of messages in accordance with their own interests, needs, and fantasies. For instance, a message which was intended to be objective and informative may be interpreted by a viewer as supporting her own pet prejudice, or the theme of a persuasive message may be missed entirely by a viewer who is ogling the speaker's beautiful figure or costume.

With these distinctions and cautions in mind, let us examine some of the research on mass communication, and on personal communication, and see what effects they have on the various stages of persuasion.

PERSUASIVE EFFECTS OF THE MASS MEDIA

What is the effect of the mass media on public opinion? In the early days of opinion research this was viewed as a simple question with a simple answer, but now we know that it is a very complex question with many different answers, depending on the circumstances.

In the first place, mass communication rarely serves as a necessary and sufficient cause of persuasive effects. Instead it operates in conjunction with other variables in the audience and the situation to produce combined or interaction effects (McGuire, 1985). Second, the six different types of dependent variables in communication studies can produce six different answers to the question of media influence. Third, one medium of communication can have markedly different effects from other media.

There is widespread agreement that the various media have differing advantages and disadvantages. **Print** media (books, magazines, and newspapers) allow readers to determine the time and pace of their exposure and also permit easy reexposure if desired. Research suggests that print media produce better comprehension and retention of *complex* material than other media, but that this advantage does not hold for simple material. The **broadcasting** media (radio and television) now reach nearly everyone in the industrialized nations, including groups such as the aged, young children, and people with low education, who are not easily reached by other media and who may be more persuasible. Moreover, they are harder to escape than the print media, since exposure can occur whenever they are within view or earshot, without any conscious action of the recipient. The **visual** media (television and films) are unique in the "you are there" immediacy conferred by their combined audio and visual nature. As a result, they typically receive more complete attention and are better liked than other media, particularly by children (Lichty, 1982). Also, they produce more yielding and retention than print media when their message is relatively simple, but less when the message is complex (Chaiken & Eagly, 1976). However, despite these advantages of the visual media, people's knowledge of current affairs is more closely related to their use of print media—see the discussion of comprehension below (Roberts & Maccoby, 1985).

We will now consider each of the communication dependent variables in turn and report a few of the studies which have found results relevant to each.

Studies of Exposure

There is a great deal of exposure to the mass media in the United States and other industrialized nations. The Nielsen ratings of television programs measure this variable by recording the times and channels when TV sets are tuned in. The average U.S. television set is turned on about seven hours per day—but up to 40% of the time no one is watching it (Allen, 1965). Children typically watch TV from two to four hours per day, depending on their ages, and by the end of high school they will have accumulated about 20,000 hours of TV viewing—far more time than they have spent in school classrooms (Adler et al., 1980). The average U.S. adult also watches TV between two and three hours per day, though there are wide individual differences related to age, sex, education, social class, and employment (Roberts & Maccoby, 1985). In many of the world's developing nations, movies (very often American movies) provide much of the information about life and conditions in other countries (Gerbner, 1977).

Despite the time dominance of television, reading in the United States has not yet become a lost art. True, daily newspaper readership has dropped off substantially in the last 20 years, from about 80% to about 60% of all U.S. adults (Robinson, 1980). Moreover, younger adults who grew up in the television era are much less likely to read newspapers regularly than older adults. However, there has been a moderate increase in the reading of magazines and books over the same time period, and younger adults report more increase in such reading than older adults (Robinson, 1980). Though many general-interest newspapers and magazines have declined or ceased publication since the advent of TV, the circulation of special-interest magazines and books has climbed sharply (Roberts & Maccoby, 1985). In general, there is little evidence that time devoted to television has displaced time spent reading, though it has reduced comic book reading, radio listening, and movie attendance (Anderson & Collins, 1988).

In the advertising area, it is well known that people often try to avoid commercial messages, for instance by taking bathroom breaks or making refrigerator raids. However, advertisements are so ubiquitous in our society, not only on TV and radio, but also on billboards, bus and train placards, and in newspapers and magazines, that most people are exposed to over 1000 every day. This high level of exposure, though, emphatically does not mean that attention and comprehension are also high.

Studies of Attention

In the United States most news events are first learned about through the mass media. A summary study of several major events showed that about 35% of people first heard of them on TV compared with about 25% each for radio and the print media (Ostlund, 1973). However, sensational events such as the shooting of President Kennedy or the start of a ghetto riot showed a different pattern—about half of the population first learned of them through word-of-mouth contact with another person, and then most people turned to the media for further information (e.g., Sheatsley & Feldman, 1965). In such calamities news travels very fast—virtually 100% of the U.S. adult population knew of the assassination within six hours of its occurrence.

Even children attend to a substantial amount of media news information (e.g., Egan, 1978). Most Americans report that they learn more about news and politics from television than from newspapers, and they perceive television as the fairest and most objective news source (Comstock, 1988). Yet roughly three times as many adults read the newspaper each day as watch the evening TV news, and people's knowledge about government and current affairs (i.e., comprehension) is more strongly related to newspaper reading than to TV news viewing (Robinson & Levy, 1986b). In particular, people tend to use the print media more as sources of information on complex topics such as science and health.

In contrast to the breadth of public attention to the mass media, the quality of attention generally leaves much to be desired. Though most people "read" a newspaper, the average reader looks at no more than one-quarter of the stories, and less than half of the readers even examine the front-page stories (Cutlip, 1954). Among the most popular sections of the paper are the comics, entertainment, and sports sections (Frank & Greenberg, 1980). Similarly with television, entertainment generally takes precedence over information. Viewing is often a secondary activity, being combined with such other daily events as cooking, eating, conversation, sorting wash, playing games, disciplining children, and reading. Such interrupted or sporadic viewing contributes to very low levels of recall of news stories that have been viewed (Neuman, 1976). Moreover, only 25% of American adults watch a national network news program on any given evening, and over half of the population doesn't see even one such program in a two-week period (Robinson, 1971).

These figures demonstrate that about 20% of the population are regular, almost daily viewers of network TV news, while the rest are very sporadic or complete nonviewers. There is a circular relationship involving attention to the media; attention leads to more knowledge and interest in the topic, but also high levels of knowledge and interest stimulate further attention to the media (Atkin, Galloway, & Nayman, 1973).

In the area of advertising, it has been found that frequency of presentation of ads *per se* does not lead to higher levels of attention, but the quality of the ads does. Ads are better attended to if they are entertaining, usefully informative,

Photograph courtesy of Columbia University.
Reprinted by permission.

Box 8–1   PAUL LAZARSFELD, *Pioneer Communication Researcher*

Probably the most famous figure in the field of communication research, Paul Lazarsfeld was founder and director of the Bureau of Applied Social Research at Columbia University, and Professor of Sociology there since 1940. Born in Austria in 1901, he took his Ph.D. at the University of Vienna, and taught and published sociological research there before coming to the U.S. in the 1930s. Before moving to Columbia, he taught briefly at the University of Newark and Princeton University.

Lazarsfeld was known for many research volumes on the mass media, such as Radio and the Printed Page, Radio Research, *and* Communications Research. *He pioneered many new approaches to interviewing, attitude measurement, and survey research, including the panel technique of repeated surveys. His research on personal influence and opinion leadership is cited later in this chapter. Chapter 13 describes his famous work as the originator of large-scale voting studies, reported in* The People's Choice *and* Voting. *Among his many honors were the first distinguished achievement award of the American Association for Public Opinion Research (AAPOR), presidency of AAPOR and the American Sociological Association, and election to the National Academy of Sciences. Following retirement, he continued a vigorous research career until his death in 1976.*

humorous, professional in appearance, or feature novel or "catchy" elements (Atkin, Bowen, Nayman, & Sheinkopf, 1973). In a landmark study, Bauer and Greyser (1968) found that the average consumer only notices about 75 ads each day out of the more than 1000 that impinge on his or her eyes, ears, and nose. Out of the number that are noticed, only one-sixth are important enough to be classified as enjoyable, informative, annoying, or offensive. These authors also found that advertising which offends or annoys some people entertains or informs others, so that the effects of ads are rarely if ever consistent across all members of the mass audience.

These findings of audience indifference to most persuasive messages and varied reactions to any given message help to explain the fact that mass information and persuasion campaigns so often fail, as pointed out long ago by Hyman and Sheatsley (1947). However, despite general public disinterest, information campaigns can be relatively successful if they carefully consider specific target audiences and their lifestyles, value systems, and media habits (Roberts & Maccoby,

1985). Though only a small proportion of the total population may be reached by such campaigns, that audience may still comprise a great many people in a major metropolitan area such as Los Angeles or New York.

Studies of Comprehension

Comprehension of mass communication has been less studied than attention. Most studies have focused on news or educational programs, measured comprehension with objective tests of knowledge, and investigated the amount of self-determined exposure to a particular area of information, a design which allows the findings to be confounded by many other viewer characteristics such as education, interests, etc. Some studies (e.g., Mendelsohn, 1973) have shown successful communication of knowledge, for instance through television special programs such as "The National Drivers Test." However, numerous studies have also found either no effects or limited effects, with more impact on comprehension than on attitude change (e.g., Peterson, Jeffrey, Bridgwater, & Dawson, 1984). Some other investigations have documented examples of widespread misunderstanding of messages.

It has often been shown that public comprehension is increased when the conclusion or moral of a communication is explicitly stated rather than left implicit or subtly suggested (Weiss, 1969). Lang and Lang (1984) similarly found that interpretive comments in TV news coverage of a political convention influenced audience perceptions of the events.

As mentioned earlier, amount of current affairs knowledge is usually more closely related to use of print media than to amount of television news viewing. Two reasons for this are that network TV news uses a short-snippet "headline" format featuring 20-second "sound bites" (Sawyer, 1988), and that it searches for exciting visual images, a process which leads to an emphasis on action, events, and peripheral "human interest" aspects of the news rather than on substantive issues and policy positions. Patterson and McClure (1976, p. 54) have summed this up: "Television news may be fascinating. It may be highly entertaining. But it is simply not informative."

In the area of political information, many studies have found that amount of media exposure to relevant messages is either unrelated to knowledge gained or has only a low positive relation to it (Roberts & Maccoby, 1985). However, attention to messages is rather closely related to knowledge gain (Atkin, Galloway, & Nayman, 1973). Patterson and McClure (1976) found that televised political ads had marked effects on voters' beliefs (that is, they were well comprehended), but they had practically no effects on voters' attitudes (they did not produce yielding).

Other variables such as demographic background, political interests, or particular motivations can interact with media variables to affect the amount of comprehension of messages. For instance, it has been shown that highly educated individuals grasp new information presented by the media more quickly than do less-educated ones. This finding has given rise to the **knowledge gap hypothesis**— that higher-status individuals, who typically have more knowledge to start with, will gather information from the media faster than low-status individuals, thus increasing the gap between the two groups (Donohue, Tichenor, & Olien, 1975). As one example, Cook et al. (1975) have demonstrated this effect in the differential amount of learning from *Sesame Street* by relatively advantaged and disadvantaged children.

Studies of Acceptance

Yielding, or acceptance of the persuasive message, is the dependent variable studied most extensively in the voluminous research on attitude change and conformity. Though yielding cannot occur without reception of the message (that is, attention and comprehension, the two variables previously discussed), the amount of yielding is not necessarily positively related to the amount of reception. Indeed, the most common finding is a lack of any clear relationship between reception and attitude change (Fishbein & Ajzen, 1972).

McGuire (1968a) has developed a theory which may help to account for this lack of relationship by using the target person's personality characteristics, for example self-esteem, as an intervening variable. In general, the theory states that "any personality characteristic which has a positive relationship to reception, tends to be negatively related to yielding, and vice versa" (p. 182). Thus, yielding should be negatively related to self-esteem while reception should be positively related to self-esteem, at least in the medium range of message difficulty. McGuire (1968a) has reported some experimental research results which generally tend to support this theory. In the area of political attitudes, Zaller (1987) has summarized support for the theory, showing that political involvement increases exposure to political messages but decreases acceptance of them.

Types of Yielding.   An important distinction was made by Kelman (1958), who described three types of attitude change which have different underlying bases: compliance, identification, and internalization. **Compliance** is public yielding to an influence attempt without private acceptance; its basis is the expectation of gaining rewards or avoiding punishment. **Identification** is yielding to influence in an attempt to emulate an individual or group; its basis is satisfaction in being like the admired other(s). **Internalization** is yielding to influence in situations where the new attitude is intrinsically rewarding, useful, or consistent with one's value system; its basis is the intrinsic value of the new attitude to oneself. Different characteristics of the source of the influence attempt will help to determine which of these types of yielding will occur. A source who is powerful (and who has continuing surveillance over one's activities) will be likely to produce compliance. An attractive source will be more likely to produce identification, and a credible source to produce internalization. Experimental results which generally support this theory have been summarized by Moscovici (1985).

Importance of the Social Setting.   Research on attitude change has most often been done in an experimental laboratory situation, using audiences of selected individuals, compulsory exposure situations, and single communications. These conditions are desirable for their control of experimental variables, but they are far different from the typical situation in which an individual is exposed to mass communication in everyday life. There the audience is mostly self-selected, the message can easily be turned off or avoided, and communications are frequently repeated. In this chapter we are focusing mostly on factors affecting the typical mass communication situation, whereas the following two chapters will deal more with experimental attitude change research findings.

Even in the real-world mass communication situation, there can be considerable control of the communication conditions if the media content is highly standardized, as is frequently the case in totalitarian nations. In that case the influence of the mass media on individual attitudes can be great, though even in oppressive dictatorships there are usually underground and foreign sources of competing information and attitudes. However, in nations with relatively free mass communication systems, there will be many conflicting viewpoints expressed in the media on almost any topic. Consequently the influence of the media on yielding is apt to be much smaller there than in totalitarian societies.

Three Models of Media Influence. Since the early part of this century, when research on the mass media began, three successive views concerning media effects have held sway. The first, a **powerful effects** model, was dominant from the 1920s through the 1940s, as illustrated in the deep fear of the possibly irresistible effects of propaganda on a defenseless public described at the beginning of this chapter. It was followed by the **minimal effects** model, articulated by Klapper (1960), based on the many empirical studies which found no effects or very limited effects of the media in changing people's beliefs, attitudes, and behavior. More recently, a model of **powerful effects under limiting conditions** has gained more adherents (Roberts & Maccoby, 1985). It denies the early all-powerful view of the media, but stresses that they have important effects in particular circumstances and with particular individuals. Thus current research is apt to focus on the interacting variables and contingent conditions under which media effects will emerge most clearly (McLeod & Reeves, 1980)—for instance, under conditions of heavy viewing and weak prior predispositions. Furthermore, current conceptions include a wide range of media effects—not just changing attitudes, but also forming new attitudes, beliefs, or behaviors, reinforcing already existing ones, and crystallizing previously vague or unstated beliefs or attitudes.

A number of general principles about the mass media's effects on attitudes have been well stated by Klapper (1960, 1963) and are summarized in Box 8–2. The fifth principle, concerning creation of attitudes and opinions on new issues, has been dealt with in the preceding chapter. The other four principles may be illustrated by citing the results of a few key studies.

1. Other Factors Mediate Mass Communication Effects. In a classic study, Peterson and Thurstone (1933) found that the famous pro-Klan film *Birth of*

Box 8-2 *Five General Principles Concerning the Influence of Mass Media*

1. *The influence of mass communication is mediated by factors such as personal predispositions, personal selective processes, group memberships, etc.*
2. *Because of these factors, mass communication usually serves to reinforce existing attitudes and opinions, though occasionally it may serve as an agent of change.*
3. *When mass communication does produce attitude change, minor change in the extremity or intensity of the attitude is much more common than is "conversion" from one side of an issue to the other side.*
4. *Mass communication can be quite effective in changing attitudes in areas where people's existing opinions are weak, as in much of commercial advertising.*
5. *Mass communication can be quite effective in creating opinions on new issues where there are no existing predispositions to reinforce.*

Source: Adapted from Klapper (1960, p. 15; 1963, pp. 70, 76).

---

a Nation had its strongest effects on children who had had little or no contact with blacks. More recently, a similar effect occurred in the 1984 election debates between Reagan and Mondale. The first debate, in which Reagan appeared old and confused, led to a definitely improved public image for Mondale, but the effect was mostly limited to the previously undecided voters.

2. Mass Communication Usually Reinforces Existing Attitudes.   That is, the net effect of many mass media campaigns is often no overall change (McGuire, 1986). This point is also illustrated by the presidential campaign debates. In each of the elections where they have been studied, their main effect was to reinforce viewers' prior candidate preferences and to increase the consistency of their attitudes about the various issues and aspects of the campaign (Sigelman & Sigelman, 1984; Kinder & Sears, 1985).

3. Mass Communication Can Produce Minor Changes in Attitudes, but It Rarely Produces Conversion to an Opposite Viewpoint.   Examples of minor change have been shown both with adolescents' traditional sex-role attitudes and with their racial attitudes, which can be shifted in either direction by appropriate television portrayals (Graves, 1980; Johnston, Ettema, & Davidson, 1980; Christenson & Roberts, 1983). Similar findings of minor shifts in the area of political attitudes started with the pioneering study of Lazarsfeld et al. (1948). More recently, a large-scale panel study of television's influence in British elections showed again that attitude changes of most voters were either small or absent altogether. Only about 10% of voters changed their intended vote from one party to another during the campaign (Blumler & McQuail, 1969). Even such a major political upheaval as the Watergate scandal, with its massive media coverage, caused relatively small changes in political attitudes among the American public (Robinson, 1974).

4. Mass Communication Is Most Effective Where Attitudes Are Weak. This principle applies particularly to advertising, where most people's product preferences are weakly held, but also to politics and many other opinion areas. In politics, many studies have shown that the least-involved voters are most apt to change opinions and most likely to be influenced by TV campaigning (Patterson, 1980). In advertising, research as well as common parental experience indicates that children can be more strongly influenced by TV commercials than adults usually are (Goldberg & Gorn, 1974).

Studies of Retention

Retention has been and still is the least-studied dependent variable in attitude change research. Much of the research which does exist was done in classroom experimental settings, so its generalizability to more typical media exposure settings is unclear. There is a particular need for research on the continuing, cumulative impact of the media over a prolonged period of time (see Comstock, 1985).

Two types of retention are of interest: retention of message content, and retention of attitude change. In general, these two variables usually show a low-to-moderate positive correlation ($r = +.2$ to $+.5$), though some studies have shown that recall of specific message content is not essential to attitude change (e.g., Cacioppo & Petty, 1979a). Often media presentations are not well-learned, in part because they may have received only sporadic attention. For instance, one study showed that only a couple of hours after a network news broadcast, the average viewer could recall only 1.2 of the 20 stories in the broadcast, though about half of the stories were correctly recognized when respondents were given a list of potential story headlines (Neuman, 1976). Moreover, as is true of any learned information, retention of message content tends to drop off rather sharply in the first hours and days after exposure, and then gradually to level off. After a period of four to six weeks, retention of newly learned material may range from a low of about 10% (Watts & McGuire, 1964) to a high of about 75% (Fitzsimmons & Osburn, 1968)—the wide range being due partly to differences in messages (printed selections vs. TV) and partly to differences in methodological procedures for measuring recall or recognition. However, some experimental studies have shown substantial amounts of information retention for periods as long as six months; and oft-repeated exposure to a message, as in media advertising campaigns, may make it almost impossible to forget a product slogan.

Retention of any attitude change which may have occurred tends to follow a rather similar declining pattern. After four to six weeks, the amount of attitude change retained may be from one-third to two-thirds of the original change (Watts & McGuire, 1964). In their study of five different TV documentaries shown to college students, Fitzsimmons and Osburn (1968) found that only one retained a significant attitudinal effect after four weeks. Many experiments have found attitude changes lasting as long as six months (McGuire, 1969), and a very impressive classroom study by Rokeach (1971) showed significant attitude changes lasting well over one year. Keep in mind that all of these findings stem from studies where the persuasive message was delivered only once, and that fact makes it hard to achieve long-lasting attitude change (Cook & Flay, 1978).

Research has shown that repeated re-exposures to a persuasive message will strengthen and prolong any prior opinion change (Cook & Insko, 1968). A dramatic example of this principle may be seen in the 25-year follow-up of Newcomb's Bennington College students whose attitudes had been changed in a liberal direction by their college experiences (Newcomb et al., 1967). The authors found that many of these women had chosen a supportive postcollege environment of husbands and associates, and as a result they retained much of the attitude change which had been created 25 years before.

Studies of Action

The final dependent variable to be considered in studies of mass communication is behavioral—taking overt action as a result of the persuasive message. The relationship between attitudes and behavior may range from zero to very strongly positive, and we will consider the nature of this relationship between attitudes and behavior at length in Chapter 11. In this section we will describe some of the typical behavioral effects of the mass media.

We know that occasionally the mass media can have very dramatic effects on people's behavior. Perhaps the most famous example is Orson Welles's 1938 radio broadcast dramatizing an invasion of Earth by Martians, a broadcast so realistic and compelling that over a million people were driven to panic and many fled their homes (Cantril, 1940). Of course, in realistic situations involving imminent danger, such as hurricane warnings along the Gulf Coast, we take it for granted that millions of people will be influenced by media warning messages. However, what are the more typical behavioral effects of the media?

Allocation of Time. Roberts and Maccoby (1985) have summarized studies of the amount of time that people spend with the mass media, particularly television. American children, from the age of three onward, spend one-sixth or more of their waking hours watching television. However, despite fears and claims that children's television attention would sharply reduce their reading, outdoor play, hobbies, or social activities, careful research has shown very little evidence of such effects—except perhaps some decrease in organized outdoor activities (Timmer et al., 1985; Anderson & Collins, 1988). Both children and adults often find time for media attention by coordinating viewing or listening with other household activities such as cooking, cleaning, and meals, and even with more demanding cognitive activities such as reading or homework.

Alleged Passivity. A number of authors have claimed that availability of TV, and earlier of radio, has increased the passivity of their audiences, perhaps even causing them to behave like "zombies." However, Anderson and Collins's (1988) careful research review concluded that there is no evidence of any such effect. An elaborate study in England found no evidence that children's TV viewing produced any of the five different sorts of passivity which concerned school teachers (Himmelweit, Oppenheim, & Vince, 1958). In fact, viewing in their early years may give children a faster start in school due to a larger vocabulary and a larger store of knowledge. Among teenagers, school achievement is somewhat lower among heavy TV viewers than among light viewers, but this relationship drops to zero when demographic and other background characteristics are controlled (Gaddy, 1986).

Social Behavior. Research on the media and social behavior has focused most heavily on aggressive behavior, and the overall findings on this topic as well as on prosocial behavior have been summarized in a massive meta-analysis by Hearold (1986). The amount of violence shown on U.S. TV entertainment programs is horrendously high, and it is by far the highest on Saturday morning programming for children, where it averages 18 or more violent episodes per hour (Signorielli, Gross, & Morgan, 1982). Many studies have shown links between watching these very high levels of violence and the likelihood of increased aggressive behavior (National Commission on the Causes and Prevention of Violence, 1969; Scientific Advisory Committee on Television and Social Behavior, 1972; Pearl, Bouthilet, & Lazar, 1982), though a few studies have concluded that the relationship is so small as to have no practical importance (Milavsky, Kessler, Stipp, & Rubens, 1982; Freedman, 1984). Careful experimental studies have demonstrated that watching violent media presentations has larger effects on initially aggressive youngsters, and that viewers are more likely to respond aggressively when the violence is portrayed as rewarded, useful, or justified (Roberts & Maccoby, 1985).

The other side of the coin—much less studied—is that television can also stimulate prosocial behavior and behavioral intentions (Rushton, 1982), and that the effects of intentional prosocial programming can be quite strong (Hearold, 1986). Viewing programs such as *Sesame Street* and *Mister Rogers' Neighborhood* has been shown to encourage children's sharing, cooperation, and self-control (Friedrich & Stein, 1975). Similarly, preschool children who watched selected prosocial episodes of programs like *Lassie* later displayed increased levels of helping behavior (Ahammer & Murray, 1979). However, there is very little prosocial programming available on U.S. television, and Fairchild (1988) has given an interesting account of the difficulties involved in pioneering and producing a TV program that was aimed primarily at prosocial themes.

Political Behavior. The huge amount of political material broadcast on U.S. television in a presidential election year includes half a billion dollars of paid political ads plus all the unpurchased time devoted to election news, predictions, interviews, and debates (McGuire, 1985). Nevertheless, the major effects of the mass media which are evident during election campaigns are *reinforcement* of voters' current attitudes, and *activation* of any latent motivational predispositions (such as party loyalty or strong issue commitments) which would lead people to vote in the desired direction. There is also some suggestive evidence that media exposure can help to increase voter turnout (Weiss, 1969).

Most research has not given the media much credit for ability to change voting intentions from one party to another. Paid political advertisements have quite small effects on voting decisions, affecting mostly the small group of still unde-cided voters (Kaid, 1981), and they fairly often influence decisions *against* rather than for the advertised candidate (Raj, 1982). However, it is clear that candidates' expenditures for media ads are related to their overall vote totals, particularly where the candidates are not already well known, so advertising is not useless (Grush, 1980).

Whereas the broadcast media in the U.S. have been required to follow the FCC's "fairness doctrine," which mandates equal coverage of both sides of contro-versial issues, the print media have historically been free to editorialize and even to slant the news on behalf of their preferred candidates. In almost every election, the great majority of newspapers support the Republican presidential candidate. For instance, 80% of newspapers backed Nixon in 1968 and 90% supported him in 1972. In keeping with the minimal effects conclusion discussed in an earlier section, such editorials may influence only a few percent of voters. However, when other factors are held constant, careful research has shown that these lopsided newspaper endorsements have led several million readers to follow their paper's editorial advice—far more than needed for the winning margin in a close election such as the one in 1968 (Robinson, 1972; Coombs, 1981). Thus newspapers can sometimes have a crucial influence on elections.

In Chapter 13 we will return to a more extensive discussion of factors affecting political behavior and voting.

Advertising. In developing countries, where mass media availability is new and information about products and fashions is not widespread, advertising in the media may be very effective (Schramm, 1964). Likewise, with child audiences, who haven't yet learned to discount the persuasive impact of commercials, the 20,000 TV ads that they are exposed to each year may both influence specific product preferences and also carry the broader message that "to consume is to be happy" (Adler et al., 1980; Roberts et al., 1980).

In the United States and other media-saturated countries, much advertising is directed at maintaining the share of the market already held by a particular tooth-paste, automobile, or detergent (that is, it is aimed at reinforcing existing prefer-ences). Frequently research has shown no relationship between advertising budgets and sales, while other studies have shown small increases in sales resulting from advertising campaigns (Gorn & Goldberg, 1982; Assmus, Farley, & Lehmann, 1984). Paradoxically, though a major ad campaign may cost millions of dollars, it does not have to influence large percentages of people in order to be successful. A highly successful sales campaign may increase a brand's share of the market by only one per cent, and it may even alienate more people (not current buyers) than it wins over as new buyers (Bauer, 1964; Raj, 1982). Thus small percentage effects may have a great dollar value, and yet the advertiser may not care at all what you or I think of his "pitch" or his product, as long as somebody likes them.

PERSUASIVE EFFECTS OF PERSONAL COMMUNICATION

There is general agreement that personal communication usually has a stronger influence on people's attitudes and behavior than does mass communication. Initial evidence for this conclusion came from studies of face-to-face speeches versus radio versus printed messages (Cantril & Allport, 1935), and similar conclusions were reached in the early election surveys, which failed to find the expected strong mass media effects (Lazarsfeld et al., 1948; Berelson et al., 1954). As a result of their findings of greater exposure to personal political conversation than to the mass media, the authors proposed the hypothesis that communication follows a **two-step flow**: from media to "opinion leaders" to other citizens. We will discuss this two-step flow concept in more detail later in this section.

Critics have pointed out that the early data only suggested but did not prove that personal communication had a stronger influence on voting than did the media (O'Keefe & Atwood, 1981). However, Katz and Lazarsfeld (1955) showed that personal contacts were more effective than the media in influencing women's decisions about marketing, fashion, and movie-going. Similarly, there is very convincing evidence that personal contact increases voter turnout, though it does not seem generally successful in changing people's voting choice (Kramer, 1970; Kraut & McConahay, 1973; Yalch, 1976; Traugott & Katosh, 1981).

Many reasons can be given to explain the apparent superiority of personal communication. Because it is a face-to-face situation, attention is likely to be higher than with the media, and the message can be given at an appropriate moment and planned to be relevant to the recipient's motives and attitudes. Because such communication is two-way, feedback from the recipient can be used to increase comprehension, counter any objections, and select particularly effective arguments. The communicator will probably have many traits and interests in common with the recipient, and (s)he can repeat part or all of the message, if necessary. The personal relationship may cause the recipient to relax any defenses against being influenced, and it may encourage yielding (compliance) in the interests of maintaining smooth social relations. Finally, if the recipient is also partici-

Photograph courtesy of Elihu Katz.
Reprinted by permission.

Box 8–3   ELIHU KATZ, *Authority on Communication Research*

Elihu Katz is simultaneously Professor of Sociology and Communication at the Hebrew University of Jerusalem and Professor at the Annenberg School of Communications of the University of Southern California. Born in 1926 in New York City, he served in the U.S. Army and then earned a B.A., M.A., and Ph.D. in sociology at Columbia University. He taught briefly at Columbia and 15 years at the University of Chicago before moving to Jerusalem, where he directed the Communications Institute for many years.

Transferring his academic experience to national service, Katz was the founding director of Israel television from 1967 to 1969. He has authored about 100 articles and 10 books, including Personal Influence, The Uses of Mass Communications, Mass Media and Social Change, *and* Broadcasting in the Third World. *He has been research consultant to CBS and the British Broadcasting Corporation and has won many awards and honors, including the McLuhan-Teleglobe Canada Award and the Israel Prize. His research on personal influence in communication is discussed in this chapter.*

pating actively in the conversation, (s)he may occasionally express agreement with the communicator—a form of public commitment—and such commitments have been found to increase attitude change and retention (e.g., Pallak, Cook, & Sullivan, 1980).

Studies of Personal Communication

Though all of these advantages do seem to be available, personal communication rather seldom makes use of them. Any political or buying influence which does take place is apt to be just part of an ordinary everyday conversation rather than a planned influence attempt. Though research studies usually focus on *changes* in opinion or behavior, personal conversations are much more apt to *reinforce* currently held views. Berelson et al. (1954) found about 30% of political conversations did not involve voting preferences (they concerned predictions of who would win, exchange of information, etc.), and over 60% involved reinforcing comments about mutual views on the candidates or the issues. That left only 6% of political conversations which involved any argument or attempt to change opinions!

There have been three major methods used to determine which citizens are

opinion leaders in personal communication with others. The original method used was *self-designation* as an advice-giver in response to questions like "Have you recently tried to convince anyone of your political ideas?" Many later studies used one or the other of two nomination approaches. In the *sociometric* method, all members of a group (for instance, all local doctors) are asked to list the group members who are most influential in giving information and advice (for instance, about the merits of new drugs). In the *key informant* approach, a limited number of knowledgeable individuals are asked to list the group members who are most influential concerning a given topic, such as choice of fashions. In some studies these "influentials" have also been interviewed to determine who or what had influenced them. Using any one of these methods, about 20% to 25% of a group are typically found to be opinion leaders on any given topic. Though there are some differences in the individuals identified as leaders by the several methods, there does appear to be substantial consistency in the methods' results (Jacoby, 1974).

What are the characteristics of opinion leaders which have been found in research? First of all, they are very like those people whom they influence— usually from the same social class, though perhaps with a bit more status and a bit more contact with the media (Katz, 1957). The finding that opinion leaders are more likely than others to split their vote suggests that they may be unusually independent and self-reliant in making up their own mind on political questions (Kingdon, 1970). The breadth of their leadership across different areas of decision making is somewhat at issue. Early studies found no generalization of opinion leadership across different areas such as public affairs and fashion (Katz & Lazarsfeld, 1955), but more recent studies have shown considerable overlap of leadership, particularly across somewhat similar product categories such as clothing and cosmetics (Jacoby, 1974).

There are a number of sequential steps in the process by which a person adopts an innovation such as a new farming method or cosmetic product. First, awareness of the innovation must occur, and next, interest must be developed and information obtained. Third, this information must be evaluated for its usefulness, and fourth, the person may try out the innovation in his or her own situation. If this proves successful, full-scale and continuing adoption may follow. In general it has been found that mass media sources are most important in the early stages of the adoption process (awareness and perhaps also information gathering), while personal sources are more important in the later stages, particularly in evaluation and final decision (Rogers, 1982).

This finding returns us to our earlier question about the direction of flow of communication in the influence process.

The Flow of Communication

Two-Step?   The original two-step-flow hypothesis postulated that communication about public affairs flowed first from the media to attentive "opinion leaders," who in turn passed it on to other citizens, but that most average citizens did not attend to the media sources directly. Though Katz (1957) reported considerable evidence supporting this sequence, additional findings cited by Katz and later authors make the picture much more complicated.

Multi-Step? A multi-step theory posits that information flows from the media to opinion leaders and then down through several levels of individuals having decreasing amounts of interest and knowledge concerning the topic. For instance, Katz and Lazarsfeld (1955) proposed that opinion leaders were most interested in the topic, but the people they talked with were moderately interested rather than completely uninterested. More recent studies have shown quite definitively that most opinion-givers are also opinion-receivers (Robinson, 1976). For instance, Troldahl and Van Dam (1965) found that 30% of their respondents had asked someone about their opinion on a major news topic in the previous two weeks, and two-thirds of those individuals had also been asked for such an opinion. From these data it appears clear that opinion leaders are also listeners, but that generally no one talks to or listens to a great many citizens (63% in this study had not discussed any major news topic with anyone, while the comparable figure in a more recent study was 40%—Robinson & Levy, 1986a). These noninteractive individuals do get a certain amount of information directly from the media, however (Robinson, 1976).

Circular Flow. Probably the most accurate view of persuasive communication is that its flow is circular, involving much alternation between media sources and personal sources. For instance, we have described above the important finding that different sources are dominant at different stages of the innovation adoption process. In addition, even though one source may be predominant at a given stage, other sources are usually involved (Rogers, 1982).

Several studies illustrate the close alternating or circular relation between obtaining information from the media and from interpersonal discussion (Chaffee, 1982). People's comprehension of news events depends as much or more on discussion of the news with other people as on the amount of media news exposure (Robinson & Levy, 1986a). The same pattern is found in election campaigns, where watching the presidential debates on television is normally associated with personal discussions of them, but the interpersonal communication is apt to contribute more heavily to people's understanding of campaign issues and to their later voting decisions (McLeod, Durall, Ziemke, & Bybee, 1979; Kennamer, 1985). In calamities, such as the assassination of President Kennedy, diffusion of the news is largely achieved by word-of-mouth (over two-thirds of the population learned of it within half an hour), but then people turn to the media for confirmation and further details (Greenberg, 1964).

The circular flow of communication can be summarized as follows:

> Personal influence may be more effective than persuasive mass communication, but at present mass communication seems the most effective means of stimulating personal influence. (Klapper, 1960, p. 72)

FIGURE 8-2 Combining media presentation and personal communication on the same topic can have a stronger effect than either alone.

Combining Media and Personal Influence. As a result of research findings about the mutual importance of both methods of communication, a number of attempts have been made to combine them in order to achieve greater persuasive effect. An approach which proved effective for developing community action programs in rural areas was to bring groups of citizens together for a media presentation, immediately followed by a group discussion and consideration of possible action (UNESCO, 1960). With children, following up a TV episode from *Mister Rogers' Neighborhood* with a discussion by the teacher which focused on the same message about helpfulness proved successful in increasing cooperative behavior (Friedrich & Stein, 1975). Similar cumulative effects of media presentations plus discussion have been found in encouraging preschoolers' helping behavior, reducing sex-role stereotyping among grade school students, and deterring smoking by adolescents (Ahammer & Murray, 1979; Johnston et al., 1980; Evans et al., 1981). These studies illustrate the potential practical importance of some of the research on persuasive communication.

SOME POSSIBLE EXPLANATIONS
OF COMMUNICATION EFFECTIVENESS

We will look at four different ideas that have been proposed in attempts to explain the relative effectiveness of the media and of personal communication in influencing attitudes. The first of these is **selective exposure**, the notion that people actively avoid information that is inconsistent with or threatening to their beliefs and attitudes, and that they seek supportive information.

Is There Selective Exposure to Communications?

The hypothesis of selective exposure has had an honored history. Hyman and Sheatsley (1947) were among the first public opinion researchers to stress the concept in their explanation of "Some reasons why information campaigns fail." It was invoked as a major explanatory concept in the first major voting study (Lazarsfeld et al., 1948) and in Klapper's (1960) widely cited review of the effects of mass communication, and it assumed an important place in Festinger's (1957) influential theory of cognitive dissonance, as we will see in Chapter 10.

With this unanimity of opinion from many famous attitude researchers, is there any point in asking further questions? Well, yes; there is. This is a good example of the maxim that a universally accepted belief is very unlikely to be completely true and is therefore most in need of critical scrutiny. Following this advice, Sears and Freedman (1967) made a careful summary of the research evidence concerning selective exposure and reached some surprising conclusions.

First of all, Sears and Freedman distinguished two different aspects of the concept: **de facto** selectivity, and **motivated** selective exposure. *De facto* selectivity means a greater than chance agreement of opinion between an audience and a communication directed to that audience. For instance, it is mostly Republicans who take the trouble to go to Republican campaign rallies. Similarly, readers of *National Review* are likely to be people who already agree with the editor's conservative viewpoint, whereas most readers of *Mother Jones* are apt to be liberal in their political and social attitudes. However, for actions as easy to perform as reading a newspaper editorial favoring one candidate or listening to the President speak on TV, there is probably much less of a tendency for the audience to be biased in favor of the communicator's position. In fact, political campaigning on television has been transformed in the last two decades—changing from long televised speeches to 5-minute commercials in the 1970s, and most recently to 30-second and 1-minute spots which are sandwiched in with other commercials, and thus are almost impossible to avoid intentionally.

These examples are consistent with the conclusions reached by Sears and Freedman. In many situations and for many people, *de facto* selectivity of communication audiences is an established fact, though this tendency is not nearly as general a phenomenon as had earlier been thought.

By contrast, there is very little firm evidence of a *motivated* search for supportive information or avoidance of opposing information. This is the kind of selectivity which most previous writers have postulated, perhaps partly because it fits so well into a Freudian defense-mechanism perspective. Despite that fit, selective exposure was not at all verified by Sears and Freedman's review of the evidence. For example, in a study on smoking and lung cancer, Feather (1962) found that neither smokers nor nonsmokers showed a significant preference for reading either of two articles, one of which argued that smoking causes lung cancer and the other of which claimed that it does not. Further, when smokers were divided according to whether they believed that the evidence linking cancer and smoking was convincing or not convincing, both groups preferred the article which *opposed* their own viewpoint—a surprising preference for nonsupportive information by these ego-involved subjects.

Other studies which cast serious doubt on the hypothesis of motivated selective exposure include research on decision-making processes (Janis & Mann, 1977), Trenaman and McQuail's (1961) British election study, and studies of responses to political campaign ads in the United States (Atkin, Bowen, et al., 1973; Ziemke, 1980). In explaining these findings, several other determinants of exposure to information have been stressed: (1) As mentioned earlier, supportive information is much more extensively available than nonsupportive information in most people's normal environments. (2) *Refutability* of information may be a factor, weak opposing information being desired but strong opposing arguments being avoided. (3) Even more important, the *usefulness* of information will make it desired, whether it is supportive or not (as in obtaining knowledge about a potentially dangerous defect in one's new car). (4) A person's recent exposure history is important because people who are aware of having received one-sided information generally will seek exposure to the other side (as in many simulated jury studies). (5) Educational level is a very powerful predictor of increased exposure to all kinds of information, both supportive and nonsupportive.

A recent review of research on motivated selective exposure (Frey, 1986) concluded that it does sometimes occur in particular media-use situations. For example, research shows that during the 1973 Watergate hearings, strong supporters of President Nixon actively avoided information about the scandal and the hearings, whereas people who had voted for his opponent, McGovern, sought out such information (Sweeney & Gruber, 1984). Thus the topic of audience selectivity is a very complicated one. However, it is encouraging that research does not show evidence for any general head-in-the-sand avoidance of all information which challenges one's presuppositions or attitudes. At the same time, we must realize that most people most of the time are surrounded by a higher proportion of supportive information than of opposing information.

The Media Define "Reality"

Though the mass media have not been found to be very effective in changing public attitudes, they have other effects which are important to consider. The first of these has been termed the creation of "second-hand reality"—that is, the definition of what is really happening in the world beyond one's own first-hand experience. Each one of us has a very limited range of experiences which we have actually participated in first-hand. Beyond that range, all of our knowledge, beliefs, and attitudes come from others, and the great majority probably come from some mass communication medium (ranging from books to billboards to radio and television).

If you have ever participated in an event which was written up in the press or described in broadcasts, you have probably discovered how different the media's "second-hand reality" is from what you have experienced first-hand. Inevitably the media select certain details to mention and omit many others. In this process they highlight and emphasize some aspects of the event and obscure others. Often this results in distortion and misleading reports even when there is no intention to mislead the public at all. When the personal beliefs, values, and motives of the reporters or of the editorial staff enter into the reporting process, as they often do, the resulting picture can be far from an objective, complete, and unbiased account. In fact, careful research in recent U.S. presidential elections has shown that some TV network news anchorpersons displayed systematically different amounts of positive facial expressions when they were mentioning different candidates (Friedman, DiMatteo, & Mertz, 1980), and that the smiles they bestowed on candidates had a favorable impact on viewers' voting on election day (Mullen et al., 1986). These smiles are very subtle stimuli—probably outside the usual awareness of both newscasters and viewers—but they dramatically indicate how potent television's effects can sometimes be.

The ways in which media selectivity occurs in the reporting process have been described in many empirical studies. Cutlip (1954) demonstrated that only about 10% of the news copy stemming from national news agencies ends up in small-town daily newspapers, so obviously the editors' biases and interests play a very strong part in determining what is available to the public to read. Even large-city dailies have limited numbers of reporters, especially in distant areas, so for many stories they have to rely on the news items selected by the national agencies' staffs. The three major weekly news magazines, *Time, Newsweek,* and *U.S. News & World Report,* have been strongly criticized for the amount of bias and slanted editorial opinion which creeps into their news reporting (Bagdikian, 1962). The titles of several in-depth scholarly volumes clearly highlight the reality-defining nature of the news media: *Deciding What's News* (Gans, 1979), *Making News: A Study in the Construction of Reality* (Tuchman, 1978), and *Creating Reality: How TV News Distorts News Events* (Altheide, 1976).

Television news broadcasts are particularly prone to creation of their own "reality" because of limitations on what is possible and easy to put on the air and what will attract audience attention (Epstein, 1973). The TV network camera crews are normally located in only a handful of major U.S. cities and a few foreign capitals, so their geographic coverage is sharply limited. Buying film footage from other sources is expensive, as is satellite transmission, so they are reserved for occasional major "lead" stories. Consequently, most of what we see as supposedly up-to-the-minute network "news" is confined to events which happen in those major cities. The only usual inputs from other locations are human interest stories or continuing events such as strikes and warfare, where footage from several recent days can be spliced together to make a coherent story. News organizations, both in

Europe and the U.S., exercise much selectivity in deciding what events are "newsworthy" and in trying to highlight a theme or pattern in the events that are broadcast (Gurevitch & Blumler, 1982).

Political news on American television is limited, due to the FCC's fairness doctrine, to stories which can be presented as having two sides, and the networks thus emphasize controversy more than consensus. They also stress the horse-race aspect of "who's ahead" in campaigns much more than the substantive issues and policy questions of the campaign (Patterson, 1980; Arterton, 1984). The nightly newscasts constantly strive to present flashy pictures—"hecklers, crowds, motorcades, balloons, rallies and gossip" (Patterson & McClure, 1976, p. 22). The result, as Lang and Lang (1984) have pointed out in numerous research examples, is that the picture on the TV tube is often much different from the reality on the streets of the city or the battlefield overseas. Particularly clear examples of this TV creation of reality occurred in selective coverage of natural disasters around the world (Adams, 1986), and in reporting of the Vietnam War.

However, this creation of second-hand reality by TV should not be confused with polemical slanting of the news. Despite the claims of antiadministration bias in TV reporting of the Vietnam War, Russo's (1971) careful content analysis study concluded that, on the average, network newscasts of the war did not present any noticeable bias against administration policies. Such claims of partisan bias are an inescapable aspect of media coverage of any highly controversial issue, for research shows that people with extreme views on the issue will always tend to see the media as biased against them (Vallone, Ross, & Lepper, 1985).

The broadest aspect of the media's creation of reality is the very widespread effect known as **enculturation**. This is the process of "instilling and reinforcing the values, beliefs, traditions, behavioral standards, and views of reality that are held by most members of a given culture" (Oskamp, 1984, p. 310). As far back in human history as Homer and other oral story tellers, this has always been one of the main functions of the media. Because this effect is so pervasive in any given culture and so consistent with the existing cultural patterns, it can easily be overlooked, and it is very hard to study objectively. Nevertheless, it is extremely important, and it has received considerable research attention in recent years.

One example of enculturation is what George Gerbner and his colleagues have called the **cultivation effect** of television—that is, that it "cultivates" or inculcates in its viewers a set of shared assumptions about the nature of social reality (e.g., Gerbner, Gross, Morgan, & Signorielli, 1980). These assumptions are shown, for instance, in commonly held beliefs about which individuals and groups are important and powerful, about what we should believe in ("the free enterprise system") and what we should fear ("crime in the streets"), etc. An example of TV's cultivation effects is its pervasive negative stereotyping and underrepresentation of low-power groups in society, such as women, ethnic minorities, and the elderly. Another example is its overemphasis on crime, in comparison to the actual amount in our society—a TV picture of a "mean" or "scary" world. Though there has been criticism of the cultivation hypothesis (Hirsch, 1980), there seems to be considerable empirical support for it when it is carefully operationalized—e.g., viewers who watch mostly situation comedies would not be expected to perceive a scary world (Hawkins & Pingree, 1982).

The Media Determine the Public Agenda

Probably the most important effect of the mass media is their **agenda-setting** function (McCombs, 1981). There is clear evidence that people attend to, are interested in, and talk about the information and ideas that they receive through the media. Since the media do not reflect reality completely and faithfully, it follows that their selectivity has a marked effect on what most people learn about and respond to.

The selectivity shown by the media in determining the public agenda has been demonstrated in several studies. Funkhouser (1973) found that coverage of major public issues in the three major U.S. news magazines from 1960 to 1970 did not show a close correspondence to the occurrence of important actual events. For instance, coverage of the Vietnam War reached its peak and began to decline before the war itself reached a peak. However, media coverage showed a close relationship to, and probably largely determined, people's responses to poll questions about the most important national problem. In a similar study, MacKuen (1981) found strong agenda-setting effects of media coverage on four different issues: the Vietnam War, race relations, campus unrest, and energy problems. On the local scene, also, media investigative reporting on an issue such as police brutality has been found to influence citizens' judgments about the importance of the issue (Leff, Protess, & Brooks, 1986).

The causal direction of agenda-setting effects is an important question. If both media content and the public's concerns were measured at only one point in time, it could be the case that public concerns or interests determine media coverage, rather than vice versa—or both might be reacting to the external reality of events in the world. However, a number of careful longitudinal studies have shown that the direction of influence is primarily from media coverage to the public agenda (McCombs, 1977; MacKuen, 1981; Behr & Iyengar, 1985) and, interestingly, that the print media seem to have stronger agenda-setting effects than does television (Patterson & McClure, 1976; McCombs, 1977). Moreover, definitive experimental studies have recently been done which subtly manipulated the amount of coverage of various topics in TV newscasts by unobtrusively combining stories from previous news programs. When these specially structured programs were shown, the viewers' judgments of the importance of various issues mirrored the amount of coverage in the programs, thus clearly establishing that the programs were the causal factor. In fact, the program content even helped to determine what specific issues the President would be judged on when viewers rated his overall performance in office (Iyengar, Kinder, Peters, & Krosnick 1984; Iyengar & Kinder, 1986). Thus television works to "prime" viewers' notions about what topics are important, and in so doing it can even influence the outcomes of national elections.

In sum, it appears clear that the various mass media all fulfill the agenda-setting function described by Cohen (1963, p. 16):

> The mass media may not be successful much of the time in telling people what to think, but the media are stunningly successful in telling their audience what to think *about*.

The Media Confer Prestige

A final major effect of the media is that, by their very mention of people, events, and issues, they confer importance upon them in the public eye (Lazarsfeld & Merton, 1948). In politics, the previously unknown candidates who win early presidential primary elections in small and atypical states (and often even nonwinners who did better than expected) get massive media attention, which gives their campaigns a major though often short-lived boost (Adams, 1984). Some media celebrities, such as Bill Cosby and Johnny Carson, have become so famous that they have been widely credited with personal persuasive power in selling products or ideas. But even formerly obscure nonentities whose actions or thoughts are picked out for coverage by TV or in print are suddenly invested with a seeming importance out of all proportion to their status in life. As a result, the media audience will pay attention to them and their ideas. Dramatic examples of this process have occurred with individuals who attempted to assassinate Presidents and then were featured on the covers of news magazines. As Lazarsfeld and Merton (1948, p. 102) put it:

> The audiences of mass media apparently subscribe to the circular belief: "If you really matter, you will be at the focus of mass attention and, if you *are* at the focus of mass attention, then surely you must really matter."

SUMMARY

Early studies of communication and propaganda were motivated by the fear that demagogues could easily sway the gullible audience. Since then, research has shown that persuasive communication is much less successful and much more complicated in its effects than had first been thought.

The main *independent* variables in persuasive communication are factors related to the source, the message, the medium (the topic of this chapter), the audience, and the target behavior. The main *dependent* variables involve the sequential steps of audience exposure, attention, comprehension, acceptance (yielding), retention, and action. Each of these stages may display different findings about communication effects because different independent variables may be important at each stage. Though the mass media often have minimal effects, they can have powerful effects under certain conditions, and personal and situational characteristics are important mediators of any media effects.

Personal communication is generally agreed to have stronger effects than mass communication. However, most personal communication is reinforcing or informative rather than persuasive in nature. The *two-step flow* of communication (from mass media to opinion leaders to other citizens) was proposed by early studies to help account for the low direct effectiveness of the media. However, it appears that communication flow tends to be circular, alternating between media sources and personal sources.

Selective exposure to communications has frequently been proposed as a mechanism by which people avoid persuasion. Research shows little evidence of *motivated* selectivity in seeking or avoiding information, but there is usually considerable *de facto* selectivity in a person's normal environment. Though the mass media are generally not very effective in changing public attitudes, they define "reality" for us in areas beyond the limited range of our first-hand personal experience, and in so doing, they *enculturate* or instill in their audience the shared beliefs and values of their society. Also, by their selection of events to cover, the mass media determine the public agenda, and they confer prestige and apparent importance on the people, events, and issues which they decide to cover.

9

Attitude Change Theories and Research
Methodology, Learning and Judgment Approaches

We are incredibly heedless in the formation of our beliefs, but find ourselves filled with an illicit passion for them when anyone proposes to rob us of their companionship.—James Harvey Robinson.

*Some praise at morning what they blame at night
But always think the last opinion right.*—Alexander Pope.

If you give me any normal human being and a couple of weeks . . . I can change his behavior from what it is now to whatever you want it to be, if it's physically possible.—James McConnell.

These three statements about attitudinal and behavioral change illustrate the widely discrepant viewpoints that different authors have held on this subject. The topic of attitude *change* has probably occupied the attention of psychologists more than all the other aspects of attitudes put together. One reason for this is the great importance of attitude changes in human affairs—for example, in events such as religious conversions, political persuasion, commercial advertising campaigns, and changes in personal prejudices. Another major reason for interest in attitude change was expressed by Kurt Lewin: to really understand something, such as the concept *attitude*, one must study it as it changes—not while it remains stable. For instance, in studying gravity, it is not enough to know that all objects fall toward the earth; to learn more we must study situations where the amount of gravitational force differs. Similarly, studying prejudiced attitudes per se is less illuminating than studying factors that can increase or decrease prejudice.

This chapter and the following one will summarize the major theories about attitude change and some selected portions of the huge body of research evidence in this field. We will organize our discussion primarily around six broad theoretical

Photograph courtesy of M.I.T. Historical
Collections. Reprinted by permission.

Box 9–1   KURT LEWIN, *Theorist, Researcher, and Founding Father*

The most influential single figure in shaping modern social psychology, Kurt Lewin was born in Prussia in 1890. After studying in Freiburg and Munich and receiving his Ph.D. at Berlin in 1914, he served in the German Army in World War I. As Professor of Philosophy and Psychology at the University of Berlin, he was a member of its influential group of Gestalt psychologists until he left Germany in 1932 to escape Nazism. After teaching briefly at Stanford and Cornell, he settled at the University of Iowa. In 1944 he founded the Research Center for Group Dynamics at M.I.T., where he died suddenly in 1947.

As a theorist, Lewin is known for his development of psychological field theory. As a researcher, he introduced methods which allowed scientific study of groups in real-life situations. He was famous for studies of democratic and autocratic group leadership methods and group discussion and decision processes. Advocating "action research," he pioneered in practical projects to lessen prejudice, reduce wartime attitude problems, and introduce group participation methods in industrial management. He helped found the National Training Laboratories, where his group dynamic principles were put to work in "T-groups" designed to improve social adjustment and group effectiveness.

orientations toward attitude change—learning, judgment, consistency, dissonance, attribution, and cognitive-response approaches. However, before beginning those topics, we will devote some attention to the various kinds of attitude change research and to the methodological problems involved in doing research in this area.

TYPES OF ATTITUDE CHANGE RESEARCH

There are two common settings for attitude change research, the classroom and the laboratory, and research done in these settings is apt to differ in many respects (McGuire, 1985). Both types of research have their advantages and their liabilities, and we will see many examples of each in the topics to follow.

Classroom research, which may be typified by the work of Carl Hovland, usually uses a large number of subjects who are run in groups. For instance, several classes of students might be given several different versions of a persuasive appeal in order to study how different arguments affect the amount of attitude change. This type of research is generally planned by beginning with a *dependent* variable of interest (such as the effects of persuasive messages) and searching for several independent variables to manipulate (such as the trustworthiness of the message source) which will influence the dependent variable. Thus it has been termed the *unidirectional convergent* style of attitude change research (McGuire, 1985). It concentrates more on careful measurement of the dependent variable and less on sophisticated procedures to control or manipulate other variables. Normally many variables are manipulated or measured at the same time, and complex statistical designs are necessary to analyze the data, which often show complicated interactions between variables. Because of less-complete controls and weak manipulations of independent variables, there is apt to be much error variance, which in turn necessitates large groups of subjects to obtain significance.

By contrast, laboratory research, typified by the work of Leon Festinger, usually uses a relatively small number of subjects who are run individually. For instance, half of the subjects may undergo a failure experience which temporarily lowers their self-esteem, and the effects of this experience on their acceptance of a persuasive message may be compared with other subjects who did not have a failure experience. This type of research is generally planned by beginning with an *independent* variable of some theoretical interest (such as cognitive dissonance) and searching for many different situations where it can be applied (such as self-exposure to new information, or the results of taking actions which are inconsistent with one's attitudes). Thus it has been termed the *unidirectional divergent* style of research (McGuire, 1985). It concentrates on manipulation of one independent variable and control of other variables, but much less on measurement techniques for the dependent variable. The manipulation procedures are apt to be complicated and precise, with careful checks on their success, so that a relatively large effect may be found. Since other contaminating variables have been controlled experimentally, a simple statistical design is sufficient, and significance may be obtained even with small groups of subjects.

Classes of Variables Studied

Another way of categorizing attitude change research is by the types of variables studied. In these two chapters we will be focusing primarily on four major classes of variables involved in the process of communication—namely, *source*, *message*, *audience*, and *target behavior* variables. (The fifth type of variable, the *medium* of communication, was discussed in Chapter 8.) A further account of research findings concerning attitude change in an area of great social importance can be found in Chapter 15, on racial attitudes and prejudice.

A multitude of topics has been studied in research on attitude change. To assist in orienting ourselves to the major substantive areas within the field, Table 9-1 is included, showing, within each of the five categories of communication variables, specific independent variables that have been fairly frequently studied during the last 20 years. Most of the variables listed in the table are ones which have been discussed in one or more of the review chapters on attitudes and attitude change printed in the *Annual Review of Psychology* every three years (e.g., Cialdini, Petty, & Cacioppo, 1981; Cooper & Croyle, 1984; Chaiken & Stangor, 1987; Tesser & Shaffer, 1990).

Some trends in this pattern of research are worth underlining. First, as indicated by the number of listings in the table, there has been considerably less research attention to medium variables and to target behavior variables than to the other categories. Second, though source variables and message variables have more listings, they were most studied in the 1950s and 1960s, and there has been a marked decline in this Hovland-type research since then. There was also a relative decline in concentration on dissonance-related variables in the 1970s and 1980s, and a concurrent rise of interest in attribution processes and variables. Finally, the large number of audience variables listed, particularly cognitive variables, reflects the burst of activity in social cognition research in the 1980s.

The next two chapters will discuss many of the variables listed in the table, particularly those which have had the greatest amount of research attention. Inter-

TABLE 9–1   Independent Variables Frequently Studied in Attitude Change Research

Source variables
   Prestige
   Credibility
      Expertise
      Trustworthiness
   Attractiveness
      Similarity (e.g., race vs. belief)
      Familiarity
      Liking
   Power
   Intent to persuade vs. objectivity (forewarning vs. distraction)
Message variables
   Type of appeal
      Rational, emotional, moral
      Positive vs. negative (fear appeals)
      Reinforcement within the message
      Message style, humor, etc.
      Quality of arguments
      Wording
   Inclusions and omissions
      Implicit vs. explicit conclusions
      Refuting vs. ignoring opposition arguments
      Repetition of the message (mere exposure)
      Situational information (e.g., victim's degree of responsibility for own injury)
   Order of presentation (primacy vs. recency; forgetting)
      Conclusion first or last
      Order with respect to desirability and agreement
      Climax vs. anticlimax (strongest argument last or first)
      Refuting opposition before or after own supporting arguments
   Discrepancy from audience member's attitude

TABLE 9–1 (Continued)

Medium variables

Direct experience with object vs. communication about it
  Interpersonal contact
  Modality (eye vs. ear, etc.)
  Mass media vs. face-to-face personal influence
    Group discussion
    Influence of minorities
  Relative efficacy of the different mass media

Audience variables

Active vs. passive role
    Forced compliance (counterattitudinal advocacy, insufficient justification, effects of effort)
    Selective exposure
    Actor vs. observer (self vs. other attribution)
  Generality of persuasibility
    Social support
  Demographic variables (age, sex, SES, etc.)
  Ability factors
  Personality factors in persuasibility
  Cognitive factors
    Involvement in issue (relevance, importance of issue)
    Latitudes of acceptance and rejection
    Postdecision processes
    Commitment and choice
    Syllogistic reasoning
    Consistency in inferences
    Judgment processes (use of cues, adding vs. averaging information, assimilation and contrast, perspectives)
    Disconfirmation of expectancies
    Perceived freedom
    Self-awareness
    Attitude complexity
    Accessibility of attitude
    Mere thought
  Emotional factors
    Arousal
    Symbolic attitudes
    Motives of audience
  Impression management
  Multiple modes of attitude change
    Cognitive responses (systematic processing)
    Heuristic processing

Target behavior variables

  Persistence of change
  Generalization of effects beyond specific target issue
  Immediate vs. delayed impact
  Direct impact vs. resistance to counterarguments
  Verbal attitude change vs. gross behavior change

Source: Adapted and expanded from McGuire (1972, p. 112) in *Experimental Social Psychology* by Charles G. McClintock, copyright © 1972 by Holt, Rinehart and Winston, Inc. Reprinted by permission of the publisher.

ested readers may also wish to consult the review chapters mentioned above for further detailed information.

METHODOLOGICAL PROBLEMS

Now we turn to a brief description of some of the most important methodological problems in attitude change research. It should be noted that these problems are not unique to the area of attitude change, being frequently found in most experimental and quasi-experimental research in social psychology.

Research Design

The choice of a research design which will yield valid conclusions is always an important step in research. The problem is greater when attitude change studies move from the laboratory to more natural settings, as is often the case in research on marketing, political attitudes, media influence, racism, and other important social issues. In such cases, investigators usually can't manipulate all the crucial variables, but they can control the conditions under which the dependent variables are measured. Cook and Campbell (1979, Chap. 3 & 5) have presented a thorough and helpful description of many different "quasi-experimental" designs for use in such situations.

A danger to be aware of in pretest-posttest designs is that the pretest may either sensitize subjects to the issue and promote attitude change, or alternatively it may commit them to their initial viewpoints and deter attitude change (Rosnow & Suls, 1970). Fortunately this kind of experimental artifact does not seem to occur frequently (McGuire, 1966). Another procedure requiring great caution is the use of change scores in pretest-posttest designs (Cronbach & Furby, 1970). Both of these problems can be circumvented by using posttest-only designs, in which subjects are randomly assigned to treatment and control groups and are not given pretests before the experimental manipulation, or by other more complex research designs.

Measurement Methods

The most common way of measuring attitudes, verbal self-report, has many limitations, particularly if subjects have any reason not to report accurately (e.g., laziness, defensiveness, saving face, etc.). Though seldom used, many other measurement approaches have been proposed, as we have discussed in Chapter 3 (cf. Dawes & Smith, 1985). Some of these methods are indirect or disguised verbal techniques which actually assess attitudes but appear to measure, for instance, the subjects' factual knowledge or their judgments of the plausibility of persuasive arguments. Others are unobtrusive, nonreactive methods of observation, which are particularly useful in nonlaboratory studies. In these methods, subjects are not aware of being studied; examples include observation of political bumper stickers, or of racial seating patterns in a classroom. Physiological and biochemical measures of attitudes have also been proposed (Cacioppo & Petty, 1983), as have methods which use bogus electronic instruments as a means of reducing subjects' tendencies to give socially desirable responses (Jones & Sigall, 1971). At present, little is known about the comparability of these many differing methods of measurement, and the confusion of noncomparable dependent variable measures may account for many of the conflicting findings in the attitude research literature (Fishbein & Ajzen, 1972).

Demand Characteristics

This term, coined by Orne, refers to perceptual cues which indicate what is expected of people in any given situation (Orne, 1969). Such cues may be explicit or implicit, and they are present in all situations, though it is in laboratory experiments where they are most apt to present a problem in the interpretation of the results. Orne and others have shown that subjects in experimental situations may try to "cooperate" with the experimenter and thus respond in ways which will support the experimental hypothesis. To take an extreme example, subjects who learn or are told the experimental hypothesis more often perform in ways that will support it than do other subjects (Weber & Cook, 1972). However, in addition to the "good subject" set, several other response sets have been mentioned as being common among experimental subjects (see next section).

Demand characteristic effects on research data can be minimized in several ways. Probably the most important way is through replication of studies in different laboratories and by experimenters with differing theoretical viewpoints. Also important are greater use of nonartificial settings, and detailed postexperimental inquiries about subject suspicions. Other helpful procedures include careful development of experimental procedures and "cover stories" to conceal the point of the research, separating the experimental manipulation from collection of the dependent variable measures so that subjects will not see a connection between them, and avoiding designs using pretests which may alert subjects to the focus of study (Rosenthal & Rosnow, 1984). Fortunately, there is some evidence that subjects are quite conscientious in following experimental instructions even if they are suspicious about the procedures (T. Cook et al., 1970).

Subject Effects

In addition to the set to be a cooperative "good subject," there are several other sets which experimental participants can adopt. Weber and Cook (1972) have discussed the uncooperative, "negativistic subject"; the "faithful subject" who scrupulously follows task instructions and avoids acting on any suspicions which (s)he may have; and the "apprehensive subject" who is worried about how his(her) behavior may be evaluated. Weber and Cook's extensive review of the research literature concluded that there is much evidence for the operation of **evaluation**

apprehension—that is, attempts by subjects to act in socially desirable ways because of their concern about evaluation by other people (e.g., Rosenberg, 1969). However, there is little or no clearcut evidence for operation of the other three subject roles except in certain very restricted situations (Spinner, Adair, & Barnes, 1977; Carlston & Cohen, 1980). Nonetheless, careful researchers will try to minimize the possibility that subject roles are influencing their findings. Appropriate precautions include carefully disguising the experimental hypothesis, doing research in natural settings where subjects are unaware that their behavior is being studied, and/or reducing evaluation apprehension by avoiding anxiety-arousing instructions and maintaining subject anonymity.

Another possible subject effect which has been studied stems from the frequent use of *volunteers* as experimental subjects. Many studies have found that volunteer subjects differ in various ways from nonvolunteers, and these differences may affect their experimental performance. For instance, volunteers are apt to be more educated, intelligent, and sociable, but also higher in need for approval. Two research reviews have reached conflicting conclusions about whether volunteer effects are a pervasive source of bias in experiments (Rosenthal & Rosnow, 1975), or not (Kruglanski, 1975). Because of the possibility of such effects, it is wise to avoid use of volunteer subjects whenever that is feasible.

As you are undoubtedly aware, college students are the type of subjects most commonly used in social psychological research. Despite long-standing recommendations for use of a wider and more representative pool of subjects, the use of college students tested in laboratory situations has actually increased in the last two decades to a large majority of all published social psychological studies (Higbee, Millard, & Folkman, 1982; Sears, 1986; Vitelli, 1988). College students are not only younger, better educated, more intelligent, and more affluent than the average citizen, but they are also more likely than older adults to have less-crystallized attitudes, self-concepts, and peer relationships. The result of overreliance on such an unrepresentative data base may be to distort some of our scientific findings about human nature in the direction of overemphasizing compliance, inconsistency, easy attitude change, and cognitive processes, and underemphasizing emotions, personality characteristics, and group norms (Sears, 1986). This potential danger needs to be considered in interpreting research findings and particularly in planning future studies.

Experimenter Effects

Distortions of research results produced by biases of the experimenter have been extensively studied by Rosenthal (1969, 1976). These biases can lead to errors in observation, recording of data, or computation of results, but the most-studied type of experimenter bias is **expectancies** which affect the subjects' behavior. The experimenter's expectancies are apparently transmitted to subjects by subtle cues of voice tone, gestures, and facial expressions that display warmth and provide feedback (Rosenthal, 1976; Snodgrass & Rosenthal, 1982). Though there have been vigorous criticisms of some of Rosenthal's research conclusions (e.g., Barber & Silver, 1968), there is widespread agreement that experimenter effects can occur under some conditions (Fishbein & Ajzen, 1972). Thus, attempts to eliminate or minimize them are desirable. Some of the best ways to do so include cutting down on experimenter-subject contact by mechanizing as much of the procedure as possible, using several different experimenters and testing for differences in their results, ensuring that the experimenter cannot reinforce subjects' behavior differentially, keeping experimenters "blind" to the research hypothesis and/or to the experimental condition assigned to specific subjects, and using extra control groups which differ only in the expectancies given to their members about the research hypothesis.

Deception and Suspicion

Because of the many extraneous variables, such as those discussed above, which can affect the results of attitude change studies, investigators in this area have often felt it necessary or desirable to increase their control of conditions by deceiving subjects during the course of experiments (Stricker, 1967). Indeed, in the 1960s and 1970s, the percentage of studies published in the major social psychological journals that used deception rose significantly to about 60% (Gross & Fleming, 1982), though it has since dropped back to about 35% (Vitelli, 1988). Deception itself, and the subjects' suspicion which may result, can become additional confounding variables which sometimes bias research results (Stricker, Messick, & Jackson, 1969; Rubin & Moore, 1971). On the other hand, an equal number of studies have shown that prior deception and/or current suspiciousness do not necessarily bias subjects' responses (Fillenbaum & Frey, 1970; Holmes & Bennett, 1974). Thus, situational differences and the carefulness of the researcher are apt to determine whether use of deception poses a threat to valid conclusions.

One approach which has been suggested instead of deception is the **simulated experiment** (sometimes also called an interpersonal replication, or passive role-playing), in which a written or tape-recorded description of the experimental situation is given to observer-subjects instead of actually placing them in the situation (Bem, 1967; Kelman, 1967). However, extensive criticisms of simulated experiments or role-playing studies have indicated that they may create more problems in the interpretation of research results than they solve (A. Miller, 1972; Spencer, 1978—see also the evidence on actor-observer differences cited in Chapter 2).

Another reason which has been stressed for avoiding experimental deception wherever possible involves questions of ethical propriety (Kelman, 1967, 1972; Baumrind, 1985). The American Psychological Association (1973, 1982) has established ethical guidelines for all aspects of research, and when deception is used in psychological studies, it is generally of a mild and innocuous sort. Indeed, studies show that most psychologists would impose more stringent ethical safeguards in research than are advocated by typical citizens or by college undergraduates (Sullivan & Deiker, 1973; Wilson & Donnerstein, 1976; Christensen, 1988). Ethical issues in research will be described further in Chapter 11.

Having discussed research methods and methodological problems, we turn now to theories of attitude change, beginning in this chapter with learning theories and judgment theories.

WHY HAVE THEORIES?

In considering theories of attitude change, we should first ask: What good are theories? Why do we have them? A number of answers have been given to this question. First, theories provide a path to guide our steps in research; they suggest factors that are important to study, ones that we might not think of otherwise. Second, theories help us to understand research findings by putting them into a context; they explain the meaning of the facts which have been discovered—how and why they fit together. Third, theories allow us to predict what will happen under various conditions in the future. In turn, correct prediction of events provides a stringent test of the adequacy of any theory. As Deutsch and Krauss (1965) have put it: "Theory is the net man weaves to catch the world of observation—to explain, predict, and influence it" (p. vii).

Another point which should be stressed is that theories are never proven. They can be disproven at crucial points by negative evidence, but an accumulation of positive evidence merely adds support to a theory rather than proving it in any final sense. These supportive data may also be compatible with another, different theory. When a theoretical relationship between two variables has been confirmed so many times that all authorities agree on its correctness, it is usually called a **law** (such as the gas laws, which describe the relationship between the temperature, pressure, and volume of gas in a closed container). Even with scientific laws, there are often exceptions and limits to the breadth of their applicability (for instance, the gas laws are less accurate at extremely low temperatures). In the social sciences there are very few relationships which have been so thoroughly established that we would call them laws. Consequently, our theories are held tentatively rather than with certainty. They are more like road maps, which display some of the connections between major points, than like detailed topographic maps, which show every feature of the landscape.

There are also different types or levels of theories which vary in their scope or range of applicability. At the narrowest end are miniature theories which deal with very limited subareas within the field of attitude change (for instance, McGuire's (1964) theory of inoculation against persuasion). At the other extreme are broad, general orientations toward ways of thinking about and explaining attitude change (for example, learning theory approaches, and consistency theory approaches). In between are numerous mid-range theories with varying degrees of scope.

There is no classification of attitude theories which is generally agreed upon.

Shaw and Costanzo (1982) describe 38 different social psychological theories, while McGuire (1985) has presented a systematic matrix of 16 possible theoretical viewpoints concerning key processes in attitude change. It is important to realize that these theoretical approaches, though stressing different processes, can only rarely be pitted against each other in opposing predictions. Different theories sometimes make similar predictions, and often they stress different independent variables and different areas of applicability. As McGuire (1969, p. 271) put it:

> these broad theories are complementary rather than contentious (though the theorists who have advocated them are often contentious rather than complimentary).

Or to use a more-critical simile, these theories are often like ships that pass in the night, without making contact with each other (Suedfeld, 1971).

LEARNING APPROACHES TO ATTITUDE CHANGE

Learning approaches to attitudes have been the subject of much research. We have presented a summary of some of this research in Chapter 7, which dealt with the formation of attitudes. There we described seven learning processes (e.g., instrumental conditioning) which can be involved in initial attitude formation. Here we should note that any of these processes can also be involved in attitude change.

The key feature of **learning approaches** to attitude change is their stress that learning processes are responsible for attitude change. Though this may seem obvious, it has several less-obvious corollaries. First, since all learning theories are based on the principles of **reinforcement** and/or temporal **contiguity** as being responsible for learning, there is much stress on reinforcement and, to a lesser extent, on association through contiguity in explaining attitude change. Second, because learning theories emphasize **stimulus-response** connections, their application in the field of attitude change has focused much attention on the characteristics of the persuasive stimulus—particularly on the source of the message and on its content. Third, researchers with a learning orientation have tended to emphasize the learning part of the communication process (that is, attention and comprehension) more than other researchers and to be less concerned with the acceptance or yielding stage of the process (Eagly & Chaiken, 1984). Fourth, since much of learning theory has been established through research with animals, a good deal of extension and translation of concepts and procedures was often needed to make them applicable to humans and to the kind of intangible intervening variable which we call an attitude. The gap between animal learning and human attitudes has led to many questions about what extensions and translations were reasonable and proper and what conclusions could be drawn if previously supported findings with animals failed to be duplicated with humans. In a word, was it the original theories or their translations and applications which were at fault?

A final consequence of applying learning theory to human attitudes has been the profusion of approaches. There are several major competing theories of learning, and there are even more ways of translating and applying them to new situations. As a result, many different attitude researchers claim a "learning theory" orientation, but the details of their approaches often have little in common other than the underlying concern with learning, reinforcement, and S-R associations. Among the best-known theorists adopting a social learning approach to attitude change are Berkowitz (e.g., 1962), Bandura (e.g., 1973), and Byrne (1971).

Out of this profusion of approaches we can describe and illustrate only a few of the most influential ones. If you would like to read further in this area, more detailed treatments can be found in Petty and Cacioppo (1981), Lott and Lott (1985), and McGuire (1985).

Conditioning Theories of Attitude Change

One of the first authors to propose the application of conditioning and learning principles to the attitude area was Doob (1947). His approach was derived from Hullian learning theory and suggested that attitudes are a type of implicit (nonobservable) response and are learned and modified through reinforcement just like all other responses. Other researchers who have investigated attitudes within a framework of classical conditioning and/or instrumental conditioning have described their approaches in the volume by Greenwald, Brock, and Ostrom (1968). These writers' views as they pertain to attitude *formation* have been presented in Chapter 7. Here we will give three examples of the relationship of conditioning to attitude *change*.

Reward for Advocating a Position.   Scott (1959) studied this subject in a debate context, where some college students were assigned to take the side opposite to their own attitudes ("counterattitudinal advocacy"), while others argued for a position less distant from their own, and still others supported their own real viewpoint in the debate. "Winners" and "losers" were randomly determined by the experimenter, though the debaters thought the decision reflected their classmates' votes. In all conditions, the reward of winning produced attitude change toward the position which the student had advocated, while the losers showed no change in attitude as a result of participating in the debate.

Verbal Reinforcement of Opinions.   Students' existing opinions were directly reinforced in an experiment by Insko (1965). Undergraduates in a psychology course were telephoned at home by student interviewers and reinforced with comments like "good," half being rewarded for stating opinions favorable to a possible new campus festival, and half for unfavorable opinions. A week later in class the students participated in an apparently unconnected activity, filling out a long questionnaire, one item of which asked for opinions on the creation of the same proposed festival, thus providing a delayed test of attitude change in a completely different setting from the experimental manipulation. Results showed that the telephone verbal reinforcement had a significant effect on the students' attitudes. Many other studies have provided ample evidence that reinforcement can have a strong effect in modifying attitudes and opinions.

Attitude Accessibility. A modern attitude conception that relies on conditioning principles is Fazio's (1986a) viewpoint that an attitude is an association in memory between an object (e.g., horses) and an evaluation (e.g., "good"). Based on past conditioning, the strength of this association determines the degree to which the attitude will be activated if one is exposed to or thinks about the object. Two factors that have been found to increase the attitude strength are direct (rather than vicarious) experience with the attitude object, and the number of times that the attitude has been expressed (Fazio, Chen, McDonel, & Sherman, 1982). As in some other conditioning approaches, attitude strength in this system is measured in terms of the reaction time when a person is asked evaluative questions about the object—that is, a quick evaluative reaction indicates a strong attitude.

Bem's Behavioral Theory

Daryl Bem (1965) has suggested another learning approach to attitude change, stemming from Skinnerian behavioristic principles. Though he uses cognitive concepts such as beliefs, attitudes, and self-awareness, he attempts to give them rigorously objective definitions, following the behavioristic tradition. Furthermore, as previously discussed in Chapter 2, he proposes that the way that people know about their own internal processes, such as attitudes, is the same way they learn about other people's attitudes and feelings—through observation. That is, a person's cues for *self-perception* are primarily the same publicly observable responses by which (s)he perceives and evaluates the feelings and attitudes of other people.

Since we have described Bem's theory at some length in Chapter 2, we will not expand further on it here. One rather uncommon feature which it shares with dissonance theory is its emphasis that attitude change often follows from behavior change, rather than the opposite sequence which many theories suggest. However, another important aspect of Bem's theory is its critique of dissonance theory concerning the underlying reasons for attitude change (Bem, 1967). This dispute will be described when we discuss dissonance theory in Chapter 10.

Hovland's Communication Research Program

At Yale University after World War II, Carl Hovland gathered a gifted and productive group of researchers, whose work dominated the attitude area in the 1950s and continues to be highly influential to this day. This group published many volumes of research findings, the most important of which in outlining their conceptual approach was *Communication and Persuasion* (Hovland, Janis, & Kelley, 1953).

Photograph copyright 1958 by the
American Psychological Association.
Reprinted by permission.

Box 9–2   CARL HOVLAND, *Leading Persuasion Researcher*

One of the most outstanding researchers on attitude change, Carl Hovland was born in Chicago in 1912 and died an untimely death in 1961. Following a B.A. and M.A. at Northwestern, he took his Ph.D. at Yale in 1936 and joined the Yale faculty, where he remained for the rest of his life. For many years he was chairman of the psychology department and director of the Yale Communication Research Program.

During World War II, Hovland directed the Research Branch of the U.S. War Department's Information and Education Division. There he studied the effectiveness of Army training films and morale problems. His many years of communication research led to volumes on Experiments on Mass Communication, Communication and Persuasion, The Order of Presentation in Persuasion, Personality and Persuasibility, Attitude Organization and Change, *and* Social Judgment. *He was honored by election to the National Academy of Sciences, and in 1957 he was one of the first recipients of the American Psychological Association's highest honor, the Distinguished Scientific Contribution Award.*

Hovland and his coworkers were very explicit in stating that they were not presenting a systematic theory, but rather an initial framework of working assumptions about factors affecting attitude change. However, it is clear that their working assumptions derived primarily from a learning and reinforcement point of view. They likened the process of attitude change to the learning of a habit or skill. Just as with learning, they postulated, attitude change will only occur if there is (a) practice ("mental rehearsal" or thinking about the new attitude), and (b) an incentive (a reward or reinforcement) for accepting it. Also they stressed the sequential process described in Chapter 8: attention to the persuasive stimulus is necessary before there can be comprehension, and comprehension is necessary before there can be acceptance of the new attitude.

Because of their stimulus-response viewpoint, Hovland et al.'s (1953) research concentrated heavily on variables in the stimulus situation which might help to determine the amount of attitude change (the response). In particular, they studied aspects of the source of the message, many elements of the content of the message, some characteristics of the audience, and a few target behavior variables. Here we will briefly mention a few of the specific variables which they investigated and their key findings, while in the following sections four of the most important of these research topics will be described in more detail.

Source Variables.   The **credibility** of the communicator was the major source variable studied, and it was found to be positively related to degree of acceptance of the message, though not very closely related to attention, comprehension, or later retention of the message. Other studies analyzed credibility into two separate aspects: the source's *expertness* (degree of knowledge), and its *trustworthiness* (lack of intention to deceive or manipulate the audience). Later research studied the **power** of the source over the audience, and its **attractiveness**, which was operationalized in several ways, including the audience's *liking* for the source, the source's *similarity* to the audience, and its *familiarity*. The three main variables of source power, attractiveness, and credibility parallel Plato's classic behavioral-affective-cognitive distinction, and they are closely related to Kelman's (1958) three processes of attitude change; that is, compliance stems primarily from the power of the source, identification from its attractiveness, and internalization from its credibility.

Message Variables.   Effects due to the content of the message were quite extensively studied by Hovland et al. One variable which has stirred continuing interest, the presence of fear-inducing arguments in the message, is discussed below. Other message content factors studied by the Hovland group included where to place the strongest argument in a persuasive communication, and whether to use only arguments on one side of the issue or to include and refute a few of the opposing arguments. In general, this "two-sided" presentation was found to be more effective, especially with intelligent audiences or subsequent contrary messages. Related studies showed that drawing conclusions explicitly was more effective than leaving them implicit.

A great deal of work has been done on the question of whether the first side of a controversy to be presented, or the most recent side, has a persuasive advantage. This **primacy-recency** question involves two opposing messages. Early research results appeared to support a universal "law of primacy," both in debate-type situations (Lund, 1925) and in forming first impressions of other people on the basis of a few bits of information (Asch, 1946). However, Hovland's work and other related research effectively challenged this conclusion and showed that recency effects were regularly obtained under some conditions (Hovland, Mandell, et al., 1957; Anderson, 1959).

Subsequent research has shown that recency effects are more likely as the time interval between the two opposing messages is increased (Miller & Campbell, 1959; Wilson & Miller, 1968). Though these results were predicted from a learning framework, they do not seem to depend heavily on forgetting of the first message during the following time interval. In general, research on order effects has found many variables which interact with each other to determine whether primacy effects or recency effects or neither will occur (Rosnow, 1966; Anderson & Farkas,

1973). We can safely conclude that there is no universal law of primacy nor of recency in persuasion.

Audience Variables.   Personality factors which are related to persuasibility were extensively studied by Hovland et al. (1953) and by Janis, Hovland, et al. (1959). Another important audience variable which they studied is active participation in stating or making up arguments for a persuasive message. Personality and persuasibility is discussed later in this chapter, while research on active participation is summarized in Chapter 10 in the section on dissonance theory research.

Target Behavior Variables.   Several types of target behavior were also studied by the Hovland group. Persistence of attitude change was investigated in a number of studies by including repeated posttests or several groups having posttests after different periods of time. A related issue, the surprising occurrence of delayed rather than immediate attitude change—dubbed the "sleeper effect"—attracted considerable interest, and studies on this topic are described in a later section. In addition, generalization of changes beyond the specific target issue to other related topics was studied by McGuire (1960) and Rosenberg (1960). Finally, though most research concerned the direct impact of persuasion, a few early studies were directed at creating *resistance* to future persuasion (e.g., McGuire, 1964).

In summary, though Hovland and his colleagues did not present a systematic theory, their approach was very influential in expanding the interest in attitude research among U.S. psychologists. Their research was prolific and well-done, and they opened up many productive areas of inquiry. Their concepts of attention, comprehension, and acceptance have provided a fertile way of analyzing attitude change effects, even though the interrelationships of these concepts are still not fully understood.

In the next four sections of this chapter we will summarize some of the research evidence concerning four topics which have been studied mainly within a learning framework: source credibility, fear appeals in messages, audience personality and persuasibility, and persistence of attitude change.

Research on Source Credibility

Variables concerning the communication source have most often been studied by presenting a given message to several groups of subjects and telling each group that the message comes from a different source (for instance, Thomas Jefferson or Karl Marx; a Nobel Prize-winning physiologist or the director of a local YMCA). The **credibility** of a source such as these has been subdivided into two aspects: *expertness*, and *trustworthiness* or objectivity. Though both aspects of credibility are usually positively related to the amount of attitude change, the findings for expertness are typically stronger and more consistent (Hass, 1981), so we will confine this discussion mostly to the expertness aspect of credibility. In experiments, expertness is usually manipulated by ascribing to the source a high degree of knowledge, intelligence, age, prestige or social status, or a relevant professional or occupational background.

A large body of research indicates that a message from a highly credible source will produce more attitude change than one from a low-credibility source (McGuire, 1985). However, this greater acceptance of the message is not due to greater reception, for the arguments of low-credibility sources are remembered as well as those of highly credible sources. Even minimal cues about the source's credibility, such as the communicator's height or erect posture, can have some persuasive effect (Weisfeld & Beresford, 1982; Hastie, Penrod, & Pennington, 1984).

Though in general an expert source produces more opinion change, there are a number of interesting exceptions and special conditions limiting this conclusion. A source who is only somewhat more knowledgeable, older, etc., such as a somewhat older child, may have more influence than a greatly superior expert. The expertise usually must be relevant to the topic being addressed (not, for instance, an eminent physiologist giving advice on dressmaking). However, sometimes high status can increase a source's persuasiveness even in irrelevant areas (Aronson & Golden, 1962). In order for the source's expertise to be most effective, it must be known to the audience before the message is delivered—a good reason for the practice of introductions which describe the speaker's qualifications (Mills & Harvey, 1972).

Research findings suggest that people often use source credibility as a basis for accepting or rejecting message conclusions, without paying much attention to the supporting arguments (Chaiken, 1980). If the message does not contain evidence to support the conclusion, the source's credibility is apt to have a greater effect than when adequate evidence is presented. On the other hand, if there is no credibility information available, then people are forced to pay more attention to the arguments that are presented (McGuire, 1985).

The source's credibility is most likely to influence people's attitudes when they are not highly involved in the issue, whereas when people are highly involved in the issue, the credibility of the source may not increase persuasion (Johnson & Scileppi, 1969). Also, credibility alone, if not supported by cues indicating trustworthiness, is apt to have relatively little effect on many attitudes (McGinnies & Ward, 1980). A strong cue for trustworthiness, leading to greater persuasive effect, is communicators who advocate a position contrary to their own personal interests (such as a sales clerk recommending the cheaper of two products—Eagly, Wood, & Chaiken, 1978; Harmon & Coney, 1982). An important cue to lack of trustworthiness is *forewarning* of the source's intention to persuade the audience, which can produce either direct persuasion or reverse (boomerang) effects, depending on other variables. Under some circumstances, forewarning of persuasion produces anticipatory attitude change in the expected direction of the communication. Under other conditions, such as a receiver's high commitment to his or her original viewpoint, forewarning leads to resistance to the persuasive message and rehearsal of arguments favoring one's original beliefs (McGuire, 1985; Petty & Cacioppo, 1979a).

Research on Fear Appeals

One of the most provocative early studies on message content was Janis and Feshbach's (1953) experiment in which they varied the extent of fear-arousing information about tooth decay in persuasive messages about proper dental care. With three levels of fear arousal, they found that a very weak fear appeal produced the most reported change in toothbrushing practices a week later, whereas the least change was produced by the strongest fear appeal (containing gruesome pictures of diseased jaws and personalized threatening information). Their interpretation of this finding stressed that arousal of negative emotions can produce avoidance and defensive reactions to a communication.

Despite this early evidence, Madison Avenue advertising copy writers have continued to use fear appeals in abundance (avoid body odor, watch out for tattle-tale gray, beware of flaky dandruff, etc.—see Figure 9-1). And in this case, subsequent research has shown that their approach could be effective in producing the desired attitude change. In fact, the bulk of the evidence shows strong fear appeals producing more attitude change than weak ones (Higbee, 1969; Evans et al., 1970; Leventhal, 1970; Beck, 1979). Many of these studies have dealt with important real-life issues such as cutting down on smoking, using seat belts, getting chest X-rays, or taking tetanus inoculations.

To explain the conflicting findings of an occasional negative relationship between fear appeals and attitude change and the more commonly found positive relationship, **curvilinear** theories have been proposed (e.g., McGuire, 1968b). According to this viewpoint, there is an inverted-U-shaped relation between amount of fear arousal and attitude change, with the greatest attitude change at moderate fear levels. Accordingly, a positive relationship to attitude change might be found for conditions low on the fear continuum, but a negative relationship for higher fear conditions. McGuire's theory relates this curvilinear pattern to the intermediate processes of reception of and yielding to the persuasive message. Thus, at very low fear levels, audience interest and reception will be low. At higher fear levels, interest and reception will be good, and credible fear appeals will also increase yielding. However, at very high fear levels, the aversive affect created by the message motivates audience members to defensively avoid the situation and/or to discount the message—mechanisms which reduce both reception and yielding, so that attitude change is sharply lower (Axelrod & Apsche, 1982; Leventhal & Nerenz, 1983). In order to test such a theory, an independent method of scaling degrees of fear arousal in different messages is needed, but no satisfactory method of accomplishing this has yet been devised.

A curvilinear theory of fear-arousal effects also implies a number of interactions with other variables. One example of an interaction which has received some empirical support is that a higher level of fear arousal is optimal when highly specific and detailed recommendations are made concerning actions to be taken to reduce the fear—for instance, directions about where to go and what to do to get a tetanus inoculation (Leventhal, 1970; Rogers & Mewborn, 1976; Leventhal, Meyer,

FIGURE 9–1 Advertising copy writers often use scare techniques.

Source: Photograph courtesy of Public Media Center, San Francisco. Reprinted by permission.

& Nerenz, 1980). Fear appeals are also more effective if the receiver knows that his(her) compliance with the message can be monitored (Evans et al., 1981).

Another fascinating finding in this area is that fear appeals fairly often have differential effects on different dependent variables, such as beliefs, attitudes, behavioral intentions, and actual behavior (Evans et al., 1970; Leventhal, 1970). For instance, in two studies by Leventhal and his colleagues, the level of fear appeal markedly affected attitudes and behavioral intentions (to stop smoking, or to get a tetanus shot) but did not have any differential effect on the actual behavior. On the other hand, specific instructions on how to perform the recommended act did not affect subjects' intentions to do so, but did markedly increase the number of people who actually followed through on the recommendation. A combination of immediately relevant fear appeals with specific behavioral instructions had the strongest positive effects on both attitudes and actual behavior in a study by McArdle (1972).

Research on Personality and Persuasibility

Another research topic of interest concerns audience personality characteristics which are related to susceptibility to persuasion. Early work by Hovland and his colleagues sought to determine to what extent persuasibility is a general personality trait which holds across various topics and situations (Hovland et al., 1953; Janis, Hovland, et al., 1959). Their hypothesis, and the general tenor of their findings, was that there is a significant but small degree of general persuasibility which is topic-free.

Early studies of persuasibility searched for linear relationships between attitude change and personality traits such as self-esteem (Janis & Field, 1959). More recently, McGuire (1968b) proposed a more complex theory involving the multiple processes which mediate between personality characteristics and attitude change— particularly reception (including both attention and comprehension), and yielding (acceptance). We have referred to this theory briefly above in relation to fear appeals, and also in Chapter 8 in discussing these mediating processes as some of the dependent variables of communication studies. The complexity of the theory stems from the fact that any personality characteristic (such as intelligence or self-esteem) which is positively related to reception is expected to be negatively related to yielding, and vice versa. Thus, a more intelligent person may comprehend a message better than a less intelligent one, but be less inclined to yield to it.

An example of this predicted relationship and the expected combined result of reception and yielding on opinion change is shown in Figure 9-2. Though McGuire suggests that very simple or very complex messages might produce linear relationships to the amount of opinion change, the curvilinear, inverted-U relationship between self-esteem and opinion change is the one which would be expected to occur in the majority of situations, rather than the linear relationship sought by earlier investigators.

There is a rather large body of research reporting interaction effects which

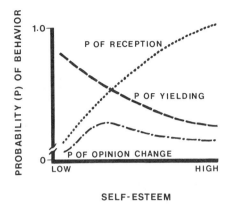

FIGURE 9-2
Predicted relationship of the personality variable of self-esteem to the mediating processes of reception and yielding and to the resulting amount of opinion change.

Source: Adapted from McGuire (1968b, p. 1151).

are supportive of McGuire's viewpoint (e.g., Lehmann, 1970). For example, Nisbett and Gordon (1967) showed that simple but poorly substantiated messages produced most attitude change in lower self-esteem subjects, whereas complex but well-substantiated messages were most effective with high self-esteem subjects. In addition to self-esteem, other frequently studied personal characteristics such as anxiety, dogmatism, and intelligence should be expected to show curvilinear relationships to amount of attitude change.

There has also been much research on gender differences in persuasibility, where the early findings showed women generally to be more persuasible than men (McGuire, 1969). However, later research has demonstrated that finding to be an artifact of the types of topics or issues usually used in influenceability studies. When the studies concern "feminine" issues (ones in which women have more interest and knowledge), men have been found to be more persuasible, and vice versa for male-oriented topics (Sistrunk & McDavid, 1971; Cacioppo & Petty, 1980; Karabenick, 1983).

Research on Persistence of Attitude Change

In Chapter 8 we discussed research on retention of both message content and attitude change, so we will not repeat that information here. A learning theory approach postulates that attitude change should be based on the new information learned or on rewards or incentives presented to the audience member. Thus it implies that there should normally be a positive relationship between the amount of message content remembered and the amount of attitude change that persists over time. However, the time course and the shape of the decay curves for content memory and attitude change are often so different that it is clear that there is no simple relationship between message learning and attitude change (McGuire, 1985).

This pattern of findings has cast doubt on the adequacy of a learning theory approach to attitude change and has encouraged work on several of the cognitive approaches that we will discuss in Chapter 10. Also, research on the persistence of attitude change has shown that it interacts in complex ways with many other variables such as source, message, medium, or audience characteristics. For instance, attitudes that people consider personally unimportant change more over time than ones that are important to their holders (Krosnick, 1988). One of the most interesting of these interaction effects involves a surprising interaction of time passage and source credibility, which has been quite extensively studied and named the "sleeper effect."

The **sleeper effect** refers to delayed attitude change in the direction advocated by a noncredible communicator (such as a convict arguing for lighter court sentences). Such a noncredible source or, alternatively, inclusion of a warning that the persuasive message is not necessarily factual, is considered a **discounting cue** that signals the receiver not to be influenced by the message. Early studies (e.g., Kelman & Hovland, 1953) found that the amount of attitude change produced by a credible source decreased over a period of several weeks, but that attitude change produced by the same message from a noncredible source *increased* and eventually reached the same level as that for the credible source. This effect was found to be due, not to the subjects' forgetting the source per se, but apparently to their ceasing to connect the source with the message content (i.e., "dissociating" the message content from the source).

These "sleeper effect" findings were fascinating because they were originally unexpected and yet seemed plausible on further consideration. However, the sleeper effect was almost "laid to rest" by several studies in the 1970s which failed to replicate the finding (e.g., Gillig & Greenwald, 1974). These studies showed that, though a gradual decrease in attitude change produced by a credible source is customary, a delayed *increase* in attitude change produced by a noncredible source is a rare and fragile phenomenon (Pratkanis, Greenwald, Leippe, & Baumgardner, 1988). More recently, though, careful research has revived the sleeper effect, demonstrating that such delayed increases in attitude change can be found, at least if (a) the persuasive message is strong and plausible, (b) the discounting cue is a strong warning that the message content is inaccurate, and (c) the discounting cue is delivered *after* the message itself, thus allowing the message a better chance of reception and acceptance (Gruder et al., 1978; Cook, Gruder, Hennigan, & Flay, 1979; Greenwald, Pratkanis, Leippe, & Baumgardner, 1986; Pratkanis et al., 1988). Under those conditions any initial persuasive effect of the message is suppressed, but later on it is apt to be displayed in delayed attitude change in the direction advocated by the message. Pratkanis et al. (1988) have interpreted this effect, not in terms of dissociation of the message and the discounting cue, but as being due to the faster forgetting of the discounting cue—thus keeping the sleeper effect firmly within a learning theory framework.

Evaluation of Learning Approaches

As mentioned earlier, there is no single unified learning theory of attitude change, and each of the approaches we have discussed is at best a partial, incomplete theory. Some, like the Hovland group's approach, are not theories at all in the technical sense of the word. Despite their common characteristics, these approaches do not really build together toward a unified theory. They differ among themselves in many details, such as their procedures and operational definitions of their concepts; they apply most clearly to different types of situations; and they all fail to cover some other types of attitude change situations.

McGuire, who was a member of the Hovland group of researchers, has concluded that learning-theory approaches to attitude change may have been "a fertile error" (McGuire, 1969, p. 266). They were fertile in suggesting areas and procedures for research, but they have often been wrong in the details of their experimental predictions. Clearly, theories of conditioning and learning can explain many attitude change phenomena, and particularly also findings in the area of attitude formation. Yet even in this area of their greatest applicability, they are vulnerable to the criticism that subjects' *awareness* of the conditioning procedures may be responsible for much of the effect obtained. If so, then cognitive or judgment theories would be more appropriate ways of understanding and explaining attitude changes. In a recent review, Jones (1985, p. 75) has stressed the value of learning and reinforcement concepts as providing "an ever-present alternative to more subtle, cognitive explanations."

We turn now to a discussion of judgment theories, and in the following chapter we will examine cognitive theories of attitude change in some detail.

JUDGMENT APPROACHES TO ATTITUDE CHANGE

Judgment theories are ones which give central attention to how people make judgments about other people and objects in their environment. They postulate that all stimuli can be arranged in a meaningful order on various dimensions (hot-cold, good-bad, etc.), and they aim to describe the principles according to which people make such comparative judgments.

Probably the best-known judgment theory is Helson's (1964) **adaptation level theory**. Its central concept, the **adaptation level**, is a person's psychological neutral point on any given dimension—that is, the level that (s)he has gotten used to, or "adapted" to. Other stimuli are judged in terms of how far they depart from this adaptation level. A concrete example will clearly illustrate that such judgments are relative. If you simultaneously put your left hand in a bucket of cold water and your right hand in a bucket of hot water, each hand will gradually adapt to the temperature of the water that it is in, with the result that the temperature will soon feel less extreme than at first. Then, if you take both hands out and put them in a pail of water at an intermediate temperature, your left hand will feel the water as being warm while your right hand will feel it as cool. This example is dramatic because we usually are adapted to only one level at a time, so experiencing two apparently different temperatures in the same pail of water vividly demonstrates that such judgments are relative.

The adaptation level constitutes an **anchor** or reference point to which stimuli are compared. When a stimulus is judged as more different from the adaptation level than it actually is, as in the water temperature judgments above, we have a **contrast effect**. On the other hand, sometimes a stimulus may be judged as closer to the adaptation level than it actually is, and that is termed an **assimilation effect**. Most of the research on adaptation level theory has dealt with judgments of physical stimuli on dimensions such as temperature, weight, brightness, or noise of objects. However, the same principles apply to judging the friendliness, intelligence, attractiveness, or any other characteristic of people, or aspects of abstract concepts, such as the humor of a story. For instance, Kenrick and Gutierres (1980) demonstrated contrast effects in ratings of the attractiveness of women after the male raters had been exposed to pictures of extremely beautiful women—e.g., after watching *My Three Angels*, men rated pictures of average-looking potential dates as less attractive than if they had not watched the TV program.

Adaptation level theory clearly illustrates the approach of judgment theory. However, since it has rarely been applied in attitude change research, we will move on to another judgment theory that has been used more extensively in attitude studies.

Sherif and Hovland's Social Judgment Theory

We have described the structural aspects of this theory at some length in Chapter 4. To recapitulate briefly, Sherif and his coworkers have presented the concept of three attitude latitudes—the latitudes of acceptance, rejection, and noncommitment. They have also concluded that the size of a person's latitude of rejection on an attitude issue is the best indicator of his(her) ego-involvement in that issue.

The attitude-change aspects of the theory, as presented in Sherif and Hovland's (1961) major theoretical statement, emphasize the principles of assimilation and of contrast. The theory postulates, first, that a person's own attitude on any given issue serves as an anchor, or reference point, for judging other people's attitudes or persuasive messages on that issue; and second, that the boundaries of the individual's latitudes of acceptance and rejection will determine what kind and amount of attitude change will result from exposure to persuasive messages. Regarding attitude change, the principle of assimilation states that social stimuli such as persuasive messages which are *within a person's latitude of acceptance* will be assimilated: that is, they will produce some attitude change in the direction advocated. On the other hand, the principle of contrast states that social stimuli which are *within a person's latitude of rejection* will be contrasted: that is, they will produce no attitude change or else attitude change opposite to the direction advocated (a "boomerang effect"). The relationship of amount of attitude change to the discrepancy between the person's attitude and the position advocated by the message will be positive in the latitude of acceptance and negative in the latitude of rejection—a curvilinear relationship (Freedman, 1964). Both assimilation and contrast effects on *judgment* will be greater for highly ego-involved individuals than for uninvolved ones, but their effects on *attitude change* will be smaller for involved individuals.

Research Related to Social Judgment Theory

Chapter 4 presented an example of assimilation and contrast effects involving *judgment* of the positions of U.S. presidential candidates on the issue of school busing in relation to the respondent's position on that issue. Here we will briefly describe some of the social judgment theory research that involves *attitude change*. The theoretical topics which have received most research attention are the discrepancy of the message from the recipient's position and the ego-involvement of the recipient.

Message Discrepancy. When a persuasive message is quite discrepant from the recipient's own attitude, (s)he may change the attitude, or (s)he may resolve the incongruity in one or more of several other ways: perceptual distortion of the message, derogation of the source, increased counterarguing, disparagement of the message, or under-recall of its contents. Several studies have shown the functional equivalence of these mechanisms, indicating that they may be used interchangeably as alternatives to attitude change, or they may be used in combination, depending on the situation (McGuire, 1969; Sears & Abeles, 1969).

Two different relationships have been postulated to hold between message discrepancy and attitude change. Some researchers have predicted and found an approximately linear rising relationship (e.g., Zimbardo, 1960; Eagly, 1967). However, the more frequent finding is the inverted-U curve predicted by social judgment theory, with the curve's downturn occurring in the latitude of rejection (e.g., Hovland, Harvey, & Sherif, 1957; Peterson & Koulack, 1969). Since the peak of the curve usually occurs at a high discrepancy level, the studies that obtained roughly linear findings may not have used messages which were extreme enough to produce a downturn in influence. With either linear or curvilinear findings, the amount of attitude change obtained is apt to be markedly less than the amount advocated by the message, though in the same direction.

An interaction between message discrepancy and source credibility has often been found, as predicted by both social judgment theory and consistency theories. The rationale behind this interaction is that source derogation and message disparagement are less likely with a highly credible source, and therefore attitude change continues to increase up to higher levels of message discrepancy than it does with a less-credible source who can be more easily disparaged.

Figure 9-3 illustrates this pattern of findings in a study where the same basic message was attributed to a Nobel Prize-winning physiologist (the highly credible source) for half of the subjects, or to the director of the Fort Worth YMCA (the less-credible source) for the other half (Bochner & Insko, 1966). The message gave reasons to support the view that the average young adult needed only a given number of hours of sleep a night, and nine different groups of subjects received messages saying that the number of hours needed was either 8, 7, 6, or on down to 2, 1, or 0 hours per night (whereas the average subject had indicated that 7.9 hours per night were needed). Consistent with the theory, both communicators had inverted-U-shaped curves of attitude change, and the peak of the curve for the high-credibility communicator was at a greater discrepancy than for the lower-credibility communicator. Note, however, that for both message sources the amount of attitude change was positive, and that for all but the small discrepancies it was much less than the amount advocated (peaking at roughly 2 hours of change in the recipient's belief about how much sleep was needed). In this experiment, even with the most-extreme messages, there was no boomerang effect leading to inverse attitude change. However, boomerang effects are sometimes found with very extreme messages, or when the source and the recipient are on opposite sides of a psychological neutral point, as with a Democratic communicator soliciting votes from a Republican audience (Lange & Fishbein, 1983).

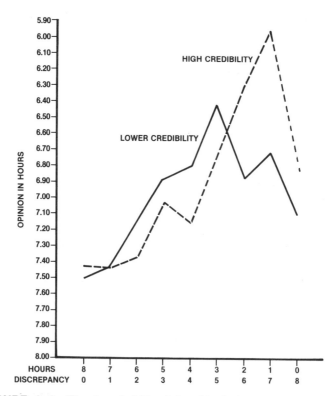

FIGURE 9–3 The inverted-U relationship between message discrepancy and attitude change, for high- and lower-credibility communicators.

Source: Reprinted from Bochner & Insko (1966, p. 618). Copyright 1966 by the American Psychological Association. Reprinted by permission.

Some research findings have not supported the predictions of social judgment theory concerning message discrepancy. For example, Eagly (1974) was unable to replicate Bochner and Insko's (1966) results, though using rather similar messages and procedures. However, neither study's dependent variable measure was exactly identical to the belief advocated in its persuasive message, and this difference may have been crucial to the obtained results.

Ego-Involvement. Research on ego-involvement has had rather mixed results. Though some relationships to attitude change have been found, the specific details of Sherif's theory have not been well-supported, and many of the research results seem contradictory.

Zimbardo (1960) attempted to clarify this situation by distinguishing between **issue** involvement (interest and concern about the issue) and **response** involvement (concern about making a desirable response—appearing well-adjusted, acceptable to the experimenter, etc.). Zimbardo's results showed that high response involvement produced more attitude change. This finding is opposite to Sherif's theory, but it appears that the theory really concerns issue involvement rather than response involvement. Chaiken and Stangor (1987) have suggested a still finer breakdown of types of involvement, citing findings that people for whom the topic of a message is important ("personal relevance") may often be more open-minded and ready to be persuaded by good arguments than Sherif's issue-involvement hypothesis suggests (Petty & Cacioppo, 1984; Leippe & Elkin, 1987). However, such individuals are still somewhat biased by their initial attitudes (Howard-Pitney, Borgida, & Omoto, 1986), and people who have a strong vested interest in their initial opinion ("position involvement") generally confirm Sherif's hypothesis of low attitude change (Sivacek & Crano, 1982; Abelson, 1986).

There is active debate in the research literature about many different proposed ways of conceptualizing involvement and about their effects on the amount of attitude change (Johnson & Eagly, 1990; Petty & Cacioppo, 1990). Though these new concepts seem plausible and useful, they are increasingly *ad hoc* in nature and distant from Sherif's original theory.

The topic of ego-involvement is rather closely related to the concept of commitment, which we will discuss in the section on dissonance theory in the next chapter (Rhine & Polowniak, 1971). People who are high in issue involvement (especially if it is position involvement) are also high in commitment to their opinion on the issue. Ego-involvement is also an important variable in the cognitive-response approaches to attitude change that are discussed in the next chapter.

Evaluation of Social Judgment Theory

Appraising this theory fairly is not easy. On one hand, it has stimulated quite a bit of research, though many studies were aimed at resolving controversies between it and dissonance theory. Its concepts of latitudes of acceptance and rejection have proved useful in resolving disputes between dissonance theory and self-perception theory (Fazio, Zanna, & Cooper, 1977). Also, much of the social judgment research has dealt with important real-world issues in a field setting (e.g., a referendum on prohibition in Oklahoma, and voter attitudes in a presidential election). On the other hand, its assimilation and contrast principles can also be derived from consistency theories and from dissonance theory, as can some of its attitude change predictions. Social judgment theory as it concerns *attitude change* is quite narrow in scope, dealing mainly with the variables of the person's ego-involvement and the message's discrepancy from the person's attitude, whereas dissonance theory has the advantage of much broader applicability and inclusion of additional variables like amount of incentive and degree of perceived choice. Also, much of the theory has been empirically derived from the results of experiments, so it has some undesirable gaps, inconsistencies, and *ad hoc* aspects.

The theory has been more successful in dealing with human judgment than with attitude change. In general, studies are consistent with the theory in showing that people's own attitudes influence their judgments about the extremity of social stimuli, but they have not supported many of the theory's more specific predictions about attitude change (Zavalloni & Cook, 1965; Eiser & Stroebe, 1972). In fact, it is possible that judgmental assimilation or contrast effects may sometimes substitute for the attitude change effects predicted by the theory—for instance, a large assimilation effect could make a message appear identical to one's own opinion and thus prevent the need for any attitude change (Lammers & Becker, 1980).

The relation found between attitude change and message discrepancy has most often been the curvilinear one predicted by social judgment theory, but there are many exceptions in the literature, and the theory's postulates about the latitudes of acceptance and rejection as determining the effects of discrepancy on attitude change do not seem to be supported (Eagly, 1981). In the area of ego-involvement the theory is somewhat confusing in predicting opposite effects of involvement on judgment and on attitude change, and predictions about involvement have suffered many set-backs in experimental studies, leading to a rash of *ad hoc* concepts and modifications of the theory. In applied research, however, Varela (1971) has claimed good success in using Sherif's notion of the latitude of acceptance in producing planned attitude change—for instance, in creating a script by which salesmen could persuade resistant customers to buy more lavishly.

All in all, despite social judgment theory's intriguing aspects and the research that it has generated, it has not yet established a claim to a leading place in the attitude change area.

Other Judgment Theories

Two more recent judgment theories that pertain to attitudes and opinions are *perspective theory* (Upshaw, 1969) and *accentuation theory* (Eiser & Stroebe, 1972; Eiser & van der Pligt, 1984). Both of these theories view assimilation and contrast effects in judgment as shifts in the way that an object or issue is *described*, rather than in how it is actually perceived. By contrast, social judgment theory and adaptation level theory share the view that assimilation and contrast represent fundamental changes in how a person perceives an object or issue. More details about these theories can be found in Petty and Cacioppo (1981).

SUMMARY

The topic of attitude change has generated much more research than other aspects of attitudes, inspiring a profusion of competing theories. This chapter has discussed many of the methodological problems that are met in attitude research, such as demand characteristics, experimenter effects, subject effects, and problems related to use of deception. However, alternative research designs and attitude measurement methods can often be used in order to overcome those problems and obtain more valid data.

Though all current theories of attitude change have serious limitations and none has achieved a predominant position, they still have an important role to play. Theories guide our research efforts, provide a context for understanding observed facts, and help us to predict future events. Theories are always held tentatively and never considered proven in any final sense, though they may be disproved by contrary evidence. The many theories discussed in this and the following chapter are largely complementary—i.e., they often have different areas of applicability, and they rarely make directly opposing predictions.

The many different *learning* approaches to attitude change have generated a great deal of research. They all stress stimulus-response connections, the importance of reinforcement or contiguity in learning, and extension or translation of concepts from animal learning experiments. Among the important topics studied within this research tradition are the credibility of the communication *source*, order effects and the use of fear appeals in the *message*, the persuasibility of *audience* members, and the *target behavior* of persistent, long-lasting attitude change. The various learning approaches to attitude change conflict with each other in many details and do not approach the status of a unified theory. Though they have been fertile in stimulating research on attitude change as well as attitude formation, many of their specific predictions have not been supported.

Judgment approaches to attitude change focus on the principles by which people make judgments by placing objects along any given dimension. The major example is Sherif and Hovland's social judgment theory, which has been used to study some important real-world issues, though it is quite narrow in scope. It has generated a good deal of research on message discrepancy and ego-involvement, but enough of this research has been nonsupportive that the theory cannot be considered a primary one in the attitude area.

10

Attitude Change
Cognitive Theories and Research

Americans have, more than any other people I know, a willingness to change their opinions.—Gunnar Myrdal.

Most of our so-called reasoning consists in finding arguments for going on believing as we already have.—James Harvey Robinson.

It requires ages to destroy a popular opinion.—Voltaire.

Attitudes can sometimes change very rapidly, whereas in other situations they may prove very resistant to change. It is the goal of theories of attitude change to define the conditions under which attitudes will change and the ways in which this will occur. It is unlikely that any single theory will ever provide all of these answers, and our current theories are merely first approximations to the answers we are seeking.

Before we become too disillusioned with the state of our current theoretical knowledge, it may be well to recall a statement by Thomas Edison: "I have constructed *three thousand* different theories in connection with the electric light. . . . Yet in only two cases did my experiments prove the truth of my theory."

In that spirit of continual searching for closer approximations of the truth, this chapter discusses several kinds of cognitive theories of attitude change—ones stressing consistency or dissonance or reactance as explanatory variables, ones emphasizing people's cognitive responses to persuasive messages, and attitude change research stemming from attribution theories.

CONSISTENCY THEORIES

Over the years, **consistency theories** of attitude change have drawn a great deal of attention and inspired much research. These theories are, first of all, cognitive theories; that is, they emphasize the importance of people's beliefs and ideas. As their name implies, their key feature is the principle that people try to maintain consistency among their beliefs, attitudes, and behaviors. Awareness of one's own inconsistency is viewed as an uncomfortable situation which every person is motivated to escape. Thus, attitude change should result if individuals receive new information which is inconsistent with their previous viewpoints or if existing inconsistencies in their beliefs and attitudes are pointed out to them.

Consistency theories view people as essentially thoughtful and rational, adjusting their attitudes and behavior in accordance with incoming information. However, they do not assume a strict logical consistency, but rather a value- and emotion-tinged "**psycho-logic,**" to use Abelson and Rosenberg's (1958) clever term. For instance, strict mathematical logic does not lead to the conclusion that "My enemy's enemy is my friend," but psycho-logic does (McGuire, 1969). Also, consistency theories have room for such "illogical" ways of maintaining consistency as **denial** of the truth of new information which conflicts with a person's present viewpoints, or searching for supportive data to **bolster** present attitudes when they have been challenged by new information (Abelson, 1959).

The original idea of consistency theory is usually credited to Fritz Heider's (1946) short paper, which he followed with a major book twelve years later (Heider, 1958). In the meantime, Festinger (1957) had launched dissonance theory, which is a form of consistency theory, but which is sufficiently different that we will discuss it separately in the following section. Soon many other variants of consistency notions arose so that, just as with learning theory, there sometimes seem to be as many different consistency theories as there are consistency theorists. The major ones which we will discuss in this section are Heider's balance theory and Osgood and Tannenbaum's (1955) congruity theory. More detailed information on these and other consistency theories can be found in books by West and Wicklund (1980) and Shaw and Costanzo (1982).

Heider's Balance Theory

Heider's theory concerns the way in which people perceive other people, objects, and ideas in their environment. For simplicity, he limits his discussion to three elements: the perceiver, P; another person, O; and some object or idea, X. Between each pair of elements there can be two types of relationships: a liking relationship, L (either positive or negative); or a unit relationship, U (also either positive or negative). The liking relationship is self-explanatory; the unit relationship refers to elements that are perceived as belonging together, for instance, due to ownership of one by the other, or similarity, or membership in the same group, etc.

With three elements in a system and either a positive or a negative relationship between each pair of elements, there are eight possible patterns. These eight patterns are shown in Figure 10-1. The characteristics of the relationships determine whether the pattern is balanced or unbalanced. A **balanced** state is one in which the relationships are in harmony so that there is no cognitive stress in the perceiver's view of the system, and consequently the system is stable and resists change. Conversely, an **unbalanced** system is unstable because it produces psychological tension in the perceiver which pushes toward change in the perceived

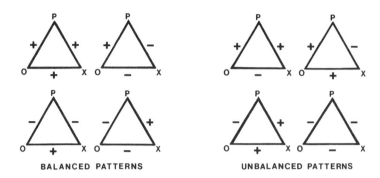

BALANCED PATTERNS   UNBALANCED PATTERNS

FIGURE 10–1   Balanced and unbalanced patterns according to Heider's theory. The lines between elements represent either liking or unit relationships. Positive relationships are shown by +, negative relationships by −.

relationships. Specifically, triadic systems are balanced when they have an odd number of positive relationships (either 3 or 1); otherwise they are unbalanced. As shown in Figure 10-1, the system is balanced if all three relationships are positive (P likes O, P likes X, O likes X) or if only one is positive (e.g., P likes O, P dislikes X, O dislikes X). However, when two relationships are positive and one negative (e.g., P likes O, P likes X, O dislikes X), the situation is cognitively uncomfortable and presses toward change. The definition of balance is less clear when all three relationships are negative (P dislikes O, P dislikes X, O dislikes X), but Heider states that this situation is unstable, so it is usually also considered as unbalanced.

Heider also discusses *dyadic* situations involving either two people or one person and one object. He states that balance exists if both the liking and the unit relationship have the same sign (e.g., P owns X, and P likes X). Also, with two people, balance requires that liking or disliking be reciprocated (that is, P likes O and O likes P is balanced; P likes O and O dislikes P is unbalanced). Again, unbalanced states "induce" or press for a change toward balance.

Heider's theory has been very influential in stimulating other cognitive consistency approaches. Its greatest limitation is its rather extreme degree of simplicity. It has no provision for degrees of liking or for degrees of balance. Systems with more than three elements are not considered. In the *triadic* system, only unidirectional relationships are discussed (e.g., from P to O, but not from O to P) and the possibility of having both liking and unit relationships between a single pair of elements is not allowed. The opposites of liking and unit relationships have different implications which the theory does not consider: disliking is negative, whereas lack of a unit relationship is neutral in character. Also there is no specification of *which* changes will be made in order to restore balance in any given situation.

Some other theorists have modified Heider's basic formulation. Most notably, Cartwright and Harary (1956) applied mathematical graph theory to problems of cognitive balance and made many valuable revisions in Heider's theory. In particular, they extended it to any number of elements, allowed nonreciprocated relationships and different types of relationships simultaneously, took neutral relationships into consideration, and presented a way to determine degrees of balance. Feather (1967) used some of the same improvements suggested by Cartwright and Harary, and applied his more precise theory specifically to persuasive communication and resulting attitude change. Wiest (1965) quantified each of the three relationships between P, O, and X on a 7-point scale and used Heider's principles to derive a complex "tetrahedron" model of balance, which has received good support in empirical research by Tashakkori and Insko (1981).

Despite the influential impact of Heider's thinking, his theory has not generated a great deal of research. In part this has been due to its roughness and lack of precision, the same factors that stimulated revisions and extensions of the theory. The most common form of research in this area has been to obtain ratings or other indications of the pleasantness or unpleasantness of hypothetical situations to test the theory's underlying postulate that balanced situations are more pleasant than unbalanced ones. This research has not been consistently supportive, and it has suggested a number of needed revisions in the theory (e.g., Morrissette, 1958; Price, Harburg, & Newcomb, 1966).

The most important findings from this research have demonstrated that people have other cognitive preferences (or biases—cf. Chapter 2) that are often just as strong or stronger than their preference for consistency. Specifically, people tend to prefer (a) **positivity** in personal relationships (i.e., a positive P-O relation), and (b) **agreement** rather than disagreement of opinions (i.e., the same sign for the P-X and O-X relations); and either of these two tendencies can often override the tendency to prefer balanced cognitive structures (Zajonc, 1968b; Sears & Whitney, 1973). For instance, contrary to balance theory, people may often disagree with their friends, find their opponents likable, or be pleased that an opponent agrees with them. Recent research has shown that the positivity or attraction preference is common because it is the simplest of these three cognitive tendencies, while agreement is somewhat more complex, and balance is the most complex of the three (Cottrell, 1975; Mower-White, 1979; Cacioppo & Petty, 1981a).

Another kind of revision to Heider's theory has been proposed by Rosenberg and Abelson (1960; Rosenberg, 1960). They gave a clearcut classification of different ways of resolving imbalance and predicted the order in which these methods would be used. Their general principle is that the easiest ways of restoring balance will be tried first and used most frequently, and they presented experimental evidence supporting this principle (Rosenberg & Abelson, 1960). In addition, Rosenberg (1960) emphasized the importance of consistency between the cognitive and the affective components of an attitude. Whenever these two components are not consistent, Rosenberg postulated, a homeostatic process will operate to bring them back into equilibrium. Several experiments have shown that a change in either the cognitive or affective component can produce a change in the other component (e.g., Carlson, 1956). More recently, Chaiken and Baldwin (1981) have used degree of affective-cognitive consistency as an index of well-defined attitudes. We have discussed research findings on affective-cognitive consistency of attitudes at greater length in Chapter 4.

Osgood and Tannenbaum's Congruity Theory

Among consistency theories, Osgood and Tannenbaum (1955) have been unique in the degree of quantification of their approach. They have measured attitudes by means of the evaluative dimension of the semantic differential (see Chapter 3), and they have made precise predictions about the direction and amount of attitude change. However, in compensation for its increased precision, the theory has a narrower scope than most other approaches. It deals solely with the results of communications in which a source (S) makes an evaluative assertion about some attitude object (O), and its predictions are based on the **congruity**—i.e., the degree of similarity—of an individual's evaluation of the source, the object, and the message (M).

An example will help to clarify the details of this approach. Let us suppose that the U.S. President (S) said something favorable about Fidel Castro (O). The attitude toward each of these men which is held by a particular individual must have been previously measured, normally on a scale from $+3$ to -3. If the person's prior attitude toward the source is different from his attitude toward the object, the theory makes several predictions:

1. The person's attitudes toward *both* the source and the object will change (rather than only the attitude toward the object, as many theories would expect).
2. The amount of change in each attitude will be inversely related to the polarization (extremity) of the attitude. In other words, the more extreme attitude will change less than the milder attitude.
3. If S said something good about O, the person's final attitudes toward both S and O will be the same.
4. If S said something bad about O, the person's final attitudes toward S and O will be equidistant from zero (one positive and one negative).

In our example, if the person's prior attitude toward the President was $+1$ and toward Castro was -2, and the message was favorable, the final equilibrium point would be -1, with the rating of the President decreasing two points and the rating of Castro increasing one point. The same result would occur if Castro had said something good about the President. However, if one said something bad about the other, then their ratings would end up on opposite sides of zero, the President at $+1\frac{2}{3}$ and Castro at $-1\frac{2}{3}$. (The fact that, in the latter case, both ratings would increase following an unfavorable assertion is one of the most paradoxical consequences of the theory.)

Congruity theory indicates that this amount of attitude change will occur as the result of a single communication, though it would not be expected to happen instantaneously. However, the theory also has some escape hatches. One is the *correction for incredulity*, which becomes necessary when a communication tries to bridge too large a discrepancy in attitudes (e.g., "U.S. President praises world Communist conspiracy," or "the Pope condemns official Catholic doctrine"). In such instances, an incredulous recipient of the message will just reject it as false. Another correction is the *assertion constant*, which is necessary because attitudes toward the object of a message have been found to change somewhat more than attitudes toward the source (about ⅙ of a point more, according to the findings of Tannenbaum, 1953). Further details about the theory and formulas for computing the attitude change may be found in Kiesler et al. (1969).

How adequate is the theory? On one hand, with the corrections mentioned above, Tannenbaum (1953) found a correlation of $+.91$ between the predicted and observed attitude change in response to specially made-up newspaper stories—nearly perfect prediction. On the other hand, later research has shown that the theory does better at predicting the *relative amount* of change of attitudes toward S and O than the absolute amount of change (Tannenbaum, 1967). Also the extensive research literature on "prestige suggestion" has demonstrated many other factors, in addition to the prestige of the source, which can affect the amount of attitude change. For example, Rokeach and Rothman (1965) showed that considering the importance of S and O to the message recipient could markedly improve the predictions of attitude change. Similarly, Kerrick (1958) showed that the theory predicted better when the prestigeful source was relevant to the topic of the message than when the source wasn't relevant (e.g., a professional football star commenting on American foreign policy). The artificial simplicity of the theory in not allowing for degrees of positiveness or negativeness in the message is another major limitation.

In spite of these limitations, congruity theory seems to have performed quite well in its narrow goal of predicting attitude change in response to a persuasive communication from a relevant source (Tannenbaum, 1967).

Research on Consistency Principles

If we focus on the general ideas underlying consistency theories, rather than the specific details of a particular version, we can find many areas where consistency theory has proved fruitful in research and applied work. For instance, consistency principles have been used to explain attitudes toward political candidates (Kinder, 1978), jurors' confidence in their verdicts (Fischoff, 1979), and international attitudes of people from different nations (Moore, 1979). Cialdini (1988) has cited consistency as one of the six central principles that direct human behavior—a principle which salesmen, advertisers, and fund raisers use extensively in trying to influence you and me.

The Foot-in-the-Door Effect. One well-established application of consistency principles which salesmen and charitable organizations frequently use is the foot-in-the-door phenomenon (named for the old door-to-door salesman's trick of putting a foot in the door to prevent it from being closed and thus allow time for completion of the sales pitch and promotion of a sale). The principle involved is that if you can persuade an individual to perform a small requested action, consistency pressures and a feeling of commitment will make it more likely that the person will later perform a larger request of the same general sort. The initial research in this area by Freedman and Fraser (1966) had volunteers go door to door, asking people to display a tiny sign saying "Be a safe driver" in their window (the small action). Since it was such a trivial request, almost all of them did so. Two weeks later, a different volunteer came by and asked them to allow a very large and unattractive billboard saying "DRIVE CAREFULLY" to be installed on their front lawn. Over three-quarters of them complied with this large request, compared to only 17% of a control group who had not received the first small request. In another condition where the initial request was to sign a petition supporting "keeping California beautiful" (an entirely different topic), about half of the people consented to erection of the DRIVE CAREFULLY sign. Since the small-request groups complied with both of the large requests so much more than the control group did, the authors concluded that performing the small request had changed their self-image, and that they complied with the large request because of a pressure to be consistent with their new self-image as someone who supported public-spirited campaigns.

Reviews of many later foot-in-the-door studies have shown that the effect, though not always easy to create, does often increase compliance with large requests; and research has supported the consistency-based explanation of the effect in terms of changes in the individual's self-image (DeJong, 1979; Beaman et al., 1983). For instance, people whose initial compliance is explicitly labeled as helpful or generous become even more likely to accede to the later large request. However, it is also possible that performing the initial small request serves as a commitment, which in turn induces later consistent behavior without any necessary change in self-image.

Liking for the Source of a Message. According to consistency principles, one's degree of liking for a person who is the source of a persuasive message should be positively related to the amount of one's resulting attitude change. In general, many studies have provided support for the theory by reporting such findings (e.g., Janis, 1983). However, a number of exceptions have also been found which fit better into other theoretical frameworks (McGuire, 1983).

One exception which follows an adaptation-level type of pattern is the "praise from a stranger" phenomenon. Praise from a stranger has more effect than praise from a family member or friend, probably because it is more novel and unexpected. Following the same principle, criticism has more impact when it comes from a friend than from a stranger (e.g., A. Miller et al., 1980). Aronson and Linder (1965) have suggested a gain-loss miniature theory of interpersonal attraction, specifying that an *increase* in praise from another person will produce greater liking for that person than will continuing high levels of praise, while a decrease in praise will lead to much lower liking.

Another exception to the normal relationship between liking and persuasiveness is the case of a disagreeable communicator delivering an unpopular message— a situation which follows dissonance-theory predictions (see next section). More acceptance of unpopular messages may be produced by a disliked source than by an attractive one (presumably because liking for the source cannot be used as a reason for listening and therefore dissonance is reduced by increasing the acceptance of the message). For example, Army reservists were persuaded to eat fried grasshoppers—definitely a counterattitudinal behavior—by an officer who behaved in an unpleasant, officious manner or a pleasant, friendly manner. Though equal numbers of men ate the disliked food in the two conditions, the men who did so for the unpleasant communicator showed more increase in liking for the grasshoppers than those who ate them for the pleasant communicator (Zimbardo, Weisenberg, Firestone, & Levy, 1965).

Similarity of the Source.   Just as with liking, source-audience similarity normally tends to produce more attitude change, and that is one reason that so many TV commercials now use testimonials from average-appearing people, who are presumably like the viewers, rather than from celebrities (Simons, Berkowitz, & Moyer, 1970; Stoneman & Brody, 1981). However, various exceptions to this principle have also been demonstrated. In the area of race relations, many studies have been directed to the issue of whether ethnic similarity or attitudinal similarity ("race or belief") is more important in determining liking for and persuasion by another person (e.g., Robinson & Insko, 1969). The results show that attitudinal similarity is more important for abstract evaluation of another person, but ethnic similarity carries more weight in determining behavioral acceptance; however, attitudinal similarity has gained increasing weight in the U.S. in recent years (Insko, Nacoste, & Moe, 1983).

It is also important to distinguish between similarities which are relevant or irrelevant to the topic of the message. Relevant *attitudinal* similarities generally produce positive effects on attitude change, relevant dissimilarities produce negative effects, and irrelevant similarities have little or no effect. However, the effect of relevant *group-membership* similarities is determined by the relative status of the source and the audience. For instance, if the source is expert on the topic and the audience is not (e.g., T. S. Eliot giving his opinion on the merits of a poem), this *dis*similarity will produce more attitude change than a similar but nonexpert source (Simons et al., 1970).

Evaluation of Consistency Theories

The popularity of consistency theories has waned since the 1960s, but they still continue to stimulate research and practical applications (Harary, 1983). The profusion of consistency approaches and their individual incompleteness have already been mentioned. Osgood and Tannenbaum's congruity theory is the most detailed and explicit in its predictions (and also one of the narrowest in its applications). Though it has had relatively good success in some experimental research, the *ad hoc* corrections which it requires and the many factors which it does not consider demonstrate its limitations and cast some doubt on the value of its quantifications. The many other consistency approaches, though less precise in their predictions, have generally had less empirical support when put to experimental tests, though they have been fruitful in suggesting many new and interesting areas of research. McGuire (1969) concluded that consistency theories have been heuristically provocative but not distinguished for their empirical validity.

Whatever the value of consistency theories, it can reasonably be suggested that man does not live by consistency alone. Probably psychologists and other highly educated people are much more concerned with maintaining consistency in their thoughts, feelings, and actions than are the great majority of humankind. Bem (1970) has stated this viewpoint vividly:

> Inconsistency is probably our most enduring cognitive commonplace. . . . I suspect that for most of the people most of the time and for all the people some of the time inconsistency just sits there. (p. 34)

In corroboration of this viewpoint, we have seen in Chapter 6 that most citizens display a great deal of inconsistency in their political attitudes and opinions.

A theoretical viewpoint which helps to explain this widespread inconsistency has been suggested by Abelson (1968). He proposes that much of our knowledge and attitudes exist in isolated "opinion molecules," each of which contains one or a few facts, feelings, and sources of support. These opinion molecules serve us well in social conversation by giving us something to say on many topics (for instance, the national budget deficit, or the dangers of nuclear energy). However, when not brought out for such use, they are generally kept in "logic-tight compartments" where we do not need to think about them in relation to other topics which might contain contradictory facts or feelings. Thus, most of us probably tolerate a great deal of inconsistency among our attitudes and beliefs all the time, and yet we are hardly ever even aware of it.

DISSONANCE THEORY

Our next major topic, cognitive dissonance theory, is a type of consistency theory. However, it has some unique aspects, and it has received so much attention and stimulated so much research that it deserves separate treatment. Conceived by Leon Festinger (1957), it has been modified by Brehm and Cohen (1962), Festinger (1964), Aronson (1968), and Wicklund and Brehm (1976), and studied experimentally by a whole generation of social psychologists. Without doubt, dissonance theory has aroused more controversy and received more praise and criticism than any other current theory in social psychology.

Nature of Dissonance Theory

The theory deals with the relations between "cognitive elements." These elements are items of knowledge, information, attitude, or belief that a person holds about himself or about his surroundings. Two elements can either be **consonant** with each other (that is, compatible or consistent), or dissonant, or irrelevant. The definition of a **dissonant** relationship is that *the opposite of one element would follow from the other element*—that is, *x* and *y* are dissonant if non-*y* follows from *x*. What "follows from" a cognitive element is determined by the person's expectations; thus dissonance can be the result of logical inconsistency, of the person's past experience concerning what things go together, or of cultural norms and values. The basic principles of the theory are that:

1. Dissonance, being psychologically uncomfortable, will motivate the person to try to reduce the dissonance and achieve consonance . . . [and to] avoid situations and information which would likely increase the dissonance.
2. The magnitude of the dissonance (or consonance) increases as the importance or value of the elements increases.
3. The strength of the pressure to reduce dissonance is a function of the magnitude of the dissonance. (Festinger, 1957, pp. 3 & 18)

To use one of Festinger's examples, the cognition "I know I smoke" is consonant with the cognition "I know I enjoy smoking" but dissonant with "I believe smoking is bad for my health." (It would also be irrelevant to many other cognitions, such as "I know that I live in the United States.") Faced with such a dissonant situation, if the elements are personally important to him or her, the individual will try to reduce the dissonance in one or more of the following ways: (1) She may change a cognition about the behavior, for instance by giving up smoking, or by deciding "I only smoke a little." (2) She may change a cognition about the environment, for instance by deciding that smoking is not harmful, or that only heavy smoking is harmful. (3) She may add new cognitions to bolster one or the other of the dissonant elements, which reduces the dissonance by lowering the proportion of elements that are dissonant: for instance, "I know most of my friends smoke," or "I believe the evidence linking smoking and cancer isn't conclusive," or "I know the dangers from smoking are no greater than the dangers from driving a car," etc. (4) Since the amount of dissonance depends on the importance of the cognitions, she may reduce dissonance by deciding that one or more cognitions are less important, e.g., "It really isn't very important that smoking is bad for my health. I'm going to live fast and die young." Though it is not always possible to reduce dissonance successfully, if the amount of dissonance is

Photograph courtesy of Leon Festinger.
Reprinted by permission.

Box 10–1 LEON FESTINGER, *Eminent Theorist and Experimentalist*

Leon Festinger was probably the most famous of Kurt Lewin's many renowned students. Born in New York in 1919, he studied at CCNY and took his M.A. and Ph.D. with Lewin at Iowa. He taught briefly at the University of Rochester before rejoining Lewin at M.I.T. Following Lewin's death, he moved with the Research Center for Group Dynamics to the University of Michigan. At the age of 32 he became a full professor at Minnesota, subsequently moving to Stanford in 1955, and back to New York at the New School for Social Research in 1968.

Festinger's famous theoretical contributions include articles on social communication and social comparison processes, and his 1957 book, A Theory of Cognitive Dissonance, *which stimulated a prolific outpouring of research on attitude change. His fame as a clever experimentalist and a role model for productive students is also widespread. In addition to theoretical and experimental writings, his work includes field and observational research and statistical contributions. He was elected to the National Academy of Sciences, and he received the American Psychological Association's Distinguished Scientific Contribution Award in 1959. In the early 1960s, he left social psychology and concentrated his research on the area of perception until his death in 1989.*

great enough, one or more cognitive elements will be changed. Moreover, cognitions are generally responsive to reality, so it is hard to change a cognition about one's behavior without also changing the behavior.

Areas of Application of the Theory

That is the basic skeleton of the theory, but it does not do justice to the richness of its applications. As Markus and Zajonc (1985) have pointed out, the theory is basically an open one which can be applied to many different situations (in contrast, for instance, to congruity theory which only concerns communications in which a source makes an evaluative assertion about an object). Dissonance theory is stated in broad conceptual terms and does not make specific predictions about particular situations until additional assumptions are stated. For instance, in any situation it is necessary to specify the dissonant cognitions which are present and the feasible and infeasible ways of reducing the dissonance. When such additional assumptions are specified, the theory can be applied to countless situations, including many beyond the realm of attitude change research. It has even been applied to an understanding of partial reinforcement effects in rats as well as in human beings, and to participant observation studies of religious cultists!

In spite of the fact that it is a cognitive theory, dissonance theory has focused many hypotheses and experiments on people's overt behavior. It has been innovative in emphasizing that attitude change often *results from* a person's behavior rather than causing the behavior. In his original statement of the theory, Festinger suggested four major areas of its application. We will review each of those areas and very briefly summarize the relevant recent evidence on them.

The Consequences of Decisions. The theory posits that dissonance is aroused by making a decision between two or more alternative objects or courses of action. The dissonant elements are the negative features of the chosen alternative and the positive features of the unchosen alternative(s). The resulting dissonance is greater when: (a) the decision is an important one, (b) the unchosen alternative(s) is(are) nearly as attractive as the chosen one, and (c) there is low similarity between the various alternatives (e.g., choosing between going to an enjoyable sports event or reading an enjoyable book would create more dissonance than choosing which of two enjoyable books to read, because the two similar alternatives have many of the same positive aspects and the same negative aspects). Ways of reducing postdecision dissonance are decreasing the subjective attractiveness of the unchosen alternative, increasing the subjective attractiveness of the chosen alternative, or, occasionally, increasing the perceived similarity of the alternatives in other ways (e.g., deciding that both sports events and reading are forms of recreation).

In this area of postdecision dissonance, the experimental findings have generally supported the theory (e.g., Festinger, 1964) though there have been some contrary reports (e.g., Harris, 1969). An intriguing real-world study done at a race track showed that bettors' confidence in their chosen horse increased markedly immediately after they placed their bet—clearcut support for the theory (Knox & Inkster, 1968).

Revisions of the Theory. In the course of these studies revisions were made to the theory, stressing the importance of **commitment** and **volition (choice)** as necessary conditions for dissonance arousal to occur (Brehm & Cohen, 1962). If people do not feel committed to (bound by) their decisions, there is no reason for them to experience dissonance, and the research findings show no evidence of dissonance reduction (Kiesler, 1968). Similarly, if they feel that they had little or no choice in their actions, then their dissonance is apt to be minimal (e.g., Linder, Cooper, & Jones, 1967), though some evidence suggests that choice is not always necessary for the arousal of dissonance (Insko, 1967).

Other revisions of dissonance theory were suggested by Aronson (1968), who proposed that inconsistency of cognitions with a person's *self-concept* was the crucial factor leading to dissonance. Thus, for anyone with a positive self-concept, doing or saying something embarrassing or nonsensical or immoral would be dissonance-arousing. Similarly, Steele and Liu (1983) posit that dissonance is aroused by threats to the self-image, and that it can be reduced by any action that affirms one's important values (not just by attitude change). In much of the recent dissonance research the self-concept has become so central that Greenwald and Ronis (1978) have argued that the theory is now focused mostly on ego defense or self-esteem maintenance rather than on preserving cognitive consistency.

Aronson (1968) also suggested that there are individual differences between people in their ability to tolerate dissonance and in their preferred ways of reducing dissonance when it occurs, and this individual-difference viewpoint has been accepted by later theorists (e.g., Wicklund & Brehm, 1976). Wicklund and Brehm also stressed the idea that a key factor in arousing dissonance is a person's feeling of *responsibility* for some negative consequences to someone. This aspect of the theory is particularly applicable to research on counterattitudinal behavior (see that topic below).

Voluntary and Involuntary Exposure to Information.   Dissonance theory holds, in general, that dissonance-reducing information will be sought out and dissonance-increasing information will be avoided. However, it is often difficult or impossible to avoid contact with information which is being spread by the mass media or by one's acquaintances. If such new information were opposite to cognitions which one already held, then dissonance would result, and efforts would be made to reduce that dissonance. That might be accomplished in many different ways: by defensive misperception or misunderstanding, discrediting the information or its source, seeking other consonant information, or changing one's attitude. There are studies which provide evidence for each of these processes occurring under some conditions. However, there are also many reasons that one might want to receive supposedly dissonant information: It may be valuable to know what the opposition is saying, especially on personally important issues; one may be highly confident of one's own position and expect the opposition arguments to be weak; one may want to appear open-minded; or one may not care much about the issue and be interested in hearing divergent viewpoints. There are research findings supporting all of these processes as well (McGuire, 1985).

For a time, reviews of these conflicting findings generally stressed lack of support for the dissonance theory predictions regarding selective exposure (e.g., Greenwald & Ronis, 1978). As we discussed in Chapter 8, there is much less evidence for *motivated* selective exposure to information than for de facto selective exposure (Sears & Freedman, 1967). However, in recent years, a number of studies have found more support for general selectivity and also pinpointed conditions under which it is less likely (Cotton, 1985; Frey, 1986). For instance, dissonant information is valuable if the decision might be reversible or if its consequences are very great (e.g., Frey, 1982), but people who avoid threatening information ("repressors") are most likely to display selective exposure (Olson & Zanna, 1979). A newsworthy example of selectivity was demonstrated during the Watergate hearings, when supporters of President Nixon tended to avoid information about the hearings while citizens who had favored his campaign opponent, George McGovern, sought out the information (Sweeney & Gruber, 1984).

Dissonance and Social Support.   Disagreement with other people is another source of dissonance, and agreement with people can reduce dissonance. This part of the theory was foreshadowed by Festinger's (1954) theory of social comparison processes, which emphasized that people very often compare their opinions with those of others around them. Dissonance theory posits that dissonance will be high if a disagreement is (a) extensive; on a topic which is (b) important and (c) difficult to verify through observation; and if the disagreeing persons are (d) many, (e) attractive, and/or (f) credible. In such situations dissonance can be reduced either by changing one's own opinion, or persuading the disagreeing person(s) to change their opinions, or by discrediting or derogating the other person(s). Alternatively, one may seek out others who agree with one's views, or try to obtain social support by communicating with and persuading others who are currently uninvolved in the issue. Festinger (1957) gave several examples of such group social support phenomena, including mild denial of reality ("it isn't really going to rain on our picnic"), spread of rumors, and mass proselyting for causes. The book *When Prophecy Fails* (Festinger, Riecken, & Schachter, 1956) illustrates how dissonance theory can explain the initiation of proselyting by a formerly secretive religious cult. However, Hardyck and Braden (1962) studied a somewhat similar religious group and pointed out additional conditions which were necessary in order for proselyting to occur.

Because of the difficulties of such field studies (Thompson & Oskamp, 1974), and also because of the many ways in which dissonance can be resolved in social situations, there is relatively little clearcut evidence concerning this part of dissonance theory. However, some recent laboratory experiments on induced counterattitudinal behavior have shown that the presence of social support (i.e., other people performing the same counterattitudinal acts) reduces the resulting attitude change, as dissonance theory predicts (White, 1980; Stroebe & Diehl, 1981, 1988; Zanna & Sande, 1986).

Effects of Forced Compliance.   This area of research is the most controversial one and, in recent years, by far the most active one spawned by dissonance theory. It is also misleadingly named for, as the above comments concerning volition indicate, it is important for the creation of dissonance that subjects not feel "forced" to comply. A better name for this research area would be **induced compliance** or **counterattitudinal behavior**. The typical research procedure is to induce subjects to do or say something contrary to their opinions, using two or more levels of inducement for different subjects. The experimental prediction is that maximum dissonance (and dissonance reduction) will be created by the *mini-*

mum successful inducement, whereas larger inducements will create less dissonance because their very size offers a reason for having performed the behavior. In the famous Festinger and Carlsmith (1959) study, subjects were paid either $1 or $20 to act briefly as assistants to the experimenter (and to be available for similar future assistance) by falsely telling another subject that a very dull experiment had been enjoyable and interesting. As predicted, the $1 group of subjects subsequently resolved their dissonance by changing their actual attitude toward the experiment to a more favorable level than did the $20 group. This is an effect of perceived amount of choice ("If I said that for only $1, I must really believe it" vs. "I said it because I was paid so much").

The controversy over this area of research is not primarily concerning the effects of perceived choice, but rather it stems from the role-playing task which the subject typically has to perform. One group of researchers, following learning theory principles, has proposed and done experiments to show that the size of *incentive* for role-playing is positively related to the amount of attitude change— directly opposite to the dissonance prediction (e.g., Elms, 1967). However, it was soon pointed out that the occasional findings which supported incentive theory did not thereby disprove dissonance theory, and attention shifted to a search for *conditions* under which one or the other theory was upheld. Carlsmith, Collins, and Helmreich (1966) offered one resolution by showing a dissonance effect in interpersonal role-playing but an incentive effect in counterattitudinal essay writing. However, Linder, Cooper, and Jones (1967) showed that even essay writing could produce a dissonance effect under high-choice conditions. Freedman (1963) supported dissonance theory in showing greater enjoyment of boring tasks when there was relatively little justification given for complying. However, Collins (1969) failed to find dissonance effects in most of a long series of forced-compliance experiments.

Recent research findings in the induced-compliance area have converged on the following conclusions. Dissonance effects are very likely to occur when counterattitudinal behavior is performed under conditions of (a) low incentive, (b) high perceived choice, with (c) unpleasant consequences of the behavior (for someone), and (d) awareness by the actor of personal responsibility for the consequences (Collins & Hoyt, 1972; Wicklund & Brehm, 1976; McGuire, 1985). The question of whether the unpleasant consequences must be foreseen in order for the dissonance effect to occur has been answered by research showing that dissonance is aroused even if the person realizes retrospectively that (s)he could have foreseen them (Goethals, Cooper, & Naficy, 1979). A major reappraisal of the forced-compliance literature from a nondissonance perspective also seems to be quite consistent with these conclusions (Nuttin, 1975). However, recent research has demonstrated that effects of commitment to proattitudinal behavior can be predicted by dissonance theory, even in situations which have no aversive consequences (Aronson, 1990).

An offshoot of the research on induced compliance is the topic of **overjustification**, which involves using rewards, threats, or surveillance to induce a person to perform an *attitude-congruent* action rather than a counterattitudinal one. The usual effects of this procedure are to "undermine" or weaken the person's former attitude toward the action (Lepper & Greene, 1975; Scott & Yalch, 1978). Since there is no reason for dissonance in doing something that one likes, this effect has been interpreted in attribution terms (cf. Kelley, 1972a) as due to discounting of the attitudinal cause for the action because of the presence of another possible cause (the reward or threat)—"If I'm getting paid to do this, it must not be such an enjoyable thing to do after all." This analysis stresses that the undermining effect is due to the controlling aspect rather than the informational aspect of the external pressures (Deci & Ryan, 1980), and it has important implications for teachers and parents who want to maintain children's interest in various intrinsically enjoyable activities, such as school learning or musical or athletic participation— don't force, bribe, or threaten!

Bem's Critique of Dissonance Theory

Bem (1967) has suggested a different approach to the forced-compliance area and to the postdecision attitude change area, based on his theory of **self-perception**. As we described in Chapter 2, his theory postulates that one learns about one's own attitudes through observation of one's behavior. Thus, in the experimental situation with large vs. small rewards for counterattitudinal perform-ance, Bem does not question the basic experimental predictions from dissonance theory, but instead gives a different theoretical explanation for them. He posits that people will observe the fact that they have said something unusual for them, and the size of the inducement, and will interpret their true attitude in light of the size of reward (e.g., "I only said it because I was paid a lot; I don't really believe it").

Bem's method for studying his theory was to perform an "interpersonal replication," in which observer-subjects were simply told about the procedures experienced by a subject in one of the classic dissonance studies (e.g., Festinger & Carlsmith, 1959) and asked to estimate the original subject's true attitude. In general, these simulated replications quite closely paralleled the results of the earlier experiments.

However, R. A. Jones et al. (1968) pointed out that some crucial information about subjects' initial attitudes was not provided to Bem's observer-subjects; and when they did "interpersonal replications" incorporating that information, the results no longer paralleled the original experimental findings. Thus they concluded that observers and involved subjects were not always comparable and that "To explore the processes by which the attitudinal responses of involved subjects are determined it appears necessary to study involved subjects" (p. 267).

In his original theoretical statement, Bem (1967) had stated that involved participants in a behavioral episode and observers of the same episode are "isomor-phic" (that is, identical) in their inference processes and conclusions about behav-ior. By 1970, Bem had retreated from this viewpoint and only claimed: "In identifying his own internal states, an individual *partially* relies on the same external cues that others use when they infer his internal states" (1970, p. 50, italics added). This is a much harder hypothesis to disprove—almost impossible, in fact—so the controversy has mostly been waged over Bem's earlier, more extreme formulation. Despite an occasional finding of actor-observer similarity, the research evidence is quite conclusively opposed to the hypothesis that their perception is similar (E. E. Jones & Nisbett, 1972; Nisbett, Caputo, Legant, & Marecek, 1973; Storms, 1973).

Though Bem's theory of a passive process of self-perception was not disproven by these results, it was also not clearly supported. Moreover, if passive observers can replicate experimental findings, it is quite possible that they are doing so because of their intuitive understanding of common ways of dissonance reduction. As Zajonc (1968b, p. 375) comments: "Most subjects are also able to guess the trajectory of an apple falling from a tree, without doing serious damage to the laws of classical mechanics." Thus it has proven difficult to find situations which clearly pit the two theories against each other.

However, one clear difference between the theories is that dissonance theory posits motivational arousal in the form of an unpleasant emotional state arising from counterattitudinal actions, whereas self-perception theory does not make such motivational assumptions. Starting from this difference, Zanna and Cooper (1974) demonstrated support for dissonance theory by showing that counterattitudinal advocacy did produce emotional arousal. Later research has largely resolved the conflict between the two theories by concluding that dissonance theory applies to behavior and ideas in the person's latitude of rejection (i.e., ones that are counterattitudinal), whereas self-perception theory applies to behavior and ideas within the latitude of acceptance (i.e., attitude-congruent ones)—Fazio, Zanna, and Cooper (1977). Thus Bem's theory is applicable to the overjustification effect described in the preceding section. We may conclude that Bem's theory has been provocative and heuristically useful, but that he has understated people's use of internal cues about their attitudes and overstated their use of external cues (see Fazio, 1986b, for a recent review).

Impression Management Theory

Another theoretical viewpoint that has arisen to challenge dissonance theory is **impression management theory** (Tedeschi, Schlenker, & Bonoma, 1971; Schlenker, 1980; Tedeschi, 1981). Its major principle is that people try to manage their self-presentations so as to maintain a favorable public image—the same basic motive posited in the concept of social desirability response set (see Chapter 3). A closely related motive in self-presentation is to maintain a public image consistent with *one's own* ideal (Baumeister, 1982). When people have done something inconsistent or socially undesirable, they make excuses or deny responsibility or look for justifications that minimize the negative consequences. Attitude statements are one form of social communication that people try to manage for purposes of self-presentation. Accordingly, the theory views attitude change following counterattitudinal behavior as being just an attempt to maintain a favorable impression in the eyes of the experimenter or other witnesses by not appearing inconsistent—not a true change of views. That is, people are more concerned about *looking* consistent than being consistent.

Since the theory views purported attitude change as false and self-presentational in nature, it has generally been tested by comparing the usual paper-and-pencil attitude change measures to techniques intended to tap people's "true" attitudes, such as the "bogus pipeline" (refer to Chapter 3 for details). A number of studies of induced compliance have found much less dissonance-based attitude change using the bogus pipeline than when using standard attitude question methods (e.g., Gaes, Kalle, & Tedeschi, 1978). In addition, there is much evidence of other sorts that people are concerned about the impressions they make in self-presentation (Jones & Pittman, 1982). However, that does not mean that impression management is people's only concern or even their main focus when they have acted counterattitudinally. Recent studies have continued to support the dissonance findings and explanation (e.g., Rosenfeld, Giacalone, & Tedeschi, 1983; Stults, Messe, & Kerr, 1984); and it is quite likely that both dissonance reduction and impression management are jointly involved in much of the induced compliance research. At this point, more studies are needed to pinpoint the factors determining which mechanism operates, when, and with whom (e.g., Paulhus, 1982; Baumeister & Tice, 1984; Chaiken & Stangor, 1987).

Recent developments in impression management theory have made it more compatible with dissonance theory and reduced much of the conflict between the two approaches. Schlenker (1980, 1982) has proposed an *identity-analytic* approach which grants that induced-compliance attitude change can be real, but explains it in terms of people's attempts to avoid being held responsible for the negative consequences of their actions. This is very similar to the view of current dissonance theory, which stresses that awareness of personal responsibility for someone's negative consequences is crucial to attitude change. Tedeschi, also, has conceded that self-presentation can be accompanied by arousal in the form of discomfort, anxiety, and embarrassment, which brings his views much closer to the concepts of cognitive dissonance theory (Tedeschi & Rosenfeld, 1981).

Other Research Related to Dissonance Theory

According to dissonance theory principles, two techniques which should have an effect on attitude change are: making a public commitment to a particular viewpoint, and active participation in stating persuasive arguments. Let us briefly examine some of the research on these topics.

Commitment.   Interest in the topic of commitment goes back to the theory and research of Kurt Lewin (1947), who proposed that making a decision would "freeze" a person's beliefs and make them resistant to future counterpressures. Bennett (1955) confirmed that both private and public decisions had that effect, though most studies have found public commitment more effective (e.g., Wicklund & Brehm, 1976; Pallak, Cook, & Sullivan, 1980).

More complex effects of commitment have been studied by Kiesler (1971) and his colleagues, usually in situations involving commitment to consonant positions, but allowing subjects no choice about the commitment. Their results often parallel dissonance research findings for commitment to counterattitudinal positions. For instance, defense of one's beliefs for a small reward produces more resistance to later attacks than does defense of one's beliefs for a large reward. When individuals have made a public commitment, they tend to become more extreme in their position and to avoid thinking about the implications of their behavior. Commitment also makes people more responsive to extreme but reputable messages which agree with them, and more inclined to act on their beliefs if they are disputed (Kiesler & Munson, 1975). Being reminded of attitudes to which they are committed makes people act in ways more consistent with their attitudes (Aronson, 1990).

Active Participation. Early studies by the Hovland group showed that active participation in improvising persuasive arguments produced more attitude change than did passive listening to the same arguments (King & Janis, 1956). Also, active participation produces longer-lasting attitude change (Watts, 1967).

An extension of this method is the technique of **role-playing**—that is, acting out the feelings and behavior that another person might display in a particular situation. This technique was shown to be effective in reducing the prejudice of whites who played the role of an advocate of peaceful racial integration (Culbertson, 1957). Another study had smokers play the part of a lung-cancer victim who had to undergo surgery. This dramatic emotional experience was found to reduce smoking significantly, an effect which lasted for at least 18 months (Mann & Janis, 1968). Undoubtedly the emotional impact of imagining, and in a sense experiencing, consequences which could happen to oneself is a powerful factor in producing attitude change through role-playing.

But why should active participation be effective in the less-emotional situation where a person merely improvises or states arguments for a position which (s)he disagrees with? A variety of research studies have suggested several different explanations, any or all of which may apply in a particular situation. Preparing to argue against one's own position stimulates open-minded and unbiased evaluation of controversial information. Actually stating the arguments produces more attitude change than just preparing them, perhaps because greater effort is involved. People also remember their own improvisations better and judge them more favorably than others' improvisations. We will return to these points in more detail in the final section of this chapter, on cognitive-response approaches to attitude change.

Despite all the evidence for greater attitude change stemming from active participation, there are also situations where the opposite effect is found. Primarily this is true in the area of "cultural truisms" or beliefs which are so common that people have rarely ever heard them challenged (e.g., "you should brush your teeth after every meal"). In such situations, a person may be unmotivated or unable to improvise supportive arguments, and thus passive reception of someone else's arguments may have more effect than active participation (McGuire, 1964, 1969). Notice that these situations are generally ones where individuals are arguing for their own beliefs, which may later be attacked, whereas in situations where they are arguing *against* their own beliefs, active participation generally produces more attitude change.

Evaluation of Dissonance Theory

Dissonance theory must be given credit, first of all, for being exciting and influential enough to stimulate research by hundreds of followers and opponents. This in itself is perhaps the most important function of a theory. It is also much broader in its applications than other consistency theories. Because of its unique way of defining inconsistency, it is particularly applicable to choice behavior in conflict situations, an arena which other consistency theories do not enter. Moreover, dissonance theory is particularly intriguing for its numerous "nonobvious" hypotheses—for instance, the inverse relationship of dissonance to incentive size in the $1 vs. $20 forced-compliance situation. Dissonance experimenters also became known for their ingenious experimental procedures, some of which require a high degree of theatrical talent and stage-setting, though they also raise the problems of believability and the ethics of deception.

Dissonance theory has also been severely criticized, most notably by Chapanis and Chapanis (1964), and defended just as stoutly by others (Silverman, 1964; Aronson, 1969). Many of the criticisms revolve around dubious methodological practices such as the discarding of some subjects or the citation of marginally significant findings—what Suedfeld (1971) termed "inviting weaknesses" in the research. These criticisms are well-taken, but there are many supportive findings to which they don't apply. Another set of criticisms proposes alternative theoretical interpretations of the experimental findings (for instance, based on subject suspiciousness, or anxiety, or degree of reinforcement, or expectation of future unpleasant consequences, etc.). One or another of these explanations may seem plausible in any given experiment, but they are almost always after the fact interpretations. Moreover, they rarely have the parsimony, and never the broad range of applicability, of the dissonance predictions. Because of these kinds of criticisms the Chapanises concluded their critique by stating that, after five years of dissonance research, they must return "a verdict of NOT PROVEN" (1964, p. 21, capitals in original). However, critics should be aware that no theory is ever proven! Theories can be disproved by contrary data, but at most they can only be supported by confirming data, never proven in any final or ultimate sense. As Aronson replied,

> Happily, after more than 10 years, it is still not proven; all the theory ever does is generate research. (1969, p. 31)

Some more crucial criticisms of the theory can be made, however. Most important is the difficulty in making clearcut predictions from the theory for a specific situation. This difficulty arises from two facts: that the same situation may create different amounts of dissonance in two individuals who have different prior cognitions, and especially that dissonance can be reduced in many different ways and even in several ways at once. These difficulties are usually overcome in experiments by contriving a situation in which the crucial cognitions are relatively clearcut and in which most of the ways of reducing dissonance are blocked or are unlikely, so that clearcut predictions can be made and tested. But in everyday life situations, it is usually very difficult to tell what important cognitions a person has or what ways of reducing dissonance may be most likely. Thus specific predictions are on shaky ground except in relatively rare or artificially controlled situations. This problem could be greatly reduced if an independent, quantitative measure of the amount of a person's dissonance could be developed, or if objective manipulation checks could be devised in experiments to verify the approximate amount of dissonance aroused. However, we would still have to deal with the problem of individual differences in the tolerance for dissonance (or ambiguity), which McPherson (1983) has measured and shown to be important in selective exposure behavior.

Other criticisms and strengths of dissonance theory are presented at greater length by Shaw and Costanzo (1982) and Markus and Zajonc (1985). Following the great impact of the theory and its domination of social psychological research in the 1960s, interest then shifted to other approaches, particularly attribution theory. However, in the 1980s dissonance theory had a substantial resurgence, and recent reviews have emphasized its central and important contributions to understanding attitude change as well as its numerous practical applications (Cialdini et al., 1981; Cooper & Croyle, 1984; Chaiken & Stangor, 1987).

REACTANCE THEORY

An indirect offshoot of dissonance theory was J. W. Brehm's (1966) reactance theory. The key principle of the theory is that people are motivationally aroused whenever they feel some aspect of their freedom is being threatened or restricted. This arousal, called **psychological reactance**, motivates the person to try to restore the threatened freedom, with the result that the potentially restricted behavior becomes more attractive to the person. For example, if one is told, "Sorry, that item is already sold, and no more are available," it suddenly becomes even more attractive to the would-be buyer. A large-scale example of reactance was seen in 1985 when the Coca-Cola Company decided to stop selling original-flavored Coke, resulting in widespread public rejection of "New Coke" (Ringold, 1988).

Threats to an individual's freedom can occur through the actions of a powerful other person or group, such as the government or the police, or through the mere implication that someone else is attempting to influence one's behavior or attitudes ("eat this lovely eggplant; you'll like it"). Also, the restrictions can be social in origin or nonsocial, as when the physical environment prevents an action. When a freedom is threatened, the magnitude of the psychological reactance is determined by the importance of the freedom, the proportion of freedoms that are threatened, the person's subjective confidence that (s)he really had that freedom to begin with, the degree of restriction experienced, the illegitimacy or lack of justification of the restriction, and the absence of any available similar alternative actions. The consequences of reactance can be observed in verbal reports of attitudes or perceptions, or sometimes in behavior directed at exercising the threatened freedom or attacking the source of the restriction.

Reactance theory is relatively simple and logically consistent, but it is not precisely quantified, so statements about the degree of reactance, the importance of a freedom, the amount of confidence concerning its possession, and the consequences of reactance have to be phrased in relative (more than/less than) terms (Shaw & Costanzo, 1982). However, considerable research has supported the principles of the theory (e.g., Wicklund, 1974; S. Brehm & J. Brehm, 1981), sometimes even finding a "boomerang effect" of reverse attitude change (Heller, Pallak, & Picek, 1973). As one example, housewives whose freedom to use detergents containing phosphates was eliminated by a local law expressed more favorable attitudes toward those detergents than did a nondeprived control group in a nearby

Photograph courtesy of Jack W. Brehm.
Reprinted by permission.

Box 10–2   JACK W. BREHM, *Originator of Reactance Theory*

Widely known for his contributions to cognitive theory, Jack W. Brehm is Professor of Psychology at the University of Kansas. Following high school, he served in the U.S. Navy and then took his B.A. at Harvard and his Ph.D. at the University of Minnesota. During three years as a faculty member at Yale, he was a member of the highly creative communication research program under Carl Hovland. Then he moved to Duke University, where he taught for 17 years until moving to Kansas in 1975.

Brehm was one of the earliest researchers on Festinger's cognitive dissonance theory, to which he made major contributions in books entitled Explorations in Cognitive Dissonance *and* Perspectives on Cognitive Dissonance. *In 1966 he published* A Theory of Psychological Reactance, *describing the original theory for which he is best known.*

city (Mazis, 1975). The theory further suggests that *forewarning* of a communicator's persuasive intent will arouse reactance motivation, thus producing less attitude change; and some studies have supported this general hypothesis (e.g., Petty & Cacioppo, 1979a).

As with dissonance theory research, impression management theory has challenged reactance findings as being due, not to concern about the actual loss of freedom, but to attempts to maintain the outward appearance of being free (e.g., a politician claiming, "No, I haven't changed my viewpoint; I've always believed that . . .") (Baer, Hinkle, Smith, & Fenton, 1980; Schlenker, 1980). However, Wright and S. Brehm (1982) have disputed the impression-management view by showing that reactance effects are found even when the resulting behavior could not be interpreted by others as a sign of autonomy.

ATTRIBUTION THEORIES AND ATTITUDE CHANGE

We have discussed attribution theories at some length in Chapter 2, noting that they replaced dissonance theory as the most frequently studied topic in the social psychological research literature of the 1970s and 1980s. However, most of the research discussed in Chapter 2 did not deal with attitude *change*, and in general, attribution theories have not been widely applied to the traditional topics of attitude change research (Kiesler & Munson, 1975). However, this situation has altered somewhat in the last decade, and in this section we will summarize several attitude change research topics where attribution theories have made useful contributions.

One such area, which we have discussed in previous sections, is the research on Bem's self-perception theory which pitted it against dissonance theory in explaining attitude change following counterattitudinal advocacy. Another topic utilizing attributional explanations, also discussed above, is the overjustification or undermining effect which is found when rewards or threats are offered for performing attitude-congruent behavior. Either Bem's theory or Kelley's (1972a) discounting principle is applicable to that situation. A third topic where attribution principles were invoked was in research on the foot-in-the-door effect, which was discussed earlier as an example of consistency motivation. One of the popular explanations of that effect adds an attributional element to the consistency interpretation, specifying that a person who complies with the first small request is influenced to make a self-attribution of helpfulness, and consequently is more likely to comply with a later large request.

Attribution of Physiological Responses.   A number of attributional studies of physiological responses involved the variable of attitude change. One was the classic experiment of Schachter and Singer (1962), in which they injected subjects with physiologically arousing epinephrine and then put them in a waiting room with an accomplice of the experimenter who began to act either euphoric or angry.

The subjects who had not been given an explanation of the drug's arousing effects apparently used the cue provided by the accomplice's behavior as the basis for self-attribution, for they later reported themselves as being either happy or angry, depending on which condition they had experienced.

An experiment by Valins (1966) extended this principle to false physiological feedback—specifically sounds which the male subjects believed were their own heartbeats. The results showed that *Playboy* pictures which were accompanied by either increased or decreased "heartrates" were later judged as more attractive than the other pictures. However, this *misattribution* of attitudes due to physiological information has limits. Taylor (1975) showed that bogus physiological feedback did not significantly influence women's ratings of men's pictures in the condition where they expected there would be future consequences of their ratings (i.e., that they would be able to meet one of the men).

Recent research has utilized misattribution of physiological arousal for therapeutic ends in treating anxiety, insomnia, and phobias (Reisenzein, 1983). For instance, in a laboratory setting, Brodt and Zimbardo (1981) increased social responsiveness and emotional comfort among very shy college women by misattributing their shyness symptoms to the environmental impact of bombardment by high-frequency noise in the experiment. More clinically feasible examples of attribution-based treatments have been used to reduce anxiety and improve performance in mixed-sex social interactions and in college examinations (Wilson & Linville, 1982; Haemmerlie & Montgomery, 1984; Noel, Forsyth, & Kelley, 1987).

Communicator Credibility. An attributional analysis of persuasion has been offered by Eagly, Chaiken, & Wood (1981), based on inferences that people make about the credibility of communicators. Credibility is seen as being determined by recipients' inferences about the *causes* of a communicator's advocacy of a particular position. The cause of the communicator's message may be a strong commitment to that position (referred to as a **knowledge bias**), or situational pressures such as trying to please a particular audience (implying a **reporting bias** on the part of the communicator), or simply a veridical view of the issue. Recipients are less likely to be persuaded if premessage cues give them an expectancy that the communicator has a knowledge bias or a reporting bias. However, if that expectancy is disconfirmed by the communicator advocating an unexpected position, persuasion is likely because then the recipient attributes the message as being based on the true weight of evidence on the issue (Eagly, Wood, & Chaiken, 1978). This analysis helps to explain why statements that appear contrary to the speaker's self-interest are apt to be quite persuasive to the hearer. Cialdini (1988) has used this principle to point out the social-influence effects of self-deprecating humor, and of waiters who suggest one of the cheaper dishes to diners (and then use the credibility conferred by that action to recommend expensive wines or fancy desserts).

A related topic is the way in which people decide about a communicator's true viewpoint. People generally attribute a statement as being due to the author's true attitude, even when they are told that the person had no choice about making the statement (Jones & Harris, 1967). This is an example of the *fundamental attribution error*, and a notable instance was the public condemnation of Patti Hearst for her statements and actions supporting her terrorist captors, the Symbionese Liberation Army. It is only when the background information about a speaker is unambiguous *and* inconsistent with his(her) statement that this attributional tendency is reduced (Ajzen, Dalto, & Blyth, 1979).

Minority Influence in a Group. A topic that has been pioneered by Serge Moscovici (cf. 1985) is the influence that can be exerted by numerical minorities in group decision or discussion situations. This European perspective represents a contrast with American social psychology's preoccupation with conformity of minorities in a group to the majority opinion (e.g., Asch, 1956). According to Moscovici and Nemeth's (1974) attributional account, single individuals or small subgroups in a group can have considerable influence on the group's decisions if they state positions that are *consistent* and *distinctive*. Such a stance leads other group members to attribute certainty and confidence to the minority, and this in turn may influence the majority decision. This general finding is quite well-established, though there are still several differing attributional explanations that have been offered for the effect (Maass & Clark, 1984; Chaiken & Stangor, 1987).

Evaluation of Attribution Approaches. It is clear that attribution theories have recently been applied productively to many different aspects of attitude change. There are some areas where they provide the best or only explanation, other areas where they have been less successful than other theories such as dissonance, and quite a few areas where they offer a useful alternative viewpoint or a needed complement to other theories in explaining a phenomenon more completely. Attribution theorists have modestly granted that some social situations may engage other social motives more than (or rather than) attribution, and also that attribution processes, which are relatively thoughtful, may be more typical among college students, the most commonly used research subjects, than among other people (Jones et al., 1972). Despite their limitations, attribution theories have stimulated a great deal of research and will undoubtedly continue to be extended to new research topics and additional practical applications (Harvey & Weary, 1985).

COGNITIVE RESPONSE THEORIES

One of the newest major theoretical viewpoints about persuasion emphasizes the cognitive responses that people make when they are exposed to persuasive messages (Petty, Ostrom, & Brock, 1981; Petty & Cacioppo, 1981). These **cognitive responses** are thoughts which recipients themselves generate, and they can be favorable to the message, or opposing counterarguments, or neutral or irrelevant thoughts. Usually there will be some mix of these different types of thoughts, and the relative balance of favorable and unfavorable thoughts is a key variable.

How can these self-generated thoughts be measured and studied empirically? They are a subjective concept, and they vary with each individual instead of being directly linked to the objective characteristics of the message. Thus their measurement presents serious problems, and a number of methods have been suggested to obtain an objective and useful measure (Cacioppo & Petty, 1981b). However, the most frequently used method is called the **thought-listing technique**. In it, subjects are given a specified period of time, such as three minutes, and asked to write down brief statements of the thoughts they had as they listened to or read the persuasive message. Later, judges code these thoughts as being favorable, unfavorable, or neutral to the position advocated in the persuasive message.

Theoretical Principles

The cognitive response viewpoint assumes that when people receive (or even anticipate) a persuasive message, they are likely to try to relate its arguments to knowledge, beliefs, and attitudes they already hold on that topic, and in doing so they generate a number of thoughts that are not part of the message itself. As one authority put it,

> What people do to messages is more important than what messages do to people. (Baumwoll, quoted in Gordon, 1987, p. 25)

The theory holds that the balance of favorable or unfavorable self-generated thoughts will determine the success of the persuasive message. That is, the cognitive responses *mediate* between characteristics of the message or the recipient and the effect of the message, and they are considered to be crucial in determining what effect the message will have. They represent a step between comprehension of the message and yielding to or acceptance of it, as described in McGuire's (1985) fine-grain analysis of the communication process.

The first ideas contributing to the cognitive response viewpoint developed from the early research on *active participation* in persuasion (see the section on dissonance research earlier in this chapter). There, studies found that people who improvised their own persuasive talk based on a written counterattitudinal communication displayed more attitude change than ones who read the written message silently or read it aloud into a tape recorder (King & Janis, 1956). The difference was not due to satisfaction with their own performance, which was higher in the read-aloud group, but rather to the element of improvising their own statement of the arguments. Later studies showed two factors that contributed to this improvisation effect. First, when people know what position they are going to have to defend, they engage in a *biased information search*, which selectively concentrates on arguments that favor that position, and this process encourages more attitude change in that direction (O'Neill & Levings, 1979). Second, people *value* the arguments that they generate themselves more than other people value them and more than they value other people's arguments (Greenwald & Albert, 1968).

Another key conclusion is that active participation in generating a talk on an assigned topic produces longer-lasting attitude change than does passive exposure to the same or equivalent arguments (Watts, 1967). An underlying reason for this difference is that people are able to *recall* their own arguments on a topic better than arguments presented by someone else (Greenwald & Albert, 1968).

Research Findings

Effects of Mere Thought. One of the areas of research that supports the cognitive response viewpoint is studies of people merely thinking about an issue without being exposed to any persuasive communication. In a series of studies, Tesser (1978) has come to the conclusion that mere thought about an issue generally results in a person's attitude becoming more extreme than it was before (termed a **polarization effect**). This effect occurs because on many topics people have viewpoints or schemas that make some aspects of the issue salient and provide guides for inferences about other aspects. Thought under the direction of such a schema leads to changes in beliefs, which are generally in the direction of greater belief consistency. Mere thought leads to more extreme attitudes only when people have such a schema or bias to guide their thinking (Tesser & Leone, 1977).

In a typical study of mere thought, subjects were introduced to either a likable partner or a dislikable partner through a tape recording. The likable partner was pleasant, describing himself self-confidently but without bragging, whereas the dislikable partner was arrogant and insulting. Then half the subjects were instructed to think about their partner, while the other half were given a distracting task to perform which would prevent their thinking about the partner very much. Next, subjects rated their partner on a series of scales and listed their thoughts about him. The results showed that subjects who thought about their partner were more favorable to the likable partner than were distracted subjects, and those who thought about the dislikable partner were more negative toward him than were the distracted subjects (Sadler & Tesser, 1973). Further research demonstrated that giving people a few more minutes for thinking resulted in more polarization of attitudes, but that after a relatively brief time all the thinking possible on the topic had been done and no further polarization occurred (Tesser, 1978).

Forewarning of Persuasion. The topic of forewarning is somewhat like mere thought in that attitude change often occurs even before the persuasive message is delivered (an **anticipatory attitude change**). The direction of the change depends on whether the recipient is highly involved in the issue or not (Cialdini & Petty, 1981). People who expect to receive a message on an issue that is not very personally relevant to them generally become more moderate (less extreme) in their attitudes. On the contrary, people who expect to receive a message on a highly relevant topic usually become more polarized in their attitudes (i.e., more extreme in the direction of their original views). The motives behind these differing changes also differ. Uninvolved individuals may moderate their views in the service of impression management—trying to present an acceptable appearance to the communicator and other recipients—and if they do not receive the message, their attitudes will "snap back" to their original position. However, individuals who are involved in the topic will be motivated to defend their true opinion, and they will rehearse arguments supporting their own viewpoint, resulting in more extreme attitudes. If the message they expect is proattitudinal, their rehearsal of favorable arguments can be explained by self-perception theory, whereas if it is counterattitudinal, their counterarguing may be seen as motivated by psychological reactance (Cialdini et al., 1976).

Resistance to Persuasion.   The above research shows that forewarning can produce resistance to persuasion by encouraging counterarguing. However, it does so only if the forewarning comes long enough before the message (e.g., 2–3 minutes) to allow time for counterarguing (Hass & Grady, 1975). Another study showed that the anticipatory thoughts involved in counterarguing are responsible for the forewarning effect, because forewarned subjects displayed the same amount of resistance to persuasion as subjects who were not forewarned but were merely instructed to list their thoughts on the topic before they heard a message (Petty & Cacioppo, 1977).

A famous early study on resistance to persuasion was McGuire's (1964) research on "inoculation" against persuasion. He used the medical analogy of creating resistance to a disease by inoculating a person with a weak form of the disease-producing germ and thus producing antibodies against the disease. The beliefs that he aimed to protect from attack were "cultural truisms"—beliefs so common in our culture that people have rarely ever heard them attacked (for instance, "mental illness is not contagious"). With such beliefs, people do not have supportive arguments readily at hand, so they need some help in defending them from attack. McGuire accomplished the inoculation by presenting subjects with some weak arguments against the truisms followed by refutations of those arguments, and he showed that this approach produced more resistance against a later attacking message than did a "supportive defense" which merely presented some arguments for the truisms before receipt of the attacking message. Consistent with a cognitive-response viewpoint, subjects listed more thoughts supportive of the truisms in the inoculation condition than in the supportive defense condition.

Issue Involvement.   We have seen in Chapter 9 that ego-involvement is an important variable in social judgment theory, and it is also a key concept in cognitive response theory. People who are highly involved in an issue will be more motivated to generate thoughts on the topic, and so their attitudes will normally become more extreme, as noted above in regard to forewarning. That means they will usually shift toward a strong proattitudinal message but become more extreme in the direction opposite to a counterattitudinal message. However, an exception to this common pattern is based on the quality of the arguments in the message. If a counterattitudinal message presents many strong arguments on an issue in which they are highly involved, people will tend to generate thoughts favorable to these strong arguments, but if the message arguments are weaker, they will generate mostly counterarguments (Petty & Cacioppo, 1979b, 1984; Leippe & Elkin, 1987). Thus, research shows that high issue involvement produces more careful processing of the message content—but not always biased processing, though that often occurs (Abelson, 1986; Howard-Pitney et al., 1986).

Central Versus Peripheral Routes to Persuasion

The complex pattern of interactions that we have discussed above can be much better understood by using a concept of two different routes to attitude change (Petty & Cacioppo, 1986). The **central route** is based on the *information* that a person has about the attitude topic or issue. It stresses the individual's prior knowledge and interest in the topic, the degree of comprehension and learning of arguments in a message, and the self-generated thoughts of the individual in reaction to a message. Thus it involves a relatively rational process of considering facts, arguments, and thoughts, though it is not completely logical for it often considers a biased group of thoughts or arguments and combines them in psychological rather than logical ways. Its hallmark is a *thoughtful* consideration of information.

The **peripheral route** to persuasion is far less thoughtful, and it ensues when a person's motivation or ability to process message content or other information is low. It relies on cues peripheral to the content of the message instead of on the arguments in the message and the thoughts which it arouses. The peripheral cues provide a *shortcut procedure* by which a person can decide how to react to a message without taking the trouble to think about all the pros and cons. For instance, one type of peripheral cue is the source's credibility or likability or power, and a recipient may rely on any one of these to determine his(her) response without thinking about the message in detail. Another type of cue is message characteristics that have been associated with rewarding or punishing experiences in the past, as in product commercials or political ads that develop a mood of sexual arousal or happy relaxation or patriotism. Also, recipient characteristics, such as low issue involvement, often lead to response by the peripheral route, as illustrated by findings in the preceding sections of this chapter. Though the peripheral route is cognitively "lazy," it is not necessarily illogical. You cannot possibly think in detail about every persuasive message, advertisement, or commercial that you are exposed to, and it may often make sense to rely on the recommendation of an expert or on the feelings of pleasure or threat which a message arouses, particularly if the topic is not important to you.

Figure 10-2 presents a schematic diagram of the main factors involved in determining whether the central route or the peripheral route will be followed and the consequences of the two routes. Petty and Cacioppo (1986) have emphasized that persuasion via the peripheral route is apt to be weak, temporary, and susceptible to counterpressures, whereas persuasion via the central route is apt to be

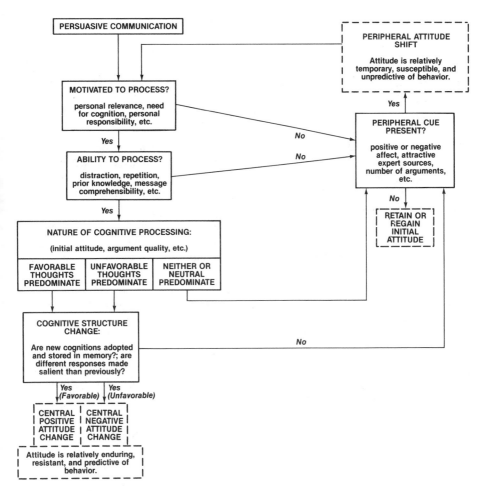

FIGURE 10–2 Schematic diagram of major factors involved in the central route and the peripheral route to persuasion, according to the elaboration likelihood model.

Source: Reprinted from Petty & Cacioppo (1986, p. 4).

stronger, relatively persistent, and resistant to counterattack. They call their theory of attitude change the **elaboration likelihood model** because it stresses that an individual's cognitive elaboration of issue-relevant arguments plays a crucial role in attitude change and persistence.

Rather similar concepts have been proposed by other researchers working in the fields of attitude change and social cognition. For instance, Petty and Cacioppo's distinction between central and peripheral routes to persuasion has considerable similarity to distinctions between systematic versus heuristic processing (Chaiken,

1980), thoughtful versus "scripted" or "mindless" processing (Abelson, 1976; Langer, Blank, & Chanowitz, 1978), and cognitive versus affective evaluation of information (Zajonc, 1980). The use of simple heuristic decision cues (e.g., "more is better," "experts can be trusted") and unthoughtful mindless reactions are special cases of the peripheral route, which is typified by the energy-saving "cognitive miser" approach (Fiske & Taylor, 1984).

In addition to the research cited in the preceding section, several other areas of research support the value of the central-peripheral distinction. For example, the effect of *distraction* during receipt of a message is to reduce cognitive elaborations and thus to weaken what would otherwise be the person's reaction to the message. Ironically, this means that distraction can lead to some favorable attitude change toward the viewpoint of a counterattitudinal message which would otherwise be rejected if the recipient were not being distracted (Petty, Wells, & Brock, 1976; Lammers & Becker, 1980). On the other hand, *message repetition* allows an opportunity for more cognitive elaboration, and if the arguments in the message are strong ones, this can lead to more favorable attitudes toward either a proattitudinal or a counterattitudinal message (Cacioppo & Petty, 1979a). However, if the message is repeated more times in a relatively short period, boredom and reactance are likely, resulting in more counterarguing and reduced attitude change. If the message arguments are weak ones, repetition can quickly lead to counterarguing and unfavorable attitude change (Petty & Cacioppo, 1981). Presenting a larger *number of arguments* in a message also allows for more cognitive elaboration. As with message repetition, if the arguments are strong ones, more favorable thoughts and more attitude change will result, but if the arguments are weak, more counterarguing and less attitude change occur (Calder, Insko, & Yandell, 1974; Harkins & Petty, 1981).

Finally, *persistence of attitude change* is explained by the cognitive response viewpoint as being due to favorable thoughts being rehearsed and remembered over a period of time. However, importantly, it is not recall of the arguments in the message that is crucial, but rather recall of the self-generated thoughts about the message that is significantly predictive of persisting attitude change (Love & Greenwald, 1978). This finding presents a major quandary for a message-learning theory of attitude change, but it is quite consistent with cognitive response theory (Cook & Flay, 1978; Chaiken, 1980).

Evaluation of Cognitive Response Approaches

Cognitive response viewpoints see attitude change largely as a process of **self-persuasion**, holding that "a person's own thoughts are a more powerful determinant of persuasion than is information that originates externally" (Petty & Cacioppo, 1981, p. 251). As demonstrated in the discussion above, this principle has received support in research on a wide variety of topics. However, questions can be raised about the thought-listing technique, which is the most common measure of the mediating process of self-generated thinking. Because results of this measure typically are closely related to measures of attitude change, it is possible that the thought-listing measure is just an alternate measure of attitude change, rather than an index of an intervening process (Sears, 1988b). If so, the obtained relationships would be far less important, and thus alternative methods of measurement are needed to validate findings with the thought-listing technique.

The distinction between central and peripheral routes to attitude change has gone far in making sense out of a diverse and often apparently conflicting set of research findings. Thus, this approach is a hopeful step toward a truly general theory of attitude change, and it is closely in tune with the recent growth of a cognitive emphasis in social psychology. In addition, it has been applied to various practical topics such as advertising and counseling (Brock & Shavitt, 1983; Heesacker, 1985).

However, even cognitive response theory proponents admit that it is not sufficient in itself to explain all attitude change (Petty & Cacioppo, 1981). Cognitive responses tell us *how* a person thinks about a message or an issue, but other (motivational) theories are necessary to tell us *why* a person generates favorable or unfavorable thoughts in response to a message. Examples of such other theories are ones discussed in this chapter, stressing motivational concepts such as a need for consistency, dissonance due to feeling responsible for some unpleasant consequences, or reactance against threats to one's freedom of action or thought. The principles of cognitive response theory provide an important explanatory link between the arousal of such motives and resulting changes in people's attitudes and behavior.

A FINAL COMMENT ON THEORIES

It is obvious from our discussion in this chapter that all theories of attitude change have limitations. Some have greater problems than others, but all have rather crucial failings. Does that mean that we should abandon them, in effect saying "a plague on both your houses"? No, definitely not. Though that course might be emotionally satisfying, it would not be good science. The scientific reasons for developing and using theories have been presented earlier in Chapter 9. As scientists, when we are faced with the inadequacies of our theories, our job is two-fold: first, to try to determine the range of conditions under which each theory holds, and second, to endeavor to construct better theories which will more fully explain the existing research evidence. This is an exciting and an urgent task.

SUMMARY

Cognitive *consistency* theories have generated a great deal of research, but they are fractionated into many partially conflicting mini-theories. The basic principle of all consistency theories is that awareness of inconsistency among one's ideas is an uncomfortable situation which will motivate cognitive changes, though not necessarily strictly logical ones. In general, consistency theories have been heuristically provocative but relatively low in the empirical validity of their research predictions. In part, this is probably due to the common and pervasive occurrence of *in*consistency in human psychological functioning.

Festinger's *dissonance* theory is a type of cognitive consistency theory but is unique in both its form and its ability to stimulate controversy and research. The theory is stated in an open way which allows it to be applied to many diverse areas. With later revisions that stressed the importance of volition and commitment and the centrality of the self-concept in the dissonance-arousal process, the theory has done quite well in predicting the consequences of making decisions, but there is less complete support for its predictions about selective exposure to information, the role of social support in reducing dissonance, and the effects of induced counterattitudinal behavior.

Brehm's *reactance* theory posits that people are motivationally aroused whenever they feel some aspect of their freedom is being threatened, and consequently they try to restore the threatened freedom. The theory has had relatively good success in predicting research findings, including the topic of forewarning of persuasive intent. *Attribution* theories, in recent years, have been increasingly applied to attitude change issues such as research on overjustification effects and the foot-in-the-door phenomenon.

Cognitive response theories are a major new approach, which emphasizes that attitude change is based largely on people's self-generated thoughts in reaction to persuasive messages, rather than on the message content itself. Support for this principle comes from many research topics: effects of active participation in improvising arguments, polarization of attitudes due to mere thought, anticipatory attitude change due to forewarning of persuasion, resistance to persuasion developed by methods such as the inoculation procedure, and effects of issue involvement on attitude change. Petty and Cacioppo's elaboration likelihood model posits two contrasting routes to persuasion: The central route depends on information and thought about the message content, whereas the peripheral route uses noncontent cues to arrive at attitude changes which are apt to be weaker and less persistent.

Though each of these theoretical approaches has had some success in predicting and explaining research findings, each is a partial theory in that it explains only certain phenomena. Other theories are complementary in explaining other findings, and much of the research cited in this chapter shows that, if used in combination, they can take us closer to the eventual goal of an adequate general theory of attitude change.

Attitude-Behavior Consistency and Related Issues

Attitude and action are linked in a continuing reciprocal process, each generating the other in an endless chain.—Herbert C. Kelman.

We have too many high sounding words, and too few actions that correspond with them.—Abigail Adams, 1774.

What I want is to get done what the people desire to have done, and the question for me is how to find that out exactly.—Abraham Lincoln.

The politician who sways with the polls is not worth his pay.—Richard Nixon.

This chapter takes up several key issues in the study of attitudes and opinions. First we will consider two long-standing questions that are still being debated—how are attitudes related to personality, and how are they related to behavior? Next we will explore some methodological problems and ethical issues—what differences are there between the findings of laboratory research and field research, and what ethical problems are raised in attitude and opinion research? Finally, extending our examination of attitudes and behavior into the public arena, we will look at the relationship of public opinion to public policy.

ATTITUDES AND PERSONALITY

The major issue here is whether or not attitudes have a systematic and close relationship to personality traits. Note that this is a different question than whether attitude *change* is related to personality, a topic discussed in Chapter 9 under the heading of Personality and Persuasibility.

Classic Studies of Attitudes and Personality

There are several classic studies that link attitudes and personality. One of the best-known of all attitude studies—*The Authoritarian Personality* (Adorno et al.,

1950)—began as a study of anti-Semitic attitudes. As the project developed, the focus broadened to include conservatism, ethnocentrism (a generalized attitude of prejudice toward many ethnic groups), and finally authoritarianism, which was conceptualized as a basic personality characteristic. Each of the major topics of the research, in turn, was studied through the development of a scale to measure it. The authors reported that the Anti-Semitism (A-S) Scale correlated +.53 with the first version of the F (for Fascism) Scale, which was their measure of authoritarian personality tendencies. This relationship was at least partly due to the fact that each successive measurement scale was constructed by using the correlations of its items with the preceding scales as a basis for item selection. However, despite this methodological problem, the point here is that this highly influential research project both assumed and found a close relationship between personality characteristics and certain attitudes.

Some of the relationships that were reported, using methods of personality testing and intensive depth interviews, were as follows: Highly prejudiced individuals were found to have rigid personality characteristics; they were highly conventional in values and standards; they rejected any negative implications about themselves or their parents; and they projected socially unacceptable impulses or characteristics onto other people. They typically reported having had parents who were concerned about status, who were cold and unloving, who used harsh physical punishment for infractions of family rules, and who gave love only for "proper" behavior.

Similar patterns of relationships between personality characteristics and attitudes have been reported in studies of political conservatism (McClosky, 1958), of international attitudes (Smith et al., 1956), and of prejudice (Martin & Westie, 1959). Another study of prejudice showed that in both Greece and the United States insecure individuals were generally high in prejudice, though the typical target groups for prejudice differed in the two cultures (Triandis & Triandis, 1962).

Methodological Critiques

Individual Prejudice versus Social Conformity.   Though personality-based theories of prejudice have received some empirical support, they by no means account for all prejudice. Since they deal with *individual* prejudice, they are least applicable in situations where social norms prescribe prejudiced and discriminatory behavior from all members of the dominant group—i.e, situations of **institutional racism**—as has been true in the American South. Despite the high degree of racial prejudice in the South, Southerners in general are no higher than Northerners on measures of authoritarian personality traits. Instead of personality being the source of most prejudiced attitudes, the evidence suggests that social conformity may be the more potent source of prejudice in those cultural settings where there are such clearcut norms of discrimination (Pettigrew, 1959). (See Chapter 15 for more information on racial prejudice.)

The Authoritarian Personality. Methodological critiques of the authoritarian personality research have been extensive and varied (Christie & Jahoda, 1954; Kirscht & Dillehay, 1967). Here we can mention only a few of the points most relevant to our discussion of personality and attitudes. For a thorough review of the topic which reads almost like a mystery novel, see the chapter on authoritarianism by Brown (1965).

Four major criticisms of the authoritarian personality research are most important. First, the sampling procedures were far from representative since most subjects were obtained through organized groups such as labor unions, Kiwanis clubs, and university classes. However, Martin and Westie (1959) and McClosky (1958) studied representative samples of adults living in a major U.S. city, and their results also showed clear connections between attitudes and personality traits. Second, the interviewers, who were allowed wide discretion in their choice of questions, were shown the subjects' F-Scale scores before the interview, and thus they may have consciously or unconsciously tried to obtain interview responses consistent with the questionnaire data. However, again, this criticism is not applicable to Martin and Westie's and McClosky's similar findings because they used questionnaires for collecting their data.

A third methodological criticism of authoritarianism research is the problem of acquiescence response set (yea-saying), which occurred because all the items of the F-Scale were worded in the authoritarian direction (as discussed in Chapter 3). However, Martin and Westie's research methods did not suffer from this problem, and their results were highly similar to Adorno et al.'s. The fourth criticism of authoritarianism research is that demographic characteristics such as education and social class are quite strongly correlated with F-Scale scores, in a negative direction (Selznick & Steinberg, 1969). There is no escaping this fact, but it does not vitiate the relationship between personality and attitudes. It appears that underprivileged groups in the United States and many other countries are more likely to develop authoritarian personality structures and the typical pattern of accompanying attitudes than are middle- or upper-class groups.

Interaction Effects. A final methodological consideration relevant to all personality and attitude studies is one which moves beyond the **main effects** of a single personality or attitude variable considered in isolation. In addition to such main effects, studies are likely to find **interaction effects**, in which two or more stimulus situations differentially affect people who have different personality or attitude characteristics. For example, we might find that authoritarian individuals display more prejudice than do nonauthoritarians when dealing with a low-status minority person, but not when dealing with a high-status minority person. The pervasiveness and importance of such interaction effects have been stressed by Cronbach (1975) and Secord (1977), among others, and greater attention to them is needed in research.

More Recent Findings

Despite these criticisms of the methodology used in previous research relating attitudes and personality variables, later studies have continued to report clearcut relationships (e.g., Wilson, 1973). A major program of research conducted over 20 years by Altemeyer (1988) has focused on right-wing authoritarianism, conceptualized as a personality trait that includes three main aspects: authoritarian submission, authoritarian aggression, and conventionalism. Altemeyer's carefully developed scale of right-wing authoritarianism has been found to correlate strongly with attitudes of acceptance of governmental injustice and illegality, punitiveness toward common criminals, ethnocentric prejudice, true-believer religiosity, and conservative political views among people interested in politics.

Conservative ideology has been studied in a particularly interesting and influential group—U.S. Senators—by Tetlock (1983a). He classified them as liberal, moderate, or conservative on the basis of their voting record, and he analyzed their published policy statements with his systematic coding measure of "integrative complexity"—a characteristic which is usually low in authoritarian personalities (see Chapter 4 for other related research). The findings showed that conservative senators were significantly less complex in their thinking than their liberal or moderate colleagues. Similarly, Tetlock (1981) found that senators who were consistently isolationistic in their foreign policy votes made policy statements that showed several features of the authoritarian personality: low complexity of thought, unusually positive ingroup attitudes, and negative affect toward outgroups.

Questionnaire research on political intolerance among a broad sample of Americans has similarly concluded that intolerance is most common among those who are "psychologically insecure"—dogmatic, misanthropic, authoritarian, low in self-esteem, and anxious about personal safety (Sullivan, Marcus, Feldman, & Piereson, 1981). Other recent research on personality and attitudes has linked relatively low ego-development among a national sample of adolescents and young adults to a variety of authoritarian attitudes (Browning, 1983). In the area of racial prejudice, study of a representative sample of white urban adults showed that the personality trait of punitiveness was significantly correlated with seven different indices of prejudiced racial beliefs and unsympathetic attitudes toward blacks (Hesselbart & Schuman, 1976). Thus, recent studies continue to provide evidence that attitudes and personality are often linked in meaningful ways.

ATTITUDES AND BEHAVIOR

The topic of attitude-behavior consistency has been a subject of debate since the early days of social psychology (e.g., LaPiere, 1934), and in more recent years whole books have been written on the subject (e.g., Deutscher, 1973; Zanna, Higgins, & Herman, 1982; Canary & Seibold, 1984). In the few pages available here we will highlight the most important aspects of this issue.

The question of what relationships exist among the cognitive, affective, and behavioral components of attitudes (or between beliefs, attitudes, and behavioral intentions as separate concepts) was discussed in Chapters 4 and 10. Now our attention shifts from the components or aspects of attitudes to the link between attitudes and behavior (that is, overt responses).

Is what we say always consistent with what we do? Obviously not, as Abigail Adams noted in 1774, before the American Revolution, in the quotation at the beginning of this chapter. We can all think of cases of discrepancy between our own words and deeds, just as between the statements and actions of others. Since attitudes are usually measured through a person's verbal report, there is a likelihood that attitudes and actions often may not correspond. Let's suppose for a moment that we pushed this idea to its extreme and asserted that attitudes were completely unrelated to actions. If that were the case, what would be the value of having the concept of "attitude"? Upon reflection, it should be clear that there would be very little value to it, for as an intervening variable, "attitude" is only a useful concept if it conveniently summarizes, predicts, or is related to patterns of actual behavior. (For instance, recall Allport's definition that an attitude is a state of readiness which influences an individual's responses to objects and situations.)

Thus it can be seen that the verdict about the usefulness of the concept "attitude" depends largely on the empirical evidence regarding its relationship to behavior. What is the evidence? From the great mass of research in this area, we will mention a few studies which illustrate important points.

A Famous Early Study

In the early 1930s, when racial prejudice toward blacks, Orientals, and most other foreigners was at a high level in the U.S., LaPiere (1934) traveled extensively around the country with a young, foreign-born Chinese couple. In a careful empirical manner he kept records on their acceptance and the quality of service they received in hotels, "auto camps," and restaurants. In addition, LaPiere attempted to vary the conditions experimentally by frequently having his Chinese friends enter restaurants first or do the negotiation for rooms. The results were dramatic: in about 10,000 miles of travel, the party was served (often with great hospitality) at 250 establishments and rejected at only one (a "rather inferior auto camp"). That was the behavioral measure.

To determine these establishments' attitudes toward Chinese as guests, La-Piere waited six months after the time of their visit and then sent each one a questionnaire asking, "Will you accept members of the Chinese race as guests in your establishment?" With persistence, he was able to get replies from 128, of which one auto camp replied "Yes," nine respondents said it would depend on the circumstances, and 118 said "No." Identical questionnaires sent to 128 similar businesses which they had not visited produced exactly the same distribution of responses. As a result of this massive discrepancy between questionnaire responses and actual behavior, LaPiere concluded that in many social situations questionnaire data cannot be trusted, and that attitudes generally must be studied through observation of actual social behavior. Results highly similar to LaPiere's have also been obtained in other studies, such as one involving racially mixed parties of diners in New York restaurants (Kutner, Wilkins, & Yarrow, 1952).

Can we conclude from these findings that these businesspeople's attitudes and actions were inconsistent? No, we cannot! Though at first glance it would appear so, there are major methodological problems involved, which are causing what we may term "pseudo inconsistency."

Pseudo Inconsistency

One important point about the question of consistency has been made by Campbell (1963), who has emphasized the importance of **situational thresholds.** He stresses that often the verbal attitude statements and the overt behavioral measures have quite different thresholds, or levels of probability of occurrence. The reason for this discrepancy may be any of a number of factors which will be discussed a bit later in this section. As an example, take a political party member who doesn't contribute financially to his party. For convenience, let us say that about 50% of the adult registered voters belong to the party; yet we know that the number of financial contributors is never more than about 5%. Campbell points out that it would be grossly unfair to call the 45% who don't contribute "inconsistent." They are merely doing the easy (or common) thing and avoiding the difficult (or uncommon) behavior. The only true case of inconsistency would be a person who did the difficult, uncommon thing but failed to perform the easy, common action—in this example, one who contributed to the party but was not a member (e.g., one who gave money to "Democrats for Reagan"). Such individuals are not only rare, but their behavior after the election is over often suggests that their attitude (stated party affiliation) was misclassified. For instance, consider the case of former Texas Governor John Connally—he headed Democrats for Nixon in 1972 and then declared himself a Republican not too long after the election.

This analysis of **pseudo inconsistency** clearly applies to the LaPiere study of the Chinese couple's acceptance in restaurants and hotels. Its famous "inconsistency" was probably primarily a matter of differences in situational thresholds, for discrimination against members of another race is much harder in the face-to-face personal situation than in the abstract written-letter situation. Another example of this point is shown in Box 11-1. However, not all attitude-behavior comparisons display such differences in situational thresholds (Raden, 1977).

Other methodological critiques of the famous "inconsistency" studies have also been made. Dillehay (1973) has pointed out that in phoning or sending questionnaires to a restaurant or hotel, there is no certainty that the attitude measure was provided by the *same person* whose behavior was earlier observed. Also, the base rate or commonness of the behavior can markedly affect the attitude-behavior correlation—where almost everyone chooses one response (as in the LaPiere study), a single inconsistent case can lower the attitude-behavior correlation to nearly zero; whereas if the base rate is closer to 50%, one inconsistent

Box 11–1 *Pseudo Inconsistency of Attitude Measures: Differing Situational Thresholds*

Minard (1952) described a group of white and Negro coal miners who worked together in the same mines, but whose interaction patterns were very different in the mines than in the town where they lived. Campbell (1963) has clarified the misleading analyses which have been made of this supposed inconsistency, as follows:

Minard's . . . comments on the Pocahontas coal miners involves two items which can be diagramed as [below]. His report clearly indicates that the settings of mine and town have markedly different situational thresholds for nondiscriminatory reactions of white miners, only 20 percent being friendly in town, 80 percent being friendly in the mines. He reports no instances of true inconsistency, i.e., being friendly in town and hostile in the mines. From this point of view, . . . [it is] clearly wrong to conclude that the middle 60 percent are persons "whose overt behavior provides no clue as to their attitudes." Their behavior clearly indicates that they have consistently middling attitudes. The two items, mine and town, correlate perfectly.

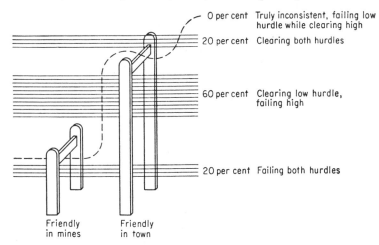

0 per cent Truly inconsistent, failing low hurdle while clearing high

20 per cent Clearing both hurdles

60 per cent Clearing low hurdle, failing high

20 per cent Failing both hurdles

Friendly in mines   Friendly in town

Source: Campbell, 1963, p. 161.

case will have very little effect on the correlation (Fishbein & Ajzen, 1975, p. 373).

We can conclude that much (but by no means all) of the alleged inconsistency in the attitude-behavior research literature is actually pseudo inconsistency.

How Much Consistency?

But what about cases of real inconsistency between attitudes and behavior? How common are they, and what explanations can be found for them? Considerable attention has been directed to these questions in recent years. In one important review article, Wicker (1969) examined more than 30 studies bearing on the attitude-behavior relationship and concluded pessimistically that in most cases verbal measures of attitudes were only slightly related or were even unrelated to the expected behaviors. In only a minority of cases was the correlation coefficient between attitude and behavior higher than .30, and even this high a relationship indicates that the two measures have only about 10% of their variance in common; that is, they show only a small degree of overlap or similarity. Thus Wicker concluded that it is risky to conceptualize attitudes as a latent process underlying behavior and/or to try to predict behavioral responses from verbal attitude measures.

However, some of the articles reviewed by Wicker suffered from the pseudo-inconsistency problems which we have described above, while others did not really have a genuine measure of attitude or an actual behavioral criterion (Fishbein & Ajzen, 1975, pp. 359–361). One reanalysis of the same studies concluded that only seven of them had adequate measures of both attitudes and behavior, and these studies found substantially higher attitude-behavior correlations (M. E. Shaw, cited in Severy, 1974). Also, we may consider that correlations from .30 up to over .60, as found in the more successful studies, actually represent a high degree of accuracy in predicting a complex social behavior. Donald Campbell has pointed out that the correlation between two different *behaviors* (for instance, willingness to serve a minority group member, and sitting beside the same person on a bus) is probably lower still (cited in A. G. Miller, 1972). Indeed, Triandis (1964) has shown that behaviors involved in social distance and prejudice do not all cluster together with high positive correlations, but rather form five relatively distinct factors. Behaviors indicating general respect may be largely uncorrelated with acceptance into friendship relations, which in turn may be unrelated to marital acceptance. Similarly, low correlations might often be found between the same behavior in two different situations; for instance, Dutton (1971) found that enforcement of stated dress regulations in some Canadian restaurants was often different depending on whether a white couple or a black couple were the first ones to arrive informally dressed—interestingly, enforcement was often more lenient for black customers.

Despite some low correlations, there is much evidence of general attitude-behavior similarity. The election campaign opinion polls almost always show a close correspondence between *aggregate* public opinion and voting behavior, and Crespi (1971) has described other examples where polls have shown good ability to predict movie attendance and food brand preference. Similarly for *individual-level* comparisons, most recent reviews of the research literature have concluded that attitudes and behavior are generally related (e.g., Schuman & Johnson, 1976; Cialdini et al., 1981; Cooper & Croyle, 1984).

Methodological Improvements

There are several methodological refinements which have been shown to yield higher attitude-behavior relationships. Two are broader methods of measurement: a multi-item attitude scale instead of measurement by a single item (e.g., Snyder & Kendzierski, 1982), and a behavioral criterion scale made up of several actions instead of just one (Fishbein & Ajzen, 1975, pp. 359–363; Jaccard, 1979). Provided that the several items in a scale are positively correlated, this procedure will necessarily increase the scale's reliability and the size of the attitude-behavior correlation (Dawes & Smith, 1985).

Two other methodological improvements are to measure attitudes toward situations (Rokeach, 1968) or attitudes toward a particular action (with a particular person) rather than using the traditional measure of attitudes toward a person or a whole category of persons such as "blacks" in general (e.g., Schwartz & Tessler, 1972). For instance, in predicting how often students will cut a particular course, we should achieve better prediction by measuring the students' attitudes concerning the importance of the course and the act of cutting class than by measuring only the students' attitudes toward the instructor.

The conditions under which attitudes and behavior are measured should be as similar as possible—for instance, *not* an anonymous measure of attitude and a public observation of behavior (Green, 1972). Also, the time interval between measurement of the attitude and the criterion behavior should be short. Another key methodological requirement that has often been ignored is that the attitude and the behavior should be measured at corresponding (i.e., similar) levels of **specificity** in terms of the object, the action, the situation, and the time involved (Fishbein & Ajzen 1975; Ajzen & Fishbein 1977). For instance, in order to have a chance of accurately predicting a person's sexual behavior, we would need to specify the type of action (intercourse?, fondling?), the partner, the situation (a dormitory room?, a romantic vacation trip?), and the time (this weekend?, sometime this summer?). Lack of congruent specification of the attitude object was obviously a problem in LaPiere's (1934) study, where the attitude questionnaire asked about Chinese guests in general, but the behavioral decision was made regarding *a particular* Chinese couple, well-dressed, well-spoken, smiling, and accompanied by a middle-class white companion. Many studies have confirmed that the more similar these key aspects of the attitudinal and behavioral measures are, the greater will be the amount of consistency.

> A person's attitude has a consistently strong relation with his or her behavior when it is directed at the same target and when it involves the same action. (Ajzen & Fishbein, 1977, p. 912)

Explanations of Inconsistency

Despite any methodological improvements, there may still remain many instances of genuine and substantial inconsistency between attitudes and behavior. Wicker (1969) and Fishbein and Ajzen (1975) have suggested many factors which can help explain such inconsistency, among which are:

1. Instability of attitudes and intentions over time. Many studies have shown that attitudes and intentions shift over time, sometimes quite sharply. Conse-

quently, the longer the time between attitude measurement and behavioral observation, the greater the chances for inconsistency (Schwartz, 1978).

2. Other competing attitudes, motives, or values. A person might have a favorable attitude toward her political party but not contribute to it financially (the behavior measure) because she had a stronger favorable attitude toward other organizations seeking her donations, or because she had a strong motive to save money. This principle has been demonstrated to apply regarding attitudes toward racial discrimination (Schuman, 1972) and toward smoking (Canon & Mathews, 1972), among other areas.

3. Inadequate intellectual, verbal, or social skills. If a person lacks the intelligence or the information to recognize that his behavior does not match his attitude, inconsistency would not be surprising. This might happen, for instance, with a poorly informed voter backing a candidate whose views are actually contrary to his own.

4. Lack of volitional control over the behavior. Some behaviors, such as a mother's ability to breast-feed her newborn baby, are not completely under voluntary control. In one study about 25% of mothers with positive attitudes were nevertheless unsuccessful at breast-feeding (Newton & Newton, 1950). Also, habitual behaviors that we perform without thinking about them are generally not under our voluntary, intentional control—this is why Triandis (1977) included habit as well as intentions as factors in his system for predicting behavior.

5. Unavailability of alternative behaviors. A good example is the person who regularly buys a daily newspaper even though he detests it, because it is the only one conveniently available in his city.

6. Situations involving normative prescriptions of "proper" behavior. A very familiar example is that we are taught to be polite to people even though we don't like them. Also, the norms held by other people present in the situation are important: a strong racist would be less likely to walk out of a racially mixed gathering if she knew that most of the others present supported social integration of the races.

7. Important expected consequences of the behavior. It has been well-established that many restaurant and hotel managers, despite strong antiblack attitudes, nevertheless began serving black customers following the passage of antidiscrimination laws when they were faced with the prospect of legal punishment for racial discrimination. In a weaker form, this consideration of likely consequences is probably also involved in the preceding category (norms regarding proper behavior).

8. Unforeseen extraneous events. For instance, even a family with a strongly favorable attitude toward church attendance might miss Sunday service if they had a seriously ill child, or if their car wouldn't start, or if a heavy thunderstorm intervened.

We may conclude from this list that attitudes are by no means the only factors necessary in order to predict behavioral responses, and sometimes they are not even among the most important factors. Thus a certain amount of inconsistency between attitudes and behavior is to be expected, the amount depending on the particular situation.

Zanna and Fazio (1982) have characterized the history of research on attitude-behavior consistency as passing through three stages. The first stage, in the 1960s, asked the "Is" question—Is there a relation between the two? Though the answers suggested were often pessimistic, as in Wicker's (1969) review, many studies did report high correlations between the two concepts. Therefore, research moved on to the second stage, asking the "When" question—Under what conditions are certain attitudes related to certain behaviors? During the 1970s, studies of this type identified many situational, personality, and attitudinal factors that moderated (i.e., helped to determine) the attitude-behavior relationship. (Most of these factors have been or will be discussed in this section of the chapter.) Finally, in the 1980s, many studies moved on to the "How" question, examining the process by which attitudes guide behavior. Most recent research has concentrated on one of

Photograph courtesy of Allan Wicker.
Reprinted by permission.

Box 11–2 ALLAN WICKER, *Critic of Attitude-Behavior Consistency*

Widely known for his research on attitudes and behavior, Allan Wicker is also an authority on environmental psychology. He grew up in Kansas and received his B.A., M.A., and Ph.D. from the University of Kansas. Following four years of teaching psychology at the University of Wisconsin-Milwaukee and the University of Illinois, he moved to Claremont Graduate School in California in 1971. He has remained there ever since except for brief periods as a visiting professor at Cornell University, the University of Tübingen in Germany, and the University of Zimbabwe in Africa.

Wicker is the author of An Introduction to Ecological Psychology, *and much of his research revolves around the topic of behavior-environment congruence. He has been elected President of the Division of Population and Environmental Psychology and has carried on his research in widely varying behavior settings, including the psychological laboratory, churches, national parks, and small business establishments.*

two approaches: either investigating systems to predict behavior, or trying to understand the process linking attitudes and behavior. The next two sections briefly summarize the highlights of this research.

Systems for Predicting Behavior

Fishbein was the first author to try to combine several factors systematically in predicting behavior. As we detailed in Chapter 4, he proposed a mathematical formula which contains both attitudinal and normative factors. They include: (a) the person's beliefs about the consequences of performing a particular behavior, (b) her evaluation of those consequences, (c) her normative beliefs regarding the expectations of relevant others, and (d) her motivation to comply with those expectations. These two pairs of factors are combined mathematically, multiplying each pair together, weighting them appropriately, and then adding the two products. This equation is used to predict behavioral intentions, rather than behavior, and in 13 studies the average multiple correlation found was a very high figure of +.75 (Fishbein & Ajzen, 1975, p. 310), while a similar analysis of 10 later studies found an even higher average multiple correlation of +.80 (Ajzen, 1988, p. 119). Moreover, many studies have shown that, in turn, behavioral intentions which are carefully measured are usually good predictors of overt behaviors, with correlation coefficients ranging from +.4 as high as +.9 (Kothandapani, 1971b; Fishbein & Ajzen, 1975, pp. 373–374; Davidson & Jaccard, 1979; Ajzen & Fishbein, 1980; Ajzen, 1988, p. 114). For instance, a person's intention to attend church on Sunday morning is likely to be highly correlated with the behavior of actually attending.

More research on this and other prediction systems is needed in order to determine whether and when they are successful in improving the prediction of behavior from attitudinal data. As an example, several studies have shown improved prediction from use of the factor of extraneous events (Wicker, 1971; Brislin & Olmstead, 1973). For instance, prediction of a person's actual church attendance can be improved if we know what he would probably do if he were confronted by unexpected events, such as a heavy thunderstorm, or his car not starting.

Some studies have challenged such prediction systems by suggesting that their measurement methods can cause respondents to construct an attitude on topics where they had none before (e.g., Budd, 1987). Other studies have looked for additional variables that influence behavior, particularly ones whose effects do not operate through behavioral intentions, as the theory of reasoned action specifies they should. One such variable that often independently predicts future behavior is *recent past behavior*, which can also be thought of as *habit* (Bentler & Speckart, 1979, 1981; Bagozzi, 1981; Fredricks & Dossett, 1983; Ajzen & Madden, 1986). Another is the person's feeling of *perceived control* over the behavior, which was shown to be a major factor in studies of difficult goals such as attempted weight loss or achieving high college grades (Schifter & Ajzen, 1985; Ajzen & Madden, 1986). As a result, Ajzen (1987) has incorporated perceived behavioral control in his recent "theory of planned behavior," and other researchers have confirmed that it adds substantially to prediction of behaviors such as problem drinking (Schlegel, d'Avernas, Zanna, & Manske, 1988). Some studies have also challenged the theory of reasoned action by finding that attitudes can influence behavior directly, rather than through their effect on intentions (Bentler & Speckart, 1981; Manstead, Proffitt, & Smart, 1983).

As described in Chapter 4, Triandis (1977) and Sheth (1974), among others, have proposed systems for predicting behavior which incorporate some of these additional variables such as habits, affect, social norms, facilitating conditions, the anticipated situation, unexpected events, and so on. Some studies with each system have also produced reports of high correlations with relevant behaviors. Taken together, these studies clearly show that in order to predict people's behavior it is not enough simply to know their attitudes. Though attitudes are one important determinant of behavior, there are many other important determinants as well.

Understanding the Attitude-Behavior Linkage

The other major current stream of research in this area has concentrated on exploring variables that clarified the *process* by which attitudes influence behavior. In contrast to the predictive approach, which typically uses correlational methods and often studies important real-world behavior (e.g., contraceptive use, voting, or energy conservation behavior), the process studies have usually been experiments conducted in laboratory settings, and often with attitudes that were trivial or developed solely during the experiment. In addition, much of the process research stems from a cognitive psychology background and consequently uses a response-latency operationalization of attitude strength. That is, instead of using self-report questionnaire responses to define attitude direction and extremity, this approach typically uses an evaluative judgment task and defines attitude strength as the speed of a person's evaluative response when presented with an attitude object. Thus, findings of the two streams of research are hard to compare because they use quite different tasks and different operational definitions of "attitude."

Nevertheless, very useful light has been shed on the attitude-behavior relation by some of the process studies. As mentioned in Chapter 9, much of this work has been done by Fazio (cf. 1986a) and his colleagues, using a conditioning concept of attitudes. In this view, an attitude is a conditioned (learned) association between an object and an evaluation (e.g., apple pie is good); and the stronger this association is, the more quickly the attitude will be "activated" or "accessed" (i.e., brought to mind or stated) when one is asked about the object.

If the association between the object and the evaluation is strong, the evaluation is very likely to come to mind when one is exposed to, or thinks about, the object—and as a result, the attitude is likely to influence subsequent behavior. (An easily accessed attitude will also be likely to influence current perception and processing of new information about the object—Fazio & Williams, 1986; Houston & Fazio, 1989.) However, if the association is weak, the evaluation may not be accessed—and in that case attitude-behavior consistency should be much less than

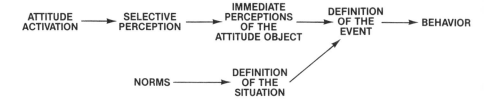

FIGURE 11-1   A diagram of the attitude-to-behavior process.

Source: Fazio (1986a, p. 212).

with strong associations. Figure 11-1 shows the sequence of steps in Fazio's (1986a) proposed model of the attitude-to-behavior process. The two lines in the figure show two components involved in determining behavior, quite similar to Fishbein and Ajzen's (1975) model: an attitude component and a normative component. However, if the person's attitude is not activated (because the association is weak or is blocked in some way), the attitude will not enter into the immediate perceptions of the object, and the resulting behavior may be quite inconsistent with the attitude. Thus, for researchers in this tradition, the interesting process-oriented question is: What factors will strengthen the learned association (i.e., the accessibility of the attitude)?

In the process studies, several variables have been found to moderate the attitude-behavior relationship, because they influence the accessibility and thus the activation of attitudes. They include: (a) direct rather than vicarious experience with the attitude object (Fazio & Zanna, 1981; Borgida & Campbell, 1982), (b) the number of times that the attitude has been expressed (Fazio et al., 1982; Houston & Fazio, 1989), (c) attitude objects which are prototypical rather than unusual members of their category (Lord, Lepper, & Mackie, 1984), (d) attitude topics that are central or involving to the respondents (Sivacek & Crano, 1982), (e) respondents who are in a state of introspective self-awareness (Gibbons, 1978), and (f) respondents who are low self-monitors, because they tend to be consistent in their attitude expression, regardless of the situation (Snyder & Kendzierski, 1982; Zanna & Olson, 1982). Each of these variables increases an attitude's accessibility, and hence they increase the consistency between the attitude and subsequent behavior.

One other feature of this approach is that it applies both to routine, habitual behavior (i.e., what Langer, 1978, called "mindless" actions), and to voluntary, nonhabitual behaviors. In contrast, recall that Fishbein and Ajzen's theory of reasoned action applies only to behavior that is under volitional control—its name as well as its formulas indicate that a person's behavior is determined in a reasoned, thoughtful way by summing his(her) salient beliefs about any object to form an attitude and combining the attitude with information about relevant social norms. This rationalistic approach has been noted as a limitation of the theory of reasoned action (Fazio, 1986a). In addition to the fact that this theory doesn't apply to habitual behavior, much of human voluntary behavior seems far less deliberate and carefully reasoned than the theory implies. By contrast, Fazio's model in Figure 11-1 indicates that if and when an attitude is activated, it leads relatively automatically to selectively biased perception of the object in the immediate situation, and this influences behavior without any necessary conscious reasoning process. Thus, Fazio's model may better capture the phenomenology of individuals as they act in relatively automatic ways in routine situations, whereas the Fishbein and Ajzen approach may be most applicable to more major, carefully thought-out decisions.

The Effect of Behavior on Attitudes

Finally, much reseach has shown that people's behavior also has a reciprocal effect on their attitudes. For example, Lieberman (1956) showed that being promoted to (or demoted from) the positions of foreman or union shop steward had clearcut effects on workers' job-related attitudes. Other prominent examples include the effects of "forced compliance" or counterattitudinal advocacy (discussed in Chapter 10 in relation to dissonance theory and impression-management theory), effects of commitment and of active participation on attitude change (also discussed in Chapter 10), and the prointegration attitudinal changes that followed U.S. school desegregation (described in Chapter 15).

Thus we may conclude with Kelman (1974) that "attitudes are alive and well and gainfully employed in the sphere of action," for we have good evidence of

> the engagement of attitude and action in a continuing, reciprocal, circular process. Not only is attitude an integral part of action, but action is an integral part of the development, testing, and crystallization of attitudes. (p. 324)

LABORATORY RESEARCH VERSUS FIELD RESEARCH

We turn next to a topic which has received increasing attention in recent years—what differences are there, if any, between the results of experimental, laboratory research and those of studies done in real-life field settings? One initial clarification may be needed: though most research in field settings uses survey methods and correlational (nonmanipulative) designs, these are not necessary characteristics of **field research**. Swingle (1973) and Reich (1982) have presented collections of field research studies, most of which are true experiments, with all of the advantages in manipulation, control, precision, and stronger causal inferences which the term "experiment" implies. (For a discussion of the advantages and disadvantages of different types of research methods, together with examples of each method, see Oskamp, 1984.)

Many of the differences between laboratory and field studies of attitudes have been summarized by Hovland (1959) and McGuire (1969). In research on persuasion and attitude change it is usually found that laboratory studies show stronger effects than field studies. For instance, this has been demonstrated in research on the size of the attitude-behavior relationship (Hanson, 1980) and on effects of TV violence on viewers' aggressiveness (Freedman, 1984). However, this contrast is probably due largely, if not entirely, to a number of methodological differences which are frequently *confounded* with the laboratory-field distinction. To clarify this point, here is a list of some of the typical methodological characteristics of laboratory studies—ways in which they are apt to differ from field studies (also see Figure 11-2):

1. An authoritative, prestigious situation. The experimenter or other communicator is in a position of power and authority, and demand characteristics encourage attitude change.
2. No distractions. In contrast, mass media communications often have to compete with many other distracting stimuli.
3. Less ego-involving or important topics. These are chosen so as to maximize

FIGURE 11-2 Some differences between laboratory and field research settings.

attitude change, whereas field research has often studied more important issues such as political attitudes.

4. College students as subjects. Students are better informed, quicker to understand, and more responsive to rational persuasion than the average citizen.

5. Disguised persuasive intent. Often experiments cover up their true purpose, while commercial advertisers, politicians, and other real-world communicators usually make a direct persuasive appeal, thus allowing the recipients to evade the message if they are so inclined.

6. No counterpersuasion. In everyday life there are almost always messages from competing products, groups, or individuals, which tend to lessen the original message's effect.

7. Better measures of attitude. The laboratory situation allows more extensive and careful attitude measurement than most real-world situations.

8. Attitude change is usually measured immediately. By contrast, in field research the measurement of change may be many days or weeks after the message, thus showing a diminished effect due to the passage of time.

The Importance of Field Research

The issue of *generalizability* is one where field research usually has an advantage due to the real-world nature of the tasks and settings involved. The degree of similarity of a research situation to circumstances in the outside world has been termed its **mundane realism**. When laboratory research uses highly unusual tasks and settings, and particularly when the participants are very aware of performing as subjects under the experimenter's scrutiny, its results may not be applicable to most situations in the world outside of the laboratory. However, well-known experimentalists have emphasized that the supposed artificiality of experimental situations need not be an obstacle to the generalizability of results as long as the situation is convincingly constructed to have **experimental realism** (believability and impact) for the subjects (Berkowitz & Donnerstein, 1982; Aronson, Brewer, & Carlsmith, 1985). These authors have also pointed out many of the challenges and difficulties inherent in conducting field research.

The lab-versus-field issue is by no means a one-sided one. Even dedicated laboratory researchers usually grant the importance and necessity of field research and recognize its relation to their own investigations. For instance, Leon Festinger, one of the most noted laboratory experimenters in social psychology, wrote:

> Laboratory experimentation, as a technique for the development of an empirical body of knowledge, cannot exist by itself. Experiments in the laboratory must derive their direction from studies of real-life situations, and results must continually be checked by studies of real-life situations. (1953, pp. 169–170)

Since the 1970s many behavioral scientists have issued calls for more field research and broader application of scientific theory and methods to a variety of social problems in the real world (e.g., McGuire, 1973; Rodin, 1985). As a result, increased attention has been directed toward field methods, as illustrated in various recent research reviews (e.g., Reich, 1982; Oskamp, 1984; Rodin, 1985). In keeping with this verbal attention to field research, its small share of the research literature published in the major American social psychology journals has increased somewhat—it was around 5% of the articles in the 1960s (Fried, Gumpper, & Allen, 1973), but it was still only a bit over 20% in the mid-1980s (Sears, 1986), and laboratory research shows a similar predominance in British journal articles (Potter, 1981). Still, the trend is encouraging, and it has been predicted that

> the next decade will see even more vigorous efforts to apply, test, and develop social psychological knowledge through the study of important human concerns, and the emergence of more creative ways to use both laboratory and field settings. (Rodin, 1985, p. 866)

ETHICAL PROBLEMS IN ATTITUDE RESEARCH

Ethical questions arise in any kind of research activity, and attitude and opinion research is no exception. Psychologists and other attitude researchers have been attentive to ethical questions for many years, and ever since 1953 they have published and updated thorough guidelines to protect the interests of research subjects and of society in general (American Psychological Association, 1953, 1967, 1973, 1981, 1982; Field, 1971). Empirical studies of ethical issues in social science research have been growing rapidly (Korn, 1984; Adair, Dushenko, & Lindsay, 1985; Adair, 1988), and Kelman (1982) has offered a scheme for classifying these issues and their specific manifestations in different types of research. Many recent volumes have analyzed, criticized, and proposed solutions for potential ethical problems in the social and behavioral sciences (e.g., Bower & de Gasparis, 1978; Beauchamp, Faden, Wallace, & Walters, 1982; Kimmel, 1982; Sieber, 1982, 1984).

The recent history of concerns about scientific research ethics is a fascinating one. In the 1960s, media publicity and a resulting public outcry led to congressional investigations of occasional ethical lapses in *biomedical* research involving failure to protect research subjects from possible harm—for example, injecting senile patients with live cancer cells without their understanding what was being done, or observing the long-term progression of syphilis in destitute black males while misleading them into believing they were being treated (Pattullo, 1984). Consequently, the U.S. Surgeon General issued an order in 1966 requiring that procedures for federally funded research projects be reviewed and approved in advance by an impartial committee at the research institution, and more extensive regulations were later promulgated by the U.S. Department of Health, Education, and Welfare (1971). Though biomedical research was the main target of the regulations, all social and behavioral science research was also included until 1981, when the federal rules governing it were greatly simplified and redirected toward the few such studies that do carry potential risks for the participants (Fields, 1981).

Though most attitude and opinion studies do not pose major ethical problems, the following important issues must be considered by any worker in this field.

Harmful Consequences. This is the most serious ethical problem in research, but it arises mostly in medical research, or in behavioral research involving administration of drugs, emotional situations such as encounter groups, or use of painful stimuli like electric shock. Only rarely does the risk of harmful consequences occur in attitude and opinion research, though it is possible in studies of the effects of stress (e.g., Berkun, Bialek, Kern, & Yagi, 1962) or of threats to subjects' self-esteem (e.g., Bramel, 1963; Walster, 1965). However, these few atypical cases have generated a great deal of comment and concern (Warwick, 1982).

Deception. Far more common in attitude and opinion research than the problem of harmful consequences is the issue of deception of research subjects by giving them false information. One survey of the social psychological literature published in the 1960s and 1970s showed that about 60% of articles used some deception (Gross & Fleming, 1982), though the figure dropped to about 35% in the mid-1980s (Vitelli, 1988). Questions have been raised not only about the morality of deceiving subjects, but also about the effect this will have over the long run on public attitudes toward psychology and sociology as disciplines, and the possible impact on society of an erosion of public trust in its institutions (Kelman, 1967, 1982).

On the other hand, in order to obtain valid results in experimental studies, it is often essential that the research subjects not be aware of the hypotheses being tested. Thus some secrecy is usually necessary, and often this can only be accomplished by actively misleading the participants, though various alternatives to deception have been proposed (Geller, 1982). In general, the currently accepted ethical principles prescribe that deception should only be used if there are no other legitimate ways to accomplish the same research goal, if the importance of the research warrants the amount of deception used, if participants are allowed to withdraw from the research at any time without penalty, and if they are fully debriefed at the end of their participation (Elms, 1982). In actual practice, some surveys have shown that psychologists are more concerned about the use of deception than are research subjects (Sullivan & Deiker, 1973; Christensen, 1988). And even when subjects have had previous experience with deception in research, it does not necessarily bias their responses in later studies (see the discussion of deception and suspicion in Chapter 9).

Informed Consent. Since 1966, it has become an essential ethical requirement of experiments that the subjects have consented to participate in an informed and knowledgeable way, after an explanation of any possible risks or unpleasant aspects of participation (American Psychological Association, 1973, 1982). If subjects agree to take part after a full and open explanation of the attendant risks and benefits, it is generally felt that they are doing so as free agents and that the researcher's ethical obligation in this area has been satisfied. However, in survey studies of public opinion, the risks involved in participation are limited to minor inconvenience at most; and consequently the requirement for informed consent has generally been considered to be fulfilled by obtaining implicit consent (i.e., the respondent answering the questions instead of refusing), and perhaps also by telling respondents that any bothersome question can be skipped (Schuman & Kalton, 1985). And in observational studies of public behavior, such as marching in a demonstration or buying a particular product, the informed consent of participants is hardly ever obtained—largely because it would be very difficult or impossible to do so, and it might be more of a bother than a service to the subjects (Aronson et al., 1985).

Invasion of Privacy. A related question concerns when and how subjects' privacy must be protected. Of course, anonymity and confidentiality of data are essential—participants' names or identification must never be linked with their behavior or opinions in reporting research results. But particularly in observational studies, the line where invasion of privacy begins is apt to be very fuzzy. Is concealed tape recording of an interview acceptable? What about listening to shoppers' conversations as they examine the merchandise? Or how about checking the number of liquor bottles in people's trash (Webb et al., 1981)? Probably the line which most researchers would draw is that public behavior or behavior in public places may legitimately be observed and/or recorded, whereas private behavior in private places must be protected from observation through invasive techniques such as "bugging," high-powered microphones, etc.

Inconvenience to Participants. Though most attitude studies involve only minor inconvenience at most, researchers must be vigilant to avoid any unnecessary inconvenience. For example, in survey interviews, questions must be worded so that embarrassment is minimized, time requirements must be reasonable, and repeated calls or inconvenient hours should be avoided (Crossley, 1971). A deplorable example of respondent inconvenience is the misleading tactics of some salesmen who disguise their initial approach as a consumer survey; one study found that very recent experience with such a deceptive practice lowered response rates to a legitimate survey interview *by 75%* (Sheets, Radlinski, Kohne, & Brunner, 1974).

Debriefing of Participants. In experimental research it has been a traditional requirement that subjects are interviewed and informed at the end of the experimental session. This accomplishes several goals: The investigator usually thanks them and gives them information about the research topic in return for their cooperation; any deception is carefully explained, the need for it described in detail, and its effectiveness checked on; participants' questions are answered and any remaining anxiety which they may have is allayed; and appeals for secrecy about the research procedure are often made so that future subjects will not learn information which might invalidate the research results. Detailed and helpful suggestions for debriefing procedures have been offered by Aronson et al. (1985). If this debriefing is done thoroughly and sensitively, most investigators feel that subjects come to appreciate the value of the research, accept the need for any deception, and leave with a positive feeling about their experience (Aronson et al., 1985; Christensen, 1988).

In field research, by contrast, it is rare and often impossible to debrief individuals after their participation in a study. Usually there is little or no deception which needs to be explained and no reason for participants to have been upset or anxious; so debriefing is less necessary. Particularly in observational research, such as a study of traffic violations, if individuals did not know they had been observed, informing them about it might only raise their concern rather than lowering it (Sieber, 1984, pp. 74–75).

Reporting of Results. In scientific publication, standards for reporting research results are carefully specified and overseen by journal editors. However, studies involving important social issues, particularly survey research findings, are often reported in the public press without the careful details and safeguards which reputable scientists would insist on. In fact, some unscrupulous pollsters have been known to slant their data collection or reporting for devious political ends (Roll & Cantril, 1980). To help eliminate these unfortunate instances, the American Association for Public Opinion Research (AAPOR) in 1968 made an important addition to its code of professional ethics and practices (Field, 1971). The added standards specify that any report of survey or poll results which is made public should contain information on the sponsor of the survey, the wording of questions, the method and dates of interviewing, the population sampled and sample size, and the likely amount of sampling error in the results. Adherence to these standards will not prevent all abuses of polls, but it will make their interpretation much more open to the scrutiny of other investigators and informed citizens.

The Obligation to Do Research. Though researchers must give careful thought to all of the ethical problems discussed above, they cannot just throw up their hands in defeat and give up the research enterprise. The duty of the trained scientist to gather information and knowledge which can be put to public use is also an ethical obligation. To withdraw from that responsibility would be just as unethical as to do research in ways which ignored the rights of participants.

> The distinctive contribution of scientists to human welfare is the development of knowledge and its intelligent application to appropriate problems. Their underlying ethical imperative, thus, is to conduct research as well as they know how. (American Psychological Association, 1982, p. 15)

PUBLIC OPINION AND PUBLIC POLICY

Related to ethical issues in attitude research are the questions about uses and abuses of opinion polls in practical politics which we considered in Chapter 5. Now, as the final major topic in this chapter, we turn to broader policy questions concerning whether and how public opinion affects or is reflected in public policy. First, *should* public opinion affect public policy? Second, *does* it do so, and if it does, in what ways and under what circumstances? And finally, what uses are there for social science research in the public policy arena?

Should Public Opinion Affect Public Policy?

This is a question which has been asked by political philosophers for centuries. In general, we can distinguish three main types of answers which have been given. One position, which we may call the "will of the people" viewpoint, holds that legislators and political administrators should make their decisions entirely in accordance with the opinion of their constituents. This view was stated before the French Revolution by Jean Jacques Rousseau in his treatise *The Social Contract*, and it was strongly supported by Thomas Jefferson. Later Abraham Lincoln expressed it well in the quotation at the beginning of this chapter: "What I want is to get done what the people desire to have done, and the question for me is how to find that out exactly."

By contrast, another viewpoint holds that the calm, reasoned "judgment of the representative" should guide his vote rather than the popular clamor or the shifting winds of public opinion. This position was prominently espoused by the British parliamentarian Edmund Burke and by Alexander Hamilton in *The Federalist Papers*. A later and less elegant statement of the same principle is seen in Richard Nixon's admonition against "swaying with the polls."

A third viewpoint might be called the "party responsibility" approach. It became popular after the rise of strong national parties, and it holds the representative responsible, not to his own local constituents, but to the program developed by his party, designed to satisfy the needs of the whole nation. Clearly, in this approach, national public opinion is an important determinant of the party platform.

Another dimension of the question about the role of public opinion is: *which* public opinion? As we discussed in Chapter 6, mass public opinion may differ greatly from elite public opinion. On any given political issue, a large majority of the whole population is usually unconcerned and/or uninformed. Therefore, is it reasonable to guide policy by overall public opinion, with its weak preferences and shifting viewpoints? Or, on the other hand, should the "involved public," the minority who are concerned over a particular issue, be the ones who guide official policy? But if that approach is followed, how can we avoid giving undue weight to vocal pressure groups and self-interested lobbyists?

These are difficult questions, and no final philosophical answers can be given to them. However, it is clear that, if public opinion is to be consulted, modern

FIGURE 11–3
Should political leaders be guided by the "will of the people"?

opinion polls give us a greatly improved method of doing so. Before the 1930s, political leaders had to seek the "will of the people" through newspaper editorials, through letters from the few involved citizens who took the trouble to write them, or through discussion with their highly selective circle of acquaintances. Now, with modern polling techniques, national leaders can learn with great accuracy the views of the total electorate *or* the opinions of the most concerned citizens, and they can balance these against the claims and demands of pressure groups and lobbyists (Gallup, 1965; Bogart, 1972a).

The type of issues on which public opinion should be consulted is also a question. Many authorities have concluded that the public should determine the decisions on broad, general questions having to do with the goals of public policy, rather than the specific means of achieving these goals. As Childs (1965) expressed it, the public is most competent

> to determine the basic ends of public policy, to choose top policy makers, to appraise the results of public policy, and to say what, in the final analysis is fair, just, and moral. On the other hand, the general public is not competent to determine the best means for attaining specific goals, to answer technical questions, to prescribe remedies for political, social, and economic ills, and to deal with specialized issues far removed from the everyday experience and understanding of the people in general. (p. 350)

Clearly, official policy cannot follow opinion poll results or specific questions in detail because the results are often unclear, shifting, uninformed, or ill-considered. For instance, in 1954 during the Korean War, over 60% of respondents to a Gallup Poll said they favored using atomic artillery shells against the Chinese army, and one-third advocated dropping hydrogen bombs on China (Bogart, 1972a, p. 19). Fortunately, such simplistic and genocidal "ultimate solutions" were not adopted by the U.S. government. However, polls inherently have great difficulty in focusing on the more complex and varied alternative policies which have to be considered by diplomats and statesmen.

Though there are dangers in public opinion influencing national policy too greatly, there are also undesirable consequences when government has so much power that it can readily manipulate public opinion. An extreme instance was the use of propaganda in Hitler's Germany, but a trend in the same direction seems to have occurred in the United States with the increase in presidential power and official secrecy—one example is the clandestine attempts to gain public support for the "Contras" fighting against the Nicaraguan government, which came to light during the Iran-Contra hearings.

Though social scientists have studied public opinion extensively, there have been relatively few studies of what effects it actually has on government actions and the process by which it is or is not translated into public policy. We will look next at some studies which bear on these questions.

Does Public Opinion Affect Public Policy?

Research in this area has shown, not one typical pattern, but many different ones, depending largely on the issue involved. Some issues have displayed a direct effect of public opinion on government policy, others no effect, and still others a reverse effect (policy influencing public opinion).

Direct Effects of Public Opinion. One of the issues where public opinion had its greatest effect on policy was the civil rights struggle of the 1950s and 1960s. A famous study of this topic by Miller and Stokes (1963) compared the attitudes, perceptions, and roll call votes of a sample of 116 Congressmen with the attitudes of their election opponents and of a sample of their constituents, district by district. The correspondence between constituents' attitudes and the legislator's roll call votes on civil rights questions was shown by a correlation of almost + .6, much the highest of the three issues studied. Moreover, additional analyses indicated that Representatives by and large correctly perceived their constituents' attitudes and chose to vote accordingly, regardless of their own attitudes (Cnudde & McCrone, 1966). This pattern is quite different from the ones found on some other issues. A similar, but improved, study of congressional voting patterns in 1977-78 showed relatively high correlations with constituents' opinions in the areas of social welfare, women's rights, and racial issues (Page, Shapiro, Gronke, & Rosenberg, 1984).

Two large-scale studies have investigated all the U.S. public issues for which there were poll data on citizens' policy preferences *and* clear subsequent federal policy actions. Studying 222 issues during the period from 1960 to 1974, Monroe (1978) found that the federal actions were consistent with public preferences 64% of the time—70% of the time for *salient* issues where there was a high level of public concern. Page and Shapiro (1983) studied quantitative *changes* in public preferences over the whole period from 1935 to 1979 and found 357 issues for which there was a significant amount of change. Like Monroe, they reported a fairly high correspondence in subsequent federal policy actions—66% of the actions taken within one year after the public opinion change were congruent, and the figure was 90% in cases where public opinion changed by 20% or more. Page and Shapiro found more congruence on salient *social* issues than on economic or welfare policies or foreign policy issues.

Even where public opinion does not determine government policy, it may set limits on the policy options which leaders feel free to consider (Roll & Cantril, 1980). This appears to have been true both in the Vietnam War, when Lyndon Johnson was forced to withdraw from the 1968 presidential race, and in the gradual U.S. mobilization before World War II. Starting in 1939, President Franklin D. Roosevelt was probably the first national leader to use poll results in a planned, programmatic way. He commissioned the noted psychologist Hadley Cantril to do repeated public opinion polls, and endeavored very successfully to manage the buildup in aid to Britain so that a majority of citizens would continue to respond that the pace was "about right."

Lack of Effect of Public Opinion. A common case where public opinion does not get translated into national policy is where one or both houses of Congress throw up roadblocks against a popularly endorsed proposal. For instance, Congress turned down Medicare legislation for many years in the 1960s (Childs, 1965) and refused to pass national health insurance in the 1980s, even though both of those programs have had strong public support. In 1970 there were sharp discrepancies between general public opinion and congressional attitudes on treatment of suspected criminals, family income maintenance approaches to welfare programs, and wage and price controls (Backstrom, 1972). Even more extreme is Congress's 40-year record of disregarding the very large majority of the population who favor gun control laws (Erskine, 1972; Schuman & Presser, 1981a).

Though the House of Representatives was planned as the branch of government which would be directly responsive to public opinion, that has often not been the case. In the Miller and Stokes (1963) study, it was shown that House roll call votes on foreign policy were essentially unrelated to constituents' attitudes. Similarly, Page et al. (1984) found no significant relationship on the issues of abortion and legal rights of accused individuals. Monroe (1978) found the greatest discrepancies between public opinion and federal action in the areas of defense issues and internal governmental reforms. Page and Shapiro (1983) pointed to public-governmental disagreement concerning foreign military and economic aid in the 1950s and on the issue of U.S. adoption of the metric system in the 1970s.

Reverse Effects—Policy Influences on Public Opinion. It is in the field of foreign affairs that public opinion most often follows rather than leads official policy (Etzioni, 1969). This is probably because public ignorance of and indifference to policy issues tends to be proportional to their geographic distance from home, so most foreign affairs engage little citizen attention and develop public attitudes which are weakly held and rather easily changed. A specific example can be seen in the many twists and turns of public opinion which followed changing administration decisions regarding nuclear testing from 1954 to 1963 (unilateral suspension of tests, an international nuclear moratorium, resumption of testing, preparation for atmospheric tests, and finally the test-ban treaty with Russia). Through all these events public opinion rather faithfully followed official policies (Childs, 1965; Rosi, 1965). Other similar cases show continuing public approval for the tremendously mounting U.S. military budget since 1945 and for President Kennedy's firm response in the 1962 Cuban missile crisis, but also for conciliatory actions such as President Nixon's easing of tensions with mainland China. Monroe (1978) reported by far the highest level of agreement between public opinion and government actions (92%) in the area of foreign policy.

Despite public willingness to follow the administration lead in foreign affairs, there are some limits to public acquiescence. The most clearcut example is the Vietnam War. Early in the war it appeared that President Johnson could lead and influence popular opinion at will (Lipset, 1966); but as U.S. casualties, budgets, and impatience with the military stalemate increased, popular approval of the war gradually changed to disapproval and finally forced a change in administrations and a withdrawal from the war (Mueller, 1973).

The fact that political leaders can often sway public opinion may encourage abuses of democratic procedures. President Nixon's attempts to cover up the Watergate deceptions are well-known examples. Ironically, political propagandists may often use slanted opinion polls in their attempts to mold public opinion in their favor. A particularly flagrant example is cited by Bogart (1972a, pp. 10-12) concerning the congressional debate over President Nixon's antiballistic missile (ABM) proposals in 1969. At a time when less than half of the public favored development of an ABM system, a later-repudiated private poll was publicized in full-page newspaper ads by a pro-ABM "Citizens Committee," purporting to show that 84% of the nation backed the ABM system.

Uses for Social Science Research

In the public policy arena there are many uses for social science research. Though it gets far less attention and funding than the physical sciences, engineering, and economics, social science research is still generally acknowledged to have substantial applied value. For instance, note this passage from an official report of the National Science Foundation (1969):

> Policies for handling the nation's most pressing issues and problems—whether they relate to the cities, pollution, inflation, or supersonic transport—must rest not only on knowledge drawn from the physical and biological sciences, but also on the best available knowledge about human individual and social behavior. Many of our most urgent domestic policy issues, indeed, are more closely related to the social sciences than to the other sciences. (pp. xiii–xiv)

Abt (1980) has provided a list of major social science research projects sponsored by the federal government, in areas ranging from child care to housing to criminal justice; and Oskamp (1984, Chap. 15) has summarized many of the findings about how social research has been used in the public policy arena. Tornatzky, Solomon, et al. (1982) have provided examples to suggest that even larger investments in social science research would pay major dividends in increasing U.S. innovation and productivity. Since a large part of the problem concerns how to ensure that available knowledge is *used* by policy makers, various proposals have been made, such as establishing a presidential Council of Social Science Advisors, parallel to the influential Council of Economic Advisors (Kiesler, 1980).

George Gallup (1965) and other pollers have long insisted that more attention to legitimate scientific opinion polls could improve the processes of government. A sad example was provided by the abortive Bay of Pigs Cuban invasion attempt in 1961, which was apparently based on the assumption that many Cubans were ready to rise up against the Castro regime. However, in 1960 Lloyd Free had conducted a careful opinion poll of 1000 urban Cubans which showed that they backed Castro overwhelmingly, and attention to those findings could have avoided the Bay of Pigs debacle (Cantril, 1967, pp. 1–5). Somewhat similarly, Ralph White (1970) has suggested that a careful analysis of South Vietnamese public opinion toward the Viet Cong versus the Saigon government could have kept the United States from its disastrous military involvement in Vietnam.

A recent government report concluded that survey research has become "indispensable in the public and private sectors" (Cordes, 1982, p. 40), and estimates indicate that over $4 *billion* is spent each year in the U.S. for survey studies intended to aid decision making in business and government (Tornatzky et al., 1982). An area where poll information is widely used is in political election campaigns for state and federal offices, as discussed in Chapter 5. Specialized governmental agencies also have many uses for social science research. One interesting example was the report of the Committee on Community Reactions to the Concorde (1977), ordered by the U.S. Secretary of Transportation in order to assess the amount of disturbance to nearby residents caused by that extremely loud supersonic aircraft. Also, a whole series of U.S. presidential commissions have sponsored and/or cited social science research (cf. Scott & Shore, 1979).

In general, many high-level federal administrators are quite receptive to the use of social science research, according to a widely cited study by Caplan, Morrison, and Stambaugh (1975). However, the way in which they use it often leaves much to be desired. A majority of policy-relevant research data is gathered by each agency's own staff, with their obvious biases and vested interests in the outcome; and even when the research is done by an outside agency, it may be commissioned and used for its political impact rather than its objective value (Weiss, 1978). Also there are cases where good research is done but then largely ignored by the government. For instance, the Supreme Court has sometimes disregarded and sometimes badly misunderstood social science research findings in several important cases (Saks, 1974; Grofman, 1980). The recent Attorney General's Commission on Pornography drew conclusions in its final report that misrepresented the social science research findings on which they ostensibly were based (Wilcox, 1987). A different, but equally sad, fate befell the social research done for the earlier Surgeon General's Advisory Committee on Television and Social

Behavior (Bogart, 1972b), and the President's Commission on Obscenity and Pornography. The latter commission's findings, gathered at a cost of $2 million, were not just ignored but were actively repudiated by many Congressmen and by President Nixon, who called them "morally bankrupt" (*Los Angeles Times*, 1970).

Obviously, this is not the sort of research utilization which one would hope for. By contrast, Campbell (1971) has advocated that we become an "experimenting society," in which new social and political programs will be tried out as planned scientific experiments with careful evaluation of their effects. Such an honest, nonpartisan, and accountable approach would be a great improvement over today's typical extremes of complete lack of evaluation of government programs or overadvocacy of programs whose value has not been established. In fact, some very large-scale policy experiments of this sort have been carried out, notably on income-maintenance programs to combat poverty (Rossi & Lyall, 1976; Heclo & Rein, 1980) and housing-assistance programs to help low-income families upgrade their housing (Field, 1980; Friedman & Weinberg, 1983).

Training for social scientists to participate in policy issues is not usually included in most behavioral science curricula, and there should be more attention to the need for such preparation. One useful example is Brayfield and Lipsey's (1976) description of a graduate training program which aims at preparing psychologists to play a responsible scientific role in the field of public affairs. However, in giving advice to policy makers, we should keep in mind the earlier section of this chapter on attitude-behavior discrepancies. As Deutscher (1965) underlined, social scientists should be very cautious about giving such advice unless they have studied behavioral outcomes as well as people's attitudes and opinions. And, in proposing or carrying out interventions in any kind of social situation, they should give careful thought to the ethical principles regarding such interventions suggested by Bermant, Kelman, and Warwick (1978).

SUMMARY

This concluding chapter of Part I has discussed five important continuing areas of controversy in the field of attitudes and opinions. A close link between personality and attitudes has been expected and found in many well-known research studies. Similarly, though there is often real inconsistency between people's verbal attitude statements and their actions, the typical pattern is one of a moderate positive relationship. Research has demonstrated numerous factors which can misleadingly produce an appearance of attitude-behavior inconsistency.

Laboratory experimental studies of attitudes generally show stronger effects than field studies, largely because of a number of methodological differences which are frequently confounded with the laboratory-field distinction. Though field research is still much less common, its popularity has been growing gradually. Ethical issues in attitude research have received much attention over the years, and guidelines have been developed to protect research participants while simultaneously affirming the scientist's societal obligation to provide new knowledge.

The relation of public opinion to public policy is also controversial. It appears that the public is most competent to determine broad questions of the goals of government policy rather than the means for achieving them. Modern survey methods provide reliable ways of determining both mass and elite public opinion, but there are dangers in political leaders either following public opinion too slavishly or leading it too manipulatively. On some issues, government policy has followed public opinion, on others it has ignored majority viewpoints for decades, and in the area of foreign affairs official policy tends to lead and shape public opinion. In addition to attitude survey data, there are many other important uses for social science research in the public policy arena.

12

Political Attitudes I

[The President] is the last person in the world to know what the people really want and think.—James A. Garfield.

Our government rests on public opinion. Whoever can change public opinion can change the government practically as such.—Abraham Lincoln.

Popular opinion is the greatest lie in the world.—Thomas Carlyle.

Political attitudes and behavior have received far more attention than any other area of public opinion. As the quotes above show, they have been the subject of great controversy as well as great interest. Some authorities, like Abraham Lincoln, have claimed that government decisions were based firmly upon public opinion. Others, such as George Gallup (1965), have doubted that they were, but felt that they should be. Still others, like Thomas Carlyle, have scoffed at the concept of public opinion and the notion that it could or should affect governmental decisions.

The political attitude area is almost unique among areas of public opinion in having an easily measured behavioral concomitant, the vote. Therefore voting behavior is frequently used as the criterion in political attitude surveys, or as the dependent variable of greatest interest. However, voting only occurs periodically, and it is only rarely that a specific political issue is presented directly to the public for their vote, as in a referendum or constitutional amendment or bond issue, etc. Therefore, we cannot confine our interest to voting behavior alone, but we must also consider public attitudes on various important political issues.

This chapter and the next one are organized in three major sections, based on the dependent variable being studied. In this chapter we will consider political attitudes per se, particularly attitudes on important issues which are not put to public vote. In the following chapter we will first consider factors influencing *individuals'* voting behavior and then shift the focus to **aggregate** voting as a dependent variable, adding together all the individual votes and studying the patterns which occur within an election and the changes from one election to the next.

PRESIDENTIAL POPULARITY

Probably the most familiar single index in all of political polling is the presidential "popularity" rating or, more accurately, the rating of people's approval of the President's performance in office. For decades, stretching back to the administration of Franklin D. Roosevelt, the Gallup Poll has been asking a question such as "Do you approve or disapprove of the way George Bush is handling his job as President?" More recently, the Harris Poll has also reported regular results of a similar question. It is widely known that fluctuations in these poll results can send shivers up and down the backs of White House staff members, or raise presidential spirits (and campaign dollars) when the results are favorable.

What do these approval ratings demonstrate about presidential popularity? Generally they start relatively high when a President comes into office and decline later as his actions or inaction displease various subgroups of the populace. For instance, Jimmy Carter's approval rating as President began around 70% but declined quite steadily to 40% in his second year in office. It had two brief periods above 50% following his Camp David peacemaking between Egypt and Israel and again following the Iranian seizure of U.S. hostages and the Soviet invasion of Afghanistan. But it quickly fell below 40% when the attempted U.S. rescue of the hostages failed, and briefly skidded to a low of 21% before hovering in the mid-30s for the rest of his term (*Gallup Opinion Index*, 1980, No. 182). President Reagan's approval rating began at 55%, climbed briefly into the 60s following his attempted assassination, but then sank to below 40% in the 1982–1983 recession. Later it rebounded above 50% for the last year of his first term and into the 60s for the first half of his second term. Following the congressional Iran-Contra investigation of the clandestine U.S. arms sales to Iran and secret government funding of the Nicaraguan rebels, Reagan's approval dropped back into the 40s, staying there throughout 1987 and rising into the low 50s during his final year in office (*Gallup Report*, 1987, No. 260; 1988, No. 270; 1989, No. 280). George Bush's approval hovered around 70% for much of his term but briefly soared to a record 89% after the Persian Gulf War (*Gallup Poll Monthly*, 1991, No. 307).

In addition to their usual tendency to decline over a President's term in office, these approval ratings are apt to rise markedly for a short while after a decisive presidential action in international affairs, such as Carter's peacemaking initiative between Israel and Egypt—sometimes even after an unsuccessful action. Mueller (1973) has dubbed this the "rally-round-the-flag phenomenon." For instance, Kennedy's popularity rose from 72% to 83% following the Cuban Bay of Pigs invasion fiasco, and from 62% to 76% after his successful handling of the Cuban missile crisis. Similarly, Johnson's approval rating rose 10 points after he ordered bombings of North Vietnamese targets near Hanoi which had formerly been off-limits to U.S. bombers. But it also rose markedly, from 36% to 49%, when he declared a moratorium on the North Vietnam bombings in 1968 (Gallup, 1972). As other examples, Carter's approval rating briefly rose 30 points when the

U.S. hostages were seized by Iran and the USSR almost simultaneously invaded Afghanistan, and Reagan's popularity jumped 8 points to its all-time high of 68% shortly after his attempted assassination.

In contrast to these rally effects, presidential popularity sags markedly during economic recessions but may not rebound as much during economic booms (Kinder, 1981; Adams, 1984). Wars can also depress public approval of the President, as shown by the fact that presidential popularity dropped steadily in close relationship to the increasing cumulative number of U.S. combat deaths in both the Korean and Vietnam Wars (Mueller, 1973; Kernell, 1978). Careful quantitative studies have shown that the following types of events, in addition to economic conditions and wars, all have clear and predictable effects on presidential approval ratings: international crises, diplomatic meetings and agreements, sympathy concerning personal events such as health problems or attempted assassinations, government scandals, domestic unrest, and policy initiatives (Ostrom & Simon, 1985). However, dramatic presidential speeches and foreign travel have much less effect on public approval than commonly thought (Simon & Ostrom, 1989).

A politically important fact about presidential approval ratings is that they are strongly predictive of success in the subsequent election. Specifically, an approval rating of 50% or above during the summer preceding a presidential election seems to be enough to ensure the subsequent electoral victory of the incumbent President or of whatever candidate his party nominates (Brody & Sigelman, 1983).

Consistent with our discussion in Chapter 8, these public perceptions of the President are influenced by the agenda-setting power of the mass media, particularly television. A single news commentary on network television can sometimes stimulate as much as four percentage points of opinion change (Page, Shapiro, & Dempsey, 1985). Content analysis of television campaign stories shows that they focus largely on the candidates' personal traits, rather than on policy issues, and they present these traits in small, easily understood packages, which are repeated with slight variations, night after night (Graber, 1987).

Researchers in the field of social cognition consider this media agenda-setting power an example of **priming**. That is, presenting certain topics in campaign news stories makes those topics more accessible in viewers' thinking (primes them), and as a result these topics assume more weight in viewers' judgments about the candidates. An extreme example of this occurred in the last few days of the 1980 campaign, when the unresolved problem of the U.S. hostages in Iran was constantly emphasized in the news, and President Carter's standing with the voters took a sharp last-minute tumble. To show that this kind of effect is really due to the content of the news stories, rather than to other concurrent events, carefully controlled experiments have been done, using actual network news stories that had been unobtrusively modified by adding segments on a particular national problem, such as defense capabilities, pollution dangers, or economic problems. These studies have shown conclusively that viewers exposed to a TV news diet emphasizing a particular national problem used that problem area heavily in their evaluations of the President's overall performance (Iyengar & Kinder, 1986).

Despite the eye-catching headline appeal of presidential approval ratings, they are at best a very crude indication of popular political attitudes. They cannot be relied on as a guide for governmental decisions because of their oversimplicity and the fact that they can be quickly changed by the impact of events. A particularly dramatic example of their rapid fluctuation is the fact that less than a year before his unexpected victory over Dewey in the 1948 election, President Truman's rating stood at a dismal figure of only 36%.

CONCERNS OF CITIZENS

A better indicator of political attitudes would focus on the *issues* and concerns that are uppermost in people's minds, for instance by asking a question such as "What do you think is the most important problem facing this country today?" Questions similar to this have been repeatedly asked of national samples by many polling organizations. It may surprise you to realize how much the answers have varied from time to time, depending on the course of national and international events. Some examples will illustrate the range of responses.

In July 1986, the Gallup Poll asked this question to a representative nationwide sample of about 1500 people, and a summary of their answers is shown in Table 12-1. At that point in time, a rather wide variety of problems was mentioned, with unemployment and fear of war/international tensions leading the list with 23%

TABLE 12–1   Responses of a National Sample to a Question About Our Nation's Most Important Problem, July 1986

Problem		% **Mentioning**
Economic problems (summary)		54%
Unemployment	23	
Budget deficit	13	
Economy (general)	7	
Poverty, hunger	6	
High cost of living, taxes	4	
Trade deficit	1	
Fear of war, international tensions		22
Drug abuse		8
Moral, religious decline		3
Crime		3
Dissatisfaction with government		2
AIDS		1
All others		18
No opinion		3
Total (some people gave multiple responses)		114%

Source: Reprinted by permission from *Gallup Report* (1987, No. 260, p. 7).

and 22% respectively (*Gallup Report*, 1987, No. 260). Many of the other problems listed, though less salient in 1986, were high on the list of people's concerns in some other years. For instance, concern over drug abuse doubled to 16% by May 1988 (*Public Opinion*, 1988, No. 2); the U.S. budget deficit worried more respondents (18%) in January 1985 (*Gallup Report*, 1985, No. 235); unemployment reached a peak level of concern of 62% in October 1982; whereas less than two years earlier, inflation was the primary worry of 73% in February 1981 (*Gallup Report*, 1983, No. 219).

An overview of trends in these public concerns since the end of World War II shows some clear patterns. From the late 1940s to the early 1960s, the greatest public worry was foreign affairs and threats to world peace. Between 1963 and 1965 the focus shifted to the civil rights struggle, including problems of racial strife and racial discrimination. Then the Vietnam War claimed the bulk of public concern until about 1970, when economic problems took over the spotlight and kept it quite continuously up through the late 1980s (Smith, 1985).

These trends in public concerns over a 43-year period since 1947 are clearly shown in Figure 12-1. The graph lumps together all mentions of war, peace, and foreign affairs as the nation's single most important problem, and it compares their level with that of racial problems and of all economic problems such as unemploy-

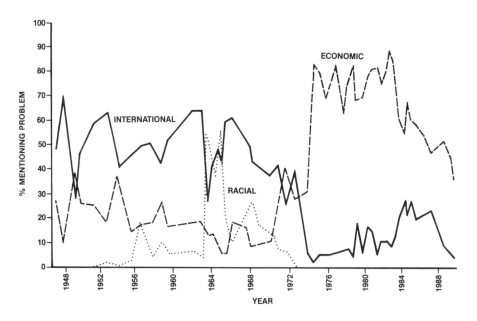

FIGURE 12–1 A 43-year summary of the public's view of our nation's most serious single problem, comparing international, economic, and racial problems from 1947 to 1989.

Source: Data are from the Gallup Poll.

ment, cost of living, taxes, and government spending. The data are from the Gallup Poll (e.g., Gallup, 1972; *Gallup Opinion Index*, 1976, No. 127; 1980, No. 181; *Gallup Report*, 1983, No. 219; 1985, No. 235; 1987, No. 260). This graph shows dramatically how briefly racial problems held center stage as the greatest American concern and how quickly both racial and international problems were forgotten when economic worries increased in the early 1970s.

It is also interesting to remember back to other serious national problems which have sporadically reared their ugly heads and then been displaced as new problems came to the fore. For instance, in 1953, 54% of respondents mentioned the Korean War as our worst problem; in 1954, 17% said it was internal Communism in the U.S.; and in 1963, 24% mentioned danger from Cuba. More recently, after the civil rights struggle of the 1960s, the nation's most important problem was seen as crime and riots in 1968 and 1969 (by 17% of respondents), college demonstrations and unrest in 1970 (by 27%), the energy crisis in early 1974 (by 46%) and again in May 1979 (by 33%), and lack of integrity in government just before President Nixon's resignation as a result of the Watergate scandal in mid-1974 (by 27%). However, in between these occasional unusual worries, the recurrent twin problems of foreign affairs and of economic conditions were generally the focus of most people's concern (see Smith, 1985, for more details).

In comparing research findings such as those just described, readers should be alert to the fact that they are influenced by the type of response required, the wording of the question, and the basis used in tabulating responses. Different findings may sometimes be obtained with free-response questions (e.g., "What are our biggest problems?") than with ones where a list of problems is read or handed to the respondent (e.g., "How worried are you about each of the following problems?"). For instance, using the latter format in a January 1987 Roper Poll, a much higher level of public concern was indicated about the problems of drug abuse and of crime and lawlessness than in the free-response question of the Gallup Poll during the same month (*Public Opinion*, 1987, No. 4; *Gallup Report*, 1987, No. 260). Additionally, in comparing studies, it is important to note not only the question wording, but also the basis of tabulating responses. When several responses per person are requested (e.g., "What are our nation's two or three biggest problems?"), the resulting percentages of mentions are not comparable with studies which report only the first or most important response, such as those summarized in Table 12-1 and Figure 12-1.

TRUST IN GOVERNMENT

Another aspect of political attitudes is how much the citizens trust their government—not the current administration, but the government as a whole. The Survey Research Center has been measuring this topic since 1958, and its findings raise doubts about the prospects for political stability in the United States. One index of trust in government is based on five questions about the federal government's performance. Historically, many more citizens have shown a "high" level of trust than a "low" level—in 1958, the difference between these two percentages was about 50, and in 1964 it was over 40. However, by 1970 only 35% of citizens had a high level of trust while 37% had a low level, a difference of -2. By fall of 1973 this sharp downward trend had continued to the point where about twice as many Americans had low trust in their government as had high trust, and the index stood at about -25 (Institute for Social Research, 1972, 1974). Research has shown that this sharp decline in the early 1970s was partly due to the Vietnam War and partly to the impact of the Watergate scandal. However, Americans' trust in government continued to fall after those events were past, and it reached its all-time low point of about -40 in 1980 (Abramson, 1983; Institute for Social Research, 1983). Since then, it increased rather steadily until 1984, but then dropped a bit again by 1986 under the combined impact of national economic problems and the publicity surrounding the Iran-Contra investigation.

As these findings show, trust in government is sensitive to national events such as economic cycles, and it is partially an evaluation of the incumbent administration (Abramson & Finifter, 1981; A. Miller, 1983; Citrin, Green, & Reingold, 1987). Further confirmation of its sensitivity to political and economic reality is shown by the fact that black Americans, who were more trusting during the 1960s era of civil rights progress, have displayed markedly lower trust in government than whites ever since 1968 (Howell & Fagan, 1988). These findings have been linked to the research on social cognition by results showing that the greatest cynicism or distrust of government occurs in those individuals who think about politics in terms of *schemas* about issues or leaders *and* who feel their own position is far from that of the policies and leaders on the current political scene (Erber & Lau, 1986).

Trust in government can also be shown by examining citizens' ratings of how good a job various branches of the government are doing compared with their ratings of other institutions in our society. What would you guess to be the most-approved institutions in our country?

The results of such a comparison in the fall of 1988 are shown in Figure 12-2. Interestingly, the two most-approved institutions of the ten included were the church/organized religion and the U.S. military, with the Supreme Court running a close third. During the last two decades, the church and the military have typically held the top places in public confidence, though the Supreme Court has sometimes been a bit lower in the ranking. Next in the 1988 distribution came banks and public schools, and well below them were newspapers and Congress. Finally, lowest among the ten institutions were television, organized labor, and big business. These three have usually been near the bottom of the distribution, though the ranking of some of the middle group has varied a bit over time (*Gallup Report*, 1988, No. 279). Other studies which have included a different list of institutions have generally found medicine and higher education also to be at or near the top in public confidence (Harris, 1981). Of the three branches of our government, the

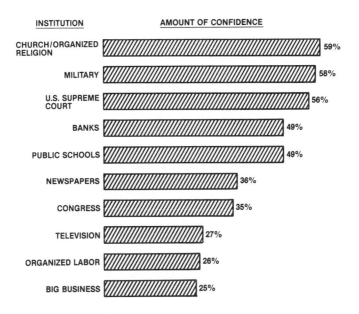

FIGURE 12–2 Public confidence in ten American institutions (percent of respondents saying they themselves have "a great deal" or "quite a lot" of confidence).

Source: Adapted from *Gallup Report* (1988, No. 279, p. 30).

Supreme Court has typically been in the middle of the distribution, with the executive branch and Congress both near the very bottom of public confidence (Ladd, 1976).

Comparative data regarding changes in public trust since the 1960s show that all the institutions measured *declined* in public confidence during that time, most of them quite markedly, with the sole exceptions of the military and the Supreme Court, which increased (*Gallup Report*, 1988, No. 279). This substantial drop in Americans' trust in almost all institutions, including the executive and legislative branches of our government, plus business, labor, and many other aspects of our society, raises serious questions whether citizens will continue to believe in the legitimacy of our social and political order (Lipset & Schneider, 1983). However, to keep this picture in perspective, it is helpful to know that even after this decline in trust, the American public was more confident in every one of its major institutions than were the citizens of West Germany, France, Great Britain, and Spain (Parisot, 1988). Research has shown that this disaffection with government does not generally cause people to withdraw from political participation and voting, though it does often lead to a more confrontational style of political activity, including protests, demonstrations, boycotts, and even violence (Kinder & Sears, 1985).

THE QUALITY OF LIFE

A fascinating trend in measuring political attitudes is to develop standardized **social indicators** as indices of the quality of life in various spheres, analogous to the well-known economic indicators such as gross national product, unemployment rate, and the cost of living index. This development is part of a general trend toward increased consideration of human values and personal satisfactions in business and industry and in economic and political decision making. Interest in the development of social indicators began in the early 1960s and was fostered by support from various foundations and government agencies (Bauer, 1966; U.S. Department of Health, Education, and Welfare, 1969). After nearly 30 years, many volumes of research have been produced based on time-series data examining public attitudes as they changed over time (e.g., Converse, Dotson, Hoag, & McGee, 1980).

The first large-scale national surveys of this sort were conducted in 1971 and 1972 by several different research organizations. They focused on a variety of areas which affect people's satisfaction with their lives, including marriage and family, health, satisfaction with job and income, leisure activities, race relations, civil liberties, women's rights, political alienation, and general happiness (Wilcox, Brooks, Beal, & Klonglan, 1972). The intent of such studies was to construct meaningful measures of the psychological and sociological aspects of our national life patterns (for instance, such measures might include an index of Gross National Happiness, or Work Satisfaction, or even a "Cost of Loving Index" to measure marriage and family satisfaction). Once developed, these indices would be measured at regular intervals to show trends and changes in our national quality of life.

Unfortunately, there are no reliable psychological survey data to tell us whether the "good old days" were really so good for most people as we often think they were in retrospect. Certainly today's assembly-line jobs, high divorce rate, urban crowding, and air pollution are factors which diminish general satisfaction. Yet the past century had problems of equal or greater impact, such as child labor, high death rates, slum tenements, and unpaved roads covered with horse manure. In fact, objectively,

> The nation's health (as measured by life expectancy, which has increased by 20 years in the last century); standard of living (as measured by real income, which has doubled since the war); cultural development (as measured by mean years of education); and family life (as measured by the proportion of people who are married or who expect to marry) are higher than they have ever been in the past. (Greeley, 1981, p. 16)

However, a major goal of the social indicators movement is to supplement these objective measures with carefully constructed indicators of the subjective side of life, such as happiness and well-being. An example of survey findings on the quality of life comes from a Survey Research Center study (Campbell, Converse, & Rodgers, 1976). Interviews were conducted with a national sample of over 2100 persons 18 years of age and older. In general, respondents were more likely to say that life was getting worse in this country than that it was getting better, a finding very similar to the ones cited above about citizens' trust in government. About half of the sample saw no change in the quality of life, about one-third felt it was deteriorating, and only about one-sixth saw it as improving. The most common complaints cited were increasing alienation, public protests and disorders, crime, drug usage, declining morality, behavior of young people, inflation, government policies, taxes, and environmental problems.

Though many of these problems are still worrisome, recent data show that public satisfaction with "the way things are going in the U.S." increased greatly from the 1970s to the late 1980s. This measure of *satisfaction with national affairs* is quite sensitive to economic and political events, reaching its highest recent levels (66% satisfied) during the prosperity of early 1986, and then dropping sharply in reaction to the revelations at the Iran-Contra hearings, before rebounding to a moderately high level (56% satisfied) in late 1988 (*Gallup Report*, 1989, No. 280).

In contrast to people's satisfaction with national affairs, their *satisfaction with personal life* is always much higher, recently ranging from 73% satisfied in 1979 to 87% satisfied in 1988. When personal satisfaction is divided into different do-

Photograph courtesy of Seymour M. Lipset.
Reprinted by permission.

Box 12–1   SEYMOUR M. LIPSET, *Political Attitudes Researcher*

Credited as being the most-cited living political scientist, Seymour M. Lipset is Professor of Political Science and Sociology and Senior Fellow of the Hoover Institution at Stanford University. He received his higher education at the City College of New York and Columbia University and taught for many years at Harvard University before moving to Stanford in 1975.

Lipset has served as President of the American Political Science Association, the International Society of Political Psychology, the Sociological Research Association, and the World Association for Public Opinion Research. He has been honored by election to the National Academy of Sciences and the American Academy of Arts and Sciences. He has authored, co-authored, or edited nearly 400 articles and nearly 50 books, among which Political Man *and* The Politics of Unreason *are particularly well-known. In this chapter we mention his research on political attitudes, including the book* The Confidence Gap.

mains, satisfaction with marriage and family life is typically highest (only 5% were dissatisfied in 1988). Levels of dissatisfaction with one's job, free time, and health were intermediate, while the highest levels of dissatisfaction were reported for household income (30%), standard of living (14%), and housing (13%) (*Gallup Report*, 1989, No. 280). The domains most closely related to overall personal life satisfaction are satisfaction with self, with standard of living, and with family life (Campbell, 1981). Levels of personal satisfaction have been found to change very little in response to economic and political conditions (Greeley, 1981; Caplow, 1982). However, U.S. citizens' enjoyment of work decreased notably between 1955 and 1980 (Glenn & Weaver, 1982).

The individuals most extremely dissatisfied with public aspects of American life were identified by a 3-item "index of political alienation" in the 1971 Survey Research Center study. During that Vietnam War era, this 2% of the sample were much more likely to be found among the young, well-educated, metropolitan residents, and blacks than among other population subgroups (Campbell, Converse, & Rodgers, 1976). However, by 1978, far fewer of the most-alienated individuals were young, and disaffection had also decreased among blacks, city residents, and the well-educated (Campbell, 1981).

ATTITUDES OF POPULATION SUBGROUPS

These findings about alienation bring us to another very important topic, the differing political attitudes of various subgroups in the population. In this area there is a great mass of demographic information, so we can only summarize some of the major trends.

The commonly accepted beliefs about the relationship of demographic factors to political attitudes and behavior are partly a mythology and partly based on depression-era political alignments which have changed markedly in more recent elections. For instance, the Republican Party was traditionally considered the party of older people, farmers and rural residents, the well-to-do, and upper educational and occupational groups; while the Democratic Party was supposed to be favored by the opposite groups, particularly by union members, blacks, and Catholics. Though many of these conclusions were correct during the great depression and World War II, they largely lost their validity during the Eisenhower era of the 1950s (W. Miller, 1960). Since then, the process of change has continued, so that most of the "traditional wisdom" is no longer applicable.

Recent Research Findings

Table 12-2 illustrates these changes from the 1950s through the 1980s by displaying patterns of expressed party identification for the major population groups which had supported FDR's New Deal voting coalition. The figures in the table show the degree of Republican advantage, so a negative number means a Democratic advantage in party identification for a particular group. The findings

TABLE 12–2   Degree of Republican Preference in Party Identification of Major New Deal Support Groups, 1952–1986

Group	1952-1960	1964-1968	1972-1976	1980	1984	1986
WASPs	28	18	20	15	26	26
White Southerners	-48	-36	-20	-21	-2	18
Catholics	-32	-34	-33	-18	-9	0
Union members	-30	-37	-30	-22	-16	-7
Jews	-59	-68	-58	-76	-53	-35
Blacks	-37	-74	-74	-73	-67	-75

Note. Numbers = Republican percentage minus Democratic percentage. Among WASPs in 1986, for example, Republicans enjoyed a 26 percentage point edge.
Source: Petrocik & Steeper in *Public Opinion* (1987, *10*(3), p. 41). Reprinted with the permission of the American Enterprise Institute for Public Policy Research, Washington, D.C.

demonstrate that white Anglo-Saxon Protestants (WASPs) maintained their previous Republican preference, but white Southerners moved from a strong Democratic preference to a moderate Republican one. Concurrently, Catholics, union members, and Jews all sharply decreased their Democratic preference, though the latter two groups still remained somewhat on the Democratic side. Only blacks countered this trend, becoming much more overwhelmingly Democratic during this period (Petrocik & Steeper, 1987). Other analyses show that the poor and central-city dwellers moved to a strong Democratic loyalty during this period (Axelrod, 1986), while women also adopted a 6–8% Democratic preference (Stanley, Bianco, & Niemi, 1986). In contrast, regular churchgoers changed from a moderate Democratic preference to a moderate Republican one (Petrocik & Steeper, 1987), and married Americans also adopted a 10% or greater Republican preference (Weisberg, 1987). In general, these changes in party identification were paralleled by changes in actual voting patterns in the elections of the 1980s (Kohut & Ornstein, 1987).

Age.   The "traditional wisdom" holds that as people get older, an increasing percentage of them tend to identify with the Republican Party, and there is some empirical evidence for the correctness of that conclusion during the 1950s (Crittenden, 1962). However, people's political attitudes are influenced not only by their age, but also by the specific political experiences of each successive generation, such as living through depressions, wars, etc. The effects of these differing experiences on different generations can be determined through a **cohort analysis**—an analysis which follows each generation, or cohort, longitudinally as they get older. (In contrast, the more common cross-sectional analysis collects data at a single point in time and compares the responses of 50-year-olds with those aged 60, 70, and so on, thus comparing people who were born in different eras and who consequently had very different early political experiences.) Cohort analyses which have been done on the variable of party identification have demonstrated less linkage between age and increasing conservatism than commonly thought (Cutler, 1969; Converse, 1976). During the 1980s, an increasing proportion of young people (traditionally expected to be liberals) became Republican supporters (Axelrod, 1986). Similarly, on many issues of morality and lifestyle, the "generation gap" in attitudes between older Americans and young adults diminished markedly in the 1980s (*Gallup Report*, 1989, No. 282/283).

Geographic Region. Despite the "melting pot" notion of social homogenization in the United States, very great regional differences persisted through the 19th century. Since then, most of these differences have decreased greatly (e.g., per-capita income in the various regions has become much more similar), though some differences still remain prominent (Ladd, 1983b). Politically, the southern states as far west as Texas and Oklahoma used to be nearly 75% Democratic in party identification, but by 1986 they were below 50% Democratic (about 32% of their residents considered themselves Republicans and about 18% Independents). There are still fairly large regional differences on many religious and moral views, and on racial and occupational attitudes, with people in the old South often being from 10% to 20% more conservative than the rest of the country (*Public Opinion*, 1988, No. 5). On some issues, such as women working and integrated schooling, the whole nation has become markedly more favorable in the last 40 years, but the attitude gap between various regions has diminished little (cf. Glenn & Simmons, 1967).

Social Class. Though upper-income and upper-occupation groups still tend to be more conservative politically than other subgroups, these differences have blurred over the decades. In a careful examination of social-class trends between 1936 and 1969, Glenn (1973) found two interesting and conflicting patterns. He showed that class-based differences in *party identification* remained strong during that period, lower-class individuals tending to identify with the Democratic Party and upper-class ones with the Republican Party. However, class-based differences in actual *voting* declined steadily during the 1950s and 1960s, except in the South where the recent emergence of a viable two-party system has led to an increase in class-based voting.

It is an interesting fact that over 70% of Americans reject the notion that U.S. society is divided into two district groups, the "haves" and the "have-nots" (*Gallup Report*, 1988, No. 276). Nevertheless, analyses of data from the 1950s through the 1980s have shown a striking new trend in class-based politics. Starting in the 1970s and accelerating during the years of Reagan's administration, the relationship of income to party identification became much stronger than before (see Table 12-3). Both upper- and middle-income groups have become much more strongly Republican. As Petrocik and Steeper (1987, p. 42) describe it:

> By 1986 upscale white voters shifted from being a marginally Democratic to a clearly Republican constituency; middle-class voters moved from an average 17 percentage

TABLE 12–3 Change in Degree of Republican Preference in Party Identification of Three Income Groups, 1952–1986

Income Group	1952-1960	1964-1968	1972-1976	1980	1984	1986
Lower	−16	−25	−20	−25	−12	−6
Middle	−17	−23	−16	−7	0	14
Upper	−3	−5	6	15	20	25

Note. Numbers = Republican percentage minus Democratic percentage.
Source: Petrocik & Steeper in *Public Opinion* (1987, *10*(3), p. 42). Reprinted with the permission of the American Enterprise Institute for Public Policy Research, Washington, D.C.

point Democratic plurality to a 14 percent Republican plurality in 1986. In concert with a shift to the Republicans across all income levels, even lower-income voters became less Democratic. Even so, the polarization of partisanship by income has become much greater.

Another phenomenon related to social class is the recent discussion of *yuppies* (young upwardly mobile professionals) as a possible new force in politics. Research has shown that these well-educated and well-paid young people tend to be fairly conservative on economic issues, like other members of the postwar "baby boom" generation, but quite markedly liberal on social issues such as school prayer, school integration, women's rights, and abortion (Hammond, 1986; Institute for Social Research, 1986). This mixture, as well as their affluence and political activism, make the yuppies a prized potential target group for both political parties.

White Ethnic Groups. In recent years it has become common to think of American white ethnic groups (the second- and third-generation descendents of non-Anglo-Saxon European immigrants) as racists, hawks, and "hard hats." Greeley (1972) examined this stereotype and found very little truth in it. Taking data from various national polls, he studied the attitudes of respondents who were Jewish, Polish, Irish, German, Italian, Scandinavian, and Slavic in relation to those of WASPs. In general, these white ethnic groups were more likely to be doves on the Vietnam War than the average respondent was, were more sympathetic to government welfare programs and to racial integration, were more concerned about pollution problems, and so on. Thus the results showed that the "hard-hat" stereotype of white ethnics as bigots is inaccurate and dysfunctional for our society.

Psychographic Groupings. Instead of looking just at single variables, such as age or social class, many recent analyses of political attitudes have focused on patterns of key values, attitudes, and demographic factors in combination—a procedure that has been called **psychographics** because it involves a psychological profile of voting groups. One example of this approach was based on in-person interviews by the Gallup Poll with over 4200 respondents. It used the statistical technique of cluster analysis to classify the American electorate into 11 relatively distinct groups, each of which has many characteristics in common and as few similarities as possible to the other ten groups (Times Mirror, 1987). Kohut and Ornstein (1987) have summarized the voting pattern of these groups in President Reagan's election victories. Without going into detail on the method or the findings, here are brief descriptions of the 11 groups:

> Bystanders (11% of adults): Almost no interest in politics and no voting history. Tend to be young, white, and poorly educated.
>
> Enterprise Republicans (10% of adults): Probusiness and antigovernment. Affluent, educated, and white.
>
> Moral Republicans (11% of adults): Swayed by moral issues and anticommunism. Middle-aged, middle-income, conservative, many Southerners.
>
> New Deal Democrats (11% of adults): Older blue-collar, union members, moderate income, fairly traditional and anticommunist.
>
> Sixties Democrats (8% of adults): Upper-middle-class, tolerant, committed to social justice and peace, many women.
>
> Partisan Poor (9% of adults): Low-income, heavily black, highly politicized, concerned with social justice, vote Democratic.
>
> Passive Poor (7% of adults): Low-income, less politicized, older, less critical of America, vote Democratic.
>
> Upbeats (9% of adults): Young, optimistic, strong believers in America, middle-income, lean toward Republicans.
>
> Disaffecteds (9% of adults): Middle-aged, pessimistic, distrust business and government, middle-income, lean toward Republicans.
>
> Seculars (8% of adults): Nonreligious, affluent, well-informed, tolerant, peace-oriented, lean toward Democrats.
>
> Followers (7% of adults): Poor, young, uninformed, little faith in America, little interest in politics, lean toward Democrats.

Sources of Political Attitudes

As indicated in Chapter 7, there are many possible sources of people's political attitudes in addition to general ideological principles, which were discussed at length in Chapter 6. Kinder and Sears (1985) have suggested six different types of sources. First, some attitudes may stem from self-interest (e.g., voting against higher taxes), but much research has shown that political attitudes are often symbolic (e.g., reverence for the flag or the military) rather than directly linked to one's self-interest. Second, many people's attitudes are strongly related to the views or concerns of salient social groups that they belong to or identify with (e.g., political parties, the middle class, or ethnic minorities). Third, people are often influenced by opinion leaders that they respect, especially the nation's President. Fourth, some attitudes seem based on the expression of individuals' central values (e.g., individualism or equalitarianism); this value-expressive function of attitudes was discussed in Chapter 4. Other attitudes may be rooted in personality needs or motives (this seems to be particularly true of attitudes based on authoritarian tendencies or political intolerance). Finally, political history may help to shape attitudes, as in public reactions to economic recessions, wars, government scandals, hostage dramas, and other foreign and domestic events.

ATTITUDES TOWARD CIVIL LIBERTIES

A particularly important area of political attitudes is people's views on civil rights—a topic so central to our democratic form of government that it is enshrined in the Bill of Rights. In the early 1950s, during the anti-communism witchhunt period fostered by Senator Joseph McCarthy, this topic was the subject of a classic study by Stouffer (1955). His findings demonstrated in great detail Americans' unwillingness to grant basic constitutional rights to avowed communists and to other dissenters such as atheists. Based on a careful probability sample of nearly 5000 respondents, Stouffer showed that two-thirds to three-fourths of Americans would not allow communists to speak publicly and would favor tapping their telephone conversations and revoking their citizenship, while 90% would not allow them to teach in public schools. One-third of the respondents even favored jailing communists for their private beliefs—a far cry from the protections for unpopular beliefs supposedly guaranteed by the Bill of Rights!

To what extent has this public intolerance changed since the 1950s? One hopeful sign in Stouffer's study was that the well-educated young adult generation was much more tolerant of dissent than was the less-educated older generation. If people's tolerance does not change as they age, the process of generational replacement should automatically increase the overall level of public tolerance (McClosky, 1964). In fact, some later studies have confirmed this expectation. In the 1970s, nearly twice as many Americans were willing to grant constitutional rights to communists and to atheists as in the 1950s (Davis, 1975; Nunn, Crockett, & Williams, 1978). The increase in tolerance continued at a slow pace in the 1980s (*Public Opinion*, 1987, No. 2; Mueller, 1988), and community leaders are markedly more tolerant than the average citizen (Nunn et al., 1978; McClosky & Brill, 1983).

However, some questions still remain. Since internal communism is no longer seen as such a sinister danger to our form of government, the apparent increased tolerance for communists may merely reflect the decreased threat of communism. This view suggests that Americans may merely have redirected their intolerance at other groups rather than becoming genuinely more tolerant. Sullivan, Piereson, and Marcus (1979) tested this notion by asking a probability sample of respondents who their least-liked group was (examples included communists, the Ku Klux Klan, the John Birch Society, the Black Panthers, and proabortionists), and then they determined tolerance toward that group. Findings from this methodological approach demonstrated that respondents were less tolerant toward their least-liked group than they were toward communists or atheists, though both tolerance figures were higher in the 1970s than Stouffer's data from the 1950s. For instance, only half of the respondents were willing to allow members of their least-liked groups to make a public speech, 40% favored tapping of their telephones, and 70% thought the group should be outlawed completely. The authors concluded that "although tolerance of communists and atheists has increased, the overall extent of tolerance may not have changed much" (p. 788). Not a heartening conclusion about the preservation of civil rights in America!

A recent intensive analysis of political tolerance by McClosky and Brill (1983) has shown that Americans express much higher levels of support for tolerance in the abstract than when they are asked about possible restrictions on specific groups or individuals. And they are even less tolerant of rights on "emerging issues" (e.g., abortion, or sexual preference) than on well-established issues. Among the more-tolerant people in our society are most elites; those who are well-educated, well-informed, and politically active; people who are younger, less religious, more liberal religiously and politically; and ones who are psychologically more secure and flexible. Among the least tolerant are advocates of "law and order," superpatriots, and foreign-policy hawks.

LIBERAL-CONSERVATIVE IDEOLOGY

One of the most basic aspects of people's political attitudes is their ideological viewpoint. We have discussed political ideology extensively in Chapter 6, but a few additional issues will be examined here. The first issue is what people mean when they answer the poller's question about whether they consider themselves "liberal" or "conservative." When they are given an in-between option, about 30% to 40% of respondents typically choose it, and when they are asked a filter question such as "or haven't you thought much about this?", roughly one-third tend to agree that they haven't (Robinson & Fleishman, 1988). When they are asked a series of questions on different issues, many people give conservative answers on some and liberal answers on others, and Kerlinger (1984) has done careful measurement work leading to the conclusion that liberalism and conservatism are two separate (and only somewhat negatively correlated) factors, rather than opposite ends of a single continuum.

Nevertheless, for respondents willing to classify themselves, you might assume that the liberal-conservative question would give very similar results to the question about Democratic versus Republican party identification; however, that is not the case. For the past 50 years, the number of Americans stating a Democratic identification has almost always been at least 1.5 times the number of Republican identifiers, whereas in recent years the number of self-reported conservatives has been nearly twice as high as the number calling themselves liberals (*Public Opinion*, 1987, No. 4; *Gallup Report*, 1988, No. 276). Thus, though the two measures are positively correlated, there are many people who respond inconsistently on them (i.e., conservative Democrats, and liberal Republicans). Moreover, whereas party identification is the best predictor of actual voting, "self-identified liberals and conservatives differ more meaningfully and significantly on political issues than do self-identified Democrats and Republicans" (Robinson & Fleishman, 1988, p. 137).

Changes over time in the liberal-conservative balance in America have been the subject of much discussion and no little misinformation. Over a 50-year period, it is clear that most social and political attitudes of Americans have moved in an increasingly liberal direction *(Gallup Report*, 1985, No. 241; Glenn, 1987). Here are a few examples: In 1937 only 33% of the U.S. population said they would be willing to vote for a woman for President, whereas in 1985 78% said they would. As recently as 1969, 68% of Americans said premarital sex was wrong, compared to 39% in 1985. In 1972, 35% of Americans disapproved of married women holding a paid job, while in 1986 the figure was only 22%. In the 1950s, only 37% said they favored allowing an atheist to speak in their community, compared to 65% in 1985. Superimposed on this long-term trend, there have been conflicting shorter-term changes on different social issues in the last 20 years. Some issues have changed in a conservative direction (e.g., increases in complaints that income taxes are too high, in support for capital punishment, and in approval of making divorces harder to obtain). At the same time, other issues have changed in a liberal direction (e.g., increases in approval of euthanasia, of making birth control information available to teenagers, and of the items on premarital sex and working wives stated above)—(Robinson, 1984).

What about changes in self-reported liberalism or conservatism? On this measure, the balance of liberals and conservatives in the U.S. population was approximately equal from the 1930s through the 1960s, but by 1970 the balance changed sharply, and through the end of the 1980s the figure remained quite stable, with nearly twice as many conservatives as liberals. It has often been claimed that there was a strong trend toward more conservatism accompanying Ronald Reagan's presidency, but this is a great exaggeration. The major change occurred by 1970, and though there was a short-lived spurt in conservative self-identification from 1980 to 1982, the figure then returned to its 1970s level for the rest of Reagan's term in office *(Public Opinion*, 1987, No. 4; Robinson & Fleishman, 1988).

Another question is: What differences distinguish conservatives from liberals? People who call themselves conservatives are, in fact, more likely to take conservative stands on various issues, but on many issues the differences are quite small (Ladd, 1981; Robinson, 1984). Examples of issues where the liberal-conservative difference in agreement is usually less than 10% include the following: The courts are not hard enough on criminals; divorce should be more difficult to obtain; the federal income tax is too high; and the U.S. should stay out of world affairs. Somewhat larger differences (less than 20%) are found on these items: approval of the death penalty for murder; there should be laws against pornography; whites have a right to exclude blacks from their neighborhoods; and the country spends too much on solving urban problems. The few items with the largest differences between liberals and conservatives (more than 20%) are morality and lifestyle issues, such as approval of the Equal Rights Amendment, legalization of marijuana, and premarital sex. Even on these issues, the majority of both groups are often on the same side of the neutral point (Robinson, 1984). Moreover, there are usually much greater differences among demographic subgroups *within* the conservative camp or the liberal camp than *between* the two groups; for instance, differences between the most-educated and the least-educated conservatives on an issue like abortion or spending for space exploration may be as large as 40%—roughly twice as large as the difference between the average conservative and the average liberal (Ladd, 1981).

Ideological Conservatism but Operational Liberalism

An important point about ideological positions was made by Free and Cantril (1967). In their study of a national sample of over 3000 respondents, they found that, ideologically, Americans tend to lean in a conservative direction. Using five

Photograph courtesy of Princeton University Archives. Reprinted by permission.

Box 12–2   HADLEY CANTRIL, *Pioneer Survey Researcher*

Best known for his studies of public opinion, Hadley Cantril was also a researcher in perceptual psychology. Born in Utah in 1906, he attended Dartmouth College, and received his Ph.D. from Harvard. After a few years of teaching, he joined the faculty of Princeton in 1936, later becoming chairman of the psychology department. He founded Princeton's Office of Public Opinion Research but left in 1955 to form the Institute for International Social Research. He died of a stroke in 1969.

Before World War II, Cantril was asked by President Roosevelt to assess Americans' feelings about involvement in the war, and later he advised both Eisenhower and Kennedy. His text Gauging Public Opinion *is a classic, and he wrote 17 other books and over 100 articles, including* The Invasion from Mars, *a study of panic reactions to Orson Welles's famous radio drama. He directed the Tensions Project of UNESCO, edited* Tensions That Cause Wars, *and conducted survey research in at least 14 nations, from Nigeria to Poland to Brazil.*

questions on abstract, general views regarding federal interference in state and local matters, government regulation of business, local solutions of social problems, belief in economic opportunity in America, and belief in individual initiative, they constructed an index of **ideological** liberalism or conservatism. The results showed that the American public fell in the following categories:

Completely or predominantly liberal	16%
Middle of the road	34%
Completely or predominantly conservative	50%

However, the results were markedly different for an index of **operational** liberalism or conservatism, which involved attitudes toward five specific government programs—federal aid to education, Medicare, the federal low-rent housing program, urban renewal, and federal efforts to reduce unemployment and poverty. At this specific, or operational, level the public leaned strongly in the liberal direction, as follows:

Completely or predominantly liberal	65%
Middle of the road	21%
Completely or predominantly conservative	14%

When scores on these two scales were cross-tabulated, a fascinating picture emerged: 78% of the ideological middle-of-the-roaders and 46% of the ideological conservatives were operational *liberals*! These results demonstrate that New Deal-type government programs aiming at the welfare of all citizens have gained very wide public support, even among professed conservatives. The authors concluded that the operational dimension is "the most significant (one) from any functional point of view" (p. 50), since it indicates the kind of specific government programs that people will support.

In more recent years, the same general pattern holds true: Many ideological conservatives support government policies and programs that are liberal in nature, such as Social Security, Medicare, farm price supports, and pollution control. Even "welfare," which has recently become a pejorative term to Americans, is supported by a substantial majority of Americans if it is called "assistance to the poor" (Smith, 1987). The combination of ideological conservatism and operational liberalism is even clearer in the following quotation:

> At the very moment three-fourths of the people are saying tax money spent for human services is poorly used, three-fourths are arguing that the federal government should provide medical care and legal assistance for everyone who can't afford them. While seven Americans in ten think government has gone too far in regulating economic life, the same proportion believes that government should make sure everyone has a good standard of living. Overwhelming majorities say federal spending is too high—but majorities just as big say even more should be spent for basic services like education and social security. (Ladd, 1983a, p. 2)

LEADING PUBLIC OPINION VERSUS FOLLOWING IT

We have mentioned at several points above that public attitudes change from time to time in response to events. The growing acceptance over the years of operationally liberal government programs is one example of such attitude change. Another example is the frequent fluctuations in presidential popularity, and particularly the typical increases in the President's ratings after he takes some decisive action in international affairs.

As these examples show, the public is usually more concerned with reaching a goal (stopping a war, ending a recession, etc.) than with the methods whereby the goal is reached. Thus, as far as the public is concerned, the President has a rather wide latitude in choosing specific programs, as long as they seem to be directed toward the important goal of that period. Because of most people's lack of information, low level of involvement in specific issues, and eagerness to believe that progress is being made, the public will usually give a favorable rating to any newly proposed presidential solution to national problems, even to programs which it had formerly rated unfavorably, such as greater recognition for Communist China, or invasion of another country such as Panama.

These conclusions are doubly true in the unfamiliar and mysterious (to most Americans) area of foreign affairs. Lipset (1966) illustrated this point with many examples from the Vietnam War era. During that period of national frustration and discontent, President Johnson was able to present clearcut escalations of the conflict (e.g., extensions of U.S. bombing raids, mining of Haiphong harbor) as attempts to bring peace closer, and a majority of Americans accepted this rationale. In the long run, as American casualties climbed to painfully high levels, public opinion gradually shifted and produced pressures to end the war (Mueller, 1973). But in the short run at least, as Lipset stressed, the President can lead public opinion very effectively rather than following it:

> the opinion data indicate that national policy-makers, particularly the President, have an almost free hand to pursue any policy they think correct and get public support for it. (1966, p. 20)

In domestic affairs also, George Gallup (1965) has emphasized, citizens are often ready to accept new and unfamiliar programs. In fact, because of their lower degree of ideological commitment, the public is often way ahead of the politicians in this regard. Charles Farnsley, a U.S. Congressman and former mayor of Louisville, Kentucky, agreed with this view, as he stated in this back-stage glimpse of political life:

> I found surveys particularly helpful, when I was Mayor, in overruling my advisors. Political advisors have a lot of stereotyped "don'ts": don't do thus and so; the public's against it; it'll be fatal to you if you do. But my surveys would frequently show me that such timidity and caution were unwarranted. The public was not only willing to go along with unorthodox and presumably politically dangerous actions, they were ready and eager for them. (Farnsley, 1965, p. 464)

However, it is not just the public at large that politicians have to be responsive to. As we have seen in this chapter and in Chapter 6, a large proportion of the mass public are so uninformed and uninvolved in public affairs that their views may be termed "nonattitudes" rather than consistent political beliefs and attitudes (Converse, 1974). Consequently, it is various "elite" segments of the population— ones having more clearcut views on particular issues—that help to shape overall public opinion and influence public policy. Moreover, the political process involves the interactions of competing and cooperating *groups and organizations*, and the political attitudes of any individual are largely irrelevant unless they are expressed through group pressures (Goldner, 1971). Keeping these qualifications in mind, however, many studies of election campaigns have clearly demonstrated the value to candidates of reliable polling information. Undoubtedly, the future will see many more candidates planning and modifying their campaigns in the light of poll information on their familiarity to voters, their popularity, the image which the public has of them, and the current importance of various issues to the voters in their area.

SUMMARY

Presidential approval ratings are the most familiar measure of public political attitudes. They tend to decline during a President's term in office, especially in response to economic recessions or international problems, but they often rise for a time after decisive presidential actions. Concerns of citizens about problems facing the country are a better index than presidential popularity because they help to identify the source of people's discontent or satisfaction. In successive eras, the most serious U.S. public concerns have been foreign affairs and war–peace issues from the late 1940s to the early 1960s, racial problems from 1963 to 1965, then the Vietnam War until the early 1970s, and economic worries almost continuously since 1974.

Another useful measure is the index of public trust in our government, which declined sharply and steadily from the late 1960s to an all-time low in 1980, and only recovered a small part of its loss by the late 1980s. Among important American institutions, organized religion, the military, medicine, and higher education usually have the highest degree of public confidence, while Congress and the executive branch of the federal government are generally near the bottom of the rating. An important trend in measuring political attitudes is the recent development of standard social indicators of the quality of life, analogous to the familiar economic indicators such as gross national product. Findings indicate a generally high level of satisfaction for most people in most areas of their personal lives, but a marked dissatisfaction about national affairs in the 1970s, which then improved substantially in the 1980s.

Traditional patterns of political attitudes among population subgroups, based on depression-era alignments, began to change rather markedly during the Eisenhower era of the 1950s. For instance, age differences and regional differences on many issues have decreased greatly. However, social class differences, which had diminished in the 1950s and 1960s, increased again in the 1970s and 1980s, with middle- and upper-income groups becoming much more strongly Republican than before.

Americans' attitudes about granting civil liberties to dissenters are not nearly as tolerant as the principles specified in the Bill of Rights, though they seem to have become somewhat more tolerant since the anticommunist scares of the 1950s. Over the last 50 years, the long-term trend of most social and political attitudes of Americans has moved in a strongly liberal direction, though since about 1970 attitudes on some issues have become somewhat more conservative. Though most Americans tend toward a conservative position on ideological issues, on operational questions concerning specific government programs they are generally liberal. The President can often lead public opinion very effectively rather than following it in his choice of specific programs and operational procedures, but the viewpoints expressed by pressure groups and organizations can have an influence on public policy.

13

Political Attitudes II
Voting

Democracy substitutes selection by the incompetent many for appointment by the corrupt few.—George Bernard Shaw.

Our government is a government of political parties under the guiding influence of public opinion. There does not seem to be any other method by which a representative government can function.—Calvin Coolidge.

I always voted at my party's call,
And I never thought of thinking for myself at all.—W. S. Gilbert.

In this chapter we will discuss two aspects of voting behavior: *individual* voting decisions and *aggregate* voting patterns. Since many of the demographic factors that influence voting behavior as well as political attitudes per se were examined in the preceding chapter, those factors will not be repeated here. Instead, we will focus on several other major determinants of individual voting decisions that have been discovered in a series of major election studies.

SOME DETERMINANTS OF INDIVIDUAL VOTING DECISIONS

Cross-Pressures

Historically, the first such factor to be analyzed came from the first large-scale scientific election study (Lazarsfeld, Berelson, & Gaudet, 1948). This research on the 1940 election, reported in a landmark volume called *The People's Choice*, was a **panel study** in which 600 residents of Erie County, Ohio, were each interviewed seven times between May and November to investigate factors involved in changing voting preferences. (Interestingly, and unexpectedly, nearly 70% of the respondents showed *no changes* in voting intentions from start to finish of the study.)

In this research, predictions of the respondents' voting patterns were made using a score called the Index of Political Predisposition (IPP), based on a combination of three demographic variables—religion, social class, and urban or rural residence. At the various levels of this index the proportion of respondents voting Democratic ranged from 26% at one extreme to 83% at the other, indicating a strong relationship of the index to voting decisions. (However, as mentioned in the preceding chapter, most demographic variables no longer relate as closely to voting behavior as they did in the 1930s and 1940s.)

In this study **cross-pressures** were defined as contradictory voting predispositions on the three variables (e.g., being a middle-class Catholic, or a working-class rural resident). Respondents who were under such conflicting pressures were also found to fluctuate in their voting intentions, to show less interest and attention to the campaign, to be more influenced by other persons' views, and to reach their voting decision later than other citizens. These results of political cross-pressures, however defined, still seem generally to hold true (Sears, 1969). However, in the 1960 election, Pool, Abelson, and Popkin (1964) found that cross-pressured voters did not display lower turnout than other voters.

Personal Influences

Following the Erie County study, a very similar panel study of the 1948 election was conducted by the same research group in Elmira, New York (Berelson, Lazarsfeld, & McPhee, 1954). Here a major variable of interest was the personal influence stemming from the voting intentions of the respondents' closest friends and family members. The investigators found this kind of influence to be strongly associated with the person's own voting intentions (Kitt & Gleicher, 1950). For instance, in this heavily Republican area the following relationships were found between the voting intentions of the respondent and those of his(her) three closest friends:

3 friends Republican	93% intended to vote Republican
2 Republican, 1 Democratic	68% " " " "
2 Democratic, 1 Republican	50% " " " "
3 friends Democratic	19% " " " "

The same kind of pattern held for differences of voting intentions between the respondent and his(her) immediate family and changes in the respondent's voting intentions between June and August. In cases where all of the family agreed with the respondent, 80% to 90% held to their original voting intention in August. But where some but not all family members were in agreement, about 70% remained unchanged in August; and where all family members disagreed with the respondent's voting plans, nearly half changed their intentions by August.

These findings underline the importance of personal communication, as discussed in Chapter 8.

Party Identification

Party identification as a determinant of voting decisions has been emphasized in the highly influential series of studies conducted by the University of Michigan's Survey Research Center (Campbell, Gurin, & Miller, 1954; Campbell et al., 1960). Measurement of the concept does not involve official party membership, registration, or campaign activity, but depends entirely on the respondent's self-classification as a strong or not-so-strong Republican or Democrat or as an Independent. Party identification, so measured, is quite a stable personal characteristic (e.g., a correlation of about +.85 over a two-year interval), and the changes that do occur are mostly ones in and out of the Independent category rather than from one major party to the other (Converse, 1964; Converse & Markus, 1979). Among major-party identifiers, 82% retained the same party identification in three

Photograph courtesy of Angus Campbell.
Reprinted by permission.

Box 13–1   ANGUS CAMPBELL, *Noted Survey Researcher*

Director of the Survey Research Center at the University of Michigan for over 20 years, Angus Campbell has been a trail-blazer in attitude and opinion research. Born in Indiana in 1910, he attended the University of Oregon and took his Ph.D. at Stanford in 1936. After teaching at Northwestern, he assisted Rensis Likert in the Division of Program Surveys of the U.S. Department of Agriculture during World War II, and moved with him to Michigan when the Survey Research Center was founded in 1946. In 1970 he succeeded Likert as Director of the Institute for Social Research, and he continued as an active researcher until his death in 1980.

    Best known for his research on political attitudes and voting, Campbell led survey studies of U.S. elections since 1948, resulting in pace-setting volumes such as The Voter Decides, The American Voter, *and* Elections and the Political Order. *More recently he published influential work on racial attitudes (cited in Chapters 2 and 15) and on social indicators of the quality of life (described in Chapter 12). His many achievements were honored by his receipt of the Distinguished Contribution Awards from both AAPOR and APA.*

interviews between 1956 and 1960; however, by contrast, only 40% of Independents kept the same self-classification over the four-year period.

In elections from 1956 to 1968, party identification was found to be more highly correlated with voting behavior than any other factor studied, such as attitudes toward campaign issues or toward the candidates (Declercq, Hurley, & Luttbeg, 1975). In 1952, party identification correlated nearly + .6 with presidential choice, whereas the other attitude measures correlated only in the range of + .2 to + .5 (Campbell & Stokes, 1959). In both 1952 and 1956, about 83% of major-party identifiers ended up voting for their party's presidential candidate, and those were years when Democratic defectors were relatively numerous (Campbell et al., 1960). In elections for Congress and other less-important offices, party loyalty was usually even higher; its peak was over 88% in the 1958 congressional election (Stokes & Miller, 1962).

However, in more recent elections, particularly 1964, 1972, and subsequently, there has been a notable decrease in the importance of party identification in determining voting behavior (Declercq et al., 1975; Wattenberg, 1987). One reason for this is the increase in the number of citizens who identify themselves as **Independents**; from about 20% in the 1950s, this figure rose to well over 30% in the 1970s and only declined slightly to about 30% in the 1980s (Glenn, 1987; *Gallup Report*, 1988, No. 276). This group can be divided into those who admit "leaning" toward Republicans or Democrats and the "pure" Independents (currently about 12%); the latter group are less well-informed and less likely to vote, and they swing widely in their voting from one election to another in accordance with short-term forces (Kinder & Sears, 1985). The increase in these politically uninvolved pure Independents parallels and reflects the rise of disillusionment and lack of trust in our government and institutions, described in the preceding chapter.

A second factor is that voting loyalty of party identifiers also declined, from 83% in the presidential races of the 1950s to 75% or less in the 1970s; and party loyalty in congressional races dropped even further to about 70% (Nie, Verba, & Petrocik, 1979; Abramson, 1983). Moreover, **ticket-splitting** (an individual not voting a straight party ticket for all offices) has also increased sharply, and as a result amazing proportions of all congressional districts have elected a Congressperson of the opposite party from their presidential vote—45% in 1972 and 44% in 1984 (Pomper, 1975; Wattenberg, 1987). These processes have gone so far as to lead some analysts to refer to the "decomposition" or "disintegration" of the party system (Burnham, 1970, 1985). Though weakened, however, party identification still remains the strongest predictor of voters' presidential choice in most elections.

Candidate Images

Next to party identification, the candidate's characteristics can also have a major impact, particularly in certain elections. In 1960, Kennedy's Catholic religion became the most crucial issue of the campaign, and studies estimated that about 4 1/2 million anti-Catholic voters switched to Nixon while about 3 million normally Republican Catholics voted for Kennedy (Pool et al., 1964). The public's personal images of Barry Goldwater in 1964, George McGovern in 1972, and Jimmy Carter in 1980 all had negative values on various important characteristics, which contributed substantially to their electoral defeats (Field & Anderson, 1969; A. Miller et al., 1976). In fact, Carter's image was so negative that many analysts concluded that, rather than Reagan winning the election (he received less than 51% of the votes in the three-way race), Carter *lost* it (e.g., *Gallup Opinion Index*, 1980, No. 183). (A similar event occurred in Britain's 1983 election when the Labour Party under an unpopular leader, Michael Foot, lost to the Conservatives and Margaret Thatcher, who got only 44% of the vote—Worcester, 1984.)

Election studies have compared the relative contribution of party identification, candidate images, and issue positions to individuals' voting decisions, using techniques such as multiple regression analysis. Whereas research on earlier elections showed party identification to be the strongest factor, in 1964 and again in 1972, a measure of candidate images was the best predictor of people's votes (RePass, 1971; Declercq et al., 1975). In rather similar analyses for 1980 and 1984, the candidate characteristic of presidential approval was the strongest predictor of voting decisions (Wattenberg, 1987). Contrary to Converse's (1964) conclusion that only the less educated and less politically involved citizens focus on candidate personal characteristics, recent studies have shown that well-educated voters give more attention to candidate characteristics, and that their judgments are centered on performance-relevant traits such as competence, integrity, and reliability (Glass, 1985; A. Miller, Wattenberg, & Malanchuk, 1986). The greatly increased emphasis on candidate characteristics instead of party positions in campaigns over a 30-year period is dramatically shown in Figure 13-1.

An interesting series of studies has demonstrated how people's images of political candidates can influence their perceptions of the candidates' issue positions (Granberg & Brent, 1980; Judd, Kenny, & Krosnick, 1983; Granberg, Nanneman, & Kasmer, 1986). Their findings support the principles of Heider's (1958) balance theory and also of social judgment theory (Sherif & Hovland, 1961) concerning the assimilation or contrast of persuasive messages. In all of the presidential elections from 1968 through 1984, American voters tended to assimilate the issue positions of their preferred candidate and preferred party—that is, they perceived them as being closer to their own views than they actually were. For example, an environmentalist who favored Reagan for President would typically perceive Reagan's stand on issues as being more proenvironmental (i.e., closer to the voter's own position) than it actually was, as objectively measured. People were also found to contrast the positions of their nonpreferred presidential candidates, but less than they assimilated the position of their preferred candidate. As social judgment theory would predict, voters who were very involved in and concerned about an election campaign showed especially strong tendencies to assimilate the positions of their preferred candidate. Other related research has supported the dissonance theory prediction that people whose expectations are not fulfilled by the election outcome change their attitudes in the direction of the outcome (Granberg & Nanneman, 1986).

Most research that has examined candidate images has considered perceived

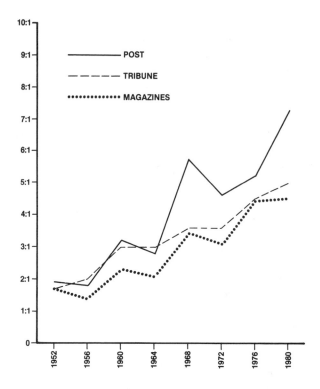

FIGURE 13–1   Ratio of mentions of candidates to parties in campaign stories in the *Washington Post, Chicago Tribune,* and three news magazines, *Newsweek, Time,* and *U.S. News and World Report,* from 1952 to 1980.

Source: Wattenberg (1984, p. 94). Reprinted by permission of the publishers from *The Decline of American Political Parties* by M. P. Wattenberg, Cambridge, Mass.: Harvard University Press, copyright 1984 by the President and Fellows of Harvard College.

personality traits such as honesty, warmth, and competence; but some recent research has also studied voters' affect toward the candidates (e.g., hope, pride, anger, or fear—Abelson, Kinder, Peters, & Fiske, 1982). These authors found that, unlike personality trait ratings, summary scores of good feelings toward a candidate and bad feelings toward the same candidate were nearly independent, indicating that candidates often arouse simultaneous conflicting emotions in voters. Moreover, the summary affect measures strongly predicted voting preferences, and their contribution was greater than and independent of trait ratings. This research is consistent with other findings about the relation of cognitive and affective judgments (Zajonc, 1980—see Chapter 7), and it provides a new methodological approach for studying candidate images.

Issue Positions

If you ask them, most citizens and most politicians will tell you that "the issues" are the key factor in people's voting decisions, but such self-reports have doubtful validity because respondents may just be giving the socially desirable or expected answer. In fact, the early election studies disputed the importance of issues in determining people's voting behavior (e.g., Campbell et al., 1960). However, since 1964 that picture has changed quite markedly.

In the 1964 election, Goldwater's strongly conservative stand on issues gave a marked ideological tone to the campaign and was clearly a factor in his low vote total (Field & Anderson, 1969). In 1968, George Wallace's third-party candidacy stressed racist and nationalist issues, and he won 13% of the total vote—enough to reverse the winning party in eight states and give the presidency to Richard Nixon instead of Hubert Humphrey (Mitofsky, 1969). In 1972 McGovern stressed the issues of the Vietnam War, urban unrest, and government aid to the poor; and in this election for the first time people's issue orientation had as much impact on their vote as did party identification (Declercq et al., 1975).

The cumulative effect of these three elections introduced a "new era of issue politics" in America (A. Miller et al., 1976; Nie et al., 1979), and this trend has continued, particularly in Reagan's strongly ideological campaign in 1980 (Abramson, Aldrich, & Rohde, 1982). In turn, this polarization of the electorate on important current issues seems to have contributed substantially to the soaring public distrust of government—a feeling that politicians are apt to be dishonest and unconcerned about the common citizen's welfare. This is a paradoxical drawback which was not anticipated by those who called for distinctive ideological stands in party platforms (A. Miller, 1974).

The central importance of economic issues in presidential campaigns has been dramatized by the creation of the **misery index**—the sum of the unemployment rate plus the inflation rate. Carter popularized the concept in his 1976 campaign criticisms of Republican handling of the economy, and Reagan turned it against him very effectively in 1980. In the 1984 and 1988 elections, a major factor in the Republican victories was considered to be the low level of the misery index; and similar relationships have been found in elections in many other industrialized nations (Lipset, 1982; *Public Opinion*, 1987, No. 4; *Gallup Report*, 1988, No. 278).

Emphasis on economic issues such as the misery index suggests that voters primarily follow their own self-interest and "vote their pocketbook," thus throwing out the incumbent party whenever times are bad and returning it to office when times are good. At the aggregate level, this generalization has held true in all the elections of the 1970s and 1980s; and it appears that voters do give strong weight to the *overall performance* of the administration—more so than to the fine-grain detail of campaign issues and policies (Fiorina, 1981). However, rather than voting primarily in terms of their own individual pocketbook situation (e.g., personal unemployment), citizens seem to vote in accordance with their view of the national economic conditions—a viewpoint that has been termed **sociotropic voting** (Kinder

& Kiewiet, 1981; but see Rosenstone, Hansen, & Kinder, 1986). Some of the evidence for this view has come from studies of **symbolic politics**, which show that individual self-interest (e.g., having a relative in the Vietnam War, or an unemployed family member) is usually less important in people's policy preferences and voting decisions than are long-standing symbolic attitudes such as anticommunism or liberal-conservative ideology (Sears, Lau, Tyler, & Allen, 1980; Sears & Citrin, 1985). This conclusion brings our discussion of determinants of voting full-circle because, for most voters, party identification is one of their long-term symbolic attachments.

EFFECTS OF POLITICAL PERSUASION ON VOTING

The other major element influencing voting decisions is all of the persuasive communication which abounds during an election campaign—political propaganda, candidate oratory, editorials, personal appeals from acquaintances, and local "grassroots" political activity. In Chapter 8 on Communication of Attitudes and Opinions, we have discussed the general findings concerning persuasive communication. Here we will only consider a few of the most salient influences which affect political voting decisions.

Kinder and Sears (1985) have pointed out that most studies of political propaganda have shown relatively little resulting attitude change—often no change at all. However, this finding does not mean that propaganda is ineffective. In many cases the most important effect of political persuasion may be **reinforcement**, that is, strengthening people's already existing attitudes (Mendelsohn & O'Keefe, 1976). In occasional elections, like 1980, the number of undecided voters remains unusually large through most of the campaign and even right up to election day, and then persuasive messages may have an unusually great effect (Wattenberg, 1984). In other cases, less than half of the change in partisan preference from one election to the next may actually occur during the campaign period (Blumler & McQuail, 1969). Thus a major function of campaign propaganda may be to support people's already changed attitudes and to extend the amount of change where possible.

Problems in Political Persuasion

In order for persuasive arguments to have any effect on attitudes and/or behavior, they must be first received and then accepted, at least to some extent; and both of these processes pose problems for the political communicator.

Reception of persuasive arguments is a problem mainly because of low levels of public exposure and attention to political information. As we have pointed out in Chapter 6, many citizens are political "know-nothings," and most of the rest are relatively uninterested in political issues. As a result, most people simply do not "catch" the available political information, even when it is presented in a highly novel or dramatic way.

Another potential problem in the reception of political arguments is people's general tendency to expose themselves selectively to communicators and channels of information with whom they already tend to agree. As we have discussed in Chapter 8, this effect seems to be largely due to people following customary and convenient modes of information-exposure, rather than to any strongly motivated search for supportive ideas or avoidance of contradictory ideas (Sears & Freedman, 1967). In recent elections, campaign managers have combatted that tendency by purchasing time for short 1-minute or even 30-second campaign "ads" in popular prime-time shows. Thus it is almost impossible to avoid exposure to many campaign messages, but the public's low level of interest and attention still pose problems for reception of their content.

Acceptance of persuasive arguments, once they are received, is also a problem for the political communicator. Where people are committed to their party identification, or have strong loyalties to racial, religious, or ethnic groups, or see clear bases of economic self-interest, it is unlikely that contrary political arguments will be effective in changing their attitudes or votes. Longitudinal panel studies of both U.S. and British election campaigns have shown that a large majority of the public—as much as 80% in some elections—has made up their minds how to vote before the formal campaign even starts. In most elections no more than 10% of citizens change their voting preferences from one side to the other during the campaign—the other changers move from undecided to some candidate preference, or vice versa (Lazarsfeld et al., 1948; Benham, 1965; Blumler & McQuail, 1969). However, it is also true, as Converse (1964) has stressed, that most people are not strongly committed to any position on most political issues. Thus, if a clear and effective argument can be presented to them on any given issue, it may be easy to sway their attitude—and even their vote if the issue is an important one.

The result of the above factors is that in elections where people's enduring commitments are relevant, political propaganda generally serves merely to reinforce their preexisting attitudes. But in elections where enduring commitments are not called into play, attitudes and votes are more labile, and political persuasion may have major effects. This is especially true in nonpartisan and primary elections where party identification does not provide a guide for voting. It is also applicable to partisan elections where economic, racial, or religious issues are not centrally involved because the candidates have taken "me-too" positions.

The greatest amount of attitude change in national election campaigns occurs in individuals who have relatively weak party identification (Abramson, 1983). It also occurs among people with a relatively low level of interest in the campaign and a resulting low level of exposure to political propaganda. Thus, surprisingly, amount of attitude change is often negatively related to amount of exposure to the mass media (Dreyer, 1971).

Some interesting recent research findings on the effects of *particular kinds* of influences are presented in the following pages.

Photograph courtesy of David Sears.
Reprinted by permission.

Box 13–2   DAVID SEARS, *Authority on Political Psychology*

Widely known for his research on political and racial attitudes, David Sears grew up in California, received his B.A. from Stanford, and earned his Ph.D. at Yale in 1962. He then became a faculty member at UCLA, where he still remains as Professor of Psychology and Political Science and Dean of Social Sciences.

Sears authored or co-authored chapters on political behavior in two successive editions of The Handbook of Social Psychology, *as well as a widely read textbook on* Public Opinion *and several other volumes. This chapter discusses his work on political attitudes and voting, previous chapters have referred to his research on political persuasion and on selective exposure to information, and Chapter 15 describes his studies of symbolic racism.*

Campaign Expenditures

"Money is the mother's milk of politics," according to a well-known politician. The truth of this statement is easy to demonstrate. In the 1984 presidential campaign alone, an estimated $345 million was spent by the candidates and their parties. To keep this figure in perspective, the nation's leading commercial advertiser, Procter & Gamble, spends about twice that much each year to promote its products (Desruisseaux, 1984).

Candidates for the U.S. Senate and House of Representatives in 1984 reported total spending of over $320 million, with the record spenders being North Carolina's Jesse Helms and his challenger Jim Hunt, who laid out more than $25 million between them—over $25 for every vote cast in the state. Special-interest political action committees (PACs) gave about $100 million to candidates for the U.S. House and Senate in the 1984 election (Baldwin, 1986; Sorauf, 1987). A large majority of these campaign funds go for TV commercials, and in recent years there has been a strong and unfortunate tendency toward negative caricatures of the opposition candidate, or "mud-slinging" ads (Baldwin, 1986).

Though not every heavily financed candidate wins, in 1982 the bigger spender won 27 of the 33 races for the U.S. Senate (Church, 1982). A more complex analysis of multicandidate presidential primary elections in 1976 reached the same conclusion: campaign expenditures were usually the strongest factor in predicting the winner (Grush, 1980). Since most of the 18 candidates who competed in one or more of these primaries were relatively unfamiliar to most voters, these results support Zajonc's (1968a) theory of the effects of repeated exposure to previously unfamiliar stimuli (discussed in Chapter 7). On the level of individual-voter attitudes toward candidates, similar exposure effects have been found for amount of exposure to political advertising (Atkin & Heald, 1976). However, such repetitive political advertising may be more successful in changing voting intentions in low-involvement elections such as local or state legislature races, but not very effective in high-involvement elections such as presidential campaigns (Rothschild & Ray, 1973).

Television

One of the main effects of TV coverage of elections has been to make the candidates' personality and "image" more crucial factors in the campaign (Wattenberg, 1984; Keeter, 1987). Since its first large-scale use in the 1952 presidential election, television advertising has leaped to an expenditure level in the early 1980s of half a billion dollars for all candidates in a presidential election year. This approach is clearly the most efficient way of reaching a large proportion of the electorate, but there are conflicting views about its effects.

In Chapter 8 we summarized the research findings about television's impact on political information as well as on political attitudes and voting behavior. Television viewing adds only a marginal amount to citizens' political knowledge during campaigns (e.g., Patterson, 1980; Zukin & Snyder, 1984). A major reason that it is uninformative about the issues of the campaign is that it focuses very largely on the candidates' personal style and trivia such as campaign tactics and blunders, rather than important ideological and policy positions of the parties and the candidates. By constantly presenting the latest poll standings and emphasizing who is ahead in the race, television campaign coverage has justly earned its description as "horse-race journalism" (Sears & Chaffee, 1979; Arterton, 1984; Stovall & Solomon, 1984). In the words of one research report, the networks

> devote most of their election coverage to the trivia of political campaigning that make for flashy pictures. Hecklers, crowds, motorcades, balloons, rallies and gossip—these are the regular subjects of network campaign stories. (Patterson & McClure, 1976, p. 22)

Typical findings concerning attitude change, both in Britain and the U.S., indicate that televised ads also have quite small persuasive effects, mostly limited to undecided voters with a low interest in the campaign and a high level of customary television usage (Blumler & McQuail, 1969; Patterson, 1980; Kaid, 1981).

Several studies have examined the process by which television influences voters. Atkin, Bowen, Nayman, and Sheinkopf (1973) found that a large number of TV ads for a candidate produced greater viewer *exposure*, apparently overcoming any tendencies toward selective exposure. However, the quantitative frequency of advertising did not influence viewer *attention* levels; instead, attention was related to the ads' qualitative characteristics, such as informative or entertainment value. These same qualitative factors influenced voting intentions also, particularly among undecided voters. More than half of them reported that the political ads for their chosen candidate helped them reach their decision, and many also mentioned the other candidates' ads as a factor weighing against them (this agrees with the findings of Raj, 1982). Similarly, many of the already decided partisans reported that their decision was reinforced by seeing the campaign advertisements— positively by their own candidate's ads and/or negatively by the opponent's. Though many campaign managers might disagree, the authors concluded that

> a moderate number of high-quality, substantively informative advertisements may be more effective than a saturation presentation of superficial image-oriented spots. (Bowen, Atkin, Sheinkopf, & Nayman, 1971, p. 458)

The greatest overall effects of television exposure might be expected to come from dramatic events with very high viewership, such as the "great debates" between presidential candidates. The first such debates between Kennedy and Nixon in 1960 reached a huge audience (55% or more of the adult population), but this was partly because they were broadcast by all three television networks; in one city where an alternative TV program was also on the air the debate audience was reduced to 35%—still an exceptionally high figure (Katz & Feldman, 1962). The candidate debates in 1976 and each subsequent election were also watched by very large audiences, but far fewer people watched the whole of any debate, and research showed that their main effect was to reinforce the preexisting preferences of viewers (Sears & Chaffee, 1979; Sigelman & Sigelman, 1984; Kinder & Sears, 1985). Nevertheless, there were key events in each series of debates, involving gaffes or weaknesses by a candidate, that were given heavy negative publicity by the media and were considered by many commentators and voters to be crucial to the final election outcome. Following the final 1980 debate between Carter and Reagan, one week before the election, Reagan's effective emphasis on the poor economy and the year-long unresolved hostage situation were highlighted by the media as the campaign came to a climax, and they led to a massive shift in people's voting intentions, from an election that was "too close to call" to a severe loss for Carter. Over one-third of voters said they decided whom to vote for in that last week *(Gallup Opinion Index,* 1980, No. 183; *Public Opinion,* 1980/1981, No. 6).

Other instances of TV's political power can also be cited. Recently, televised facial expressions of political leaders have been found to influence the attitudes and emotional responses of viewers, so news departments' choices of which film clips to show can potentially affect audience reactions (Lanzetta, Sullivan, Masters, & McHugo, 1985). Rather similarly, studies of network news programs noted that the anchor person of one network (Peter Jennings of ABC) smiled more when referring to President Reagan than when mentioning his campaign opponent, Fritz Mondale. Surprisingly, this subtle and probably unconscious cue was found to be significantly related to the presidential votes of viewers of that network's news programs (Mullen et al., 1986). Though this particular election outcome was not close, the researchers raised a provocative question: Can a newscaster's smile elect a President? These findings go even further in emphasizing the potential power of the network news programs than did the study by Iyengar and Kinder (1986), which demonstrated their agenda-setting power in determining the issues on which viewers would judge the performance of a President (see Chapters 8 and 12).

Newspapers

Though newspapers were strongly preferred as a source of campaign information in earlier years, newspaper reading in the U.S. has declined since the 1950s, especially among young adults (Robinson, 1980), and the public's increasing trust in television as a news source made it the preferred political news medium by the 1970s. However, as we discussed in Chapter 8, people's knowledge of current affairs and politics is more closely related to newspaper reading than to television news viewing (Robinson & Levy, 1986b). There is also research evidence that newspapers have a greater agenda-setting effect than television, that they influence audience attitudes more, and that they are particularly influential on local issues (Palmgreen & Clarke, 1977; Patterson, 1980). People tend to rely on newspapers more for information on complex topics, and newspaper readers pay less attention to political candidates' personal traits than do TV viewers (Keeter, 1987).

Concerning influence on voting, newspapers have a historical tradition of backing their preferred candidates with editorial endorsements and even, at times, with slanted news coverage, whereas U.S. television and radio have been required by the FCC's "fairness doctrine" to give roughly equal coverage to both sides of controversial issues. Accordingly, in the 1968 election, though respondents ranked television as their most important source of campaign news, they were more likely to *vote* in accordance with their newspaper's election preference than with their impressions from TV (Robinson, 1972). Since 1968 was a very close election, and since about 80% of the nation's newspapers were pro-Nixon, this effect may have played an important role in the election outcome. Robinson found that, when other factors were held constant, voters exposed to pro-Nixon papers were about 6% less likely to vote for Humphrey than voters who read pro-Humphrey papers. As might be expected, this effect was strongest among Independents and undecided voters, where such differential voting reached levels of 35% to 40%. In total, Robinson concluded that the pro-Nixon newspaper endorsements had swayed about 3% of the overall vote to Nixon—enough to give him the election, since his winning margin was only 1% of the total vote.

Studies of newspaper editorials in other elections have reached similar conclusions about their potentially crucial influence, especially in local elections (Mason, 1973; Erikson, 1976; Scarrow & Borman, 1979; Coombs, 1981).

Personal Contact

In Chapter 8 we discussed general findings about the persuasive effects of personal communication. In the area of voting, some researchers have claimed that personal contact is a more effective influence on political decisions than any of the mass media (e.g., Katz & Lazarsfeld, 1955), while others have disputed that conclusion (e.g., Pool, 1959; Mendelsohn & O'Keefe, 1976). The original study of this topic (Lazarsfeld et al., 1948) found that less than half of their respondents mentioned personal contact as a campaign influence, and only one-fourth mentioned it as the most important factor. In a British study (Milne & Mackenzie, 1958) only about 12% of the respondents mentioned personal discussions as their most important source of election information, while over 80% mentioned one of the mass media. In the 1972 election O'Keefe (1973) found young first-time voters relied on personal sources of information much more than did older voters.

Media exposure to political messages is likely to be accompanied by personal discussion of them, but some studies have found the personal interaction to be a stronger influence on people's understanding of the campaign and their voting decisions (McLeod et al., 1979). However, Deutschmann (1962) has pointed out that discussions are very often held with like-minded individuals, and so they may serve more to reinforce existing voting intentions than to change them.

Several studies have shown clearcut effects of personal contact. Rossi and Cutright (1961) found that contacts by political workers had only a slight effect on voting in presidential elections, but they were absolutely crucial to the outcome of primary elections and very important in local partisan elections. Both field experiments and national survey findings have shown that *turnout* on election day was markedly higher for voters contacted by telephone or in person than for voters who received only a mailed appeal to vote or ones who were not contacted at all (Clausen, 1968; Yalch, 1976; Adams & Smith, 1980).

Dramatic support for this conclusion was found in a careful experimental test by Kraut and McConahay (1973). Exposure to a short political-opinion interview, without any appeals to vote, more than doubled the voting turnout rate at a primary election held two weeks later. Even more surprising, the effect persisted strongly to another primary election four months after the interview, where turnout was still 60% above that of the uninterviewed control group. Another study found that people who had taken part in several lengthy research interviews were more likely to vote than those who had been surveyed only once—that is, several interviews had a cumulative effect on turnout (Traugott & Katosh, 1979). These research findings corroborate political lore about the importance of canvassing to get out the vote, and they point to a potent method of increasing citizen involvement in politics.

Other Types of Public Exposure

Several other factors affecting individual voting decisions should be briefly mentioned. As several social psychological theories predict, the *familiarity* of the candidate, either in terms of having a regional reputation, or more previous media coverage, or name exposure through advertising, adds to the probability of a favorable vote (Grush, 1980; Schaffner, Wandersman, & Stang, 1981). Top *positions on the ballot* also add a bit to a candidate's vote, both in the U.S. and

FIGURE 13-2
A way to increase citizen involvement.

Australia, and honorary titles confer a voting advantage in Britain (Mueller, 1970; Kelley & McAllister, 1984). *Endorsements* by activist groups also yield an electoral bonus. All of these factors were clearly demonstrated in a study of an unusual election for positions on a newly created junior college board of trustees, where there were no incumbents, no party labels, and 133 eager candidates, about most of whom voters knew very little (Mueller, 1970). Other evidence of the advantage conferred by celebrity status can be seen in the election of Clint Eastwood and Sonny Bono as mayors of California cities, and of *Loveboat's* "Gopher" as a Congressman from Iowa. These influences on voting results, which can be seen so clearly in these unusual elections, are probably also operative to a lesser degree in many other campaigns.

FACTORS AFFECTING AGGREGATE VOTING

Before the development of public opinion surveys allowed us to study factors influencing individuals' voting decisions, the only way to analyze election outcomes was in terms of aggregate voting results for different geographic areas. This is still a useful analytic approach, and it has produced some interesting findings. Since 1920 the Census Bureau has published data on the demographic and social characteristics of each small census tract in the United States, and these data can be very illuminating when linked with aggregate voting results for the same areas.

Other facts about our society can also be tied to aggregate voting trends; for instance, Campbell (1962) has shown that the advent of radio as a nearly universal household possession was accompanied by a dramatic rise in voter turnout for elections in the 1930s. Undoubtedly this was at least partly due to radio's ability to carry political information and appeals to the less-educated and less-involved portions of the populace who were unlikely to get the same type of information by reading. By contrast, the advent of nationwide television in the 1950s was not accompanied by any clear increase in voter turnout. Though television has replaced radio as a major source of information and has increased the importance of candidates' visual images, Campbell's data show that it did not produce any noticeable increase in the information level or political involvement of the electorate.

Typical Aggregate Voting Patterns

Some of the facts about aggregate voting patterns are relatively well-known. First, voter **turnout** in presidential election years is markedly higher than in the intervening "off-year" congressional elections. The percentage of the electorate voting in presidential elections since World War II has ranged between approximately 50% and 63%, while it has been only about 36% to 45% in the off-year elections. The difference in turnout at successive elections has always been at least 10% of the electorate, so the dropoff in voting after each presidential election ranges from one-fifth to one-third of the previous election's voters. It is also well-known that the party in power typically loses seats in the House of Representatives at the off-year election; this has happened at every off-year election in this century except 1934.

Two less-well-known facts about voting patterns are related to the above observations. In presidential elections the variation in percentage of voters choosing a given party is about twice as great as in off-year elections (Stokes & Miller, 1962); that is, there are larger swings in party dominance of the vote in presidential years. Also, when there are large increases in voter turnout, the added votes usually go very heavily to one party rather than being split more equally.

Campbell (1964) offered an explanation for these facts of aggregate voting, based on two important characteristics of individual voters, their *party identification* and their degree of *interest in politics*. Survey Research Center panel studies have shown that these two attributes are both quite stable over time for most individuals. What's more, they are related; in general, people who are highly interested in politics are likely to have a strong party identification. Such people tend to vote regularly in every election, whereas less-interested individuals only vote when strong situational forces push them to do so. Thus voters in the lower-interest off-year elections tend to be the core group of politically interested citizens with strong party identifications. They are rather unlikely to shift parties, so the division of the vote is quite stable from election to election. By contrast, the greater ballyhoo and hullabaloo of presidential elections bring many additional voters to the polls, most of whom are only marginally interested in politics.

Moreover, at any given time there are a variety of **short-term forces** which influence people's voting intentions—such factors as important recent events, the candidates' personal characteristics, the public images of the majority parties, and current issues developed in the campaign. When these short-term forces are approximately balanced in the degree to which they favor one party or the other, the division of the total vote will be determined mainly by the pattern of **long-term political characteristics** in the population, that is, by political interest and party identification. However, the short-term forces often build up and favor one candidate and party over the other—"an honest man," "end the war," "get the government off our backs," "no new taxes," etc. When that occurs, strongly committed voters may not shift their vote, but marginal voters are attracted to the favored party in droves.

Thus it sometimes happens that in high-interest presidential elections which stimulate a high voter turnout there is a dramatic surge to the favored candidate. But in the next congressional election, most of those off-and-on voters stay home, the division of the vote returns close to its normal level, and the party that is in the White House loses seats in Congress.

Several other aspects of voter turnout are also of interest here. Overall turnout increased markedly from 1920, when women gained the right to vote, through 1940 and reached new peaks in 1952 and 1960. However, a topic of concern to many analysts has been the steady decrease in turnout at each presidential election since 1960 (Abramson, 1983; Burnham, 1985). In 1980 and 1984 this figure was only 54%, and in 1988 it fell to a new low of 49%, meaning that over half the adult citizens—94 million people—failed to vote (Institute for Social Research, 1988). It also means that, even in this landslide election, the winner received the votes of only 29% of the American electorate. Voter turnout in the U.S. is strikingly lower than in many other industrialized democracies (for instance, turnout in Britain averages 75%), but that is partly because those countries have automatic registration or allow registration right up to election day (Powell, 1986). The American post–World War I maximum turnout figure, 63% of the electorate in 1960, is misleadingly low due to the multiplicity of state registration laws which prevent many citizens from voting if they are ill or disabled, traveling or living abroad, or have recently moved. In 1984, the election turnout of citizens who had met all the state registration requirements was actually 74% (Burnham, 1985). However, the federal law which established a later registration deadline for presidential elections has not succeeded in increasing voter turnout at all (Teixeira, 1987).

A final important trend in aggregate voting is the steady increase in ticket-splitting, which has been going on throughout this century. The number of people who voted for different parties for President and House of Representatives averaged 14% in the 1952–1964 period and then spurted to an average of 28% for the 1968–1984 elections, with a peak of 34% in 1980 (Wattenberg, 1987). This trend is part of the process of party dealignment discussed earlier, and it has two notable corollaries. First, it has allowed the Democrats to keep control of the House continuously since 1948, and usually of the Senate too, despite Republican landslides for President in 1972 and 1984. Second, it is closely linked to the electoral advantage of being an **incumbent**, that is, holding the office for which one is running. A huge majority of people who split their tickets vote for incumbents, and as a consequence incumbent representatives almost always win, often by very heavy margins (Mann & Wolfinger, 1980). In the years 1950–1978, on average, less than 2% of House incumbents were defeated in primary elections, and only 6% lost in the general election. In 1984, less than 4% lost their seats in the general election, and in 1986 and 1988 less than 2% (Jones, 1985; Rothenberg, 1989). This pattern gives a stability to congressional membership that would otherwise have been lost in the trend toward party dealignment.

Switchers and Standpatters

One way of classifying groups of voters is to lump together all those who switched their party vote from one presidential election to the next, the **switchers**, and compare them with those who voted for the same party at both elections, the **standpatters**. There is also a third group, whom we can call **new voters**, consisting of young adults who have reached voting age since the last election *and* of older individuals who did not vote then, for whatever reason. Key and Cummings (1966) made a thorough analysis of these three groups, based on Gallup Poll and National Opinion Research Center (NORC) national survey findings for the period from 1936 to 1960.

The switchers are the group most responsible for changing patterns of party victory and defeat. How many such voters are there, and what are they like? First of all, they are much more numerous than you might think, based on changes in the division of the overall vote. For instance, in 1984 Reagan got about 59% of the vote, an increase of about 8% over his winning margin in 1980 (Burnham, 1985). However, far more than 8% of voters switched their choice that year. The 8% figure is a net change, made up of many individuals who switched their vote from Democratic to Republican and many others who switched from Republican to Democratic. Historically, the proportion of vote switchers has ranged from about 10% to about 20% in various elections, but in 1968 it reached an unprecedented 33% (Converse, Miller, Rusk, & Wolfe, 1969).

The standpatters are a much larger group, about 60% to 75% of total voters, making up the backbone of support of each party. However, standpatters alone would rarely ever be numerous enough to win an election, and the out-of-office party in particular is compelled to direct its appeals at potential switchers and new voters. The "new voters" (who include many older people with low political interest) generally number from 15% to 20% of the voters at each presidential election.

Typically, switchers come more from the ranks of Democratic Party identifiers than from the Republican Party, partly due to the lower average interest in politics of Democrats, and partly because there are more registered Democrats. However, in elections following a major Republican victory such as Reagan's in 1984, there are apt to be more defections from those who voted Republican in the past election than from Democratic ranks. Of course, many of these "defectors" from the Republican ranks were actually Democratic party identifiers returning "home" after previously defecting to vote Republican.

Let us look at a recent election to examine the nature of the switchers, who often determine the overall outcome. In Reagan's landslide victory in 1984, when he won 59% of the vote, the groups that displayed the largest percentage shifts to Reagan included the following: white born-again Christians (a 14% shift to 80% support), voters aged 18–29 (a 10% shift to 57% support), people with family income of $12,500 to $25,000 (10% shift), women (7% shift to 55% support—still 8% less than men), voters 60 and over (7% shift to 57% support), whites, Midwesterners, and conservatives (each shifted 6%). In contrast, the groups which switched most strongly to voting for the Democratic candidate, Mondale, included: Jews (13% shift to 69% support), the unemployed (12% shift), blacks (3% shift to 91% support), voters aged 30–44 (2% shift), Hispanics (2% shift), Westerners (1% shift to 42% support), and union households (1% shift to 57% support)— (Burnham, 1985; Wattenberg, 1987). As Burnham pointed out, this picture of the Republican coalition shows that

> Reagan's strength is concentrated among people most completely rooted in the "have" segments of the American social structure, and those who—like born-again Christians and white Protestants more generally—are most linked to traditional white social mores. . . . The Mondale citadels are populated . . . [by] marginalized and "have-not" groups. (1985, pp. 217–218)

The "Normal" Vote

Consider the contrast between the 1976 election, where Carter won with 51% of the total vote, and the 1984 election, where Reagan won with almost 59% of the vote. These figures lead us to another important question: What is the **"normal" vote**, that is, the most likely division of the popular vote? Since there are two major parties, and since they frequently succeed each other as election winners, you might assume that the normal state of affairs is a 50-50 division of party strength. However, that is not the case. Statistics show that since 1936 the "normal" Democratic Party proportion of the vote has been 54% (Converse, 1966; A. Miller, 1979). An even higher proportion of party identifiers are Democratic, but Republican party identifiers, on the average, are higher in political interest, and in turnout, and lower in voting defection. Also, the increasingly large group of Independents tend to divide their votes, somewhat unevenly, between the two parties. The net result of these group loyalties and interests is that, in national elections where short-term forces do not favor either party, the Democrats can expect to receive about 54% of the votes cast.

In the preceding period of Republican Party ascendancy, from 1896 to 1928, the "normal" expected Republican proportion of the vote was also 54%. The fact that these two percentages are identical has led Sellers (1965) to speculate that this level of partisanship may represent a natural limit within our political system. He concluded that

> there seems to be at work a constant tendency toward equilibrium that is built into the structure of the American two-party system. The persistent narrowness of the margin between the parties is one of the most striking characteristics of the system. . . . There is a tendency not only for a minority party to readjust its image so as to detach groups from the majority coalition, but also for a party with an oversized majority to

FIGURE 13–3 The "normal" division of the vote.

force out groups in the process of deciding which part of its coalition its policies will favor. (pp. 28, 30)

In their current status as a minority party, the Republicans have to seek issues and candidates that will appeal to the nonideological marginal voters (weakly committed Democrats and Independents) who can swing the election to them. Clearly, in the last three decades they have been very successful in doing that, except for 1964 when Goldwater was viewed as an ideological extremist by a large majority of the populace. After the Eisenhower era, the Republicans won five of the next eight elections, several of them by landslides.

Cycles of Party Dominance

The historian Charles Sellers (1965) has analyzed changes in the electoral fortunes of U.S. political parties all the way back to the nation's first election in 1789. On the basis of his careful quantitative study, he concluded that

oscillations from one party to the other do not occur in random fashion, from one election to another. Instead, the parties supplant each other by blocks of elections, both presidential and congressional, each block extending over a period of some years. Moreover, there is a tendency for a party's majorities within a block to rise and fall by regular, graded steps, rather than bouncing up and down in a random fashion. (p. 19)

To explain this sequence of gradual voting changes, he proposed that there is an underlying gradual oscillation in the pattern of party identification in the electorate.

A period of **ascendancy** of one party (typically 12 years or less) is followed by a period of **equilibrium** (sometimes as long as 16 years) in which the difference between the two parties' share of the presidential and congressional vote is small and shifting in direction. Then forces in the nation or the world lead to a period of **realignment** (ranging from 2 to 10 years in length) "in which the underlying pattern of party identifications is substantially and durably altered" (Sellers, 1965, p. 22). The realignment phase is usually accompanied by a third-party movement or even multiple parties, which provide a temporary home for many of the voters whose party identifications are shifting. Surprisingly, the end result of the pressures toward realignment may just as often be a renewed ascendancy of the previously dominant party as a shift to ascendancy of the former minority party. A rather similar analysis has been made by Burnham (1970).

Another historian, Arthur Schlesinger (1939), has also described cyclical "tides of American politics"; however, he ascribed them to alternating periods of liberal and conservative public sentiment. By contrast, Campbell (1964) has emphasized that most fluctuations of party electoral success in the U.S. have not been based on shifts in ideological views among the electorate, but on a simple desire for a change in leadership. An example of this principle was Reagan's election in 1980, even though it has been painted as a conservative mandate by some political commentators. Remember that Reagan won with less than 51% of the total vote in a year when the economic "misery index" was exceedingly high and the fate of the U.S. hostages in Iran was continually in the news every day before the election. Political researchers are in general agreement that the 1980 election outcome was a judgment on Carter's poor performance as President and on the sad state of the economy, rather than a mandate for conservative governmental policies (e.g., *Gallup Opinion Index*, 1980, No. 183; A. Miller & Wattenberg, 1985; Schlozman & Verba, 1987). In fact, nonvoters partially determined the election results in 1980, for that year registered voters who failed to go to the polls favored Carter by a large margin (Petrocik, 1987).

Classification of Elections

The three phases of the party voting cycle described by Sellers are paralleled by three basic types of presidential elections. Campbell (1966) has termed these types maintaining, deviating, and realigning elections.

Maintaining Elections.   These are elections in which the underlying pattern of party identifications is maintained and is reflected in the distribution of the vote. In other words, the majority party of that era retains power or is returned to power. Carter's victory in 1976 is an example, though that has also been termed a reinstating election since the majority party had previously been out of power. It is typical of maintaining elections that there are no overriding policy issues nor particularly attractive candidates impelling marginal voters disproportionately toward one party. It is also typical for voter turnout to be relatively low because of the lackluster campaign.

Deviating Elections. These are campaigns in which the pattern of party identification remains unchanged, but short-term forces lead to the defeat of the majority party. These forces may be strong candidate personalities or important events or issues which impel many citizens to shift their vote temporarily away from their basic party allegiance. After these personalities or events have passed from the current political scene, the balance of the vote reverts back to an advantage for the current majority party. Examples of deviating elections occurred in 1980 and 1984, when Carter's poor performance and a bad economy, and then Reagan's personality and a healthy economy, exerted a major effect on the vote; also in 1968, when controversies over the Vietnam War and George Wallace's third-party candidacy led to the defeat of Hubert Humphrey and the Democratic Party. Another example was the 1916 election, where Woodrow Wilson was elected during a period of Republican dominance as the majority party.

Sellers (1965) has shown that throughout U.S. history, in every election which displayed a particularly strong surge of voters to one candidate in a two-party race, the winners—

> Washington, Jackson, Harrison, Taylor, Grant, and Eisenhower—were "popular hero" candidates who were widely revered for their military achievements and personal characteristics before entering politics. . . . Apparently, only such candidates have the power to draw to the polls the previously apathetic citizens who mainly create the surge effect. (p. 22)

Since Reagan was not a military hero, his massive victory in 1984 does not seem to fit this description—unless perhaps he can qualify as a hero based on his movie star roles (?).

Realigning Elections. In a period of realignment, popular political feelings are so intense and issues and/or events have such an impact that there is a shifting of the basic party loyalties of part of the electorate. Such periods are rare, but very important to our political system. Since the emergence of the Republican Party in 1856–1860 in the conflict over slavery, there have been only two other clear periods of basic political realignment: the reascendance of the Republicans with McKinley's election in 1896, and the shift to Democratic dominance during the depression with Roosevelt's victories in 1932–1936 (Campbell, 1964). The differences between these three periods and the deviating "surge" elections are fascinating:

> Neither Lincoln, McKinley nor Roosevelt, it may be noted, was a military figure and none of them possessed any extraordinary personal appeal at the time he first took office. The quality which did distinguish these elections was the presence of a great national issue and the association of the two major parties with relatively clearly contrasting programs for its solution. In some degree, national politics during these realigning periods did take on an ideological character. The flow of the vote was not a temporary reaction to a heroic figure or a passing embarrassment of the party in power; it reflected a reorientation of basic party attachments growing out of a conflict regarding governmental policies. (Campbell, 1964, p. 753)

The issues which lead to major political realignment leave their effects, not just on individual citizens, but on the party loyalties of whole groups within society. In 1856 and 1896 the groups that changed their political views were mostly regional ones; in 1936 the depression-induced issues led to political changes related to voters' social class status. During the depression, and probably also in earlier realignments, it was largely the young, first-time voters who switched party identification permanently, whereas older voters who switched their votes tended to change back again in subsequent elections (Campbell et al., 1960).

Another Realigning Period?

Based on the above findings it is interesting to speculate on the nature of recent presidential elections. 1964 was clearly a maintaining election, with an extra surge of votes related to candidate images and policy issues. Nixon's victory in 1968 is a bit harder to classify. It was probably a deviating election, but the presence of a viable third-party challenge and the importance of circumstances and issues rather than candidate images raise the possibility that 1968 may have been the beginning of a period of realignment. The 1972 election, with its landslide victory for the former minority party and the great importance of ideological issues in the campaign, was a further indication of strong realigning forces at work in the electorate (A. Miller et al., 1976). However, just as with Goldwater in 1964, the negative candidate image of McGovern in the 1972 election was a factor which suggests classifying it not as a realigning election, but as a deviating one. Then Carter's victory in 1976 would appear to be a maintaining (or reinstating) election.

Reagan's two victories in the 1980s raise the same questions as Nixon's in 1968 and 1972. The 1980 campaign was highly ideological, and there was a third-party challenge from John Anderson, a Republican Congressman—both possible indicators of a realigning trend—but Carter's negative candidate image suggests the likelihood that it was a deviating election. The 1984 landslide for the former minority party and the increasing proportion of young adults identifying and voting Republican are consistent with the realignment hypothesis (Norpoth, 1987; *Public Opinion*, 1985, No. 5); but Reagan's great personal popularity and the lack of ideological emphasis in the campaign are more indicative of another deviating election. However, with Bush's substantial win in 1988, when he received 54% of the vote despite lacking Reagan's popularity and despite the absence of strong ideological issues in the campaign, the series of Republican victories began to look like a developing realignment toward a Republican majority. And yet, in 1988 the Democratic party identification advantage had rebounded from its 1984–1985 low back to its traditional 3:2 ratio, thus contradicting the anticipated Republican trend, so the shift in alignment, if real, was still "soft" (*Gallup Report*, 1988, No. 276).

It is clear that the coalitions of groups supporting the two parties have changed quite markedly in recent decades (Petrocik, 1981). If the 1980s were indeed realigning elections, Seller's analysis of electoral cycles reminds us that we still cannot tell what the ultimate shape of the realignment will be, for despite the Republican victories a realigning period may end with either party in the ascendancy. In the 1970s, the twin blows of Watergate and recession thwarted Republican hopes to build a new dynasty based on the "silent majority." Likewise, Reagan's popularity was dimmed considerably by the Iran-Contra scandal, but it was aided by the nation's continuing economic health and by foreign-policy rapprochement with the USSR. Probably the success of Bush's administration and the hopes of Republican political dominance will rest heavily on the national economic condition in the 1990s and on any major scandals or policy successes that occur in that era.

However, there is another alternative future other than realignment, which is getting increasing attention by political researchers. It is **dealignment**, or decomposition of the party system. Burnham (1985), a noted authority on this topic, believes that dealignment started about 1968 with the decline in party identification and turnout, an increase in vote-switching and ticket-splitting, the precipitous drop in trust in government, heightened attention to candidate images, and the importance of incumbency in congressional races. Other features include greater importance of short-term situational forces, a lessened value of presidential coattails to other candidates of the same party, and a smaller shift to the opposition party in off-year congressional elections (Tuckel & Tejera, 1983). The net result has been a substantial disintegration of party coalitions—erosion of the role of parties and increased prominence of individual candidates and of the media, through which they wage a "permanent campaign" to woo increasingly fickle supporters (Blumenthal, 1982). Burnham refers to this dealignment situation as an "interregnum state," which is increasingly difficult to govern because of the impotence of party platforms and party discipline, the proliferation of many special-interest groups trying to obtain or buy influence, the spurt of single-issue campaigning which ignores all other policy concerns, and the sharp polarization of the electorate along class lines of "haves" versus "have-nots." Thus, dealignment is a marked change in our political system, but not the expected one of a political party achieving a newly dominant position.

Not everyone is as pessimistic about the effects of dealignment as Burnham. Warren Miller, one of the original SRC researchers who stressed the primacy of party identification, agrees that there was a dealignment in the 1970s, with many of the consequences discussed above (W. Miller, 1987). However, in the 1984 election, he has found evidence of some countervailing trends which may restore some of the centrality of political parties. In 1984 the Democratic advantage in party identification was the smallest ever recorded in an election year, and the move toward Republican identification occurred in most age groups, especially those over 60 and those in their 30s. However, at the same time, young cohorts in their 20s and 30s became more polarized ideologically— that is, they showed increases in the number identifying with the Democratic Party as well as the Republican Party. Whether these changes presage an increase in party-line voting and in ideological elections, only time will tell (Wattenberg, 1987).

Predicting the Vote

Is it possible to predict electoral outcomes successfully using polling methods? There are several ways to answer this question. First, we know that in U.S. presidential elections the major commercial polls have not "come a cropper" since their failure to predict the 1948 election. They correctly noted Humphrey's last-minute comeback in 1968, pronouncing the outcome "too close to call," and they all reflected Reagan's final surge in 1980. In 20 congressional and presidential elections from 1950 to 1988, the Gallup Poll's average error in predicting the outcome was only 1.5%, a figure well within the poll's expected margin of sampling error (*Gallup Report*, 1988, No. 279). However, looking at national poll predictions in nine countries over the last 40 years, 15% of published predictions have gone astray in close elections (Buchanan, 1986).

Studies of many different elections have shown that, quite typically, 80% of voters have their minds made up by August and do not change their voting intentions in the three months between then and election day. This was true in the first major scientific election study by Lazarsfeld et al. (1948) in the small area of Erie County, Ohio. It was also true for representative national samples in the photo-finish election of 1960 and the landslide election of 1964 (Benham, 1965). And it was true in the Reagan landslide of 1984 (Cronin, 1985), though not in the unique surge toward Reagan in 1980, when 35% of voters made up their minds in the final week of the campaign after the last debate (*Gallup Opinion Index*, 1980, No. 183). Thus in most elections, except for the closest ones,

> the campaign for the underdog becomes nothing more than running out a pop fly and hoping his opponent will drop the ball. (Benham, 1965, p. 188)

A variety of techniques have been developed to predict the results of elections in elaborate detail. Pioneering a technique somewhat like the psychographic analysis of voter groups described in Chapter 12, Pool et al. (1964) demonstrated that computer simulations of the electorate could be quite accurate in predicting the vote of many voter groups. The accuracy of the computer predictions also helped to demonstrate the fictitious nature of potential "hidden feelings" which respondents were unwilling to divulge to interviewers. Neither prejudiced anti-Catholic voting in 1960, nor pro-Goldwater racial "white backlash" in 1964, exceeded the amount readily reported to interviewers. Again prediction from the polls was shown to be basically accurate (Abelson, 1968).

Another system for forecasting election results has been based on separate predictions for the 50 states, because the states' electoral college votes, not the overall popular vote, are the final determinant of the outcome (Rosenstone, 1983). This system has performed excellently in predicting presidential elections. Only recently have forecasting schemes been proposed for House and Senate elections (e.g., Tufte, 1975), using relatively simple predictor variables such as the state of the economy and of presidential popularity. Though these systems performed well in their early trials, they overpredicted Republican House losses in 1982 and 1986 and underpredicted Republican Senate losses in 1986 (Lewis-Beck, 1987). These errors are consistent with our previous discussion of dealignment, and they suggest that more complex models are needed for predicting outcomes of congressional races.

One major reason that both national and state or district elections are hard to predict accurately is the crucial importance of *turnout* and of *undecided voters* in determining the outcome (see the discussion in Chapter 5). Consequently, elaborate systems have been devised for predicting the overall level of turnout and which poll respondents will actually vote. Though not always successful, these methods have greatly improved the accuracy of polls' election predictions (Perry, 1979; Traugott & Tucker, 1984; Crespi, 1988).

Two kinds of election situations have proved to be particularly hard to predict correctly—i.e., primary elections and referendum campaigns. This is true partly because the efforts of local political workers are very influential in these campaigns, and partly because the overarching factor of party identification is irrelevant to voters' decisions, so other less-stable voting determinants are called into play. However, development of careful procedures has helped the state polls to predict primary results quite accurately, particularly when the polling is done just a few days before the election (Felson & Sudman, 1975).

Thus research indicates that high levels of predictive accuracy can often be reached using survey data. In most voting situations there are relatively few issues and psychographic factors that actually affect voters' decisions. If the few crucial issues can be identified and the major voter types who respond to them can be specified, relatively simple combinations of these data should usually produce predictions that are very close to the final vote results (Pool et al., 1964; Rosenstone, 1983).

The television election-night predictions have used this kind of rationale, and their success demonstrates the validity of this approach. In the 1960s and 1970s, before the development of "exit polling," the television projections of election winners were made after the polls closed, based on counts of the first few ballots from "key districts," carefully chosen to be representative of the voting patterns of the state. In 1964 and 1966 the predictions made in this way by both NBC and CBS Television proved to be over 99% correct—a sensational batting average in any league (Skedgell, 1966; Abelson, 1968).

However, not content with these results, the networks extended their competition with the goal of continually being earlier in broadcasting projections of the election outcome. To this end, by 1980 they changed their prediction method and began to rely on exit polls (described in Chapter 5), which potentially allow them to predict the results of apparently lopsided contests many hours before the close of voting. Though the inaccuracy of sampling inherent in this method caused incorrect network predictions in a number of 1982 contests, by and large their early projections have continued to be predominantly accurate (Levy, 1983; Roper, 1983). However, a serious question remains as to how much these early afternoon election projections discourage voters from going to the polls and thus diminish public involvement in the electoral process (e.g., Wolfinger & Linquiti, 1981).

A final issue concerning prediction of voting is how well *individual* voters' decisions, rather than aggregate outcomes, can be predicted. Among the many studies on this topic, ones using Fishbein and Ajzen's theory of reasoned action are probably most numerous, and a summary of their approach to predicting voting behavior is provided by Fishbein, Ajzen, and Hinkle (1980). Their theory emphasizes voters' cognitive beliefs about and affective evaluations of candidates as predictors of voting intentions, and they report a high correlation of +.80 between voting intention and voting behavior, with very little addition to this figure when other more-traditional political variables were added to the prediction equation. Jaccard, Knox, and Brinberg (1980) offer an example of use of this theory, in which voting intentions correctly predicted 97% of the respondents' presidential votes, 85% of their senatorial votes, and 76% of their congressional votes. In turn, the theory's formulas correctly predicted the voting intentions of over 85% of the respondents; and voters' beliefs predicted their attitudes toward the candidates with a multiple correlation of about +.75. A similar study using the theory to predict voting on statewide "bottle deposit bill" referendum measures also reported very high relationships between voting intentions and voting behavior (Gill, Crosby, & Taylor, 1986). These findings show an excellent ability to predict a group of voters but at least a modest margin of error in predicting individuals' votes.

SUMMARY

Individual voting decisions are affected by several major determinants, including personal influences from friends or family members and cross-pressures due to a person's noncongruent demographic characteristics. An individual's party identification is often the most important determinant in voting; however, in some recent elections, the public's image of the candidates has become an even more important factor, and since the 1960s, many campaigns have been more ideological in nature, with more attention given to issue positions.

Political persuasion is generally much more likely to reinforce existing attitudes than to change contrary attitudes, for both reception and acceptance of political persuasion attempts are limited. Campaign expenditures, largely for television commercials, are typically the strongest factor in determining election winners. The advent of television in politics in the 1950s made the personality and "image" of a candidate more important in the campaign, and major events such as the presidential debates can sometimes swing election outcomes in close races. Newspapers' political endorsements frequently have a noticeable effect on readers' voting, while personal contact is particularly effective in local or primary elections. In low-interest elections, even factors such as order on the ballot or a familiar name can markedly affect vote totals.

Aggregate voting patterns in presidential elections reflect the turnout of many marginally interested voters, who are more influenced than regular voters by the short-term forces favoring one party or the other at that time. Citizens who switch their vote at successive elections make up only 10% to 20% of the electorate, but they often determine the election outcome, particularly during the post-1968 period of decomposition or dealignment of the U.S. party system.

The "normal" or average division of the vote has been 54% Democratic since 1936, whereas between 1896 and 1928 it was 54% Republican. Historically, a period of ascendancy by one party is usually followed by a period of rough equilibrium, and then eventually by a period of realignment when the electorate's pattern of party identifications is markedly altered.

Since 1950 the major U.S. polling organizations have had a remarkably good record in predicting the division of the popular vote, and a variety of more complex methods have been developed to predict the results for specific voter groups and special types of elections.

14

International Attitudes

Wars begin in the minds of men.—UNESCO Charter.

Our images of Italy, of Turkey, and of Austria are formed of biased history texts and loaded newspaper stories. . . . Similarly the legend of the crude, materialistic, uneducated American goes unchallenged in much of the world.— Ross Stagner.

O wad some Power the giftie gie us
To see oursel's as ithers see us!—Robert Burns.

This chapter discusses how people develop their attitudes toward other nations and their images of foreign peoples. To what extent are their sources of information limited and/or biased? As a result, are their international attitudes stereotyped, or are they sensitive to reality factors? What kinds of people tend to develop warlike attitudes, for instance, or isolationistic viewpoints? Finally, how can international attitudes be changed?

If you agree that wars begin in people's minds, the importance of international attitudes is clear. Since a nuclear war could devastate the whole planet and possibly wipe out all human life, nations' warlike actions and the beliefs and attitudes that lead up to them are literally life-and-death issues for all of us. In addition, nations' preparations for preventing or fighting a war have an overpowering impact on everything else they do or don't do, as illustrated in these quotations:

> The money required to provide adequate food, water, education, health and housing for everyone in the world has been estimated at $17 billion a year. It is a huge sum of money—about as much as the world spends on arms every two weeks. *(World Federalist Newsletter, 1980)*

> By 1990, nearly enough will have been spent on defense during the Cold War—$3.7 trillion in constant 1972 dollars—to buy everything in the U.S. except the land: every house, factory, train, plane and refrigerator. (Hiatt & Atkinson, 1985)

Much of what we have already learned about political attitudes applies directly to international affairs. However, there are some special ways in which international attitudes are unique. One characteristic feature is that many people's attitudes are formed despite their having little or no direct contact with other nations, foreigners, or issues of foreign affairs. As a result, the attitudes may be quite unrelated to the realities of world affairs. Of course all of our attitudes are based on our perception of the environment rather than on the actual, objective situation. But in the field of foreign affairs the gap between perception and reality is apt to be especially large.

Images.   A number of authors from different disciplines have emphasized the gap between international attitudes and international reality by using the term **images** to describe our often-distorted views of other nations and peoples (e.g., Jervis, 1970; Fiske, Fischhoff, & Milburn, 1983; Holt & Silverstein, 1989). The following quotation clearly conveys that point of view:

> Americans do not know Russia; they know an image of Russia, subject to many errors and misconceptions. In fact, they do not know America, but only an image thereof; and it is sometimes amazing to find how we differ among ourselves as to the attributes of our nation. (Stagner, 1967, p. 12)

THE IGNORANT PUBLIC

Even more than in the area of political attitudes, public information about world affairs is sharply limited. For example, in the area of basic geographic knowledge, half of Americans are unaware that Nicaragua is the country where Sandinistas and American-backed Contras have been fighting; 45% don't know that apartheid is a government policy in South Africa; 32% can't name any of the member nations of NATO; and half can't name any of the Warsaw Pact countries. When given an outline map of Europe, the average American high school graduate can correctly name only slightly more than three of 12 European nations, whereas 40 years ago Americans could name almost twice as many (*Gallup Report*, 1988, No. 277). As recently as 1979, three-fourths of the public incorrectly thought that the U.S. had a fairly effective defense against nuclear weapons, and in 1984 81% falsely believed that the U.S. had a no-first-use policy for nuclear weapons in case of war. In 1985, only about one-third of a national sample had heard of the ABM/SALT I treaty, and 28% of another sample thought that the Soviet Union had fought *against* the U.S. in World War II (Public Agenda Foundation, 1984; Graham & Kramer, 1986; Silverstein & Flamenbaum, 1989).

Many other compilations of public ignorance have been made (e.g., Erskine, 1963b). The implications of this lack of public information are clear: many people in our society are "know-nothings," and if you ask their opinions, especially about world affairs, you will very likely be measuring what Converse has called "non-attitudes," based on a complete lack of information and understanding. Thus, it is important for attitude surveys to eliminate or isolate such respondents by the use of careful screening questions so that their "attitudes" are not lumped together with those of more knowledgeable citizens. The best-informed group, the "issue publics" in Converse's terminology, are the ones whose attitudes are more likely to be meaningful and stable. However, in between the two extremes, a large middle group with limited knowledge nevertheless display an understandable pattern of foreign policy preferences and beliefs (Jervis, 1986; Hurwitz & Peffley, 1987). One indication of this is the amount of attention given to foreign affairs, both by candidates and by voters, in many presidential election campaigns (Aldrich, Sullivan, & Borgida, 1989).

CHILDREN'S VIEWS OF FOREIGN PEOPLES

How do our international attitudes originate and develop? When do children begin to become aware of foreign nations and peoples, and how do their attitudes change with increasing age?

A classic study of these questions was conducted by Lambert and Klineberg (1967), following a research plan developed by the United Nations Educational, Social, and Cultural Organization (UNESCO). The study used a careful cross-cultural approach in eleven different areas of the world: the United States, Bantu children in South Africa, Brazil, English Canada, French Canada, France, Germany, Israel, Japan, Lebanon, and Turkey. In each area 300 children at three age levels (6, 10, and 14) were interviewed at length by native interviewers. The sample was carefully selected from among lower-class and middle-class urban children, but was not representative of the whole nation's child population.

The structured interviews with the children concentrated on their conceptions of their own national groups, on which foreign peoples were similar to or different from them, and on liked and disliked nationalities. Table 14-1 shows a sample of the findings, comparing children's descriptions of their own nationality with the most typical descriptions of their nations by other national groups.

Of course, these national descriptions are stereotypes, frequently based on little information and having doubtful validity at best. Nevertheless, this glimpse of children's national images provides intriguing food for thought. For instance, nearly all nations' children regarded their own people as "good," but (in 1959, when the interviewing was conducted) the Bantu and the Japanese did not—perhaps the result of racial oppression and disastrous defeat in war, respectively. Similarly, positive evaluations were foremost in descriptions of almost all other nations, though Russians were seen as "good" less often than they were seen as "aggressive" (keep in mind that this study was done during the cold war period and almost entirely in nations allied to the United States rather than to Russia). The other descriptive terms showed much greater differences—from wealthy and free, to intelligent, cultured, and happy. Undoubtedly some of these stereotypes have changed substantially since then with the flow of international events (economic recovery, wars, superpower agreements, etc.).

TABLE 14-1   Most Typical Descriptions of Various National Groups as Seen by Children of Their Own and Other Nations

Nationality	Self-description	Description by other nations
American	good, wealthy, free	good, wealthy, intelligent, aggressive
Bantu	factual statements (e.g., dark-skinned) and similarity references (e.g., like us)	(description of "Negroes from Africa") good, uncultured, unintelligent, dominated, poor, bad, aggressive
Brazilian	good, intelligent, cultured, happy, unambitious	good (no other terms)
French	good, intelligent, cultured, happy, bad	(not obtained)
German	good, ambitious, wealthy, intelligent	good, aggressive, intelligent, bad
Israeli	good, religious, peaceful, intelligent	(not obtained)
Japanese	poor, intelligent, bad	(not obtained)
Turkish	good, peaceful, ambitious, religious, patriotic, clean	(not obtained)
Chinese	(not interviewed)	good, poor, aggressive, bad
Indians from India	(not interviewed)	good, poor
Russians	(not interviewed)	aggressive, good, intelligent, bad, dominated

Note. Terms are listed in approximate order of their frequency of usage in each national description.

Source: Adapted from W. E. Lambert & O. Klineberg, *Children's Views of Foreign Peoples*, 1967, pp. 102, 143. Reprinted by permission of Irvington Publishers, Inc.

Development of Children's Attitudes

The process of development and change in these attitudes toward foreign peoples is particularly important. At age 6 many of the children could give only very sparse responses about foreign peoples—mostly simple factual information and evaluations of "good" or "bad." At ages 10 and 14 there was a progressive increase in the range of evaluative categories used, such as intelligent, aggressive, poor, wealthy, peaceful, dominated, and ambitious. At the same time there was a change in the type of descriptive statements—from physical characteristics, clothing, and language, to a greater emphasis on personality traits, habits, political and religious characteristics, and material possessions. Interestingly, children described well-liked nations with many factual, descriptive terms and with relatively few evaluative terms, whereas less-liked nations were characterized with many evaluative terms (often negative) and few factual descriptions.

Lambert and Klineberg (1967) concluded that the stereotyping process gets its start in children's early conceptions of their own group, and that between the ages of 6 and 14 children develop increasingly stereotyped views of foreign peoples. A basic finding of many studies is that children as young as 6 generally express strong positive feelings for their own nation and for traditional national symbols (e.g., Hess & Torney, 1967). By about age 10, many children develop fairly strong negative feelings for enemy or rival nations (Middleton, Tajfel, & Johnson, 1970).

These early national preferences and aversions are based largely on ingroup-outgroup relationships and are fostered by consistency motives—preferences for "us" and related groups, and aversions for groups that are seen as different from or opposed to "us." In a long series of experimental studies, Tajfel and his colleagues have shown that ingroup-versus-outgroup, "we-versus-they," feelings can be generated simply by separating people into categories, even on characteristics as unimportant as their estimation of the number of dots in a random pattern (Tajfel, 1981). Once such cognitive distinctions are established, they take on emotional significance as well, and people come to consider them important as a basis for self-esteem as well as personal consistency (e.g., "It's great to be an American"). Furthermore, these stereotypes serve as guides for assessing new information, so actions of an outgroup are usually remembered and interpreted in ways consistent with a person's existing stereotype of the group (e.g., Howard & Rothbart, 1980).

Principles of attribution theory are also relevant here, and Pettigrew (1979) has described a common tendency which he calls the **ultimate attribution error**—that is, attributing negative behavior by outgroup members to their dispositions ("They're just naturally aggressive"), while ignoring or explaining away their positive behavior as situationally determined (e.g., "Our threats made them behave properly"). Other recent discussions of the development of international images have been offered by Coles (1986) and Hesse (1988), and a collection of research papers on enemy images is contained in Holt and Silverstein (1989).

ADULTS' VIEWS OF FOREIGN PEOPLES

In adulthood, attitudes toward foreign nations and peoples tend to remain fairly stable unless influenced by strong pressures or events. However, studies in life-span developmental psychology have shown that important changes can occur at any stage of life if the pressures are strong enough (Kinder & Sears, 1985).

A pioneering study of adult attitudes, rather similar to the one with children described above, was conducted under UNESCO sponsorship in 1948–1949 (Buchanan & Cantril, 1953). At that time, shortly after World War II, only the more industrialized nations had public opinion polling organizations, so the study was carried out in nine relatively advanced nations: Australia, Britain, France, parts of West Germany, Italy, the Netherlands, Norway, Mexico (only in cities), and the United States. A quota sample of about 1000 adults was interviewed in each country. Instead of using open-ended questions, as in the study with children, a list of 12 adjectives was presented for respondents to choose from in describing two foreign peoples (Americans and Russians) and natives of their own country. Thus the sampling was broader and more representative than in the Lambert and Kline-berg children's study, but the interview content was much less extensive.

The results of this study largely reflected alignments in the recently con-cluded World War II and the subsequent "cold war" between the eastern and western blocs of nations. When the survey was taken in 1948, the United States was clearly the best-liked foreign country in the eight western nations studied (an average of 33% of respondents so listed it), while Russia was least-liked (by an average of 36% of respondents). Of the countries surveyed, only France departed from this pattern, choosing the Swiss as the best-liked people and the Germans as least-liked. Britain was second best-liked, with an average mention of 12%, and the Scandinavian countries as a whole were third with 8%. In the least-liked category, Germany was second with 16% and Japan third with 7%. America was mentioned as least-liked by 3%, and the same number listed Russia as most-liked. Nations that shared a common language and/or culture in most cases had strongly friendly feelings for each other, but sharing a common boundary was slightly more likely to lead to disliking than to liking. Interestingly, the bordering countries which were well-liked were all smaller than the country which liked them, and thus unlikely to be a military or economic threat.

TABLE 14–2   Percentage of Countries Using Various Adjectives to Describe Them-selves and Other Nations

	People described					
Adjective	*Russians*	*Americans*	*British*	*French*	*Chinese*	*Own countrymen*
	(8)[a]	*(7)*	*(3)*	*(3)*	*(3)*	*(8)*
Hardworking	69[b]	43	33	33	100	62
Intelligent		14	67	67	11	62
Practical		86	17			
Conceited		14	50	67		
Generous		43		33		38
Cruel	75				44	
Backward	62				100	
Brave			33	33	11	62
Self-controlled			67			
Domineering	94	14		17		
Progressive		86				
Peace-loving			33	50	33	75

Note. The three most frequently used adjectives were tabulated for each combination of describing country and people described.
[a] The number in parentheses is the number of describing countries.
[b] Ties for third-place adjectives resulted in percentages not evenly divisible by the number of describing countries.

Source: Adapted from Buchanan & Cantril (1953, p. 50).

Table 14–2 shows the characteristics most commonly ascribed to foreign peoples. As with the Lambert and Klineberg study of children's attitudes, it must be remembered that the data all came from western, noncommunist countries and represent very gross stereotypes of the peoples described. However, each nation's stereotype was relatively clearcut. Russians were seen in mostly unflattering terms: domineering, cruel, hardworking, and backward. Americans (in that era of the Marshall Plan for aid to Europe) were generally viewed as practical, progressive, hard-working, and generous. The respondents' own country, no matter which one it happened to be, was usually seen in highly favorable terms: peace-loving, hardworking, intelligent, and brave.

Of course, these national stereotypes can sometimes change quite rapidly, as the Russian image had changed for the worse in the few years since the end of World War II. This fact led Buchanan and Cantril to conclude that national images are more likely to be determined by the relationship between nations than to be a major determinant of such relationships. An illustration of this process can be seen in a series of studies conducted in western European countries for the U.S. Information Agency (USIA) between 1952 and 1965, which in effect extend Buchanan and Cantril's original UNESCO study and enable us to see changes in international attitudes over a period of years (Merritt & Puchala, 1968). In each survey a representative national sample in each of several countries was interviewed by a polling organization located in that country.

Some results of the USIA studies are presented in Figure 14-1, which shows changes in composite attitudes toward six different countries over the period 1954-

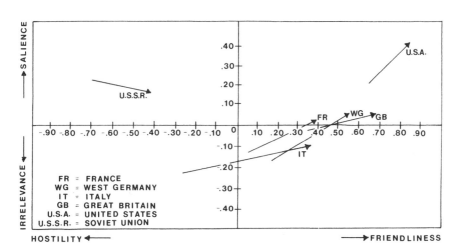

FIGURE 14–1 Changes from 1954 to 1964 in the composite attitudes of four western European countries toward six nations.

Source: From Western European Perspectives on International Affairs: Public Opinion Studies and Evaluations, Richard L. Merritt and Donald J. Puchala (Eds.), p. 133. Data in part II © 1968 by Frederick A. Praeger, Inc., New York. Reprinted by permission.

1964. The attitudes plotted are those of a composite group made up of random samples of citizens from four western European countries, France, West Germany, Italy, and Great Britain. The method of plotting emphasizes long-term underlying trends and largely discounts short-term fluctuations in attitudes toward each country by citizens of the other three countries, over the 10-year period. The starting and ending points are shown on the graph by linear arrows stretching from the 1954 position to the 1964 position. The coordinates of the graph represent the two most important dimensions of attitudes toward other nations, the degree of friendliness on the horizontal axis, and on the vertical axis the degree of importance or salience of the nation (based on the percentage of respondents having firm opinions about it).

The attitude changes between 1954 and 1964 shown in Figure 14-1 are remarkably parallel. First, all six countries registered gains in the friendliness toward them shown by the other three western European nations. Second, all countries except the USSR also displayed gains in their importance to the other nations. Third, all countries maintained their same relative position over the 10-year period, with the United States receiving most friendliness, Great Britain next most, and Russia least, while the United States and Russia remained first and second in importance to the others. Finally, all the countries except Italy ended up at least slightly above zero on the importance dimension, and Italy moved considerably in that direction. Thus, the graph reflects and quantifies the international trends of the early 1960s such as increased U.S.-Soviet détente and growing integration of the European Economic Community (Merritt & Puchala, 1968).

It would be highly desirable to have a continuing series of international measurements such as the USIA surveys, but unfortunately they were abandoned after 1964 in budget-cutting moves by later Presidents. However, a variety of other techniques have been applied to measuring international attitudes (e.g., Wish, Deutsch, & Biener, 1970), and changes in the degree of favorability of American samples toward various other nations have been tracked from the 1950s through the 1980s (e.g., *Gallup Opinion Index*, 1976, No. 136; 1980, No. 176; de Boer, 1980; *Gallup Report*, 1985, No. 237; *Public Opinion*, 1988, No. 3).

FOREIGNERS' VIEWS OF THE U.S.

Other nations' attitudes toward the United States have varied quite markedly over time. Since the era of favorability depicted in the USIA surveys, there have been two main periods when our major allies were much less favorable to us: during the Vietnam War, and early in the 1980s when President Reagan was seen as a dangerous warmonger, partly for his bellicose rhetoric and partly for sending U.S. troops to Grenada and Lebanon, bombing Libya, and sending arms to the Contras in Nicaragua. In 1982, respondents in six western European countries were asked how much confidence they had in the ability of the U.S. to deal wisely with present world problems. In five of the countries (Switzerland, France, Denmark,

Belgium, and Britain—all except West Germany) the percentage saying they had "little" or "very little" confidence exceeded the percentage saying "considerable" or "very great" confidence (Wybrow, 1984).

The attitudes of the British toward the U.S. provide a key example, since they have been our strongest allies all through this century. On the above question about confidence in the U.S. to deal wisely with world problems, a relatively stable average of only 30-34% of Britons expressed at least considerable confidence during the presidencies of Nixon, Ford, and Carter, but this figure sank to 25% during the first six years of Reagan's administration. On more specific items, majorities of about 70%–75% of Britons agree with statements like these:

The United States is as great a threat to world peace as is the USSR.

The United States forces its policies too much on Britain and other European countries.

The military and organizations like the CIA have too much influence on United States policies.

Moreover, these anti-American attitudes are much stronger in the younger generation (age 18–35) than in older ones (Crewe, 1987, p. 52). By 1986 the U.S. and USSR were seen by Britons as about equally unresponsive in trying to prevent a third world war, whereas only a few years earlier the difference between the two nations had been much more in America's favor.

However, it is important to note that these criticisms are primarily of U.S. government policies—not mainly of the U.S. people, for whom Britons still retain a reservoir of goodwill. For instance, majorities of over 80% and over 60% respectively agreed with the following items:

Americans are, on the whole, pleasant and friendly people.

The United States does much good for poor countries in the world by food and other aid. (Crewe, 1987, p. 52)

And when asked how trustworthy people from 17 other countries were, Britons placed Americans fourth, only behind citizens of three nearby, small, and peaceable nations, Switzerland, the Netherlands, and Denmark.

The Meaning of "Socialism" and "Capitalism"

Another aspect of disagreement between the U.S. and our European allies— the differing meanings attached to the words "socialism" and "capitalism"—was studied by White (1966) using the USIA surveys of public opinion in Britain, France, West Germany, and Italy. When representative samples in these four countries were asked to rate the United States on a scale from completely capitalistic (0) to completely socialistic (10), an amazing 63% of them said the United States was completely capitalistic (0 on the scale) while 25% more put it at 1 or 2 on the scale. By contrast, in groups of Americans whom White has asked the same question, no one ever rated the United States at 0, and the typical response was usually about 5—roughly halfway between complete capitalism and complete socialism.

When the USIA surveys asked western Europeans how much capitalism or socialism they wanted for their own countries, by far the most common answer was 5 on the 0-10 scale, given by 35% of the respondents; 65% chose answers in the range from 3 to 7, with 23% higher and 12% lower. White cites this and other evidence to show that in many countries "capitalism is on balance a slightly dirty word" and "that in most of the world the word socialism is more unequivocally positive than the word capitalism is negative" (p. 219).

White points out that when Americans speak of socialism, they often refer to government ownership of industry, whereas in most other countries the term is used much more to refer to government responsibility for social welfare and government regulation of industry and labor. Similarly, to Americans, capitalism primarily means private ownership of industry, whereas in most other countries it means excessive political power for the rich (capitalists) and lack of social welfare for poor people. In addition, most other peoples dislike communism, which they associate with dictatorship and violence, and make a sharp distinction between it and socialism. (Indeed the dominant party in many countries is named Democratic Socialists or some variation thereof.) In contrast, many Americans use the words communist and socialist almost interchangeably as pejorative terms.

An important substantive lesson can be drawn from these semantic distinctions. White concludes that American social welfare programs and government regulative laws have given us an intermediate level of socialism (probably not far from the level preferred by many Europeans). However, there is a great ignorance of that fact overseas, and Americans compound that problem by often referring to our system as capitalistic and by "confusing socialism with Communism and condemning both in the same breath" (p. 228). White recommends, in the interest of clearer communication and understanding with other nations, that we should try

> to avoid needless emphasis on issues in the area of socialism that we and they may disagree on, and to emphasize instead the principles of democracy that we and they have in common. . . . We can then define what America stands for unambiguously as a maximum of democracy, a minimum of government ownership, and a medium-to-high amount of social welfare. (White, 1966, p. 228)

U.S. IMAGES OF THE USSR

Another important aspect of international attitudes is the views of each other's country held by Americans and Soviets, the major cold war protagonists. The attitudes of Soviet citizens are rather hard to estimate for several reasons. Though public opinion polling is gradually becoming an accepted tool of Soviet social scientists, very little of it deals with political or foreign policy issues (Welsh,

1981). Westerners attempting to interview Russian citizens often receive very cautious answers, which raise questions of their validity, and the views of Russian defectors are obviously biased and unrepresentative. In spite of these problems, several researchers investigating this area have reached remarkably similar conclusions.

A unique opportunity to study Russian attitudes came to Urie Bronfenbrenner, a social psychologist who was one of the first American scientists to visit Russia during a thaw in U.S.-Russian relations in 1960. He was allowed to travel quite freely without a guide in a number of cities, and since he spoke fluent Russian, he was able to converse with many of the common citizens. He held conversations with many people whom he chose in a semirandom manner and talked with systematically, and he returned with some fascinating observations and conclusions.

The Mirror Image

Bronfenbrenner's (1961) main conclusion was that Soviet citizens view the world almost exactly as American citizens do, but with a reversed evaluative direction—a **mirror image** in international perceptions. For instance, each nation sees itself as peace-loving and can give many reasons and arguments to support that view. Similarly, both Americans and Russians view the other nation as aggressive and threatening to foment a war at any moment, as evidenced by its huge expenditures for armed forces and military weapons. Consequently each nation feels that it must arm itself heavily for "defensive" purposes—to prevent the warlike other from carrying out its aggressive plans. In these respects the two countries hold exact mirror images of each other. The major common themes in the international viewpoints of Soviet and American citizens noted by Bronfenbrenner are listed and illustrated in Box 14–1.

Many other aspects of the mirror image have been described by Ralph White (1965, 1984) and documented by quotations from official statements or government leaders, and by interviews with foreigners who have visited each country. (In fact, Holsti, 1962, in a careful content analysis study, has shown that a prime example of mirror-image beliefs is contained in the public statements of John Foster Dulles, the U.S. Secretary of State during the Eisenhower administration.) White points out that most Americans and most Russians view the vast bulk of the other country's citizens as good, peace-loving individuals. But each country has a "black-top" image of the other—a belief that their leaders are evil, aggressive, and reckless. Though each country lives in constant fear of reckless aggressive actions by the other, neither is able to see that the other's actions are often motivated by fear rather than by hostile intent. Surprisingly enough, each side uses similar standards in judging themselves and the other side—truthfulness, strength, material advancement, courage, unselfishness, etc.—but since they do not see any given event from the same viewpoint, they apply these standards to an entirely different perception of world affairs. Finally, each side claims that the other's statements are propaganda, intended to deceive, and therefore it pays little attention to them.

Box 14–1 *Mirror Images of the U.S.A. and U.S.S.R.*

American Image of Russia

1. *They are the aggressors.*
   They have imposed communist regimes on many countries by force.

   They prevent disarmament by refusing to allow inspection.

2. *Their government exploits and deludes the people.*
   Communist party members, though a small part of the population, control the government.
   Russian elections are a travesty since only one party is on the ballot.

   The Russian radio and press are controlled by the government.

3. *Their people are not really sympathetic to the regime.*
   The Russian people distrust their government propaganda.
   They praise communism only because they have to in order to avoid getting in trouble.
   They would prefer to live under our system of government.

4. *Their leaders cannot be trusted.*
   Though they claim to favor disarmament, they are probably carrying on secret nuclear tests.
   Everything they do is part of an aggressive communist plan.

5. *Their policy verges on madness.*
   The Soviet position on such issues as Berlin and disarmament is completely unrealistic.
   They carry their actions even to the brink of war.
   Only Western restraint and coordinated reaction to the Russian provocations over Berlin avoided World War III.

Russian Image of America

1. *They are the aggressors.*
   They have established American bases and troops on every border of the U.S.S.R.
   They turn down our disarmament proposals and even send spy planes illegally over our country.

2. *Their government exploits and deludes the people.*
   A capitalist-militarist clique controls the American government.

   American voting is a farce since both parties' candidates are chosen by the same powerful interests.
   The American radio and press are controlled by the capitalist-militarist interests.

3. *Their people are not really sympathetic to the regime.*
   The American people disapprove of their government's aggressive actions.
   Most of them don't say anything controversial in order to avoid sanctions against liberal elements.
   If they knew what communism is really like, they would choose it as their form of government.

4. *Their leaders cannot be trusted.*
   Though they claim to favor disarmament, they insist on inspection only to discover our secrets.
   They take advantage of our hospitality by sending in spies disguised as tourists.

5. *Their policy verges on madness.*
   The American position on such issues as East Germany and disarmament is completely unrealistic.
   They carry their actions even to the brink of war.
   Only Soviet prudence and restraint in reacting to the American U-2 plane provocations avoided World War III.

Source: Extracts from Bronfenbrenner (1961, pp. 46–48).

In spite of these many similarities, U.S.-Russian perceptions are not a perfect reflection of each other. The mirror image has "flaws"—points where the reciprocal perceptions don't match exactly. One such wrinkle in the mirror is the Russians' strong feeling of warmth and friendliness for the American people, which is only feebly reciprocated by Americans. Another is the Russians' admiration for America's wealth and material progress, whereas Americans view Russia as poor, drab, and inefficient. Though both nations highly value "democracy," they hold quite different meanings of that term: Americans emphasize free elections and individual freedoms, whereas Russians stress citizens' responsibilities to serve the common good.

The Double Standard

Despite these and other small discrepancies, the mirror image in U.S. and Soviet attitudes seems to be a well-established fact. If Russians and Americans observe the same world events and emerge with opposite conclusions, then it follows that both sides are probably using a **double standard** for evaluating international affairs. Oskamp (1965; Oskamp & Hartry, 1968; also see Mickolus, 1980) demonstrated that a double standard of evaluation does indeed underlie the mirror image. He developed a list of 50 international actions which had been taken in substantially equivalent forms by both the United States and the USSR—both countries had increased their military budgets, blockaded foreign areas, made disarmament proposals, signed joint treaties, sent great musicians to perform in the other country, etc. When American college students were asked to indicate how favorable they felt toward these identical actions by the two countries, they were markedly more favorable toward almost every one of the U.S. actions than to the comparable Russian action. Some of the differences were as large as 4 points on a 6-point scale; for instance, the students felt quite favorable to the U.S. blockading a nearby area but quite unfavorable toward Russia blockading an area near her.

This double standard in evaluating international events makes possible the mirror-image phenomenon. People generally see any action by their own country, whether warlike or peaceful, in a much more favorable light than similar actions which are taken by an opposing country (Burn & Oskamp, 1989). This view is maintained by attributions in which the actions of one's own country are ascribed to altruistic motives whereas the similar actions of an enemy are attributed to self-serving motives. Later research (Oskamp, 1972; Sande, Goethals, Ferrari, & Worth, 1989) showed, as predicted, that students in Britain and Canada have much less of a double standard in evaluating U.S. and Russian actions. (Of course, they would be expected to show a clearcut double standard in evaluating actions of their own country in relation to those of another nation, such as France. In fact, laboratory studies have shown that a mirror-image evaluative attitude toward two fictitious national groups can be easily created in an internation simulation experiment—Streufert & Sandler, 1971.)

Though the double standard in international affairs is pervasive, it is not impervious to events. The protest movement which developed in the United States during the Vietnam War at first had little effect on the size of subjects' preference for U.S. actions, but by 1971 the size of students' double standard had decreased by more than half (Oskamp, 1972). In particular, U.S. warlike or hostile actions and U.S. nonmilitary sanctions against other nations were evaluated less favorably in 1971 than in 1968 or 1963, while Russian peaceful statements were evaluated more favorably than earlier.

Recent Changes in Images of the USSR

Representative national samples of Americans have also displayed changing attitudes toward the Soviet Union. From the peak of cold war hostility in the early 1950s until about 1975 there was a gradual decline in Americans' negative views, but three subsequent events were each followed by successively higher levels of unfavorability to the USSR: namely, the North Vietnamese takeover of Saigon and South Vietnam in 1975, the Soviet invasion of Afghanistan at the end of 1979, and the Russian shooting down of a Korean airliner in 1983. However, despite President Reagan's March, 1983, speech describing the Soviet Union as an "evil empire," a substantial *decrease* in American antipathy occurred from 1984 to 1988 (Yatani & Bramel, 1989).

Looking beyond measures of general favorability, U.S. attitudes toward the USSR are highly complex and ambivalent. On the one hand, in a representative national sample, a very large majority of Americans stated that the Soviets are constantly testing us and quick to take advantage of weakness; that they used détente with the U.S. to build up their military strength; and that they would attack us or our allies if we were weak. On the other hand, equally large majorities believed that the Russian people are potentially friendly to us; that the U.S. has to accept some of the blame for the recent tensions in U.S.-Soviet relations; and that we often blame the Soviets for troubles in other countries that are really caused by poverty, hunger, political corruption, and repression (Public Agenda Foundation, 1984; Yankelovich & Doble, 1984). Concerning how to deal with the USSR, large majorities of respondents in the same study agreed that the Soviets only respond to military strength, and that we should continue to develop new and better nuclear weapons. On the other hand, they also stated that if we and the Soviets keep building missiles instead of negotiating to get rid of them, they will eventually be used; that the U.S. can't be the policeman of the world; that we should live and let live, allowing each side to have its own system; and that we can get along with communist countries, for we do so all the time. This complicated and partially conflicting set of beliefs shows that Americans have not achieved a consensus about relations with the Soviet Union (Public Agenda Foundation, 1984).

However, a major factor in the increasing general favorability toward the USSR has been the policies and statements of Mikhail Gorbachev since he became the Soviet leader in 1985. In late 1987, following his signing of a treaty with the U.S. banning intermediate-range nuclear missiles, he became the first Russian ever to be named by Americans to their list of ten most-admired men, and in 1988 he was second only to President Reagan in popularity (*Gallup Report*, 1987, No. 267;

Photograph courtesy of Ralph K. White.
Reprinted by permission.

Box 14–2   RALPH K. WHITE, *Authority on U.S.-Soviet Relations*

Ralph White has devoted nearly 50 years to studying the psychological aspects of international affairs, especially the causes and prevention of war. He took his Ph.D. with Kurt Lewin at the University of Iowa and later spent 17 years of service in the U.S. government, with first-hand experience in Berlin, Saigon, and Moscow. Subsequently he taught for many years at George Washington University, where he is now Professor Emeritus of Psychology.

*   Much of White's research and writing deals with attitudes concerning the East-West conflict. His books include* Nobody Wanted War: Misperception in Vietnam and Other Wars, Fearful Warriors: A Psychological Profile of U.S.-Soviet Relations, *and* Psychology and the Prevention of Nuclear War. *He has been honored by election as President of Psychologists for Social Responsibility and the International Society of Political Psychology.*

1989, No. 280). In national sample studies comparing him with President Reagan, respondents in the U.S. regarded Gorbachev almost as favorably, in France about equally, and in Britain and West Germany much more favorably than Reagan (*Public Opinion*, 1988, No. 6). The key basis of Gorbachev's popularity was the perceived degree of his efforts to stop the arms race; in a poll of citizens of nine European nations, three times as many respondents (32%) named him as working harder toward this goal than the 11% who named Reagan (Church, 1987).

ATTITUDES CONCERNING WAR

Some beliefs about war are agreed on by almost all Americans: 96% assert that "picking a fight with the Soviet Union is too dangerous in a nuclear world"; 89% agree that "there can be no winner in an all-out nuclear war; both the U.S. and the Soviet Union would be completely destroyed"; 83% say that "we cannot be certain that life on earth will continue after a nuclear war"; and 83% believe that "if either superpower were to use nuclear weapons, it would turn into all-out nuclear war" (Public Agenda Foundation, 1984). A 1983 Harris poll found that 86% of U.S. adults are worried about the prospect of a future nuclear war, and 67% believe that there is a likelihood of a "third world war breaking out in the next 20 years" (Plous, 1985).

Indeed, in studies comparing nationwide samples in many countries, U.S. beliefs in the likelihood of a major war in the next five or ten years were much higher than in any of 13 European countries and 15 non-European countries, with over half the U.S. sample above the midpoint of the scale (*Gallup Report*, 1986, No. 255; Listhaug, 1986). In a pioneering study in 1987 comparing the beliefs of Americans with a sample of Moscow residents, nearly five times as many Americans as Russians predicted a high chance of a world war, and only about half as many Americans were optimistic about the possibility of totally eliminating all nuclear weapons (*Gallup Report*, 1987, No. 258; 1987, No. 266). A unique study comparing random samples of urban Russian and American teenagers showed that the Russian school children were much better informed on various facts about nuclear war; for instance, 68% of them versus only 17% of the Americans knew that the U.S. had not pledged "no first use" of nuclear weapons, and differences on some other information items were even greater (Andreyenkov, Robinson, & Popov, 1989). An earlier study of a sample of Soviet children found they were much more worried than American children about the idea of nuclear war, and twice as pessimistic about national survival in a nuclear war, but much more optimistic about the possibility of preventing such a war (Chivian, Mack, & Waletzky, 1983).

Americans' beliefs about the devastating consequences of a nuclear war are much stronger than they were 30 years ago, when a majority said that the hydrogen bomb had made another world war less likely, and only 27% believed that all mankind would be destroyed in a nuclear war (Public Agenda Foundation, 1984). A thorough summary of changes in Americans' nuclear attitudes since the end of World War II found a moderate increase in personal worry about nuclear war and expectations of nonsurvival, and large increases in disapproval of the arms race and of U.S. readiness to use nuclear weapons if its allies were attacked (Kramer, Kalick, & Milburn, 1983). Some of the facts about nuclear war that the U.S. public has been gradually absorbing are as follows (Oskamp, 1985b, pp. 9-10):

> Increasing numbers of Americans are learning that our Pershing II nuclear missiles now installed in Germany can reach the U.S.S.R. in six minutes, which is less time than it took our officials to discover that several nuclear alerts in 1979 and 1980 were false alarms caused by computer errors (Caldicott, 1980). If a full-scale nuclear war should occur, the estimated number of deaths in the United States within the first 30 days ranges from 75 million to 145 million (that is, from one-third to two-thirds of the population), even in the highly unlikely case of the population being sheltered as fully as possible. "However, deaths from burns, injuries, and radiation sickness can be expected to continue far beyond this particular [30 day] interval" (U.S. Congress, 1979, p. 97). In fact, even in the most limited nuclear war, in which "only one city is attacked, and the remaining resources of the nation are available to help, medical facilities would be inadequate to care for the injured" (U.S. Congress, 1979, p. 6). Even in such a limited attack, the entire amount of U.S. blood supplies for a year might be needed within the first 24 hours (Chivian et al., 1982).

Horrifying facts such as these, together with the increased danger of war accompanying the installation of Pershing II nuclear missiles in Europe, and the belligerent rhetoric of President Reagan's first term, led to an unprecedented upsurge of international support for a "nuclear freeze" in the early 1980s (de Boer, 1985; Rochon, 1988). Many psychologists made important research and theoretical contributions to this peace movement (e.g., Deutsch, 1983; Janis, 1985; Nevin, 1985; White, 1985). Klineberg (1984) has written a useful summary of factors in the rise of this movement and psychological contributions to it. In 1982, a Harris poll found huge majorities of Americans supporting arms control: 73% favored banning the production, storage, and use of nuclear weapons; 86% wanted the U.S. and the USSR to negotiate a nuclear arms reduction agreement; and 81% favored an agreement not to produce any new nuclear weapons as long as the two superpowers had a rough nuclear equivalence (Klineberg, 1984). The U.S. experienced a number of enormous antinuclear rallies, and nuclear freeze resolutions were adopted by hundreds of town meetings and some city councils and state legislatures; but the movement was even stronger in several European countries, where it led to the rise of antinuclear political parties and the election of a number of antinuclear members of various parliaments.

Since 1983 the nuclear freeze movement has declined in public prominence, though Americans' attitudes on nuclear issues have remained essentially as described above (Gilbert, 1988). The movement did succeed in passing a nuclear freeze resolution in the U.S. House of Representatives and influencing the stands of several Democratic presidential candidates (Klineberg, 1984). Most important, in his second term, President Reagan began to espouse arms control proposals and eventually negotiated and signed a treaty with the USSR banning intermediate range nuclear missiles. Thus, in the U.S. as well as in Europe, many of the goals of the nuclear freeze movement were accepted by more mainstream groups, indicating that in some cases such grass-roots movements can have an effect on public policy.

Public Opinion About the Vietnam War

Another instance in which public opinion eventually affected U.S. government policy was during the Vietnam War, which has been called the most divisive and bitter American experience since the Civil War. To investigate that claim scientifically, Mueller (1971, 1973) summarized national poll data about attitudes toward the war from start to finish, and compared them with the progression of similar attitudes during the course of American involvement in the Korean War of 1950–1953. His findings will probably surprise you.

Many times during the Vietnam and Korean Wars citizens were asked, "Do you think the U.S. made a mistake sending troops to fight in Vietnam (Korea)?" The changing patterns of support over time for the Korean War and the Vietnam War are plotted graphically in Figure 14-2. In reading this graph, note that the figures shown can be below 50% and still be pluralities, since usually 10%–18% of respondents were undecided. Since the Vietnam War had no clear starting point, and was initially given little attention by U.S. public opinion, Mueller chose as its

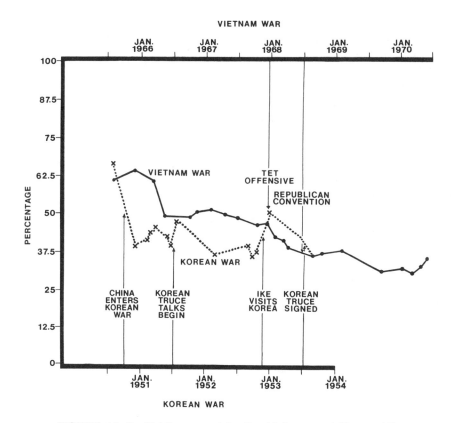

FIGURE 14–2 Public support for the Vietnam and Korean Wars.

Source: Adapted from Mueller (1971, pp. 362, 364).

beginning date mid-1965 when American troops and bombers were being committed to the war in large numbers.

These data demonstrate several points. First, both wars began with high public support (over 60% pro and less than 25% con)—what Mueller called a "rally-round-the-flag phenomenon." Then, fairly quickly, there was a marked drop in public enthusiasm, followed by a slow decline in support over a period of years. There were also fluctuations in attitudes related to a few highly dramatic events—particularly in the Korean War, when the Chinese entry into the war caused a huge early drop in support and President Eisenhower's visit to Korea to speed up the truce talks produced a clear increase in public support. However, in general, most events do not seem to have had much effect on the underlying trend of public support for the wars.

Comparing support for the two wars, it is clear that the Korean War was lower in public support for almost its whole course of time. This finding is sharply contrary to the many claims that the Vietnam War was "the most unpopular war in

[U.S.] history" (Wise, 1968). However, Mueller pointed out that the Korean War started abruptly and involved much higher early casualties than the Vietnam War. Using the statistical technique of regression analysis, he was able to demonstrate that

> In each war, support . . . started at much the same level and then every time American casualties increased by a factor of 10 (i.e., from 100 to 1,000 or from 10,000 to 100,000) support for the war dropped by about 15 percentage points. (1971, p. 366)

Thus, Mueller concluded that patterns of public support for the two wars were very similar. It is true, of course, that approval of the Vietnam War eventually dropped lower than the Korean War levels, but it only did so after the war had gone on longer and American casualties had climbed much higher than in Korea.

ISOLATIONISM VERSUS INTERNATIONALISM

Though the U.S. public's opposition to the Vietnam War eventually ended it, that does not mean that most Americans have become isolationists. **Isolationism** is a national policy of withdrawing from and avoiding treaties and commitments with foreign nations; in contrast, **internationalism** means a policy of active involvement in foreign relations, including international trade, treaties, and cooperation (Foster, 1983). The continuum between these two extreme viewpoints represents probably the most important dimension of foreign policy attitudes (Oldendick & Bardes, 1982).

There have been immense changes in American public opinion about foreign relations during this century. Public revulsion over World War I, which was supposed to be "a war to end all wars," led to an extreme degree of American isolationism in the 1930s. For instance, a Gallup Poll in 1937 asked, "If another war like World War I developed in Europe, should America take part again?" and 95% of Americans said "No"! As late as 1939, 66% of Americans said the United States should not help either side if Germany and Italy went to war against England and France (Free & Cantril, 1967, p. 63). Congress shared this revulsion toward war and "foreign entanglements"; consequently it had defeated President Wilson's efforts to have the U.S. join the League of Nations, and it had passed legislation prohibiting U.S. sales of military supplies to other countries. That restriction on military sales was the reason that, when aid to Britain became clearly necessary to prevent her defeat by Hitler, it took the form of "lend-lease" supplies. It was only after Hitler's conquest of Holland, Belgium, and France in the spring of 1940 that a majority of Americans became convinced that the U.S. might have to become involved in the European war and should aid Britain despite that risk (Foster, 1983).

With that background of pre–World War II isolationism, the extent of U.S. internationalism after the war is nothing short of amazing. Large majorities of the public approved of joining the United Nations and of the Marshall Plan for aid to European countries, the founding of NATO for mutual national defense, the airlifts sending supplies to Berlin when it was blockaded by Soviet troops, U.S. entry into the Korean War as the major component of the United Nations forces opposing the North Korean invasion of South Korea, and many other activist measures. Despite some setbacks stemming from public discouragement over the long-protracted Korean War and from Senator Joseph McCarthy's investigations in the early 1950s of alleged Communist Party subversion of our government, U.S. internationalism not only persisted but reached a high point about 1965 (Page & Shapiro, 1982).

In 1964 a landmark study of internationalism interviewed two national probability samples totaling over 3000 respondents (Free & Cantril, 1967). Using a scale of five items, respondents were classified as "completely internationalist" if they agreed that the United States should cooperate fully with the United Nations and take into account the views of its allies, and disagreed with the statements that the United States should go its own way in international matters, mind its own business internationally, and concentrate more on its own national problems. Respondents who varied from this pattern on only one item were classified as "predominantly internationalist." There were parallel categories on the isolationist side and an intermediate "mixed" category. The distribution of respondents was as follows:

Completely internationalist	30%
Predominantly internationalist	35
Mixed	27
Predominantly isolationist	5
Completely isolationist	3

This very high level of internationalism was a dramatic and important finding, particularly in comparison with the extreme levels of isolationism in America before World War II. Indeed, in 1964, all population subgroups which were analyzed had at least a majority of members who were internationalistic.

However, by 1968 the U.S. level of internationalism had begun to recede as public protest over the Vietnam War increased, and by 1974 the picture was substantially different, though not reversed (41% on the internationalistic side of the spectrum, 38% mixed, and 21% on the isolationistic side). Other items showed a corresponding drop since 1964 in endorsement of the U.S. "even going to the brink of war" if necessary to maintain its dominant position in the world, but an *increase* in agreement that (a) U.S. economic aid to foreign countries and (b) U.S. defense spending should be maintained or increased (Watts & Free, 1974). Thus the legacy of the Vietnam War seemed to be a modified internationalism—less willingness to send American troops abroad, but even more willingness to send economic aid and to invest in national defense (Foster, 1983). Supporting this conclusion, there was a massive 87% agreement that "The U.S. should continue to play a major role internationally, but cut down on some of its responsibilities abroad" (Watts & Free, 1973, p. 204).

By 1980 another change occurred, involving reactions to the Iranian capture of U.S. hostages and American opposition to the Soviet occupation of Afghanistan. At this point American internationalism climbed markedly again and reached a level close to its 1964 high point (Free & Watts, 1980—see Figure 14-3). The general public approval of U.S. activism in foreign affairs but disapproval of military intervention has continued with little change into the 1980s (Benson, 1982; *Public Opinion*, 1989, No. 6).

Nationalism Versus Patriotism

A concept that is often contrasted with the viewpoint of internationalism is the attitude of nationalism, or predominant devotion to the interests of one's own country. However, these two viewpoints are not diametrically opposed, for the best interests of one's country may often demand international trade or cooperation, as in the World War II alliance against the Axis powers. A useful empirical analysis of nationalism has been made by Kosterman and Feshbach (1989), who differentiated between **nationalism** (belief that one's nation is superior and should be dominant) and **patriotism** (positive attachment to one's nation). They developed scales to measure these two attitudes as well as internationalism, and results

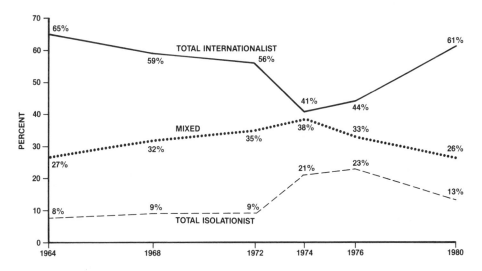

FIGURE 14–3 Trends in internationalism versus isolationism from 1964 to 1980.

Source: Free & Watts in *Public Opinion* (1980, 3 (2), p. 49). Reprinted with the permission of the American Enterprise Institute for Public Policy Research, Washington, DC.

showed that the three concepts were in fact quite distinct. That is, one can have strong feelings of love for one's country (patriotism) without believing that it is necessarily right or best (nationalism), and neither of these viewpoints is necessarily connected with isolationism (the opposite of internationalism). The fact that these three attitudes are empirically distinct and hardly correlated with each other illustrates the multidimensionality of attitudes in the international arena.

WHO HOLDS WHICH ATTITUDES?

In this section we will discuss the **correlates** of isolationist and internationalist attitudes. That is, we will ask: What subgroups of people tend to hold specific types of international attitudes? Though there is considerable agreement among research studies in this area, an important caution to keep in mind here is that significant differences which are reported usually represent at most a moderate degree of relationship—i.e., one that would allow for many exceptions in individual cases.

Isolationism

Three major national survey studies of isolationist versus internationalist attitudes have reported findings which are largely complementary. One survey study, by Free and Cantril (1967), was described previously in this chapter, and another was a very similar follow-up study in 1980 (Free & Watts, 1980). The third study (McClosky, 1967), conducted in the late 1950s, was unique in using long paper-and-pencil questionnaires with large representative samples, including a national cross-section of about 1500 people and a mail survey of over 3000 political leaders who had been delegates and alternates to the 1956 Democratic and Republican conventions. A key measure used by McClosky was a carefully constructed and validated 9-item scale of isolationism including items such as the following:

> Most of the countries which have gotten economic help from America end up resenting what we have done for them.

> George Washington's advice to stay out of agreements with foreign powers is just as wise now as it was when he was alive.

Demographic Correlates of Isolationism. All three studies agreed that poorly informed individuals and those with little education were more likely to be isolationists, as were rural residents. Persons age 60 and over and non-labor-force members (mostly retired people) tended toward isolationism, as did women in general (see also Bardes, 1986). Protestants were more likely to be isolationistic than Catholics, and Jews were least so. The Southern states which voted Republican in 1964 were most isolationistic, while the East and Midwest showed the opposite trend. The poor and blue-collar workers were much more likely to be isolationistic than were those better off financially, including white-collar workers and professional and business people. However, in 1980 there was no difference in isolationism between Republicans, Democrats, and Independents in the general population.

Personality Correlates of Isolationism.   McClosky (1967) reported findings on over 70 different scales, most of them measures of personality characteristics. His results can be briefly summarized as follows: Isolationists showed many of the characteristics of authoritarianism, such as ethnocentric and anti-Semitic beliefs, and tendencies to acquiesce to authority. They were also typified by intolerance of ambiguity, obsessive tendencies, rigidity, and inflexibility. They tended to be low in democratic convictions and commitment, and high in political alienation (cynicism, suspiciousness, and a sense of political futility).

Another prime characteristic of isolationists, according to McClosky's findings, was misanthropy. They tended toward hostile and paranoid views of the world, including lack of faith in people, contempt for weakness, and intolerance of human frailty. Yet at the same time they were low in ego strength themselves, suffering from anxiety, guilt feelings, frustrations, and lack of satisfaction in life.

As a final refinement, McClosky was able to divide isolationists empirically into two subtypes: peaceful, and aggressive (or jingoistic). The *peaceful* isolationist wants the nation to withdraw into its shell and avoid most contacts with other nations, including any threats or use of force. The *jingoistic* isolationist, on the other hand, relies on power and the threat of force to ensure the nation's safety behind its impregnable defenses. McClosky showed that peaceful isolationists are less driven by aversive psychological needs like hostility and alienation, and therefore are more like nonisolationists than are jingoistic isolationists.

Attitudes Concerning War

Reviews of studies on hard-line cold-war attitudes versus conciliatory viewpoints have reported findings closely resembling those for isolationism (Scott, 1965; Rosenberg, 1967).

Though government policy makers are much better informed than the average citizen about foreign policy issues, they are not immune from these attitudinal influences. Two opposing images of international conflict tend to predominate among policy officials: the deterrence image is typical among "hard-liners," who criticize appeasement and cite the pre-World War II Munich agreement as their key analogy; whereas the conflict-spiral image is typical among "conciliators," who cite the pre–World War I build-up of world tensions as their most pertinent example (Tetlock, 1983b). These two types of policy makers have been shown to have personality differences similar to those described above for isolationists versus internationalists (Etheredge, 1978). For example, content analysis of speeches in the U.S. Senate showed that isolationistic Senators presented foreign policy issues in more simple, rigid, and emotionally charged terms than did their nonisolationistic colleagues (Tetlock, 1981).

Attitudes of the Mass Public Versus Elites

Several studies of international attitudes have contrasted average citizens with elite groups (e.g., Oldendick & Bardes, 1982; Schneider, 1983; Public Agenda Foundation, 1984). Elites have often been defined as being senior leaders in fields including government, business, labor, education, religion, journalism, and civic service. Though such elites agree with the mass public on many issues, there are moderate-to-extreme differences between them on other issues.

The most striking of these differences in 1978 was that much higher percentages of the elites were internationalistic (e.g., 38% higher on the U.S. taking an active role in world affairs, 33% higher on expanding economic aid to other countries, 49% higher on eliminating tariffs, and 27% higher on the goal of improving the world's standard of living—Oldendick & Bardes, 1982). On the dimension of militarism, the elites were 24% higher on defending our allies' security, 33% higher in favor of selling military equipment and giving military aid, 38% higher on using U.S. troops if western Europe was invaded, but 18% *lower* on the goal of containing communism in general. There were somewhat smaller differences on desirable American goals (elites were 14% lower on bringing democracy to other nations, 16% lower on protecting the value of the dollar, 21% lower on protecting American business abroad, and 46% lower on protecting jobs of American workers); also on moving toward détente with the USSR (elites were 34% higher on opposing trade restrictions, 34% higher on favoring exchange of scientists, 22% higher on favoring joint energy efforts, and 21% higher on limiting some nuclear weapons). There were mixed differences on international diplomacy (elites were 26% lower on the goal of strengthening the UN, 15% higher on not interfering in Soviet treatment of Jews, but 22% higher in favoring more active opposition to apartheid—Oldendick & Bardes, 1982; Foster, 1983). These major differences between the public and elites continued on into the 1980s. In addition, elites became 40% higher than the public in favoring diplomatic negotiations with Cuba, and 21% higher in favoring a mutual nuclear freeze with the USSR (Schneider, 1983).

HOW DO INTERNATIONAL ATTITUDES CHANGE?

Though views about foreigners and other nations are typically developed without any direct contact with the attitude object, once formed, international attitudes are usually quite resistant to major changes, even through relevant personal experience. What factors can produce changes in people's international attitudes?

Contact with Foreigners.   Foreign travel is often thought to influence attitudes of both the traveler and those host country citizens with whom the visitor comes in contact. For instance, foreign student programs and cultural exchanges have often assumed that getting to know foreigners will lead to greater liking for them and increase international goodwill. However, review of empirical studies of such programs shows that these assumptions are much too simple and are frequently in error (Pool, 1965). The purpose of the travel (study, tourism, business trip, military assignment, etc.) must be considered, as well as the social and cultural situation which travelers meet in relation to their backgrounds and expectations. Foreign contact will usually increase detail and differentiation in attitudes, but it may cause either favorable or unfavorable changes, no change at all, or a change from either extreme toward a more moderate view. A common finding is a U-shaped curve of favorability toward the host country over the time period of the visit—a low point in the middle when initial enthusiasm has worn off and everyday complications and annoyances are salient, followed by increasing favorability as the time to leave approaches. Some research has shown a second U-shaped pattern of readjustment upon return to one's own country (Selltiz & Cook, 1962; Gullahorn & Gullahorn, 1963).

Personal Experiences. Other than contact with foreigners, personal experiences of other sorts can sometimes affect international attitudes. A prime example is Rappoport and Cvetkovich's (1968) report on attitude changes in a group of Vietnam veterans. Though hardly any of them had felt negative toward the war before their own overseas duty, most of the veterans who had been in intense combat had become much more critical of the war; by contrast, a majority of the light-combat and rear-echelon noncombat groups had become more positive toward the war while in Vietnam. These findings are particularly interesting because they run counter to predictions which would be made from the dissonance theory principle that one comes to like what one has suffered for.

Impact of Events. Thorough reviews of this topic have been made by Deutsch and Merritt (1965) and Page and Shapiro (1982). Attitude change can result from spectacular events, which receive much media coverage, or from "cumulative events" which take place gradually over a long time (e.g., increasing industrialization of a country). However, often even spectacular events have no effect on attitudes, or they may cause only a brief fluctuation followed by a return to the preexisting attitude. For instance, following the failure of the Cuban Bay of Pigs invasion attempt, the events of the Cuban missile crisis in 1962 did not change the level of public opposition to an American invasion of Cuba (about 65% opposed). When rapid attitude shifts occur, they are usually related to major events international affairs or in the economy, such as the improvement in U.S.-Soviet relations that took place under Gorbachev. As a contrasting example, after the Chinese army's massacre of student protesters in Tiananmen Square in 1989, the percentage of American who expressed favorable opinions of China plunged briefly from 72% to 31% (*Gallup Report*, 1989, No. 287). However, even the most dramatic changes in political alignments usually involve attitude changes by only 20% to 30% of the population, and such changes almost always involve a combination of spectacular events and cumulative events. Either type of event alone is apt to produce attitude changes of no more than 10%.

Education and Persuasion. A review of research on education and persuasion attempts to influence international attitudes (Janis & Smith, 1965) indicates that there are many sources of resistance to such approaches. For instance, both group affiliations and personality needs are likely to reinforce people for maintaining their current attitudes. For this reason, intended audiences often do not receive adequate exposure to the message, let alone take the further steps of attention, comprehension, and acceptance (e.g., Star & Hughes, 1950). Little research has been done specifically on persuasion regarding international attitudes, but a few studies have shown that significant attitude changes can be achieved under the right conditions (e.g., Putney & Middleton, 1962; Nelson, 1988).

Government or Media Programs. Governments and the mass media manage much of the public presentation of information which is relevant to international attitudes. By giving special attention to (or withholding it from) certain events, developments, or programs, they are in a position of potential influence over public attitudes (Deutsch & Merritt, 1965). A recent report described how commercial public relations campaigns in the U.S. media have been successful in improving the image of various foreign countries in Americans' minds (Manheim & Albritton, 1984). Conversely, the U.S. news media usually ignore developments in major areas of the world, such as the Arab world of the Middle East and North Africa, except for events which threaten U.S. or Israeli interests (Adams, 1982). The way in which the emphasis of news programs can determine the topics that influence American public opinion has been convincingly demonstrated by Iyengar and Kinder (1986—see Chapter 8).

In the era of the cold war between the United States and Russia, some proposals were advanced for ways to break the vicious circle of mutual distrust, suspicion, and hostility. For instance, Osgood (1962, 1986) proposed what he called the GRIT strategy (the initials stand for "Graduated and Reciprocated Initiatives in Tension-reduction"). In this strategy one of the two superpowers would begin a preannounced program of small unilateral steps to reduce world tensions, which the other major power would be urged to reciprocate in ways which it felt would further reduce tension. This approach would reverse the upward spiral of the arms race and break the typical logjam of intransigence in negotiations which allows each nation to prevent any beneficial movement by the other. Experimental tests of the GRIT strategy have shown that it works well in laboratory situations (Lindskold, 1978). Moreover, Etzioni (1967) has described the actions and statements of the Kennedy administration between June and November, 1963, as a partial test of this gradualist approach to détente, which he called the "Kennedy experiment." He concluded that these actions did lead to a reduction of world tensions and to less hostile international attitudes. In the late 1980s, Soviet leader Gorbachev appears to have followed parts of this strategy in his arms reduction initiatives, which had a dramatic effect on U.S. public opinion and on actions of the Reagan and Bush administrations.

RESEARCH ON INTERNATIONAL ATTITUDES

Most research on international attitudes is unsophisticated and descriptive in nature. Sometimes it only presents item responses for the whole sample of respondents, and most studies provide data for only one point in time and one nation (or, frequently, for one subgroup within a nation, such as students). Such descriptive surveys are valuable in aiding communication of public viewpoints and letting decision makers know in some detail about public beliefs and feelings. However, there is a real need for more sophisticated studies comparing attitudes across several periods of time, and in several countries, and using statistical analyses to show the significance and stability of trends (Etzioni, 1969). The USIA surveys of western European countries (Merritt & Puchala, 1968) provide some of the best examples of such comparative research, which has unfortunately been discontinued by later administrations.

To achieve a causal understanding of factors in attitude change, experimental and quasi-experimental research designs are needed to test and verify hypotheses developed from anecdotal and descriptive studies. In the field of international attitudes, experimental research on attitude change has hardly begun, but testable hypotheses have been offered, for example, about the factors that inhibit arms control activism on the part of American citizens (Gilbert, 1988). In quasi-experimental, time-series research, Tetlock (1985) has demonstrated how the level of complexity of official U.S. and Soviet foreign policy rhetoric responds to the other country's behavior and to important current events. Good experimental research has been done by Lindskold (1978) on effects of Osgood's GRIT strategy on conflict and cooperation, and by Iyengar and Kinder (1986) on the way that TV network newscasts can prime public responses to international issues. Similarly, an experimental study of internation simulations, in which American citizens take the roles of policy makers from other nations, revealed factors that prevented their goal of improved international attitudes from occurring (Trost, Cialdini, & Maass, 1989). There is a wide-open field for more experimental research of this sort on international attitudes.

SUMMARY

Our images of foreign nations and peoples are often incomplete and distorted. Particularly in the area of world affairs, public information is sharply limited. Children's views of foreign peoples begin to be formed as early as age 6, based largely on ingroup-outgroup relationships and on shaping by parents and teachers. Adults' stereotypes of other nations also seem to be based largely on national alliances or competition.

Other nations' attitudes toward the U.S. have varied considerably with events, being highly favorable during our post–World War II aid to Europe but much less positive during the Vietnam War and the first part of the Reagan administration. The cold war competition between the United States and Russia has developed mirror-image perceptions of world affairs in which each side sees itself as peace-loving and virtuous and sees the other side as aggressive and reckless, its powerless people unwillingly being controlled by their exploitive leaders.

Americans support arms control measures by very large majorities, but they are relatively pessimistic about the possibility of avoiding a future nuclear war, despite its devastating consequences. In the 1960s Americans were strongly internationalistic, in stark contrast to their views before World War II. In the 1970s internationalism became less popular in the U.S., but by 1980 it had returned almost to its 1964 high level. Thus the Vietnam War did not permanently reduce U.S. internationalism, and in general, much higher percentages of elite groups than of the mass public tend to be internationalistic.

Though international attitudes are often formed without any direct contact with the attitude object, these attitudes are usually quite resistant to major changes, even through personal experience. The main factors which (on occasion) are effective in influencing international attitudes are: contact with foreigners, personal experiences such as combat participation, spectacular or cumulative world events, education and persuasion campaigns, and government or media programs combining international actions and public statements.

15

Racism
and Prejudice

There is no more evil thing in this present world than race prejudice, none at all. . . . It justifies and holds together more baseness, cruelty, and abomination than any other sort of error in the world.—H. G. Wells.

No State shall make or enforce any law which shall abridge the privileges or immunities of citizens of the United States; nor shall any State deprive any person of life, liberty, or property, without due process of law; nor deny to any person within its jurisdiction the equal protection of the laws.—The Fourteenth Amendment to the U.S. Constitution.

The status of black Americans today can be characterized as a glass that is half full—if measured by progress since 1939—or as a glass that is half empty—if measured by the persisting disparities between black and white Americans since the early 1970s.—Gerald D. Jaynes & Robin M. Williams, Jr., 1989.

Americans like to think of the U.S. as "one nation . . . with liberty and justice for all." However, despite these high ideals, our nation has a long history of intolerance and injustice—first toward the native Americans, and then toward a succession of immigrant groups, each of which had to struggle to gain the freedom, equality, and justice guaranteed to them by the Constitution. To cite just one example, anti-Catholicism was rampant in all of the American colonies settled by Protestants, even leading to the execution of priests. It grew even stronger when large numbers of Catholic immigrants began arriving in the 19th century. Powerful groups formed the violently anti-Catholic Know-Nothing Party, and later the Ku Klux Klan persecuted Catholics as well as blacks and Jews. Though the Irish, Italians, Poles, and other immigrant groups gradually gained local political power, on the national scene New York Governor Alfred Smith's Catholicism doomed his presidential bid in 1928 and stirred up more anti-Catholic violence. Even in 1960, John F. Kennedy nearly lost the election due to anti-Catholic sentiment and votes. Since then, those passions have mostly evaporated, but it wasn't until 1979 that a Pope could be entertained in the White House and welcomed as a visitor by Americans of all religious persuasions (Morrow, 1979).

BACKGROUND OF RACE RELATIONS IN THE U.S.

This chapter deals mostly with racial prejudice and discrimination against black Americans, who were stigmatized most severely by slavery in America and later by legalized "Jim Crow" segregation. However, it is important to realize that fairly similar accounts could be written about religious persecution, not only against Catholics but also Jews, Muslims, and others, and about ethnic and racial prejudice against Hispanics, Orientals, native Americans, and many other groups. To provide a context for recent developments, we will recap a few of the key events of black history in America. Former Secretary of Health, Education, and Welfare John Gardner (1984) has written about the black struggle for civil rights as follows:

> In 1776 we proclaimed to the world that "all men are created equal." Eighty-seven years elapsed before Lincoln issued his Emancipation Proclamation. That's a long time to wait.
>
> We fought a tragic and bloody war to free the slaves, and their rights as free citizens were embedded in the Thirteenth, Fourteenth, and Fifteenth Amendments to the Constitution. After the Civil War, Congress passed rudimentary civil rights legislation, but the Supreme Court invalidated much of it, and it left no mark whatever after the period of Reconstruction. Worse yet, the Court chose to interpret the post-Civil War amendments in such a way as to minimize their impact on civil rights. More than three quarters of a century passed before the Court faced up to the post-Civil War amendments. That's a long time too.—Gardner, J. W. (1984, p. 38). W. W. Norton & Company Inc., New York, NY.

After the end of Reconstruction, most Southern states passed laws prohibiting most Negroes from voting, and segregation soon spread to public transportation, education, hospitals, government employment, hotels and restaurants, and other public facilities. In its *Plessy v. Ferguson* ruling of 1896, the Supreme Court for the first time interpreted the Fourteenth Amendment as allowing "separate but equal" facilities. During the depression years of the 1930s there were many lynchings of blacks in the South, and the Ku Klux Klan held considerable political power. With the urgent need for national unity in World War II, there was a beginning of racial integration in some parts of the armed forces and industry, but full integration of the armed forces didn't occur until President Truman's order in 1948 (Oskamp, 1984).

Soon afterward the cause of integrated education was pressed in many communities. For instance, Topeka, Kansas had a separate school system for black children even though Kansas had been a free state ever since its admission to the Union. Black parents there and elsewhere filed lawsuits demanding integrated education on the grounds that separate schools were inherently unequal (Smith, 1988). The Supreme Court agreed and ordered desegregation of education in its 1954 *Brown v. Board of Education of Topeka, Kansas* decision, but practically no action followed until 1964, when 99% of black children were still attending segregated schools (Edelman, 1973).

Thus in the 1960s "Jim Crow" segregation still persisted, with separate restrooms, separate water fountains, and separate facilities of all kinds for blacks throughout the South. The civil rights movement in the South sprouted when local black people refused any longer to sit only in the back of buses and demanded to be served at lunch counters in drugstores and variety stores. When black protest marchers were beaten by local gangs and by police, the national publicity drew thousands of whites to the South to aid the civil rights movement, but there were also protest riots with huge fires, many deaths, and much destruction of property in a number of Northern cities. In 1964, Congress passed the first civil rights act since Reconstruction, and since then other laws have guaranteed access to public accommodations, voting rights, nondiscrimination in housing, and equal employment opportunity for all Americans. Blacks and other racial minorities have been voting in larger and larger numbers, and with greater political power they have also been able to exercise their rights to equal treatment in most localities and establishments (Schuman, Steeh, & Bobo, 1985).

The progress in American race relations during recent decades has been extensive, and a source of justifiable pride. American black leaders have served in Congress and in the United Nations, have been elected mayors of many American cities and run for the presidency of the U.S., and have made great progress in business as well as sports and entertainment. And yet evidence shows that racism is still a fact of American life, so more progress is needed. This chapter summarizes some of the past progress and the present remaining problems in race relations.

WHAT IS RACISM?

The term **racism** is a broader one than "racial prejudice," and it is generally used to include not only prejudice, but also "hostility, discrimination, segregation, and other negative *action* expressed toward an ethnic group" (Marx, 1970, p. 101, italics added). **Prejudice**, in turn, can be defined as an intolerant, unfair, or irrational unfavorable *attitude* toward another group of people (Harding et al., 1969). Most authorities agree that racism can be found at both the individual level and the institutional level. A person might be considered an individual racist if prejudiced attitudes and discriminatory behavior against another racial group were important and central parts of his or her life—shown, for instance, by frequently talking about them, acting upon them, or trying to persuade other people to share the same attitudes and behavior patterns.

Institutional racism is a new term in our language, but it describes an age-old pattern of behavior. It refers to formal and explicit laws and regulations which discriminate against certain ethnic groups, as well as to informal, but powerful, social norms which limit the opportunities and choices available to certain ethnic groups. Examples of formal institutional racism include the recent dual school systems in the South, housing covenants which formerly prohibited the sale of homes in certain areas to "undesirable" minority groups, and laws which prohibited interracial marriages. On the informal level, colleges and universities have had quotas to admit only a small percentage of minority applicants no matter how good their qualifications. Similarly, many business firms hire only the "right" sort of person—one who would be acceptable at the club. Real estate agents and lending institutions still often "steer" minority group members away from purchasing homes in certain areas (DeMott, 1986). On a subtler level, the use of certain standardized procedures like aptitude testing for job selection or college admission can be a form of institutional racism if it unfairly or invalidly discriminates against minority group members who could actually succeed on the job or in the college if given a chance (Jones, 1972).

Individual and institutional racism are mutually reinforcing. It is doubtful that institutional racism could develop or survive without support from many individual racists, nor is it likely that individual racism would thrive without strong social support. This chapter concentrates on individual racism and particularly on racial attitudes regarding black people. However, keep in mind that the focus of the civil rights movement was on combatting institutional racism, which was seen as the most important factor in the oppression of ethnic minorities.

CHILDREN'S RACIAL ATTITUDES

Bigots are made, not born. As described in Chapter 7, we learn about the world not only through personal experience, but also through social interaction with parents, teachers, and peers, and through the influence of the media. As Allport (1954) pointed out in his classic volume on prejudice, many of our attitudes and opinions toward groups of people are *adopted*, i.e., learned from our family and culture, rather than *developed*, i.e., learned through life experiences that lead us to fear or dislike minority groups.

Attitudes cannot exist without awareness of the attitude object, and racial awareness has been found to develop quite early. Children as young as three years old can identify their own race and the race of others. By seven years of age, almost 100% can accurately discriminate between their own and other racial groups, and they also display clear affective reactions to them (Clark & Clark, 1947; Goodman, 1964; Aboud, 1987).

A number of ingenious methods have been used to elicit racial preferences and attitudes from very young children. The best known is the doll technique developed by Kenneth B. and Mamie P. Clark (1947). Children are shown two dolls (or sometimes more), one representing a black child, the other a white child, and asked to respond to a number of questions by choosing one of the dolls. The questions include: Which doll is most like you? Which is the black (white, Negro, colored) doll? Which is the good (bad) doll? Which is the doll you would like to play with? On the basis of the doll choices, it was established that white children had a strong preference for the white dolls. Further, white children tended to attribute good qualities to the white dolls and bad qualities to the black dolls (e.g., Clark & Clark, 1947; Asher & Allen, 1969). There has been little disagreement in the interpretation of the results of these studies for white children. White children appear to learn racial discrimination early in life. They generally have strong positive attitudes toward themselves and other members of their race, and they have negative reactions to blacks.

Until the late 1960s, the results for black children seemed equally unambiguous. They too preferred and identified with *white* dolls and rejected black dolls. These data, from the studies cited above and many others, were interpreted to mean that black children developed the same racial attitudes as white children (prowhite, antiblack). The result was a diminished self-concept coupled with an unrealistic and self-defeating wish to be white (Chethick, Fleming, Meyer, & McCoy, 1967; Coles, 1968).

In the late 1960s, new studies began to challenge the earlier findings. Greenwald and Oppenheim (1968) argued that black children may have misidenti-

Photograph courtesy of Kenneth B. Clark. Reprinted by permission

Box 15–1   KENNETH B. CLARK, *Pioneer Racial Attitude Researcher*

Kenneth B. Clark, Distinguished Professor of Psychology Emeritus at the City College of New York, has had a real impact on the position of minority groups in the United States. Born in Panama in 1914, he grew up in Harlem, attended Howard University, and earned a Ph.D. at Columbia University in 1940. After brief periods of teaching and wartime research, he joined the faculty at CCNY, where he remained for the rest of his career. In later years he also served as President of the Metropolitan Applied Research Center, and upon retirement he founded a consulting firm dealing with human relations and affirmative action issues.

The early research of Clark and his wife on the self-images of Negro children was cited in the 1954 U.S. Supreme Court decision regarding school desegregation, Brown v. Board of Education. *Since then he has served as consultant to many organizations and written books such as* Prejudice and Your Child, Dark Ghetto, The Negro American, A Relevant War Against Poverty, *and* Pathos of Power. *He was a member of the New York State Board of Regents for 20 years, and in 1971 he was elected President of the American Psychological Association.*

fied themselves as white in earlier studies because experimenters failed to take account of the range of skin color of black Americans. From the light-skinned black child's point of view, the white doll may in fact have looked more like him(her)self than the black doll. It was found that in earlier studies, the percentage of misidentification was much higher among light-skinned than dark-skinned blacks (80% versus 23% in the Clarks' study). There were also data-based arguments about whether black children's apparent preferences for white dolls were statistically different from a chance distribution (Banks, 1976; Williams & Morland, 1979).

In addition to these possible experimental artifacts, two developments in U.S. society seemed to be having an impact on black children's self-images. Both the black pride movement, with its emphasis on positive cultural traditions and values, and the sharply increased amount of racial integration in public schools were expected to improve black children's self-concepts. Consistent with these expectations, Hraba and Grant (1970) found that black children in integrated schools in Lincoln, Nebraska were as problack in their doll choices as white children were prowhite. Similarly, Crooks (1970) reported that black children in Halifax, Nova Scotia, who had just completed an enriched, integrated, preschool program identified themselves as black and chose black dolls as the ones they preferred more frequently than a control group of black children who had not experienced the program. These results seemed to indicate that for some black children under some conditions racial preferences were changing.

However, in spite of these societal trends, more recent research findings seem to have reverted to the earlier picture of prowhite doll preference among most black children (Toufexis, 1987). Also, school desegregation has too often been carried out under unfortunate conditions which decreased rather than increased black pupils' self-esteem and led to increased prejudice by whites toward blacks and vice versa (Stephan, 1978; Cook, 1979, 1984; Gerard, 1983). In sum, it is clear that both black children and white children can and do learn racial prejudice early. Though some children of both races may have profited from the black pride movement and from increased cross-racial contact in desegregated schools, the majority of black and white children still remain both the holders and the targets of racial prejudice.

RACIAL AND ETHNIC STEREOTYPES

What are "they" like, anyway? Most of us, whether we care to admit it or not, hold many ethnic stereotypes: the "crafty" Jew, the "lazy" black, the "gentlemanly" Briton, the "drunken" Irishman, the "stupid" Pole. Even if we reject the accuracy or appropriateness of stereotypes, we can laugh when Archie Bunker uses them, for we have learned that many other people in our society believe them (Vidmar & Rokeach, 1974). In Chapters 2 and 7 we have described the nature and development of stereotypes in general.

In the racial area, as with international attitudes (see Chapter 14), the degree of stereotyping is usually measured in terms of the amount of consensus in people's choice of traits as typical of members of an ethnic group—for instance, by having them check pertinent adjectives from an offered list. If the percentage of agreement is high, a stereotype is said to exist. A classic study of this sort done by Katz and Braly in 1933 found that Princeton undergraduates showed very high agreement (above 75%) in describing Negroes as superstitious and lazy, and more than 25% agreement in viewing them as happy-go-lucky, ignorant, ostentatious, and musical.

Over the next 35 years, the specific adjective *content* of students' stereotypes of blacks remained quite similar, but the amount of *consensus* on these terms declined quite markedly. Thus in the late 1960s more than 25% of Princeton students agreed that blacks were musical, happy-go-lucky, pleasure-loving, lazy, and ostentatious (Karlins et al., 1969), while a 1976 sample of California college students agreed more than 25% only on the traits of "musical" and "aggressive" (Borden, 1977). This fading of social stereotypes has been accompanied by greater reluctance on the part of many raters to attribute traits to whole racial groups. However, in the current era, there are much higher levels of agreement when raters are asked what traits *others* attribute to blacks than when they are asked about their *own* perceptions (e.g., Apostle, Glock, Piazza, & Suelzle, 1983).

In fact, college students are probably less likely than older and less-educated citizens to make such stereotypic attributions. A 1936 report by high-ranking officers at the Army War College illustrates that invidious stereotypes of blacks were common throughout American society:

> The Negro is docile, tractable, light-hearted, care-free, and good-natured. . . . He is careless, shiftless, irresponsible, and secretive. He resents censure and is best handled with praise and ridicule. He is unmoral, untruthful, and his sense of right doing is relatively inferior. (National Science Foundation, 1969, p. 18)

It is obvious that awareness of such extremely negative stereotypes can damage the self-concept of their target groups, and that they can be invoked to rationalize all sorts of harmful discrimination and injustice (cf. Porter & Washington, 1979; Crocker & Major, 1989). However, since stereotyping in its milder forms is apparently a universal cognitive tendency that helps people to simplify environmental complexity, it is an important question whether cognitive stereotypes are necessarily carried over into discriminatory behavior. The mere availability of stereotypes may often contribute to prejudice and discrimination, but it is also possible that people can possess stereotypes of groups without letting them affect their behavior and attitudes toward *individuals* (Brewer & Kramer, 1985).

Racial Stereotypes in the Mass Media

The mass media not only reflect a society's stereotypes but greatly contribute to them as well. Since the heyday of radio and the later advent of television, there have been dramatic changes in the depiction of ethnic minorities in the media. Three major stages have been described: first, nonrecognition of their existence, then a period of ridicule which highlighted the most extreme stereotypes (as in *Amos and Andy*'s eye-rolling, shuffling, and fractured English), and later a modicum of inclusion (Clark, 1969).

In the 1950s less than 1% of all TV prime-time characters were black and only 2% were Hispanic. With the civil rights movement of the 1960s, pressure on the networks increased the percentage of black roles to 7%, including a few starring roles (as on *Mission: Impossible*) and notably excluding the old dim-witted, servile stereotypes. In the 1970s TV adopted the "black pride" theme by pioneering some all-black sitcoms such as *The Jeffersons* and *Sanford and Son*, often in ghetto settings. The characters in these shows were presented as having strengths, but also flaws and foibles which highlighted some other stereotypes: "The shows substituted jivin' and struttin' for grinnin' and shufflin'. This was seen by many as no great improvement" (Lichter, Lichter, Rothman, & Amundson, 1987, p. 14). Concurrently the range of parts for blacks expanded to include a much wider variety of occupations, including a greater number of negative roles and some criminals and villains; but almost all of the few Hispanics on TV were still portrayed as hustlers, criminals, or drug lords. In the 1980s blacks comprised nearly 10% of television prime-time characters (still well below their percentage of the population), while the number of Hispanics had not advanced from the 2% level, with characters spanning "a narrow spectrum from villains to second bananas" (Lichter et al., 1987, p. 16). In this era, *The Cosby Show* became the most popular program for several years, and depicted blacks as having positive roles and values similar to those of the white middle class.

Despite this progress in combatting old stereotypes of blacks on prime-time TV, other racial groups continue to be underrepresented and portrayed much less realistically. Also, the many reruns of old movies and former TV serials continue to present the derogatory racial images of past decades: the drunken or bloodthirsty Indian, the sinister, inscrutable Oriental, and the shuffling, happy-go-lucky "darkie" (U.S. Commission on Civil Rights, 1977b).

The *effects* of these stereotypic media presentations are hard to measure because they are confounded with so many other factors. Studies of single programs, even one as phenomenally popular as *Roots*, have generally found relatively minor effects, if any, on the racial attitudes of viewers (Ball-Rokeach, Grube, & Rokeach, 1981). However, research suggests that the cumulative effects of many repeated media presentations of stereotypic information may be very powerful in establishing and maintaining racial attitudes—an example of the media's enculturation function (see Chapter 8). Moreover, a meta-analysis of all available research on television effects has concluded that the effects of stereotyping in single programs are consistently larger than those of programs that feature *anti*stereotyping content (Hearold, 1986). Though unfortunate, this is not surprising since the stereotyping messages are consistent with the overall cultural impact, whereas the antistereotyping programs have to combat it.

WHITE RACIAL ATTITUDES

"This is our basic conclusion: Our nation is moving toward two societies, one black, one white—separate and unequal" *(Report of the National Advisory Commission on Civil Disorders,* 1968, p. 1). This prophetic statement, made in the wake of the racial disorders of the mid-1960s, summarized the despair of many about the future of race relations in the United States. Is there good reason for such despair, or were the members of the Commission simply overwhelmed by the events of the 1960s? There is no simple answer to this question.

It has become popular among white liberals and black militants to describe the United States as a racist society. Yet, the status of race relations in the United States is so complex that no simple summary statement, no catch phrase such as white racism, can do justice to the complexity. In fact, even within a given individual, there are very often conflicting and inconsistent racial attitudes on different aspects of the topic. Moreover, this has been true since the founding of our nation, as shown in the lives of two of our most famous Presidents, Jefferson and Lincoln. Jefferson wrote that "all men are created equal" and avowed that he ardently wished for the abolition of slavery, yet he owned many slaves and did not free them. Though Lincoln opposed slavery for many years, he did not believe that blacks and whites could live as equals, and he hesitated long before initiating the Emancipation Proclamation. Even then, he restricted it only to the rebellious Southern states, not including the slave-holding border states fighting on the Union side (Bobo, 1988).

Three Aspects of Racial Attitudes

Social Distance.   One important aspect of racial attitudes is the first area that was measured scientifically, the amount of social distance that people desire to maintain from any given ethnic group (Bogardus, 1925). Recall that in Chapter 3 we summarized later research by Triandis (1964) which showed that there were five relatively separate dimensions of social distance, such as exclusion, respect, and marital acceptance. Various activities in our lives involve different degrees of intimacy, and it is common for members of a particular racial group to be accepted for some of these activities but not for others.

In general, white Americans resist interracial relationships most strongly when intimacy is greatest (as in dating or marriage) and least in situations where interaction is limited and formal (as in many job situations or customer-salesperson relationships). For instance, in one major study of white racial attitudes, only 12% of the respondents said they would mind a lot or a little if they had a qualified black supervisor on their job, while 44% would mind a lot or a little if a black family of the same income and education moved next door (A. Campbell, 1971). In the same era over 70% of Americans said they disapproved of "marriage between whites and nonwhites" (and note that the wording of "nonwhites" is probably less threatening than if the item said "blacks")—Schuman et al. (1985).

Thus, as the intimacy of relationships increases, prejudice against blacks increases (Jaynes & Williams, 1989). While some small proportion of the white population may be opposed to any kind of racial equality, most people are willing to accept equality in some spheres of their lives, if not in all of them.

Furthermore, white Americans' social distance measures have changed markedly toward greater racial acceptance over the several decades since systematic survey studies began. By the early 1980s 40% of respondents expressed approval of white-nonwhite intermarriage, compared to only 4% in 1958. In roughly the same time period, acceptance of having a family member bring a black friend home to dinner rose from 52% to 78% of the population. Similarly, on a more impersonal item, acceptance of sending one's children to a school where a few children are black climbed from 75% to 95% of respondents. Over an earlier time period from 1942 to 1972, willingness to have a black family with the same income and education as oneself move into one's block rose from 36% to 85% (Schuman et al., 1985). Though items describing different degrees of intimacy have reached different levels of acceptance, almost without exception all items have shown marked increases in white acceptance of blacks (that is, less social distance) in the last 40 years or so.

Principles of Equal Treatment.   Another racial attitude area involves support for general principles of equal treatment and nondiscrimination. Just as with the area of social distance, white attitudes here have shown very large, parallel increases in favorability over the last several decades. Figure 15-1 dramatically displays these trends for a large selection of poll questions that have been repeated frequently over the years. The authors summarize these findings as follows (Schuman et al., 1985, p. 93):

FIGURE 15–1   Trends in Americans' attitudes toward principles of equal treatment over a 40-year period. Symbols represent the following items:
EJ (Equal Jobs): "Do you think Negroes should have as good a chance as white people to get any kind of job, or do you think white people should have the first chance at any kind of job?" (% As good a chance)
ST (Segregated Transportation): "Generally speaking, do you think there should be separate sections for Negroes in streetcars and buses?" (% No)
SA (Same Accommodations): "Do you think Negroes should have the right to use the same parks, restaurants, and hotels as white people?" (% Yes)
RC2 (Residential Choice, 2 alternatives): "Which of these statements would you agree with: White people have a right to keep black people out of their neighborhoods if they want to, or, black people have a right to live wherever they can afford to, just like anybody else?" (% Blacks have rights)
SS (Same Schools): "Do you think white students and black students should go to the same schools or to separate schools?" (% Same)

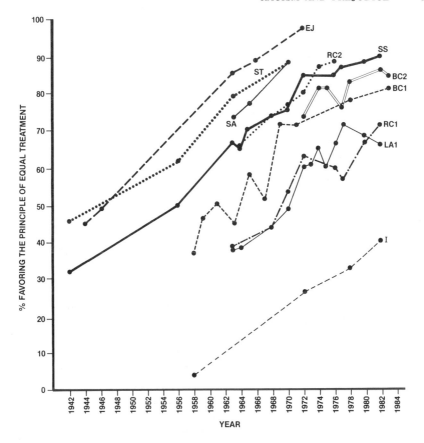

BC2 (Black Candidate, NORC): "If your party nominated a black for President, would you vote for him if he were qualified for the job?" (% Yes)

BC1 (Black Candidate, Gallup): "If your party nominated a generally well-qualified man for president and he happened to be a black, would you vote for him?" (% Yes)

RC1 (Residential Choice, 1 alternative): "Here are some opinions other people have expressed in connection with black-white relations. Which statement on the card comes closest to how you yourself feel? White people have a right to keep blacks out of their neighborhoods if they want to, and blacks should respect that right." (% Disagree strongly + Disagree slightly)

LA1 (Laws Against Intermarriage): "Do you think there should be laws against marriages between blacks and whites?" (% No)

I (Intermarriage): "Do you approve or disapprove of marriage between whites and nonwhites?" (% Approve)

Source: Reprinted by permission of the publishers from *Racial Attitudes in America* by Howard Schuman, Charlotte Steeh, and Lawrence Bobo, Cambridge, Mass.: Harvard University Press, Copyright © 1985 by the President and Fellows of Harvard College.

It appears that segregation of and discrimination against black Americans were accepted as *principles* by a majority of white Americans in the early 1940s. . . . By the early 1970s, however, support for overt discrimination in employment had nearly vanished . . . and in most other public spheres of life—public accommodations, public transportation, and even public schools—the proportion of the white population insisting on segregation in principle was both small and shrinking.

The only exception to heavy majority support for racial integration shown in Figure 15-1 is the item on approval of intermarriage (discussed above under "social distance"). Thus, based on acceptance of principles of equal treatment, it appears that by the early 1980s our society had largely become "color-blind." Certainly these data do not support the conclusion of the presidential Commission on Civil Disorders quoted at the beginning of this section that American society was becoming more separate and unequal. However, a third aspect of racial attitudes must still be considered, and it presents quite a different picture.

Implementation of Principles of Equality. This attitude area deals with steps that the government might take to combat segregation or discrimination or to reduce racial inequality in status or income. In this area, the general picture shows very little if any change in Americans' attitudes from the 1960s to the 1980s (Schuman et al., 1985). Of the nine poll questions of this sort that have been repeated frequently over the years, only two showed clear increasing trends: (1) Agreement that the government should "support the right of black people to go to any hotel or restaurant they can afford" increased from 44% to 66% from 1964 to 1974, and the question has not been repeated since then. (2) Approval of laws "that a homeowner cannot refuse to sell to someone because of their race or color" increased from 34% to 46% from 1973 to 1983.

However, counterbalancing those increases, two items showed decreasing public support of government implementation actions: (3) In the early 1970s, support for correcting "the problems of poverty and unemployment that give rise to urban unrest and rioting" decreased from 51% to 41% (perhaps because riots were no longer occurring), while support for the alternative response of using "all available force to maintain law and order, no matter what results" remained at about 40%. (4) Over the longer time period from 1964 to 1978, agreement that "the government in Washington should see to it that white and black children go to the same schools" decreased from 42% to 25%. Five other questions in this area showed essentially no change from the 1960s to the early 1980s: they included items about government intervention to ensure fair treatment in jobs, government spending to improve the conditions of blacks and other minorities, and approval of busing to achieve racial integration (Schuman et al., 1985).

Thus, in the area of government implementation of programs to promote racial equality, only a minority of Americans favor such actions, and the size of that minority has not been increasing. What are we to make of this paradox of massive and increasing endorsement of principles of racial equality, but no increase in support for implementation of those principles? Is this an indication of vast

American hypocrisy and racism? Or are there other explanations? We will discuss several of the viewpoints on this issue which different researchers have advanced.

Modern Racism

One persuasive explanation of the above contradictory findings is that the nature of racism and prejudice has changed since the early part of this century (McConahay, Hardee, & Batts, 1981). Examples of "old-fashioned" racist attitudes include support for segregation laws and beliefs in the intellectual and moral inferiority of blacks. Since the civil rights movement of the 1960s, such blatant prejudice has been abandoned, first by elite, trend-setting groups in society and then by most other citizens, except for a few die-hard segregationists such as members of the KKK or White Citizens Party. However, the concept of **modern racism** emphasizes that the affective aspects of racial attitudes are usually acquired in childhood and are harder to change than the cognitive belief aspects. Thus, many people who have given up the old-fashioned racist beliefs and attitudes nevertheless still harbor negative, aversive feelings toward blacks (for related evidence, see Crosby, Bromley, & Saxe, 1980; Gaertner & Dovidio, 1986).

The result of these contrasting tendencies is that, for many people, their negative racial feelings come to influence new issues of the era, including ones that are not overtly racial on their face. However, whites generally do not perceive their attitudes on these new issues as racist, and they tend to justify their positions on nonracial grounds. Examples of such new issues include beliefs as to whether there is continuing racial discrimination in U.S. society, attitudes toward busing of school children, and support for various government programs to aid the poor. McConahay and his colleagues (1981) have developed scales to measure both old-fashioned and modern racism in order to study their relationship. Some of their old-fashioned racism items (with the racist answer in parentheses) are:

Black people are generally not as smart as whites. (agree)
Generally speaking, I favor full racial integration. (disagree)

Examples of more subtle, modern racism items are:

The streets are not safe these days without a policeman around. (agree)
It is easy to understand the anger of black people in America. (disagree)
Over the past few years the government and news media have shown more respect to blacks than they deserve. (agree)

Research findings showed that respondents recognized the old-fashioned items as being more indicative of prejudice than the modern racism items, though the latter were not perceived as racially neutral. Also, in a situation where faking lack of prejudice was socially desirable, respondents moderated their answers only on the obvious, old-fashioned racism items. Other findings have shown that the modern racism scale predicts antiblack voting and degree of preferred racial social distance, and that it correlates with other measures of negative feelings toward blacks (McConahay et al., 1981). Thus it provides a measure for the extent of subtle racial prejudice, which may not be uncovered by the more-obvious, old-fashioned racism items.

Symbolic Racism

Rather closely akin to the modern racism viewpoint, this concept adds another element. **Symbolic racism** is defined as a blend of antiblack affect and belief in traditional American values related to the Protestant Ethic:

> a form of resistance to change in the racial status quo based on moral feelings that blacks violate such traditional American values as individualism and self-reliance, the work ethic, obedience, and discipline. (Kinder & Sears, 1981, p. 416)

Measurement of this concept has used almost exactly the same kind of items as those in the modern racism scale. However, its proponents emphasize that these items have an abstract, symbolic character which is quite unrelated to respondents' personal lives, but closely connected to their moral code and social ideals (Sears, 1988a).

As a result of this conceptualization, research has generally contrasted symbolic racism (and more broadly, symbolic politics) with behavior based on threats to respondents' personal *self-interest* (see the related discussion in Chapter 13). For instance, studies have shown that symbolic racism was a stronger predictor of voting against a black political candidate than were realistic personal racial threats stemming from crime, local school or neighborhood integration, or job competition (Kinder & Sears, 1981). Similarly, several studies have found opposition to busing of school children more closely related to symbolic racism scores than to self-interest varables, such as living in impacted neighborhoods or having children who would be affected by such busing (Sears & Allen, 1984).

However, you can see that these research findings use a narrow definition of self-interest in terms of individual impact on the respondent. If individuals who have no young children vote against busing, based on what they feel is best for their community, they will not be classified as following self-interest by this definition. Indeed, Kinder and Kiewiet (1981) have suggested the term **sociotropic voting** for this kind of broader community or national focus in voting. Clearly, citizens' general values and ideological commitments will be important in such voting, which is why Sears and his colleagues have stressed the importance of traditional American values in their concept of symbolic racism. But traditional values are not enough to predict or explain voters' rejection of a black candidate or a school busing plan; empirical findings of several studies have shown that an important predictor is the kind of antiblack feeling that is tapped by items measuring modern racist beliefs and affect.

Though people differ in the strength of their symbolic racist feelings, Sears

(1988a) has suggested .aat in our society it is probably almost impossible for anyone of any race to escape some degree of antiblack feeling based on centuries-long cultural patterns of deeply ingrained racist assumptions. Thus it is common for people to believe that blacks deserve to have all the rights of citizenship, but also to agree that they "should not push themselves where they're not wanted" or that "white people have a right to keep blacks out of their neighborhoods" (*Public Opinion*, 1987, No. 2).

Realistic Group Conflict

Another possible basis for antiblack feelings is the idea that different racial groups are in realistic conflict over the distribution of limited economic and political resources (Bobo, 1983, 1988). This view deemphasizes the symbolic aspects of prejudice and racism, though it does not deny them entirely, and it gives more attention to *group* struggles to gain political power, educational and job opportunities, and so on. Supporting this viewpoint are findings that racial attitudes have several distinguishable dimensions, and that the dimension which best predicts opposition to school busing is a person's attitude toward black political activism (Bobo, 1983). In fact, group interests are clearly reflected in both whites' and blacks' responses to a poll question about whether blacks are pushing for change "at about the right speed" or not. In the civil rights era of 1964, 74% of whites said blacks were moving "too fast," compared to only 9% of blacks. However, in 1980, a period of much less civil rights activism, the number of whites saying "at about the right speed" had doubled from 25% to 51%, whereas blacks giving that response had dropped from 63% to 49% (Bobo, 1988).

Thus the group conflict viewpoint interprets the lack of change over the last several decades in whites' limited support for implementing equalitarian principles as being based in group self-interest—a "go-slow" philosophy that aims to hold on to group privilege as long as possible within the bounds of the law and political reality.

Opposition to Government Intervention

A final possible explanation of why responses to implementation items have changed little in recent decades is that such items confound attitudes toward integration with more general attitudes toward government intervention (Kuklinski & Parent, 1981). During the 1980s, the theme of "getting government off our backs" was a popular one with many voters, so opposition to government intrusion or activism might cause such people to oppose concrete steps toward implementing racial equality even though they sincerely believed in the principles of integration and equality. There may be some truth to this claim, but there is also some contradictory evidence. For example, on two implementation items, particularly the one about federal intervention to desegregate public accommodations such as hotels and restaurants, there have been strong positive trends in public opinion over time. Thus, in some circumstances, there is increasing white support for government intervention. However, over roughly the same time period, there was a marked drop in public support for federal intervention to enforce school integration. Therefore, these opposing trends do not seem logically related to concern over government intervention per se, but rather to the more threatening nature of integration in neighborhood schools than in less personal spheres of interaction.

These findings seem quite consistent with the discussion of social distance above: People are more opposed to government intrusion in areas which involve greater intimacy of contact than in areas where social interaction is more limited and formal (Schuman et al., 1985). Also, people are less inclined to act on the basis of abstract principles that they believe in *if* those principles conflict with other valued principles (such as individualism) or goals (such as a high-quality school for one's children). Of course, one result of this widespread opposition to government action in enforcing equality is that minority groups are largely forced to rely on their own meager resources in trying to assert their rights to equal treatment and opportunity, and this happens most often in exactly those areas where they need the most help because of general public resistance.

Attitudes Toward School Integration and Busing

If there is a single event in the last 40 years which stands out in the battle for equal rights, it is the 1954 decision of the Supreme Court of the United States in *Brown v. Board of Education.* This decision, which held that separate educational facilities for blacks were inherently unequal, was the basis for new social policy which began to change the structure of race relations in this country. While desegregation efforts were concentrated on the dismantling of *de jure* (by law) dual school systems of the South, support in the North was high. Surprisingly to many, support for desegration also grew in the South as newly integrated school systems proved that they could function very satisfactorily (cf. Coleman et al., 1966). In the South, the amount of busing in school systems, particularly in rural areas, was often *reduced* as a result of the dismantling of dual school systems. It was no longer possible to bus black and white children past each other to reach segregated schools, as had been done in Topeka, Kansas, as described by Linda Brown Smith (1988), the named plaintiff in the *Brown* case.

Nevertheless, two problems have hounded the school desegregation process. The first problem is "white flight." Survey studies show that acceptance of school integration decreases markedly when the proportion of blacks in a school increases beyond half (Schuman et al., 1985). Even before that level is reached, in the first year of desegregation many white parents remove their children from the public schools or move away to a neighborhood or a suburb where there are fewer minorities. This flight usually decreases or stops in later years of school integration, but in some cities the total loss of white enrollment in the school district has been as high as 50% (Armor, 1988). In many large cities, such as Los Angeles, the growing population of minority children combined with the shrinking base of white children has made district-wide school integration numerically impossible. In such cases, the only way to accomplish full-scale desegregation would be to combine the city school district with the largely white suburban districts in a metropolitan desegregation plan, involving large-scale busing back and forth (Coleman, 1975). Such plans have been tried in a few cities, but a later Supreme Court decision discouraged creation of mandatory metropolitan plans (Oskamp, 1984).

A second area of controversy is busing. Historically, more than 40% of American children were bused to school prior to court desegregation decisions which required busing to achieve racial balance in schools, and busing was viewed almost universally as a way to improve education, by consolidating resources and facilities. Nevertheless, up until the 1980s, busing to achieve desegregation was supported by less than 20% of Americans, with majority disapproval by every segment of white Americans and also by many blacks (Ladd & Lipset, 1975).

It seems clear that the busing issue may bring many values into painful conflict within individual citizens. On one hand, most people value equal opportunity and integration, and on the other hand, they value quality of education, local control of schools, monetary savings, children's time and safety, etc. (McClendon, 1985). It is not usually possible to predict attitudes toward busing from other racial attitudes—they are not related among the general public. Only among highly educated elite groups is opposition to busing seen as related to racial prejudice (Kelley, 1974). This finding has been offered as supporting evidence for the symbolic racism viewpoint, but it is also consistent with Converse's general findings about the greater degree of interrelationship among political attitudes in elite groups than in the mass public (see Chapter 6).

In the 1980s, attitudes toward busing took a surprising turn. By 1986, the former heavy opposition was reduced to 53% of Americans opposing busing for desegregation and 41% favoring it, according to a Harris survey (*Equal Justice*, 1987). Not only that, but entering college students, who are the first generation to have grown up with desegregated schools, actually favored busing to achieve racial balance in schools by a 54% majority (Meyer & Evans, 1986). These changes seem to be due to two major trends: nationwide, the number of families whose children have been bused to school has roughly doubled in the 1980s, and a large majority of the parents in these families, both black and white, report that they feel good about their children's school experiences (Hawley & Smylie, 1988). For many people, apparently, the anticipation of busing was much worse than its reality when they experienced it. Thus, even the busing controversy, which had seemed perhaps the most intractable issue concerning implementation of racial integration, no longer appears as formidable a cause of racial conflict.

WHICH WHITES HOLD WHICH ATTITUDES?

Personality

During the 1950s, the book called *The Authoritarian Personality* (Adorno et al., 1950) provided an explanation of prejudice based on psychoanalytic theory (see Chapter 11). The authors concluded that prejudiced individuals were the product of authoritarian child-rearing practices (strict physical punishment, reverence for parents and other authority figures, denial of sexuality, and so on). Among the consequences of these child-rearing practices was an inability to accept negative feelings about one's self or one's own group. Denial of self-blame led to the attribution of blame for bad thoughts and deeds to scapegoats—usually minority groups, who could not defend themselves and who occupied a low status in the community. Everything that could not be accepted in oneself was "projected" onto a weaker target. Thus prejudice was seen, in effect, as a personality disorder—a viewpoint termed the **scapegoat theory of prejudice**. In this theoretical view, people use prejudice as a crutch to hold up their low self-esteem, and they blame minority groups as scapegoats for poor economic or social conditions. Research based on this viewpoint has also found prejudice to be related to dogmatic opposition to women's liberation, opposition to civil liberties in general, a rigidly punitive view of law enforcement, and a conservative ideological position (Maykovich, 1975).

While *The Authoritarian Personality* provided some important insights into the dynamics of prejudice, later research has produced other explanations of prejudice in terms of conformity to social norms and of limited education (e.g., Pettigrew, 1971). These findings indicate that it is often more fruitful to look for understanding of prejudice at the level of the social context rather than at the personality level. Let us consider some of these demographic and group factors.

Demography

Generally, there are three important correlates of racial prejudice for whites: region of the country, education, and age (Maykovich, 1975). Southerners hold generally less favorable attitudes toward blacks than do northerners. It is now agreed that the regional difference is not a function of differences in personality between people in the North and South but a difference in social norms (Pettigrew, 1959). In the South, important social institutions like the churches and schools were (and still are) more likely to support segregation than similar institutions in the North. Therefore, racial prejudice in the South was a sign that a person was well integrated into his(her) community—conforming to its social norms—whereas in a more equalitarian social system racial prejudice might be a sign of personality disturbance, as proposed by Adorno et al. (1950).

Some of the specific changes in racial attitudes over the last several decades have been parallel in the North and the South, with both regions becoming more favorable toward integration but the gap between them remaining about the same. However, on several specific topics, people in the South changed faster so that the gap decreased, and on some items the two regions became almost identical by the 1980s (Schuman et al., 1985). The most remarkable example of a trend toward identical scores is the Gallup item asking if respondents would "have any objection to sending your children to a school where half of the children are black?" The changing percentages of white respondents in the two regions saying "no objection" over two decades are shown in Figure 15-2.

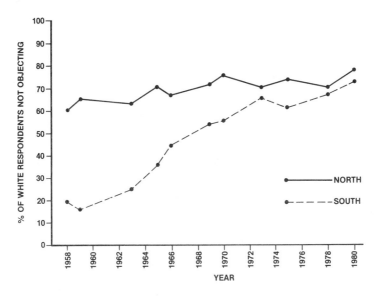

FIGURE 15–2 Comparison of North and South on trends in acceptance of sending one's own children to a school where half of the children are black.

Source: Schuman et al. (1985, p. 64). Reprinted by permission of the publishers from *Racial Attitudes in America* by Howard Schuman, Charlotte Steeh, and Lawrence Bobo, Cambridge, Mass.: Harvard University Press, copyright © 1985 by the President and Fellows of Harvard College.

People with more education, particularly those who have attended college, are less prejudiced on the average than those who have less education. The difference is largest on items describing general principles of equality and is usually smaller on items involving implementation of principles or social distance preferences (Schuman et al., 1985). Campbell (1971) has suggested that it is primarily an individual's *personal* experience with college in recent years that results in a more liberal racial attitude. Parents' education does not seem to matter; thus it is not the child's background that is responsible for the difference.

Younger people hold more positive racial attitudes than older people. During the 1960s and early 1970s the changes in white Americans' racial attitudes occurred almost as strongly among older respondents as among younger ones. However, since then, the slower changes in overall population attitudes have been almost entirely due to the gradual replacement of older cohorts by younger, more liberal cohorts (Schuman et al., 1985). A portion of the relationship between youth and positive racial attitudes seems to be due to the steady increase in the proportion of young people who attend college (Taylor, Sheatsley, & Greeley, 1978). There are fewer differences in racial attitudes between young and old for those who have not attended college.

RACIAL ATTITUDES OF BLACK AMERICANS

Early surveys of racial attitudes did not usually include black respondents for several reasons. Often survey samples excluded racial minorities, and even if they were included, there were usually too few respondents of a given minority group to yield reliable estimates of their attitudes. Also, race relations was seen basically as a white issue that whites would have to solve (Schuman et al., 1985). Thus it was not until the early 1960s that large samples of blacks were interviewed about their racial attitudes, so the available data on their time trends cover only about 20 years, and in addition they are sparser because the same survey questions have not been repeated as often with large black samples. We will discuss the data that are available on black attitudes after presenting a brief sketch of black demographic conditions.

The Circumstances and Goals of Blacks

Everyone realizes that blacks have been at the bottom of the U.S. economic and social hierarchy ever since they were first brought to this country as slaves. Their disadvantage still exists late in the 20th century despite many important social changes (Jaynes & Williams, 1989). In 1976, black men rated well below white men, and black women generally below white women, on ten different indices of economic and social status—e.g., percentage completing high school, average earnings, unemployment rates, etc. (Jones, 1981). However, major changes have occurred in some of these figures since the civil rights movement of the 1960s. The median amount of education completed by blacks rose from 9 years in 1968 to 12 years in 1985, and the proportion of black adults who have completed high school doubled from 30% to 60%. Half of all black American families now own their own homes, and the number of blacks in high-status jobs has risen sharply (Zinsmeister, 1988).

Yet the problems of poverty and deprivation remain acute for much of the black populace. Economic inequality among American blacks is substantially greater than among whites. This means that the upper third of black households are comfortably middle-class (or higher) with an annual income above $25,000 in the mid-1980s, while another third are working-class, employed families with incomes over $10,000. However, the remaining third are mired in poverty, most of them dependent on some form of government financial aid, many of them single parents with young children, and living under conditions of high crime, poor health, and widespread hopelessness. The contrasts within the black community are paradoxical: In the two decades since 1968, the number of black elected officials nationwide increased six-fold to 7000, including the mayors of many of our largest cities, and the number of black managers, business executives, and professionals increased to 1 1/2 million. Yet at the very same moment, only 56% of black men were employed, *down* 14% from 1968 (Zinsmeister, 1988). As a result, blacks still have many justified doubts about equality in America, but they also differ among themselves on some key questions of social policy.

In general, blacks and whites in America share many of the same aspirations. They want the same things for themselves and for their children—a good income (and the comforts that brings), good schools, freedom from fear of repression and crime, opportunity to get ahead, and so on. However, blacks and whites do not agree as much on how blacks might best achieve the goals of middle America, nor do they always agree on which goals are most important (Wilson, 1970). Nationwide, many more blacks than whites (58% to 17%) score high on the value of social justice, which stresses the role of government in providing for the needy, whereas more whites than blacks (28% to 11%) score high on a belief in America's boundless ability to solve its problems (Colasanto, 1988).

In judging civil rights progress, whites and blacks have shown opposing opinion trends since the 1960s. Over these years, an increasing percentage of whites said they perceived "a lot" of positive change in the circumstances of blacks, but decreasing percentages of blacks have agreed. A similar disagreement is evident in responses about whether "civil rights leaders are trying to push too fast, are going too slowly, or are moving at about the right speed." Over the years since the heyday of the civil rights movement in 1964, greatly increasing proportions of whites have been saying "about right," and far fewer have been saying "too fast." In contrast, increasing proportions of blacks have been saying "too slow" and fewer "about right." Less than 10% of whites say "too slow," and less than 10% of blacks say "too fast" (Schuman et al., 1985, p. 142). On another question, a majority of 61% of blacks (versus 39% of whites) attribute the continuing black poverty to societal reasons such as discrimination, whereas a plurality of 49% of whites (versus 30% of blacks) attribute it to characteristics of blacks themselves (Colasanto, 1988). These conflicting views are a good illustration of how realistic group conflict can lead to contrasting perceptions of the same events.

Principles of Equality and Their Implementation

On some principles of equal treatment, blacks are practically unanimous in their views. Very close to 100% of nationwide black samples agree that "white students and black students should go to the same schools" rather than separate schools, and that "black people have a right to live wherever they can afford to, just like anybody else" rather than that "white people have a right to keep black people out of their neighborhoods if they want to." Moreover, the unanimity on these items has not changed at all over 20 years—in contrast, about 90% of whites agree with these items, and that figure increased about 25% since the 1960s (Schuman et al., 1985, pp. 74–75, 144–145—see Figure 15-1 for item wording and responses of whites).

Blacks support school integration because they believe that whites get a better deal in the schools: more experienced teachers, more funds, newer schools and materials, expectations of success, and so on. It is perhaps for those reasons that a majority of blacks did not favor black principals, even in predominantly black schools, nor did they believe that black students were better taught by black teachers (Schuman & Hatchett, 1974).

On other principles, blacks are more divided. Nearly 80% approve of marriage between whites and nonwhites, and that figure has remained steady (compared with 40% of whites). Only 56% say they favor desegregation rather than "strict segregation, or something in between," and that figure has dropped 22% since 1964, while those favoring "something in between" have increased 22% to 39%. In comparison, whites have increased about 10% on each of these options—to 35% for desegregation and 60% for something in between (Schuman et al., 1985).

On implementation items, blacks, like whites, are less favorable than they are on the corresponding general principles. For blacks, the gap between support of principles and of their implementation is only about half as large as for whites, but in recent years their percentage of approval for government intervention has declined substantially on some issues. For instance, blacks express 82% support for federal action to ensure fair treatment on jobs (down 10% from 1964); 60% support for federal action to assure school desegregation (down 22%); 49% support for federal help to improve the social and economic position of minorities (down 29%); and 64% support for solving the problems of poverty and unemployment that led to urban unrest, rather than using force to maintain law and order (down 10%). Blacks' highest level of support on implementation items is 91%, for federal action to keep hotels and restaurants open to blacks; 80% are supportive of government spending to improve the condition of blacks; 75% favor federal laws to ensure open housing; and none of these items has changed much since they were first asked. Finally, black support for busing to achieve integration is one of the lowest of any of these implementation items, 56% of those expressing an opinion—about where it was in the early 1970s but a bit lower than its peak in the mid-1970s (Schuman et al., 1985).

Thus there are some parallels between black racial attitudes and those of whites. Though blacks' approval of both general principles of equality and actions to implement those principles is generally higher than whites' approval—sometimes much higher—both racial groups are less enthusiastic about the implementation actions than about the principles. Also, the drop in support since the 1960s was quite parallel for both groups on the issue of federal intervention to ensure school integration, and black decreases in support for several other implementation actions have brought them somewhat closer to average white attitudes on those issues. The large minority of blacks who oppose busing for integration mention reasons including school quality, safety, inconvenience, freedom of choice, and preference for neighborhood schools; and the overlap of these reasons with those of white busing opponents provides further evidence that opposition to busing is not just a smokescreen for white racism (Schuman et al., 1985).

Job Discrimination and Alienation

Affirmative action and equal-opportunity employment are phrases often seen in advertisements for employment. How do blacks feel about progress in eliminating job discrimination? Blacks in Detroit in 1971 did not believe job discrimination had disappeared; 63% believed that a white would be hired before a black even if qualifications were equal. Yet, more than two-thirds believed that young blacks could get ahead if they worked hard enough, despite prejudice and discrimination. More than 80% preferred to work in racially mixed groups, and a majority believed the "work situation" was improving. A very great majority of blacks work with whites (in the Detroit survey, the figure was 91%). Of those who worked with whites, 69% reported that they got together with whites frequently for lunch while only 9% reported that they never did. Of those with white supervisors, 82% reported equal treatment of blacks and whites (Schuman & Hatchett, 1974). Thus, despite the belief that blacks are often discriminated against in obtaining employment, most blacks did not report discrimination in *their own* job situation.

The most careful and objective study of black **alienation** was made by Schuman and Hatchett (1974). Eleven survey items, which tapped responses of Detroit blacks concerning perception of discrimination in various domains and willingness to take action or support policies to correct discrimination, formed an *alienation from white society index.* Of the 11 items, only two displayed even a plurality of alienated responses in 1971: beliefs that many places will hire a white before a black with the same qualifications, and that whites want to keep blacks down. On the other hand, only four items yielded less than 20% of alienated responses: beliefs that the U.S. is not worth fighting for in a world war, that violence is the best way to gain black rights, that no white people can be trusted, and a personal preference to live in an all-black or mostly black neighborhood.

The mean score on the index indicated that an average of about 40% of the respondents were alienated on each item—a distressingly high proportion. Following the assassination of Martin Luther King, Jr. in 1968, the average level of black alienation increased until 1971, but then dropped again by 1976. Limited evidence suggests that it has remained roughly stable since then (Schuman et al., 1985). There has been relatively little black racial protest activity since 1971 and no repetition of the wave of urban violence of the 1960s. On the other hand, whites have taken to the streets in Boston and Louisville to protest busing. It is understandable that these actions on the part of whites would increase the percentage of blacks who believe whites want to keep blacks down and who are disenchanted with peaceful protest as a means to achieve racial equality.

The Distribution of Black Racial Attitudes

Like the racial attitudes of whites, black racial attitudes can be related to region of the country, education, and age. However, the findings are not always as clear as they are for whites. In general, southern blacks are slightly more conservative (or less alienated or less radical) than northern blacks, but the differences are small (Goldman, 1970). The data do not support any notion that southern blacks are more passive, compliant, or docile than northern blacks.

Riot participants (self-reported) in northern urban centers were more often long-term residents of the city, relatively better educated than nonrioters, higher in their job aspirations, more likely to have voted, and more favorable in their self-perceptions and perceptions of their race. In short, these data sharply dispute the "riff-raff theory" of rioting and protest. To quote Caplan (1970, p. 71):

> The militant is a viable creature in search of practical responses to arbitrary institutional constraints and preemptions which deny him the same freedom and conventional opportunities as the white majority. He is the better educated but underemployed, politically disaffected but not the politically alienated. He is willing to break laws for rights already guaranteed by law, but under ordinary circumstances he is no more likely to engage in crime than his nonmilitant neighbor.

For whites, a college education is apt to be linked to positive racial attitudes; but for blacks the opposite result is found. As of 1971, well-educated blacks (with 16 or more years of education) were the most alienated subgroup of blacks, and the general picture has not changed much since then (Schuman & Hatchett, 1974; Schuman et al., 1985). Almost as alienated from white society were blacks without high school diplomas (if questioned by black interviewers). One study of black college students (Banks, 1970) found that black students were becoming less authoritarian (perhaps less ready to accept society's view of them) and more negative in their attitudes toward the white majority. If education helps to create a critical awareness of our society, it is not surprising to find that, during college, blacks become more alienated toward white society while whites become more sympathetic toward black protest.

Young blacks are generally more radical than older blacks—for instance, more likely to support militant and separatist action (Caplan, 1970). Though younger whites are more tolerant of blacks, younger blacks are less tolerant of whites. However, it would be incorrect to infer that many blacks of any age group hate whites. As Marx (1967) concluded, "They don't hate (whites), but they don't like them either" (p. 179). In fact, those lowest in antiwhite feeling are most militant in their support of civil rights actions (Marx, 1967; Caplan, 1970). The changes in black attitudes that have occurred since 1971, particularly the decrease in support for a number of government implementation activities, have been fairly general across all demographic groups (Schuman et al., 1985).

CHANGING RACIAL ATTITUDES

Over the past 50 years, whites' racial attitudes have generally become much more positive. The many civil rights marches, sit-ins, and protests have dramatized the issues of discrimination and led to laws mandating racial equality. In turn, it is clear that the changes in laws and segregation practices have often led to more favorable racial attitudes, rather than more favorable attitudes preceding the changes in laws and practices. Thus, though whites often complain about civil rights changes being too rapid, when a new law is passed or a new desegregation step is taken, people's attitudes soon adjust, and more and more people express favorable opinions toward the new practice. One clear example, discussed above, is the positive change in attitudes concerning school integration which followed the Supreme Court decision ordering school desegregation, and which has continued into the 1980s. Another example is favorable racial attitude changes which often occur in suburban neighborhoods some months after the first black family moves into the neighborhood (Hamilton, Carpenter, & Bishop, 1984).

Of course there have been occasional local setbacks, as in the violence and protest over school busing in Boston in 1975 and 1976. Usually these violent episodes have occurred when important community leaders publicly opposed the changes, as happened in Boston, thus making it easier for firebrands to whip up disorder and violence. On the other hand, when community leaders (whatever their private feelings) unite in advocating orderly and nonviolent procedures, even major social changes have usually been made with little public disturbance (U.S. Commission on Civil Rights, 1977a). These findings again show the greater importance of social norms, compared to the impact of private attitudes, in the area of race relations (Pettigrew, 1969).

Black racial attitudes have also shown marked changes, both up and down, in the course of the last 30 years. During the early 1960s blacks were generally more optimistic about progress toward racial equality and about whites' willingness to assist in that progress than they are currently. In general, it has been shown that U.S. attitudes toward integration, among both whites and blacks, are most positive in people who have experienced integration and much less favorable in people who have not had interracial contact (Pettigrew, 1969). Thus, the racial separatist movements among blacks, if long continued, would be likely to lead to less-favorable racial attitudes among both blacks and whites.

Of course, not all contact has led to reduced interracial hostility. Just as in the area of international contact (see Chapter 14), a number of conditions must be met before contact with other races will improve racial attitudes (see below). Having one or a few black friends or acquaintances, especially if they are of lower social status, is not enough to overcome prejudice (Jackman & Crane, 1986). However, with the transformation of racial practices in the U.S., types of contact which were impossible in the past have become commonplace today. Americans of all ethnic origins share public accommodations, work together, and, in many places, go to the same schools in relative peace and harmony. If this trend continues, the fear of many white Americans about interracial neighborhoods and perhaps even interracial marriage will also become a thing of the past.

Experimental Studies of Racial Attitude Change

In this section we will examine briefly some of the methods which social scientists have tried in experimental attempts to change prejudiced racial attitudes.

Interracial Contact.   One of the prevailing hypotheses about race relations is that contact between groups who dislike each other, under favorable conditions, will lead to increased liking and decreased prejudice. Amir (1969) argued that the following conditions must be met: (a) the members of each group must be of equal status, *or* (b) the members of the minority group of a higher status than the majority group members; (c) there must be a favorable climate for intergroup contact, (d) the contact must be of an intimate rather than casual nature, (e) the contact must be rewarding and pleasant, and (f) the two groups should have a mutual goal which requires interdependent and cooperative action.

Unfortunately, all of these conditions are seldom met completely in "real life." However, one of the first empirical studies of changing black-white relations observed what happened when some public housing developments were desegregated after World War II. In this quasi-experimental situation there was an unbiased system of assignment to apartments and equal-status contact among the new neighbors, and the result was that white tenants became much more favorable to equal-housing policies (Deutsch & Collins, 1951).

Moving on to fully controlled experimental research, Cook (1969) created contact conditions like those listed above in a laboratory study. Black and white college women met together over a one-month period to participate in a simulation exercise (a game used as a management training device). The black women and half of the white women were experimental confederates; the other white women, unbeknownst to themselves, were chosen for their highly negative attitudes toward blacks. The game required a high degree of cooperation, provided a basis for fairly close contact (two hours per day for 20 work days), equal-status contact (since the subject and the two confederates rotated jobs), and a superordinate goal (winning and earning a bonus). Also, during each two-hour session, breaks occurred which provided planned opportunities for pleasant interracial contact, discussion of race-related topics, and personal comments which allowed the black confederate to establish herself as an individual and to weaken racial stereotypes held by the subject.

A comparison of the subjects' racial attitudes before and after the contact experience showed a significant positive change in racial attitudes by about 40% of the women, whereas in an untreated control group of prejudiced women only 12% showed significant favorable attitude change. There was also some evidence that the change was generalized beyond the experimental situation. These results are encouraging, though the monetary cost to achieve this amount of attitude change was very great. However, the findings leave open two major questions: (a) In view of these ideal conditions, why didn't the other prejudiced women change? (b) Could similar results be obtained in a real-life field situation?

Many studies have demonstrated that induced cooperation can weaken hostility between rival groups (e.g., Sherif et al., 1961), and several groups of researchers have applied this principle to reduction of interracial animosity. In newly desegregated junior and senior high schools, Weigel, Wiser, & Cook (1975) established some experimental classrooms where small groups of students of mixed ethnic composition (black, Hispanic, and white) worked interdependently. They found these students were more likely to engage in cross-ethnic helping behavior and to have greater relative respect for each other than students taught in regular classrooms where individual competition was stressed. Similar principles of cooperative learning were emphasized in an influential series of studies using a technique termed the "jigsaw classroom" in elementary schools (Aronson, Blaney, Stephan, Sikes, & Snapp, 1978). The authors reported increased cross-racial liking within the small cooperative learning groups, as well as improved self-esteem and liking for school, higher school performance by the minority students, decreased competitiveness, and more willingness to learn from other students. In other states and nations, several other research teams have demonstrated favorable results for equal-status, cooperative-learning methods, sometimes combined with intergroup competition between the small cooperative groups (Sharan, 1980; Slavin, 1980; Johnson, Johnson, & Maruyama, 1983).

All of these results provide support for the conclusion that administrative arrangements involving properly structured intergroup contact can affect racial attitudes favorably. The question of exactly how the intergroup contact should be established and explained has been analyzed carefully by Brewer and Miller (1984, 1988). They conclude that it is important to emphasize the individual, *personalized* characteristics of team members rather than their racial category membership, and this conclusion has implications for methods of assigning members to teams and for avoiding intergroup competition, which detracts from the cooperative atmosphere.

Experiencing Discrimination.   Weiner and Wright (1973) demonstrated that white children who were given a planned experience of arbitrary discrimination in their classrooms were more willing to interact with black children and showed decreased prejudice as compared to a control group who had not undergone the experience. Role-playing the part of a minority group member has become a regular part of many human relations training programs which attempt to increase the sensitivity of public officials (particularly police officers) to minority problems (e.g., Pfister, 1975; Sata, 1975).

Spotlighting Value Conflicts.   Rokeach (1971) and his colleagues demonstrated that the exposure of value-attitude-behavior inconsistencies can produce changes in race-related attitudes and behaviors. Rokeach's typical experimental procedure highlighted inconsistencies between ratings of two values (freedom and equality) and the relationship of these values to civil rights attitudes and behavior. For instance, subjects were shown a table which indicated the relative importance of 18 values for Michigan State University students. The table showed that "freedom" was ranked first, "equality" eleventh; and the experimenter interpreted this discrepancy for the subjects as follows: "Michigan State University students, in general, are much more interested in their own freedom than they are in freedom for other people" (1971, p. 454). The subjects were given time to compare their own responses with those in the table, and later they were shown a second table which indicated that students who ranked "equality" high were more likely to

Photograph courtesy of Sandra J.
Ball-Rokeach. Reprinted by permission.

Box 15–2   MILTON ROKEACH, *Crusader for Equality*

One of the most creative contributors to social psychology, Milton Rokeach was born in 1918 in Poland and emigrated to the U.S. at age 7. He grew up in Brooklyn and graduated from Brooklyn College in 1941. Following service in the Army Air Force in World War II, he earned his Ph.D. at the University of California at Berkeley, working as an assistant on the Authoritarian Personality project and writing his dissertation on ethnocentrism. He taught at Michigan State University for 23 years, moved briefly to the University of Western Ontario, and spent 14 years as Professor of Sociology and Psychology at Washington State University, before a final move to the Annenberg School of Communications at the University of Southern California, where he died in 1988.

Rokeach is known as both an outstanding conceptualizer and researcher. He introduced the concept of dogmatism in his book The Open and Closed Mind, *and he conducted the most extensive social science study of values in his volumes* Beliefs, Attitudes, and Values, The Nature of Human Values, *and* Understanding Human Values. *These contributions converged in his research on prejudice, racial attitudes and behavior, experiments on value change, and advocacy of equality as a key value, which are discussed in this chapter. Among his many honors are election as President of the Society for the Psychological Study of Social Issues and receipt of the Kurt Lewin Memorial Award.*

participate in or sympathize with civil rights demonstrations. The experimenter pointed out that people who were against civil rights valued their own freedom, but not the freedom of others.

Rokeach (1971) found relatively long-lasting value and attitude changes as a result of this brief and simple experimental procedure, and he also found clearcut changes in behavior. Experimental subjects were more likely than control subjects, who had not received information about inconsistencies within their value-attitude system, to respond favorably to a NAACP solicitation for memberships 15-17 months after the experimental treatment and to register for courses in ethnic relations 21 months after the treatment. Though the absolute number of subjects who responded in these ways was not large, these results are still very impressive for such a simple and straightforward procedure. In later years, many other studies have essentially replicated these findings (Rokeach & Grube, 1979), though one study in the 1970s, when the civil rights movement was no longer so prominent, found that favorable changes in the ranking of "equality"were not carried over into joining the NAACP (Sanders & Atwood, 1979).

Rokeach and McLellan (1972) extended the above findings by showing that examining normative information about others without comparable information about oneself can also have a long-term impact on values, attitudes, and behaviors. Subjects who saw the two tables but did not rank the values for themselves, as well as ones who experienced Rokeach's original procedure, displayed significant changes in their rankings of the values "freedom" and "equality," and also were more willing to support a campus civil rights group four months after the experiment. Though such value-change procedures could have ominous effects if they were extensively used by the mass media, a distinction must be drawn between results obtained with a captive audience of introductory psychology students and the mass media audience. As we have discussed in Chapters 8 and 11, the mass media audience can refuse to read, to watch, or to listen to appeals which might upset their sense of self-satisfaction. Also, in a democratic society, there are apt to be other powerful media presenting opposite appeals to the public. Consistent with this view, further experimental research has supported the **unidirectional hypothesis** of value change—i.e., that values can only be modified in a direction that *reduces the individual's self-dissatisfaction* and increases consistency with the self-concept (Rokeach & Grube, 1979; Ball-Rokeach, Rokeach, & Grube, 1984).

In sum, these studies by Rokeach and his colleagues are exciting and promising demonstrations of ways of making attitude change research relevant to socially important issues. They suggest possible approaches toward resolving the "new American dilemma"—the conflict between Americans' beliefs in justice and equality and their resistance to implementing them fully (Taylor & Katz, 1988).

SUMMARY

Many have argued that racism is pervasive in the United States, as demonstrated by the necessity for sweeping court decisions and civil rights laws. At the individual level, *racism* means a pattern of prejudiced attitudes and discriminatory behavior which is important and central in a person's life. *Institutional racism* refers to formal, explicit laws and regulations which discriminate against certain ethnic groups, and also to informal social norms which limit the opportunities and choices available to certain ethnic groups. Individual and institutional racism operate so as to support and bolster each other.

Children learn racial discriminations and preferences early in life from early socializers (parents, school, church) more often than from personal experience. The specific content of racial stereotypes has remained fairly similar over the past 60 years, but the degree of consensus about stereotypes and willingness to stereotype have decreased substantially. Yet stereotyped images of minorities are still very common in our mass media.

Whites' racial attitudes depend in part on social distance. Most are willing to grant equality to blacks and other minority groups in areas of interaction (such as employment) that do not require close personal contact, but many whites strongly resist more intimate contact—mixed neighborhoods, dating, and marriage, and even school integration when the proportion of blacks in schools is more than half. Since the civil rights movement of the 1960s, the proportion of whites supporting principles of equal treatment has increased to very large majorities, but the number favoring various government actions toward implementation of those principles has risen little. Among the viewpoints proposed to explain this contrast are the concepts of modern racism or symbolic racism, realistic group conflict, and opposition to government activism.

Overall, blacks have made much economic and social progress in the last 30 years, but the acute poverty and deprivation of the bottom third of black Americans have produced a substantial amount of alienation. In general, blacks support rapid desegration, largely because they believe that whites control access to the good things in life rather than because they are eager for social integration. Since the 1960s increasing proportions of blacks have stated that civil rights progress is too slow, but they are not unanimous in their views on some implementation programs, especially busing. Young and well-educated blacks are apt to be more militant than others.

Positive changes in racial attitudes since the 1950s have been caused largely by changes in the law and in public practices brought about through peaceful protest. Though whites often complain about civil rights changes being too rapid, they have adjusted and become increasingly favorable to new laws or practices. People who have experienced racial integration, both whites and blacks, are much more favorable to it than those who have not.

Experimental studies of racial attitude change have been carried out by social scientists in attempts to pinpoint the conditions which will facilitate positive attitude change. In particular, studies of interracial contact with equal-status, cooperative activities and of spotlighted value inconsistencies have shown ways of making attitude change research relevant to important social issues.

16

Gender Role Attitudes

Women are our property. . . . They belong to us, just as a tree that bears fruit belongs to a gardener.—Napoleon Bonaparte.

God put both sexes on earth and each has its own purpose. I'd hate like hell to wake up next to a pipefitter.—Barry Goldwater.

The only position for women in SNCC is prone.—Stokeley Carmichael, head of Student Nonviolent Coordinating Committee (SNCC).

Both men and women have one main role—that of a human being.—Edmund Dahlström.

The negative quotes above could be paralleled scores of times, but positive ones are rare. A predominant theme in reference to women throughout history is that women are different from, less than, and subordinate to men. A German proverb states: "A woman has the form of an angel, the heart of a serpent, and the mind of an ass." Because women have been viewed in these stereotyped ways, their "place" in society has been prescribed on the basis of their sex rather than individual characteristics. At the same time, the range of allowable behavior for men has also been limited by related stereotypes of appropriate masculine conduct.

Research and writing related to sex and gender have been expanding at a rapid pace in the last two decades (Deaux, 1985). Two journals specifically covering these topics were introduced in the mid-1970s, *Sex Roles* and *Psychology of Women Quarterly*, women's studies curricula were established on many college and university campuses, and interdisciplinary contributions to understanding of women's roles were published in the journal *Signs* and in countless books and magazine articles. Subsequently, a parallel but much smaller resurgence of interest in men's roles also developed (e.g., David & Brannon, 1976; Pleck, 1981), and social science findings about changing male and female roles have influenced public policy debates and decisions in our government and judicial systems (Russo & Denmark, 1984).

Usage of the terms *sex* and *gender* has been shifting in recent years. **Sex** refers to biological differences between males and females, while *gender* once referred mainly to grammatical classification of nouns into masculine, feminine, and neuter categories. However, recently **gender** has been adopted by many authors as a term denoting *socially determined* psychological and behavioral characteristics of males and females, as opposed to biologically determined sex differences such as genitalia and behavior related to procreation and child-bearing (e.g., Deaux, 1985). We will use the term in that way, though many differing usages are still current (e.g., Unger, 1979; Archer & Lloyd, 1985). Thus we will consider **gender roles** as social expectations—learned cultural prescriptions for sex-appropriate personality and behavior.

SEXISM AND RACISM

The 1970s added a new word to the language of prejudice: **sexism**, a prejudiced attitude or discriminatory behavior based on the presumed inferiority or difference of women as a group. It is no semantic accident that this word is a first cousin to "racism." In the United States the link between the struggle, on the part of blacks and women, for equality and self-determination is historically rooted. In the 19th century, the abolitionist and feminist movements were closely interrelated; many suffragist leaders, both men and women, had honed their political skills in the slavery abolition movement (Myrdal, 1944).

The women's movement of the 20th century is also linked to black equality. In 1964, Title VII of the Civil Rights Act was passed prohibiting discrimination on the basis of race and sex. The "sex" provision was added as an intended stumbling block to the bill's passage, according to Bird (1968, pp. 4–10). Subsequent neglect of that provision by the Equal Employment Opportunities Commission led in 1966 to the formation of the National Organization for Women, which has since spearheaded the moderate wing of the women's movement (Freeman, 1973).

The parallel between the struggle of blacks and that of women is not only historical, but based on a similar ideology and experience of subordination. Thomas made this point as early as 1907 in a penetrating analysis titled "The mind of woman and the lower races." Myrdal (1944) pointed out the paternalism basic to our society, which provides a rationale and arguments favoring inequality. Kirkpatrick (1963) discussed the analogous situation of blacks and women, listing 36 parallel items. These ranged from rationales for subordination (biological inferiority and religious prescriptions), to discriminatory practices in education, sexuality, and occupations, to the minimizing of individuality through stereotyping (as emotional, infantile, and sly). Similarly, Hacker (1951) described various accommodating attitudes (such as deference, concealment of feelings, and subtlety in getting one's way) which are defense mechanisms employed by both groups. Finally, there were great personal and political advantages to white males in keeping both blacks and women in the subordinate status of servants.

However, several major differences can be traced in the subordination of women and that of blacks. First, blacks were a numerically small minority in most places outside the South, and thus many whites might never see or contact them and might have only an abstract conception of the realities of racism. In contrast, since women comprise over half the population, it would be impossible for a male to grow up without contact with them and without personal experience of the differential treatment of women (Reid, 1988). Second, blacks were separated out as a group, whereas women's lives have been individually and intimately intertwined with members of the dominant male group. Women have known far greater informal power through liaison with individual men, but little strength as a group.

Third, blacks were literally owned and sold as property on the auction block, whereas women were "wards" by law. The influence of British common law in American history gave husbands custody of the wife's person, property, earnings, and children; yet, ironically, one of the ways of "keeping woman in her place" was to put her on a pedestal (Lewin, 1984). A Madonna view of womanhood, at its height in the 19th century, contrasted with a coarser image of men, supported the sexual double standard, and restricted women's activities. Man's "better half" was kept in the kitchen or nursery, unsullied by the evils of the labor market and the sordidness of politics. The "weaker sex" was protected from the physical strain of employment and the mental and emotional stress of higher education. Women found it harder to object to subjugation when it was combined with veneration! Yet, ironically, though black men who had once been slaves received the right to vote after the Civil War, American women had to wait until 1920 to win that badge of full citizenship.

A final difference between the subordination of blacks and women is that the type of racism directed at blacks in the U.S. is a unique result of American historical, political, and social conditions—differing in important details from racism in other nations and times—whereas the characteristics of sexism in America are very like the practices and beliefs of many other nations (Rogers, 1981; Blackwell, 1985). In fact, sexism may be the most deeply rooted prejudice of the human race, since it is founded on the fundamental dichotomization of the human race into male and female, with "Adam's Rib" as the second sex. Like all prejudice it cuts two ways, and men's behavior is limited by the reverse of the stereotypes evolved for women. The study of gender roles will be incomplete until equal attention has been given to the problems involved for men.

The facts of discrimination against women in many realms of life have been very thoroughly documented by statistical data, gathered by sources such as the U.S. Department of Labor (e.g., 1980; Nieva & Gutek, 1981). Also, the literature of the feminist movement is now prolific and readily available, though its thrust tends to be more polemical than empirical. To complement these well-established bodies of literature, this chapter aims to fill a major gap by focusing on research into gender role attitudes and their origins.

ORIGINS OF GENDER ROLES—BIOLOGICAL OR CULTURAL?

There is no question that the roles of men and women have differed throughout history, but it is important to clarify whether the differences are inevitable or optional. The traditional assumption has been that biological sex and gender roles are inevitably linked in human life. To examine this assumption, we will look at evidence from research on gender identity and from cross-cultural studies.

Gender Identity

Perhaps the most determining statement for one's future occurs in the delivery room when the nurse or doctor pronounces "It's a boy" or "It's a girl." The question of "how do they know?" seldom occurs—after all, it's obvious. However, it's not as simple as that, according to Money and Ehrhardt (1972), who have spent decades studying hermaphrodites—individuals whose physiological sex as male or female is ambiguous. As examples, occasionally a genuine penis may resemble a clitoris, or a child may appear to be male and yet test chromosomally as female. When such an anomaly is recognized early, a gender is assigned, usually on the basis of chromosomal sex. Hormonal treatments, operations, etc., may be performed so that the gender is clarified for the child and for society. The assigned gender greatly affects people's attitudes toward the child and the way that it is reared. If, on the other hand, a sexual anomaly goes unrecognized for a period of time, the psychological impact of an attempted change of gender identity after age two can be devastating to the child.

Money maintains that research with hermaphrodites demonstrates that the gender assigned and accepted (**gender identity**) can have more impact than physiological sex. Though Money believes that there are some inherent psychosexual differences between men and women, he says that there are only four biological imperatives: menstruation, gestation, and lactation for women; impregnation for men—all other behavior is possible for both sexes. In short, physiological sex apparently determines some predispositions, but a person's behavior is extensively modifiable by learning and culture (cf. Matlin, 1987).

Cross-Cultural Studies

Another way of determining whether behavior is biologically linked is through cross-cultural examination of gender roles. Universality of such roles would argue for biological determinism; variability would demonstrate the power of learning. Stephens (1963) found definite regularities in the division of labor in several hundred societies, but there was no task which was exclusive to one sex in all of the cultures.

Margaret Mead (1935) startled the world with her early study of three New Guinea tribes which showed marked variation in role differentiation and expression. Mead found that Arapesh men and women were both typically "feminine" in western terms: considerate, gentle, and cooperative. Mundugumor men and women both displayed "masculine" traits of aggressiveness and the absence of tenderness. The Tchambuli displayed differential personality traits, but they reversed the western patterns: men were dependent and nurturant, while the women were impersonal and managerial. Though there have been critiques of Mead's research procedures

(Freeman, 1983), her underlying conclusion of wide cultural variability is well-established. A thorough study of ethnographic reports on 110 primitive societies found many varying patterns of gender roles; some matched, others reversed, and still others blurred our typical dichotomous patterns (Barry, Bacon, & Child, 1957).

In explanation, D'Andrade (1966) theorized that the typical division of labor, and related personality traits, are extensions of primitive biological necessity. Women, by nature less strong than men and encumbered by pregnancy and lactation, tended to center their activities near their living area; men, stronger and not thus burdened, were freer to travel, hunt, and handle dangerous situations. Therefore, in most societies, men had the most strenuous and dangerous tasks (which were also apt to be considered most important), and their appropriate temperaments were aggressive and dominant. Since women were generally home-centered in their

Photograph courtesy of Margaret Mead.
Reprinted by permission.

Box 16–1 MARGARET MEAD, *Pioneer Researcher on Gender Roles*

Both by her research and her example, Margaret Mead has been uniquely influential in expanding the role of women in our society. Retired as Curator Emeritus of Ethnology at the American Museum of Natural History in New York after 43 years of continuous service, she continued to lecture, go on anthropological expeditions, and work for causes she believed in until her death in 1978.

Born in 1901 in Philadelphia, Mead attended Barnard College and earned her Ph.D. in anthropology at Columbia in 1929. By then she had already been on an expedition and written her first famous book, Coming of Age in Samoa. *It was quickly followed by* Growing Up in New Guinea, Sex and Temperament in Three Primitive Societies, *and eventually by 40 other books.*

In addition to her curator duties, Mead held over 20 short-term lectureships at universities in five different countries, made 24 anthropological expeditions, accepted over 20 honorary degrees and 30 special awards, and served on innumerable boards, committees, and councils. Notable among her honors were membership in the National Academy of Sciences and election as President of the American Anthropological Association and the American Association for the Advancement of Science.

tasks, their personalities accordingly became more passive and nurturant. This minimal division of labor was an aid to survival at first. However, maternal child care, which was essential during lactation, was extended beyond the mandatory period; and those who hunted became the "obvious" persons to make weapons and tools. Such social roles have been further elaborated throughout history. Their original rationale now long forgotten, gender roles became normative patterns. Strong attitudes supporting them were perpetuated in succeeding generations by culturally prescribed customs and child-rearing patterns (cf. Lee & Stewart, 1976). Moreover, the activities prescribed for males in any given society, whatever they might be, were virtually always valued more than the prescribed female activities (Rosaldo, 1974).

Developments during the last quarter of the 20th century should help untangle issues of biological versus cultural causation, at least for women in industrialized nations. They have been freed by the population boom and the pill from the mandate of motherhood, and they can now choose whether or not to enter an automated work world where physical strength is no longer a prerequisite. Their handling of these options will powerfully affect gender role attitudes in the future.

TRADITIONAL GENDER ROLES AND STEREOTYPES

Let us briefly sketch the traditional stereotypes of gender roles in American society. In doing so we must recognize that any brief description has to be a caricature of the full detail of gender expectations and behavior. We should also realize that there have been variations of these themes in different historical eras as well as in different nations and subcultures. However, a recent study of current gender stereotypes in 30 nations ranging from Peru to Malaysia has shown a surprising degree of similarity in their major themes in practically all of those nations (Williams & Best, 1982).

Gender stereotypes have at least four main aspects: personality traits, role behaviors, physical characteristics, and occupations that are expected of women or of men (Deaux & Lewis, 1984). One major theme that appears over and over again in descriptions of gender roles is that women tend to have more **expressive** traits (e.g., being more emotional or sentimental) while men have more **instrumental** traits (e.g., acting to reach a goal)—(Parsons, 1955). A closely related theme is that women are more **communal** (selfless and concerned with others) while men display more **agency** (being self-interested, self-assertive, and motivated toward mastery)—(Block, 1973). Thus, among the trait terms that are stereotypically feminine are affectionate, gentle, appreciative, and sensitive, but also complaining, weak, and prudish. In contrast, stereotypically masculine traits are forceful, aggressive, independent, and ambitious, but also boastful, coarse, and disorderly (Williams & Bennett, 1975; Cowan & Stewart, 1977).

You might think that these gender stereotypes have been changing rapidly in recent years, due to much higher numbers of women being employed and the general effects of the women's movement. However, research has shown that the specific characteristics which were seen as typically female or male in our society were almost identical in the 1970s and in the 1980s (e.g., Spence, Helmreich, & Stapp, 1974; Ruble, 1983).

The Female Role

A detailed description of the traditional American female gender role of this century has been presented in a book entitled *Fascinating Womanhood* (Andelin, 1980), which sounds as if it might be a parody, but is actually the foundation of an organization aimed at teaching women how to live out this pattern. Its portrayal of desirable "feminine dependency" includes the following description:

> Dispense with any air of strength and ability, of competence and fearlessness, and acquire instead an attitude of frail dependency. . . .
>
> Be submissive: . . . To be feminine, a woman must be yielding to her husband's rule. . . .
>
> Don't try to excel him: . . . Don't compete with men in anything which requires masculine ability. . . .
>
> Need his care and protection: Let him open doors for you, help you on with your coat, pull up your chair. . . . (pp. 241–244)

The Male Role

A central aspect of the American male role is a man's work. His job and his role as breadwinner typically take precedence over other aspects of the husband and father roles, such as caring for children, helping with housework, and sharing intimacy with his wife. David and Brannon (1976) have suggested the following four themes as comprising the core requirements of the stereotypical male role:

> No sissy stuff: A stigma on all stereotyped feminine characteristics and qualities, including openness and vulnerability.
>
> The big wheel: Striving for success and status; the need to be looked up to.
>
> The sturdy oak: A manly air of toughness, confidence, and self-reliance.
>
> Give 'em hell!: An aura of aggression, violence, and daring. (p. 12)

Influences of Gender Stereotypes on Behavior

Believing in such gender stereotypes, even in part, or interacting with other people who do, can have far-reaching effects on the behavior of men and women. A very typical effect has been termed the **self-fulfilling prophecy** (Merton, 1957). Many studies have demonstrated that people tend to behave in ways that confirm other people's expectations of them (e.g., Berger, Rosenholtz, & Zelditch, 1980; Darley & Fazio, 1980). In one study, undergraduate women applying for a part-time job were led to believe that the interviewer had a concept of the ideal job applicant that either closely matched or markedly differed from the traditional feminine gender stereotype. The women in the traditional condition presented themselves in a substantially more "feminine" manner. For instance, they dressed more conservatively and talked much less than the women in the nontraditional condition (von Baeyer, Sherk, & Zanna, 1981).

However, despite the pervasiveness and power of gender roles' impact on people's behavior, research has also shown that their influence can be overcome in some situations. In laboratory experiments on social cognition, where subjects are given a file of information about several people and asked to make decisions about them (e.g., which one to hire as a kindergarten teacher), the influence of information about their gender may be greatly outweighed by other information that is logically related to the decision (e.g., their performance as a practice teacher, or their love of young children)—(Locksley, Borgida, Brekke, & Hepburn, 1980). However, in the actual world such characteristics are apt to be positively correlated and, even when they are not, judges making decisions *expect* them to be. Hence, the relative influence of gender labels and other characteristics cannot normally be teased apart in real-world situations, and gender stereotypes are apt to play a major role in such decisions as job hiring and evaluation (Deaux, 1985).

SOURCES OF GENDER ROLE ATTITUDES

How do gender roles originate and develop? A great deal of research has examined influences which may be responsible for current gender role views. These socializing pressures are the "attitudes behind our attitudes." Among these sources of influence are all of the socializing agents that we discussed in Chapter 7—parents, teachers, peers, and the mass media—plus some others that are particularly relevant to transmission of gender attitudes. These include clinicians who treat our minds and bodies, social scientists who describe our place in society, writers of children's literature who shape early attitudes, and even the everyday language that we speak and hear. Here are some brief examples of each of these types of influence on gender role attitudes.

Parents, Teachers, and Peers

Parents treat infant boys and girls differently starting from the very day of their birth. American mothers and fathers tend to describe their day-old girls as tiny, soft, delicate, and the like, whereas they describe their newborn boys as strong, alert, firm, and bigger—despite the fact that the infants in the research were not objectively different in size or muscle tone (Rubin, Provenzano, & Luria, 1974). In the first six months of life, boys in our society receive more physical contact (being touched, held, nursed, etc.), while girls get more nonphysical attention (being looked at, talked to, etc.—Lewis, 1972; Maccoby & Jacklin, 1974). These differences in treatment set the stage for the children's expected gender role behavior. Lest you think that the treatment differences are elicited by different characteristics of the infants, some studies have found these differential patterns of treatment toward *the same infant*, when it was dressed and introduced to adults as a boy versus as a girl (e.g., Smith & Lloyd, 1978; Sidorowicz & Lunney, 1980). Adults talked quietly to a 6-month-old "girl" and offered "her" a doll to play with, whereas the same child dressed as a boy was typically given a toy hammer and encouraged to engage in large-scale vigorous play.

Parents make more demands on boys in their first few years than on girls, and they reprimand boys more severely than girls for acting in gender-inappropriate ways (Hartley, 1974). Though American parents often deny that they pick baby clothes according to the child's sex, the clothing usually identifies the infant as a boy or a girl (Shakin, Sternglanz, & Shakin, 1985). Most clothing for infants designates their sex not only by its color and direction of fastening, but also by style of collars, type of trim, patterns and embroidery, etc. Boys' clothes tend to be durable and give more freedom of movement, while girls' costumes usually have more delicate prints and dainty fabrics (Richardson, 1988).

Toys, too, are highly gender-typed, as demonstrated by an analysis of a Sears toy catalogue, shown in Table 16-1. Toys on a page section illustrated with a boy model or drawing were almost entirely manipulatory (e.g., blocks, Lego assembly units, or vehicles), while those grouped with a girl illustration were mostly related to marriage and child-rearing (e.g., dolls, kitchen toys). Cultural and educational toys were more equitably illustrated—most often with no models or mixed genders (Richardson, 1988). As a result of parental and societal conditioning, children as young as two tend to show preferences for gender-appropriate toys (Blakemore,

TABLE 16-1 Percent and Number of Half Pages in 1986 Sears *Toys* Catalogue Displaying Various Types of Toys with Child Models

	Types of Toys			
Sex of model	Preparation for spouse/parent roles	Manipulatory toys and vehicles	Cultural and educational	Number of half pages
Male	4% (1)	57% (37)	46% (17)	55
Mixed genders	8% (2)	40% (26)	35% (13)	41
Female	88% (21)	3% (2)	19% (7)	30
Total	100% (24)	100% (65)	100% (37)	126

Note. Number of half pages in parentheses.

Source: Adaptation of table from page 48 of THE DYNAMICS OF SEX AND GENDER, 3rd ed., by Laurel Richardson. Copyright © 1988 by Harper & Row, Publishers, Inc. Reprinted by permission of the publisher.

LaRue, & Olejnik, 1979), as do older children in their requests to Santa Claus (Richardson & Simpson, 1982).

Teachers are no more immune than parents to gender role stereotyping. For instance, in one study nursery school teachers were found to reward boys more for aggressive behavior and girls more for dependency. They also tended to help girls perform tasks, whereas they more often gave boys verbal instructions for carrying out tasks on their own. Such interactions encourage boys to be capable and independent and girls to feel helpless and dependent (Serbin & O'Leary, 1975).

In nursery school and elementary school, children's peers become increasingly strict monitors and enforcers of gender role norms in activities, toy preferences, friendships, and so on (Langlois & Downs, 1980; Pitcher & Schultz, 1983; Carter & McCloskey, 1983-1984). Even in college, when gender role options become broader and less restrictive, peers still remain major influences on students' gender role attitudes and behavior (Komarovsky, 1985).

Psychotherapists

The writings of psychotherapists have had a profound impact on social attitudes toward the personality and role of women. Freud's view of woman—that her anatomy was her destiny—assigned her firmly to her place in the home. Freud defined woman biologically and psychologically as an incomplete male, who envied the man's penis and superior creative capacities. Her sexuality was pronounced as immature unless orgasm was achieved through vaginal intercourse with a male. This view went relatively unchallenged until Masters and Johnson (1966) proved that the clitoris is the center of sexual stimulation and that an orgasm is an orgasm, however triggered.

Weisstein (1971) pointed out that other leaders in the psychiatric field (Bettelheim, Erikson, and Rheingold) have described the well-adjusted woman as defining herself in terms of men—in the roles of wife, mother, and homemaker. Chesler (1972) asserted that this kind of viewpoint among "healing" professionals has contributed greatly to pathological diagnoses of women who do not fit the mold, and to the fact that about twice as many women as men are hospitalized for emotional disturbance in the U.S.

A frequently cited study suggested that clinicians still viewed women patients much as Freud did (Broverman, Broverman, Clarkson, Rosenkrantz, & Vogel, 1970). Male and female psychiatrists, psychologists, and social workers were asked to describe mentally healthy men, women, and adults on a list of behavioral and personality traits. Results showed that a double standard of mental health was held by both male and female practitioners. Trait ratings of the healthy man and the healthy adult were highly similar, but ratings of the healthy woman differed from both. She was described as more dependent, submissive, easily influenced, emotional, and subjective, and less competitive, aggressive, and adventuresome—all characteristics otherwise attributed to unhealthy adults.

Results of this study imply that, if these clinicians practice what they preach, they may encourage women patients to adjust to norms that are opposed to increasing maturity and individuality. However, it is well to note that the dichotomous way that ratings were reported in this study tended to exaggerate the relatively small differences that the therapists saw between the healthy man and the healthy woman. Also, when rating the "healthy adult," the judges may have thought of that person as a man, and if so, the results would be very logical and not a sign of an invidious view of women as less mentally healthy than men. It is encouraging that later studies of a similar sort have found little or no stereotypic bias in therapists' ratings of the mental health of men and women (e.g., Gomes & Abramowitz, 1976; M. Smith, 1980; Hare-Mustin, 1983).

Nevertheless, in response to reports and concerns about sexist practices in psychotherapy, the American Psychological Association established a Task Force on Sex Bias and Sex-Role Stereotyping in Psychotherapeutic Practice. Its report (APA, 1975) warned of the potential dangers of sexism in four aspects of psychotherapy: fostering of traditional gender roles, bias in expectations and devaluation of women, sexist use of psychoanalytic concepts, and responding to women in treatment as sex objects. Going beyond these proscriptions, new groups of feminist therapists have begun to offer clients nonsexist, individualized treatment approaches which aim at equality between men and women and seek to change society in that direction (Gilbert, 1980).

Gynecologists

Gynecologists are expected to be medical experts on female physiology and sexuality, but their training may not have kept up with recent research findings that have disproved traditional sex stereotypes such as the following:

- Man's sexual drive versus woman's urge to procreate
- Vaginal versus clitoral orgasm, the former being described as the "mature" response

One study examined 12 gynecology texts that were published since Masters and Johnson's research, hoping to find that these myths were no longer being taught (Scully & Bart, 1973). However, analysis regarding the first stereotype revealed that three of the 12 texts did not even index female sexuality, three characterized women as generally nonorgasmic, six stressed their primary interest in sex for procreation, and 8 of the 12 emphasized the stronger male sex drive. None mentioned women's capacity for multiple orgasms. Concerning the second stereotype, vaginal versus clitoral orgasm, the study found that 8 of the 12 texts did not even index orgasm. None mentioned that portions of the vagina have no nerve endings and therefore lack sensation. One specified that the clitoris is the focus of sensation, but two continued affirmation of vaginal orgasm as the only mature response. This research article on the training of gynecologists ended with the thought, "With friends like that, who needs enemies?"

No follow-up studies of more recent gynecology texts have come to light, but even if they have corrected all of their former misconceptions, there will still be a large group of practicing gynecologists who were brought up on the former inaccurate ideas.

History, Sociology, and Marriage and Family Textbooks

The writings of social scientists may be more influential on public opinion than literary writings because of people's faith in the objectivity and factuality of scientific findings. However, attitudes toward gender roles revealed by writers in the social sciences are characterized by androcentrism (a focus on men), stereotyping, and a bipolar view of gender roles. Research into history books has illustrated these biases.

> Sexism in historical writing is much like sexism in daily life. For the most part women are made invisible. When discussed at all, women . . . appear as part of the domestic scenery behind the real actors and action of national life. (Rosen, 1971, p. 541)

Even writers who have tried to focus on women have found it difficult to examine their activities in history without reference to domestic roles. One author, for example, called the work and friends of suffragists "spouse surrogates," as if women were incomplete in themselves.

Sociology, often defined as the study of man in society, might be more accurately described as the study of *males* in society. An examination of 10 introductory sociology texts published in the late 1960s revealed that only half of these books indexed any reference to women (Kirschner, 1973). Half mentioned the increasing equalitarianism of the American family, usually with scant reference to either the causes or consequences of this important phenomenon. Only 2 of the 10 texts mentioned the significantly lower wages earned by women, a factor which Kirschner regarded as the key to understanding women's place in the economy. Even though this study was done in the early years of the women's movement, this degree of neglect of women in society is an astounding omission.

The textbooks used in marriage and family classes, above all sources, would be expected to present a realistic picture of gender roles as they are and as they may develop. However, they have been shot through with unsubstantiated "facts" and prescriptive judgments. Ehrlich (1971) analyzed the content of six leading marriage and family texts on several important dimensions, and her findings were a serious indictment of family writers' scientific objectivity. Examining sexual attitudes, she found women typically described as asexual. The active, aggressive male was depicted as normal; the woman with a high sexual drive was a "nymphomaniac," needed "psychiatric attention," and/or "endangered her marriage" with her demands. Traditional homemaker/breadwinner roles were upheld as natural, proper, and expedient. The textbooks suggested that a woman might take a job (preferably part-time) to add to family income, *provided that her husband agreed and her work did not interfere with her household obligations.*

Examination of current marriage and family textbooks shows encouraging efforts to avoid these past deficiencies. Many of them now emphasize the recent changes in expected roles for American men and women and highlight the resulting greater latitude in occupational choices, personality traits, sexual behavior, and everyday social interactions. However, there are others that still do not mention the concept of gender roles, give relatively little space to "sex roles," and tend to discuss them as if they were biologically or ethically mandated rather than broadly variable and produced by social expectations and pressures.

Children's Literature

An important critique of books for children is contained in a small paperback called *Dick and Jane as Victims* (Women on Words and Images, 1975). A carefully documented content analysis of 134 elementary school readers revealed a consistent pattern of stereotypic messages to the nation's children. The differential treatment accorded boys and girls in the 2760 stories studied illustrates some assumptions underlying gender role attitudes which may be learned in school. Boys in these school readers were more clever than girls by a four to one ratio. They were more heroic (ratio 4:1)—e.g., saving others from fires, stampedes, storms, and rampaging buffaloes. They had far-flung adventures (ratio 3:1) such as panning for gold, weathering tornados, and catching cattle rustlers. By contrast, girls stood passively, hands behind their backs, admiring the feats of their brothers. They carried out domestic work (ratio 3:1 compared to boys) and did so cheerfully while boys more grudgingly helped Mother with "her" chores. In the stories, father was the fun person, the problem-solver and adventure-promoter. Mother was colorless and unimaginative as she obsessively cleaned, cooked, and scolded.

A similar study of 83 later readers showed a possible trend toward a more even male-female balance, but still there were two to three times as many male occupations, biographies, and illustrations as female ones. The researchers also felt that there was a trend toward more realism in the stories. Females were depicted with a wider range of individuality, and males were shown less often than before as exhibiting impossible standards of heroism and emotional strength (Women on Words and Images, 1975).

Another important research project (Weitzman, Eifler, Hokada, & Ross, 1972) examined the socialization of preschool children through prize-winning picture books. The Caldecott Medal is given yearly by the American Library Association to the best preschool book; it may mean 60,000 sales for the book, and it is influential in setting standards for other children's literature. The study analyzed 18 Caldecott winners and runners-up for the period 1967–1971. The gender roles portrayed were similar to those described in the previous study. There was an active/passive, outdoor/indoor, task-oriented/person-oriented dichotomy between males and females.

A prototypical example from an earlier preschool book titled *The Very Little Girl* is an illustration showing a fragile little girl being dragged along by a tiny dachshund on a leash. A companion book called *The Very Little Boy*, by the same author and illustrator, contains a parallel drawing of a boy of the same age successfully giving commands to and caring for a dog twice his size (Weitzman et al., 1972). Perhaps the most flagrant fallacy in the Caldecott award books concerned the occupational picture presented. During a period when close to half of American women worked, the *only* occupational roles portrayed for women were wife and mother, *fairy, fairy godmother, and underwater maiden!* Hardly a realistic set of options!

More recent studies of children's books have reported similar patterns of lopsided concentration on male characters, and active, adventurous, problem-solving roles for males versus passive, fantasy, or home-centered activities for females (e.g., St. Peter, 1979; Stockard & Johnson, 1980). However, in contrast to this general picture, some recent preschool books and school readers have begun to reflect the goals of the women's movement and to show greater male-female equality, less dominance for males, and a much wider range of roles for girls and women. A helpful list of such equalitarian books is presented by Pitcher, Feinberg, and Alexander (1984), and a few of their titles convey their character: *Girls Can Be Anything, Jennifer Takes Over*, and *Mommies at Work.*

Everyday Language

Just like children's literature, our everyday speech often expresses and reinforces gender role stereotypes. As Henley (1989) has summarized, our use of language treats men and women unequally:

1. Language deprecates women. For instance, there are from 6 to 10 times more feminine terms than masculine terms for various negative concepts (e.g., a sexually promiscuous person) and, conversely, many more masculine terms for prestigeful concepts. As another example, the common use of "girl" to refer to a mature woman is infantilizing, in the same way that using "boy" to address a mature black man is insulting.

2. Language use reflects gender stereotypes. For instance, phrases like "woman doctor" or "male nurse" show our society's normal expectations about the sex of individuals in those occupations. Similarly, the differentiation of marital status in our traditional terms of address for women (*Miss, Mrs.*) but not for men (*Mr.*) indicates that marriage is considered more crucial to women's status.

3. Language treats the male as normative and ignores women. The most widespread example of this is use of the masculine as a generic form, as in *chairman, man in the street, workman's compensation*, or *he* or *him* used to include persons of both sexes.

Some defenders of the linguistic status quo have argued that these common usages are just a matter of convenience and do not matter in terms of women's treatment in society. However, in recent years, much research contradicting that view has accumulated. For instance, a story about a woman political candidate using sexist terms such as "lady candidate" and "girl" made readers more negative to the candidate's seriousness and competence than did reading the same story purged of sexist language (Dayhoff, 1983). All of the many studies on the generic masculine form have shown that it introduces a bias in people's thinking because it does not call to mind females as readily as males (e.g., Martyna, 1980; Henley, 1989). Furthermore, information written in the generic masculine form gives males an advantage, for research has shown that men remember such material better than gender-neutral material, whereas women remember it less well (Crawford & English, 1984). Moreover, job descriptions written in the generic masculine (e.g., "The professor is expected to. . . . He also must. . . .") cause females to be less interested in considering such jobs, and cause readers to deprecate females' ability to perform the jobs (Bem & Bem, 1973; Briere & Lanktree, 1983; Hyde, 1984). Thus the linguistic form may influence highly consequential social and behavioral choices, and use of the generic *he* is a subtle way of brainwashing women (and men) about their place in society.

In view of these detrimental effects of sexism in language, the recent efforts to eliminate it should be applauded and extended. The American Psychological Association (1977) has published guidelines for nonsexist use of language and incorporated them in its *Publication Manual,* which applies to articles in all APA journals and most other psychological journals. However, many undergraduates are still unconvinced that sexist language is offensive or that it has damaging consequences (Matlin, 1987). Therefore, a demonstration by Adamsky (1981) can be a useful classroom device. In some of her classes she made a point of using the generic *feminine* form for a few days (always using "she" as the generic pronoun), and she found that it not only raised everyone's awareness of the issue, but also made some of the women students feel proud and powerful, and motivated them to continue that usage in their written papers. Though it is difficult to get people to change their linguistic habits, our society's general adoption of the term "black" to replace "Negro" shows that it can be done.

The Mass Media

The mass media which pervade modern life generally present consistent stereotyped messages about gender roles. The extensiveness of bias may be demonstrated by analysis of popular songs, television, and magazines.

You might think that popular music, which is predominantly created and consumed by young people, would be the medium most likely to challenge traditional gender roles. Indeed, in recent decades, popular songs have prominently protested against war, pollution, racism, and restrictive middle-class lifestyles. However, in most respects, they still reflect traditional gender role stereotypes (Chafetz, 1974; Hyden & McCandless, 1983). A majority of popular songs are about males, and a large majority are sung by males. Characteristics that typify men but not women in these songs include being aggressive, rational, demanding, a breadwinner, sexually aggressive, nonconformist, rigid, egotistical, adventuresome, and using drugs. By contrast, women are depicted as domestic, passive, flirtatious, idealistic, dependent, and childlike. The only ways that these songs depart from traditional gender stereotypes are in portraying a large minority of women as secure, and many men as sensitive, emotional, loving, and gentle.

In television entertainment programs, gender role stereotypes are very pervasive (Butler & Paisley, 1980; Downs, 1981). In general, men are depicted as smarter, more powerful, rational, and stable, but also more violent and evil; women characters are generally younger, more attractive, warmer, and happier than men (Tedesco, 1974). A similar pattern is found on children's television shows: aggressive and constructive men, ineffective and deferential women (Sternglanz & Serbin, 1974; Williams, LaRose, & Frost, 1981). However, a fascinating exception to this pattern occurs on the daytime "soap operas," the audience for which is mostly women. There, women are depicted as much more equal to men in power and in professional occupations, and housewives are generally shown as intelligent, self-reliant, and articulate (Katzman, 1972; Downing, 1974).

In television commercials, women are also subordinate. They appear much less frequently than men, and are most often shown as housewives being advised or persuaded to use a household product, while the advice-giver is usually a man, and the authoritative off-screen voice summarizing the product's benefits is almost always a man (Women's Action Alliance, 1981; Courtney & Whipple, 1983). Similar depictions of women occur in British TV commercials (Manstead & McCulloch, 1981), and gender role stereotypes are particularly prevalent in commercials for children's toys (Feldstein & Feldstein, 1982).

In popular women's magazine fiction of the 1960s and 1970s, almost all heroines were portrayed as "happy housewives," without careers or intellectual interests of their own, and dependent on men in most aspects of their lives (Lefkowitz, 1972; Ray, 1972; Franzwa, 1974). Meanwhile, men were depicted as well-rounded, active, independent husbands and providers (Chafetz, 1974). However, there has been some movement away from these stereotypes, especially in magazine and newspaper ads for soft drinks and cigarettes, which have been showing many more women in nontraditional activities and occupations (Sexton & Haberman, 1974). For men in ads, the chief change has been away from portraying them in traditional "manly" activities and toward more depictions in purely "decorative," nonfunctional roles (Skelly & Lundstrom, 1981).

Since such changes in gender role presentations have been occurring in some television entertainment shows (e.g., *The Cosby Show, Moonlighting, L.A. Law*) and in some TV commercials as well as magazine ads, it is important to know what their effect may be. Experiments which have exposed women to a few vivid commercials showing nontraditional gender role activities have shown that they can have clear short-term effects on career aspirations and social behavior (Geis, Brown, Jennings, & Porter, 1984). Similarly, studies of a children's TV series called *Freestyle* which highlighted nontraditional occupational possibilities for girls and boys found that viewers displayed a broadened set of career viewpoints and gender role beliefs (Johnston & Ettema, 1982). Given results such as these, it seems certain that American children must be powerfully influenced by the cumulative impact of traditional gender role portrayals in the 20,000 hours of television programs and 350,000 commercials that they see, on the average, while they are growing up (Adler et al., 1980).

Enculturation. As discussed in Chapter 8, the most widespread effect of the mass media is *enculturation* (or *cultivation*)—the process of instilling and reinforcing the attitudes and views of reality that are held by most members of a given culture. The studies cited in the sections above show that this process has begun to receive the research attention that its importance merits. A major review of mass communication effects concluded:

> Work on sex-role socialization supports a cultivation effect interpretation. The media appear to contribute to the continuance of sex-stereotyped perceptions, but are capable of establishing new perceptual sets when nonstereotypic content is introduced. (Roberts & Bachen, 1981, p. 346)

PAST TRENDS IN GENDER ROLE ATTITUDES

We have examined the major influences which help to shape current gender role attitudes. Now let's look back about 50 years and trace the historical pattern of attitudinal shifts on certain key topics: the idea of a woman President for the U.S. (as reflected in opinion poll data), the Equal Rights Amendment, views of women and work, and attitudes toward women's roles.

A Woman for President?

Public attitudes toward the employment capabilities of women are perhaps most stringently tested by the question: "If your party nominated a woman for President, would you vote for her if she were qualified for the job?" The Gallup Poll has posed this question, with slight variations in wording, to citizens since 1937 (Erskine, 1971). Combining data for both sexes, public opinion changed dramatically between 1937 and 1987 from 33% positive to 82% positive. The changes over time are shown, separately for men and women respondents, in Figure 16-1.

Over the years, there has been a roughly linear increase in positive attitudes. A sharp rise followed the end of World War II, possibly because of women's competency in war work; but there was a surprising decline in women's favorability to a woman President during the 1960s. This decline may have been related to the era of the "feminine mystique"—the idealization of the "wife-mother" role described by Friedan (1963). In the 1960s men for the first time became more favorable to a woman President than women were, but women caught up with them again in 1971. The issues of the women's liberation movement and the status of women did not receive public attention through major news media coverage until after 1969 (Morris, 1973), and this may have been an influential factor in women's 1971 increase. Since then, favorability has continued to rise steadily, and men's and women's attitudes have been essentially identical.

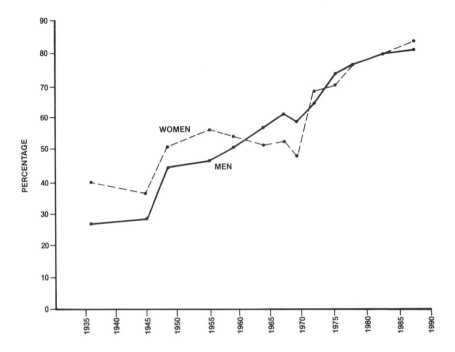

FIGURE 16–1 Historical trends in percentages of American men and women who say they are willing to vote for a woman for President of the U.S.

Source: Data from Erskine (1971); Gallup (1972); *Los Angeles Times* (1976); and *Gallup Report* (1987, No. 262).

The Equal Rights Amendment

The unsuccessful struggle to ratify the Equal Rights Amendment (ERA) to the U.S. Constitution was the symbolic peak of the modern American women's movement. The amendment was passed by an overwhelming majority in Congress in 1972, and it merely said: "Equality of rights under the law shall not be denied or abridged by the United States or by any state on account of sex." Initially, this was a very popular position, but a small group of dedicated opponents of the amendment led by Phyllis Schlafly raised issues such as the likelihood that unisex bathrooms would be required, that husbands would no longer have to support their wives, and that women would be drafted for military combat duty.

The opposition was based very largely on beliefs that traditional gender roles were biologically determined and should not be tampered with, and many opposing legislators were outspoken in stating their antifeminist sentiments, calling ERA supporters "bra-less brainless broads" and declaring that women would "rather be loved than liberated" (Mansbridge, 1986). Thus, the opposition to the ERA had a strong symbolic, value-laden character, similar to the symbolic racism discussed in

Chapter 15, but the openly sexist nature of their arguments was more extreme than the public reactions to blacks that are heard in this era of modern, subtle racism.

Over the next ten years, legislatures in most of the states voted approval of the amendment, but after bitter battles in the remaining states, the final total of support fell a few states short of the three-quarters needed for its ratification. As a result, the amendment died in 1982, though there have been sporadic attempts to reintroduce it in Congress and begin the ratification process all over again.

What did the public think about the ERA? There has been substantial majority support for it ever since it was passed by Congress. The lowest percentage of support that it received in Gallup Polls was 57% in 1976, with only 24% opposed and 19% expressing no opinion. Also noteworthy is the fact that up until 1980 women were about 7% *less* in favor of the ERA than men were. Ironically, in 1981, less than a year before the amendment's demise, and despite President Reagan's opposition to it, nationwide public support rose to 63% (32% opposed, and 5% no opinion), with women and men equally favorable, and even conservatives supporting it 58% to 38% (*Gallup Report*, 1981, No. 190). Finally, by 1988, long after the ERA was a dead letter, public support for it had increased to 73% (16% opposed, 11% no opinion), and by this time women were 7% *more* favorable than men (*Gallup Report*, 1988, No. 274). These fascinating changes are statistically significant, and the history of the ERA demonstrates once again that heavy public support for a policy does not ensure its governmental adoption (cf. Chapter 11).

Women and Work

As everyone knows, the last 50 years have brought profound changes in American women's roles, particularly in employment. Between 1940 and 1981, the number of women employed outside the home more than tripled, and the number of working *mothers* increased more than ten-fold. In the 1980s, well over 50% of adult women were in the American labor force, and the figure was equally high for women with children. In 1982, 59% of women who had children under 18 years of age were employed, and even 50% of women with preschool-age children (U.S. Department of Labor, 1982). Concurrent changes in family marriage and divorce patterns have led to about 17% of American families being supported by a woman. Because of women's usual low wages, this pattern is very often linked to a poverty situation; among poor families, 47% are supported by a woman (Russo & Denmark, 1984).

With passage of the Equal Pay Act in 1963 and Title VII of the Civil Rights Act in 1964, equal opportunity in employment for men and women of all races became the national policy. However, in the mid-1980s the pay of full-time working women averaged only about 63% of what employed men made, and that percentage had not increased at all since 1955 (Blau & Ferber, 1985). As one example, women with a bachelor's degree earned $616 *less* per year than men who had not completed high school (Bergmann, 1983). As a result of this and many other types of gender discrimination, the women's movement has vigorously supported laws and court rulings requiring affirmative action in hiring and promotion, equal pay for equal work and, more recently, comparable worth as a basis for computing appropriate pay for women (for background information, see Blanchard & Crosby, 1989; Lowe & Wittig, 1989).

How have Americans' attitudes about working women changed during recent decades? In 1938, only 23% of respondents to a Gallup Poll supported the idea of women's employment, whereas by 1978 the positive responses had soared to 77% (Spitze & Huber, 1980). When the question concerned a married woman working "if she has a husband capable of supporting her," only 18% of respondents approved in 1936, while by 1986 77% approved (Gallup, 1972; Simon & Landis, 1989). There has also been increasing support for the idea that there are no types of work that should be closed to women, though this view was still held by a minority of the public in the 1970s (Duncan & Duncan, 1978). On the topic of equal pay for women doing the same work as men, public approval was already 78% in 1942 (during the war), and it increased to 94% in 1977 (Erskine, 1971; Simon & Landis, 1989).

Gender stereotypes about traits relevant to employment have also been changing. Shortly after World War II, men were credited with more ability than women by both sexes, and as late as 1970, 49% of men and 40% of women believed that women could not run businesses as well as men (Erskine, 1971). However, these stereotypic gender role attitudes have been declining (de Boer, 1977). For example, in a cross-sectional sample, Agassi (1982) found that over 90% of both men and women said that women can manage or supervise just as well as men, and even higher numbers said that women can do mathematics just as well as men.

Despite such favorable reports, there is still evidence of more subtle unfavorable attitudes toward women on the part of supervisors and managers (e.g., Martin, Harrison, & Dinitto, 1983). In one study of nearly 900 male supervisors, men workers were rated as significantly more likely than women workers to approach problems rationally, have leadership potential, be independent and self-sufficient, be capable administrators, and understand the "big picture" of the organization. In contrast, women workers were rated as significantly more likely to enjoy doing routine tasks, cry easily, be good at detail work, and be jealous (Rosen & Jerdee, 1978).

Though the data reported in this section generally show major improvements in the favorability of attitudes toward women workers, there still remains a great deal of behavioral discrimination against them. This is evident in their substantially higher unemployment rates, occupational segregation into jobs and work groups that are mostly female, lower pay even for identical jobs and responsibilities, and widespread exposure to sexual harassment on the job (Kahn & Crosby, 1985). A majority of American women are aware of the widespread discrimination against women workers, but a surprisingly large percentage of them deny being aware of any individual disadvantage in their personal job situation (*Gallup Report*, 1987, No. 256–257; Crosby, Pufall, Snyder, O'Connell, & Whalen, 1989).

The contrast between generally favorable attitudes and frequent discriminatory behavior against women workers parallels the findings in Chapter 15 about the more subtle, modern forms of racism. The discriminatory behavior that occurs is often not the result of individual prejudice against women workers, but rather of situational and organizational norms that perpetuate unequal treatment (e.g., paying men higher starting wages, favoring them for management training, or evaluating them more favorably for promotion—cf. Schrank & Riley, 1976). Both unfavorable individual attitudes and inequitable institutional norms are likely to operate as self-fulfilling prophecies that hinder the advancement of women (e.g., Rice, Bender, & Vitters, 1980).

> Most people do not make it a point to exclude or oppress working women. People may, at the same time, continue in their work-force behaviors to favor this man or that in one situation or another. . . . Many discrete individual actions, each perpetuating a seemingly insignificant male advantage in one place or another, accumulate and the aggregate effect becomes one of keeping women severely at a disadvantage. (Kahn & Crosby, 1985, p. 228)

Questionnaire Studies of Women's Roles

Most of the studies cited above have used interview methods and representative samples of men and women to collect their data. An alternative approach is to use written questionnaires, and these are usually given to local samples (e.g., of workers in a particular company or city), who are apt to be less representative of the whole population. However, carefully developed questionnaires have the advantages of reliability and repeatability, which are important in tracking trends in gender role attitudes.

As far back as the 1930s, Kirkpatrick (1963) developed his Belief-Pattern Scale, containing 40 feminist and 40 antifeminist statements. Giving it to college students and their parents, he found the students to be more liberal, especially the girls. A gradual ensuing trend toward liberality in gender role attitudes was interrupted by a sharp drop in the 1960s, similar to that for women respondents on the woman-for-President question discussed above.

Spence and Helmreich (1972) took up where Kirkpatrick left off, using similar questionnaire categories with updated content. They administered an Attitudes towards Women Scale (AWS) to large samples of college students and their parents. Like Kirkpatrick, they found students significantly more liberal than the older generation and women significantly more liberal than men for both generations. By 1980, both the students and their parents had become markedly more egalitarian than in 1972 (Helmreich, Spence, & Gibson, 1982). In 1974, Spence et al. introduced the Personal Attributes Questionnaire (PAQ) as a measure of gender roles, and at least 10 other scales measuring gender roles have been proposed (Stapp, 1978). Other related questionnaires, such as those by Sandra Bem (1974) and Berzins, Welling, and Wetter (1978), are discussed in the following section.

In summary, both poll data and questionnaire studies have indicated a trend over time toward liberalization of U.S. gender role attitudes. However, due to persisting subtle prejudice and opposing institutional norms and pressures, there has been less change in widespread societal patterns of discrimination against women in various realms.

ASPECTS OF CURRENT GENDER ROLE ATTITUDES

Since gender roles are social prescriptions for sex-appropriate personality and behavior, they involve expectations about other people. A famous early sociologist, Thomas (1923), recognized that what we expect often influences our view of "reality" more than objective facts do. If we define women as illogical and men as insensitive, we will "see" these traits in individual women or men, whether or not they are there. Furthermore, gender role stereotypes provide a rationale for rigidly prescribing role behavior without allowing for individuality. They restrict societal options as well as personal flexibility. However, in the late 1960s, the impact of the American women's movement began to change many formerly fixed expectations and norms about women's and men's behavior, and similar changes also occurred in many other countries (e.g., Steinmann, 1975).

Sex-Typed Personality Traits

Psychological gender role stereotypes have most often been studied through the use of adjective check lists. As described earlier in this chapter, typical findings are that men are viewed as more aggressive, independent, and ambitious (instrumental traits), while women are seen as more affectionate, gentle, and sensitive (expressive traits). Moreover, in the 1970s and 1980s, traits seen as typical of men and women have remained essentially unchanged (Spence, Deaux, & Helmreich, 1985).

However, changes have occurred in the way that masculinity and femininity are conceptualized and measured. Until the 1970s, most measures used a bipolar organization of items along a single continuum from masculine at one end to feminine at the other end. This approach is rooted in the assumption that femininity is the opposite, the absence, or even the negative of masculinity (Constantinople, 1973).

More recently, researchers have broken with this stereotypic approach and have conceptualized masculine characteristics and feminine characteristics as two relatively independent dimensions, so that it is possible for a person to score high on both or low on both. In addition they have avoided another fallacy of early research, the labeling of persons not scoring in the "appropriate" masculine or feminine range on the scale as confused or ambivalent about their sexuality. Sandra Bem (1974) and Berzins, Welling, and Wetter (1978) have developed rather similar approaches to measure psychological **androgyny**, meaning the balanced possession of both typically masculine and typically feminine characteristics. Within their systems, an individual who scores high on just the masculine or feminine scale can be referred to as **sex-typed** or **sex-reversed**, depending on the person's sex. An individual who scores high on both scales is called androgynous, while one who scores low on both is often referred to as undifferentiated.

These new instruments have encouraged improved research into the relationship between personality types and gender role behavior. For instance, Bem (1975) compared the comfort and flexibility of sex-typed, sex-reversed, and androgynous individuals on some experimental tasks which required independence of judgment and other tasks which required nurturance and expressive behavior (such as interacting with a young baby). A number of early studies indicated that sex-typed persons are typically somewhat less flexible, creative, intellectual, and socially poised, and have greater anxiety and lower self-esteem than androgynous individuals. These findings confirmed that psychological masculinity and femininity can be measured as relatively separate traits rather than opposite ends of one continuum, and they suggested that gender-stereotypic personalities are not as socially functional for men and women as our society has assumed.

However, more recent research findings have introduced complications (Cook, 1985). For one thing, the content and scoring methods of the various scales, such as those of Bem, Berzins et al., and Spence et al., are different, and as a result they agree only about 50% of the time in their classification of individuals into the four gender role categories. Second, the research findings have not convincingly demonstrated the hypothesized greater flexibility of androgynous individuals in both masculine and feminine tasks. In her later writings, Bem (1981) has deemphasized the behavioral flexibility interpretation of androgyny in favor of a cognitive gender schema theory, which posits that sex-typed individuals are particularly likely to process incoming information in terms of culturally based definitions of masculinity and femininity, and to shape their self-concepts and behavior accordingly.

The stereotypically masculine traits are valued in American society, but many of the stereotypically feminine traits are also valued in both men and women (Spence et al., 1974). Accordingly, androgynous individuals have generally been found to be high in self-esteem, adjustment, sociability, leadership, and many other positive characteristics. However, high masculinity alone (for men or for women) may be as socially important as androgyny, for many studies have found it also to be predictive of self-esteem, adjustment, emotional stability, assertiveness, and so on. Persons scoring high on femininity typically are lower on those characteristics but, as expected, higher on nurturance, empathy, friendliness, and conformity. Undifferentiated individuals (those scoring low on both dimensions) are worst off; they report more psychological problems, poor social interactions, and few positive characteristics (Cook, 1985).

Criticisms have also been raised about the measurement characteristics and scoring methods of masculinity-femininity scales, particularly the Bem Sex-Role Inventory (BSRI). Its 60 adjectives were chosen on the basis of Stanford University undergraduates' judgments that they were more desirable in American society for men or for women. Several studies replicating its construction or testing its

Photograph courtesy of University of Texas News and Information Service. Reprinted by permission.

Box 16–2   JANET T. SPENCE, *Authority on Gender Roles*

After earning her B.A. from Oberlin College and her Ph.D. in psychology from the University of Iowa, Janet T. Spence joined the faculty of Northwestern University. She subsequently spent several years as a research psychologist at the Iowa City Veterans Administration Hospital because the nepotism rules of that time prevented her and her husband from both being on the university psychology faculty. In 1964 she moved to the University of Texas at Austin, where she remains as Professor of Psychology and Educational Psychology.

A central theme in Spence's research is how motivation, personality, and attitudes are related to observable behaviors. In her early research she became famous as author of the Taylor Manifest Anxiety Scale. More recently she has focused on gender role attitudes and behavior, where she is noted for developing the Attitudes towards Women Scale and other objective measures which are discussed in this chapter. Among her many scientific and professional honors, she has been elected President of both the American Psychological Association and the American Psychological Society.

validity have concluded that many of the BSRI adjectives are not differentially desirable for American men and women (e.g., Edwards & Ashworth, 1977; Pedhazur & Tetenbaum, 1979; Myers & Gonda, 1982). Consequently, it seems possible either that Bem's undergraduate judges were different in their gender norms from judges elsewhere, or that American standards of gender role behavior have been changing rapidly enough to partially outdate the BSRI. A revised 30-item form of the scale was developed later in response to some critiques (Bem, 1979), but questions about its item content and validity have continued.

Gender Role Ideals

Most of the gender role scales discussed above have been administered primarily to samples of college students, so generalization of their findings to other populations is hazardous. However, a set of scales that has been used with much larger and more varied samples is the Maferr inventories (Steinmann, 1975). The Maferr Foundation (Male-Female Role Research) of New York has focused for 30 years on the perceptions of both men and women regarding gender roles. Close to 30,000 persons (generally younger, better educated, and of higher socioeconomic status than average, permitting wider role choice), have been included in samples from 17 cultures (Steinmann & Fox, 1974). The Maferr male and female inventories contain 34 items, half of which emphasize family orientation and half, self-orientation. Respondents answer the questions three times—for perception of their own gender role, their own ideal, and their perception of the ideal held by the opposite sex.

Findings with this instrument were surprisingly consistent across time and culture until the late 1960s. Women saw themselves as having a balanced emphasis on family nurturance and self-realization, and their ideal woman was a little more domestic; however, they believed that men's ideal woman was *much* more passive, submissive, and family-centered. In a pattern partially mirroring that of women, men saw themselves as fairly balanced in orientation, giving self-achievement needs slight priority over the needs and desires of their families. Their ideal male was a bit more committed to achievement, but they perceived women as idealizing a strongly family-oriented male. In other words, both sexes saw a small gap between what they were and wanted to be, but a much larger gap between what they were and what the opposite sex wished of them.

Did this perceived gap really exist? The fascinating fact is that both sexes denied it! Men's "ideal woman" was almost identical to women's own ideal, with roughly equal nurturant and self-actualization components. Women's "ideal male" was even more aggressive and self-oriented than the men's ideal. Thus, neither sex was trying to force the other into the family-centered mold. At least, so they said! (Similar findings have been reported more recently by Gilbert, Waldroop, & Deutsch, 1981.)

In the 1970s, the extent of the perceptual discrepancy increased (Steinmann, 1975). Since about 1968, women have been laying increasing stress on their own self-achievement rather than on the familial role (though emphasis on both remains). Data for six countries (United States, Czechoslovakia, Brazil, England, Greece, and Israel) have supported this finding cross-culturally. Except in Greece, men were giving at least token support to women's aspirations. However, in *every* country surveyed, the women seriously distrusted male "liberalism," and the greater their education, the stronger was women's belief that men wanted them back in the home. Similarly, Parelius (1975) found a marked shift away from the traditional gender role attitudes among college women between 1969 and 1973, but little change in their perception of men as relatively conservative in this area. Steinmann concluded that both men and women must learn to balance family and achievement values in order to close their perceptual gap and bring about the companionship which both sexes rate as the most desired trait in a spouse.

Marital Roles

Several times since 1974 the Roper Poll has asked large national samples of Americans about their preference for a traditional marriage where the "husband assumes responsibility for providing for the family and the wife runs the house and takes care of the children" versus a marriage where husband and wife "both work and share housekeeping and child care responsibilities" (Simon & Landis, 1989, p. 273). In 1974, almost exactly 50% of both men and women preferred the traditional marriage, but by 1985 only 37% of the women and 43% of the men stated that preference. Meanwhile the number preferring the marriage of shared responsibilities increased to 57% of the women and 50% of the men (a few percent stated other preferences or expressed no opinion). In a similar finding in 1987, only 34% of women said that their ideal lifestyle was to be married without a full-time job (*Gallup Report*, 1987, No. 267).

Though these data show a clear shift in a liberal direction (that is, away from traditional gender roles), there are still large minorities of both men and women who prefer the traditional marriage arrangement. That point is underlined further by national poll responses to the item: "It is much better for everyone involved if the man is the achiever outside the home and the woman takes care of the home and family" (Simon & Landis, 1989, p. 275). In 1977 the percentage of respondents saying "strongly agree" or "agree" was 62% of women and 68% of men; by 1986 these figures had decreased significantly to 47% of both men and women— still a high figure. Rather parallel decreases occurred in agreement with the item: "It is more important for a wife to help her husband's career than to have one herself," and by 1986 only 37% of women and 33% of men agreed with that statement (p. 273).

Marital happiness is influenced by the gender role characteristics of the two partners. Both men and women whose spouses are high in expressiveness are generally more satisfied with their marriage than those whose spouse is relatively nonexpressive (Antill, 1983). Moreover, high instrumentality is associated with good adjustment for both men and women. Thus, couples where both members are androgynous (i.e., high in instrumentality *and* expressiveness) are most likely to be satisfied with their marriage. By contrast, and contrary to popular beliefs, couples in which both partners are traditionally sex-typed are apt to be low in marital satisfaction (Spence et al., 1985). Whatever a wife's own gender role attitudes, her marital happiness tends to be greater if her husband has egalitarian role attitudes. However, husbands who have traditional role attitudes express *less* marital satisfaction if their wives have egalitarian attitudes (Antill, Cotton, & Tindale, 1983).

Another aspect of marital roles that has been studied is the division of household duties and the amount of time that each spouse spends doing housework (Miller & Garrison, 1982). Traditionally in America, the division of household duties has been highly sex-typed—husbands typically do repairs, auto maintenance, and lawn care, while wives do cooking, cleaning, marketing, and child care (Blood & Wolfe, 1960). Of course some families disregard this pattern altogether, and many minor variations occur within families. However, this normative pattern of types of activities has changed very little in the 1980s, despite the large changes in Americans' stated gender role attitudes (Geerken & Gove, 1983).

There have been substantial changes in the amount of time that husbands and wives spend in household duties, however. Between 1965 and 1985, women's time devoted to housework decreased nearly 8 hours per week (from 27 to less than 20), while men's housework time increased about 5 hours per week (from less than 5 to almost 10). Thus women now spend twice as many hours as men in housework, compared to six times as many as men in 1965 (Robinson, 1988). However, these figures do not include child care, which is largely done by women. Husbands of working wives do *proportionally* more of the household duties traditionally assigned to women than do husbands of full-time homemakers. However, the reason for this is *not* that the husband spends more time, but rather that the working wife spends *less* time doing housework (Blau & Ferber, 1985; Pleck, 1985; Antill & Cotton, 1988).

There is a striking contrast between the current gender attitudes expressed by many Americans and their behavior concerning housework. A majority of married couples believe that household tasks should be shared responsibilities, but very few couples share them equally (Hiller & Philliber, 1986). Similarly, in a national sample of high school seniors, a majority stated that child care and housework should be shared equally by both spouses, but at the same time they expected men to be the primary family breadwinners and women not to work full-time when their children were preschoolers (Herzog, Bachman, & Johnston, 1983). Behaviorally, women as well as men conform to the traditional gender norms concerning housework more than they do in their expressed attitudes, and equality in family and household activities is far from being attained by most couples. More housework is typically done by husbands who are younger, have children, work in jobs without long hours, or do not work a day shift (Staines & Pleck, 1984; Coverman, 1985).

Dual-Career Couples. As recently as 1920, only 12% of women with professional careers ever married (Chafe, 1976). Today, in contrast, couples where both partners have professional careers (not just routine jobs) are common and have been widely studied, though they comprise only 2% of American couples (Gilbert, 1985). Dual-career marriages face extra problems in integrating work and family life because of the heavy work commitments of both partners (Rapoport & Rapoport, 1977; Bryson & Bryson, 1978). They undergo especial stress in cases where the wife's career success outpaces the husband's, and such marriages rarely survive unless both partners are egalitarian in their role attitudes (Hiller & Philliber, 1982). Maintaining the relationship often requires sacrifices in both spouses' careers, but in most cases the woman's career is affected more, for even egalitarian couples often end up making traditional role choices (e.g., Foster, Wallston, & Berger, 1980). In fact, dual-career couples do not share household tasks any more equally than other dual-worker couples, though their higher incomes do allow many of them to hire outside help for some household responsibilities (Gilbert, 1985).

Changes in the Male Role. As the women's movement has transformed the situation for women in this country, men's expected roles have also been changing, but there has not been the same kind of an organized movement to help men adapt to the new reality. The result of these changes has been called **role strain** (Pleck, 1981). The traditional male gender role and the modern one are partially contradictory, and some aspects of the traditional one are maladaptive in today's world. For instance, aggressiveness and hostility are counterproductive in modern society, and physical strength and dominance are often irrelevant to the tasks that men perform in their work or home lives. Also, some of the expressive aspects that are expected in the modern male role—being a warm, sensitive, loving husband and father—are hard to learn and to perform if one has been socialized in opposite patterns. Therefore many men are confused about what is expected of them, and their plight is made worse because, traditionally, violations of gender roles are frowned on and punished more for males than for females (Costrich, Feinstein, Kidder, Marecek, & Pascale, 1975). These confusions and contradictions concerning the modern male role may be one reason for the gap between men's expressions of support for equalitarian role behavior and their frequent failure to carry it into action.

Attitudes Toward Women's Liberation

Since the 1960s, the women's movement has fought against personality and behavioral stereotyping and has spearheaded the campaign for changes in women's roles. In examining attitudes toward gender roles, therefore, it is especially informative to look at people's opinions of this movement, which is also referred to as the women's liberation movement.

Though the women's movement gained prominence only in the late 1960s, it quickly made a notable impact on American society. By 1973, approximately half of a very large sample of *Redbook* magazine's women readers credited the women's movement with having made them aware of society's discrimination against women. However, research in the 1980s suggests that most women have not become personally aggrieved by their lack of power in society, and consequently they have not become dedicated to group organizing and collective action to remedy their grievances. More women favor an individual approach to social change—working separately for their own benefit—rather than a collective approach (Institute for Social Research, 1982).

In the last two decades, there have been great increases in public approval of the goals of the women's movement. In 1970, when a representative nationwide sample was asked, "Do you favor or oppose most of the efforts to strengthen and change women's status in society today?", 40% of women and 44% of men stated approval. Throughout the 1970s more men than women continued to state their support, but by 1985 women had overtaken men and the approval figures had increased to 73% of women and 69% of men (Wilkins & Miller, 1985). However, when the phrase "women's liberation" was included in the question, approval was markedly reduced (Institute for Social Research, 1974). Similarly, there is considerable public opposition to the concept of affirmative action in employment, which is one of the movement's key goals (*Gallup Report*, 1987, No. 260).

The responses of men to the women's movement were studied by Tavris (1973), in a self-selected sample of respondents who were younger, better educated, and more liberal than the general public. She concluded that more than three-quarters of this male sample were "unliberated liberals" because they "support women's liberation as long as it stays somewhere else" (p. 196). Their *attitudes* were equalitarian but their *behavior* was traditional. For example, 73% approved of equality in household and child-care responsibilities, but only 15% of married men actually shared these tasks.

Sex Differences.   An intriguing fact is that, on many different measures of gender role attitudes, men presented themselves as more liberal than women during the 1970s (e.g., Chandler, 1972). However, in the 1980s, women's attitudes have moved farther in the nontraditional direction, so this gap has closed and, in some instances, slightly reversed (e.g., Wilkins & Miller, 1985). For women, egalitarian gender role attitudes are associated with being employed after marriage (Mason, Czajka, & Arber, 1976; Houser & Beckman, 1980). Surprisingly however, for men, having wives or mothers who are employed does not lead to more liberal gender attitudes (Crosby & Herek, 1986). For women, experiences of occupational or sexual exploitation are strong factors increasing support for the women's movement, whereas for men, a sense of sexual or occupational threat from "equal" women is a negative factor diminishing support for the women's movement (Tavris, 1973).

The recent trend in gender roles is clearly in the direction of broader possibilities and loosening of past constraints. Changing legislation, expanding opportunities, and novel personal experiences are alerting both women and men to previously unavailable options. Yet society in general and men in particular have a major stake in maintaining the past traditions of family and work life. It remains to be seen how far the current open attitudes will be carried into far-reaching social change.

SUMMARY

In the United States, there has been a link between the struggles against racism and sexism in both the 19th and 20th century. Women as well as blacks have faced parallel forms of stereotyping and discrimination which have prevented fulfillment of their individual potential. Gender roles are culturally determined, and traditional gender stereotypes in most modern societies picture women's personalities and behavior as being largely expressive and communal, whereas men are expected to display more instrumentality and agency.

Among the early influences on children's gender role development are parents' behavior toward the child and their choice of clothing and toys, as well as teachers' and peers' monitoring of gender role norms. Other important influences which help to enculturate society's dominant gender role attitudes include biased presentations by psychotherapists, historians, and sociologists, texts in gynecology and marriage and the family, and authors of children's literature. Even our everyday language often deprecates and/or ignores women and reflects biased gender stereotypes, and the mass media also feature the predominant presence, authority, and positive presentation of men as compared to women.

Over the past 50 years, a strong trend toward more liberal gender role attitudes is evident, though large pay differentials and subtle discrimination directed at employed women still remain common. In the 1970s new approaches to measuring the gender-related personality traits of men and women were proposed, leading to a burst of research on "androgynous" individuals—ones who are high on both masculine (instrumental) and feminine (expressive) characteristics.

Studies of gender role ideals have revealed large communication gaps between the sexes, and also much ambivalence—i.e., desire for more equalitarian relationships, but reluctance of both men and women to relinquish old attitudes and behavior patterns. Similarly, research on attitudes toward women's liberation has demonstrated large increases since 1970 in public approval of the goals of the women's movement, but many people (especially men) who express liberal attitudes do not carry them into more egalitarian behavior in their everyday lives.

References

Abelson, R. P. (1959). Modes of resolution of belief dilemmas. *Journal of Conflict Resolution, 3*, 343–352.

Abelson, R. P. (1968). Computers, polls and public opinion—Some puzzles and paradoxes. *Trans-action, 5*(9), 20–27.

Abelson, R. P. (1976). A script theory of understanding, attitude, and behavior. In J. Carroll & T. Payne (Eds.), *Cognition and social behavior*. Potomac, MD: Erlbaum.

Abelson, R. P. (1981). The psychological status of the script concept. *American Psychologist, 36*, 715–739.

Abelson, R. P. (1986). Beliefs are like possessions. *Journal for the Theory of Social Behaviour, 16*, 223–250.

Abelson, R. P., Kinder, D. R., Peters, M. D., & Fiske, S. T. (1982). Affective and semantic components in political person perception. *Journal of Personality and Social Psychology, 42*, 619–630.

Abelson, R. P., & Rosenberg, M. J. (1958). Symbolic psycho-logic: A model of attitudinal cognition. *Behavioral Science, 3*, 1–13.

Aboud, F. E. (1987). The development of ethnic self-identification and attitudes. In J. S. Phinney & M. J. Rotheram (Eds.), *Children's ethnic socialization: Pluralism and development* (pp. 32–55). Newbury Park, CA: Sage.

Aboud, F. E., & Taylor, D. M. (1971). Ethnic and role stereotypes: Their relative importance in person perception. *Journal of Social Psychology, 85*, 17–27.

Abrams, M. (1970). The opinion polls and the 1970 British general election. *Public Opinion Quarterly, 34*, 317–324.

Abramson, L. Y., & Martin, D. J. (1981). Depression and the causal inference process. In J. H. Harvey, W. J. Ickes, & R. F. Kidd (Eds.), *New directions in attribution research* (Vol. 3, pp. 117–168). Hillsdale, NJ: Erlbaum.

Abramson, P. R. (1972). Political efficacy and political trust among black schoolchildren: Two explanations. *Journal of Politics, 34*, 1243–1269.

Abramson, P. R. (1983). *Political attitudes in America: Formation and change*. San Francisco: Freeman.

Abramson, P. R., Aldrich, J. H., & Rohde, D. W. (1982). *Change and continuity in the 1980 elections*. Washington, DC: Congressional Quarterly Press.

Abramson, P. R., & Finifter, A. W. (1981). On the meaning of political trust: New evidence from items introduced in 1978. *American Journal of Political Science, 25*, 297–307.

Abt, C. C. (1980). Social science in the contract research firm. In R. F. Kidd & M. J. Saks (Eds.), *Advances in applied social psychology* (Vol. 1). Hillsdale, NJ: Erlbaum.

Adair, J. G. (1988). Research on research ethics. *American Psychologist, 43*, 825–826.

Adair, J. G., Dushenko, D. W., & Lindsay, R. C. L. (1985). Ethical regulations and their impact on research practice. *American Psychologist, 40*, 59–72.

Adams, W. C. (1982). Middle East meets West: Surveying American attitudes. *Public Opinion, 5*(2), 51–55.

Adams, W. C. (1984). Media coverage of campaign '84: A preliminary report. *Public Opinion, 7*(2), 9–13.

Adams, W. C. (1985, May). *Early TV calls in 1984: How western voters deplored but ignored them.* Paper presented at American Association for Public Opinion Research meeting, McAfee, NJ.

Adams, W. C. (1986). Whose lives count?: TV coverage of natural disasters. *Journal of Communication, 36*, 113–122.

Adams, W. C., & Smith, D. J. (1980). Effects of telephone canvassing on turnout and preferences: A field experiment. *Public Opinion Quarterly, 44*, 389–395.

Adamsky, C. (1981). Changes in pronominal usage in a classroom situation. *Psychology of Women Quarterly, 5*, 773–779.

Adler, R. P., Lesser, G. S., Meringoff, L. K., Robertson, T. S., & Ward, S. (1980). *The effects of television advertising on children*. Lexington, MA: Heath.

Adorno, T. W., Frenkel-Brunswik, E., Levinson, D. J., & Sanford, R. N. (1950). *The authoritarian personality*. New York: Harper.

Agassi, J. B. (1982). *Comparing the work attitudes of women and men*. Lexington, MA: Lexington.

Ahammer, I. M., & Murray, J. P. (1979). Kindness in the kindergarten: The relative influence of role playing and prosocial television in facilitating altruism. *International Journal of Behavior Development, 2*, 133–157.

Ajzen, I. (1987). Attitudes, traits, and actions: Dispositional prediction of behavior in personality and social psychology. In L. Berkowitz (Ed.), *Advances in experimental social psychology* (Vol. 20). New York: Academic Press.

Ajzen, I. (1988). *Attitudes, personality, and behavior*. Chicago: Dorsey.

Ajzen, I., Dalto, C. A., & Blyth, D. P. (1979). Consistency and bias in the attribution of attitudes. *Journal of Personality and Social Psychology, 37*, 1871–1876.

Ajzen, I., & Fishbein, M. (1970). The prediction of behavior from attitudinal and normative variables. *Journal of Experimental Social Psychology, 6,* 466–487.

Ajzen, I., & Fishbein, M. (1977). Attitude-behavior relations: A theoretical analysis and review of empirical research. *Psychological Bulletin, 84,* 888–918.

Ajzen, I., & Fishbein, M. (1980). *Understanding attitudes and predicting social behavior.* Englewood Cliffs, NJ: Prentice-Hall.

Ajzen, I., & Madden, T. J. (1986). Prediction of goal-directed behavior: Attitudes, intentions, and perceived behavioral control. *Journal of Experimental Social Psychology, 22,* 453–474.

Aldrich, J. H., Sullivan, J. L., & Borgida, E. (1989). Foreign affairs and issue voting: Do presidential candidates "waltz before a blind audience"? *American Political Science Review, 83,* 123–141.

Allen, C. L. (1965). Photographing the TV audience. *Journal of Advertising Research, 5,* 2–8.

Alley, T. R. (1981). Head shape and the perception of cuteness. *Developmental Psychology, 17,* 650–654.

Allport, F. H. (1937). Toward a science of public opinion. *Public Opinion Quarterly, 1,* 7–23.

Allport, G. W. (1935). Attitudes. In C. Murchison (Ed.), *A handbook of social psychology* (pp. 798–844). Worcester, MA: Clark University Press.

Allport, G. W. (1954). *The nature of prejudice.* Reading, MA: Addison-Wesley.

Allport, G. W. (1985). The historical background of social psychology. In G. Lindzey & E. Aronson (Eds.), *The handbook of social psychology* (3rd ed., Vol. 1, pp. 1–46). New York: Random House.

Altemeyer, B. (1988). *Enemies of freedom: Understanding right-wing authoritarianism.* San Francisco: Jossey-Bass.

Altheide, D. L. (1976). *Creating reality: How TV news distorts news events.* Beverly Hills, CA: Sage.

Altschuler, B. E. (1982). *Keeping a finger on the public pulse: Private polling and presidential elections.* Westport, CT: Greenwood.

Altschuler, B. E. (1986). Lyndon Johnson and the public polls. *Public Opinion Quarterly, 50,* 285–299.

American Psychological Association. (1953). *Ethical standards of psychologists.* Washington, DC: Author.

American Psychological Association. (1967). *Casebook on ethical standards of psychologists.* Washington, DC: Author.

American Psychological Association. (1973). *Ethical principles in the conduct of research with human participants.* Washington, DC: Author.

American Psychological Association. (1975). Report of the task force on sex bias and sex-role stereotyping in psychotherapeutic practice. *American Psychologist, 30,* 1169–1175.

American Psychological Association. (1977). Guidelines for nonsexist language in APA journals. *American Psychologist, 32,* 487–494.

American Psychological Association. (1981). Ethical principles of psychologists. *American Psychologist, 36,* 633–638.

American Psychological Association. (1982). *Ethical principles in the conduct of research with human participants* (rev. ed.). Washington, DC: Author.

Amir, Y. (1969). Contact hypothesis in ethnic relations. *Psychological Bulletin, 71,* 319–342.

Anastasi, A. (1979). *Fields of applied psychology* (2nd ed.). New York: McGraw-Hill.

Andelin, H. B. (1980). *Fascinating womanhood* (rev. ed.). New York: Bantam.

Anderson, B. A., Silver, B. D., & Abramson, P. R. (1988). The effects of the race of the interviewer on race-related attitudes of black respondents in SRC/CPS national election studies. *Public Opinion Quarterly, 52,* 289–324.

Anderson, C. A., Lepper, M. R., & Ross, L. (1980). Perseverance of social theories: The role of explanation in the persistence of discredited information. *Journal of Personality and Social Psychology 39,* 1037–1049.

Anderson, D. R., & Collins, P. A. (1988). *The impact on children's education: Television's influence on cognitive development* (Office of Research Working Paper No. 2). Washington, DC: U.S. Department of Education.

Anderson, N. H. (1959). Test of a model of opinion change. *Journal of Abnormal and Social Psychology, 59,* 371–381.

Anderson, N. H. (1971). Integration theory and attitude change. *Psychological Review, 78,* 171–206.

Anderson, N. H., & Farkas, A. J. (1973). New light on order effects in attitude change. *Journal of Personality and Social Psychology, 28,* 88–93.

Andreyenkov, V., Robinson, J. P., & Popov, N. (1989). News media use and adolescents' information about nuclear issues: A Soviet-American comparison. *Journal of Communication, 39*(2), 95–104.

Antill, J. K. (1983). Sex-role complementarity versus similarity in married couples. *Journal of Personality and Social Psychology, 45,* 145–155.

Antill, J. K., & Cotton, S. (1988). Factors affecting the division of labor in households. *Sex Roles, 18,* 531–553.

Antill, J. K., Cotton, S., & Tindale, S. (1983). Egalitarian or traditional: Correlates of the perception of an ideal marriage. *Australian Journal of Psychology, 35,* 245–257.

Apostle, R. A., Glock, C. Y., Piazza, T., & Suelzle, M. (1983). *The anatomy of racial attitudes.* Berkeley: University of California Press.

Archer, J., & Lloyd, B. (1985). *Sex and gender* (rev. ed.). Cambridge, England: Cambridge University Press.

Arkin, R. M., Appelman, A. J., & Burger, J. M. (1980). Social anxiety, self-presentation, and the self-serving bias in causal attributions. *Journal of Personality and Social Psychology, 38,* 23–35.

Armor, D. J. (1988). School busing: A time for change. In P. A. Katz & D. A. Taylor (Eds.), *Eliminating racism: Profiles in controversy* (pp. 259–280). New York: Plenum.

Aronson, E. (1968). Dissonance theory: Progress and problems. In R. P. Abelson, E. Aronson, W. J. McGuire, T. M. Newcomb, M. J. Rosenberg, & P. H. Tannenbaum (Eds.), *Theories of cognitive consistency: A sourcebook* (pp. 5–27). Chicago: Rand McNally.

Aronson, E. (1969). The theory of cognitive dissonance: A current perspective. In L. Berkowitz (Ed.), *Advances in experimental social psychology* (Vol. 4, pp. 1–34). New York: Academic Press.

Aronson, E. (1990, April). *The return of the repressed: Dissonance theory makes a comeback.* Paper presented at Western Psychological Association meeting, Los Angeles.

Aronson, E., Blaney, N., Stephan, C., Sikes, J., & Snapp, M. (1978). *The jigsaw classroom.* Beverly Hills, CA: Sage.

Aronson, E., Brewer, M., & Carlsmith, J. M. (1985). Experimentation in social psychology. In G. Lindzey & E. Aronson (Eds.), *The handbook of social psychology* (3rd ed., Vol. 1, pp. 441–486). New York: Random House.

Aronson, E., & Golden, B. W. (1962). The effect of relevant and irrelevant aspects of communicator credibility on attitude change. *Journal of Personality, 30,* 135–146.

Aronson, E., & Linder, D. (1965). Gain and loss of esteem as determinants of interpersonal attraction. *Journal of Experimental Social Psychology, 1,* 156–171.

Arterton, F. C. (1984). *Media politics: The news strategies of presidential campaigns.* Lexington, MA: Heath.

Asch, S. E. (1946). Forming impressions of personality. *Journal of Abnormal and Social Psychology, 41,* 258–290.

Asch, S. E. (1956). Studies of independence and conformities. *Psychological Monographs, 70*(9, Whole No. 416).

Asher, S. R., & Allen, V. L. (1969). Racial preference and social comparison processes. *Journal of Social Issues, 25*(1), 157–166.

Ashmore, R. D., & Del Boca, F. K. (1976). Psychological approaches to understanding intergroup conflicts. In P. A. Katz (Ed.), *Towards the elimination of racism.* Elmsford, NY: Pergamon.

Assmus, G., Farley, J. U., & Lehmann, D. R. (1984). How advertising affects sales: Meta-analysis of econometric results. *Journal of Marketing Research, 21,* 65–74.

Atkin, C. K., Bowen, L., Nayman, O. B., & Sheinkopf, K. G. (1973). Quality versus quantity in televised political ads. *Public Opinion Quarterly, 37,* 209–224.

Atkin, C. K., Galloway, J., & Nayman, O. (1973). Mass communication and political socialization among college students. *Public Opinion Quarterly, 37,* 443–444.

Atkin, C., & Heald, G. (1976). Effects of political advertising. *Public Opinion Quarterly, 40,* 216–228.

Axelrod, R. (1967). The structure of public opinion on policy issues. *Public Opinion Quarterly, 31,* 51–60.

Axelrod, R. (1986). Presidential election coalitions in 1984. *American Political Science Review, 80,* 281–284.

Axelrod, S., & Apsche, J. (1982). *The effects of punishment on human behavior.* New York: Academic Press.

Bachman, J. G., & O'Malley, P. M. (1984). Yea-saying, nay-saying, and going to extremes: Black-white differences in response styles. *Public Opinion Quarterly, 48,* 491–509.

Backstrom, C. H. (1972). Congress and public: How representative is the one of the other? *Public Opinion Quarterly, 36,* 420–421.

Backstrom, C. H., & Hursh-Cesar, G. (1981). *Survey research* (2nd ed.). New York: Wiley.

Baer, R., Hinkle, S., Smith, K., & Fenton, M. (1980). Reactance as a function of actual versus projected autonomy. *Journal of Personality and Social Psychology, 38,* 416–422.

Bagdikian, B. H. (1962). Bias in the weekly newsmagazines. In R. M. Christenson & R. O. McWilliams (Eds.), *Voice of the people: Readings in public opinion and propaganda* (pp. 148–164). New York: McGraw-Hill.

Bagozzi, R. P. (1981). Attitudes, intentions, and behavior: A test of some key hypotheses. *Journal of Personality and Social Psychology, 41,* 607–627.

Bagozzi, R. P., Tybout, A. M., Craig, C. S., & Sternthal, B. (1979). The construct validity of the tripartite classification of attitudes. *Journal of Marketing Research, 16,* 88–95.

Bain, R. (1928). An attitude on attitude research. *American Journal of Sociology, 33,* 940–957.

Baldwin, D. (1986, March/April). The mud slingers. *Common Cause Magazine,* pp. 30–33.

Ball-Rokeach, S., Grube, J. W., & Rokeach, M. (1981). "Roots: The Next Generation": Who watched and with what effect? *Public Opinion Quarterly, 45,* 58–68.

Ball-Rokeach, S. J., Rokeach, M., & Grube, J. W. (1984). *The great American values test: Influencing behavior and belief through television.* New York: Free Press.

Bancroft, G., & Welch, E. H. (1946). Recent experience with problems of labor force measurement. *Journal of the American Statistical Association, 41,* 303–312.

Bandura, A. (1973). *Aggression: A social learning analysis.* Englewood Cliffs, NJ: Prentice-Hall.

Bandura, A. (1977). *Social learning theory.* Englewood Cliffs, NJ: Prentice-Hall.

Banks, W. C. (1976). White preference in blacks: A paradigm in search of a phenomenon. *Psychological Bulletin, 83,* 1179–1186.

Banks, W. M. (1970). The changing attitudes of black students. *Personnel and Guidance Journal, 48,* 739–745.

Barber, T. X., & Silver, M. J. (1968). Fact, fiction, and the experimenter bias effect. *Psychological Bulletin Monograph Supplement, 70* (6, Pt. 2), 1–29.

Bardes, B. A. (1986, May). *Men, women and foreign policy in the 1980s: Looking inward or outward?* Paper presented at American Association for Public Opinion Research meeting, St. Petersburg Beach, FL.

Barron, F. (1959). Review of the Edwards Personal Preference Schedule. In O. K. Buros (Ed.), *The fifth mental measurements yearbook* (pp. 114–117). Highland Park, NJ: Gryphon Press.

Barry, H., III, Bacon, M. K., & Child, I. L. (1957). A cross-cultural survey of some sex differences in socialization. *Journal of Abnormal and Social Psychology*, *55*, 327–332.

Bass, B. M. (1955). Authoritarianism or acquiescence? *Journal of Abnormal and Social Psychology*, *51*, 616–623.

Bauer, R. A. (1964). The obstinate audience: The influence process from the point of view of social communication. *American Psychologist*, *19*, 319–328.

Bauer, R. A. (1966). *Social indicators*. Cambridge, MA: MIT Press.

Bauer, R. A., & Greyser, S. A. (1968). *Advertising in America: The consumer view*. Boston: Graduate School of Business Administration, Harvard University.

Bauman, K. E., & Dent, C. W. (1982). Influence of an objective measure on self-reports of behavior. *Journal of Applied Psychology*, *67*, 623–628.

Baumeister, R. F. (1982). A self-presentational view of social phenomena. *Psychological Bulletin*, *91*, 3–26.

Baumeister, R. F., & Tice, D. M. (1984). Role of self-presentation and choice in cognitive dissonance under forced compliance: Necessary or sufficient causes? *Journal of Personality and Social Psychology*, *46*, 5–13.

Baumrind, D. (1985). Research using intentional deception: Ethical issues revisited. *American Psychologist*, *40*, 165–174.

Beach, B. H. (1980). Blood, sweat and fears. *Time*, September 8, p. 44.

Beal, R. S., & Hinckley, R. H. (1984). Presidential decision making and opinion polls. *The Annals of the American Academy of Political and Social Science*, *47*, 72–84.

Beaman, A. L., Cole, C. M., Preston, M., Klentz, B., & Steblay, N. M. (1983). Fifteen years of foot-in-the-door research: A meta-analysis. *Personality and Social Psychology Bulletin*, *9*, 181–196.

Beauchamp, T. L., Faden, R. R., Wallace, R. J., Jr., & Walters, L. R. (Eds.). (1982). *Ethical issues in social science research*. Baltimore: Johns Hopkins University Press.

Beck, K. H. (1979). The effects of positive and negative arousal upon attitudes, belief acceptance, behavioral intention, and behavior. *Journal of Social Psychology*, *107*, 239–251.

Behr, R. L., & Iyengar, S. (1985). Television news, real-world cues, and changes in the public agenda. *Public Opinion Quarterly*, *49*, 38–57.

Bem, D. J. (1965). An experimental analysis of self-persuasion. *Journal of Experimental Social* Psychology, *1*, 199–218.

Bem, D. J. (1967). Self-perception: An alternative interpretation of cognitive dissonance phenomena. *Psychological Review*, *74*, 183–200.

Bem, D. J. (1970). *Beliefs, attitudes, and human affairs*. Belmont, CA: Brooks/Cole.

Bem, D. J. (1972). Self-perception theory. In L. Berkowitz (Ed.), *Advances in experimental social psychology* (Vol. 6, pp. 1–62). New York: Academic Press.

Bem, D. J., & McConnell, H. K. (1970). Testing the self-perception explanation of dissonance phenomena: On the salience of premanipulation attitudes. *Journal of Personality and Social Psychology*, *14*, 23–31.

Bem, S. L. (1974). The measurement of psychological androgyny. *Journal of Consulting and Clinical Psychology*, *42*, 155–162.

Bem, S. L. (1975). Sex role adaptability: One consequence of psychological androgyny. *Journal of Personality and Social Psychology*, *31*, 634–643.

Bem S. L. (1979). Theory and measurement of androgyny: A reply to the Pedhazur-Tetenbaum and Locksley-Colten critiques. *Journal of Personality and Social Psychology*, *37*, 1047–1054.

Bem, S. L. (1981). Gender schema theory: A cognitive account of sex typing. *Psychological Review*, *88*, 354–364.

Bem, S. L., & Bem, D. J. (1973). Does sex-biased job advertising "aid and abet" sex discrimination? *Journal of Applied Social Psychology*, *3*, 6–18.

Benham, T. W. (1965). Polling for a presidential candidate: Some observations on the 1964 campaign. *Public Opinion Quarterly*, *29*, 185–199.

Beniger, J. R. (1983). The popular symbolic repertoire and mass communication. *Public Opinion Quarterly*, *47*, 479–484.

Bennett, E. (1955). Discussion, decision, commitment and consensus in "group decisions." *Human Relations*, *8*, 251–274.

Bennett, W. L. (1975). *The political mind and the political environment*. Lexington, MA: Heath.

Bennett, W. L. (1980). *Public opinion in American politics*. New York: Harcourt Brace Jovanovich.

Benson, J. M. (1982). The polls: U.S. military intervention. *Public Opinion Quarterly*, *46*, 592–598.

Bentler, P. M., & Speckart, G. (1979). Models of attitude-behavior relations. *Psychological Review*, *86*, 452–464.

Bentler, P. M., & Speckart, G. (1981). Attitudes "cause" behaviors: A structural equation analysis. *Journal of Personality and Social Psychology*, *40*, 226–238.

Berelson, B. R., Lazarsfeld, P. F., & McPhee, W. N. (1954). *Voting: A study of opinion formation in a presidential election*. Chicago: University of Chicago Press.

Berger, J., Rosenholtz, S. J., & Zelditch, M., Jr. (1980). Status organizing processes. *Annual Review of Sociology*, *6*, 479–508.

Bergmann, B. (1983, March/April). Women's plight: Bad and getting worse. *Challenge*, pp. 22–26.

Berkowitz, L. (1962). *Aggression: A social psychological analysis*. New York: McGraw-Hill.

Berkowitz, L. (1972). Social norms, feelings, and other factors affecting helping and altruism. In L. Berkowitz (Ed.), *Advances in experimental social psychology* (Vol. 6, pp. 63–108). New York: Academic Press.

Berkowitz, L., & Donnerstein, E. (1982). External validity is more than skin deep: Some answers to criticisms of laboratory experiments. *American Psychologist*, *37*, 245–257.

Berkun, M. M., Bialek, H. M., Kern, R. P., & Yagi, K. (1962). Experimental studies of psychological stress in man. *Psychological Monographs, 76*(15, Whole No. 534).

Bermant, G., Kelman, H. C., & Warwick, D. P. (Eds.). (1978). *The ethics of social intervention.* Washington, DC: Hemisphere.

Berzins, J. I., Welling, M. A., & Wetter, R. E. (1978). A new measure of psychological androgyny based on the Personality Research Form. *Journal of Consulting and Clinical Psychology, 46,* 126–138.

Bettman, J. R., & Weitz, B. A. (1983). Attributions in the board room: Causal reasoning in corporate annual reports. *Administrative Science Quarterly, 28,* 165–183.

Bierbrauer, G. (1973). *Effect of set, perspective, and temporal factors in attribution research.* Unpublished doctoral dissertation, Stanford University.

Billiet, J., & Loosveldt, G. (1988). Improvement of the quality of responses to factual survey questions by interviewer training. *Public Opinion Quarterly, 52,* 190–211.

Bird, C. (1968). *Born female: The high cost of keeping women down.* New York: David McKay.

Bishop, G. F. (1976). The effect of education on ideological consistency. *Public Opinion Quarterly, 40,* 337–348.

Bishop, G. F., & Frankovic, K. A. (1981). Ideological consensus and constraint among party leaders and followers in the 1978 election. *Micropolitics, 1,* 87–111.

Bishop, G. F., Oldendick, R. W., & Tuchfarber, A. J. (1982). Effects of presenting one versus two sides of an issue in survey questions. *Public Opinion Quarterly, 46,* 69–85.

Bishop, G. F., Oldendick, R. W., Tuchfarber, A. J., & Bennett, S. E. (1978). The changing structure of mass belief systems: Fact or artifact? *Journal of Politics, 40,* 781–787.

Bishop, G. F., Tuchfarber, A. J., & Oldendick, R. W. (1986). Opinions on fictitious issues: The pressure to answer survey questions. *Public Opinion Quarterly, 50,* 240–250.

Blackwell, J. E. (1985). *The black community: Diversity and unity* (2nd ed.). New York: Harper & Row.

Blakemore, J. E. O., LaRue, A. A., & Olejnik, A. B. (1979). Sex-appropriate toy preference and the ability to conceptualize toys as sex-role related. *Developmental Psychology, 15,* 339–340.

Blanchard, F. A., & Crosby, F. J. (Eds.). (1989). *Affirmative action in perspective.* New York: Springer-Verlag.

Blau, F. D., & Ferber, M. A. (1985). Women in the labor market: The last twenty years. In L. Larwood, A. H. Stromberg, & B. A. Gutek (Eds.), *Women and work: An annual review* (Vol. 1, pp. 19–49). Beverly Hills, CA: Sage.

Bleda, P. R. (1976). Conditioning and discrimination of affect and attraction. *Journal of Personality and Social Psychology, 34,* 1106–1113.

Block, J. H. (1973). Conceptions of sex role: Some cross-cultural and longitudinal perspectives. *American Psychologist, 28,* 512–526.

Blood, R. O., Jr., & Wolfe, D. M. (1960). *Husbands and wives: The dynamics of married living.* New York: Free Press.

Blumenthal, S. (1982). *The permanent campaign.* New York: Simon & Schuster.

Blumler, J. G., & McQuail, D. (1969). *Television in politics: Its uses and influence.* Chicago: University of Chicago Press.

Bobo, L. (1983). Whites' opposition to busing: Symbolic racism or realistic group conflict? *Journal of Personality and Social Psychology, 45,* 1196–1210.

Bobo, L. (1988). Group conflict, prejudice, and the paradox of contemporary racial attitudes. In P. A. Katz & D. A. Taylor (Eds.), *Eliminating racism: Profiles in controversy* (pp. 85–114). New York: Plenum.

Bochner, S. (Ed.). (1982). *Cultures in contact: Studies in cross-cultural interaction.* Elmsford, NY: Pergamon.

Bochner, S., & Insko, C. A. (1966). Communicator discrepancy, source credibility, and opinion change. *Journal of Personality and Social Psychology, 4,* 614–621.

Bogardus, E. S. (1925). Measuring social distance. *Journal of Applied Sociology, 9,* 299–308.

Bogardus, E. S. (1928). *Immigration and race attitudes.* Boston: Heath.

Bogart, L. (1972a). *Silent politics: Polls and the awareness of public opinion.* New York: Wiley-Interscience.

Bogart, L. (1972b). Warning: The Surgeon General has determined that TV violence is moderately dangerous to your child's mental health. *Public Opinion Quarterly, 36,* 491–521.

Borden, B. (1977, April). *Social stereotypes among college undergraduates.* Paper presented at Western Psychological Association meeting, Seattle.

Borgida, E., & Brekke, N. (1981). The base rate fallacy in attribution and prediction. In J. H. Harvey, W. J. Ickes, & R. F. Kidd (Eds.), *New directions in attribution research* (Vol. 3). Hillsdale, NJ: Erlbaum.

Borgida, E., & Campbell, B. (1982). Belief relevance and attitude-behavior consistency: The moderating role of personal experience. *Journal of Personality and Social Psychology, 42,* 239–247.

Borgida, E., & Nisbett, R. E. (1977). The differential impact of abstract vs. concrete information on decisions. *Journal of Applied Social Psychology, 7,* 258–271.

Bowen, L., Atkin, C. K., Sheinkopf, K. G., & Nayman, O. B. (1971). How voters react to electronic political advertising: An investigation of the 1970 election campaigns in Wisconsin and Colorado. *Public Opinion Quarterly, 35,* 457–458.

Bower, R. T., & de Gasparis, P. (1978). *Ethics in social research: Protecting the interests of human subjects.* New York: Praeger.

Bradburn, N. M., & Sudman, S. (1979). *Improving interview method and questionnaire design.* San Francisco: Jossey-Bass.

Brady, H. E., & Sniderman, P. M. (1985). Attitude attribution: A group basis for political reasoning. *American Political Science Review*, *79*, 1061–1078.

Bramel, D. (1963). Selection of a target for defensive projection. *Journal of Abnormal and Social Psychology*, *66*, 318–324.

Brayfield, A. H., & Lipsey, M. W. (1976). Public affairs psychology. In P. J. Woods (Ed.), *Career opportunities for psychologists: Expanding and emerging areas*. Washington, DC: American Psychological Association.

Breckler, S. J. (1984). Empirical validation of affect, behavior, and cognition as distinct components of attitude. *Journal of Personality and Social Psychology*, *47*, 1191–1205.

Brehm, J. W. (1966). *A theory of psychological reactance*. New York: Academic Press.

Brehm, J. W., & Cohen, A. R. (1962). *Explorations in cognitive dissonance*. New York: Wiley.

Brehm, S. S., & Brehm, J. W. (1981). *Psychological reactance: A theory of freedom and control*. New York: Academic Press.

Brent, E., & Granberg, D. (1982). Subjective agreement with the presidential candidates of 1976 and 1980. *Journal of Personality and Social Psychology*, *42*, 393–403.

Brewer, M. B., & Kramer, R. M. (1985). The psychology of intergroup attitudes and behavior. *Annual Review of Psychology*, *36*, 219–243.

Brewer, M. B., & Miller, N. (1984). Beyond the contact hypothesis: Theoretical perspectives on desegregation. In N. Miller & M. B. Brewer (Eds.), *Groups in contact: The psychology of desegregation* (pp. 281–302). Orlando, FL: Academic Press.

Brewer, M. B., & Miller, N. (1988). Contact and cooperation: When do they work? In P. A. Katz & D. A. Taylor (Eds.), *Eliminating racism: Profiles in controversy* (pp. 315–326). New York: Plenum.

Briere, J., & Lanktree, C. (1983). Sex-role related effects of sex bias in language. *Sex Roles*, *9*, 625–632.

Brigham, J. C. (1971). Ethnic stereotypes. *Psychological Bulletin*, *76*, 15–38.

Brigham, J. C., & Cook, S. W. (1970). The influence of attitude and judgments of plausibility: A replication and extension. *Educational and Psychological Measurement*, *30*, 283–292.

Brinberg, D. (1979). An examination of the determinants of intention and behavior: A comparison of two models. *Journal of Applied Social Psychology*, *9*, 560–575.

Brislin, R. W., & Olmstead, K. H. (1973). An examination of two models designed to predict behavior from attitude and other verbal measures. *Proceedings, 81st Annual Convention, APA*, *8*, 259–260.

Brock, T. C., & Shavitt, S. (1983). Cognitive-response analysis in advertising. In L. Percy & A. Woodside (Eds.), *Advertising and consumer psychology*. Lexington, MA: Heath.

Brodt, S. E., & Zimbardo, P. G. (1981). Modifying shyness-related social behavior through symptom misattribution. *Journal of Personality and Social Psychology*, *41*, 437–449.

Brody, R., & Sigelman, L. (1983). Presidential popularity and presidential elections: An update and extension. *Public Opinion Quarterly*, *47*, 325–328.

Bronfenbrenner, U. (1961). The mirror image in Soviet-American relations: A social psychologist's report. *Journal of Social Issues*, *17*(3), 45–56.

Broverman, I. K., Broverman, D. M., Clarkson, F. E., Rosenkrantz, P. S., & Vogel, S. R. (1970). Sex-role stereotypes and clinical judgments of mental health. *Journal of Consulting and Clinical Psychology 34*, 1–7.

Brown, R. (1965). *Social psychology*. New York: Free Press.

Browning, D. L. (1983). Aspects of authoritarian attitudes in ego development. *Journal of Personality and Social Psychology*, *45*, 137–144.

Bryson, J. B., & Bryson, R. B. (Eds.). (1978). Dual-career couples. *Psychology of Women Quarterly*, *3*, 5–120.

Buchanan, W. (1986). Election predictions: An empirical assessment. *Public Opinion Quarterly*, *50*, 222–227.

Buchanan, W., & Cantril, H. (1953). *How nations see each other: A study in public opinion*. Urbana: University of Illinois Press.

Budd, R. J. (1987). Response bias and the theory of reasoned action. *Social Cognition*, *5*, 95–107.

Budd, R. J., & Spencer, C. (1984). Latitude of rejection, centrality and certainty: Variables affecting the relationship between attitudes, norms and behavioural intentions. *British Journal of Social Psychology*, *23*, 1–8.

Burger, J. M. (1986). Temporal effects on attributions: Actor and observer differences. *Social Cognition*, *4*, 377–387.

Burn, S. M., & Oskamp, S. (1989). Ingroup biases and the U.S.-Soviet conflict. *Journal of Social Issues*, *45*(2), 73–89.

Burnham, W. D. (1970). *Critical elections and the mainsprings of American politics*. New York: Norton.

Burnham, W. D. (1985). The 1984 election and the future of American politics. In E. Sandoz & C. V. Crabb, Jr. (Eds.), *Election 84: Landslide without a mandate?* (pp. 204–260). New York: New American Library.

Busch, R. J., & Lieske, J. A. (1985). Does time of voting affect exit poll results? *Public Opinion Quarterly*, *49*, 94–104.

Butler, M., & Paisley, W. (Eds.). (1980). *Women and the mass media: Sourcebook for research and action*. New York: Human Sciences Press.

Byrne, D. (1971). *The attraction paradigm*. New York: Academic Press.

Cacioppo, J. T., & Petty, R. E. (1979a). Effects of message repetition and position on cognitive responses, recall, and persuasion. *Journal of Personality and Social Psychology*, *37*, 97–109.

Cacioppo, J. T., & Petty, R. E. (1979b). Attitudes and cognitive response: An electrophysiological approach. *Journal of Personality and Social Psychology*, *37*, 1281–1299.

Cacioppo, J. T., & Petty, R. E. (1980). Sex differences in influenceability: Toward specifying the underlying processes. *Personality and Social Psychology Bulletin*, *6*, 651–656.

Cacioppo, J. T., & Petty, R. E. (1981a). Effects of extent of thought on the pleasantness ratings of P-O-X triads: Evidence for three judgmental tendencies in evaluating social situations. *Journal of Personality and Social Psychology, 40,* 1000–1009.

Cacioppo J. T., & Petty, R. E. (1981b). Social psychological procedures for cognitive response assessment: The thought-listing technique. In T. V. Merluzzi, C. R. Glass, & M. Genest (Eds.), *Cognitive assessment.* New York: Guilford.

Cacioppo, J. T., & Petty, R. E. (1983). *Social psychophysiology: A sourcebook.* New York: Guilford.

Cahalan, D. (1968). Correlates of respondent inaccuracy in the Denver validity study. *Public Opinion Quarterly, 32,* 607–621.

Cahalan, D. (1989). The *Digest* poll rides again! *Public Opinion Quarterly, 53,* 129–133.

Calder, B. J., Insko, C. A., & Yandell, B. (1974). The relation of cognitive and memorial processes to persuasion in a simulated jury trial. *Journal of Applied Social Psychology, 4,* 62–93.

Caldicott, H. (1980). *Nuclear madness: What can you do?* New York: Bantam.

Campbell, A. (1962). Has television reshaped politics? *Columbia Journalism Review, 1*(2), 10–13.

Campbell, A. (1964). Voters and elections: Past and present. *Journal of Politics, 26,* 745–757.

Campbell, A. (1966). A classification of presidential elections. In A. Campbell, P. E. Converse, W. E. Miller, & D. E. Stokes, *Elections and the political order* (pp. 66–77). New York: Wiley.

Campbell, A. (1971). *White attitudes toward black people.* Ann Arbor: Institute for Social Research, University of Michigan.

Campbell, A. (1981). *The sense of well-being in America: Recent patterns and trends.* New York: McGraw-Hill.

Campbell, A., Converse, P. E., Miller, W. E., & Stokes, D. E. (1960). *The American voter.* New York: Wiley.

Campbell, A., Converse, P. E., Miller, W. E., & Stokes, D. E. (1966). *Elections and the political order.* New York: Wiley.

Campbell, A., Converse, P. E., & Rodgers, W. L. (1976). *The quality of American life: Perceptions, evaluations, and satisfactions.* New York: Russell Sage Foundation.

Campbell, A., Gurin, G., & Miller, W. E. (1954). *The voter decides.* New York: Harper & Row.

Campbell, A., & Stokes, D. E. (1959). Partisan attitudes and the presidential vote. In E. Burdick & A. J. Brodbeck (Eds.), *American voting behavior* (pp. 353–371). Glencoe, IL: Free Press.

Campbell, B. A. (1981). Race-of-interviewer effects among Southern adolescents. *Public Opinion Quarterly, 45,* 231–244.

Campbell, D. T. (1947). *The generality of social attitudes.* Unpublished doctoral dissertation, University of California, Berkeley.

Campbell, D. T. (1963). Social attitudes and other acquired behavioral dispositions. In S. Koch (Ed.), *Psychology: A study of a science* (Vol. 6, pp. 94–172). New York: McGraw-Hill.

Campbell, D. T. (1967). Stereotypes and the perception of group differences. *American Psychologist, 22,* 817–829.

Campbell, D. T. (1971, September). *Methods for the experimenting society.* Paper presented at American Psychological Association meeting, Washington, DC.

Campbell, D. T., & Stanley, J. C. (1966). *Experimental and quasi-experimental designs for research.* Chicago: Rand McNally.

Canary, D. J., & Seibold, D. R. (1984). *Attitude and behavior: An annotated bibliography.* New York: Praeger.

Cannell, C. F., Miller, P. V., & Oksenberg, L. (1981). Research on interviewing techniques. In S. Leinhardt (Ed.), *Sociological methodology.* San Francisco: Jossey-Bass.

Canon, L. K., & Mathews, K. E., Jr. (1972). Concern over personal health and smoking-relevant beliefs and behavior. *Proceedings, 80th Annual Convention, APA, 7,* 271–272.

Cantril, H. (1940). *The invasion from Mars.* Princeton, NJ: Princeton University Press.

Cantril, H. (1967). *The human dimension: Experiences in policy research.* New Brunswick, NJ: Rutgers University Press.

Cantril, H., & Allport, G. W. (1935). *The psychology of radio.* New York: Harper.

Caplan, N. (1970). The new ghetto man: A review of recent empirical studies. *Journal of Social Issues, 26*(1), 59–73.

Caplan, N., Morrison, A., & Stambaugh, R. J. (1975). *The use of social science knowledge in policy decisions at the national level: A report to respondents.* Ann Arbor: Institute for Social Research, University of Michigan.

Caplow, T. (1982). Decades of public opinion: Comparing NORC and Middletown data. *Public Opinion, 5*(5), 30–31.

Carlsmith, J. M., Collins, B. E., & Helmreich, R. L. (1966). Studies on forced compliance: I. The effect of pressure for compliance on attitude change produced by face-to-face role-playing and anonymous essay writing. *Journal of Personality and Social Psychology 4,* 1–13.

Carlson, E. R. (1956). Attitude change through modification of attitude structure. *Journal of Abnormal and Social Psychology, 52,* 256–261.

Carlston, D. E., & Cohen, J. L. (1980). A closer examination of subject roles. *Journal of Personality and Social Psychology, 38,* 857–870.

Carter, D. B., & McCloskey, L. A. (1983–1984). Peers and the maintenance of sex-typed behavior: The development of children's conceptions of cross-gender behavior in their peers. *Social Cognition, 2,* 294–314.

Cartwright, D., & Harary, F. (1956). Structural balance: A generalization of Heider's theory. *Psychological Review, 63,* 277–293.

Ceci, S. J., & Kain, E. L. (1982). Jumping on the bandwagon with the underdog: The impact of attitude polls on polling behavior. *Public Opinion Quarterly, 46,* 228–242.

Cervone, D., & Peake, P. K. (1986). Anchoring, efficacy, and action: The influence of judgmental heuristics on self-efficacy judgments and behavior. *Journal of Personality and Social Psychology, 50*, 492–501.

Chafe, W. H. (1976). Looking backward in order to look forward: Women, work and social values in America. In J. M. Kreps (Ed.), *Women and the American economy: A look to the 1980's*. Englewood Cliffs, NJ: Prentice-Hall.

Chafetz, J. S. (1974). *Masculine/feminine or human? An overview of the sociology of sex roles*. Itasca, IL: Peacock.

Chaffee, S. H. (1982). Mass media and interpersonal channels: Competitive, convergent or complementary? In G. Gumpert & R. Cathcart (Eds.), *Inter/media: Interpersonal communication in a media world* (pp. 57–77). New York: Oxford University Press.

Chaiken, S. (1980). Heuristic versus systematic information processing and the use of source versus message cues in persuasion. *Journal of Personality and Social Psychology, 39,* 752–766.

Chaiken, S., & Baldwin, M. W. (1981). Affective-cognitive consistency and the effect of salient behavioral information on the self-perception of attitudes. *Journal of Personality and Social Psychology, 41*, 1–12.

Chaiken, S., & Eagly, A. H. (1976). Communication modality as a determinant of message persuasiveness and message comprehensibility. *Journal of Personality and Social Psychology, 34*, 605–614.

Chaiken, S., & Stangor, C. (1987). Attitudes and attitude change. *Annual Review of Psychology, 38*, 575–630.

Chandler, R. (1972). *Public opinion: Changing attitudes on contemporary political and social issues*. New York: Bowker.

Chapanis, N. P., & Chapanis, A. (1964). Cognitive dissonance: Five years later. *Psychological Bulletin, 61*, 1–22.

Chassin, L., Presson, C. C., & Sherman, S. J. (1984). Cigarette smoking and adolescent psychosocial development. *Basic and Applied Social Psychology, 5*, 295–315.

Chesler, P. (1972). *Women and madness*. Garden City, NY: Doubleday.

Chethick, M., Fleming, E., Meyer, M. F., & McCoy, J. N. (1967). Quest for identity. *American Journal of Orthopsychiatry, 37*, 71–77.

Childs, H. L. (1965). *Public opinion: Nature, formation, and role*. Princeton, NJ: Van Nostrand.

Chivian, E., Chivian, S., Lifton, R. J., & Mack, J. E. (Eds.). (1982). *Last aid: The medical dimensions of nuclear war*. San Francisco: Freeman.

Chivian, E., Mack, J., & Waletzky, J. (1983). *What Soviet children are saying about nuclear war*. Unpublished manuscript, International Physicians for the Prevention of Nuclear War and Harvard Medical School, Department of Psychiatry.

Christensen, L. (1988). Deception in psychological research: When is its use justified? *Personality and Social Psychology Bulletin, 14*, 664–675.

Christenson, P. G., & Roberts, D. F. (1983). The role of television in the formation of children's social attitudes. In M. J. A. Howe (Ed.), *Learning from television: Psychological and educational research* (pp. 79–99). London: Academic Press.

Christie, R., Havel, J., & Seidenberg, B. (1958). Is the F scale irreversible? *Journal of Abnormal and Social Psychology, 56*, 143–159.

Christie, R., & Jahoda, M. (Eds.). (1954). *Studies in the scope and method of "the authoritarian personality."* New York: Free Press.

Church, G. J. (1982, November 15). Slinging mud and money. *Time*, pp. 43–44.

Church, G. J. (1987, June 22). Back to the wall: Reagan rallies with a strong speech. *Time*, pp. 18–20.

Cialdini, R. B. (1988). *Influence: Science and practice* (2nd ed.). Glenview, IL: Scott, Foresman.

Cialdini, R. B., Levy, A., Herman, P., Kozlowski, L., & Petty, R. E. (1976). Elastic shifts of opinion: Determinants of direction and durability. *Journal of Personality and Social Psychology, 34*, 663–672.

Cialdini, R. B., & Petty, R. E. (1981). Anticipatory opinion effects. In R. E. Petty, T. M. Ostrom, & T. C. Brock (Eds.), *Cognitive responses in persuasion* (pp. 217–235). Hillsdale, NJ: Erlbaum.

Cialdini, R. B., Petty, R. E., & Cacioppo, J. T. (1981). Attitude and attitude change. *Annual Review of Psychology, 32*, 357–404.

Citrin, J., Green, D., & Reingold, B. (1987). The soundness of our structure: Confidence in the Reagan years. *Public Opinion, 10*(4), 18–19 & 59–60.

Clark, C. C. (1969). Television and social controls: Some observations on the portrayal of ethnic minorities. *Television Quarterly, 8*, 18–22.

Clark, K. B., & Clark, M. P. (1947). Racial identification and preference in Negro children. In T. M. Newcomb & E. L. Hartley (Eds.), *Readings in social psychology* (pp. 169–178). New York: Holt, Rinehart & Winston.

Clausen, A. R. (1968). Response validity: Vote report. *Public Opinion Quarterly, 32*, 588–606.

Cnudde, C. F., & McCrone, D. J. (1966). The linkage between constituency attitudes and Congressional voting behavior: A causal model. *American Political Science Review, 60*, 66–72.

Cohen, B. C. (1963). *The press and foreign policy*. Princeton, NJ: Princeton University Press.

Colasanto, D. (1988). Black attitudes. *Public Opinion, 10*(5), 45–49.

Coleman, J. S. (1975). Racial segregation in the schools: New research with new policy implications. *Phi Delta Kappan, 57*(2), 75–78.

Coleman, J. S., Campbell, E. Q., Hobson, C. J., McPartland, J., Mood, A. M., Weinfeld, F. O., & York, R. L. (1966). *Equality of educational opportunity*. Washington, DC: U.S. Government Printing Office.

Coles, R. (1968). *Children of crisis*. Boston: Faber.

Coles, R. (1986). *The political life of children*. Boston: Atlantic Monthly Press.

Collins, B. E. (1969). The effect of monetary inducements on the amount of attitude change produced by forced compliance. In A. C. Elms (Ed.), *Role playing, reward, and attitude change* (pp. 209–223). New York: Van Nostrand Reinhold.

Collins, B. E., & Hoyt, M. F. (1972). Personal responsibility-for-consequences: An integration and extension of the forced compliance literature. *Journal of Experimental Social Psychology, 8,* 558–593.

Committee on Community Reactions to the Concorde. (1977). *Community reactions to the Concorde: An assessment of the trial period at Dulles Airport.* Washington, DC: National Academy of Sciences.

Comstock, G. (1985). Television and film violence. In S. Apter & A. Goldstein (Eds.), *Youth violence: Programs and prospects.* New York: Pergamon.

Comstock, G. (1988). Today's audiences, tomorrow's media. In S. Oskamp (Ed.), *Television as a social issue: Applied social psychology annual 8* (pp. 324–345). Newbury Park, CA: Sage.

Comstock, G., Chaffee, S., Katzman, N., McCombs, M., & Roberts, D. (1978). *Television and human behavior.* New York: Columbia University Press.

Conger, J. J. (1981). Freedom and commitment: Families, youth and social change. *American Psychologist, 36,* 1475–1484.

Constantinople, A. (1973). Masculinity-femininity: An exception to the famous dictum? *Psychological Bulletin, 80,* 389–405.

Converse, J. M. (1984). Strong arguments and weak evidence: The open/closed questioning controversy of the 1940s. *Public Opinion Quarterly, 48,* 267–282.

Converse, J. M. (1987). *Survey research in the United States: Roots and emergence, 1890–1960.* Berkeley: University of California Press.

Converse, J. M., & Presser, S. (1986). *Survey questions: Handcrafting the standardized questionnaire.* Beverly Hills, CA: Sage.

Converse, P. E. (1964). The nature of belief systems in mass publics. In D. Apter (Ed.), *Ideology and discontent* (pp. 206–261). New York: Free Press.

Converse, P. E. (1966). The concept of a normal vote. In A. Campbell, P. E. Converse, W. E. Miller, & D. E. Stokes, *Elections and the political order.* New York: Wiley.

Converse, P. E. (1974). Comment: The status of nonattitudes. *American Political Science Review, 68,* 650–660.

Converse, P. E. (1975). Public opinion and voting behavior. In F. Greenstein & N. Polsby (Eds.), *Handbook of political science* (Vol. 4, pp. 75–169). Reading, MA: Addison-Wesley.

Converse, P. E. (1976). *The dynamics of party support: Cohort analyzing party identification.* Beverly Hills, CA: Sage.

Converse, P. E. (1980). Comment: Rejoinder to Judd and Milburn. *American Sociological Review, 45,* 644–646.

Converse, P. E., Dotson, J. D., Hoag, W. J., & McGee, W. H., III. (Eds.). (1980). *American social attitudes data sourcebook 1947–1978.* Cambridge, MA: Harvard University Press.

Converse, P. E., & Markus, G. B. (1979). Plus ça change. . . .The new CPS election study panel. *American Political Science Review, 73,* 32–49.

Converse, P. E., Miller, W. E., Rusk, J. G., & Wolfe, A. C. (1969). Continuity and change in American politics: Parties and issues in the 1968 election. *American Political Science Review, 63,* 1083–1105.

Converse, P. E., & Pierce, R. (1985). *Political representation in France.* Cambridge, MA: Harvard University Press.

Conway, M. M. (1984). The use of polls in congressional, state, and local elections. *Annals of the American Academy of Political and Social Science, 472,* 97–105.

Conway, M. M., Wyckoff, M., Feldbaum, E., & Ahern, D. (1981). The news media in children's political socialization. *Public Opinion Quarterly, 45,* 164–178.

Cook, E. P. (1985) *Psychological androgyny.* New York: Pergamon.

Cook, S. W. (1969). Motives in a conceptual analysis of attitude-related behavior. *Nebraska Symposium on Motivation, 17,* 179–231.

Cook, S. W. (1979). Social science and school desegregation: Did we mislead the Supreme Court? *Personality and Social Psychology Bulletin, 5,* 420–437.

Cook, S. W. (1984). The 1954 Social Science Statement and school desegregation: A reply to Gerard. *American Psychologist, 39,* 819–832.

Cook, S. W., & Selltiz, C. (1964). A multiple-indicator approach to attitude measurement. *Psychological Bulletin, 62,* 36–55.

Cook, T. D., Appleton, H., Conner, R. F., Shaffer, A., Tamkin, G., & Weber, S. J. (1975). *"Sesame Street" revisited.* New York: Russell Sage Foundation.

Cook, T. D., Bean, J. R., Calder, B. J., Frey, R., Krovetz, M. L., & Reisman, S. R. (1970). Demand characteristics and three conceptions of the frequently deceived subject. *Journal of Personality and Social Psychology, 14,* 185–194.

Cook, T. D., & Campbell, D. T. (1979). *Quasi-experimentation: Design & analysis issues for field settings.* Chicago: Rand McNally.

Cook, T. D., & Flay, B. R. (1978). The persistence of experimentally induced attitude change. In L. Berkowitz (Ed.), *Advances in experimental social psychology* (Vol. 11, pp. 1–57). New York: Academic Press.

Cook, T. D., Gruder, C. L., Hennigan, K. M., & Flay, B. R. (1979). History of the sleeper effect: Some logical pitfalls in accepting the null hypothesis. *Psychological Bulletin, 86,* 662–679.

Cook, T., & Insko, C. (1968). Persistence of attitude change as a function of conclusion re-exposure: A laboratory-field experiment. *Journal of Personality and Social Psychology, 9,* 322–328.

Coombs, C. H. (1950). Psychological scaling without a unit of measurement. *Psychological Review, 57,* 145–158.

Coombs, S. L. (1981). Editorial endorsements and electoral outcomes. In M. B. MacKuen & S. L. Coombs (Eds.), *More than news* (pp. 145–230). Beverly Hills, CA: Sage.

Cooper, J., & Croyle, R. T. (1984). Attitudes and attitude change. *Annual Review of Psychology, 35*, 395–426.

Cordes, C. (1982). NAS gives behavioral research a boost: Study calls the benefits "significant and lasting." *APA Monitor, 13*(8), 40–41.

Costrich, N., Feinstein, J., Kidder, L., Marecek, J., & Pascale, L. (1975). When stereotypes hurt: Three studies of penalties for sex-role reversals. *Journal of Experimental Social Psychology, 11*, 520–530.

Cotter, P. R., Cohen, J., & Coulter, P. B. (1982). Race-of-interviewer effects in telephone interviews. *Public Opinion Quarterly, 46*, 278–284.

Cotton, J. L. (1985). Cognitive dissonance in selective exposure. In D. Zillman & J. Bryant (Eds.), *Selective exposure to communication* (pp. 11–33). Hillsdale, NJ: Erlbaum.

Cottrell, N. B. (1975). Heider's structural balance principle as a conceptual rule. *Journal of Personality and Social Psychology, 31*, 713–720.

Couch, A., & Keniston, K. (1960). Yeasayers and naysayers: Agreeing response set as a personality variable. *Journal of Abnormal and Social Psychology, 60*, 151–174.

Courtney, A. E., & Whipple, T. W. (1983). *Sex stereotyping in advertising.* Lexington, MA: Lexington.

Coverman, S. (1985). Explaining husbands' participation in domestic labor. *Sociological Quarterly, 26*, 81–97.

Cowan, M. L., & Stewart, B. J. (1977). A methodological study of sex stereotypes. *Sex Roles, 3*, 205–216.

Cox, A. (1983, October). The business of attitudes. *United*, p. 11.

Crawford, M., & English, L. (1984). Generic versus specific inclusion of women in language: Effects on recall. *Journal of Psycholinguistic Research, 13*, 373–381.

Crespi, I. (1971). What kinds of attitude measures are predictive of behavior? *Public Opinion Quarterly, 35*, 327–334.

Crespi, I. (1980). Polls as journalism. *Public Opinion Quarterly, 44*, 462–476.

Crespi, I. (1988). *Pre-election polling: Sources of accuracy and error.* New York: Russell Sage Foundation.

Crewe, I. (1987). Why the British don't like us anymore. *Public Opinion, 9*(6), 51–56.

Crittenden, J. (1962). Aging and party affiliation. *Public Opinion Quarterly, 26*, 648–657.

Crocker, J., & Major, B. (1989). Social stigma and self-esteem: The self-protective properties of stigma. *Psychological Review, 96*, 608–630.

Cronbach, L. J. (1975). Beyond the two disciplines of scientific psychology. *American Psychologist, 30*, 116–127.

Cronbach, L. J. (1984). *Essentials of psychological testing* (4th ed.). New York: Harper & Row.

Cronbach, L. J., & Furby, L. (1970). How should we measure "change"—or should we? *Psychological Bulletin, 74*, 68–80.

Cronin, T. E. (1985). The presidential election of 1984. In E. Sandoz & C. V. Crabb, Jr. (Eds.), *Election 84: Landslide without a mandate?* (pp. 28–65). New York: New American Library.

Cronkhite, G. (1977). Scales measuring general evaluation with minimal distortion. *Public Opinion Quarterly, 41*, 65–73.

Crooks, R. C. (1970). The effects of an interracial preschool program upon racial preference, knowledge of racial differences, and racial identification. *Journal of Social Issues, 26*(4), 137–144.

Crosby, F., Bromley, S., & Saxe, L. (1980). Recent unobtrusive studies of black and white discrimination and prejudice: A literature review. *Psychological Bulletin, 87*, 546–563.

Crosby, F., & Herek, G. M. (1986). Male sympathy with the situation of women: Does personal experience make a difference? *Journal of Social Issues, 42*(2), 55–66.

Crosby, F. J., Pufall, A., Snyder, R. C., O'Connell, M., & Whalen, P. (1989). The denial of personal disadvantage among you, me, and all the other ostriches. In M. Crawford & M. Gentry (Eds.), *Gender and thought: Psychological perspectives* (pp. 79–99). New York: Springer-Verlag.

Crossley, H. M. (1971). Honesty with respondents and interviewers. *Public Opinion Quarterly, 35*, 476–478.

Crowne, D. P., & Marlowe, D. (1964). *The approval motive.* New York: Wiley.

Crusco, A. H., & Wetzel, C. G. (1984). The Midas touch: The effects of interpersonal touch on restaurant tipping. *Personality and Social Psychology Bulletin, 10*, 512–517.

Culbertson, F. M. (1957). Modification of an emotionally held attitude through role playing. *Journal of Abnormal and Social Psychology, 54*, 230–234.

Cutler, N. E. (1969). Generation, maturation, and party affiliation: A cohort analysis. *Public Opinion Quarterly, 33*, 583–588.

Cutlip, S. C. (1954). Content and flow of AP news—From trunk to TTS to reader. *Journalism Quarterly, 31*, 434–446.

D'Andrade, R. G. (1966). Sex differences and cultural institutions. In E. E. Maccoby (Ed.), *The development of sex differences* (pp. 174–204). Stanford, CA: Stanford University Press.

Darley, J. M., & Fazio, R. H. (1980). Expectancy confirmation processes arising in the social interaction sequence. *American Psychologist, 35*, 867–881.

Darley, J. M., & Gross, P. H. (1983). A hypothesis-confirming bias in labeling effects. *Journal of Personality and Social Psychology, 44*, 20–33.

David, D. S., & Brannon, R. (Eds.). (1976). *The forty-nine percent majority: The male sex role.* Reading, MA: Addison-Wesley.

Davidson, A. R., & Jaccard, J. (1979). Variables that moderate the attitude-behavior relation: Results of a longitudinal survey. *Journal of Personality and Social Psychology, 37*, 1364–1376.

Davis, J. (1975). Communism, conformity, cohorts, and categories: American tolerance in 1954 and 1972–73. *American Journal of Sociology, 81*, 491–513.

Dawes, R. M., & Smith, T. L. (1985). Attitude and opinion measurement. In G. Lindzey & E. Aronson (Eds.), *The handbook of social psychology* (3rd ed., Vol. 1, pp. 509–566). New York: Random House.

Dayhoff, S. A. (1983). Sexist language and person perceptions: Evaluation of candidates from newspaper articles. *Sex Roles, 9*, 543–555.

Deaux, K. (1985). Sex and gender. *Annual Review of Psychology, 36*, 49–81.

Deaux, K., & Lewis, L. L. (1984). The structure of gender stereotypes: Interrelationships among components and gender label. *Journal of Personality and Social Psychology, 46*, 991–1004.

de Boer, C. (1977). The polls: Women at work. *Public Opinion Quarterly, 35*, 275–290.

de Boer, C. (1980). The polls: Changing attitudes and policies toward China. *Public Opinion Quarterly, 44*, 267–273.

de Boer, C. (1985). The polls: The European peace movement and deployment of nuclear missiles. *Public Opinion Quarterly, 49*, 119–132.

Deci, E. L., & Ryan, R. M. (1980). The empirical exploration of intrinsic motivational processes. In L. Berkowitz (Ed.), *Advances in experimental social psychology* (Vol. 13). New York: Academic Press.

Declercq, E. (1978). The use of polling in congressional campaigns. *Public Opinion Quarterly, 42*, 247–258.

Declercq, E., Hurley, T. L., & Luttbeg, N. R. (1975). Voting in American presidential elections: 1956–1972. In S. A. Kirkpatrick (Ed.), *American electoral behavior: Change and stability* (pp. 9–33). Beverly Hills, CA: Sage.

DeFleur, M. L., & Westie, F. R. (1958). Verbal attitudes and overt acts: An experiment on the salience of attitudes. *American Sociological Review, 23*, 667–673.

DeFleur, M. L., & Westie, F. R. (1963). Attitude as a scientific concept. *Social Forces, 42*, 17–31.

DeJong, W. (1979). An examination of self-perception mediation of the foot-in-the-door effect. *Journal of Personality and Social Psychology, 37*, 2221–2239.

DeMott, J. S. (1986, June 30). The racism next door. *Time*, pp. 40–41.

Desruisseaux, P. (1984, March 28). Expert on campaign finance calculates the cost of presidential politics. *The Chronicle of Higher Education*, pp. 5–7.

Deutsch, F. M. (1989). The false consensus effect: Is the self-justification hypothesis justified? *Basic and Applied Social Psychology, 10*, 83–99.

Deutsch, K. W., & Merritt, R. L. (1965). Effects of events on national and international images. In H. C. Kelman (Ed.), *International behavior: A social-psychological analysis* (pp. 132–187). New York: Holt, Rinehart & Winston.

Deutsch, M. (1983). The prevention of World War III: A psychological perspective. *Political Psychology, 4*, 3–31.

Deutsch, M., & Collins, M. E. (1951). *Interracial housing: A psychological evaluation of a social experiment.* Minneapolis: University of Minnesota Press.

Deutsch, M., & Krauss, R. M. (1965). *Theories in social psychology.* New York: Basic Books.

Deutscher, I. (1965). Words and deeds: Social science and social policy. *Social Problems, 13*, 235–254.

Deutscher, I. (1973). *What we say/what we do: Sentiments and acts.* Glenview, IL: Scott, Foresman.

Deutschmann, P. J. (1962). Viewing, conversation, and voting intentions. In S. Kraus (Ed.), *The great debates* (pp. 232–252). Bloomington: Indiana University Press.

Dillehay, R. C. (1973). On the irrelevance of the classical negative evidence concerning the effect of attitudes on behavior. *American Psychologist, 28*, 887–891.

Dillman, D. A. (1978). *Mail and telephone surveys: The total design method.* New York: Wiley.

Donohue, G. A., Tichenor, P. J., & Olien, C. N. (1975). Mass media and the knowledge gap: A hypothesis reconsidered. *Communication Research, 2*, 3–23.

Doob, A. N. (1982). The role of the mass media in creating exaggerated levels of fear of being the victim of a violent crime. In P. Stringer (Ed.), *Confronting social issues: Some applications of social psychology* (Vol. 1). London: Academic Press.

Doob, L. W. (1947). The behavior of attitudes. *Psychological Review, 54*, 135–156.

Doob, L. W. (1950). Goebbels' principles of propaganda. *Public Opinion Quarterly, 14*, 419–442.

Downing, M. (1974). Heroine of the daytime serial. *Journal of Communication, 24*(2), 130–137.

Downs, A. C. (1981). Sex-role stereotyping on prime-time television. *Journal of Genetic Psychology, 138*, 253–258.

Dreyer, E. C. (1971). Media use and electoral choices: Some political consequences of information exposure. *Public Opinion Quarterly, 35*, 544–553.

Duncan, B., & Duncan, O. D. (1978). *Sex typing and social roles: A research report.* New York: Academic Press.

Dutton, D. G. (1971). Reactions of restaurateurs to blacks and whites violating restaurant dress requirements. *Canadian Journal of Behavioral Science, 3*, 298–302.

Eagly, A. H. (1967). Involvement as a determinant of response to favorable and unfavorable information. *Journal of Personality and Social Psychology Monograph Supplement, 7*, No. 643, 1–15.

Eagly, A. H. (1974). The comprehensibility of persuasive arguments as a determinant of opinion change. *Journal of Personality and Social Psychology, 29*, 758–773.

Eagly, A. H. (1981). Recipient characteristics as determinants of responses to persuasion. In R. E. Petty, T. M. Ostrom, & T. C. Brock (Eds.), *Cognitive responses in persuasion* (pp. 173–195). Hillsdale, NJ: Erlbaum.

Eagly, A. H., & Chaiken, S. (1984). Cognitive theories of persuasion. In L. Berkowitz (Ed.), *Advances in experimental social psychology* (Vol. 17, pp. 268–359). New York: Academic Press.

Eagly, A. H., Chaiken, S., & Wood, W. (1981). An attributional analysis of persuasion. In J. H. Harvey, W. J. Ickes, & R. F. Kidd (Eds.), *New directions in attribution research* (Vol. 3, pp. 37–62). Hillsdale, NJ: Erlbaum.

Eagly, A. H., Wood, W., & Chaiken, S. (1978). Causal inferences about communicators and their effect on opinion change. *Journal of Personality and Social Psychology, 36*, 424–435.

Easton, D., & Dennis, J. (1965). The child's image of government. *Annals of the American Academy of Political and Social Science, 361*, 40–57.

Edelman, M. W. (1973). Southern school desegregation, 1954–1973: A judicial-political overview. *Annals of the American Academy of Political and Social Science, 407*, 32–42.

Edgell, S. E., Himmelfarb, S., & Duchan, K. L. (1982). Validity of forced responses in a randomized response model. *Sociological Methods and Research, 11*, 89–100.

Edwards, A. L. (1964). The assessment of human motives by means of personality scales. In D. Levine (Ed.), *Nebraska symposium on motivation* (Vol. 12, pp. 135–162). Lincoln: University of Nebraska Press.

Edwards, A. L., & Ashworth, C. D. (1977). A replication study of item selection for the Bem Sex-Role Inventory. *Applied Psychological Measurement, 1*, 501–508.

Edwards, A. L., & Kilpatrick, F. P. (1948). A technique for the construction of attitude scales. *Journal of Applied Psychology, 32*, 374–384.

Edwards, C. D., & Williams, J. E. (1970). Generalization between evaluative words associated with racial figures in preschool children. *Journal of Experimental Research in Personality, 4*, 144–155.

Egan, L. M. (1978). Children's viewing patterns for television news. *Journalism Quarterly, 55*, 347–352.

Ehrlich, C. (1971). The male sociologist's burden: The place of women in marriage and family texts. *Journal of Marriage and the Family, 33*, 421–430.

Ehrlich, J. S., & Riesman, D. (1961). Age and authority in the interview. *Public Opinion Quarterly, 25*, 39–56.

Eiser, J. R., & Osmon, B. E., (1978). Judgmental perspective and value connotations of response scale labels. *Journal of Personality and Social Psychology, 36*, 491–497.

Eiser, J. R., & Stroebe, W. (1972). *Categorization and social judgement.* London: Academic Press.

Eiser, J. R., & van der Pligt, J. (1984). Accentuation theory, polarization, and the judgement of attitude statements. In J. R. Eiser (Ed.), *Attitudinal judgement* (pp. 43–63). New York: Springer.

Elms, A. C. (1967). Role playing, incentive, and dissonance. *Psychological Bulletin, 68*, 132–148.

Elms, A. C. (1982). Keeping deception honest: Justifying conditions for social scientific research stratagems. In T. L. Beauchamp, R. R. Faden, R. J. Wallace, Jr., & L. R. Walters (Eds.), *Ethical issues in social science research* (pp. 232–245). Baltimore: Johns Hopkins University Press.

Epstein, E. J. (1973). *News from nowhere: Television and the news.* New York: Random House.

Epstein, L., & Strom, G. (1984). Survey research and election night predictions. *Public Opinion, 7*(1), 48–50.

Equal Justice. (1987, Spring). Rising support for busing documented. P. 2.

Erber, R., & Lau, R. R. (1986, August). *Political cynicism revisited: The role of political schemata and the media in the decline of trust in government.* Paper presented at American Psychological Association meeting, Washington, DC.

Erikson, R. S. (1976). The influence of newspaper endorsements in presidential elections: The case of 1964. *American Journal of Political Science, 20*, 207–233.

Erikson, R. S. (1979). The SRC panel data and mass political attitudes. *British Journal of Political Science, 9*, 89–114.

Erskine, H. G. (1962). The polls: The informed public. *Public Opinion Quarterly, 26*, 669–677.

Erskine, H. G. (1963a). The polls: Textbook knowledge. *Public Opinion Quarterly, 27*, 133–141.

Erskine, H. G. (1963b). The polls: Exposure to international information. *Public Opinion Quarterly, 27*, 658–662.

Erskine, H. (1971). The polls: Women's role. *Public Opinion Quarterly, 35*, 275–290.

Erskine, H. (1972). The polls: Gun control. *Public Opinion Quarterly, 36*, 455–469.

Etheredge, L. S. (1978). *A world of men.* Cambridge, MA: MIT Press.

Etzioni, A. (1967). The Kennedy experiment. *Western Political Quarterly, 20*, 361–380.

Etzioni, A. (1969). Social-psychological aspects of international relations. In G. Lindzey & E. Aronson (Eds.), *The handbook of social psychology* (2nd ed., Vol. 5, pp. 538–601). Reading, MA: Addison-Wesley.

Evans, R. I., Rozelle, R. M., Lasater, T. M., Dembroski, T. M., & Allen, B. P. (1970). Fear arousal, persuasion, and actual versus implied behavioral change: New perspective utilizing a real-life dental hygiene program. *Journal of Personality and Social Psychology, 16*, 220–227.

Evans, R. I., Rozelle, R. M., Maxwell, S. E., Raines, B. E., Dill, C. A., Guthrie, T. J., Henderson, A. H., & Hill, P. C. (1981). Social modeling films to deter smoking in adolescents: Results of a three-year field investigation. *Journal of Applied Psychology, 66*, 399–414.

Fairchild, H. H. (1988). Creating positive television images. In S. Oskamp (Ed.), *Television as a social issue: Applied social psychology annual 8* (pp. 270–279). Newbury Park, CA: Sage.

Farnsley, C. P. (1965). Polls as a tool of government. *Public Opinion Quarterly, 29*, 463–464.

Farrell, W. (1974). *The liberated man: Beyond masculinity: Freeing men and their relationships with women.* New York: Random House.

Fazio, R. H. (1986a). How do attitudes guide behavior? In R. M. Sorrentino & E. T. Higgins (Eds.), *The handbook of motivation and cognition: Foundations of social behavior.* New York: Guilford.

Fazio, R. H. (1986b). Self-perception theory: A current perspective. In M. P. Zanna, J. M. Olson, & C. P. Herman (Eds.), *Social influence: The Ontario Symposium* (Vol. 5). Hillsdale, NJ: Erlbaum.

Fazio, R. H. (1988). On the power and functionality of attitudes: The role of attitude accessibility. In A. R. Pratkanis, S. J. Breckler, & A. G. Greenwald (Eds.), *Attitude structure and function.* Hillsdale, NJ: Erlbaum.

Fazio, R. H., Chen, J., McDonel, E. C., & Sherman, S. J. (1982). Attitude accessibility, attitude-behavior consistency, and the strength of the object-evaluation association. *Journal of Experimental Social Psychology, 18,* 339–357.

Fazio, R. H., & Williams, C. J. (1986). Attitude accessibility as a moderator of the attitude-perception and attitude-behavior relations: An investigation of the 1984 presidential election. *Journal of Personality and Social Psychology, 51,* 505–514.

Fazio, R. H., & Zanna, M. P. (1981). Direct experience and attitude-behavior consistency. In L. Berkowitz (Ed.), *Advances in experimental social psychology* (Vol. 14, pp. 161–202). New York: Academic Press.

Fazio, R. H., Zanna, M. P., & Cooper, J. (1977). Dissonance and self-perception: An integrative view of each theory's proper domain of application. *Journal of Experimental Social Psychology, 13,* 464–479.

Feather, N. T. (1962). Cigarette smoking and lung cancer: A study of cognitive dissonance. *Australian Journal of Psychology, 14,* 55–64.

Feather, N. T. (1967). A structural balance approach to the analysis of communication effects. In L. Berkowitz (Ed.), *Advances in experimental social psychology* (Vol. 3, pp. 100–166). New York: Academic Press.

Feldman, R. H. L., & Mayhew, P. C. (1984). Predicting nutrition behavior: The utilization of a social psychological model of health behavior. *Basic and Applied Social Psychology, 5,* 183–195.

Feldstein, J. H., & Feldstein, S. (1982). Sex differences on televised toy commercials. *Sex Roles, 8,* 581–593.

Felson, M., & Sudman, S. (1975). The accuracy of presidential-preference primary polls. *Public Opinion Quarterly, 39,* 232–236.

Festinger, L. (1953). Laboratory experiments. In L. Festinger & D. Katz (Eds.), *Research methods in the behavioral sciences* (pp. 136–172). New York: Dryden.

Festinger, L. (1954). A theory of social comparison processes. *Human Relations, 7,* 117–140.

Festinger, L. (1957). *A theory of cognitive dissonance.* Stanford, CA: Stanford University Press.

Festinger, L. (Ed.). (1964). *Conflict, decision, and dissonance.* Stanford, CA: Stanford University Press.

Festinger, L., & Carlsmith, J. M. (1959). Cognitive consequences of forced compliance. *Journal of Abnormal and Social Psychology, 58,* 203–210.

Festinger, L., Riecken, H. W., & Schachter, S. (1956). *When prophecy fails: A social and psychological study of a modern group that predicted the destruction of the world.* New York: Harper.

Fiedler, F. E., Fiedler, J., & Campf, S. (1971). Who speaks for the community? *Journal of Applied Social Psychology, 1,* 324–333.

Fiedler, K. (1982). Causal schemata: Review and criticism of research on a popular construct. *Journal of Personality and Social Psychology, 42,* 1001–1013.

Field, C. G. (1980). Social testing for United States housing policy: The Experimental Housing Allowance Program. In Organisation for Economic Co-operation and Development, *The utilisation of the social sciences in policy making in the United States: Case studies.* Paris: Author.

Field, J. O., & Anderson, R. E. (1969). Ideology in the public's conceptualization of the 1964 election. *Public Opinion Quarterly, 33,* 380–398.

Field, M. D. (1971). The researcher's view. *Public Opinion Quarterly, 35,* 342–346.

Field, M. D. (1983). Political opinion polling in the United States of America. In R. M. Worcester (Ed.), *Political opinion polling: An international review* (pp. 198–228). New York: St. Martin's Press.

Fields, C. M. (1981, February 2). Much research with human subjects freed from close scrutiny by panels. *Chronicle of Higher Education,* pp. 1, 16.

Fields, J. M., & Schuman, H. (1976). Public beliefs about the beliefs of the public. *Public Opinion Quarterly, 40,* 427–448.

Fillenbaum, S., & Frey, R. (1970). More on the "faithful" behavior of suspicious subjects. *Journal of Personality, 38,* 43–51.

Fiorina, M. P. (1981). *Retrospective voting in American national elections.* New Haven, CT: Yale University Press.

Fischoff, S. (1979). "Recipe for a jury" revisited: A balance theory prediction. *Journal of Applied Social Psychology 9,* 335–349.

Fishbein, M., & Ajzen, I. (1972). Attitudes and opinions. *Annual Review of Psychology, 23,* 487–544.

Fishbein, M., & Ajzen, I. (1974). Attitudes toward objects as predictors of single and multiple behavioral criteria. *Psychological Review, 81,* 59–74.

Fishbein, M., & Ajzen, I. (1975). *Belief, attitude, intention, and behavior: An introduction to theory and research.* Reading, MA: Addison-Wesley.

Fishbein, M., Ajzen, I., & Hinkle, R. (1980). Predicting and understanding voting in American elections: Effects of external variables. In I. Ajzen & M. Fishbein, *Understanding attitudes and predicting social behavior* (pp. 173–195). Englewood Cliffs, NJ: Prentice-Hall.

Fiske, S. T., Fischhoff, B., & Milburn, M. A. (1983). Images of nuclear war. *Journal of Social Issues, 39*(1), 1–180.

Fiske, S. T., & Taylor, S. E. (1984). *Social cognition.* Reading, MA: Addison-Wesley.

Fitzsimmons, S. J., & Osburn, H. G. (1968). The impact of social issues and public affairs television documentaries. *Public Opinion Quarterly, 32,* 379–397.

Fleishman, J. A. (1986). Types of political attitude structure: Results of a cluster analysis. *Public Opinion Quarterly, 50,* 371–386.

Foster, H. S. (1983). *Activism replaces isolationism: U.S. public attitudes 1940–1975.* Washington, DC: Foxhall.

Foster, M. A., Wallston, B. S., & Berger, M. (1980). Feminist orientation and job-seeking behavior among dual-career couples. *Sex Roles, 6,* 59–66.

Fox, J. A., & Tracy, P. E. (1986). *Randomized response: A method for sensitive surveys.* Beverly Hills, CA: Sage.

Fox, R. J., Crask, M. R., & Kim, J. (1988). Mail survey response rate: A meta-analysis of selected techniques for inducing response. *Public Opinion Quarterly, 52,* 467–491.

Frank, R. E., & Greenberg, M. G. (1980). *The public's use of television: Who watches and why.* Beverly Hills, CA: Sage.

Frankel, M. R., & Frankel, L. R. (1987). Fifty years of survey sampling in the United States. *Public Opinion Quarterly, 51,* s127–s138.

Franzwa, H. (1974). Working women in fact and fiction. *Journal of Communication, 24,* 104–109.

Fredricks, A. J., & Dossett, D. L. (1983). Attitude-behavior relations: A comparison of the Fishbein-Ajzen and the Bentler-Speckart models. *Journal of Personality and Social Psychology, 45,* 501–512.

Free, L. A., & Cantril, H. (1967). *The political beliefs of Americans: A study of public opinion.* New Brunswick, NJ: Rutgers University Press.

Free, L., & Watts, W. (1980). Internationalism comes of age . . . Again. *Public Opinion, 3*(2), 46–50.

Freedman, J. L. (1963). Attitudinal effects of inadequate justification. *Journal of Personality, 31,* 371–385.

Freedman, J. L. (1964). Involvement, discrepancy, and change. *Journal of Abnormal and Social Psychology. 69,* 290–295.

Freedman, J. L. (1984). Effect of television violence on aggressiveness. *Psychological Bulletin, 96,* 227–246.

Freedman, J. L., & Fraser, S. C. (1966). Compliance without pressure: The foot-in-the-door technique. *Journal of Personality and Social Psychology, 4,* 195–202.

Freeman, D. (1983). *Margaret Mead and Samoa: The making and unmaking of an anthropological myth.* Cambridge, MA: Harvard University Press.

Freeman, J. (1973). The origins of the women's liberation movement. In J. Huber (Ed.), *Changing women in a changing society* (pp. 30–49). Chicago: University of Chicago Press.

Frenkel-Brunswik, E., & Havel, J. (1953). Prejudice in the interviews of children: Attitudes toward minority groups. *Journal of Genetic Psychology, 82,* 91–136.

Frey, D. (1982). Different levels of cognitive dissonance, information seeking, and information avoidance. *Journal of Personality and Social Psychology, 43,* 1175–1183.

Frey, D. (1986). Recent research on selective exposure to information. In L. Berkowitz (Ed.), *Advances in experimental social psychology* (Vol. 19, pp. 41–80). Orlando, FL: Academic Press.

Fried, S. B., Gumpper, D. C., & Allen, J. C. (1973). Ten years of social psychology: Is there a growing commitment to field research? *American Psychologist, 28,* 155–156.

Friedan, B. (1963). *The feminine mystique.* New York: Dell.

Friedman, H. S., DiMatteo, M. R., & Mertz, T. I. (1980). Nonverbal communication on television news: The facial expressions of broadcasters during coverage of a presidential election campaign. *Personality and Social Psychology Bulletin, 6,* 427–435.

Friedman, J., & Weinberg, D. H. (Eds.). (1983). *The great housing experiment.* Beverly Hills, CA: Sage.

Friedrich, L. K., & Stein, A. H. (1975). Pro-social television and young children: The effects of verbal labeling and role playing on learning and behavior. *Child Development, 46,* 27–38.

Frieze, I. H., Bar-Tal, D., & Carroll, J. S. (Eds.) (1979). *New approaches to social problems: Applications of attribution theory.* San Francisco: Jossey-Bass.

Funkhouser, G. R. (1973). The issues of the sixties: An exploratory study in the dynamics of public opinion. *Public Opinion Quarterly, 37,* 62–75.

Gaddy, G. D. (1986). Television's impact on high school achievement. *Public Opinion Quarterly, 50,* 340–359.

Gaertner, S. L., & Dovidio, J. F. (1986). The aversive form of racism. In J. F. Dovidio & S. L. Gaertner (Eds.), *Prejudice, discrimination, and racism* (pp. 61–89). Orlando, FL: Academic Press.

Gaes, G. G., Kalle, R. J., & Tedeschi, J. T. (1978). Impression management in the forced compliance situation. *Journal of Experimental Social Psychology, 14,* 493–510.

Gallup, G. (1948). *A guide to public opinion polls* (2nd ed.). Princeton, NJ: Princeton University Press.

Gallup, G. (1965). Polls and the political process—Past, present, and future. *Public Opinion Quarterly, 29,* 544–549.

Gallup, G. H. (1972). *The Gallup Poll: Public opinion 1935–1971.* New York: Random House.

Gallup, G. (1976). *The sophisticated poll watcher's guide* (rev. ed.). Princeton, NJ: Princeton Opinion Press.

Gallup, G. H. (1978). *The Gallup Poll: Public opinion 1972–77* (Vol. 2). Wilmington, DE: Scholarly Resources.

Gallup, G. H. (1980). *The Gallup Poll: Public opinion 1979.* Wilmington, DE: Scholarly Resources.

Gallup Opinion Index. (1976, February). Most important problem. Report No. 127, p. 3.

Gallup Opinion Index. (1976, November). How Americans have rated other nations. Report No. 136, p. 4.

Gallup Opinion Index. (1978, April). Panama Canal treaties gaining more support as awareness grows. Report No. 153, pp. 15–24.

Gallup Opinion Index. (1979, April). Awareness of Three Mile Island incident. Report No. 165, p. 3.

Gallup Opinion Index. (1980, March). Ratings of nations—Trends. Report No. 176, p. 32.

Gallup Opinion Index. (1980, September). Economy overshadows other problems. Report No. 181, pp. 9–11.

Gallup Opinion Index. (1980, October/November). Carter popularity. Report No. 182, pp. 5–14.

Gallup Opinion Index. (1980, December). 1980 election one of most unusual. Report No. 183, pp. 29–30.

Gallup Poll Monthly. (1991, April). Bush approval drops from stratospheric levels. Report No. 307, pp. 19–23.

Gallup Report. (1981, July). Public support for ERA reaches new high. Report No. 190, pp. 23–25.

Gallup Report. (1983, December). Most important problem, 1981–1983. Report No. 219, p. 6.

Gallup Report. (1985, March). Aware of "Star Wars" proposal. Report No. 234, p. 13.

Gallup Report. (1985, April). Most important problem. Report No. 235, pp. 20–21.

Gallup Report. (1985, May). Religious knowledge of Americans. Report No. 236, p. 57.

Gallup Report. (1985, June). United Nations slowly grows in Americans' esteem. Report No. 237, pp. 26–27.

Gallup Report. (1985, October). Gallup Poll anniversary: Public's views and behavior have changed greatly since 1935. Report No. 241, pp. 5–6.

Gallup Report. (1986, March). How closely followed events in Philippines? Report No. 246, p. 16.

Gallup Report. (1986, March). Awareness of Halley's Comet. Report No. 246, pp. 34–35.

Gallup Report. (1986, April). Awareness of AIDS. Report No. 247, p. 20.

Gallup Report. (1986, December). Gallup international: Americans more fearful of world war than are people of other nations. Report No. 255, p.6.

Gallup Report. (1987, January/February). Women's perception of job bias grows. Report No. 256–257, p. 18.

Gallup Report. (1987, March). U.S./Soviet relations: Americans more cynical than Soviets about eliminating nuclear weapons. Report No. 258, p. 34.

Gallup Report. (1987, May). Most important problem. Report No. 260, pp. 6–7.

Gallup Report. (1987, May). Reagan's job performance 1981–1984. Report No. 260, p. 12.

Gallup Report. (1987, May). Majority opposes Supreme Court ruling in affirmative action case. Report No. 260, pp. 18–19.

Gallup Report. (1987, July). Large majorities willing to vote for woman, jew, or black for president. Report No. 262, pp. 16–20.

Gallup Report. (1987, November). Gallup international: Soviets more likely than Americans to predict a peaceful 1988. Report No. 266, p. 35.

Gallup Report. (1987, December). U.S. women endorse jobs, marriage, and children. Report No. 267, pp. 24–25.

Gallup Report. (1987, December). Gorbachev is first Soviet leader chosen among "most admired" in U.S. Report No. 267, pp. 26–27.

Gallup Report. (1988, March). Reagan's job performance—Overall. Report No. 270, p. 20.

Gallup Report. (1988, July). Equal Rights Amendment. Report No. 274, p. 15.

Gallup Report. (1988, September). Political party affiliation—Trend. Report No. 276, p. 7.

Gallup Report. (1988, September). Poverty: Most Americans reject notion that U.S. is divided into "haves," "have-nots." Report No. 276, pp. 8–12.

Gallup Report. (1988, October). Geographic knowledge deemed vital, but many lack basic skills. Report No. 277, p. 35.

Gallup Report. (1988, November). The economy: Bush campaign seen gaining from low "misery index." Report No. 278, p. 28.

Gallup Report. (1988, December). Confidence in institutions. Report No. 279, pp. 29–30.

Gallup Report. (1988, December). Gallup Poll accuracy record. Report No. 279, p. 44.

Gallup Report. (1989, January). Satisfaction levels. Report No. 280, pp. 4–8.

Gallup Report. (1989, January). ˙Reagan job performance. Report No. 280, p. 13.

Gallup Report. (1989, January). Gorbachev ranks second on Americans' list of "most admired men." Report No. 280, p. 16.

Gallup Report. (1989, March/April). Social values. Report No. 282/283, pp. 35–44.

Gallup Report. (1989, August). Ratings of foreign countries. Report No. 287, pp. 13–14.

Gans, H. J. (1979). *Deciding what's news: A study of CBS Evening News, NBC Nightly News, Newsweek, and Time*. New York: Pantheon.

Gardner, J. W. (1984). *Excellence* (rev. ed.). New York: Norton.

Garramone, G. M., & Atkin, C. K. (1986). Mass communication and political socialization: Specifying the effects. *Public Opinion Quarterly, 50*, 76–86.

Gatty, R., & Mack, J. (1979). *How body rhythms influence opinion*. Paper presented at meeting of American Association for Public Opinion Research, Buck Hill Falls, PA.

Geerken, M., & Gove, W. R. (1983). *At home and at work: The family's allocation of labor*. Beverly Hills, CA: Sage.

Geis, F. L., Brown, V., Jennings (Walstedt), J., & Porter, N. (1984). TV commercials as achievement scripts for women. *Sex Roles, 10*, 513–525.

Geller, D. M. (1982). Alternatives to deception: Why, what, and how? In J. E. Sieber (Ed.), *NIH readings on the protection of human subjects in behavioral and social science research: Conference proceedings and background papers* (pp. 39–55). Frederick, MD: University Publications of America.

Gerard, H. B. (1983). School desegregation: The social science role. *American Psychologist, 38*, 869–877.

Gerard, H. B., & Orive, R. (1987). The dynamics of opinion formation. In L. Berkowitz (Ed.), *Advances in experimental social psychology* (Vol. 20). San Diego: Academic Press.

Gerbner, G. (Ed.). (1977). *Mass media policies in changing cultures*. New York: Wiley.

Gerbner, G., Gross, L., Morgan, M., & Signorielli, N. (1980). The "mainstreaming" of America: Violence profile no. 11. *Journal of Communication, 30*(3), 10–29.

Gibbons, F. X. (1978). Sexual standards and reactions to pornography: Enhancing behavioral consistency through self-focused attention. *Journal of Personality and Social Psychology, 36*, 976–987.

Gilbert, L. A. (1980). Feminist therapy. In A. Brodsky & R. Hare-Mustin (Eds.), *Women and psychotherapy*. New York: Guilford.

Gilbert, L. A. (1985). *Men in dual-career families: Current realities and future prospects.* Hillsdale, NJ: Erlbaum.

Gilbert, L. A., Waldroop, J. A., & Deutsch, C. J. (1981). Masculine and feminine stereotypes and adjustment: A reanalysis. *Psychology of Women Quarterly, 5,* 790–794.

Gilbert, R. K. (1988). The dynamics of inaction: Psychological factors inhibiting arms control activism. *American Psychologist, 43,* 755–764.

Gilbert, W. S. (1932). *The best known works of W. S. Gilbert.* New York: Illustrated Editions.

Gill, J. D., Crosby, L. A., & Taylor, J. R. (1986). Ecological concern, attitudes, and social norms in voting behavior. *Public Opinion Quarterly, 50,* 537–554.

Gillig, P. M., & Greenwald, A. G. (1974). Is it time to lay the sleeper effect to rest? *Journal of Personality and Social Psychology, 29,* 132–139.

Ginzel, L. E., Jones, E. E., & Swann, W. B., Jr. (1987). How "naive" is the naive attributor?: Discounting and augmentation in attitude attribution. *Social Cognition, 5,* 108–130.

Glass, D. P. (1985). Evaluating presidential candidates: Who focuses on their personal attributes? *Public Opinion Quarterly, 49,* 517–534.

Glenn, N. D. (1973). Class and party support in the United States: Recent and emerging trends. *Public Opinion Quarterly, 37,* 1–20.

Glenn, N. D. (1987). Social trends in the United States: Evidence from sample surveys. *Public Opinion Quarterly, 51,* s109–s126.

Glenn, N. D., & Simmons, J. L. (1967). Are regional cultural differences diminishing? *Public Opinion Quarterly, 31,* 176–193.

Glenn, N. D., & Weaver, C. N. (1982). Enjoyment of work by full-time workers in the U.S., 1955 and 1980. *Public Opinion Quarterly, 46,* 459–470.

Goethals, G. R., Cooper, J., & Naficy, A. (1979). Role of foreseen, foreseeable, and unforeseeable behavioral consequences in the arousal of cognitive dissonance. *Journal of Personality and Social Psychology, 37,* 1179–1185.

Goldberg, L. R. (1981). Unconfounding situational attributions from uncertain, neutral, and ambiguous ones: A psychometric analysis of descriptions of oneself and various types of others. *Journal of Personality and Social Psychology, 41,* 517–552.

Goldberg, M. E., & Gorn, G. J. (1974). Children's reactions to television advertising: An experimental approach. *Journal of Consumer Research, 1,* 69–75.

Goldhaber, G. M. (1984). A pollsters' sampler. *Public Opinion, 7*(3), 47–53.

Goldman, P. (1970). *Report from black America.* New York: Simon & Schuster.

Goldner, F. H. (1971). Public opinion and survey research: A poor mix. *Public Opinion Quarterly, 35,* 447–448.

Gomes, B., & Abramowitz, S. I. (1976). Sex-related patient and therapist effects on clinical judgment. *Sex Roles, 2,* 1–14.

Goodman, M. E. (1964). *Race awareness in young children* (rev. ed.). New York: Crowell Collier.

Gordon, C. (1987). Fresh eggs and APA meet on Madison Ave. *APA Monitor, 18*(5), 25.

Gore, A. (1960). Political public opinion polls. *Congressional Record, 106,* 16958–16965.

Gorn, G. J., & Goldberg, M. E. (1982). Behavioral evidence of the effects of televised food messages on children. *Journal of Consumer Research, 9,* 200–205.

Gorsuch, R. L., & Ortberg, J. (1983). Moral obligation and attitudes: Their relation to behavioral intentions. *Journal of Personality and Social Psychology, 44,* 1025–1028.

Graber, D. A. (1987). Kind pictures and harsh words: How television presents the candidates. In K. L. Schlozman (Ed.), *Elections in America* (pp. 115–141). Boston: Allen & Unwin.

Graham, T. W., & Kramer, B. M. (1986). The polls: ABM and Star Wars: Attitudes toward nuclear defense, 1945–1985. *Public Opinion Quarterly, 50,* 125–134.

Granberg, D. (1982). Family size preferences and sexual permissiveness as factors differentiating abortion activists. *Social Psychology Quarterly, 45,* 15–23.

Granberg, D. (1984). Attributing attitudes to members of groups. In J. R. Eiser (Ed.), *Attitudinal judgement* (pp. 85–108). New York: Springer-Verlag.

Granberg, D., & Brent, E. (1980). Perceptions of issue positions of presidential candidates. *American Scientist, 68,* 617–625.

Granberg, D., & Nanneman, T. (1986). Attitude change in an electoral context as a function of expectations not being fulfilled. *Political Psychology, 7,* 753–765.

Granberg, D., Nanneman, T., & Kasmer, J. (1986, May). *An empirical examination of two theories of political perception.* Paper presented at American Association for Public Opinion Research meeting, St. Petersburg Beach, FL.

Granberg, D., & Robertson, C. (1982). Contrast effects in estimating the policies of the federal government. *Public Opinion Quarterly, 46,* 43–53.

Graves, S. B. (1980). Psychological effects of black portrayals on television. In S. B. Withey & R. P. Abeles (Eds.), *Television and social behavior: Beyond violence and children* (pp. 259–289). Hillsdale, NJ: Erlbaum.

Greeley, A. M. (1972). Political attitudes among American white ethnics. *Public Opinion Quarterly, 36,* 213–220.

Greeley, A. M. (1981). The state of the nation's happiness. *Psychology Today, 15*(1), 14–16.

Green, J. A. (1972). Attitudinal and situational determinants of intended behavior toward blacks. *Journal of Personality and Social Psychology, 22,* 13–17.

Greenberg, B. S. (1964). Diffusion of news of the Kennedy assassination. *Public Opinion Quarterly, 28,* 225–232.

Greenberg, J., Pyszczynski, T., & Solomon, S. (1982). The self-serving attributional bias: Beyond self-presentation. *Journal of Experimental Social Psychology, 18*, 56–67.

Greenwald, A. G. (1980). The totalitarian ego: Fabrication and revision of personal history. *American Psychologist, 35*, 603–618.

Greenwald, A. G., & Albert, R. D. (1968). Acceptance and recall of improvised arguments. *Journal of Personality and Social Psychology, 8*, 31–34.

Greenwald, A. G., Brock, T. C., & Ostrom, T. M. (Eds.). (1968). *Psychological foundations of attitudes*. New York: Academic Press.

Greenwald, A. G., Pratkanis, A. R., Leippe, M. R., & Baumgardner, M. H. (1986). Under what conditions does theory obstruct research progress? *Psychological Review, 93*, 216–229.

Greenwald, A. G., & Ronis, D. L. (1978). Twenty years of cognitive dissonance: A case study of the evolution of a theory. *Psychological Review, 85*, 53–57.

Greenwald, H. J., & Oppenheim, D. B. (1968). Reported magnitude of self-misidentification among Negro children—Artifact? *Journal of Personality and Social Psychology, 8*, 49–52.

Grofman, B. (1980). Jury decision making models and the Supreme Court: The jury cases from *Williams v. Florida* to *Ballew v. Georgia. Policy Studies Journal, 8*, 749–772

Gross, A. E., & Fleming, I. (1982). Twenty years of deception in social psychology. *Personality and Social Psychology Bulletin, 8*, 402–408.

Groves, R. M., & Kahn, R. L. (1979). *Surveys by telephone: A national comparison with personal interviews*. New York: Academic Press.

Groves, R. M., & Mathiowetz, N. A. (1984). Computer assisted telephone interviewing: Effects on interviewers and respondents. *Public Opinion Quarterly, 48*, 356–369.

Gruder, C. L., Cook, T. D., Hennigan, K. M., Flay, B. R., Alessi, C., & Halamaj, J. (1978). Empirical tests of the absolute sleeper effect predicted from the discounting cue hypothesis. *Journal of Personality and Social Psychology, 36*, 1061–1074.

Grush, J. E. (1976). Attitude formation and mere exposure phenomena: A nonartifactual explanation of empirical findings. *Journal of Personality and Social Psychology, 33*, 281–290.

Grush, J. E. (1979). A summary review of mediating explanations of exposure phenomena. *Personality and Social Psychology Bulletin, 5*, 154–159.

Grush, J. E. (1980). Impact of candidate expenditures, regionality, and prior outcomes on the 1976 Democratic presidential primaries. *Journal of Personality and Social Psychology, 38*, 337–347.

Gullahorn, J. T., & Gullahorn, J. E. (1963). An extension of the U-curve hypothesis. *Journal of Social Issues, 19*(3), 33–47.

Gurevitch, M., & Blumler, J. G. (1982). The construction of election news: An observation study at the BBC. In J. S. Ettema & D. C. Whitney (Eds.), *Individuals in mass media organizations: Creativity and constraint* (pp. 179–204). Beverly Hills, CA: Sage.

Guttman, L. (1944). A basis for scaling qualitative data. *American Sociological Review, 9*, 139–150.

Hacker, H. M. (1951). Women as a minority group. *Social Forces, 30*, 60–69.

Haemmerlie, F. M., & Montgomery, R. L. (1984). Purposefully biased interactions: Reducing heterosocial anxiety through self-perception theory. *Journal of Personality and Social Psychology, 47*, 900–908.

Hamill, R., Wilson, T. D., & Nisbett, R. E. (1980). Insensitivity to sample bias: Generalizing from atypical cases. *Journal of Personality and Social Psychology, 39*, 578–589.

Hamilton, D. L. (Ed.). (1981a). *Cognitive processes in stereotyping and intergroup behavior*. Hillsdale, NJ: Erlbaum.

Hamilton, D. L. (1981b). Illusory correlation as a basis for stereotyping. In D. L. Hamilton (Ed.), *Cognitive processes in stereotyping and intergroup behavior* (pp. 115–144). Hillsdale, NJ: Erlbaum.

Hamilton, D. L., Carpenter, S., & Bishop, G. D. (1984). Desegregation of urban neighborhoods. In N. Miller & M. B. Brewer (Eds.), *Groups in contact: The psychology of desegregation* (pp. 97–121). Orlando, FL: Academic Press.

Hamilton, D. L., Dugan, P. M., & Trolier, T. K. (1985). The formation of stereotypic beliefs: Further evidence for distinctiveness-based illusory correlations. *Journal of Personality and Social Psychology, 48*, 5–17.

Hamilton, D. L., & Rose, T. L. (1980). Illusory correlation and the maintenance of stereotypic beliefs. *Journal of Personality and Social Psychology, 39*, 832–845.

Hamilton, D. L., & Trolier, T. K. (1986). Stereotypes and stereotyping: An overview of the cognitive aporoach. In J. F. Dovidio & S. L. Gaertner (Eds.), *Prejudice, discrimination, and racism* (pp. 127–163). Orlando, FL: Academic Press.

Hammond, J. L. (1986). Yuppies. *Public Opinion Quarterly, 50*, 487–501.

Hammond, K. R. (1948). Measuring attitudes by error-choice: An indirect method. *Journal of Abnormal and Social Psychology, 43*, 38–48.

Hanson, D. J. (1980). Relationship between methods and findings in attitude-behavior research. *Psychology, 17*, 11–13.

Harary, F. (1983). Consistency theory is alive and well. *Personality and Social Psychology Bulletin, 9*, 60–64.

Harding, J., Proshansky, H., Kutner, B., & Chein, I. (1969). Prejudice and ethnic relations. In G. Lindzey & E. Aronson (Eds.), *The handbook of social psychology* (2nd ed., Vol. 5, pp. 1–76). Reading, MA: Addison-Wesley.

Hardyck, J. A., & Braden, M. (1962). Prophecy fails again: A report of a failure to replicate. *Journal of Abnormal and Social Psychology, 65*, 136–141.

Hare-Mustin, R. T. (1983). An appraisal of the relationship between women and psychotherapy: 80 years after the case of Dora. *American Psychologist, 38,* 593–601.

Harkins, S. G., & Petty, R. E. (1981). Effects of source magnification of cognitive effort on attitudes: An information processing view. *Journal of Personality and Social Psychology, 40,* 401–413.

Harmon, R. R., & Coney, K. A. (1982). The persuasive effects of source credibility in buy and lease situations. *Journal of Marketing Research, 19,* 255–260.

Harris, L. (1981, October 22). Confidence in institutions. *Harris Survey,* No. 85.

Harris, R. J. (1969). Dissonance or sour grapes? Post-"decision" changes in ratings and choice frequencies. *Journal of Personality and Social Psychology, 11,* 334–344.

Hartley, R. E. (1974). Sex-role pressures and the socialization of the male child. In J. Pleck & J. Sawyer (Eds.), *Men and masculinity* (pp. 7–13). Englewood Cliffs, NJ: Prentice-Hall.

Harvey, J. H., & Weary, G. (1981). *Perspectives on attributional processes.* Dubuque, IA: Wm. C. Brown.

Harvey, J. H., & Weary, G. (Eds.). (1985). *Attribution: Basic issues and applications.* New York: Academic Press.

Hass, R. G. (1981). Effects of source characteristics on cognitive responses and persuasion. In R. E. Petty, T. M. Ostrom, & T. C. Brock (Eds.), *Cognitive responses in persuasion* (pp. 141–172). Hillsdale, NJ: Erlbaum.

Hass, R. G., & Grady, K. (1975). Temporal delay, type of forewarning and resistance to influence. *Journal of Experimental Social Psychology, 11,* 459–469.

Hastie, R., Penrod, S. D., & Pennington, N. (1984). *Inside the jury.* Cambridge, MA: Harvard University Press.

Hatchett, S., & Schuman, H. (1975). White respondents and race-of-interviewer effects. *Public Opinion Quarterly, 39,* 523–528.

Hawkins, R. P., & Pingree, S. (1982). TV influence on social reality and conceptions of the world. In D. Pearl, L. Bouthilet, & J. Lazar (Eds.), *Television and behavior: Ten years of scientific progress and implications for the eighties* (Vol. 2, pp. 224–247). Washington, DC: U.S. Government Printing Office.

Hawley, W. D., & Smylie, M. A. (1988). The contribution of school desegregation to academic achievement and racial integration. In P. A. Katz & D. A. Taylor (Eds.), *Eliminating racism: Profiles in controversy* (pp. 281–297). New York: Plenum.

Hearold, S. (1986). A synthesis of 1043 effects of television on social behavior. In G. Comstock (Ed.), *Public communication and behavior* (Vol. 1, pp. 65–133). Orlando, FL: Academic Press.

Heath, L., & Petraitis, J. (1987). Television viewing and fear of crime: Where is the mean world? *Basic and Applied Social Psychology, 8,* 97–123.

Hechinger, F. M. (1979, March 13). About education: Council to fight U.S. students' parochial views. *New York Times,* p. c-5.

Heclo, H., & Rein, M. (1980). Social science and negative income taxation. In Organisation for Economic Co-operation and Development, *The utilisation of the social sciences in policy making in the United States: Case studies.* Paris: Author.

Heesacker, M. (1985). Applying attitude change theory to counseling. *Contemporary Social Psychology, 11,* 209–213.

Heider, F. (1944). Social perception and phenomenal causality. *Psychological Review, 51,* 358–374.

Heider, F. (1946). Attitudes and cognitive organization. *Journal of Psychology, 21,* 107–112.

Heider, F. (1958). *The psychology of interpersonal relations.* New York: Wiley.

Heller, J. F., Pallak, M. S., & Picek, J. M. (1973). The interactive effects of intent and threat on boomerang attitude change. *Journal of Personality and Social Psychology, 26,* 273–279.

Helmreich, R. L., Spence, J. T., & Gibson, R. H. (1982). Sex-role attitudes: 1972–1980. *Personality and Social Psychology Bulletin, 8,* 656–663.

Helson, H. (1964). *Adaptation level theory: An experimental and systematic approach to behavior.* New York: Harper & Row.

Henley, N. M. (1989). Molehill or mountain? What we know and don't know about sex bias in language. In M. Crawford & M. Gentry (Eds.), *Gender and thought: Psychological perspectives* (pp. 59–78). New York: Springer-Verlag.

Hennessy, B. C. (1970). A headnote on the existence and study of political attitudes. *Social Science Quarterly, 51,* 463–476.

Hennessy, B. C. (1975). *Public opinion* (3rd ed.). North Scituate, MA: Duxbury.

Herek, G. M. (1986). The instrumentality of attitudes: Toward a neofunctional theory. *Journal of Social Issues, 42*(2), 99–114.

Herz, M. F. (1949). Some psychological lessons from leaflet propaganda in World War II. *Public Opinion Quarterly, 13,* 471–486.

Herzog, A. R., Bachman, J. G., & Johnston, L. D. (1983). Paid work, child care and housework: A national survey of high school seniors' preferences for sharing responsibilities between husband and wife. *Sex Roles, 9,* 109–135.

Hess, E. H. (1965). Attitude and pupil size. *Scientific American, 212*(4), 46–54.

Hess, R. D. (1963). The socialization of attitudes toward political authority: Some cross-national comparisons. *International Social Science Journal, 25,* 542–559.

Hess, R. D., & Torney, J. V. (1967). *The development of political attitudes in children.* Chicago: Aldine.

Hesse, P. (1988). The development of enemy images: Universal and culture-specific themes. *Center Review, 2*(2), 6. (Center for Psychological Studies in the Nuclear Age, Cambridge, MA)

Hesselbart, S., & Schuman, H. (1976). Racial attitudes, educational level, and a personality measure. *Public Opinion Quarterly, 40*, 108–114.

Hiatt, F., & Atkinson, R. (1985, December 1). *Washington Post.*

Higbee, K. L. (1969). Fifteen years of fear arousal: Research on threat appeals: 1953–1968. *Psychological Bulletin, 72*, 426–444.

Higbee, K. L., Millard, R. J., & Folkman, J. R. (1982). Social psychology research during the 1970s: Predominance of experimentation and college students. *Personality and Social Psychology Bulletin, 8*, 180–183.

Higgins, E. T., & Bargh, J. A. (1987). Social cognition and social perception. *Annual Review of Psychology, 38*, 369–425.

Hilgard, E. R., & Payne, S. L. (1944). Those not at home: Riddle for pollsters. *Public Opinion Quarterly, 8*, 254–261.

Hiller, D. V., & Philliber, W. W. (1982). Predicting marital and career success among dual-worker couples. *Journal of Marriage and the Family, 44*, 53–62.

Hiller, D. V., & Philliber, W. W. (1986). The division of labor in contemporary marriage: Expectations, perceptions, and performance. *Social Problems, 33*, 191–201.

Himmelfarb, S., & Lickteig, C. (1982). Social desirability and the randomized response technique. *Journal of Personality and Social Psychology, 43*, 710–717.

Himmelweit, H. T., Humphreys, P., Jaegers, M., & Katz, M. (1981). *How voters decide: A longitudinal study of political attitudes and voting extending over fifteen years.* London: Academic Press.

Himmelweit, H. T., Oppenheim, A. N., & Vince, P. (1958). *Television and the child.* London: Oxford University Press.

Hippler, H.-J., & Schwarz, N. (1986). Not forbidding isn't allowing: The cognitive basis of the forbid-allow asymmetry. *Public Opinion Quarterly, 50*, 87–96.

Hirsch, P. M. (1980). The "scary world" of the nonviewer and other anomalies: A reanalysis of Gerbner et al. findings on cultivation analysis, part I. *Communication Research, 7*, 403–456.

Hoffman, L. W. (1977). Changes in family roles, socialization and sex differences. *American Psychologist, 32*, 644–657.

Hogarth, R. M. (1981). Beyond discrete biases: Functional and dysfunctional aspects of judgmental heuristics. *Psychological Bulletin, 90*, 197–217.

Holmes, D. S., & Bennett, D. H. (1974). Experiments to answer questions raised by the use of deception in psychological research: I. Role playing as an alternative to deception; II. Effectiveness of debriefing after a deception; III. Effect of informed consent on deception. *Journal of Personality and Social Psychology, 29*, 358–367.

Holsti, O. R. (1962). The belief system and national images: A case study. *Journal of Conflict Resolution, 6*, 244–252.

Holt, R. R., & Silverstein, B. (1989). The image of the enemy: U.S. views of the Soviet Union. *Journal of Social Issues, 45*(2), 1–175.

Houser, B. B., & Beckman, L. J. (1980). Background characteristics and women's dual-role attitudes. *Sex Roles, 6*, 355–366.

Houston, D. A., & Fazio, R. H. (1989). Biased processing as a function of attitude accessibility: Making objective judgments subjectively. *Social Cognition, 7*, 51–66.

Hovland, C. I. (1959). Reconciling conflicting results derived from experimental and survey studies of attitude change. *American Psychologist, 14*, 8–17.

Hovland, C. I., Harvey, O. J., & Sherif, M. (1957). Assimilation and contrast effects in communication and attitude change. *Journal of Abnormal and Social Psychology, 55*, 244–252.

Hovland, C. I., Janis, I. L., & Kelley, H. H. (1953). *Communication and persuasion.* New Haven, CT: Yale University Press.

Hovland, C. I., Lumsdaine, A. A., & Sheffield, F. D. (1949). *Experiments on mass communication.* Princeton, NJ: Princeton University Press.

Hovland, C. I., Mandell, W., Campbell, E. H., Brock, T., Luchins, A. S., Cohen, A. E., McGuire, W. J., Janis, I. L., Feierabend, R. L., & Anderson, N. H. (1957). *The order of presentation in persuasion.* New Haven, CT: Yale University Press.

Hovland, C. I., & Sherif, M. (1952). Judgmental phenomena and scales of attitude measurement: Item displacement in Thurstone scales. *Journal of Abnormal and Social Psychology, 47*, 822–832.

Howard, J., & Rothbart, M. (1980). Social categorization and memory for ingroup and outgroup behavior. *Journal of Personality and Social Psychology, 38*, 301–310.

Howard-Pitney, B., Borgida, E., & Omoto, A. M. (1986). Personal involvement: An examination of processing differences. *Social Cognition, 4*, 39–57.

Howell, S. E., & Fagan, D. (1988). Race and trust in government: Testing the political reality model. *Public Opinion Quarterly, 52*, 343–350.

Hraba, J., & Grant, G. (1970). Black is beautiful: A reexamination of racial preference and identification. *Journal of Personality and Social Psychology, 16*, 398–402.

Hurwitz, J., & Peffley, M. (1987). How are foreign policy attitudes structured? A hierarchical model. *American Political Science Review, 81*, 1099–1120.

Hyde, J. S. (1984). Children's understanding of sexist language. *Developmental Psychology, 20*, 697–706.

Hyden, P., & McCandless, N. J. (1983). Men and women as portrayed in the lyrics of contemporary music. *Popular Music and Society, 9*(2), 10–26.

Hyman, H. H. (1972). *Secondary analysis of sample surveys: Principles, procedures, and potentialities*. New York: Wiley.

Hyman, H. H., & Sheatsley, P. B. (1947). Some reasons why information campaigns fail. *Public Opinion Quarterly, 11*, 412–423.

Inglehart, R. (1985). Aggregate stability and individual-level flux in mass belief systems: The level of analysis paradox. *American Political Science Review, 79*, 97–116.

Insko, C. A. (1965). Verbal reinforcement of attitude. *Journal of Personality and Social Psychology, 2*, 621–623.

Insko, C. A. (1967). *Theories of attitude change*. New York: Appleton-Century-Crofts.

Insko, C. A., Nacoste, R. W., & Moe, J. L. (1983). Belief congruence and racial discrimination: Review of the evidence and critical evaluation. *European Journal of Social Psychology, 13*, 153–174.

Institute for Social Research. (1972, Winter). Americans' trust in government has fallen steadily. *ISR Newsletter, 1*(13), 5.

Institute for Social Research. (1974, Winter). Public asked to rank country's major institutions. *ISR Newsletter, 1*(20), 8.

Institute for Social Research. (1982, Spring/Summer). Group consciousness. *ISR Newsletter, 10*(1&2), 4–5.

Institute for Social Research. (1983, Autumn). Public more trusting? *ISR Newsletter, 11*(2), 4–5.

Institute for Social Research. (1986, Spring/Summer). Yuppie politics. *ISR Newsletter, 14*(1), 5–7.

Institute for Social Research. (1988, Winter). Voter registration. *ISR Newsletter, 16*(1), 3.

Iyengar, S., & Kinder, D. R. (1986). More than meets the eye: TV news, priming, and public evaluations of the president. In G. Comstock (Ed.), *Public communication and behavior* (Vol. 1, pp. 135–171). Orlando, FL: Academic Press.

Iyengar, S., Kinder, D. R., Peters, M. D., & Krosnick, J. A. (1984). The evening news and presidential evaluations. *Journal of Personality and Social Psychology, 46*, 778–787.

Jaccard, J. (1979). Personality and behavioral prediction: An analysis of behavioral criterion measures. In L. Kahle & D. Fiske (Eds.), *Methods for studying person-situation interactions*. San Francisco: Jossey-Bass.

Jaccard, J., & Davidson, A. R. (1975). A comparison of two models of social behavior: Results of a survey sample. *Sociometry, 38*, 497–517.

Jaccard, J., Knox, R., & Brinberg, D. (1980). Designing political campaigns to elect a candidate: Toward a social psychological theory of voting behavior. *Journal of Applied Social Psychology, 10*, 367–383.

Jackman, M. (1973). Education and prejudice or education and response sets? *American Sociological Review, 38*, 327–339.

Jackman, M. R., & Crane, M. (1986). "Some of my best friends are black . . .": Interracial friendship and whites' racial attitudes. *Public Opinion Quarterly, 50*, 459–486.

Jackson, J. E. (1983). Election night reporting and voter turnout. *American Journal of Political Science, 27*, 613–635.

Jacoby, J. (1974). The construct validity of opinion leadership. *Public Opinion Quarterly, 38*, 81–89.

James, W. (1902). *Varieties of religious experience*. New York: Longmans, Green.

Jamieson, D. W., & Zanna, M. P. (1988). Need for structure in attitude formation and expression. In A. R. Pratkanis, S. J. Breckler, & A. G. Greenwald (Eds.), *Attitude structure and function*. Hillsdale, NJ: Erlbaum.

Janis, I. L. (1983). The role of social support in adherence to stressful decisions. *American Psychologist, 38*, 143–160.

Janis, I. L. (1985). International crisis management in the nuclear age. In S. Oskamp (Ed.), *International conflict and national public policy issues: Applied social psychology annual 6* (pp. 63–86). Beverly Hills, CA: Sage.

Janis, I. L., & Feshbach, S. (1953). Effects of fear-arousing communications. *Journal of Abnormal and Social Psychology, 48*, 78–92.

Janis, I. L., & Field, P. B. (1959). Sex differences and personality factors related to persuasibility. In I. L. Janis, C. I. Hovland, et al., *Personality and persuasibility* (pp. 55–68). New Haven, CT: Yale University Press.

Janis, I. L., Hovland, C. I., Field, P. B., Linton, H., Graham, E., Cohen, A. R., Rife, D., Abelson, R. P., Lesser, G. S., & King, B. T. (1959). *Personality and persuasibility*. New Haven, CT: Yale University Press.

Janis, I. L., & Mann, L. (1977). *Decision making*. New York: Free Press.

Janis, I. L., & Smith, M. B. (1965). Effects of education and persuasion on national and international images. In H. C. Kelman (Ed.), *International behavior: A social-psychological analysis* (pp. 190–235). New York: Holt, Rinehart & Winston.

Jaspars, J., Fincham, F., & Hewstone, M. (Eds.). (1983). *Attribution theory research: Conceptual, developmental and social dimensions*. London: Academic Press.

Jaynes, G. D., & Williams, R. M., Jr. (Eds.). (1989). *A common destiny: Blacks and American society*. Washington, DC: National Academy Press.

Jennings, M. K., & Niemi, R. G. (1968). The transmission of political values from parent to child. *American Political Science Review, 62*, 169–184.

Jennings, M. K., & Niemi, R. G. (1973, September). *Continuity and change in political orientations: A longitudinal study of two generations*. Paper presented at American Political Science Association meeting, New Orleans.

Jervis, R. (1970). *The logic of images in international relations*. Princeton, NJ: Princeton University Press.

Jervis, R. (1986). Cognition and political behavior. In R. R. Lau & D. O. Sears (Eds.), *Political cognition: The 19th annual Carnegie Symposium on Cognition* (pp. 319–336). Hillsdale, NJ: Erlbaum.

Johnson, B. T., & Eagly, A. H. (1990). Involvement and persuasion: Types, traditions, and the evidence. *Psychological Bulletin, 107*, 375–384.

Johnson, D. W., Johnson, R. T., & Maruyama, G. (1983). Interdependence and interpersonal attraction among heterogeneous and homogeneous individuals: A theoretical formulation and a meta-analysis of the research. *Review of Educational Research, 53*, 5–54.

Johnson, H. H., & Scileppi, J. A. (1969). Effects of ego-involvement conditions on attitude change to high and low credibility communicators. *Journal of Personality and Social Psychology, 13*, 31–36.

Johnston, J., & Ettema, J. S. (1982). *Positive images: Breaking stereotypes with children's television.* Beverly Hills, CA: Sage.

Johnston, J., Ettema, J., & Davidson, T. (1980). *An evaluation of "Freestyle": A television series to reduce sex role stereotypes.* Ann Arbor, MI: Institute for Social Research.

Jones, C. O. (1985). The voters say yes: The 1984 congressional elections. In E. Sandoz & C. V. Crabb, Jr. (Eds.), *Election 84: Landslide without a mandate?* (pp. 86–124). New York: New American Library.

Jones, E. E. (1985). Major developments in social psychology during the past five decades. In G. Lindzey & E. Aronson (Eds.), *The handbook of social psychology* (3rd ed., Vol. 1, pp. 47–107). New York: Random House.

Jones, E. E., & Davis, K. E. (1965). From acts to dispositions: The attribution process in person perception. In L. Berkowitz (Ed.), *Advances in experimental social psychology* (Vol. 2, pp. 219–266). New York: Academic Press.

Jones, E. E., & Gerard, H. B. (1967). *Foundations of social psychology.* New York: Wiley.

Jones, E. E., & Harris, V. A. (1967). The attribution of attitudes. *Journal of Experimental Social Psychology, 3*, 1–24.

Jones, E. E., Kanouse, D. E., Kelley, H. H., Nisbett, R. E., Valins, S., & Weiner, B. (1972). *Attribution: Perceiving the causes of behavior.* Morristown, NJ: General Learning Press.

Jones, E. E., & McGillis, D. (1976). Correspondent inferences and the attribution cube: A comparative reappraisal. In J. H. Harvey, W. J. Ickes, & R. F. Kidd (Eds.), *New directions in attribution research* (Vol. 1, pp. 389–420). Hillsdale, NJ: Erlbaum.

Jones, E. E., & Nisbett, R. E. (1972). The actor and the observer: Divergent perceptions of the causes of behavior. In E. E. Jones, D. E. Kanouse, H. H. Kelley, R. E. Nisbett, S. Valins, & B. Weiner, *Attribution: Perceiving the causes of behavior* (pp. 79–94). Morristown, NJ: General Learning Press.

Jones, E. E., & Pittman, T. S. (1982). Toward a general theory of strategic self-presentation. In J. Suls (Ed.), *Psychological perspectives on the self* (pp. 231–262). Hillsdale, NJ: Erlbaum.

Jones, E. E., & Sigall, H. (1971). The bogus pipeline: A new paradigm for measuring affect and attitude. *Psychological Bulletin, 76*, 349–364.

Jones, J. M. (1972). *Prejudice and racism.* Reading, MA: Addison-Wesley.

Jones, J. M. (1981). The concept of racism and its changing reality. In B. P. Bowser & R. G. Hunt (Eds.), *Impacts of racism on white Americans* (pp. 27–49). Beverly Hills, CA: Sage.

Jones, R. A., Linder, D. E., Kiesler, C. A., Zanna, M., & Brehm, J. W. (1968). Internal states or external stimuli: Observers' attitude judgments and the dissonance-theory—self-persuasion controversy. *Journal of Experimental Social Psychology, 4*, 247–269.

Judd, C. M., Kenny, D. A., & Krosnick, J. A. (1983). Judging the positions of political candidates: Models of assimilation and contrast. *Journal of Personality and Social Psychology, 44*, 952–963.

Judd, C. M., Krosnick, J. A., & Milburn, M. A. (1981). Political involvement and attitude structure in the general public. *American Sociological Review, 46*, 660–669.

Judd, C. M., & Milburn, M. A. (1980). The structure of attitude systems in the general public: Comparisons of a structural equation model. *American Sociological Review, 45*, 627–643.

Kahle, L. R. (Ed.). (1983). *Social values and social change: Adaptation to life in America.* New York: Praeger.

Kahn, W. A., & Crosby, F. (1985). Discriminating between attitudes and discriminatory behaviors: Change and stasis. In L. Larwood, A. H. Stromberg, & B. A. Gutek (Eds.), *Women and work: An annual review* (Vol. 1, pp. 215–238). Beverly Hills, CA: Sage.

Kahneman, D., & Tversky, A. (1982). The simulation heuristic. In D. Kahneman, P. Slovic, & A. Tversky (Eds.), *Judgment under uncertainty: Heuristics and biases* (pp. 201–208). Cambridge: Cambridge University Press.

Kaid, L. L. (1981). Political advertising. In D. D. Nimmo & K. R. Sanders (Eds.), *Handbook of political communication* (pp. 249–271). Beverly Hills, CA: Sage.

Karabenick, S. A. (1983). Sex-relevance of content and influenceability: Sistrunk and McDavid revisited. *Personality and Social Psychology Bulletin, 9*, 243–252.

Karlins, M., & Abelson, H. I. (1970). *Persuasion: How opinions and attitudes are changed* (2nd ed.). New York: Springer.

Karlins, M., Coffman, T. L., & Walters, G. (1969). On the fading of social stereotypes: Studies in three generations of college students. *Journal of Personality and Social Psychology, 13*, 1–16.

Kassin, S. M. (1979). Consensus information, prediction, and causal attribution: A review of the literature and issues. *Journal of Personality and Social Psychology, 37*, 1966–1981.

Katosh, J. P., & Traugott, M. W. (1981). The consequences of validated and self-reported voting measures. *Public Opinion Quarterly, 45*, 519–535.

Katz, D. (1942). Do interviewers bias poll results? *Public Opinion Quarterly, 6*, 248–268.

Katz, D. (1960). The functional approach to the study of attitudes. *Public Opinion Quarterly, 24*, 163–204.

Katz, D., & Braly, K. (1933). Racial stereotypes of one hundred college students. *Journal of Abnormal and Social Psychology, 28,* 280–290.

Katz, D., & Stotland, E. (1959). A preliminary statement to a theory of attitude structure and change. In S. Koch (Ed.), *Psychology: A study of a science* (Vol. 3, pp. 423–475). New York: McGraw-Hill.

Katz, E. (1957). The two-step flow of communications: An up-to-date report on an hypothesis. *Public Opinion Quarterly, 21,* 61–78.

Katz, E., & Feldman, J. J. (1962). The debates in the light of research: A survey of surveys. In S. Kraus (Ed.), *The great debates* (pp. 173–223). Bloomington: Indiana University Press.

Katz, E., & Lazarsfeld, P. F. (1955). *Personal influence.* Glencoe, IL: Free Press.

Katz, P. A., & Taylor, D. A. (Eds.). (1988). *Eliminating racism: Profiles in controversy.* New York: Plenum.

Katzman, N. I. (1972). Television soap operas: What's been going on anyway? *Public Opinion Quarterly, 36,* 200–212.

Keeter, S. (1987). The illusion of intimacy: Television and the role of candidate personal qualities in voter choice. *Public Opinion Quarterly, 51,* 344–358.

Kelley, H. H. (1967). Attribution theory in social psychology. In D. Levine (Ed.), *Nebraska symposium on motivation* (Vol. 15, pp. 192–238). Lincoln: University of Nebraska Press.

Kelley, H. H. (1972a). Attribution in social interaction. In E. E. Jones, D. E. Kanouse, H. H. Kelley, R. E. Nisbett, S. Valins, & B. Weiner, *Attribution: Perceiving the causes of behavior* (pp. 1–26). Morristown, NJ: General Learning Press.

Kelley, H. H. (1972b). Causal schemata and the attribution process. In E. E. Jones, D. E. Kanouse, H. H. Kelley, R. E. Nisbett, S. Valins, & B. Weiner, *Attribution: Perceiving the causes of behavior* (pp. 151–174). Morristown, NJ: General Learning Press.

Kelley, H. H., & Michela, J. L. (1980). Attribution theory and research. *Annual Review of Psychology, 31,* 457–501.

Kelley, J. (1974). The politics of school busing. *Public Opinion Quarterly, 38,* 23–39.

Kelley, J., & McAllister, I. (1984). Ballot paper cues and the vote in Australia and Britain: Alphabetic voting, sex, and title. *Public Opinion Quarterly, 48,* 452–466.

Kelly, E. L. (1955). Consistency of the adult personality. *American Psychologist, 10,* 659–681.

Kelman, H. C. (1958). Compliance, identification, and internationalization: Three processes of attitude change. *Journal of Conflict Resolution, 2,* 51–60.

Kelman, H. C. (1967). Human use of human subjects: The problem of deception in social psychological experiments. *Psychological Bulletin, 67,* 1–11.

Kelman, H. C. (1972). The rights of the subject in social research: An analysis in terms of relative power and legitimacy. *American Psychologist, 27,* 989–1016.

Kelman, H. C. (1974). Attitudes are alive and well and gainfully employed in the sphere of action. *American Psychologist, 29,* 310–324.

Kelman, H. C. (1982). Ethical issues in different social science methods. In T. L. Beauchamp, R. R. Faden, R. J. Wallace, Jr., & L. R. Walters (Eds.), *Ethical issues in social science research* (pp. 40–98). Baltimore: Johns Hopkins University Press.

Kelman, H. C., & Hovland, C. I. (1953). "Reinstatement" of the communicator in delayed measurement of opinion change. *Journal of Abnormal and Social Psychology, 48,* 327–335.

Kennamer, J. D. (1985, May). *Debate viewing and debate discussion as predictors of campaign cognition.* Paper presented at meeting of American Association for Public Opinion Research, Great Gorge, NJ.

Kenrick, D. T., & Gutierres, S. E. (1980). Contrast effects and judgments of physical attractiveness: When beauty becomes a social problem. *Journal of Personality and Social Psychology, 38,* 131–140.

Kerlinger, F. N. (1984). *Liberalism and conservatism: The nature and structure of social attitudes.* Hillsdale, NJ: Erlbaum.

Kernell, S. (1978). Explaining presidential popularity. *American Political Science Review, 72,* 506–522.

Kerrick, J. S. (1958). The effect of relevant and non-relevant sources on attitude change. *Journal of Social Psychology, 47,* 15–20.

Kessel, J. H. (1965). Cognitive dimensions and political activity. *Public Opinion Quarterly, 29,* 377–389.

Kessel, J. H. (1968). *The Goldwater coalition.* Indianapolis: Bobbs-Merrill.

Key, V. O., Jr., & Cummings, M. C., Jr. (1966). *The responsible electorate: Rationality in presidential voting* (pp. 1936–1960). Cambridge, MA: Harvard University Press.

Kidder, L. H., & Campbell, D. T. (1970). The indirect testing of social attitudes. In G. F. Summers (Ed.), *Attitude measurement* (pp. 333–385). Chicago: Rand McNally.

Kiesler, C. A. (1968). Commitment. In R. P. Abelson et al. (Eds.), *Theories of cognitive consistency: A sourcebook.* Chicago: Rand McNally.

Kiesler, C. A. (1971). *The psychology of commitment: Experiments linking behavior to belief.* New York: Academic Press.

Kiesler, C. A. (1980). Psychology and public policy. In L. Bickman (Ed.), *Applied social psychology annual* (Vol. 1). Beverly Hills, CA: Sage.

Kiesler, C. A., Collins, B. E., & Miller, N. (1969). *Attitude change: A critical analysis of theoretical approaches.* New York: Wiley.

Kiesler, C. A., & Munson, P. A. (1975). Attitudes and opinions. *Annual Review of Psychology, 26,* 415–456.

Kimmel, A. J. (Ed.). (1982). *New directions for methodology of social and behavioral research: The ethics of human subjects research.* San Francisco: Jossey-Bass.

Kinder, D. R. (1978). Political person perception: The asymmetrical influence of sentiment and choice on perceptions of presidential candidates. *Journal of Personality and Social Psychology, 36,* 859–871.

Kinder, D. R. (1981). Presidents, prosperity, and public opinion. *Public Opinion Quarterly, 45,* 1–21.

Kinder, D. R., & Kiewiet, D. R. (1981). Sociotropic politics. *British Journal of Political Science, 11,* 129–161.

Kinder, D. R., & Sears, D. O. (1981). Prejudice and politics: Symbolic racism versus racial threats to the good life. *Journal of Personality and Social Psychology, 40,* 414–431.

Kinder, D. R., & Sears, D. O. (1985). Public opinion and political action. In G. Lindzey & E. Aronson (Eds.), *The handbook of social psychology* (3rd ed., Vol. 2, pp. 659–741). New York: Random House.

King, B. T., & Janis, I. L. (1956). Comparison of the effectiveness of improvised vs. non-improvised role-playing in producing opinion changes. *Human Relations, 9,* 177–186.

King, F. W. (1970). Anonymous versus identifiable questionnaires in drug usage surveys. *American Psychologist, 25,* 982–985.

King, M. (1977–78). Assimilation and contrast of presidential candidates' issue positions, 1972. *Public Opinion Quarterly, 41,* 515–522.

King, R., & Schnitzer, M. (1968). Contemporary use of private political polling. *Public Opinion Quarterly, 32,* 431–536.

Kingdon, J. W. (1970). Opinion leaders in the electorate. *Public Opinion Quarterly, 34,* 256–261.

Kirkpatrick, C. (1963). *The family as process and institution* (2nd ed.). New York: Ronald.

Kirkpatrick, S. A. (1970a). Political attitude structure and component change. *Public Opinion Quarterly, 34,* 403–407.

Kirkpatrick, S. A. (1970b). Political attitudes and behavior: Some consequences of attitudinal ordering. *Midwest Journal of Political Science, 14,* 1–24.

Kirschner, B. F. (1973). Introducing students to women's place in society. In J. Huber (Ed.), *Changing women in a changing society* (pp. 289–292). Chicago: University of Chicago Press.

Kirscht, J. P., & Dillehay, R. C. (1967). *Dimensions of authoritarianism: A review of research and theory.* Lexington: University of Kentucky Press.

Kitt, A. S., & Gleicher, D. B. (1950). Determinants of voting behavior: A progress report on the Elmira election study. *Public Opinion Quarterly, 14,* 393–412.

Klapper, J. T. (1960). *The effects of mass communication.* Glencoe, IL: Free Press.

Klapoer, J. T. (1963). The social effects of mass communication. In W. Schramm (Ed.), *The science of human communication* (pp. 65–76). New York: Basic Books.

Klatzky, R. L., Martin, G. L., & Kane, R. (1982). Influence of social-category activation on processing of visual information. *Social Cognition, 1,* 95–109.

Klineberg, O. (1984). Public opinion and nuclear war. *American Psychologist, 39,* 1245–1253.

Knox, R. E., & Inkster, J. A. (1968). Postdecision dissonance at post time. *Journal of Personality and Social Psychology, 8,* 319–323.

Kohut, A., & Ornstein, N. (1987). Constructing a winning coalition. *Public Opinion, 10*(4), 41–44.

Komarovsky, M. (1985). *Women in college.* New York: Basic Books.

Korn, J. H. (1984). Research ethics needs careful scrutiny. *APA Monitor, 15*(12), 36.

Kosterman, R., & Feshbach, S. (1989). Toward a measure of patriotic and nationalistic attitudes. *Political Psychology, 10,* 257–274.

Kothandapani, V. (1971a). *A psychological approach to the prediction of contraceptive behavior.* Chapel Hill: University of North Carolina, Carolina Population Center.

Kothandapani, V. (1971b). Validation of feeling, belief, and intention to act as three components of attitude and their contribution to prediction of contraceptive behavior. *Journal of Personality and Social Psychology, 19,* 321–333.

Kramer, B. M., Kalick, S. M., & Milburn, M. A. (1983). Attitudes toward nuclear weapons and nuclear war: 1945–1982. *Journal of Social Issues, 39*(1), 7–24.

Kramer, G. H. (1970). The effects of precinct-level canvassing on voter behavior. *Public Opinion Quarterly, 34,* 560–572.

Kraut, R. E., & McConahay, J. B. (1973). How being interviewed affects voting: An experiment. *Public Opinion Quarterly, 37,* 398–406.

Krech, D., Crutchfield, R., & Ballachey, E. (1962). *Individual in society.* New York: McGraw-Hill.

Krippendorff, K. (1980). *Content analysis: An introduction to its methodology.* Beverly Hills, CA: Sage.

Krosnick, J. A. (1988). Attitude importance and attitude change. *Journal of Experimental Social Psychology, 24,* 240–255.

Krosnick, J. A. (1989). Question wording and reports of survey results: The case of Louis Harris and Associates and Aetna Life and Casualty. *Public Opinion Quarterly, 53,* 107–113.

Kruglanski, A. W. (1975). The practice of environmental quality behavior: Residential, life cycle, and attitudinal effects. *Advances in experimental social psychology* (Vol. 8, pp. 101–147). New York: Academic Press.

Kuklinski, J. H., & Parent, W. (1981). Race and big government: Contamination in measuring racial attitudes. *Political Methodology, 7,* 131–159.

Kulik, J. A. (1983). Confirmatory attribution and the perpetuation of social beliefs. *Journal of Personality and Social Psychology, 44,* 1171–1181.

Kutner, B., Wilkins, C., & Yarrow, P. R. (1952). Verbal attitudes and overt behavior involving racial prejudice. *Journal of Abnormal and Social Psychology, 47,* 649–652.

Ladd, E. C., Jr. (1976). The polls: The question of confidence. *Public Opinion Quarterly, 40,* 544–552.

Ladd, E. C., Jr. (1981). Conservatism: A national review. *Public Opinion, 4*(1), 19–31.

Ladd, E. C., Jr. (1983a). Politics in the 80's: An electorate at odds with itself. *Public Opinion, 5*(6), 2–5.

Ladd, E. C., Jr. (1983b). American differences: A regional review. *Public Opinion, 6*(1), 21–40.

Ladd, E. C., & Ferree, G. D. (1981). Were the pollsters really wrong? *Public Opinion, 3*(6), 13–20.

Ladd, E. C., Jr., & Lipset, S. M. (1975, October 20). Academics: America's most politically liberal stratum. *The Chronicle of Higher Education, 20,* 1–2.

Lambert, W. E., & Klineberg, O. (1967). *Children's views of foreign peoples.* New York: Appleton-Century-Crofts.

Lammers, H. B., & Becker, L. A. (1980). Distraction effects on the perceived extremity of a communication and on cognitive responses. *Personality and Social Psychology Bulletin, 6,* 261–266.

Lane, R. E. (1962). *Political ideology: Why the American common man believes what he does.* New York: Free Press.

Lane, R. E. (1973). Patterns of political belief. In J. N. Knutson (Ed.), *Handbook of political psychology* (pp. 83–116). San Francisco: Jossey-Bass.

Lang, G. E., & Lang, K. (1984). *Politics and television re-viewed* (3rd ed.). Beverly Hills, CA: Sage.

Lang, K., & Lang, G. E. (1984). The impact of polls on public opinion. *The Annals of the American Academy of Political and Social Science, 472,* 129–142.

Lange, R., & Fishbein, M. (1983). Effects of category differences on belief change and agreement with the source of a persuasive communication. *Journal of Personality and Social Psychology, 44,* 933–941.

Langer, E. J. (1978). Rethinking the role of thought in social interaction. In J. H. Harvey, W. Ickes, & R. E. Kidd (Eds.), *New directions in attribution research* (Vol. 2, pp. 35–58). Hillsdale, NJ: Erlbaum.

Langer, E. J., Blank, A., & Chanowitz, B. (1978). The mindlessness of ostensibly thoughtful action. *Journal of Personality and Social Psychology, 36,* 635–642.

Langlois, J. H., & Downs, A. C. (1980). Mothers, fathers, and peers as socialization agents of sex-typed play behaviors in young children. *Child Development, 51,* 1217–1247.

Lanzetta, J. T., Sullivan, D. G., Masters, R. D., & McHugo, G. J. (1985). Emotional and cognitive responses to televised images of political leaders. In S. A. Kraus & R. M. Perloff (Eds.), *Mass media and political thought: An information-processing approach* (pp. 85–116). Beverly Hills, CA: Sage.

LaPiere, R. T. (1934). Attitudes vs. actions. *Social Forces, 13,* 230–237.

LaPiere, R. T. (1936). Type-rationalizations of group antipathy. *Social Forces, 15,* 232–237.

Lau, R. R., & Russell, D. (1980). Attributions in the sports pages. *Journal of Personality and Social Psychology, 39,* 29–38.

Lavrakas, P. J. (1987). *Telephone survey methods: Sampling, selection, and supervision.* Newbury Park, CA: Sage.

Lazarsfeld, P. F., Berelson, B., & Gaudet, H. (1948). *The people's choice.* New York: Columbia University Press.

Lazarsfeld, P. F., & Merton, R. K. (1948). Mass communication, popular taste and organized social action. In L. Bryson (Ed.), *The communication of ideas* (pp. 95–118). New York: Harper.

Lee, A. McC., & Lee, E. B. (1939). *The fine art of propaganda: A study of Father Coughlin's speeches.* New York: Harcourt, Brace.

Lee, P. C., & Stewart, R. S. (Eds.). (1976). *Sex differences: Cultural and developmental dimensions.* New York: Urizen.

Leff, D. R., Protess, D. L., & Brooks, S. C. (1986). Crusading journalism: Changing public attitudes and policy-making agendas. *Public Opinion Quarterly, 50,* 300–315.

Lefkowitz, M. (1972). The women's magazine short-story heroine in 1957 and 1967. In C. Safilios-Rothschild (Ed.), *Toward a sociology of women* (pp. 37–40). Lexington, MA: Xerox.

Lehmann, S. (1970). Personality and compliance: A study of anxiety and self-esteem in opinion and behavior change. *Journal of Personality and Social Psychology, 15,* 76–86.

Leippe, M. R., & Elkin, R. A. (1987). When motives clash: Issue involvement and response involvement as determinants of persuasion. *Journal of Personality and Social Psychology, 52,* 269–278.

Lepper, M. R., & Greene, D. (1975). Turning play into work: Effects of adult surveillance and extrinsic rewards on children's intrinsic motivation. *Journal of Personality and Social Psychology, 31,* 479–486.

Leventhal, H. (1970). Findings and theory in the study of fear communications. In L. Berkowitz (Ed.), *Advances in experimental social psychology* (Vol. 5, pp. 119–186). New York: Academic Press.

Leventhal, H., Meyer, D., & Nerenz, D. (1980). The common sense representation of illness danger. In S. Rachman (Ed.), *Medical psychology* (Vol. 2, pp. 7–30). New York: Pergamon.

Leventhal, H., & Nerenz, D. (1983). Representations of threat and the control of stress. In D. Meichenbaum & M. Jaremko (Eds.), *Stress reduction and prevention: A cognitive behavioral approach.* New York: Plenum.

Lever, M., & Smooha, S. (1981). A part-whole strategy for the study of opinions. *Public Opinion Quarterly, 45,* 560–570.

Levy, M. R. (1983). The methodology and performance of election day polls. *Public Opinion Quarterly, 47,* 54–67.

Levy, M. R. (1984). Polling and the presidential election. *The Annals of the American Academy of Political and Social Science, 472,* 85–96.

Lewin, K. (1947). Group decision and social change. In T. M. Newcomb & E. L. Hartley (Eds.), *Readings in social psychology* (pp. 330–344). New York: Holt.

Lewin, M. (1984). The Victorians, the psychologists, and psychic birth control. In M. Lewin (Ed.), *In the shadow of the past: Psychology portrays the sexes* (pp. 39–76). New York: Columbia University Press.

Lewis, M. (1972). State as an infant-environment interaction: An analysis of mother-infant interactions as a function of sex. *Merrill-Palmer Quarterly, 18,* 95–121.

Lewis-Beck, M. (1987). A model performance. *Public Opinion, 9*(6), 57–58.

Lichter, S. R., Lichter, L. S., Rothman, S., & Amundson, D. (1987). Prime-time prejudice: TV's image of blacks and Hispanics. *Public Opinion, 10*(2), 13–16.

Lichty, L. W. (1982). Video versus print. *Wilson Quarterly, 6*(5), 48–57.

Lieberman, S. (1956). The effects of changes in roles on the attitudes of role occupants. *Human Relations, 9,* 385–402.

Liebhart, E. H. (1979). Information search and attribution: Cognitive processes mediating the effect of false autonomic feedback. *European Journal of Social Psychology 9,* 19–37.

Lifton, R. J. (1963). *Thought reform and the psychology of totalism.* New York: Norton.

Likert, R. (1932). A technique for the measurement of attitudes. *Archives of Psychology,* No. 140.

Linder, D. E., Cooper, J., & Jones, E. E. (1967). Decision freedom as a determinant of the role of incentive magnitude in attitude change. *Journal of Personality and Social Psychology, 6,* 245–254.

Lindskold, S. (1978). Trust development, the GRIT proposal, and the effects of conciliatory acts on conflict and cooperation. *Psychological Bulletin, 85,* 772–793.

Linville, P. W. (1982). The complexity-extremity effect and age-based stereotyping. *Journal of Personality and Social Psychology, 42,* 193–211.

Lippmann, W. (1922). *Public opinion.* New York: Harcourt, Brace & World.

Lipset, S. M. (1966). The President, the polls, and Vietnam. *Trans-action, 3*(6), 19–24.

Lipset, S. M. (1982). No room for the ins: Elections around the world. *Public Opinion, 5*(5), 41–43.

Lipset, S. M., & Schneider, W. (1983). *The confidence gap: Business, labor and government in the public mind.* New York: Free Press.

Listhaug, O. (1986). War and defence attitudes: A first look at survey data from 14 countries. *Journal of Peace Research, 23,* 69–76.

Litwak, E., Hooyman, N., & Warren, D. (1973). Ideological complexity and middle-American rationality. *Public Opinion Quarterly, 37,* 317–332.

Locksley, A., Borgida, E., Brekke, N., & Hepburn, C. (1980). Sex stereotypes and social judgment. *Journal of Personality and Social Psychology, 39,* 821–831.

London, P. (1970). The rescuers: Motivational hypotheses about Christians who saved Jews from the Nazis. In J. Macaulay & L. Berkowitz (Eds.), *Altruism and helping behavior: Social psychological studies of some antecedents and consequences* (pp. 241–250). New York: Academic Press.

Lord, C. G., Lepper, M. R., & Mackie, D. (1984). Attitude prototypes as determinants of attitude-behavior consistency. *Journal of Personality and Social Psychology, 46,* 1254–1266.

Lord, C. G., Ross, L., & Lepper, M. R. (1979). Biased assimilation and attitude polarization: The effects of prior theories on subsequently considered evidence. *Journal of Personality and Social Psychology, 37,* 2098–2109.

Los Angeles Times. (1970, October 16). Nixon repudiates U.S. commission's obscenity report.

Los Angeles Times. (1973, May 18). Public opinion polls—An interference or a help in the electoral process? Part II, p. 11.

Los Angeles Times. (1976, April 22). Gallup Poll: Equality: The enemy is within. Part IV, p. 5.

Lott, B., & Lott, A. J. (1985). Learning theory in contemporary social psychology. In G. Lindzey & E. Aronson (Eds.), *The handbook of social psychology* (3rd ed., Vol. 1, pp. 109–135). New York: Random House.

Love, R. E., & Greenwald, A. C. (1978). Cognitive responses to persuasion as mediators of opinion change. *Journal of Social Psychology, 104,* 231–241.

Lowe, R. H., & Wittig, M. A. (Eds.). (1989). Approaching pay equity through comparable worth. *Journal of Social Issues, 45*(4), 1–246.

Lund, F. H. (1925). The psychology of belief: IV. The law of primacy in persuasion. *Journal of Abnormal and Social Psychology, 20,* 183–191.

Luttbeg, N. E. (1968). The structure of beliefs among leaders and the public. *Public Opinion Quarterly, 32,* 398–409.

Luttbeg, N. E. (1970). Attitude bias in community leader selection. *Social Science Quarterly, 51,* 750–754.

Maass, A., & Clark, R. D., III. (1984). Hidden impact of minorities: Fifteen years of minority influence research. *Psychological Bulletin, 95,* 428–450.

Macaulay, T. B. (1830). *Southey's colloquies.* (Cited in G. Seldes (Compiler), *The great quotations.* New York: Pocket Books, 1967, p. 706.)

Maccoby, E., & Jacklin, C. N. (1974). *The psychology of sex differences.* Stanford, CA: Stanford University Press.

MacKuen, M. B. (1981). Social communication and the mass policy agenda. In M. B. MacKuen & S. L. Coombs (Eds.), *More than news: Media power in public affairs* (pp. 17–144). Beverly Hills, CA: Sage.

Malvin, J. H., & Moskowitz, J. M. (1983). Anonymous versus identifiable self-reports of adolescent drug attitudes, intentions, and use. *Public Opinion Quarterly, 47,* 557–566.

Manheim, J. B., & Albritton, R. B. (1984). Changing national images: International public relations and media agenda setting. *American Political Science Review, 78,* 641–657.

Manis, M., Nelson, T. E., & Shedler, J. (1988). Stereotypes and social judgment: Extremity, assimilation, and contrast. *Journal of Personality and Social Psychology, 55,* 28–36.

Mann, L., & Janis, I. L. (1968). A follow-up study on the long-term effects of emotional role playing. *Journal of Personality and Social Psychology, 8*, 339–342.

Mann, T. E., & Wolfinger, R. E. (1980). Candidates and parties in congressional elections. *American Political Science Review, 74*, 617–632.

Mansbridge, J. J. (1986). *Why we lost the ERA*. Chicago: University of Chicago Press.

Manstead, A. S. R., & McCulloch, C. (1981). Sex-role stereotyping in British television advertisements. *British Journal of Social Psychology, 20*, 171–180.

Manstead, A. S. R., Proffitt, C., & Smart, J. L. (1983). Predicting and understanding mothers' infant-feeding intentions and behavior: Testing the theory of reasoned action. *Journal of Personality and Social Psychology, 44*, 657–671.

Marks, G., & Miller, N. (1987). Ten years of research on the false-consensus effect: An empirical and theoretical review. *Psychological Bulletin, 102*, 72–90.

Marks, G., & Miller, N. (1988). Perceptions of attitude similarity: Effect of anchored versus unanchored positions. *Personality and Social Psychology Bulletin, 14*, 92–102.

Markus, H., & Zajonc, R. B. (1985). The cognitive perspective in social psychology. In G. Lindzey & E. Aronson (Eds.), *The handbook of social psychology* (3rd ed., Vol. 1, pp. 137–230). New York: Random House.

Marquis, K. H. (1978). *Record check validity of survey responses: A reassessment of bias in reports of hospitalization* (R-2319-HEW). Santa Monica, CA: Rand Corp.

Marquis, K. H., Duan, N., Marquis, M. S., & Polich, J. M. (1981). *Response errors in sensitive topic surveys* (R-1710-HHS). Santa Monica, CA: Rand Corp.

Martin, J. G., & Westie, F. R. (1959). The tolerant personality. *American Sociological Review, 24*, 521–528.

Martin, P. Y., Harrison, D., & Dinitto, D. (1983). Advancement for women in hierarchical organizations: A multilevel analysis of problems and prospects. *Journal of Applied Behavioral Science, 19*, 19–33.

Martyna, W. (1980). Beyond the "he/man" approach: The case for nonsexist language. *Signs, 5*, 482–493.

Marx, G. T. (1967). *Protest and prejudice: A study of belief in the black community*. New York: Harper & Row.

Marx, G. T. (1970). Racism and race relations. In M. Wertheimer (Ed.), *Confrontation: Psychology and the problems of today* (pp. 100–102). Glenview, IL: Scott, Foresman.

Mason, K. O., Czajka, J. L., & Arber, S. (1976). Change in U.S. women's sex-role attitudes, 1964–1974. *American Sociological Review, 41*, 573–596.

Mason, W. M. (1973). The impact of endorsements on voting. *Sociological Methods and Research, 1*, 463–495.

Masters, W. H., & Johnson, V. E. (1966). *Human sexual response*. Boston: Little, Brown.

Matlin, M. W. (1987). *The psychology of women*. New York: Holt, Rinehart & Winston.

Maykovich, M. K. (1975). Correlates of racial prejudice. *Journal of Personality and Social Psychology, 32*, 1014–1020.

Mazis, M. B. (1975). Antipollution measures and psychological reactance theory: A field experiment. *Journal of Personality and Social Psychology, 31*, 654–660.

McArdle, J. B. (1972). *Positive and negative communications and subsequent attitude and behavior change in alcoholics*. Unpublished doctoral dissertation, University of Illinois.

McArthur, L. Z. (1972). The how and what of why: Some determinants and consequences of causal attribution. *Journal of Personality and Social Psychology, 22*, 171–193.

McArthur, L. Z., & Friedman, S. A. (1980). Illusory correlation in impression formation: Variations in the shared distinctiveness effect as a function of the distinctive person's age, race, and sex. *Journal of Personality and Social Psychology, 39*, 615–624.

McClendon, M. J. (1985). Racism, rational choice, and white opposition to racial change: A case study of busing. *Public Opinion Quarterly, 49*, 214–233.

McClosky, H. (1958). Conservatism and personality. *American Political Science Review, 52*, 27–45.

McClosky, H. (1964). Consensus and ideology in American politics. *American Political Science Review, 58*, 361–382.

McClosky, H. (1967). Personality and attitude correlates of foreign policy orientation. In J. N. Rosenau (Ed.), *Domestic sources of foreign policy* (pp. 51–109). New York: Free Press.

McClosky, H., & Brill, A. (1983). *Dimensions of tolerance: What Americans believe about civil liberties*. New York: Russell Sage Foundation.

McCombs, M. E. (1977). Newspapers versus television: Mass communication effects across time. In D. L. Shaw & M. E. McCombs (Eds.), *The emergence of American political issues: The agenda-setting function of the press* (pp. 89–105). St. Paul, MN: West.

McCombs, M. E. (1981). The agenda-setting approach. In D. D. Nimmo & K. R. Sanders (Eds.), *Handbook of political communication* (pp. 121–140). Beverly Hills, CA: Sage.

McConahay, J. B., Hardee, B. B., & Batts, V. (1981). Has racism declined in America? It depends on who is asking and what is asked. *Journal of Conflict Resolution, 25*, 563–579.

McEwen, C. A. (1980). Continuities in the study of total and nontotal institutions. *Annual Review of Sociology, 6*, 143–185.

McGinnies, E., & Ward, C. D. (1980). Better liked than right: Trustworthiness and expertise as factors in credibility. *Personality and Social Psychology Bulletin, 6*, 467–472.

McGuire, W. J. (1960). A syllogistic analysis of cognitive relationships. In M. J. Rosenberg et al. (Eds.), *Attitude organization and change: An analysis of consistency among attitude components* (pp. 65–111). New Haven, CT: Yale University Press.

McGuire, W. J. (1964). Inducing resistance to persuasion. In L. Berkowitz (Ed.), *Advances in experimental social psychology* (Vol. 1, pp. 191–229). New York: Academic Press.

McGuire, W. J. (1966). Attitudes and opinions. *Annual Review of Psychology, 17,* 475–514.

McGuire, W. J. (1968a). Personality and attitude change: An information-processing theory. In A. G. Greenwald, T. C. Brock, & T. M. Ostrom (Eds.), *Psychological foundations of attitudes* (pp. 171–196). New York: Academic Press.

McGuire, W. J. (1968b). Personality and susceptibility to social influence. In E. F. Borgatta & W. W. Lambert (Eds.), *Handbook of personality theory and research* (pp. 1130–1187). Chicago: Rand McNally.

McGuire, W. J. (1969). The nature of attitudes and attitude change. In G. Lindzey & E. Aronson (Eds.), *The handbook of social psychology* (2nd ed., Vol. 3, pp. 136–314). Reading, MA: Addison-Wesley.

McGuire, W. J. (1972). Attitude change: The information-processing paradigm. In C. G. McClintock (Ed.), *Experimental social psychology* (pp. 108–141). New York: Holt, Rinehart & Winston.

McGuire, W. J. (1973). The yin and yang of progress in social psychology: Seven koan. *Journal of Personality and Social Psychology, 26,* 446–456.

McGuire, W. J. (1981). The probabilogical model of cognitive structure and attitude change. In R. E. Petty, T. M. Ostrom, & T. C. Brock (Eds.), *Cognitive responses in persuasion* (pp. 291–307). Hillsdale, NJ: Erlbaum.

McGuire, W. J. (1983). A contextualist theory of knowledge: Its implications for innovations and reform in psychology research. In L. Berkowitz (Ed.), *Advances in experimental social psychology* (Vol. 16, pp. 1–47). New York: Academic Press.

McGuire, W. J. (1985). Attitudes and attitude change. In G. Lindzey & E. Aronson (Eds.), *The handbook of social psychology* (3rd ed., Vol. 2, pp. 233–346). New York: Random House.

McGuire, W. J. (1986). The myth of massive media impact: Savagings and salvagings. In G. Comstock (Ed.), *Public communication and behavior* (Vol. 1). Orlando, FL: Academic Press.

McLeod, J. M., & Becker, L. B. (1981). The uses and gratifications approach. In D. D. Nimmo & K. R. Sanders (Eds.), *Handbook of political communication* (pp. 67–99). Beverly Hills, CA: Sage.

McLeod, J. M., Durall, J. A., Ziemke, D. A., & Bybee, C. R. (1979). Reactions of young and older voters: Expanding the context. In S. Kraus (Ed.), *The great debates: Carter vs. Ford, 1976* (pp. 348–367). Bloomington: Indiana University Press.

McLeod, J. M., & Reeves, B. (1980). On the nature of mass media effects. In S. B. Withey & R. P. Abeles (Eds.), *Television and social behavior: Beyond violence and children* (pp. 17–54). Hillsdale, NJ: Erlbaum.

McPherson, K. (1983). Opinion-related information seeking: Personal and situational variables. *Personality and Social Psychology Bulletin, 9,* 116–124.

Mead, M. (1935). *Sex and temperament in three primitive societies.* New York: Morrow.

Mendelsohn, H. (1973). Some reasons why information campaigns can succeed. *Public Opinion Quarterly, 37,* 50–61.

Mendelsohn, H., & O'Keefe, G. J. (1976). *The people choose a president: Influences on voter decision making.* New York: Praeger.

Mendelson, G., & Young, M. (1972). *Network children's programming: A content analysis of black and minority treatment on children's television.* Newtonville, MA: Action for Children's Television.

Merritt, R. L., & Puchala, D. J. (Eds.). (1968). *Western European perspectives on international affairs: Public opinion studies and evaluations.* New York: Praeger.

Merton, R. (1957). *Social theory and social structure.* Glencoe, IL: Free Press.

Meyer, T. J., & Evans, G. (1986, January 15). Most of this year's freshmen hold liberal views, study finds. *Chronicle of Higher Education,* pp. 34–36.

Mickolus, E. (1980). The double standard in nation perception: Artifact versus main effect. *International Journal of Group Tensions, 10,* 38–60.

Middleton, M. R., Tajfel, H., & Johnson, N. B. (1970). Cognitive and affective aspects of children's national attitudes. *British Journal of Social and Clinical Psychology, 9,* 122–134.

Milavsky, J. R., Kessler, R. C., Stipp, H. H., & Rubens, W. S. (1982). *Television and aggression: Results of a panel study.* New York: Academic Press.

Milavsky, J. R., Swift, A., Roper, B. W., Salant, R., & Abrams, F. (1985). Early calls of election results and exit polls: Pros, cons, and constitutional considerations. *Public Opinion Quarterly, 49,* 1–18.

Milbrath, L. W. (1962). Latent origins of liberalism-conservatism and party identification: A research note. *Journal of Politics, 24,* 679–688.

Milgram, S. (1963). Behavioral study of obedience. *Journal of Abnormal and Social Psychology, 67,* 371–378.

Miller, A., Engeman, M., Polulach, J., Sweet, D., & Ullman, R. (1980). Is positive or negative prior contact a determinant of the reinforcing function of approval? *Journal of Psychology, 106,* 265–276.

Miller, A. G. (1972). Role playing: An alternative to deception? A review of the evidence. *American Psychologist, 27,* 623–636.

Miller, A. G. (Ed.). (1982). *In the eye of the beholder: Contemporary issues in stereotyping.* New York: Praeger.

Miller, A. (1974). Political issues and trust in government: 1964–1970. *American Political Science Review, 68,* 951–972.

Miller, A. H. (1979). Normal vote analysis: Sensitivity to change over time. *American Journal of Political Science, 23,* 406–420.

Miller, A. H. (1983). Is confidence rebounding? *Public Opinion, 6*(3), 16–20.

Miller, A. H., Miller, W. E., Raine, A. S., & Brown, T. A. (1976). A majority party in disarray: Policy polarization in the 1972 election. *American Political Science Review, 70,* 753–778.

Miller, A. H., & Wattenberg, M. P. (1984). Politics from the pulpit: Religiosity and the 1980 elections. *Public Opinion Quarterly, 48,* 301–317.

Miller, A. H., & Wattenberg, M. P. (1985). Throwing the rascals out: Policy and performance evaluations of presidential candidates, 1952–1980. *American Political Science Review, 79,* 359–372.

Miller, A. H., Wattenberg, M. P., & Malanchuk, O. (1986). Schematic assessments of presidential candidates. *American Political Science Review, 80,* 521–540.

Miller, C. E. (1980). Assessing the existence of "wishful thinking." *Personality and Social Psychology Bulletin, 6,* 282–286.

Miller, D. T., Norman, S. A., & Wright, E. (1978). Distortion in person perception as a consequence of the need for effective control. *Journal of Personality and Social Psychology, 36,* 598–602.

Miller, J., & Garrison, H. H. (1982). Sex roles: The division of labor at home and in the workplace. *Annual Review of Sociology, 8,* 237–262.

Miller, M. M., & Hurd, R. (1982). Conformity to AAPOR standards in newspaper reporting of public opinion polls. *Public Opinion Quarterly, 46,* 243–249.

Miller, N., & Brewer, M. B. (Eds.). (1984). *Groups in contact: The psychology of desegregation.* Orlando, FL: Academic Press.

Miller, N., & Campbell, D. T. (1959). Recency and primacy in persuasion as a function of the timing of speeches and measurement. *Journal of Abnormal and Social Psychology, 59,* 1–9.

Miller, W. E. (1960). The political behavior of the electorate. In E. Latham et al. (Eds.), *American Government Annual, 1960–1961* (pp. 40–48). New York: Holt, Rinehart & Winston.

Miller, W. E. (1987). The election of 1984 and the future of American politics. In K. L. Schlozman (Ed.), *Elections in America* (pp. 293–320). Boston: Allen & Unwin.

Miller, W. E., & Stokes, D. E. (1963). Constituency influence in Congress. *American Political Science Review, 57,* 45–56.

Mills, J., & Harvey, J. (1972). Opinion change as a function of when information about the communicator is received and whether he is attractive or expert. *Journal of Personality and Social Psychology, 21,* 52–55.

Milne, R. S., & Mackenzie, H. C. (1958). *Marginal seat, 1955.* London: Hansard Society for Parliamentary Government.

Minard, R. D. (1952). Race relations in the Pocahontas Coal Field. *Journal of Social Issues, 8*(1), 29–44.

Mirels, H. L. (1980). The avowal of responsibility for good and bad outcomes: The effects of generalized self-serving biases. *Personality and Social Psychology Bulletin, 69,* 299–306.

Mitofsky, W. J. (1969). Who voted for Wallace? *Public Opinion Quarterly, 33,* 444–445.

Money, J., & Ehrhardt, A. (1972). *Man and woman, boy and girl.* Baltimore: Johns Hopkins University Press.

Monroe, A. D. (1978). Public opinion as a factor in public policy formation. *Policy Studies Journal, 6,* 542–548.

Moore, M. (1979). Structural balance and international relations. *European Journal of Social Psychology, 9,* 323–326.

Morgan, M. (1982). Television and adolescents' sex role stereotypes: A longitudinal study. *Journal of Personality and Social Psychology, 43,* 947–955.

Morris, M. (1973). Newspapers and the new feminists: Blackout as social control? *Journalism Quarterly, 50,* 37–42.

Morrissette, J. O. (1958). An experimental study of the theory of structural balance. *Human Relations, 11,* 239–254.

Morrow, L. (1979, October 15). The rise and fall of anti-Catholicism. *Time,* pp. 36–38.

Moscovici, S. (1985). Social influence and conformity. In G. Lindzey & E. Aronson (Eds.), *The handbook of social psychology* (3rd ed., Vol. 2, pp. 347–412). New York: Random House.

Moscovici, S., & Nemeth, C. (1974). Social influence II: Minority influence. In C. Nemeth (Ed.), *Social psychology: Classic and contemporary integrations* (pp. 217–249). Chicago: Rand McNally.

Mosteller, F., Hyman, H., McCarthy, P. J., Marks, E. S., & Truman, D. B. (1949). *The pre-election polls of 1948.* New York: Social Science Research Council.

Mower-White, C. J. (1979). Factors affecting balance, agreement, and positivity biases in POQ and POX triads. *European Journal of Social Psychology, 9,* 129–148.

Mueller, J. E. (1970). Choosing among 133 candidates. *Public Opinion Quarterly, 34,* 395–402.

Mueller, J. E. (1971). Trends in popular support for the wars in Korea and Vietnam. *American Political Science Review, 65,* 358–375.

Mueller, J. E. (1973). *War, presidents and public opinion.* New York: Wiley.

Mueller, J. E. (1988). Trends in political tolerance. *Public Opinion Quarterly, 52,* 1–25.

Mullen, B., Futrell, D., Stairs, D., Tice, D. M., Baumeister, R. F., Dawson, K. E., Riordan, C. A., Radloff, C. E., Goethals, G. R., Kennedy, J. G., & Rosenfeld, P. (1986). Newscasters' facial expressions and voting behavior of viewers: Can a smile elect a president? *Journal of Personality and Social Psychology, 51,* 291–295.

Murray, J. P., & Kippax, S. (1979). From the early window to the late night show: International trends in the study of television's impact on children and adults. In L. Berkowitz (Ed.), *Advances in experimental social psychology* (Vol. 12, pp. 253–320). New York: Academic Press.

Myers, A. M., & Gonda, G. (1982). Empirical validation of the Bem Sex-Role Inventory. *Journal of Personality and Social Psychology, 43,* 304–318.

Myrdal, G. (1944). *An American dilemma: The Negro problem and modern democracy.* New York: Harper.

National Commission on the Causes and Prevention of Violence. (1969). *To establish justice, to insure domestic tranquility.* New York: Award Books.

National Science Foundation. (1969). *Knowledge into action: Improving the nation's use of the social sciences* (Report of the Special Commission on the Social Sciences of the National Science Board). Washington, DC: Author.

Nedzi, L. N. (1971). Public opinion polls: Will legislation help? *Public Opinion Quarterly, 35,* 336–341.

Nelson, L. (1988, August). *Influencing enemy perceptions and nuclear policy options with educational interventions.* Paper presented at American Psychological Association meeting, Atlanta.

Neter, J., & Waksberg, J. (1964). A study of response errors in expenditures data from household interviews. *Journal of the American Statistical Association, 59,* 18–55.

Neuman, W. R. (1976). Patterns of recall among television news viewers. *Public Opinion Quarterly, 40,* 115–123.

Neuman, W. R. (1986). *The paradox of mass politics: Knowledge and opinion in the American electorate.* Cambridge, MA: Harvard University Press.

Nevin, J. A. (1985). Behavior analysis, the nuclear arms race, and the peace movement. In S. Oskamp (Ed.), *International conflict and national public policy issues: Applied social psychology annual 6* (pp. 27–44). Beverly Hills, CA: Sage.

Newcomb, T. M. (1943). *Personality and social change.* New York: Dryden.

Newcomb, T. M., Koenig, K. E., Flacks, R., & Warwick, D. P. (1967). *Persistence and change: Bennington College and its students after 25 years.* New York: Wiley.

Newspaper Enterprise Association. (1985). *The world almanac and book of facts, 1986.* New York: Author.

Newton, N., & Newton, M. (1950). Relationship of ability to breast feed and maternal attitudes toward breast feeding. *Pediatrics, 5,* 869–875.

Nie, N. H., & Andersen, K. (1974). Mass belief systems revisited: Political change and attitude structure. *Journal of Politics, 36,* 540–591.

Nie, N. H., & Rabjohn, J. N. (1979). Revisiting mass belief systems revisited: Or, doing research is like watching a tennis match. *American Journal of Political Science, 23,* 139–175.

Nie, N. H., Verba, S., & Petrocik, J. R. (1979). *The changing American voter* (enlarged ed.). Cambridge, MA: Harvard University Press.

Nie, N. H., Verba, S., & Petrocik, J. R. (1981). Reply to Abramson and to Smith. *American Political Science Review, 75,* 149–152.

Niemi, R. G., Ross, R. D., & Alexander, J. (1978). The similarity of political values of parents and college-age youths. *Public Opinion Quarterly, 42,* 503–520.

Nieva, V. F., & Gutek, B. A. (1981). *Women and work: A psychological perspective.* New York: Praeger.

Nisbett, R. E., Caputo, C., Legant, P., & Marecek, J. (1973). Behavior as seen by the actor and as seen by the observer. *Journal of Personality and Social Psychology, 27,* 154–164.

Nisbett, R. E., & Gordon, A. (1967). Self-esteem and susceptibility to social influence. *Journal of Personality and Social Psychology, 5,* 268–276.

Nisbett, R. E., & Ross, L. (1980). *Human inference: Strategies and shortcomings of social judgment.* Englewood Cliffs, NJ: Prentice-Hall.

Nisbett, R. E., & Valins, S. (1972). Perceiving the causes of one's own behavior. In E. E. Jones, D. E. Kanouse, H. H. Kelley, R. E. Nisbett, S. Valins, & B. Weiner, *Attribution: Perceiving the causes of behavior.* Morristown, NJ: General Learning Press.

Noel, J. G., Forsyth, D. R., & Kelley, K. N. (1987). Improving the performance of failing students by overcoming their self-serving attributional biases. *Basic and Applied Social Psychology, 8,* 151–162.

Norpoth, H. (1987). Under way and here to stay: Party realignment in the 1980s? *Public Opinion Quarterly, 51,* 376–391.

Nunn, C. Z., Crockett, H. J., Jr., & Williams, J. A., Jr. (1978). *Tolerance for nonconformity.* San Francisco: Jossey-Bass.

Nuttin, J. M., Jr. (1975). *The illusion of attitude change: Towards a response contagion theory of persuasion.* London: Academic Press.

O'Keefe, G. J. (1973). A developmental analysis of political communication behavior in the young voter. *Public Opinion Quarterly, 37,* 442–443.

O'Keefe, G. J. (1985). "Taking a bite out of crime": The impact of a public information campaign. *Communication Research, 12,* 147–178.

O'Keefe, G. J., & Atwood, L. E. (1981). Communication and election campaigns. In D. D. Nimmo & K. R. Sanders (Eds.), *Handbook of political communication* (pp. 329–357). Beverly Hills, CA: Sage.

Oldendick, R. W., & Bardes, B. A. (1982). Mass and elite foreign policy options. *Public Opinion Quarterly, 46,* 368–382.

Olson, J. M., & Zanna, M. P. (1979). A new look at selective exposure. *Journal of Experimental Social Psychology, 15,* 1–15.

O'Malley, M., & Thistlethwaite, D. L. (1980). Inference in inconsistency reduction: New evidence on the "Socratic effect." *Journal of Personality and Social Psychology, 39,* 1064–1071.

O'Neill, P., & Levings, D. E. (1979). Induced biased scanning in a group setting to change attitudes toward bilingualism and capital punishment. *Journal of Personality and Social Psychology, 37,* 1432–1438.

Orne, M. T. (1969). Demand characteristics and the concept of quasi-controls. In R. Rosenthal & R. L. Rosnow (Eds.), *Artifact in behavioral research* (pp. 143–179). New York: Academic Press.

Orton, B. (1982). Phony polls: The pollster's nemesis. *Public Opinion, 5*(3), 56–60.

Osgood, C. E. (1962). *An alternative to war or surrender*. Urbana: University of Illinois Press.

Osgood, C. E. (1965). Cross cultural comparability of attitude measurement via multi-lingual semantic differentials. In I. S. Steiner & M. Fishbein (Eds.), *Recent studies in social psychology* (pp. 95–107). New York: Holt, Rinehart & Winston.

Osgood, C. E. (1986). Graduated and reciprocated initiatives in tension-reduction: GRIT. In R. K. White (Ed.), *Psychology and the prevention of nuclear war* (pp. 194–207). New York: New York University Press.

Osgood, C. E., Suci, G. J., & Tannenbaum, P. H. (1957). *The measurement of meaning*. Urbana: University of Illinois Press.

Osgood, C. E., & Tannenbaum, P. H. (1955). The principle of congruity in the prediction of attitude change. *Psychological Review, 62*, 42–55.

Oskamp, S. (1965). Attitudes toward U.S. and Russian actions: A double standard. *Psychological Reports, 16*, 43–46.

Oskamp, S. (1972). International attitudes of British and American students: A fading double standard. *Proceedings, 80th Annual Convention, APA, 7*, 295–296.

Oskamp, S. (1984). *Applied social psychology*. Englewood Cliffs, NJ: Prentice-Hall.

Oskamp, S. (Ed.). (1985a). *International conflict and national public policy issues: Applied social psychology annual 6*. Beverly Hills, CA: Sage.

Oskamp, S. (1985b). Introduction: Social psychology, international affairs, and public policy. In S. Oskamp (Ed.), *International conflict and national public policy issues: Applied social psychology annual 6* (pp. 7–18). Beverly Hills, CA: Sage.

Oskamp, S., & Hartry, A. (1968). A factor-analytic study of the double standard in attitudes toward U.S. and Russian actions. *Behavioral Science, 13*, 178–188.

Ostlund, L. E. (1973). Interpersonal communication following McGovern's Eagleton decision. *Public Opinion Quarterly, 37*, 601–610.

Ostrom, C. W., Jr., & Simon, D. M. (1985). Promise and performance: A dynamic model of presidential popularity. *American Political Science Review, 79*, 334–358.

Page, B. I., & Shapiro, R. Y. (1982). Changes in Americans' policy preferences, 1935–1979. *Public Opinion Quarterly, 46*, 24–42.

Page, B. I., & Shapiro, R. Y. (1983). Effects of public opinion on policy. *American Political Science Review, 77*, 175–189.

Page, B., Shapiro, R., & Dempsey, G. (1985, May). *The mass media do affect policy preferences*. Paper presented at American Association for Public Opinion Research meeting, McAfee, NJ.

Page, B. I., Shapiro, R. Y., Gronke, P. W., & Rosenberg, R. M. (1984). Constituency, party, and representation in congress. *Public Opinion Quarterly, 48*, 741–756.

Page, M. M. (1974). Demand characteristics and the classical conditioning of attitudes experiment. *Journal of Personality and Social Psychology, 30*, 468–476.

Pagel, M. D., & Davidson, A. R. (1984). A comparison of three social-psychological models of attitude and behavioral plan: Prediction of contraceptive behavior. *Journal of Personality and Social Psychology, 47*, 517–533.

Pallak, M. S., Cook, D. A., & Sullivan, J. (1980). Commitment and energy conservation. In L. Bickman (Ed.), *Applied social psychology annual* (Vol. 1, pp. 235–253). Beverly Hills, CA: Sage.

Palmgreen, P., & Clarke, P. (1977). Agenda-setting with local and national issues. *Communication Research, 4*, 435–452.

Paloutzian, R. F. (1981). Purpose in life and value changes following conversion. *Journal of Personality and Social Psychology, 41*, 1153–1160.

Parelius, A. P. (1975). Emerging sex-role attitudes, expectations and strains among college women. *Journal of Marriage and the Family, 37*, 146–153.

Parish, T. S., & Fleetwood, R. S. (1975). Amount of conditioning and subsequent change in racial attitudes of children. *Perceptual and Motor Skills, 40*, 79–86.

Parisot, L. (1988). Attitudes about the media: A five country comparison. *Public Opinion, 10*(5), 18–19 & 60.

Park, B., & Rothbart, M. (1982). Perception of out-group homogeneity and levels of social categorization: Memory for the subordinate attributes of in-group and out-group members. *Journal of Personality and Social Psychology, 42*, 1051–1068.

Parry, H. J., & Crossley, H. M. (1950). Validity of responses to survey questions. *Public Opinion Quarterly, 14*, 61–80.

Parsons, T. (1955). Family structure and the socialization of the child. In T. Parsons & R. F. Bales (Eds.), *Family, socialization, and interaction process*. Glencoe, IL: Free Press.

Patchen, M. (1982). *Black-white contact in schools: Its social and academic effects*. West Lafayette, IN: Purdue University Press.

Patterson, T. E. (1980). *The mass media election: How Americans choose their president*. New York: Praeger.

Patterson, T. E., & McClure, R. D. (1976). *The unseeing eye: The myth of television power in national elections*. New York: Putnam.

Pattullo, E. L. (1984). Institutional review boards and social research: A disruptive, subjective perspective, retrospective and prospective. In J. E. Sieber (Ed.), *NIH readings on the protection of human subjects in behavioral and social science research: Conference proceedings and background papers* (pp. 10–17). Frederick, MD: University Publications of America.

Paulhus, D. (1982). Individual differences, self-presentation, and cognitive dissonance: Their concurrent operation in forced compliance. *Journal of Personality and Social Psychology, 43,* 838–852.

Pavlos, A. J. (1982). *The cult experience.* Westport, CT: Greenwood.

Payne, S. L. (1951). *The art of asking questions.* Princeton, NJ: Princeton University Press.

Peake, P. K., & Cervone, D. (1989). Sequence anchoring and self-efficacy: Primacy effects in the consideration of possibilities. *Social Cognition, 7,* 31–50.

Pearl, D., Bouthilet, L., & Lazar, J. (Eds.). (1982). *Television and behavior: Ten years of scientific progress and implications for the eighties* (Vol. 1): *Summary report;* (Vol. 2): *Technical reviews.* Washington, DC: U.S. Government Printing Office.

Pedhazur, E. J., & Tetenbaum, T. J. (1979). Bem Sex Role Inventory: A theoretical and methodological critique. *Journal of Personality and Social Psychology, 37,* 996–1016.

Perlman, D., & Oskamp, S. (1971). The effects of picture content and exposure frequency on evaluations of Negroes and whites. *Journal of Experimental Social Psychology, 7,* 503–514.

Perry, P. K. (1960). Election survey procedures of the Gallup Poll. *Public Opinion Quarterly, 24,* 531–542.

Perry, P. (1979). Certain problems in election survey methodology. *Public Opinion Quarterly, 43,* 312–325.

Peterson, C. (1980). Attribution in the sports pages: Archival investigation of the covariation hypothesis. *Social Psychology Quarterly, 43,* 134–141.

Peterson, P. D., & Koulack, D. (1969). Attitude change as a function of latitudes of acceptance and rejection. *Journal of Personality and Social Psychology, 11,* 309–311.

Peterson, P. E., Jeffrey, D. B., Bridgwater, C. A., & Dawson, B. (1984). How pronutritional television programming affects children's dietary habits. *Developmental Psychology, 20,* 55–63.

Peterson, R. C., & Thurstone, L. L. (1933). *Motion pictures and the social attitudes of children.* New York: Macmillan.

Petrocik, J. R. (1981). *Party coalitions: Realignments and the decline of the New Deal party system.* Chicago: University of Chicago Press.

Petrocik, J. R. (1987). Voter turnout and electoral preference: The anomalous Reagan elections. In K. L. Schlozman (Ed.), *Elections in America* (pp. 239–259). Boston: Allen & Unwin.

Petrocik, J. R., & Steeper, F. T. (1987). The political landscape in 1987. *Public Opinion, 10*(3), 41–44.

Pettigrew, T. F. (1959). Regional differences in anti-Negro prejudice. *Journal of Abnormal and Social Psychology, 59,* 28–36.

Pettigrew, T. (1967). Social evaluation theory: Convergences and applications. In D. Levine (Ed.), *Nebraska symposium on motivation* (Vol. 15, pp. 241–311). Lincoln: University of Nebraska Press.

Pettigrew, T. F. (1969). Racially separate or together? *Journal of Social Issues, 25*(1), 43–69.

Pettigrew, T. F. (1971). Race relations. In R. Merton & R. Nisbet (Eds.), *Contemporary social problems* (pp. 407–466). New York: Harcourt Brace Jovanovich.

Pettigrew, T. F. (1979). The ultimate attribution error: Extending Allport's cognitive analysis of prejudice. *Personality and Social Psychology Bulletin, 5,* 461–476.

Petty, R. E., & Cacioppo, J. T. (1977). Forewarning, cognitive responding, and resistance to persuasion. *Journal of Personality and Social Psychology, 35,* 645–655.

Petty, R. E., & Cacioppo, J. T. (1979a). Effects of forewarning of persuasive intent and involvement on cognitive responses and persuasion. *Personality and Social Psychology Bulletin, 5,* 173–176.

Petty, R. E., & Cacioppo, J. T. (1979b). Issue involvement can increase or decrease persuasion by enhancing message-relevant cognitive responses. *Journal of Personality and Social Psychology, 37,* 1915–1926.

Petty, R. E., & Cacioppo, J. T. (1981). *Attitudes and persuasion: Classic and contemporary approaches.* Dubuque, IA: Brown.

Petty, R. E., & Cacioppo, J. T. (1984). The effects of involvement on responses to argument quantity and quality: Central and peripheral routes to persuasion. *Journal of Personality and Social Psychology, 46,* 69–81.

Petty, R. E., & Cacioppo, J. T. (1986). *Communication and persuasion: Central and peripheral routes to attitude change.* New York: Springer-Verlag.

Petty, R. E., & Cacioppo, J. T. (1990). Involvement and persuasion: Tradition versus integration. *Psychological Bulletin, 107,* 367–374.

Petty, R. E., Ostrom, T. M., & Brock, T. C. (Eds.). (1981). *Cognitive responses in persuasion.* Hillsdale, NJ: Erlbaum.

Petty, R. E., Wells, G. L., & Brock, T. C. (1976). Distraction can enhance or reduce yielding to propaganda: Thought disruption versus effort justification. *Journal of Personality and Social Psychology, 34,* 874–884.

Pfister G. (1975). Outcomes of laboratory training for police officers. *Journal of Social Issues, 31*(1), 115–121.

Phillips, D. L., & Clancy, K. J. (1972). "Modeling effects" in survey research. *Public Opinion Quarterly, 36,* 246–253.

Pierce, C. M. (1980). Social trace contaminants: Subtle indicators of racism in TV. In S. B. Withey & R. P. Abeles (Eds.), *Television and social behavior: Beyond violence and children.* Hillsdale, NJ: Erlbaum.

Pitcher, E. G., Feinberg, S. G., & Alexander, D. (1984). *Helping young children learn* (4th ed.). Columbus, OH: Merrill.

Pitcher, E. G., & Schultz, L. H. (1983). *Boys and girls at play: The development of sex roles.* New York: Praeger.

Pleck, J. H. (1981). *The myth of masculinity*. Cambridge, MA: MIT Press.

Pleck, J. H. (1985). *Working wives, working husbands*. Beverly Hills, CA: Sage.

Plous, S. (1985). Psychological and strategic barriers in present attempts at nuclear disarmament: A new proposal. *Political Psychology, 6*, 109–133.

Pomper, G. M. (1975). Impacts on the political system. In S. A. Kirkpatrick (Ed.), *American electoral behavior: Change and stability* (pp. 137–143). Beverly Hills, CA: Sage.

Pool, I. deS. (1959). TV: A new dimension in politics. In E. Burdick & A. J. Brodbeck (Eds.), *American voting behavior* (pp. 197–208). Glencoe, IL: Free Press.

Pool, I. deS. (1965). Effects of cross-national contact on national and international images. In H. C. Kelman (Ed.), *International behavior: A social-psychological analysis* (pp. 106–129). New York: Holt, Rinehart & Winston.

Pool, I. deS., Abelson, R. P., & Popkin, S. L. (1964). *Candidates, issues, and strategies: A computer simulation of the 1960 presidential election*. Cambridge, MA: MIT Press.

Poppleton, P. K., & Pilkington, G. W. (1964). A comparison of four methods of scoring an attitude scale in relation to its reliability and validity. *British Journal of Social and Clinical Psychology, 3*, 36–39.

Porter, J. R., & Washington, R. E. (1979). Black identity and self-esteem: A review of studies of black self-concept, 1968–1978. *Annual Review of Sociology 5*, 53–74.

Potter, J. (1981). The development of social psychology: Consensus, theory and methodology in the *British Journal of Social and Clinical Psychology*. *British Journal of Social Psychology, 20*, 249–258.

Powell, G. B., Jr. (1986). American voter turnout in comparative perspective. *American Political Science Review, 80*, 17–43.

Pratkanis, A. R., Greenwald, A. G., Leippe, M. R., & Baumgardner, M. H. (1988). In search of reliable persuasion effects: III. The sleeper effect is dead. Long live the sleeper effect. *Journal of Personality and Social Psychology, 54*, 203–218.

Price, K. O., Harburg, E., & Newcomb, T. M. (1966). Psychological balance in situations of negative interpersonal attitudes. *Journal of Personality and Social Psychology, 3*, 265–270.

Pryor, J. B. (1986). The influence of different encoding sets upon the formation of illusory correlations and group impressions. *Personality and Social Psychology Bulletin, 12*, 216–226.

Public Agenda Foundation. (1984). *Voter options on nuclear arms policy: A briefing book for the 1984 elections*. New York: Author.

Public Opinion. (1980/1981, December/January). Opinion roundup: 1980 results. No. 6, pp. 21–44.

Public Opinion. (1985, October/November). Is it realignment? Surveying the evidence. No. 5, pp. 21–31.

Public Opinion. (1987, July/August). The state of intolerance in America. No. 2, pp. 21–31.

Public Opinion. (1987, July/August). Political minorities. No. 2, p. 29.

Public Opinion. (1987, November/December). Party I.D.; Ideology. No. 4, pp. 22–23.

Public Opinion. (1987, November/December). Most important problems. No. 4, pp. 26–27.

Public Opinion. (1987, November/December). Economic indicators. No. 4, pp. 34–37.

Public Opinion. (1988, January/February). America: A regional review. No. 5, pp. 25–30.

Public Opinion. (1988, March/April). Attitudes toward the Soviet Union and the United States: A four-country comparison. No. 6, pp. 29–30.

Public Opinion. (1988, July/August). Most important problems. No. 2, pp. 34–35.

Public Opinion. (1988, September/October). Attitudes toward the Soviets: Stability. No. 3, pp. 26–27.

Public Opinion. (1989, January/February). The exit poll results. No. 5, pp. 24–26.

Public Opinion. (1989, March/April). Attitudes today. No. 6, pp. 30–33.

Putney, S., & Middleton, R. (1962). Some factors associated with student acceptance or rejection of war. *American Sociological Review, 27*, 655–667.

Quigley-Fernandez, B., & Tedeschi, J. T. (1978). The bogus pipeline as lie detector: Two validity studies. *Journal of Personality and Social psychology, 36*, 247–256.

Raden, D. (1977). Situational thresholds and attitude-behavior consistency. *Sociometry, 40*, 123–129.

Raj, S. P. (1982). The effects of advertising on high and low loyalty consumer segments. *Journal of Consumer Research, 9*, 77–89.

Rapoport, R., & Rapoport, R. N. (1977). *Dual-career families revisited*. New York: Academic Press.

Rappoport, L., & Cvetkovich, G. (1968). Opinion on Vietnam: Some findings from three studies. *Proceedings, 76th Annual Convention, APA, 3*, 381–382.

Rathje, W. L., & Ritenbaugh, C. (Eds.). (1984). Household refuse analysis: Theory, methods, and applications in social science. *American Behavioral Scientist, 28*, 1–160.

Ray, L. (1972). The American woman in mass media: How much emancipation and what does it mean? In C. Safilios-Rothschild (Ed.), *Toward a sociology of women* (pp. 41–62). Lexington, MA: Xerox.

Read, S. J. (1983). Once is enough: Causal reasoning from a single instance. *Journal of Personality and Social Psychology, 45*, 323–334.

Redbook. (1973, January). Pp. 67–69.

Reese, S. D., Danielson, W. A., Shoemaker, P. J., Chang, T-K., & Hsu, H-L. (1986). Ethnicity-of-interviewer effects among Mexican-Americans and Anglos. *Public Opinion Quarterly, 50*, 563–572.

Regan, D. T., & Totten, J. (1975). Empathy and attribution: Turning observers into actors. *Journal of Personality and Social Psychology, 32*, 850–856.

Reich, J. W. (1982). *Experimenting in society: Issues and examples in applied social psychology*. Glenview, IL: Scott, Foresman.

Reid, P. T. (1988). Racism and sexism: Comparison and conflicts. In P. A. Katz & D. A. Taylor (Eds.), *Eliminating racism: Profiles in controversy* (pp. 203–221). New York: Plenum.

Reisenzein, R. (1983). The Schachter theory of emotion: Two decades later. *Psychological Bulletin, 94*, 239–264.

Renshon, S. A. (Ed.). (1977). *Handbook of political socialization: Theory and research.* New York: Free Press.

RePass, D. E. (1971). Issue salience and party choice. *American Political Science Review, 65*, 389–400.

Report of the National Advisory Commission on Civil Disorders. (1968). New York: Bantam.

Rettig, S. (1966). Relation of social systems to intergenerational changes in moral attitudes. *Journal of Personality and Social Psychology, 4*, 409–414.

Rhine, R. J., & Polowniak, W. A. (1971). Attitude change, commitment and ego involvement. *Journal of Personality and Social Psychology, 19*, 246–250.

Rice, R. W., Bender, L. R., & Vitters, A. G. (1980). Leader sex, follower attitudes toward women, and leadership effectiveness. *Organizational Behavior and Human Performance, 25*, 46–78.

Richardson, J. G., & Simpson, C. H. (1982). Children, gender, and social structure: An analysis of the contents of letters to Santa Claus. *Child Development, 53*, 429–436.

Richardson L. (1988). *The dynamics of sex and gender: A sociological perspective* (3rd ed.). New York: Harper & Row.

Riddleberger, A. B., & Motz, A. B. (1957). Prejudice and perception. *American Journal of Sociology, 62*, 498–503.

Riess, M., Rosenfeld, P., Melburg, V., & Tedeschi, J. T. (1981). Self-serving attributions: Biased private perceptions and distorted public descriptions. *Journal of Personality and Social Psychology, 41*, 224–251.

Riley, R. T., & Pettigrew, T. F. (1976). Dramatic events and attitude change. *Journal of Personality and Social Psychology, 34*, 1004–1015.

Ringold, D. J. (1988). Consumer response to product withdrawal: The reformulation of Coca-Cola. *Psychology and Marketing, 5*, 189–210.

Roberts, D., & Bachen, C. (1981). Mass communication effects. *Annual Review of Psychology, 32*, 307–356.

Roberts, D. F., Christenson, P., Gibson, W. A., Mooser, L., & Goldberg, M. E. (1980). Developing discriminating consumers. *Journal of Communication, 30*(3), 94–105.

Roberts, D. F., & Maccoby, N. (1985). Effects of mass communication. In G. Lindzey & E. Aronson (Eds.), *The handbook of social psychology* (3rd ed., Vol. 2, pp. 539–598). New York: Random House.

Robinson, J. E., & Insko, C. A. (1969). Attributed belief similarity-dissimilarity versus race as determinants of prejudice: A further test of Rokeach's theory. *Journal of Experimental Research in Personality, 4*, 72–77.

Robinson, J. P. (1971). The audience for national TV news programs. *Public Opinion Quarterly, 35*, 403–405.

Robinson, J. P. (1972). Perceived media bias and the 1968 vote: Can the media affect behavior after all? *Journalism Quarterly, 49*, 239–246.

Robinson, J. P. (1974). Public opinion during the Watergate crisis. *Communication Research, 1*, 391–405.

Robinson, J. P. (1976). Interpersonal influence in election campaigns: Two step-flow hypotheses. *Public Opinion Quarterly, 40*, 304–319.

Robinson, J. P. (1980). The changing reading habits of the American public. *Journal of Communication, 30*, 141–152.

Robinson, J. P. (1984). The ups and downs and ins and outs of ideology. *Public Opinion, 7*(1), 12–15.

Robinson, J. P. (1988). Who's doing the housework? *American Demographics, 10*(12), 24–28 & 63.

Robinson, J. P., & Fleishman, J. A. (1988). The polls—A report: Ideological identification: Trends and interpretations of the liberal-conservative balance. *Public Opinion Quarterly, 52*, 134–145.

Robinson, J. P., & Levy, M. R. (1986a). Interpersonal communication and news comprehension. *Public Opinion Quarterly, 50*, 160–175.

Robinson, J. P., & Levy, M. R. (1986b). *The main source: Learning from television news.* Beverly Hills, CA: Sage.

Rochon, T. R. (1988). *Mobilizing for peace: The antinuclear movements in western Europe.* Princeton, NJ: Princeton University Press.

Rodin, J. (1985). The application of social psychology. In G. Lindzey & E. Aronson (Eds.), *The handbook of social psychology* (3rd ed., Vol. 2, pp. 805–881). New York: Random House.

Rogers, E. R. (1982). *Diffusion of innovations* (3rd ed.). New York: Free Press.

Rogers, R. W., & Mewborn, C. R. (1976). Fear appeals and attitude change: Effects of a threat's noxiousness, probability of occurrence, and efficacy of coping response. *Journal of Personality and Social Psychology, 34*, 54–61.

Rogers, S. C. (1981). Woman's place: A critical review of anthropological theory. In S. Cox (Ed.), *Female psychology: The emerging self* (2nd ed.). New York: St. Martin's.

Rokeach, M. (1960). *The open and closed mind.* New York: Basic Books.

Rokeach, M. (1967). Authoritarianism scales and response bias: Comment on Peabody's paper. *Psychological Bulletin, 67*, 349–355.

Rokeach, M. (1968). *Beliefs, attitudes, and values: A theory of organization and change.* San Francisco: Jossey-Bass.

Rokeach, M. (1971). Long-range experimental modification of values, attitudes, and behavior. *American Psychologist, 26*, 453–459.

Rokeach, M. (1979). Some unresolved issues in theories of beliefs, attitudes, and values. *Nebraska Symposium on Motivation, 27*, 261–304.

Rokeach, M., & Grube, J. W. (1979). Can values be manipulated arbitrarily? In M. Rokeach, *Understanding human values: Individual and social* (pp. 241–256). New York: Free Press.

Rokeach, M., & McLellan, D. D. (1972). Feedback of information about the values and attitudes of self and others as determinants of long-term cognitive and behavioral change. *Journal of Applied Social Psychology, 2,* 236–251.

Rokeach, M., & Rothman, G. (1965). The principle of belief congruence and the congruity principle as models of cognitive interaction. *Psychological Review, 72,* 128–142.

Roll, C. W., Jr., & Cantril, A. H. (1980). *Polls: Their use and misuse in politics* (rev. ed.). Cabin John, MD: Seven Locks Press.

Roper, B. (1983). The polls' malfunction in 1982. *Public Opinion, 5*(6), 41–42.

Roper, B. W. (1984). Are polls accurate? *Annals of the American Academy of Political and Social Science, 472,* 24–34.

Rosaldo, M. Z. (1974). Women, culture, and society: A theoretical overview. In M. Z. Rosaldo & L. Lamphere (Eds.), *Woman, culture, and society.* Stanford, CA: Stanford University Press.

Rosen, B., & Jerdee, T. H. (1978). Perceived sex differences in managerially relevant characteristics. *Sex Roles, 4,* 837–843.

Rosen, R. (1971). Sexism in history or, writing women's history is a tricky business. *Journal of Marriage and the Family, 33,* 541–544.

Rosenberg, M. J. (1960). An analysis of affective-cognitive consistency. In M. J. Rosenberg, C. I. Hovland, W. J. McGuire, R. P. Abelson, & J. W. Brehm, *Attitude organization and change: An analysis of consistency among attitude components* (pp. 15–64). New Haven, CT: Yale University Press.

Rosenberg, M. J. (1967). Attitude change and foreign policy in the cold war era. In J. N. Rosenau (Ed.), *Domestic sources of foreign policy* (pp. 111–159). New York: Free Press.

Rosenberg, M. J. (1969). The conditions and consequences of evaluation apprehension. In R. Rosenthal & R. L. Rosnow, *Artifact in behavioral research* (pp. 279–349). New York: Academic Press.

Rosenberg, M. J., & Abelson, R. P. (1960). An analysis of cognitive balancing. In M. J. Rosenberg et al., *Attitude organization and change: An analysis of consistency among attitude components* (pp. 112–163). New Haven, CT: Yale University Press.

Rosenberg, M. J., Hovland, C. I., McGuire, W. J., Abelson, R. P., & Brehm, J. W. (1960). *Attitude organization and change: An analysis of consistency among attitude components.* New Haven, CT: Yale University Press.

Rosenfeld, P., Giacalone, R. A., & Tedeschi, J. T. (1983). Cognitive dissonance vs. impression management. *Journal of Social Psychology, 120,* 203–211.

Rosenstone, S. J. (1983). *Forecasting presidential elections.* New Haven, CT: Yale University Press.

Rosenstone, S. J., Hansen, J. M., & Kinder, D. R. (1986). Measuring change in personal economic well-being. *Public Opinion Quarterly, 50,* 176–192.

Rosenthal, R. (1969). Interpersonal expectations: Effects of the experimenter's hypothesis. In R. Rosenthal & R. L. Rosnow, *Artifact in behavioral research* (pp. 181–277). New York: Academic Press.

Rosenthal, R. (1976). *Experimenter effects in behavioral research* (enlarged ed.). New York: Irvington.

Rosenthal, R., & Rosnow, R. L. (1969). *Artifact in behavioral research.* New York: Academic Press.

Rosenthal, R., & Rosnow, R. L. (1975). *The volunteer subject.* New York: Wiley.

Rosenthal, R., & Rosnow, R. L. (1984). *Essentials of behavioral research: Methods and data analysis.* New York: McGraw-Hill.

Rosi, E. J. (1965). Mass and attentive opinion on nuclear weapons tests and fall out, 1954–1963. *Public Opinion Quarterly, 29,* 280–297.

Rosnow, R. L. (1966). Whatever happened to the "law of primacy"? *Journal of Communication, 16,* 10–31.

Rosnow, R. L., & Suls, J. M. (1970). Reactive effects of pretesting in attitude research. *Journal of Personality and Social Psychology, 15,* 338–343.

Ross, L. (1977). The intuitive psychologist and his shortcomings: Distortions in the attribution process. In L. Berkowitz (Ed.), *Advances in experimental social psychology* (Vol. 10, pp. 173–220). New York: Academic Press.

Ross, L., Amabile, T. M., & Steinmetz, J. L. (1977). Social roles, social control, and biases in social perception processes. *Journal of Personality and Social Psychology, 35,* 485–494.

Ross, L., Greene, D., & House, P. (1977). The "false consensus effect": An egocentric bias in social perception and attribution processes. *Journal of Experimental Social Psychology, 13,* 279–301.

Ross, M., & Fletcher, G. J. O. (1985). Attribution and social perception. In G. Lindzey & E. Aronson (Eds.), *The handbook of social psychology* (3rd ed., Vol. 2, pp. 73–122). New York: Random House.

Rossi, P. H., & Cutright, P. (1961). The impact of party organization in an industrial setting. In M. Janowitz (Ed.), *Community political systems* (pp. 81–116). Glencoe, IL: Free Press.

Rossi, P. H., & Lyall, K. C. (1976). *Reforming public welfare: A critique of the negative income tax experiment.* New York: Russell Sage Foundation.

Rossi, P. H., Wright, J. D., & Anderson, A. B. (Eds.). (1983). *Handbook of survey research.* New York: Academic Press.

Rothbart, M., Evans, M., & Fulero, S. (1979). Recall for confirming events: Memory processes and the maintenance of social stereotyping. *Journal of Experimental Social Psychology, 15,* 343–355.

Rothbart, M., Fulero, S., Jensen, C., Howard, J., & Birrell, B. (1978). From individual to group impressions: Availability heuristics in stereotype formation. *Journal of Experimental Social Psychology, 14,* 237–255.

Rothenberg, S. (1989). Election '88: The House and the Senate. *Public Opinion, 11*(5), 8–11 & 59.

Rothschild, M. L., & Ray, M. L. (1973). Involvement and political advertising effectiveness: A laboratory repetition experiment. *Public Opinion Quarterly, 37,* 448–449.

Rotter, J. B. (1966). Generalized expectancies for internal versus external control of reinforcement. *Psychological Monographs, 80*(1, Whole No. 609).

Rubin, J., Provenzano, F., & Luria, Z. (1974). The eye of the beholder: Parents' views on sex of newborns. *American Journal of Orthopsychiatry, 44,* 512–519.

Rubin, Z., & Moore, J. C., Jr. (1971). Assessment of subjects' suspicions. *Journal of Personality and Social Psychology, 17,* 163–170.

Ruble, T. L. (1983). Sex stereotypes: Issues of change in the 1970s. *Sex Roles, 9,* 397–402.

Rushton, J. P. (1975). Generosity in children: Immediate and long-term effects of modeling, preaching and moral judgment. *Journal of Personality and Social Psychology, 31,* 459–466.

Rushton, J. P. (1982). Television and prosocial behavior. In D. Pearl, L. Bouthilet, & J. Lazar (Eds.), *Television and behavior: Ten years of scientific progress and implications for the eighties* (Vol. 2): *Technical reviews.* Washington, DC: U.S. Government Printing Office.

Russo, F. D. (1971). A study of bias in TV coverage of the Vietnam War: 1969 and 1970. *Public Opinion Quarterly, 35,* 539–543.

Russo, N. F., & Denmark, F. L. (1984). Women, psychology, and public policy: Selected issues. *American Psychologist, 39,* 1161–1165.

Rutter, M., Maughan, B., Mortimore, P., & Ouston, J. (1979). *Fifteen thousand hours: Secondary schools and their effects on children.* Somerset, England: Open Books.

Sadler, O., & Tesser, A. (1973). Some effects of salience and time upon interpersonal hostility and attraction during social isolation. *Sociometry, 36,* 99–112.

St. Peter, S. (1979). Jack went up the hill . . . but where was Jill? *Psychology of Women Quarterly, 4,* 256–260.

Saks, M. J. (1974). Ignorance of science is no excuse. *Trial, 10*(6), 18–20.

Sande, G. N., Goethals, G. R., Ferrari, L., & Worth, L. T. (1989). Value-guided attributions: Maintaining the moral self-image and the diabolical enemy-image. *Journal of Social Issues, 45*(2), 91–118.

Sanders, K. R., & Atwood, L. E. (1979). Value change initiated by the mass media. In M. Rokeach, *Understanding human values: Individual and social* (pp. 226–240). New York: Free Press.

Sargant, W. (1957). *Battle for the mind: A physiology of conversion and brainwashing.* Garden City, NY: Doubleday.

Sata, L. S. (1975). Laboratory training for police officers. *Journal of Social Issues, 31*(1), 107–114.

Sawyer, F. (1988). Realities of television news programming. In S. Oskamp (Ed.), *Television as a social issue: Applied social psychology annual 8* (pp. 30–43). Newbury Park, CA: Sage.

Saxe, L., & Dougherty, D. (1985). Technology assessment and congressional use of social psychology: Making complexity understandable. In S. Oskamp (Ed.), *Applied social psychology annual* (Vol. 6): *International conflict and national public policy issues.* Beverly Hills, CA: Sage.

Scarrow, H. A., & Borman, S. (1979). The effects of newspaper endorsements on election outcomes: A case study. *Public Opinion Quarterly, 43,* 388–393.

Schachter, S., & Singer, J. E. (1962). Cognitive, social, and physiological determinants of emotional state. *Psychological Review, 69,* 379–399.

Schaffner, P. E., Wandersman, A., & Stang, D. (1981). Candidate name exposure and voting: Two field studies. *Basic and Applied Social Psychology, 2,* 195–203.

Schifter, D. E., & Ajzen, I. (1985). Intention, perceived control, and weight loss: An application of the theory of planned behavior. *Journal of Personality and Social Psychology, 49,* 843–851.

Schlegel, R. P., d'Avernas, J. R., Zanna, M. P., & Manske, S. R. (1988). *Problem drinking: A problem for the theory of reasoned action?* Unpublished manuscript, University of Waterloo.

Schlenker, B. R. (1980). *Impression management: The self-concept, social identity, and interpersonal relations.* Monterey, CA: Brooks/Cole.

Schlenker, B. R. (1982). Translating actions into attitudes: An identity-analytic approach to the explanation of social conduct. In L. Berkowitz (Ed.), *Advances in experimental social psychology* (Vol. 15, pp. 193–247). New York: Academic Press.

Schlesinger, A. M. (1939). Tides of American politics. *Yale Review, 29,* 217–230.

Schlozman, K. L. (Ed.). (1987). *Elections in America.* Boston: Allen & Unwin.

Schlozman, K. L., & Verba, S. (1987). Sending them a message—Getting a reply: Presidential elections and democratic accountability. In K. L. Schlozman (Ed.), *Elections in America* (pp. 3–25). Boston: Allen & Unwin.

Schneider, D. J., Hastorf, A. H., & Ellsworth, P. C. (1979). *Person perception* (2nd ed.). Reading, MA: Addison-Wesley.

Schneider, W. (1983). Elite and public opinion: The alliance's new fissure? *Public Opinion, 6*(1), 5–8 & 51.

Schonbach, P. (1981). *Education and intergroup attitudes.* London: Academic Press.

Schramm, W. (1964). *Mass media and national development.* Stanford, CA: Stanford University Press.

Schrank, H. T., & Riley, J. W., Jr. (1976). Women in work organizations. In J. M. Kreps (Ed.), *Women and the American economy: A look to the 1980's.* Englewood Cliffs, NJ: Prentice-Hall.

Schuessler, K., Hittle, D., & Cardascia, J. (1978). Measuring responding desirably with attitude-opinion items. *Social Psychology, 41,* 224–235.

Schuman, H. (1972). Attitudes vs. actions versus attitudes vs. attitudes. *Public Opinion Quarterly, 36,* 347–354.

Schuman, H., & Hatchett, S. (1974). *Black racial attitudes: Trends and complexities.* Ann Arbor, MI: Institute for Social Research, University of Michigan.

Schuman, H., & Johnson, M. P. (1976). Attitudes and behavior. *Annual Review of Sociology, 2,* 161–207.

Schuman, H., & Kalton, G. (1985). Survey methods. In G. Lindzey & E. Aronson (Eds.), *The handbook of social psychology* (3rd ed., Vol. 1, pp. 635–697). New York: Random House.

Schuman, H., & Presser, S. (1981a). The attitude-action connection and the issue of gun control. *The Annals of the American Academy of Political and Social Science, 455,* 40–47.

Schuman, H., & Presser, S. (1981b). *Questions and answers in attitude surveys: Experiments on question form, wording, and context.* New York: Academic Press.

Schuman, H., Steeh, C., & Bobo, L. (1985). *Racial attitudes in America: Trends and interpretations.* Cambridge, MA: Harvard University Press.

Schwartz, S. H. (1978). Temporal instability as a moderator of the attitude-behavior relationship. *Journal of Personality and Social Psychology, 36,* 715–724.

Schwartz, S. H., & Tessler, R. C. (1972). A test of a model for reducing measured attitude-behavior discrepancies. *Journal of Personality and Social Psychology, 24,* 225–236.

Scientific Advisory Committee on Television and Social Behavior. (1972). *Television and growing up: The impact of televised violence.* Report to the Surgeon General, USPHS. Washington, DC: U.S. Department of Health, Education, & Welfare.

Scott, C. A., & Yalch, R. F. (1978). A test of the self-perception explanation of the effects of rewards on intrinsic interest. *Journal of Experimental Social Psychology, 14,* 180–192.

Scott, J. P., & Fuller, J. R. (1965). *Genetics and social behavior of the dog.* Chicago: University of Chicago Press.

Scott, R. A., & Shore, A. R. (1979). *Why sociology does not apply: A study of the use of sociology in public policy.* New York: Elsevier.

Scott, W. A. (1959). Attitude change by response reinforcement: Replication and extension. *Sociometry, 22,* 328–335.

Scott, W. A. (1965). Psychological and social correlates of international images. In H. C. Kelman (Ed.), *International behavior: A social-psychological anaysis* (pp. 71–103). New York: Holt, Rinehart & Winston.

Scott, W. A. (1968). Attitude measurement. In G. Lindzey & E. Aronson (Eds.), *The handbook of social psychology* (2nd ed., Vol. 2, pp. 204–273). Reading, MA: Addison-Wesley.

Scully, D., & Bart, P. (1973). A funny thing happened on the way to the orifice: Women in gynecology textbooks. In J. Huber (Ed.), *Changing women in a changing society* (pp. 283–288). Chicago: University of Chicago Press.

Sears, D. O. (1969). Political behavior. In G. Lindzey & E. Aronson (Eds.), *The handbook of social psychology* (2nd ed., Vol.5, pp. 315–458). Reading, MA: Addison-Wesley.

Sears, D. O. (1986). College sophomores in the laboratory: Influences of a narrow data base on social psychology's view of human nature. *Journal of Personality and Social Psychology, 51,* 515–530.

Sears, D. O. (1988a). Symbolic racism. In P. A. Katz & D. A. Taylor (Eds.), *Eliminating racism: Profiles in controversy* (pp. 53–84). New York: Plenum.

Sears, D. O. (1988b). [Review of *Communication and persuasion: Central and peripheral routes to attitude change*]. *Public Opinion Quarterly, 52,* 262–265.

Sears, D. O., & Abeles, R. P. (1969). Attitudes and opinions. *Annual Review of Psychology, 20,* 253–288.

Sears, D. O., & Allen, H. M., Jr. (1984). The trajectory of local desegregation controversies and whites' opposition to busing. In N. Miller & M. B. Brewer (Eds.), *Groups in contact: The psychology of desegregation* (pp. 123–151). New York: Academic Press.

Sears, D. O., & Chaffee, S. H. (1979). Uses and effects of the 1976 debates: An overview of empirical studies. In S. Kraus (Ed.), *The great debates, 1976: Ford vs. Carter* (pp. 223–261). Bloomington: Indiana University Press.

Sears, D. O., & Citrin, J. (1985). *Tax revolt: Something for nothing in California* (enlarged ed.). Cambridge, MA: Harvard University Press.

Sears, D. O., & Freedman, J. L. (1967). Selective exposure to information: A critical review. *Public Opinion Quarterly, 31,* 194–213.

Sears, D. O., Lau, R. R., Tyler, T. R., & Allen, H. M., Jr. (1980). Self-interest versus symbolic politics in policy attitudes and presidential voting. *American Political Science Review, 74,* 670–684.

Sears, D. O., & Whitney, R. E. (1973). *Political persuasion.* Morristown, NJ: General Learning Press.

Secord, P. F. (1977). Social psychology in search of a paradigm. *Personality and Social Psychology Bulletin, 3,* 41–50.

Seggar, J. F., & Wheeler, P. (1973). World of work on TV: Ethnic and sex representation in TV drama. *Journal of Broadcasting, 17,* 201–214.

Sellers, C. (1965). The equilibrium cycle in two-party politics. *Public Opinion Quarterly, 29,* 16–38.

Selltiz, C., & Cook, S. W. (1962). Factors influencing attitudes of foreign students toward the host country. *Journal of Social Issues, 18*(1), 7–23.

Selznick, G. J., & Steinberg, S. (1969). *The tenacity of prejudice: Anti-semitism in contemporary America.* New York: Harper & Row.

Serbin, L. A., & O'Leary, K. D. (1975, December). How nursery schools teach girls to shut up. *Psychology Today,* pp. 56–58.

Severy, L. J. (1974, December). *Procedures and issues in the measurement of attitudes* (TM Report 30). Princeton, NJ: ERIC Clearinghouse on Tests, Measurement, & Evaluation, Educational Testing Service.

Sexton, D., & Haberman, P. (1974). Women in magazine advertisements. *Journal of Advertising Research, 14,* 41–46.

Shakin, M., Sternglanz, S. H., & Shakin, D. (1985). Infant clothing: Sex labeling for strangers. *Sex Roles, 5*(2), 28–37.

Shamir, J. (1986). Preelection polls in Israel: Structural constraints on accuracy. *Public Opinion Quarterly, 50,* 62–75.

Sharan, S. (1980). Cooperative learning in small groups: Recent methods and effects on achievement, attitudes, and ethnic relations. *Review of Educational Research, 50,* 241–271.

Shavitt, S. (1988). Operationalizing functional theories of attitude. In A. R. Pratkanis, S. J. Breckler, & A. G. Greenwald (Eds.), *Attitude structure and function.* Hillsdale, NJ: Erlbaum.

Shaw, M. E., & Costanzo, P. R. (1982). *Theories of social psychology* (2nd ed.). New York: McGraw-Hill.

Shaw, M. E., & Wright, J. M. (1967). *Scales for the measurement of attitudes.* New York: McGraw-Hill.

Sheatsley, P. B. (1977). Public Opinion—A weekly journal. *Public Opinion Quarterly, 41,* 400–401.

Sheatsley, P. B., & Feldman, J. J. (1965). A national survey on public reactions and behavior. In B. S. Greenberg & E. B. Parker (Eds.), *The Kennedy assassination and the American public* (pp. 149–177). Stanford, CA: Stanford University Press.

Sheets, T., Radlinski, A., Kohne, J., & Brunner, G. A. (1974). Deceived respondents: Once bitten, twice shy. *Public Opinion Quarterly, 38,* 261–263.

Sherif, C. W., Sherif, M., & Nebergall, R. E. (1965). *Attitude and attitude change: The social judgment-involvement approach.* Philadelphia: Saunders.

Sherif, M., Harvey, O. J., White, B. J., Hood, W. E., & Sherif, C. W. (1961). *Intergroup conflict and cooperation: The Robber's Cave experiment.* Norman: University of Oklahoma Book Exchange.

Sherif, M., & Hovland, C. I. (1961). *Social judgment: Assimilation and contrast effects in communication and attitude change.* New Haven, CT: Yale University Press.

Sheth, J. N. (1974). A field study of attitude structure and the attitude-behavior relationship. In J. N. Sheth (Ed.), *Models of buyer behavior: Conceptual, quantitative, and empirical* (pp. 242–268). New York: Harper & Row.

Shively, W. P. (1971). A reinterpretation of the New Deal realignment. *Public Opinion Quarterly, 35,* 621–624.

Sidorowicz, L., & Lunney, G. S. (1980). Baby X revisited. *Sex Roles, 6,* 67–73.

Sieber, J. E. (Ed.). (1982). *The ethics of social research: Surveys and experiments.* New York: Springer-Verlag.

Sieber, J. E. (Ed.). (1984). *NIH readings on the protection of human subjects in behavioral and social science research: Conference proceedings and background papers.* Frederick, MD: University Publications of America.

Sigelman, L., & Sigelman, C. K. (1984). Judgments of the Carter-Reagan debate: The eyes of the beholders. *Public Opinion Quarterly, 48,* 624–628.

Signorielli, N., Gross, L., & Morgan, M. (1982). Violence in television programs: Ten years later. In D. Pearl, L. Bouthilet, & J. Lazar (Eds.), *Television and behavior: Ten years of scientific progress and implications for the eighties* (Vol. 2): *Technical reviews.* Washington, DC: U.S. Government Printing Office.

Silver, B. D., Anderson, B. A., & Abramson, P. R. (1986). Who overreports voting? *American Political Science Review, 80,* 613–624.

Silverman, I. (1964). In defense of dissonance theory: Reply to Chapanis and Chapanis. *Psychological Bulletin, 62,* 205–209.

Silverstein, B., & Flamenbaum, C. (1989). Biases in the perception and cognition of the actions of enemies. *Journal of Social Issues, 45*(2), 51–72.

Simmons, W. H., & Zumpf, C. (1983). The lost letter technique revisited. *Journal of Applied Social Psychology, 13,* 510–514.

Simon, D. M., & Ostrom, C. W., Jr. (1989). The impact of televised speeches and foreign travel on presidential approval. *Public Opinion Quarterly, 53,* 58–82.

Simon, R. J., & Landis, J. M. (1989). The polls—A report: Women's and men's attitudes about a woman's place and role. *Public Opinion Quarterly, 53,* 265–276.

Simons, H. W., Berkowitz, N. N., & Moyer, R. J. (1970). Similarity, credibility, and attitude change: A review and a theory. *Psychological Bulletin, 73,* 1–16.

Singer, E., Frankel, M. R., & Glassman, M. B. (1983). The effect of interviewer characteristics and expectations on response. *Public Opinion Quarterly, 47,* 68–83.

Sistrunk, F., & McDavid, J. W. (1971). Sex variables in conforming behavior. *Journal of Personality and Social Psychology, 17,* 200–207.

Sivacek, J., & Crano, W. D. (1982). Vested interest as a moderator of attitude-behavior consistency. *Journal of Personality and Social Psychology, 43,* 210–221.

Siwolop, S. (1987, February 16). Excuse me, what's the pollsters' big problem? *Business Week,* p. 108.

Skalaban, A. (1988). Do the polls affect elections? Some 1980 evidence. *Political Behavior, 10,* 136–150.

Skedgell, R. A. (1966). How computers pick an election winner. *Trans-action, 4*(1), 42–46.

Skelly, G. U., & Lundstrom, W. J. (1981). Male sex roles in magazine advertising, 1959–1979. *Journal of Communication, 31*(4), 52–57.

Skinner, B. F. (1957). *Verbal behavior.* New York: Appleton-Century-Crofts.

Skowronski, J. J., & Carlston, D. E. (1989). Negativity and extremity biases in impression formation: A review of explanations. *Psychological Bulletin, 105,* 131–142.

Slavin, R. E. (1980). Cooperative learning. *Review of Educational Research, 50,* 315–342.

Slovic, P., Fischhoff, B., & Lichtenstein, S. (1980). Facts vs. fears: Understanding perceived risk. In R. Schwing & W. A. Albers, Jr. (Eds.), *Societal risk assessment: How safe is safe enough?* New York: Plenum.

Smith, C., & Lloyd, B. (1978). Maternal behavior and perceived sex of infant: Revisited. *Child Development, 49,* 1263–1265.

Smith, E. R., & Manard, B. B. (1980). Causal attributions and medical school admissions. *Personality and Social Psychology Bulletin, 6,* 644–650.

Smith, L. B. (1988). Foreword. In P. A. Katz & D. A. Taylor (Eds.), *Eliminating racism: Profiles in controversy* (pp. xi–xiii). New York: Plenum.

Smith, M. B., Bruner, J. S., & White, R. W. (1956). *Opinions and personality.* New York: Wiley.

Smith, M. L. (1980). Sex bias in counseling and psychotherapy. *Psychological Bulletin, 89,* 392–407.

Smith, T. W. (1985). The polls: America's most important problems. Part I: National and international. *Public Opinion Quarterly, 49,* 264–274.

Smith, T. W. (1987). That which we call welfare by any other name would smell sweeter: An analysis of the impact of question wording on response patterns. *Public Opinion Quarterly, 51,* 75–83.

Snodgrass, S. E., & Rosenthal, R. (1982). Teacher suspiciousness of experimenter's intent and the mediation of teacher expectancy effects. *Basic and Applied Social Psychology, 3,* 219–230.

Snyder, M., & DeBono, K. G. (1987). A functional approach to attitudes and persuasion. In M. P. Zanna, J. M. Olson, & C. P. Herman (Eds.), *Social influence: The Ontario Symposium* (Vol. 5). Hillsdale, NJ: Erlbaum.

Snyder, M., & Kendzierski, D. (1982). Acting on one's attitudes: Procedures for linking attitudes and actions. *Journal of Experimental Social Psychology, 18,* 165–183.

Snyder, M. L., Stephan, W. G., & Rosenfield, D. (1976). Egotism and attribution. *Journal of Personality and Social Psychology, 33,* 435–441.

Sorauf, F. J. (1987). Varieties of experience: Campaign finance in the House and Senate. In K. L. Schlozman (Ed.), *Elections in America* (pp. 197–218). Boston: Allen & Unwin.

Spence, J. T., Deaux, K., & Helmreich, R. L. (1985). Sex roles in contemporary American society. In G. Lindzey & E. Aronson (Eds.), *The handbook of social psychology* (3rd ed., Vol. 2, pp. 149–178). New York: Random House.

Spence, J. T., & Helmreich, R. (1972). The Attitudes towards Women Scale: An objective instrument to measure attitudes toward the rights and roles of women in contemporary society. *JSAS Catalog of Selected Documents in Psychology, 2,* 66.

Spence, J. T., Helmreich, R. L., & Stapp, J. (1974). The Personal Attributes Questionnaire: A measure of sex role stereotypes and masculinity-femininity. *JSAS Catalog of Selected Documents in Psychology, 4,* 43. (Ms. No. 617).

Spencer, C. D. (1978). Two types of role playing: Threats to internal and external validity. *American Psychologist, 33,* 265–268.

Spinner, B., Adair, J. G., & Barnes, G. E. (1977). A reexamination of the faithful subject role. *Journal of Experimental Social Psychology, 13,* 543–551.

Spitze, G., & Huber, J. (1980). Changing attitudes toward women's nonfamily roles: 1938 to 1978. *Sociology of Work and Occupations, 7,* 317–335.

Squire, P. (1988). Why the 1936 *Literary Digest* poll failed. *Public Opinion Quarterly, 52,* 125–133.

Stagner, R. (1967). *Psychological aspects of international conflict.* Belmont, CA: Brooks/Cole.

Staines, G. L., & Pleck, J. H. (1984). Nonstandard work schedules and family life. *Journal of Applied Psychology, 69,* 515–523.

Stanley, H. W., Bianco, W. T., & Niemi, R. G. (1986). Partisanship and group support over time: A multivariate analysis. *American Political Science Review, 80,* 969–976.

Stapp, J. (1978). What's new in measurement? *SASP Newsletter, 4*(4), 10–11.

Star, S. A., & Hughes, H. McG. (1950). Report of an educational campaign: The Cincinnati plan for the United Nations. *American Journal of Sociology, 55,* 389–400.

Steeh, C. G. (1981). Trends in nonresponse rates, 1952–1979. *Public Opinion Quarterly, 45,* 40–57.

Steele, C. M., & Liu, T. J. (1983). Dissonance processes as self-affirmation. *Journal of Personality and Social Psychology, 45,* 5–19.

Steinberg, A. (1983). Off the track in California. *Public Opinion, 5*(6), 44–45.

Steinmann, A. (1975). Female and male concepts of sex roles: An overview of twenty years of cross-cultural research. *Transnational Mental Health Research Newsletter, 17*(4), 2–4 & 8–11.

Steinmann, A., & Fox, D. (1974). *The male dilemma.* New York: Aronson.

Stephan, W. G. (1978). School desegregation: An evaluation of predictions made in *Brown v. Board of Education. Psychological Bulletin, 85,* 217–238.

Stephan, W. G. (1985). Intergroup relations. In G. Lindzey & E. Aronson (Eds.), *The handbook of social psychology* (3rd ed., Vol. 2, pp. 599–658). New York: Random House.

Stephens, W. N. (1963). *The family in cross-cultural perspective.* New York: Holt, Rinehart & Winston.

Sternglanz, S., & Serbin, L. (1974). Sex role stereotyping on children's television programs. *Developmental Psychology, 10,* 710–715.

Stinchcombe, A. L., Jones, C., & Sheatsley, P. (1981). Nonresponse bias for attitude questions. *Public Opinion Quarterly, 45,* 359–375.

Stockard, J., & Johnson, M. M. (1980). *Sex roles: Sex inequality and sex role development.* Englewood Cliffs, NJ: Prentice-Hall.

Stokes D. E., & Miller W. E. (1962). Party government and the saliency of Congress. *Public Opinion Quarterly, 26*, 531–546.

Stoneman, Z., & Brody, G. H. (1981). Peers as mediators of television food advertisements aimed at children. *Developmental Psychology, 17*, 853–858.

Storms, M. D. (1973). Videotape and the attribution process: Reversing actor's and observer's points of view. *Journal of Personality and Social Psychology, 27*, 165–175.

Stouffer, S. A. (1955). *Communism, conformity, and civil liberties.* New York: Doubleday.

Stovall, J. G., & Solomon, J. H. (1984). The poll as a news event in the 1980 presidential campaign. *Public Opinion Quarterly, 48*, 615–623.

Streufert, S., & Sandler, S. I. (1971). A laboratory test of the mirror image hypothesis. *Journal of Applied Social Psychology, 1*, 378–397.

Streufert, S., & Streufert, S. C. (1978). *Behavior in the complex environment.* Washington, DC: Winston.

Stricker, L. J. (1967). The true deceiver. *Psychological Bulletin, 68*, 13–20.

Stricker, L. J., Messick, S., & Jackson, D. N. (1969). Evaluating deception in psychological research. *Psychological Bulletin, 71*, 343–351.

Stroebe, W., & Diehl, M. (1981). Conformity and counterattitudinal behavior: The effect of social support on attitude change. *Journal of Personality and Social Psychology, 41*, 876–899.

Stroebe, W., & Diehl, M. (1988). When social support fails: Supporter characteristics in compliance-induced attitude change. *Personality and Social Psychology Bulletin, 14*, 136–144.

Stryker, S., & Gottlieb, A. (1981). Attribution theory and symbolic interactionism: A comparison. In J. H. Harvey, W. J. Ickes, & R. F. Kidd (Eds.), *New directions in attribution research* (Vol. 3, pp. 425–458). Hillsdale, NJ: Erlbaum.

Stults, D. M., Messe, L. A., & Kerr, N. L. (1984). Belief discrepant behavior and the bogus pipeline: Impression management or arousal attribution. *Journal of Experimental Social Psychology, 20*, 47–54.

Sudman, S. (1967). *Reducing the cost of surveys.* Chicago: Aldine.

Sudman, S. (1982). The presidents and the polls. *Public Opinion Quarterly, 46*, 301–310.

Sudman, S. (1983). The network polls: A critical review. *Public Opinion Quarterly, 47*, 490–496.

Sudman, S. (1986). Do exit polls influence voting behavior? *Public Opinion Quarterly, 50*, 331–339.

Sudman, S., & Bradburn, N. M. (1982). *Asking questions: A practical guide to questionnaire design.* San Francisco: Jossey-Bass.

Sudman, S., & Bradburn, N. M. (1987). The organizational growth of public opinion research in the United States. *Public Opinion Quarterly, 51*, s67–s78.

Suedfeld, P. (1971). Models of attitude change: Theories that pass in the night. In P. Suedfeld (Ed.), *Attitude change: The competing views* (pp. 1–62). Chicago: Aldine Atherton.

Sullivan, D. S., & Deiker, T. E. (1973). Subject-experimenter perceptions of ethical issues in human research. *American Psychologist, 28*, 587–591.

Sullivan, J. L., Marcus, G. E., Feldman, S., & Piereson, J. E. (1981). The sources of political tolerance: A multivariate analysis. *American Political Science Review, 75*, 92–106.

Sullivan, J. L., Piereson, J. E., & Marcus, G. E. (1978). Ideological constraint in the mass public: A methodological critique and some new findings. *American Journal of Political Science, 228*, 233–249.

Sullivan, J. L., Piereson, J. E., & Marcus, G. E. (1979). An alternative conceptualization of political tolerance: Illusory increases 1950s-1970s. *American Political Science Review, 73*, 781–794.

Sweeney, P. D., & Gruber, K. L. (1984). Selective exposure: Voter information preferences and the Watergate affair. *Journal of Personality and Social Psychology, 46*, 1208–1221.

Swingle, P. G. (Ed.). (1973). *Social psychology in natural settings: A reader in field experimentation.* Chicago: Aldine.

Tajfel, H. (1981). *Human groups and social categories: Studies in social psychology.* Cambridge, England: Cambridge University Press.

Tannenbaum, P. H. (1953). *Attitude toward source and concept as factors in attitude change through communications.* Unpublished doctoral dissertation, University of Illinois.

Tannenbaum, P. H. (1967). The congruity principle revisited: Studies in the reduction, induction, and generalization of persuasion. In L. Berkowitz (Ed.), *Advances in experimental social psychology* (Vol. 3, pp. 270–320). New York: Academic Press.

Tannenbaum, P. H. (Ed.). (1980). *The entertainment functions of television.* Hillsdale, NJ: Erlbaum.

Tannenbaum, P. H., & Kostrich, L. J. (1983). *Turned-on TV/turned-off voters: Policy options for election projections.* Beverly Hills, CA: Sage.

Tashakkori, A., & Insko, C. A. (1981). Interpersonal attraction and person perception: Two tests of three balance models. *Journal of Experimental Social Psychology, 17*, 266–285.

Tavris, C. (1973). Who likes women's liberation—and why: The case of the unliberated liberals. *Journal of Social Issues, 29*(4), 175–198.

Taylor, D. A., & Katz, P. A. (1988). Conclusion. In P. A. Katz & D. A. Taylor (Eds.), *Eliminating racism: Profiles in controversy* (pp. 359–369). New York: Plenum.

Taylor, D. G. (1982). Pluralistic ignorance and the spiral of silence: A formal analysis. *Public Opinion Quarterly, 46*, 311–335.

Taylor, D. G., Sheatsley, P. B., & Greeley, A. M. (1978, June). Attitudes toward racial integration. *Scientific American, 238*, 42–51.

Taylor, D. M., & Jaggi, V. (1974). Ethnocentrism and causal attribution in a south Indian context. *Journal of Cross-Cultural Psychology, 5,* 162–171.

Taylor, J. B., & Parker, H. A. (1964). Graphic ratings and attitude measurement: A comparison of research tactics. *Journal of Applied Psychology, 48,* 37–42.

Taylor, S. E. (1975). On inferring one's own attitudes from one's behavior: Some delimiting conditions. *Journal of Personality and Social Psychology, 31,* 126–131.

Taylor, S. E. (1981). The interface of cognitive and social psychology. In J. H. Harvey (Ed.), *Cognition, social behavior, and the environment.* Hillsdale, NJ: Erlbaum.

Taylor, S. E., & Koivumaki, J. H. (1976). The perception of self and others: Acquaintanceship, affect, and actor-observer differences. *Journal of Personality and Social Psychology, 33,* 403–408.

Tedeschi, J. T. (Ed.). (1981). *Impression management theory and social psychological research.* New York: Academic Press.

Tedeschi, J. T., & Rosenfeld, P. (1981). Impression management theory in the forced compliance situation. In J. T. Tedeschi (Ed.), *Impression management theory and social psychological research.* New York: Academic Press.

Tedeschi, J. T., Schlenker, B. R., & Bonoma, T. V. (1971). Cognitive dissonance: Private ratiocination or public spectacle? *American Psychologist, 26,* 685–695.

Tedesco, N. (1974). Patterns of prime time. *Journal of Communication, 24,* 119–124.

Teixeira, R. A. (1987). *Why Americans don't vote: Turnout decline in the United States, 1960–1984.* New York: Greenwood.

Tesser, A. (1978). Self-generated attitude change. In L. Berkowitz (Ed.), *Advances in experimental social psychology* (Vol. 11, pp. 289–338). New York: Academic Press.

Tesser, A., & Leone, C. (1977). Cognitive schemas and thought as determinants of attitude change. *Journal of Experimental Social Psychology, 13,* 340–356.

Tesser, A., & Shaffer, D. R. (1990). Attitudes and attitude change. *Annual Review of Psychology, 41,* 479–523.

Tetlock, P. E. (1981). Personality and isolationism: Content analysis of senatorial speeches. *Journal of Personality and Social Psychology, 41,* 737–743.

Tetlock, P. E. (1983a). Cognitive style and political ideology. *Journal of Personality and Social Psychology, 45,* 118–126.

Tetlock, P. E. (1983b). Policy-makers' images of international conflict. *Journal of Social Issues, 39*(1), 67–86.

Tetlock, P. E. (1985). Integrative complexity of American and Soviet foreign policy rhetoric: A time-series analysis. *Journal of Personality and Social Psychology, 49,* 1565–1585.

Tetlock, P. E. (1986). A value pluralism model of ideological reasoning. *Journal of Personality and Social Psychology, 50,* 819–827.

Thistlethwaite, D. L. (1974). Impact of disruptive external events on student attitudes. *Journal of Personality and Social Psychology, 30,* 228–242.

Thomas, W. I. (1907). The mind of woman and the lower races. *American Journal of Sociology, 12,* 435–569.

Thomas, W. I. (1923). *The unadjusted girl.* Boston: Little, Brown.

Thompson, K. S., & Oskamp, S. (1974). Difficulties in replicating the proselyting effect in doomsday groups. *Psychological Reports, 35,* 971–978.

Thurstone, L. L. (1928). Attitudes can be measured. *American Journal of Sociology, 33,* 529–554.

Times Mirror. (1987). *The people, the press and politics.* Reading, MA: Addison-Wesley.

Timmer, S. G., Eccles, J., & O'Brien, K. (1985). How children use time. In F. T. Juster & F. P. Stafford (Eds.), *Time, goods, and well-being.* Ann Arbor, MI: Institute for Social Research.

Tittle, C. R., & Hill, R. J. (1967). Attitude measurement and prediction of behavior: An evaluation of conditions and measurement techniques. *Sociometry, 30,* 199–213.

Tognacci, L. N., & Cook, S. W. (1975). Conditioned autonomic responses as bidirectional indicators of racial attitude. *Journal of Personality and Social Psychology, 31,* 137–144.

Tolley, H., Jr. (1973). *Children and war: Political socialization to international conflict.* New York: Teachers College Press, Columbia University.

Tornatzky, L. G., Solomon, T., et al. (1982). Contributions of social science to innovation and productivity. *American Psychologist, 37,* 737–746.

Torney, J. V., Oppenheim, A. N., & Farnen, R. F. (1975). *Civic education in ten countries: An empirical study.* New York: Wiley.

Toufexis, A. (1987, September 14). A question of black pride. *Time,* p. 74.

Tourangeau, R., & Rasinski, K. A. (1988). Cognitive processes underlying context effects in attitude measurement. *Psychological Bulletin, 103,* 299–314.

Tracy, P. E., & Fox, J. A. (1981). The validity of randomized response for sensitive measurements. *American Sociological Review, 46,* 187–200.

Traugott, M. W., & Katosh, J. P. (1979). Response validity in surveys of voting behavior. *Public Opinion Quarterly, 43,* 359–377.

Traugott, M. W., & Katosh, J. P. (1981). Interviews may stimulate voting. *Institute for Social Research Newsletter,* p. 3.

Traugott, M. W., & Tucker, C. (1984). Strategies for predicting whether a citizen will vote and estimation of electoral outcomes. *Public Opinion Quarterly, 48,* 330–343.

Trenaman, J., & McQuail, D. (1961). *Television and the political image.* London: Methuen.

Triandis, H. C. (1964). Exploratory factor analyses of the behavioral component of social attitudes. *Journal of Abnormal and Social Psychology, 68,* 420–430.

Triandis, H. C. (1971). *Attitude and attitude change.* New York: Wiley.

Triandis, H. C. (1977). *Interpersonal behavior.* Monterey, CA: Brooks/Cole.

Triandis, H. C., & Triandis, L. M. (1962). A cross-cultural study of social distance. *Psychological Monographs, 76,* No. 21 (Whole No. 540).

Troldahl, V. C., & Van Dam, R. (1965). Face-to-face communication about major topics in the news. *Public Opinion Quarterly, 29,* 626–634.

Trost, M. R., Cialdini, R. B., & Maass, A. (1989). Effects of an international conflict simulation on perceptions of the Soviet Union; A FIREBREAKS backfire. *Journal of Social Issues, 45*(2), 139–158.

Tuchman, G. (1978). *Making news: A study in the construction of reality.* New York: Free Press.

Tuckel, P. S., & Tejera, F. (1983). Changing patterns in American voting behavior, 1914–1980. *Public Opinion Quarterly, 47,* 230–246.

Tufte, E. R. (1975). Determinants of the outcomes of midterm congressional elections. *American Political Science Review, 69,* 812–826.

Turner, A. G. (1972). *The San Jose methods test of known crime victims.* Washington, DC: National Criminal Justice Information and Statistics Service, U.S. Department of Justice.

Turner, C. F., & Martin, E. (Eds.). (1981). *Surveys of subjective phenomena: Summary report.* Washington, DC: National Academy Press.

Tversky, A., & Kahneman, D. (1974). Judgment under uncertainty: Heuristics and biases. *Science, 185,* 1124–1131.

Tversky, A., & Kahneman, D. (1982). Judgments of and by representativeness. In D. Kahneman, P. Slovic, & A. Tversky (Eds.), *Judgement under uncertainty: Heuristics and biases* (pp. 84–98). Cambridge, England: Cambridge University Press.

Tybout, A. M., & Scott, C. A. (1983). Availability of well-defined internal knowledge and the attitude formation process: Information aggregation versus self-perception. *Journal of Personality and Social Psychology, 44,* 474–491.

UNESCO. (1960). *Rural television in Japan.* Paris: UNESCO.

Unger R. K. (1979). Toward a redefinition of sex and gender. *American Psychologist, 34,* 1085–1094.

Upshaw, H. S. (1969). The personal reference scale: An approach to social judgment. In L. Berkowitz (Ed.), *Advances in experimental social psychology* (Vol. 4, pp. 315–371). New York: Academic Press.

U.S. Commission on Civil Rights. (1977a). *Reviewing a decade of school desegregation, 1966–1975.* Washington, DC: U.S. Government Printing Office.

U.S. Commission on Civil Rights. (1977b). *Window dressing on the set: Women and minorities in television.* Washington, DC: U.S. Government Printing Office.

U.S. Congress, Office of Technology Assessment. (1979). *The effects of nuclear war.* Washington, DC: Author.

U.S. Department of Health, Education, and Welfare. (1969). *Toward a social report.* Washington, DC: U.S. Government Printing Office.

U.S. Department of Health, Education, and Welfare. (1971). *The institutional guide to DHEW policy on protection of human subjects* (DHEW Publication No. (NIH) 72–102). Washington, DC: U.S. Government Printing Office.

U.S. Department of Labor. (1980). *Perspectives on working women: A databook.* Washington, DC: U.S. Government Printing Office.

U.S. Department of Labor. (1982). *20 facts on women workers.* Washington, DC: U.S. Government Printing Office.

Valins, S. (1966). Cognitive effects of false heart-rate feedback. *Journal of Personality and Social Psychology, 4,* 400–408.

Vallone, R. P., Ross, L., & Lepper, M. R. (1985). The hostile media phenomenon: Biased perception and perceptions of media bias in coverage of the Beirut massacre. *Journal of Personality and Social Psychology, 49,* 577–585.

Varela, J. A. (1971). *Psychological solutions to social problems: An introduction to social technology.* New York: Academic Press.

Vidmar, N., & Rokeach, M. (1974). Archie Bunker's bigotry: A study in selective perception and exposure. *Journal of Communication, 14*(1), 36–47.

Vitelli, R. (1988). The crisis issue assessed: An empirical analysis. *Basic and Applied Social Psychology, 9,* 301–309.

Vogel, S. R., Broverman, I. K., Broverman, D. M., Clarkson, F. E., & Rosenkrantz, P. S. (1970). Maternal employment and perception of sex roles among college students. *Developmental Psychology, 3,* 384–391.

von Baeyer, C. L., Sherk, D. L., & Zanna, M. P. (1981). Impression management in the job interview: When the female applicant meets the male "chauvinist" interviewer. *Personality and Social Psychology Bulletin, 7,* 45–51.

Walster, E. (1965). The effect of self-esteem on romantic liking. *Journal of Experimental Social Psychology, 1,* 184–197.

Wang, C. K. A. (1932). Suggested criteria for writing attitude statements. *Journal of Social Psychology, 3,* 367–373.

Ware, J. E. (1978). Effects of acquiescent response set on patient satisfaction ratings. *Medical Care, 16,* 327–336.

Warwick, D. P. (1982). Types of harm in social research. In T. L. Beauchamp, R. R. Faden, R. J. Wallace, Jr., & L. R. Walters (Eds.), *Ethical issues in social science research* (pp. 101–124). Baltimore: Johns Hopkins University Press.

Watson, D. (1982). The actor and the observer: How are their perceptions of causality divergent? *Psychological Bulletin, 92,* 682–700.

Wattenberg, M. P. (1984). *The decline of American political parties, 1952–1980.* Cambridge, MA: Harvard University Press.

Wattenberg, M. P. (1987). The hollow realignment: Partisan change in a candidate-centered era. *Public Opinion Quarterly, 51,* 58–74.

Watts, W., & Free, L. A. (1973). *State of the nation.* New York: Universe Books.

Watts, W., & Free, L. A. (1974). *State of the nation 1974.* Washington, DC: Potomac Associates.

Watts, W. A. (1967). Relative persistence of opinion change induced by active compared to passive participation. *Journal of Personality and Social Psychology, 5,* 4–15.

Watts, W. A., & McGuire, W. J. (1964). Persistence of induced opinion change and retention of inducing message content. *Journal of Abnormal and Social Psychology, 68,* 233–241.

Weary, G. (1980). Examination of affect and egotism as mediators of bias in causal attributions. *Journal of Personality and Social Psychology, 38,* 348–357.

Webb, E. J., Campbell, D. T., Schwartz, R. D., Sechrest, L., & Grove, J. (1981). *Nonreactive measures in the social sciences* (2nd ed.). Boston: Houghton Mifflin.

Webb, S. C. (1955). Scaling of attitudes by the method of equal-appearing intervals: A review. *Journal of Social Psychology, 42,* 215–239.

Weber, R., & Crocker, J. (1983). Cognitive processes in the revision of stereotypic beliefs. *Journal of Personality and Social Psychology, 45,* 961–977.

Weber, S. J., & Cook, T. D. (1972). Subject effects in laboratory research: An examination of subject roles, demand characteristics, and valid inference. *Psychological Bulletin, 77,* 273–295.

Weeks, M. F., & Moore, R. P. (1981). Ethnicity-of-interviewer effects on ethnic respondents. *Public Opinion Quarterly, 45,* 245–249.

Weigel, R. H., Wiser, P. L., & Cook, S. W. (1975). The impact of cooperative learning experiences on cross-ethnic relations and attitudes. *Journal of Social Issues, 31*(1), 219–244.

Weiner, J. J., & Wright, F. E. (1973). Effects of undergoing arbitrary discrimination upon subsequent attitudes toward a minority group. *Journal of Applied Social Psychology, 3,* 94–102.

Weisberg, H. F. (1987). The demographics of a new voting gap: Marital differences in American voting. *Public Opinion Quarterly, 51,* 335–343.

Weisfeld, G. E., & Beresford, J. M. (1982). Erectness of posture as a mediator of dominance or success in humans. *Motivation and Emotion, 6,* 113–131.

Weiss, C. H. (1978). Improving the linkage between social research and public policy. In L. E. Lynn, Jr. (Ed.), *Knowledge and policy: The uncertain connection* (Study Project on Social Research and Development, Vol. 5). Washington, DC: National Academy of Sciences.

Weiss, R. F. (1968). An extension of Hullian learning theory to persuasive communication. In A. G. Greenwald, T. C. Brock, & T. M. Ostrom (Eds.), *Psychological foundations of attitudes* (pp. 109–145). New York: Academic Press.

Weiss, W. (1969). Effects of the mass media of communication. In G. Lindzey & E. Aronson (Eds.), *The handbook of social psychology* (2nd ed., Vol. 5, pp. 77–195). Reading, MA: Addison-Wesley.

Weisstein, N. (1971). Psychology constructs the female. In V. Gornick & B. K. Moran (Eds.), *Woman in sexist society: Studies in power and powerlessness* (pp. 207–224). New York: Basic Books.

Weitzman, L. G., Eifler, D., Hokada, E., & Ross, C. (1972). Sex-role socialization in picture books for preschool children. *American Journal of Sociology, 77,* 1125–1149.

Wells, G. L., & Petty, R. E. (1980). The effects of overt head-movements on persuasion: Compatibility and incompatibility of responses. *Basic and Applied Social Psychology, 1,* 219–230.

Welsh, W. A. (1981). *Survey research and public attitudes in Eastern Europe and the Soviet Union.* New York: Pergamon.

West, S. G., & Wicklund, R. A. (1980). *A primer of social psychological theories.* Monterey, CA: Brooks/Cole.

Westie, F. R., & DeFleur, M. L. (1959). Autonomic responses and their relationship to race attitudes. *Journal of Abnormal and Social Psychology, 58,* 340–347.

Wheeler, M. (1976). *Lies, damn lies, and statistics: The manipulation of public opinion in America.* New York: Liveright.

White, G. L. (1980). Consensus and justification effects on attitude following counterattitudinal behavior. *Social Psychology Quarterly, 43,* 321–327.

White, R. K. (1965). Images in the context of international conflict: Soviet perceptions of the U.S. and the U.S.S.R. In H. C. Kelman (Ed.), *International behavior: A social-psychological analysis* (pp. 238–276). New York: Holt, Rinehart & Winston.

White, R. K. (1966). "Socialism" and "capitalism": An international misunderstanding. *Foreign Affairs, 44,* 216–228.

White, R. K. (1970). *Nobody wanted war: Misperception in Vietnam and other wars* (rev. ed.). Garden City, NY: Doubleday.

White, R. K. (1984). *Fearful warriors: A psychological profile of U.S.-Soviet relations.* New York: Free Press.

White, R. K. (1985). Ten psychological contributions to the prevention of nuclear war. In S. Oskamp (Ed.), *International conflict and national public policy issues: Applied social psychology annual 6* (pp. 45–61). Beverly Hills, CA: Sage.

White, R. K. (Ed.). (1986). *Psychology and the prevention of nuclear war.* New York: New York University Press.

Wicker, A. W. (1969). Attitudes versus actions: The relationship of verbal and overt behavioral responses to attitude objects. *Journal of Social Issues, 25*(4), 41–78.

Wicker, A. W. (1971). An examination of the "other variables" explanation of attitude-behavior inconsistency. *Journal of Personality and Social Psychology, 19,* 18–30.

Wicklund, R. A. (1974). *Freedom and reactance.* Potomac, MD: Erlbaum.

Wicklund, R. A., & Brehm, J. W. (1976). *Perspectives on cognitive dissonance.* Hillsdale, NJ: Erlbaum.

Wiest, W. M. (1965). A quantitative extension of Heider's theory of cognitive balance applied to interpersonal perception and self-esteem. *Psychological Monographs, 79*(1, Whole No. 607).

Wilcox, B. L. (1987). Pornography, social science, and politics: When research and ideology collide. *American Psychologist, 42,* 941–943.

Wilcox, L. D., Brooks, R. M., Beal, G. M., & Klonglan, G. E. (1972). *Social indicators and societal monitoring: An annotated bibliography.* San Francisco: Jossey-Bass.

Wilder, D. A. (1981). Perceiving persons as a group: Categorization and intergroup relations. In D. L. Hamilton (Ed.), *Cognitive processes in stereotyping and intergroup behavior* (pp. 213–257). Hillsdale, NJ: Erlbaum.

Wilder, D. A., & Cooper, W. E. (1981). Categorization into groups: Consequences for social perception and attribution. In J. H. Harvey, W. J. Ickes, & R. F. Kidd (Eds.), *New directions in attribution research* (Vol. 3, pp. 247–277). Hillsdale, NJ: Erlbaum.

Wilker, H. R., & Milbrath, L. W. (1970). Political belief systems and political behavior. *Social Science Quarterly, 51,* 477–493.

Wilkins, S., & Miller, T. A. W. (1985). Working women: How it's working out. *Public Opinion, 8*(5), 44–48.

Williams, F., LaRose, R., & Frost, F. (1981). *Children, television, and sex-role stereotyping.* New York: Praeger.

Williams, J. E., & Bennett, S. M. (1975). The definition of sex stereotypes via the adjective check list. *Sex Roles, 1,* 327–337.

Williams, J. E., & Best, D. L. (1982). *Measuring sex stereotypes: A thirty-nation study.* Beverly Hills, CA: Sage.

Williams, J. E., & Morland, J. K. (1976). *Race, color, and the young child.* Chapel Hill: University of North Carolina Press.

Williams, J. E., & Morland, J. K. (1979). Comment on Banks's "White preference in blacks: A paradigm in search of a phenomenon." *Psychological Bulletin, 86,* 28–32.

Wilson, D. W., & Donnerstein, E. (1976). Legal and ethical aspects of nonreactive social psychological research: An excursion into the public mind. *American Psychologist, 31,* 765–773.

Wilson, G. D. (Ed.). (1973). *The psychology of conservatism.* London: Academic Press.

Wilson, T. D., & Linville, P. W. (1982). Improving the academic performance of college freshmen: Attribution therapy revisited. *Journal of Personality and Social Psychology, 42,* 367–376.

Wilson, W. (1970). Rank order of discrimination and its relevance to civil rights priorities. *Journal of Personality and Social Psychology, 15,* 118–124.

Wilson, W., & Miller, H. (1968). Repetition, order of presentation, and timing of arguments and measures as determinants of opinion change. *Journal of Personality and Social Psychology, 9,* 184–188.

Wilson, W. R. (1979). Feeling more than we can know: Exposure effects without learning. *Journal of Personality and Social Psychology, 37,* 811–821.

Winkler, J. D., Kanouse, D. E., & Ware, J. E., Jr. (1982). Controlling for acquiescence response set in scale development. *Journal of Applied Psychology, 67,* 555–561.

Wise, D. (1968, November 3). The twilight of a president. *New York Times Magazine,* p. 27.

Wish, M., Deutsch, M., & Biener, L. (1970). Differences in conceptual structures of nations: An exploratory study. *Journal of Personality and Social Psychology, 16,* 361–373.

Wittenbraker, J., Gibbs, B. L., & Kahle, L. R. (1983). Seat belt attitudes, habits, and behaviors: An adaptive amendment to the Fishbein model. *Journal of Applied Social Psychology, 13,* 406–421.

Wolfgang, M. E., & Weiner, N. A. (Eds.). (1982). *Criminal violence.* Beverly Hills, CA: Sage.

Wolfinger, R., & Linquiti, P. (1981). Tuning in and turning out. *Public Opinion, 4*(1), 56–60.

Women on Words and Images. (1975). *Dick and Jane as victims: Sex stereotyping in children's readers.* Princeton, NJ: Author.

Women's Action Alliance. (1981). *The radio and television commercial monitoring project: Summary report.* New York: Author.

Woodmansee, J. J. (1970). The pupil response as a measure of social attitudes. In G. F. Summers (Ed.), *Attitude measurement* (pp. 514–533). Chicago: Rand McNally.

Worcester, R. M. (1980). Pollsters, the press, and political polling in Britain. *Public Opinion Quarterly, 44,* 548–566.

Worcester, R. M. (1984). The polls: Britain at the polls 1945–1983. *Public Opinion Quarterly, 48,* 824–833.

Worcester, R. M. (1987). The internationalization of public opinion research. *Public Opinion Quarterly, 51,* s79–s85.

World Federalist Newsletter. (1980, Winter). *5*(4), 8.

Wright, J. D. (1975). Does acquiescence bias the "index of political efficacy"? *Public Opinion Quarterly, 39,* 219–226.

Wright, R. A., & Brehm, S. S. (1982). Reactance as impression management: A critical review. *Journal of Personality and Social Psychology, 42,* 608–618.

Wrightsman, L. S. (1969). Wallace supporters and adherence to "law and order." *Journal of Personality and Social Psychology, 13,* 17–22.

Wybrow, R. J. (1984, May). *A view from across the Atlantic: British attitudes towards America's world role*. Paper presented at American Association for Public Opinion Research meeting, Delavan, WI.

Wyer, R. S., Jr., & Gordon, S. E. (1982). The recall of information about persons and groups. *Journal of Experimental Social Psychology, 18,* 128–164.

Wyer, R. S., Jr., & Srull, T. K. (Eds.). (1984). *Handbook of social cognition* (Vols. 1–3). Hillsdale, NJ: Erlbaum.

Wyner, G. A. (1980). Response errors in self-reported number of arrests. *Sociological Methods and Research, 9,* 161–177.

Yalch, R. F. (1976). Interview effects on voter turnout. *Public Opinion Quarterly, 40,* 331–336.

Yankelovich, D. (1981). *New rules: Searching for self-fulfillment in a world turned upside down*. New York: Random House.

Yankelovich, D., & Doble, J. (1984). The public mood: Nuclear weapons and the U.S.S.R. *Foreign Affairs, 63,* 33–46.

Yatani, C., & Bramel, D. (1989). Trends and patterns in Americans' attitudes toward the Soviet Union. *Journal of Social Issues, 45*(2), 13–32.

Youniss, J. (1980). *Parents and peers in social development*. Chicago: University of Chicago Press.

Zajonc, R. B. (1968a). Attitudinal effects of mere exposure. *Journal of Personality and Social Psychology, 9*(2, Pt. 2), 1–27.

Zajonc, R. B. (1968b). Cognitive theories in social psychology. In G. Lindzey & E. Aronson (Eds.), *The handbook of social psychology* (2nd ed., Vol. 1, pp. 320–411). Reading, MA: Addison-Wesley.

Zajonc, R. B. (1980). Feeling and thinking: Preferences need no inferences. *American Psychologist, 35,* 151–175.

Zaller, J. R. (1987). Diffusion of political attitudes. *Journal of Personality and Social Psychology, 53,* 821–833.

Zanna, M. P., & Cooper, J. (1974). Dissonance and the pill: An attribution approach to studying the arousal properties of dissonance. *Journal of Personality and Social Psychology, 29,* 703–709.

Zanna, M. P., & Fazio, R. H. (1982). The attitude-behavior relation: Moving toward a third generation of research. In M. P. Zanna, E. T. Higgins, & C. P. Herman (Eds.), *Consistency in social behavior: The Ontario Symposium* (Vol. 2, pp. 283–301). Hillsdale, NJ: Erlbaum.

Zanna, M. P., Higgins, E. T., & Herman, C. P. (Eds.). (1982). *Consistency in social behavior: The Ontario Symposium* (Vol. 2). Hillsdale, NJ: Erlbaum.

Zanna, M. P., Kiesler, C. A., & Pilkonis, P. A. (1970). Positive and negative attitudinal affect established by classical conditioning. *Journal of Personality and Social Psychology, 14,* 321–328.

Zanna, M. P., & Olson, J. M. (1982). In M. P. Zanna, E. T. Higgins, & C. P. Herman (Eds.), *Consistency in social behavior: The Ontario Symposium* (Vol. 2, pp. 75–104). Hillsdale, NJ: Erlbaum.

Zanna, M. P., & Sande, G. N. (1986). The effects of collective actions on the attitudes of individual group members: A dissonance analysis. In M. P. Zanna, J. M. Olson, & C. P. Herman (Eds.), *Social influence: The Ontario Symposium* (Vol. 5). Hillsdale, NJ: Erlbaum.

Zavalloni, M., & Cook, S. W. (1965). Influence of judges' attitudes on ratings of favorableness of statements about a social group. *Journal of Personality and Social Psychology, 1,* 43–54.

Ziemke, D. A. (1980). Selective exposure in a presidential campaign contingent on certainty and salience. In D. D. Nimmo (Ed.), *Communication yearbook 4* (pp. 497–510). New Brunswick, NJ: Transaction.

Zimbardo, P. G. (1960). Involvement and communication discrepancy as determinants of opinion conformity. *Journal of Abnormal and Social Psychology, 60,* 86–94.

Zimbardo, P. G., Weisenberg, M., Firestone, I., & Levy, B. (1965). Communicator effectiveness in producing public conformity and private attitude change. *Journal of Personality, 33,* 233–255.

Zinsmeister, K. (1988). Black demographics. *Public Opinion, 10*(5), 41–44.

Zuckerman, D. M., Singer, D. G., & Singer, J. L. (1980). Children's television viewing, racial and sex-role attitudes. *Journal of Applied Social Psychology, 10,* 281–294.

Zuckerman, M., Mann, R. W., & Bernieri, F. J. (1982). Determinants of consensus estimates: Attribution, salience, and representativeness. *Journal of Personality and Social Psychology, 42,* 839–852.

Zukin, C., & Snyder, R. (1984). Passive learning: When the media environment is the message. *Public Opinion Quarterly, 48,* 629–638.

Name Index

H

Haberman, P., 416
Hacker, H. M., 402
Haemmerlie, F. M., 253
Hamill, R., 27
Hamilton, Alexander, 284
Hamilton, D. L., 29–31, 395
Hammond, J. L., 305
Hammond, K. R., 72
Hansen, J. M., 322
Hanson, D. J., 278
Harary, F., 232–233, 237
Harburg, E., 233
Hardee, B. B., 383
Harding, J., 161, 373
Hardyck, J. A., 243
Hare-Mustin, R. T., 411
Harkins, S. G., 260
Harmon, R. R., 217
Harris, L., 16, 101, 107, 125, 298
Harris, R. J., 241
Harris, V. A., 254
Harrison, D., 420
Harrison, William H., 336
Hartley, R. E., 409
Hartry, A., 355
Harvey, J. H., 33, 44, 217, 254
Harvey, O. J., 166, 225
Hass, R. G., 216, 257
Hastie, R., 217
Hastorf, A. H., 21
Hatchett, S., 120, 391, 393–394
Havel, J., 66, 161
Hawkins, R. P., 198
Hawley, W. D., 387
Heald, G., 325
Hearold, S., 187, 378
Hearst, Patti, 26, 37, 254
Heath, Edward, 109
Hechinger, F. M., 134
Heclo, H., 290
Heesacker, M., 261
Heider, F., 33–35, 47, 231–233, 319
Heller, J. F., 251
Helmreich, R. L., 244, 407, 421–422
Helms, Jesse, 324
Helson, H., 223
Henley, N. M., 414–415
Hennessy, B. C., 102, 139
Hennigan, K. M., 222
Hepburn, C., 408
Herek, G. M., 79–80, 429
Herman, C. P., 266
Herz, M. F., 174
Herzog, A. R., 427
Hess, E. H., 73
Hess, R. D., 162, 164, 347

Hesse, P., 347
Hesselbart, S., 266
Hewstone, M., 33
Hiatt, F., 343
Higbee, K. L., 208, 218
Higgins, E. T., 20, 266
Hilgard, E. R., 122
Hill, R. J., 61
Hiller, D. V., 427
Himmelfarb, S., 119
Himmelweit, H. T., 150, 167, 187
Hinckley, R. H., 101, 124, 128
Hinkle, R., 341
Hinkle, S., 252
Hippler, H.-J., 114
Hirsch, P. M., 197
Hitler, Adolf, 173–174, 361
Hittle, D., 64
Hoag, W. J., 300
Hoffman, L. W., 161
Hogarth, R. M., 23
Hokada, E., 413
Holmes, D. S., 209
Holmes, Sherlock, 27
Holsti, O. R., 353
Holt, R. R., 344, 347
Hood, W. E., 166
Hooyman, N., 148
House, P., 25–26
Houser, B. B., 429
Houston, D. A., 275–276
Hovland, C. I., 40, 54, 88, 94–95, 97, 157,
    171, 174, 202, 204, 213–216, 220, 222–225,
    229, 248, 251, 277, 319
Howard, J., 30, 347
Howard-Pitney, B., 227, 258
Howell, S. E., 298
Hoyt, M. F., 244
Hraba, J., 376
Hsu, H-L., 120
Huber, J., 420
Hughes, H. McG., 368
Hull, C., 212
Humphrey, Hubert, 109, 122, 127, 321, 327,
    336, 339
Humphreys, P., 150
Hunt, Jim, 324
Hurd, R., 130
Hurley, T. L., 318
Hursh-Cesar, G., 121
Hurwitz, J., 345
Hyde, J. S., 415
Hyden, P., 415
Hyman, H. H., 122, 131, 180, 194

I

Inglehart, R., 150

Subject Index